# Equity

CFA® PROGRAM CURRICULUM • VOLUME 4

## LEVEL II
## 2009

PEARSON

Custom
Publishing

Cover photograph courtesy of Corbis.

10  9  8  7  6  5  4  3  2  1

ISBN 0-536-53712-7

2007160915

AG/NN

Please visit our web site at *www.pearsoncustom.com*

PEARSON CUSTOM PUBLISHING
501 Boylston Street, Suite 900, Boston, MA 02116
A Pearson Education Company

# CONTENTS

45/8 4 11/16
5½ 5½ — 3/8
5½ 20 5/8 21 13/16 — 1/16
17 3/8 18 1/8 + 7/8
6½ 6½ — ½
7¼ 6½ 31/32 — 1/8
15/16
9/16 9/16
9/16
7 15/16
7 15/16 7 13/16 7 15/16
2 5/8 2 11/32 2½ +
2¾ 2¼ 2¼
12 1/16 11 3/8 11 3/4 +
87 33¾ 33 33 1/8 —
25 5/8 24 9/16 25 5/8 +
12 11 5/8 11 5/8 +
16 10½ 10½ 10½ —
78 15 5/8 15 13/16 15 5/8 —
9 1/16 8¼ 8 1/8
430 11¼ 10 1/8

# HOW TO USE THE CFA
# PROGRAM CURRICULUM

Congratulations on passing Level I of the Chartered Financial Analyst (CFA®) Program. This exciting and rewarding program of study reflects your desire to become a serious investment professional. You are participating in a program noted for its requirement of ethics and breadth of knowledge, skills, and abilities.

The credential you seek is respected around the world as a mark of accomplishment and dedication. Each level of the program represents a distinct achievement in professional development. Successful completion of the program is rewarded with membership in a prestigious global community of investment professionals. CFA charterholders are dedicated to life-long learning and maintaining currency with the ever-changing dynamics of a challenging profession.

The CFA examination measures your degree of mastery of the assigned CFA Program curriculum. Effective study and preparation based on that curriculum are keys to your success on the examination.

## Curriculum Development

The CFA Program curriculum is grounded in the practice of the investment profession. Utilizing a collaborative website, CFA Institute performs a continuous practice analysis with investment professionals around the world to determine the knowledge, skills, and abilities that are relevant to the profession. Regional panels and targeted surveys are also conducted annually to verify and reinforce the continuous feedback. The practice analysis process ultimately defines the Candidate Body of Knowledge (CBOK™) an inventory of knowledge and responsibilities expected of the investment management professional at the level of a new CFA charterholder. The process also determines how much emphasis each of the major topic areas receives on the CFA examinations.

A committee made up of practicing charterholders, in conjunction with CFA Institute staff, designs the CFA Program curriculum to deliver the CBOK to candidates. The examinations, also written by practicing charterholders, are designed to allow you to demonstrate your mastery of the CBOK as set forth in the CFA Program curriculum. As you structure your personal study program, you should emphasize mastery of the CBOK and the practical application of that knowledge. For more information on the practice analysis, CBOK, and development of the CFA Program curriculum, please visit www.cfainstitute.org/toolkit.

## Organization

The Level II CFA Program curriculum is organized into 10 topic areas. Each topic area begins with a brief statement of the material and the depth of knowledge expected.

Each topic area is then divided into one or more study sessions. These study sessions—18 sessions in the Level II curriculum—should form the basic structure of your reading and preparation.

Each study session includes a statement of its structure and objective, and is further divided into specific reading assignments. The outline on the inside front cover of each volume illustrates the organization of these 18 study sessions.

*The reading assignments are the basis for all examination questions, and are selected or developed specifically to teach the CBOK.* These readings are drawn from CFA Program-commissioned content, textbook chapters, professional journal articles, research analyst reports, and cases. Many readings include problems and solutions as well as appendices to help you learn.

Reading-specific Learning Outcome Statements (LOS) are listed in the pages introducing each study session as well as at the beginning of each reading. These LOS indicate what you should be able to accomplish after studying the reading. We encourage you to review how to properly use LOS, and the descriptions of commonly used LOS "command words," at www.cfainstitute.org/toolkit. The command words signal the depth of learning you are expected to achieve from the reading. You should use the LOS to guide and focus your study, as each examination question is based on an assigned reading and one or more LOS. However, the readings provide context for the LOS and enable you to apply a principle or concept in a variety of scenarios. It is important to study the whole of a required reading.

## Features of the Curriculum

► **Required vs. Optional Segments** - You should read all of the pages for an assigned reading. In some cases, however, we have reprinted an entire chapter or article and marked those parts of the reading that are not required as "optional." The CFA examination is based only on the required segments, and the optional segments are included only when they might help you to better understand the required segments (by seeing the required material in its full context). When an optional segment begins, you will see an icon and a solid vertical bar in the outside margin that will continue until the optional segment ends, accompanied by another icon. *Unless the material is specifically marked as optional, you should assume it is required.* Keep in mind that the optional material is provided strictly for your convenience and will not be tested. You should rely on the required segments and the reading-specific LOS in preparing for the examination.

► **Problems/Solutions** - *All questions and problems in the readings as well as their solutions (which are provided in an appendix at the end of each volume) are required material.* When appropriate, we have included problems within and after the readings to demonstrate practical application and reinforce your understanding of the concepts presented. The questions and problems are designed to help you learn these concepts. Many of the questions are adapted from past CFA examinations.

Beginning with the 2009 exams, the selected response questions on the CFA exam will have three choices (a correct answer and two distracters). This includes both the multiple choice questions at Level I and the item set questions at Levels II and III. In many cases, the questions provided in the curriculum have been modified to match the new three-choice format.

► **Margins** - The wide margins in each volume provide space for your note-taking.

► **Two-Color Format** - To enrich the visual appeal and clarity of the exhibits, tables, and text, the curriculum is printed in a two-color format.

► **Six-Volume Structure** - For portability of the curriculum, the material is spread over six volumes.

► **Glossary and Index** - For your convenience, we have printed a comprehensive glossary and index in each volume. Throughout the curriculum, a **bolded blue** word in a reading denotes a term defined in the glossary.

▶ **Source Material** - The authorship, publisher, and copyright owners are given for each reading for your reference. We recommend that you use this CFA Institute curriculum rather than the original source materials because the curriculum may include only selected pages from outside readings, updated sections within the readings, and may have problems and solutions tailored to the CFA Program.

▶ **LOS Self-Check** - We have inserted checkboxes next to each LOS that you can use to track your progress in mastering the concepts in each reading.

## Designing Your Personal Study Program

**Create a Schedule** - An orderly, systematic approach to examination preparation is critical. You should dedicate a consistent block of time every week to reading and studying. Complete all reading assignments and the associated problems and solutions in each study session. Review the LOS both before and after you study each reading to ensure that you have mastered the applicable content and can demonstrate the knowledge, skill, or ability described by the LOS and the assigned reading. Use the new LOS self-check to track your progress and highlight areas of weakness for later review.

You will receive periodic e-mail communications that contain important study tips and preparation strategies. Be sure to read these carefully.

CFA Institute estimates that you will need to devote a minimum of 10–15 hours per week for 18 weeks to study the assigned readings. Allow a minimum of one week for each study session, and plan to complete them all at least 30–45 days prior to the examination. This schedule will allow you to spend the final four to six weeks before the examination reviewing the assigned material and taking online sample and mock examinations.

At CFA Institute, we believe that candidates need to commit to a *minimum* of 250 hours reading and reviewing the curriculum, and taking online sample examinations, to master the material. This recommendation, however, may substantially underestimate the hours needed for appropriate examination preparation depending on your individual circumstances, relevant experience, and academic background.

You will undoubtedly adjust your study time to conform to your own strengths and weaknesses, and your educational and professional background. You will probably spend more time on some study sessions than on others. You should allow ample time for both in-depth study of all topic areas and additional concentration on those topic areas for which you feel least prepared.

**Candidate Preparation Toolkit** - We have created the online toolkit to provide a single comprehensive location with resources and guidance for candidate preparation. In addition to in-depth information on study program planning, the CFA Program curriculum, and the online sample and mock examinations, the toolkit also contains curriculum errata, printable study session outlines, sample examination questions, and more. Errata that we have identified in the curriculum are corrected and listed periodically in the errata listing in the toolkit. We encourage you to use the toolkit as your central preparation resource during your tenure as a candidate. Visit the toolkit at www.cfainstitute.org/toolkit.

**Online Sample Examinations** - As part of your study of the assigned curriculum, use the CFA Institute online sample examinations to assess your exam preparation as you progress toward the end of your study. After each question, you will receive immediate feedback noting the correct response and indicating the relevant assigned reading, so you'll be able to identify areas of weakness for further study. The 120-minute sample examinations reflect the question formats, topics, and level of difficulty of the actual CFA examinations. Aggregate data indicate that the CFA examination pass rate was higher among candidates who took one or more online sample examinations than among candidates who did not take the online sample examinations. For more information on the online sample examinations, please visit www.cfainstitute.org/toolkit.

 **Online Mock Examinations** - In response to candidate requests, CFA Institute has developed mock examinations that mimic the actual CFA examinations not only in question format and level of difficulty, but also in length. The three-hour online mock exams simulate the morning and afternoon sessions of the actual CFA exam, and are intended to be taken after you complete your study of the full curriculum, so you can test your understanding of the CBOK and your readiness for the exam. To further differentiate, feedback is provided at the end of the exam, rather than after each question as with the sample exams. CFA Institute recommends that you take these mock exams at the final stage of your preparation toward the actual CFA examination. For more information on the online mock examinations, please visit www.cfainstitute.org/toolkit.

## Tools to Measure Your Comprehension of the Curriculum

With the addition of the online mock exams, CFA Institute now provides three distinct ways you can practice for the actual CFA exam. The full descriptions are above, but below is a brief summary of each:

**End-of-Reading Questions** - These questions are found at the end of each reading in the printed curriculum, and should be used to test your understanding of the concepts.

**Online Sample Exams** - Typically available two months before the CFA exam, online sample exams are designed to assess your exam preparation, and can help you target areas of weakness for further study.

**Online Mock Exams** - In contrast to the sample exams, mock exams are not available until closer to the actual exam date itself. Mock exams are designed to replicate the exam day experience, and should be taken near the end of your study period to prepare for exam day.

**Preparatory Providers** - After you enroll in the CFA Program, you may receive numerous solicitations for preparatory courses and review materials. Although preparatory courses and notes may be helpful to some candidates, you should view these resources as *supplements* to the assigned CFA Program curriculum. The CFA examinations reference only the CFA Institute assigned curriculum—no preparatory course or review course materials are consulted or referenced.

Before you decide on a supplementary prep course, do some research. Determine the experience and expertise of the instructors, the accuracy and currency of their content, the delivery method for their materials, and the provider's claims of success. Most importantly, make sure the provider is in compliance with the CFA Institute Prep Provider Guidelines Program. Three years of prep course products can be a significant investment, so make sure you're getting a sufficient return. Just remember, there are no shortcuts to success on the CFA examinations. Prep products can enhance your learning experience, but the CFA curriculum is the key to success. For more information on the Prep Provider Guidelines Program, visit www.cfainstitute.org/cfaprog/resources/prepcourse.html.

## SUMMARY

Every question on the CFA examination is based on specific pages in the required readings and on one or more LOS. Frequently, an examination question is also tied to a specific example highlighted within a reading or to a specific end-of-reading question/problem and its solution. To make effective use of the curriculum, please remember these key points:

1. All pages printed in the Custom Curriculum are required reading for the examination except for occasional sections marked as optional. You may read optional pages as background, but you will not be tested on them.

2. All questions/problems printed at the end of readings and their solutions in the appendix to each volume are required study material for the examination.

3. Make appropriate use of the CFA Candidate Toolkit, the online sample/mock examinations, and preparatory courses and review materials.

4. Schedule and commit sufficient study time to cover the 18 study sessions, review the materials, and take sample/mock examinations.

5. **Note:** Some of the concepts in the study sessions may be superseded by updated rulings and/or pronouncements issued after a reading was published. Candidates are expected to be familiar with the overall analytical framework contained in the assigned readings. Candidates are not responsible for changes that occur after the material was written.

## Feedback

At CFA Institute, we are committed to delivering a comprehensive and rigorous curriculum for the development of competent, ethically grounded investment professionals. We rely on candidate and member feedback as we work to incorporate content, design, and packaging improvements. You can be assured that we will continue to listen to your suggestions. Please send any comments or feedback to curriculum@cfainstitute.org. Ongoing improvements in the curriculum will help you prepare for success on the upcoming examinations, and for a lifetime of learning as a serious investment professional.

| | | | |
|---|---|---|---|
| | 4⅝ | 4¹¹⁄₁₆ | − ⅜ |
| | 5½ | 5½ | − |
| | 5½ | 21¹³⁄₁₆ | − ¹⁄₁₆ |
| | 20⅝ | 18⅛ | + ⅞ |
| | 17⅜ | | |
| 3½ | 6½ | 6½ | − ½ |
| 7¼ | 6½ | 3¹⁄₃₂ | − ⅛ |
| | 15⁄₁₆ | | |
| | 9⁄₁₆ | ⅝ | |
| 1⁄₃₂ | | 7¹⁵⁄₁₆ | |
| 7¹⁵⁄₁₆ | 7¹³⁄₁₆ | | |
| 2⅝ | 2¹¹⁄₃₂ | 2½ | + |
| 23¾ | 2¼ | 2¼ | |
| 6⅛ | 12¹⁄₁₆ | 11⅜ | 11¾ + |
| 87 | 33¾ | 33 | 33¼ − |
| 602 | 25⅝ | 24⁹⁄₁₆ | 25⅝ + |
| 833 | 12 | 11⅝ | 11⅝ + |
| 16 | 10½ | 10½ | 10½ − |
| 78 | 15⅝ | 15¹³⁄₁₆ | 15⅝ − |
| 4508 | 9⁹⁄₁₆ | 8¼ | 8¼ + |
| 430 | 11¼ | 10⅛ | |

# EQUITY INVESTMENTS

## TOPIC LEVEL LEARNING OUTCOME

The candidate should be able to analyze and apply concepts and techniques that are basic to the valuation of equities. Models derived from fundamental analysis are applied to estimate equity risk and return within a global context.

45⁄8 4⅛  
5½ — ⅜  
5½ 5½  
5⅛ 5½ 21³⁄₁₆ — ¼  
20⅝ 18⅛ + ⅞  
17⅜ 18⅛ +  
18½ 6½ — ½  
7¼ 6½ 6½ —  
15⁄16 31⁄32 — ⅛  
1 9⁄16  
9⁄16 9⁄16  
19⁄32 7¹⁵⁄₁₆ 7¹⁵⁄₁₆  
7¹⁵⁄₁₆ 7¹³⁄₁₆  
2⅝ 2¹¹⁄₃₂ 2½ +  
546 2¾ 2¼ 2¼  
527 12¹⁄₁₆ 11⅜ 11¾ +  
616 33¾ 33 33¼ —  
87 25⅝ 24⁹⁄₁₆ 25⅜ +  
602 12 11⅝ 11⅞ +  
833 16 10½ 10½ 10½ —  
78 15⅞ 15¹³⁄₁₆ 15⅞ —  
4608 9¹⁄₁₆ 8¼ 8⅛ +  
430 11¼ 10⅛ 10⅞  
4⅜

# STUDY SESSION 10
## EQUITY INVESTMENTS:
### Valuation Concepts

This study session examines the well-established methodologies of security analysis, the process an analyst uses in applying these models, and the limitations of each. The readings contrast the characteristics of equity markets around the world. The session ends with a presentation of alternative return concepts, theories, and calculations.

## READING ASSIGNMENTS

**Reading 33**   A Note on Asset Valuation
  by George H. Troughton, CFA

**Reading 34**   The Equity Valuation Process
  *Analysis of Equity Investments: Valuation,* by John D. Stowe, CFA, Thomas R. Robinson, CFA, Jerald E. Pinto, CFA, and Dennis W. McLeavey, CFA

**Reading 35**   Equity: Markets and Instruments
  *Global Investments,* Sixth Edition, by Bruno Solnik and Dennis McLeavey, CFA

**Reading 36**   Return Concepts
  by John D. Stowe, CFA, Thomas R. Robinson, CFA, Jerald E. Pinto, CFA, and Dennis W. McLeavey, CFA

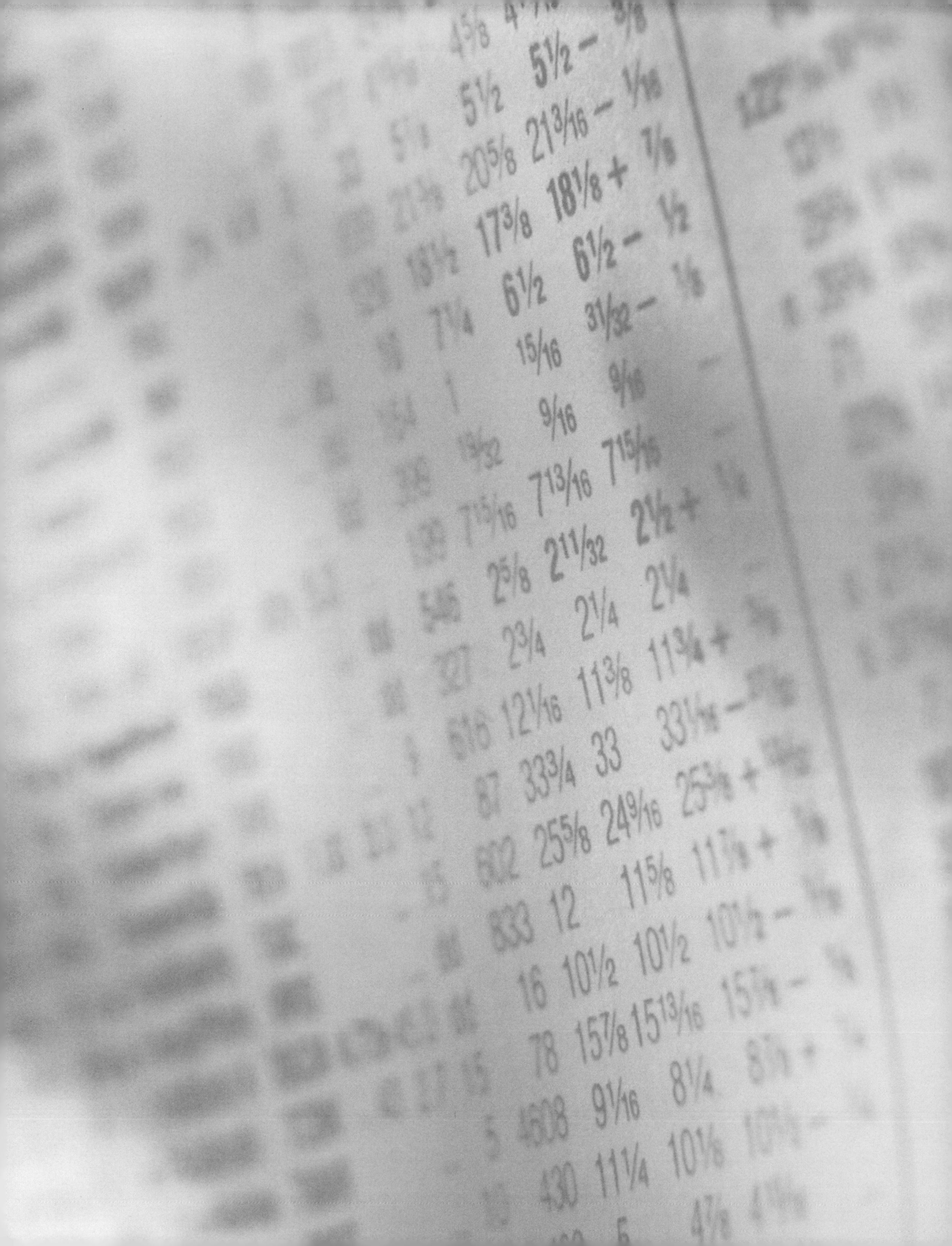

4⅞ 4⅞ ⅝
5½ 5½ −
5½ 21³⁄₁₆ − ⅛
20⅝ 21³⁄₁₆ − ⅛
17⅜ 18⅛ + ⅞
18½ 17⅜ 18⅛ + ⅞
6½ 6½ − ½
7¼ 6½ 6½ − ½
15⁄₁₆ 31⁄₃₂ − ⅛
9⁄₁₆ 9⁄₁₆
9⁄₁₆ 9⁄₁₆
19⁄₃₂
7¹⁵⁄₁₆ 7¹³⁄₁₆ 7¹⁵⁄₁₆
2½ +
2⅝ 2¹¹⁄₃₂ 2½ +
2¾ 2¼ 2¼
23¾ 2¼ 2¼
11¾ +
12¹⁄₁₆ 11⅜ 11¾ +
33¼ − 
87 33¾ 33 33¼ −
602 25⅝ 24⁹⁄₁₆ 25⅜ +
833 12 11⅝ 11⅞ +
16 10½ 10½ 10½ −
78 15⅞ 15¹³⁄₁₆ 15⅞ −
8⅜ +
4608 9¹⁄₁₆ 8¼ 8⅜ +
430 11¼ 10⅛ 10¼
4⅞

# A NOTE ON ASSET VALUATION
by George H. Troughton, CFA

## LEARNING OUTCOME

| The candidate should be able to explain how the classic works on asset valuation by Graham and Dodd and John Burr Williams are reflected in modern techniques of equity valuation. | Mastery ☐ |
| --- | --- |

In the 1940s, Benjamin Graham, often called the dean of security analysis, began championing the idea of a professional rating for security analysts. In the premier issue of the *Analysts Journal* (now the *Financial Analysts Journal*) in January 1945, Graham summarized the issue as follows: "The crux of the question is whether security analysis as a calling has enough of the professional attribute to justify the requirement that its practitioners present to the public evidence of fitness for their work."[1] It took almost two decades to decide that question in the affirmative, but in June of 1963, some 300 security analysts sat for the examination that would earn them the designation of Chartered Financial Analyst.

In the first decade of the CFA Study Program, the primary valuation text for Level II candidates was the fourth edition of the (by then) classic *Security Analysis*, co-authored by Benjamin Graham and his Columbia Business School colleague David Dodd. That epic work stressed a philosophy of investing centered on the concept of "intrinsic value."

In their early readings, Graham and Dodd discussed the common elements of analysis that applied to various asset classes. The following discussions present some of Graham and Dodd's philosophy to today's candidate. In their view, distinguishing investment from speculation is essential:

> . . . investment is grounded on the past whereas speculation looks primarily to the future. But this statement is far from complete. Both investment and speculation

---

[1] Nancy Regan, *The Institute of Chartered Financial Analysts: A Twenty-Five Year History* (Charlottesville, VA: The Institute of Chartered Financial Analysts, 1987), p. 5.

must meet the test of the future; they are subject to its vicissitudes and are judged by its verdict. But what we have said about the analyst and the future applies equally well to the concept of investment. For investment, the future is something to be guarded against rather than to be profited from. If the future brings improvement, so much the better; but investment as such cannot be founded in any important degree upon the expectation of improvement. Speculation, on the other hand, may always properly—and often soundly—derive its basis and its justification from prospective developments that differ from past performance.[2]

Graham and Dodd stipulated that investing, as opposed to speculating, requires the purchase of leading issues, such as growth stocks, at prices within a range of their intrinsic value or the purchase of secondary issues, such as cyclical stocks and medium quality bonds, at bargain prices. Intrinsic value is to be determined independently of market price. The most important factor in determining a security's intrinsic value is a forecast of "earning power."

An additional criterion that distinguished investment from speculation was that the investment asset's earning power should provide a margin of safety. When analyzing bonds and preferred stock, the analyst was to determine whether the securities had a sufficient earning power in excess of interest and preferred stock dividend requirements. When analyzing common stocks, the analyst was to forecast earning power and multiply that prediction by an appropriate capitalization factor. Earning power was the *unifying* factor in determining the attractiveness of all securities from the highest-grade bond down to the secondary common stocks that were considered investment opportunities because their prices were well below indicated minimum intrinsic values. In investing, diversification was counted on to offset the recognized risk of individual securities.

Graham and Dodd applied their philosophy to the leading asset classes at that time—common stocks, preferred stocks, high-grade fixed-income securities, senior securities of questionable quality, and warrants. In the decades that followed the publication of the last revision of Graham and Dodd's *Security Analysis* in 1962, asset classes expanded rapidly and the Level II CFA curriculum changed to reflect a wide array of assets. The asset valuation curriculum now includes readings from several sources rather than one primary text. Equity analysis, which traditionally centered on common stocks, now includes such securities as real estate, venture capital, and closely held securities. In addition, whereas the analysis of fixed-income securities once centered on credit analysis, much of the fixed-income curriculum now focuses on structured securities such as asset-backed securities. Derivative securities—options, futures, forwards, and swaps—are used for both speculation and to modify the risk and return characteristics of both debt and equity securities.

In the twenty-first century, candidates naturally tend to regard the investment valuation process as segmented, with peculiar terminology and techniques associated with particular assets. In the study sessions that follow, the candidate should realize that certain general principles underlie the valuation process regardless of asset class. The readings in corporate finance, for example, take an "inside the company" look at corporate financial performance, with emphasis on capital budgeting, leverage, cost of capital, dividend policy, and mergers and restructurings. The Porter and Hooke readings focus on industry and company factors. All of these methodologies are related to Graham and Dodd's estimate of earning power.

---

[2] Benjamin Graham, David L. Dodd, and Sidney Cottle, *Security Analysis*, 4th edition (New York McGraw-Hill, 1962), p. 52.

The Fabozzi fixed income valuation readings supplement Graham and Dodd's emphasis on credit analysis with a valuation framework that includes term structure, interest rate volatility, and embedded options.

The Stowe, Robinson, Pinto, and McLeavey readings on equity valuation and the Fabozzi readings on fixed income valuation reinforce Graham and Dodd's philosophy by emphasizing the common elements in determining the value of various asset classes. These readings emphasize that valuation models are universal, not country specific, and as such they are also applicable to markets outside the United States. Although Stowe, et al. sometimes use different terminology (such as free cash flow to firm and free cash flow to equity) in the valuation process, their methodology is consistent with Graham and Dodd's approach of determining whether earning power is sufficient to provide a margin of safety. In their reading on price multiples, Stowe et al. revive Graham and Dodd's justifiable multiple approach.

Another work, John Burr Williams' *The Theory of Investment Value,*[3] used a financial technique called discounting that was incorporated in the CFA Program within its first decade. Williams proposed that a share of common stock had an intrinsic value that could be estimated by calculating the present value of all future dividends per share. Candidates will find that Stowe et al. refine the discounted cash flow technique.

Taken together, Graham and Dodd, and John Burr Williams provided the core of the equity valuation study sessions in the early CFA Candidate Program. This work, sometimes called "blocking and tackling" is continued and updated in the readings currently assigned in the Program.

To some extent, then, as the CFA candidate curriculum approaches its sixth decade, things have come full circle.

---

[3] John Burr Williams, *The Theory of Investment Value* (Cambridge: Harvard University Press, c1938).

$4^{5}/_{8}$  $4^{...}$

$5^{1}/_{2}$  $-$  $^{...}/_{8}$

$5^{1}/_{2}$  $5^{1}/_{2}$  $-$  $^{1}/_{16}$

$20^{5}/_{8}$  $21^{3}/_{16}$  $+$  $^{7}/_{8}$

$17^{3}/_{8}$  $18^{1}/_{8}$  $+$

$18^{1}/_{2}$  $6^{1}/_{2}$  $-$  $^{1}/_{2}$

$7^{1}/_{4}$  $6^{1}/_{2}$  $6^{1}/_{2}$  $-$  $^{1}/_{8}$

$15/_{16}$  $3^{1}/_{32}$  $-$

$1$  $^{9}/_{16}$

$9/_{16}$

$^{15}/_{32}$  $7^{13}/_{16}$  $7^{15}/_{16}$

$7^{15}/_{16}$  $7^{13}/_{16}$  $7^{15}/_{16}$

$2^{5}/_{8}$  $2^{11}/_{32}$  $2^{1}/_{2}$  $+$

$2^{3}/_{4}$  $2^{1}/_{4}$  $2^{1}/_{4}$

$12^{1}/_{16}$  $11^{3}/_{8}$  $11^{3}/_{4}$  $+$

$6^{1}/_{5}$  $12^{1}/_{16}$  $11^{3}/_{8}$  $11^{3}/_{4}$  $+$

$87$  $33^{3}/_{4}$  $33$  $33^{1}/_{8}$  $-$

$602$  $25^{5}/_{8}$  $24^{9}/_{16}$  $25^{3}/_{8}$  $+$

$833$  $12$  $11^{5}/_{8}$  $11^{7}/_{8}$  $+$

$16$  $10^{1}/_{2}$  $10^{1}/_{2}$  $10^{1}/_{2}$  $-$

$78$  $15^{7}/_{8}$  $15^{13}/_{16}$  $15^{7}/_{8}$  $-$

$9^{1}/_{16}$  $8^{1}/_{4}$  $8^{1}/_{8}$  $+$

$4808$  $9^{1}/_{16}$  $8^{1}/_{4}$

$430$  $11^{1}/_{4}$  $10^{1}/_{8}$

$4^{7}/_{8}$

# THE EQUITY VALUATION PROCESS

by John D. Stowe, CFA, Thomas R. Robinson, CFA, Jerald E. Pinto, CFA, and Dennis W. McLeavey, CFA

## LEARNING OUTCOMES

| The candidate should be able to: | Mastery |
|---|:---:|
| **a.** define valuation and discuss the uses of valuation models; | ☐ |
| **b.** contrast quantitative and qualitative factors in valuation; | ☐ |
| **c.** discuss the importance of quality of inputs in valuation; | ☐ |
| **d.** discuss the importance of the interpretation of footnotes to accounting statements and other disclosures; | ☐ |
| **e.** calculate alpha; | ☐ |
| **f.** contrast the going-concern and non-going-concern assumptions in valuation; | ☐ |
| **g.** contrast absolute valuation models to relative valuation models; | ☐ |
| **h.** discuss the role of ownership perspective in valuation. | ☐ |

# INTRODUCTION                    1

Every day thousands of participants in the investment profession—investors, portfolio managers, regulators, researchers—face a common and often perplexing question: What is the value of a particular asset? The answers to this question usually determine success or failure in achieving investment objectives. For one group of those participants—equity analysts—the question and its potential answers are particularly critical, for determining the value of an ownership stake is at the heart of their professional activities and decisions. To determine value received for money paid, to determine relative value—the prospective differences in risk-adjusted return offered by different stocks at current market prices—the

Jan R. Squires, CFA, provided invaluable comments and suggestions for this reading.

*Analysis of Equity Investments: Valuation*, by John D. Stowe, CFA, Thomas R. Robinson, CFA, Jerald E. Pinto, CFA, and Dennis W. McLeavey, CFA. Copyright © 2002 by AIMR. Reprinted with permission.

analyst must engage in valuation. **Valuation** is the estimation of an asset's value based either on variables perceived to be related to future investment returns or on comparisons with similar assets. Skill in valuation is one very important element of success in investing.

Benjamin Graham and David L. Dodd's *Security Analysis* (1934) represented the first major attempt to organize knowledge in this area for the investment profession. Its first sentence reads: "This book is intended for all those who have a serious interest in security values." *Analysis of Equity Investments: Valuation* addresses candidates in the Chartered Financial Analyst (CFA®) Program of the Association for Investment Management and Research (AIMR); all readers, however, with a "serious interest in security values" should find the book useful. Drawing on knowledge of current professional practice as well as both academic and investment industry research in finance and accounting, this book presents the major concepts and tools that analysts use in conducting valuations and communicating the results of their analysis to clients.

In this reading we address some basic questions: "What is equity valuation?" "Who performs equity valuation?" "What is the importance of industry knowledge?" and "How can the analyst effectively communicate his analysis?"

The reading is organized as follows: Section 2 surveys the scope of equity valuation within the overall context of the portfolio management process. In various places in this volume, we will discuss how to select an appropriate valuation approach given a security's characteristics. In Section 3, we address valuation concepts and models and examine the first three steps in the valuation process—understanding the company, forecasting company performance, and selecting the appropriate valuation model. Section 4 discusses the analyst's role and responsibilities in researching and recommending a security for purchase or sale. Section 5 discusses the content and format of an effective research report—the analyst's work in valuation is generally not complete until he communicates the results of his analysis—and highlights the analyst's responsibilities in preparing research reports. We close with a summary of the reading.

## 2  THE SCOPE OF EQUITY VALUATION

Investment analysts work in a wide variety of organizations and positions; as a result, they find themselves applying the tools of equity valuation to address a range of practical problems. In particular, analysts use valuation concepts and models to accomplish the following:

> ► *Selecting stocks.* Stock selection is the primary use of the tools presented in this book. Equity analysts must continually address the same question for every common stock[1] that is either a current or prospective portfolio

---

[1] In the United Kingdom, *ordinary share* is the term corresponding to *common stock* (for short, *share* or *stock*)—the ownership interest in a corporation that represents the residual claim on the corporation's assets and earnings.

holding, or for every stock that he or she is professionally assigned to analyze: Is this a security my clients should purchase, sell, or continue to own? Equity analysts attempt to identify securities as fairly valued, overvalued, or undervalued, relative to either their own market price or the prices of comparable securities.

▶ *Inferring (extracting) market expectations.* Market prices reflect the expectations of investors about the future prospects of companies. Analysts may ask, what expectations about a company's future performance are consistent with the current market price for that company's stock? This question may concern the analyst for several reasons:

   ▶ There are historical and economic reasons that certain values for earnings growth rates and other company fundamentals may or may not be reasonable. (**Fundamentals** are characteristics of a company related to profitability, financial strength, or risk.)

   ▶ The extracted expectation for a fundamental characteristic may be useful as a benchmark or comparison value of the same characteristic for another company.[2]

▶ *Evaluating corporate events.* Investment bankers, corporate analysts, and investment analysts use valuation tools to assess the impact of corporate events such as mergers, acquisitions, divestitures, spin-offs, **management buyouts (MBOs)**, and leveraged recapitalizations.[3] Each of these events may affect a company's future cash flows and so the value of equity. Furthermore, in mergers and acquisitions, the company's own common stock is often used as currency for the purchase; investors then want to know whether the stock is fairly valued.

▶ *Rendering fairness opinions.* The parties to a merger may be required to seek a fairness opinion on the terms of the merger from a third party such as an investment bank. Valuation is at the center of such opinions.

▶ *Evaluating business strategies and models.* Companies concerned with maximizing shareholder value must evaluate the impact of alternative strategies on share value.

▶ *Communicating with analysts and shareholders.* Valuation concepts facilitate communication and discussion among company management, shareholders, and analysts on a range of corporate issues affecting company value.

▶ *Appraising private businesses.* Although we focus on publicly traded companies, another important use of the tools we present is to value the common stock of private companies. The stock of private companies by definition does not trade publicly; consequently, we cannot compare an estimate of the stock's value with a market price. For this and other reasons, the valuation of private

---

[2] To extract or reverse-engineer a market expectation, the analyst must specify a model that relates market price to expectations about fundamentals, and calculate or assume values for all fundamentals except the one of interest. Then the analyst calculates the value of the remaining fundamental that calibrates the model value to market price (makes the model value equal market price)—this value is the extracted market expectation for the variable. Of course, the model that the analyst uses must be appropriate for the characteristics of the stock.

[3] A **merger** is the combination of two corporations. An **acquisition** is also a combination of two corporations, usually with the connotation that the combination is not one of equals. In a **divestiture**, a corporation sells some major component of its business. In a **spin-off**, the corporation separates off and separately capitalizes a component business, which is then transferred to the corporation's common stockholders. In an **MBO**, management repurchases all outstanding stock, usually using the proceeds of debt issuance; in a **leveraged recapitalization**, some stock remains in the hands of the public.

companies has special characteristics. The analyst encounters these challenges in evaluating initial public offerings (IPOs), for example.[4]

---

### EXAMPLE 1

**Inferring Market Expectations**

On 21 September 2000, Intel Corporation (Nasdaq NMS: INTC)[5] issued a press release containing information about its expected revenue growth for the third quarter of 2000. The announced growth fell short of the company's own prior prediction by 2 to 4 percentage points and short of analysts' projections by 3 to 7 percentage points. In response to the announcement, Intel's stock price fell nearly 30 percent during the following five days.

Was the information in Intel's announcement sufficient to explain a loss of value of that magnitude? Cornell (2001) examined this question using a valuation approach that models the value of a company's equity as the present value of expected future cash flows from operations minus the expenditures needed to maintain the company's growth. What future revenue growth rates were consistent with Intel's stock price of $61.50 just prior to the press release, and $43.31 only five days later?

Using a conservatively low discount rate, Cornell estimated that the price of $61.50 was consistent with a growth rate of 20 percent a year for the subsequent 10 years (and then 6 percent per year thereafter). The price of $43.31 was consistent with a decline of the 10-year growth rate to well under 15 percent per year. In the final year of the forecast horizon (2009), projected revenues with the lower growth rate would be $50 billion below the projected revenues based on the pre-announcement price. Because the press release did not obviously point to any changes in Intel's fundamental long-run business conditions (Intel attributed the quarterly revenue growth shortfall to a cyclical slowing of demand in Europe), Cornell's detailed analysis left him skeptical that the stock market's reaction could be explained in terms of fundamentals.

Was investors' reaction to the press release therefore irrational? That was one possible interpretation. Cornell also concluded, however, that Intel's stock was overvalued prior to the press release. For example, the 20 percent revenue growth rate consistent with the pre-announcement stock price was much higher than Intel's growth rate averaged over the previous five years when the company was much smaller. Cornell viewed the press release as "a kind of catalyst which caused movement toward a

---

[4] An **initial public offering** is the initial issuance of common stock registered for public trading by a formerly private corporation. Later in this reading, we mention one issue related to valuing private companies, marketability discounts.

[5] In this reading, the shares of real companies are identified by an abbreviation for the stock exchange or electronic marketplace where the shares of the company are traded, followed by a ticker symbol or formal acronym for the shares. For example, Nasdaq NMS stands for "Nasdaq National Market System," an electronic marketplace in the United States managed by the National Association of Securities Dealers, Inc., and INTC is the ticker symbol for Intel Corporation on the Nasdaq NMS. (Many stocks are traded on a number of exchanges worldwide, and some stocks may have more than one formal acronym; we usually state just one marketplace and one ticker symbol.) For fictional companies we do not give the marketplace, but we often give the stock an acronym by which we can refer to it.

more rational price, even though the release itself did not contain sufficient long-run valuation information to justify that movement."[6] Analysts can perform the same type of analysis as Cornell did. Exercises of this type are very useful for forming a judgment on the reasonableness of market prices. It is also noteworthy that Cornell found much lacking in the valuation discussions in the 28 contemporaneous analysts' reports on Intel that he examined. Although all reports made buy or sell recommendations, he characterized their discussions of fundamental value as "typically vague and nebulous."[7] To the extent Cornell's assessment was accurate, the reports would not meet the criteria for an effective research report that we present later in this reading.

## 2.1 Valuation and Portfolio Management

Although valuation can take place without reference to a portfolio, the analysis of equity investments is conducted within the context of managing a portfolio. We can better appreciate the scope of valuation when we recognize valuation as a part of the overall portfolio management process. An investor's most basic concern is generally not the characteristics of a single security but the risk and return prospects of his or her total investment position. How does valuation, focused on a single security, fit into this process?

From a portfolio perspective, the investment process has three steps: *planning*, *execution*, and *feedback* (which includes *evaluating* whether objectives have been achieved, and *monitoring and rebalancing* of positions). Valuation, including equity valuation, is most closely associated with the planning and execution steps.

▶ *Planning.* In the planning step, the investor identifies and specifies **investment objectives** (desired investment outcomes relating to both risk and return) and constraints (internal or external limitations on investment actions). An important part of planning is the concrete elaboration of an **investment strategy**, or approach to investment analysis and security selection, with the goal of organizing and clarifying investment decisions.

Not all investment strategies involve making valuation judgments about individual securities. For example, in indexing strategies, the investor seeks only to replicate the returns of an externally specified index—such as the Financial Times Stock Exchange (FTSE) Eurotop 300, which is an index of Europe's 300 largest companies. Such an investor could simply buy and hold those 300 stocks in index proportions, without the need to analyze individual stocks.

Valuation, however, is relevant, and critical, to active investment strategies. To understand active management, it is useful to introduce the concept of a **benchmark**—the comparison portfolio used to evaluate performance—which for an index manager is the index itself. **Active investment managers** hold portfolios that differ from the benchmark in an attempt to produce superior risk-adjusted returns. Securities held in different-from-benchmark weights reflect

---

[6] Cornell (2001, p. 134).

[7] Cornell (2001, p. 131).

expectations that differ from consensus expectations (**differential expectations**). The manager must also translate expectations into value estimates, so that securities can be ranked from relatively most attractive to relatively least attractive. This step requires valuation models. In the planning phase, the active investor may specify quite narrowly the kinds of active strategies to be used and also specify in detail valuation models and/or criteria.

▶ *Execution.* In the execution step, the manager integrates investment strategies with expectations to select a portfolio (the **portfolio selection/composition problem**), and portfolio decisions are implemented by trading desks (the **portfolio implementation problem**).

# 3    VALUATION CONCEPTS AND MODELS

In Section 3, we turn our attention to the valuation process. This process includes understanding the company to be valued, forecasting the company's performance, and selecting the appropriate valuation model for a given valuation task.

## 3.1 The Valuation Process

We have seen that the valuation of a particular company is a task within the context of the portfolio management process. Each individual valuation that an analyst undertakes can be viewed as a process with the following five steps:

1. *Understanding the business.* This involves evaluating industry prospects, competitive position, and corporate strategies. Analysts use this information together with financial statement analysis to forecast performance.
2. *Forecasting company performance.* Forecasts of sales, earnings, and financial position (pro forma analysis) are the immediate inputs to estimating value.
3. *Selecting the appropriate valuation model.*
4. *Converting forecasts to a valuation.*
5. *Making the investment decision (recommendation).*

The fourth and fifth steps are addressed in detail in succeeding readings of this volume. Here we focus on the first three steps. Because common stock represents the ownership interest in a company, analysts must carefully research the company before making a recommendation about the company's stock.

An in-depth understanding of the business and an ability to forecast the performance of a company help determine the quality of an analyst's valuation efforts.

## 3.2 Understanding the Business

Understanding a company's economic and industry context and management's strategic responses are the first tasks in understanding that company. Because similar economic and technological factors typically affect all companies in an industry, industry knowledge helps analysts understand the basic characteristics of the markets served by a company and the economics of the company. An airline industry analyst will know that jet fuel costs are the second biggest expense for airlines behind labor expenses, and that in many markets airlines have difficulty passing through higher fuel prices by raising ticket prices. Using this knowledge, the analyst may inquire about the degree to which different airlines hedge the commodity price risk inherent in jet fuel costs. With such information in hand, the analyst is better able to evaluate risk and forecast future cash flows. Hooke (1998) discussed a broad framework for industry analysis.

An analyst conducting an industry analysis must also judge management's strategic choices to better understand a company's prospects for success in competition with other companies in the industry or industries in which that company operates. Porter (1998) may lead analysts to focus on the following questions:

1. *How attractive are the industries in which the company operates, in terms of offering prospects for sustained profitability?* Inherent industry profitability is one important factor in determining a company's profitability. Analysts should try to understand **industry structure**—the industry's underlying economic and technical characteristics—and the trends affecting that structure. Analysts must also stay current on facts and news concerning all the industries in which the company operates, including the following:

   ▶ industry size and growth over time;

   ▶ recent developments (management, technological, financial) in the industry;

   ▶ overall supply and demand balance;

   ▶ subsector strength/softness in the demand–supply balance; and

   ▶ qualitative factors, including the legal and regulatory environment.

2. *What is the company's relative competitive position within its industry?* Among factors to consider are the level and trend of the company's market share in the markets in which it operates.

3. *What is the company's competitive strategy?* Three general corporate strategies for achieving above-average performance are:

   ▶ **cost leadership**—being the lowest cost producer while offering products comparable to those of other companies, so that products can be priced at or near the industry average;

   ▶ **differentiation**—offering unique products or services along some dimensions that are widely valued by buyers so that the company can command premium prices; and

   ▶ **focus**—seeking a competitive advantage within a target segment or segments of the industry, based on either cost leadership (cost focus) or differentiation (differentiation focus).

   The analyst can assess whether a company's apparent strategy is logical or faulty only in the context of thorough knowledge of the company's industry or industries.

4. *How well is the company executing its strategy?* Competitive success requires not only appropriate strategic choices, but also competent execution.

One perspective on the above issues often comes from the companies themselves in regulatory filings, which analysts can compare with their own independent research.[8]

---

[8] For example, companies filing Form 10-Ks with the U.S. Securities and Exchange Commission identify legal and regulatory issues and competitive factors and risks.

## EXAMPLE 2

### Competitive Analysis

Veritas DGC Inc. (NYSE: VTS) is a provider of seismic data—two- or three-dimensional views of the earth's subsurface—and related geophysical services to the natural gas and crude oil (petroleum) industry. Oil and gas drillers purchase such information to increase drilling success rates and so lower overall exploration costs.

According to Standard & Poor's Corporation, VTS's peer group is "Oil & Gas-Geophysical Data Technologies" in Oil & Gas Equipment and Services. Competitors include WesternGeco, a joint venture of Schlumberger Ltd. (NYSE: SLB) and Baker Hughes Inc. (NYSE: BHI); Petroleum Geo-Services (NYSE: PGO) which in late 2001 announced plans to merge with VTS; Dawson Geophysical (Nasdaq NMS: DWSN); Compagnie Générale de Géophysique (NYSE: GGY); and Seitel, Inc. (NYSE: SEI).

1. Discuss the economic factors that may affect demand for the services provided by VTS and its competitors, and explain a logical framework for analyzing and forecasting revenue for these companies.

2. Explain how comparing the level and trend in profit margin (net income/sales) and revenue per employee for the above companies may help in evaluating whether one of these companies is the cost leader in the peer group.

**Solution to 1:** Because VTS provides services related to oil and gas exploration, the level of exploration activities by oil and gas producers is probably the major factor determining the demand for VTS's services. In turn, the prices of natural gas and crude oil are critical in determining the level of exploration activities. Therefore, among other economic factors, an analyst should research those relating to supply and demand for natural gas and crude oil.

- ▶ Supply factors in natural gas. Factors include natural gas inventory levels. Energy analysts should be familiar with sources for researching this information, such as the American Gas Association (AGA) for gas inventory levels in the United States.

- ▶ Demand factors in natural gas. These factors include household and commercial use of natural gas and the amount of new power generation equipment being fired by natural gas.

- ▶ Supply factors in crude oil. Factors include capacity constraints and production levels in OPEC and other oil-producing countries. Analysts should be familiar with sources such as the American Petroleum Institute for researching these factors.

- ▶ Demand factors in crude oil. Factors include household and commercial use of oil and the amount of new power generation equipment using oil products as its primary fuel.

For both crude oil and natural gas, projected economic growth rates could be examined as a demand factor and depletion rates as a supply side factor.

> **Solution to 2:** Profit margin reflects cost structure; in interpreting profit margin, however, analysts should evaluate any differences in companies' abilities to affect profit margin through power over price. A successfully executed cost leadership strategy will lower costs and raise profit margins. All else equal, we would also expect a cost leader to have relatively high sales per employee, reflecting efficient use of human resources.

## 3.3 Forecasting Company Performance

The second step in the valuation process—forecasting company performance—can be viewed from two perspectives: the economic environment in which the company operates and the company's own financial characteristics.

### 3.3.1 Economic Forecasting

Industry analysis and competitive analysis take place within the larger context of macroeconomic analysis. As an approach to forecasting, moving from the international and national macroeconomic forecasts to industry forecasts and then to individual company and asset forecasts is known as a **top-down forecasting approach**. For example, Benninga and Sarig (1997) illustrated how, starting with forecasts of the level of macroeconomic activity, an analyst might project overall industry sales and the market share of a company within the industry to arrive at revenue forecasts for the company.[9] It is also possible to aggregate individual company forecasts of analysts (possibly arrived at using various methodologies) into industry forecasts, and finally into macroeconomic forecasts; doing so is called a **bottom-up forecasting approach**. Figure 1 illustrates the two approaches.

A bottom-up forecasting approach is subject to the problem of inconsistent assumptions. For example, different analysts may assume different inflationary environments, and this may compromise the comparability of resulting individual stock valuations. In a top-down approach, an organization can ensure that all analysts use the same inflation assumption.[10]

### 3.3.2 Financial Forecasting

The analyst integrates the analysis of industry prospects and competitive and corporate strategy with financial statement analysis to formulate specific numerical forecasts of such items as sales and earnings. Techniques of financial forecasting are presented in detail in later readings of this book, and also in White, Sondhi,

---

[9] Benninga and Sarig (1997, Chapter 5). See also Chapter 19 of Reilly and Brown (2000).

[10] A related but distinct concept is **top-down investing** versus **bottom-up investing** as one broad description of types of active investment styles. For example, a top-down investor, based on a forecast that an economy is about to transition out of an economic recession, might increase exposure to shares in the Basic Materials sector, because profits in that economic sector are typically sensitive to changes in macroeconomic growth rates; at the same time exposure to recession-resistant sectors such as Consumer Non-Durables might be reduced. (The preceding would describe a **sector rotation strategy**, an investment strategy that overweights economic sectors that are anticipated to outperform or lead the overall market.) In contrast, an investor following a bottom-up approach might decide that a security is undervalued based on some valuation indicator, for example, without making an explicit judgment on the overall economy or the relative value of different sectors. Note that some forecasting and investing approaches mix top-down and bottom-up elements.

**FIGURE 1    The Top-Down and Bottom-Up Approaches
to Equity Analysis**

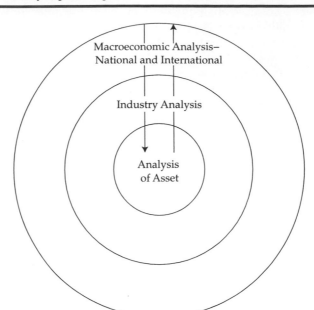

and Fried (1998), Higgins (2001), Reilly and Brown (2000), and Benninga and Sarig (1997), which are useful complementary readings.

Analysts may consider qualitative as well as quantitative factors in financial forecasting and valuation. For example, some analysts may modify their overall valuation judgments and recommendations based on qualitative factors. These may include the analyst's viewpoint on the business acumen and integrity of management as well as the transparency and quality of a company's accounting practices. Although analysts may attempt to reflect the expected direction of such considerations in their financial forecasts or to otherwise quantify such factors, no formal valuation expression can fully capture these factors.[11] We caution that qualitative adjustments to valuation opinions are necessarily subjective.

**3.3.2.1  Using Accounting Information**    In working with quantitative forecasting tools, the analyst must attempt to use the most appropriate and reliable information available. A key source of such information is a company's accounting information and financial disclosures. Equity analysts study financial results and disclosures for information bearing on the company's current and future ability to create economic value. Reports to shareholders can differ substantially, however, with respect to the *accuracy* of reported accounting results as reflections of economic performance and the *detail* in which results are disclosed.

The investigation of issues relating to accuracy is often broadly referred to as **quality of earnings analysis**. The term broadly includes the scrutiny of *all* financial statements, including the balance sheet; that is, quality of earnings analysis includes scrutiny of balance sheet management as well as earnings management. With respect to detail, more detail is almost always superior to less, particularly in

---

[11] For example, management will react to future opportunities and risks that the analyst cannot anticipate at the time of the valuation.

those areas of accounting practice (e.g., pensions, mergers and acquisitions, currency translation) where cursory examination seldom proves useful.

Equity analysts will generally benefit by developing their ability to assess a company's quality of earnings. An analyst who can skillfully analyze a company's financial statements can more accurately value a security than peer analysts with only a superficial understanding of the numbers. Also, extensive research suggests that analysts can generally expect stock prices to reflect quality of earnings considerations.[12] Skill in quality of earnings analysis, however, comes only with a thorough knowledge of financial statement analysis as well as practical experience.[13] Careful scrutiny and interpretation of footnotes to accounting statements, and of all other relevant disclosures, is essential to a quality of earnings analysis. Examples of only a few of the many available indicators of possible problems with a company's quality of earnings are provided in Table 1.

Various examples throughout this book will touch on analyst adjustments to reported financial results. Both the importance of accounting practices in influencing reported financial results and the judgment that analysts need to exercise in using those results in any valuation model are illustrated in Example 3.

## EXAMPLE 3

### Quality of Earnings Warning Signs

Livent, Inc., was a publicly traded theatrical production company that staged a number of smash hits such as Tony-award winning productions of *Showboat* and *Fosse*. Livent capitalized preproduction costs including expenses for pre-opening advertising, publicity and promotion, set construction, props, costumes, and salaries and fees paid to the cast and crew musicians during rehearsals. The company then amortized these capitalized costs over the expected life of the theatrical production based on anticipated revenues.

1. State the effect of Livent's accounting for preproduction costs on its reported earnings per share.

In the reading on free cash flow valuation and elsewhere we will encounter the popular concept of EBITDA: earnings before interest, taxes, depreciation, and amortization (interest, taxes, depreciation, and amortization are added back to earnings). Some analysts use ratios such as EBITDA/interest expense and debt/EBITDA to assess one aspect of a company's financial strength, debt-paying ability.

---

[12] The literature is vast, but see in particular Fairfield and Whisenant (2000) and the references therein. Studies have also documented the *Briloff effect* showing that when a company's accounting games are exposed in *Barron's*, its stock price declines rapidly (Abraham Briloff is an accounting professor at Baruch College, City University of New York, who has explored the subject extensively). Other literature shows that bond market participants see through attempts at smoothing earnings and in some cases (the institutional bond market) penalize it (see Robinson and Grant 1997 and Robinson, Grant, Kauer, and Woodlock 1998).

[13] Sources for our discussion on quality of earnings analysis and accounting risk factors include Hawkins (1998), Levitt (1998), Schilit (2002), and White, Sondhi, and Fried (1998), as well as American Institute of Certified Public Accountants *Consideration of Fraud in a Financial Statement Audit* (28 February 2002) and International Federation of Accountants, International Standards on Auditing 240, *The Auditor's Responsibility to Consider Fraud and Error in an Audit of Financial Statements* (March 2001).

**TABLE 1    Selected Quality of Earnings Indicators**

| Category | Observation | Potential Interpretation |
| --- | --- | --- |
| Revenues and gains | Recognizing revenue early, for example:<br>▸ bill-and-hold sales<br>▸ lessor use of capital lease classification<br>▸ recording sales of equipment or software prior to installation and acceptance by customer | Acceleration in the recognition of revenue boosts reported income masking a decline in operating performance. |
| | Classification of nonoperating income or gains as part of operations. | Income or gains may be nonrecurring and may not relate to true operating performance, in fact perhaps masking a decline in operating performance. |
| Expenses and losses | Deferral of expenses by capitalizing expenditures as an asset. For example:<br>▸ customer acquisition costs<br>▸ product development costs | May boost current income at the expense of future income. May mask problems with underlying business performance. |
| | Use of nonconservative estimates and assumptions, such as:<br>▸ long depreciable lives<br>▸ long periods of amortization<br>▸ high pension discount rate<br>▸ low assumed rate of compensation growth for pensions<br>▸ high expected return on assets for pension | Nonconservative estimates may indicate actions taken to boost current reported income. Changes in assumptions may indicate an attempt to mask problems with underlying performance in the current period. |
| Balance sheet issues (may also affect earnings) | Use of special purpose entities (SPEs).[14] | Assets and/or liabilities may not be properly reflected on the balance sheet. Income may also be overstated by sales to the special purpose entity or a decline in the value of assets transferred to the SPE. |

---

[14] A **special purpose entity** is a nonoperating entity created to carry out a specified purpose, such as leasing assets or securitizing receivables. The use of SPEs is frequently related to off-balance-sheet financing (financing that does not currently appear on the balance sheet).

**2.** If an analyst calculated EBITDA/interest expense and debt/EBITDA based on Livent's accounting for preproduction costs without adjustment, how might the analyst be misled in assessing Livent's financial strength?

**Solution to 1:** Livent's accounting for preproduction costs immediately increased reported earnings per share because it deferred expenses. Instead of immediately expensing costs. Livent reported them on its balance sheet as an asset. The warning signal—the deferral of expenses—indicates very aggressive accounting; preproduction costs should have been expensed immediately because of the tremendous uncertainty about revenues from theatrical productions. There was no assurance that there would be revenues against which expenses could be matched.

**Solution to 2:** Livent did not deduct preproduction costs from earnings as expenses. If the amortization of capitalized preproduction costs were then added back to earnings, the EBITDA/interest and debt/EBITDA ratios would not reflect in any way the cash outflows associated with items such as paying pre-opening salaries; but cash outflows reduce funds available to meet debt obligations. The analyst who mechanically added back amortization of preproduction costs to calculate EBITDA would be misled into overestimating Livent's financial strength. Based on a closer look at the company's accounting, we would properly not add back amortization of preproduction expenses in computing EBITDA. If preproduction expenses are not added back, a very different picture of Livent's financial health would emerge. In 1996, Livent's reported debt/EBITDA ratio was 1.7, but the ratio without adding back amortization for preproduction costs was 5.5. In 1997, debt/EBITDA was 3.7 based on positive EBITDA of $58.3 million, but EBITDA without the add-back was *negative* $52.6 million.[15] In November 1998, Livent declared bankruptcy and it is now defunct.

Analysts recognize a variety of risk factors that may signal possible future negative surprises. A working selection of these risk factors would include the following (AICPA, 2002):

▶ Poor quality of accounting disclosures, such as segment information, acquisitions, accounting policies and assumptions, and a lack of discussion of negative factors.

▶ Existence of related-party transactions.

▶ Existence of excessive officer, employee, or director loans.

▶ High management or director turnover.

▶ Excessive pressure on company personnel to make revenue or earnings targets, particularly when combined with a dominant, aggressive management team or individual.

▶ Material non-audit services performed by audit firm.

---

[15] Moody's Investor Services (2000). The discussion of this example is indebted to that report.

▶ Reported (via regulatory filings) disputes with and/or changes in auditors.

▶ Management and or directors' compensation tied to profitability or stock price (through ownership or compensation plans). Although such arrangements are desirable, they can indicate a risk of aggressive reporting as well.

▶ Economic, industry, or company-specific pressures on profitability, such as loss of market share or declining margins.

▶ Management pressure to meet debt covenants or earnings expectations.

▶ A history of securities law violations, reporting violations, or persistent late filings.

## EXAMPLE 4

### Benjamin Graham on Accounting

In a manuscript from 1936 (reprinted in Ellis 1991), Benjamin Graham pictures the chair of a major corporation outlining how his company will return to profitability in the middle of the Great Depression of the 20th century:

> "Contrary to expectations, no changes will be made in the company's manufacturing or selling policies. Instead, the book-keeping system is to be entirely revamped. By adopting and further improving a number of modern accounting and financial devices the corporation's earning power will be amazingly transformed."

> The top item on the chair's list gives a flavor of the progress that will be made: "Accordingly, the Board has decided to extend the write-down policy initiated in the 1935 report, and to mark down the Fixed Assets from $1,338,552,858.96 to a round *Minus* $1,000,000,000 . . . As the plant wears out, the liability becomes correspondingly reduced. Hence, instead of the present depreciation charge of some $47,000,000 yearly there will be an annual *appreciation credit* of 5 percent, or $50,000,000. This will increase earnings by no less than $97,000,000 per annum." Summing up, the chair shares the foresight of the Board: ". . . [T]he Board is not unmindful of the possibility that some of our competitors may seek to offset our new advantages by adopting similar accounting improvements . . . Should necessity arise, moreover, we believe we shall be able to maintain our deserved superiority by introducing still more advanced bookkeeping methods, which are even now under development in our Experimental Accounting Laboratory."

## 3.4 Selecting the Appropriate Valuation Model

Skill in selecting, applying, and interpreting valuation models is important in investment analysis and valuation.[16] In this section, we discuss the third step in the valuation process—selecting the appropriate model for the valuation task at hand. First we address alternative value perspectives, then we present absolute and relative valuation models, and we close with a discussion of issues in model selection.

---

[16] The remaining readings of this volume will discuss these issues in detail for the valuation approaches presented.

## 3.4.1 Value Perspectives

Several value perspectives serve as the foundation for the variety of valuation models available to the equity analyst; intrinsic value is the necessary starting point, but other concepts of value—going-concern value, liquidation value, and fair value—are also important.

**3.4.1.1 Intrinsic Value**    The quality of the analyst's forecasts, in particular the expectational inputs used in valuation models, is a key element in determining investment success. *For an active strategy to be consistently successful, the manager's expectations must differ from consensus expectations and be, on average, correct as well.* Only when accurate forecasts are combined with an appropriate valuation model will the analyst obtain a useful estimate of intrinsic value. The **intrinsic value** of an asset is the value of the asset given a hypothetically complete understanding of the asset's investment characteristics.

Valuation is an inherent part of the active manager's attempt to produce positive excess risk-adjusted return. An excess risk-adjusted return is also called an **abnormal return** or **alpha**. The manager hopes to capture a positive alpha as a result of his efforts to estimate intrinsic value. Any departure of market price from the manager's estimate of intrinsic value is a perceived **mispricing** (calculated as the difference between the estimated intrinsic value and the market price of an asset). Any perceived mispricing becomes part of the manager's expected holding-period return estimate, which is the manager's forecast of the total return on the asset for some holding period.[17] An expected holding-period return is the sum of expected capital appreciation and investment income, both stated as a proportion of purchase price. Naturally, expected capital appreciation incorporates the investor's perspective on the convergence of market price to intrinsic value. In a forward-looking (*ex ante*) sense, an asset's alpha is the manager's expected holding-period return minus the fair (or equilibrium) return on the asset given its risk, using some model relating an asset's average returns to its risk characteristics. The fair return on an asset given its risk is also known as its required rate of return.

$$\textit{Ex ante} \text{ alpha} = \textbf{Expected holding-period return} - \text{Required return} \tag{34-1}$$

In a backward-looking (*ex post*) sense, alpha is actual return minus the contemporaneous required return. Contemporaneous required return is what investments of similar risk actually earned during the same period.

$$\textit{Ex post} \text{ alpha} = \text{Actual holding-period return} - \text{Contemporaneous required return} \tag{34-2}$$

To illustrate these concepts, assume that an investor's expected holding-period return for a stock for the next 12 months is 12 percent, and the stock's required return, given its risk, is 10 percent. The *ex ante* alpha is $12 - 10 = 2$ percent. Assume that a year passes, and the stock has a return of $-5$ percent. The *ex post* alpha depends on the contemporaneous required return. If the contemporaneous required return was $-8$ percent, the stock would have an *ex post* alpha of $-5 - (-8) = 3$ percent.

---

[17] For brevity, we sometimes use *return* for *rate of return* in this discussion.

## EXAMPLE 5

### Intrinsic Value and Return Concepts (1)

As an automotive industry analyst, you are researching Fiat S.p.A. (Milan Stock Exchange: FIA.MI), a leading Italian-headquartered automobile manufacturer. You have assembled the following information and assumptions as of late March 2002:

- ▶ The current share price of FIA.MI is €15.895 (based on the closing price on 22 March 2002).
- ▶ Your estimate of FIA.MI's intrinsic value is €17.26.
- ▶ Over the course of one year, you expect the mispricing of FIA.MI shares, equal to €17.26 − €15.895 = €1.365, to be fully corrected. In addition to the correction of mispricing, you forecast additional price appreciation of €1.22 per share over the course of the year as well as the payment of a cash dividend of €0.61.
- ▶ You estimate that the required rate of return on FIA.MI shares is 10.6 percent a year.

Using the above information:

1. State whether FIA.MI shares are overvalued, fairly valued, or undervalued, based on your forecasts.
2. Calculate the expected one-year holding-period return on FIA.MI stock.
3. Determine the expected alpha for FIA.MI stock.

**Solution to 1:** Because FIA.MI's intrinsic value of €17.26 is greater than its current market price €15.895, FIA.MI appears to be undervalued, based on your forecasts.

**Solution to 2:** The expected holding-period return is the sum of expected price appreciation plus the expected return from dividends. To calculate the expected price appreciation, we add €1.365 (from the convergence of price to intrinsic value) plus €1.22 (from the additional forecasted price appreciation) and obtain €2.585. The expected dividend is €0.61. The sum of expected price appreciation plus expected dividends is €3.195. The expected holding-period return for one year is €3.195/€15.895 = 0.201 or 20.1 percent.

**Solution to 3:** The expected holding-period return of 20.1 percent minus the required rate of return of 10.6 percent gives a positive expected excess risk-adjusted return or positive expected alpha of 9.5 percent.

The equity analyst recognizes that, no matter how hard he or she works to identify mispriced securities, uncertainty is associated with realizing a positive expected alpha, however accurate the forecasts and whatever the valuation approach used. Even if the analyst is highly confident about the accuracy of forecasts and risk adjustments, there is no means of ensuring the ability to capture the benefits of any perceived mispricing without risk. Convergence of the market price to perceived intrinsic value may not happen within the investor's investment horizon, if at all.[18] One uncertainty in applying any valuation methodology concerns whether the analyst has accounted for all sources of risk reflected in an asset's price. Because competing equity risk models will always exist, there is no possible final resolution to this dilemma. Differences in valuation judgments resulting from applying alternative models of equity risk are illustrated in Example 6.

### EXAMPLE 6

**Intrinsic Value and Return Concepts (2)**

As an active investor, you have developed forecasts of returns for three securities and translated those forecasts into expected rate of return estimates. You have also estimated the securities' required rates of return using two models that we will discuss in the reading on discounted dividend valuation: the capital asset pricing model (CAPM) and the Fama–French (FF) three-factor model. As a next step, you intend to rank the securities by alpha.

#### TABLE 2    Rates of Return

|  | Expected Rate of Return | CAPM Required Rate of Return | FF Required Rate of Return |
|---|---|---|---|
| Security 1 | 0.15 | 0.10 | 0.12 |
| Security 2 | 0.07 | 0.12 | 0.07 |
| Security 3 | 0.09 | 0.10 | 0.10 |

Based on the information in Table 2:

1. Calculate the *ex ante* alphas of each security.
2. Rank the securities by relative attractiveness using the CAPM, and state whether each security is overvalued, fairly valued, or undervalued.

**Solution to 1:** The analyst can develop two sets of estimates of alpha, because the securities have different required rates of return depending on whether risk is modeled using the CAPM or FF models.

---

[18] Related to this uncertainty is the concept of a catalyst. Besides evidence of mispricing, some active investors look for the presence of a particular market or corporate event (**catalyst**) that will cause the marketplace to re-evaluate a company's prospects.

### CAPM

Alpha of Security 1 = 0.15 − 0.10 = 0.05 or 5 percent
Alpha of Security 2 = 0.07 − 0.12 = −0.05 or −5 percent
Alpha of Security 3 = 0.09 − 0.10 = −0.01 or −1 percent

### Fama–French

Alpha of Security 1 = 0.15 − 0.12 = 0.03 or 3 percent
Alpha of Security 2 = 0.07 − 0.07 = 0.00 or 0 percent
Alpha of Security 3 = 0.09 − 0.10 = −0.01 or −1 percent

**Solution to 2:** With an alpha of 5 percent, using the CAPM, Security 1 is the only security with a positive expected risk-adjusted return and is relatively most attractive. Security 3 ranks second with an alpha of −1 percent, and Security 2 is last with an alpha of −5 percent. Both Security 3 and 2 appear to be overvalued, however, because they have negative alphas.

We distinguish between market price, *P*, and intrinsic value (value for short), *V*. We accept the possibility of mispricing, which raises the question of the relationship between the analyst's efforts and the concept of market efficiency. **Market efficiency** is a finance perspective on capital markets that asserts, in the **traditional efficient markets formulation**, that an asset's market price is the best available estimate of its intrinsic value. A more modern formulation, the **rational efficient markets formulation** (Grossman and Stiglitz 1980), recognizes that no investor will rationally incur the expenses of gathering information unless he or she expects to be rewarded by higher gross returns compared with the free alternative of accepting the market price. Furthermore, modern theorists recognize that when intrinsic value is hard to ascertain (as is the case for common stock) and when trading costs exist, there is even further room for price to diverge from value.[19]

Thus the perspective of this reading is consistent with some concepts of market efficiency. Many analysts often view market prices both with respect and with skepticism. They seek to identify mispricing. At the same time, they often rely on price eventually converging to intrinsic value. They also recognize distinctions between the levels of market efficiency in different markets or tiers of markets (for example, stocks heavily followed by analysts and stocks neglected by analysts).

**3.4.1.2  Other Value Measures**  A company generally has one value if it is immediately dissolved, and another value if it continues in operation. The **going-concern assumption** is the assumption that the company will maintain its business activities into the foreseeable future. The **going-concern value** of a company is its value under a going-concern assumption. Once established as publicly traded, most companies have relatively long lives. Models of going-concern value are the focus of this reading.

In addition to going-concern value, however, the marketplace considers other values. A company's **liquidation value** is its value if it were dissolved and its

---

[19] See Lee, Myers, and Swaminathan (1999).

assets sold individually.[20] For many companies, the value added by assets working together and by human capital applied to managing those assets makes estimated going-concern value greater than liquidation value. A persistently unprofitable business, however, may be worth more "dead" than "alive." The higher of going-concern value or liquidation value is the company's fair value. If the marketplace has confidence that the company's management is acting in the owners' best interests, market prices should on average reflect fair value. **Fair value** is the price at which an asset (or liability) would change hands between a willing buyer and a willing seller when the former is not under any compulsion to buy and the latter is not under any compulsion to sell.

### 3.4.2 *Absolute Valuation Models*

The two broad types of going-concern models of valuation are absolute valuation models and relative valuation models. An **absolute valuation model** is a model that specifies an asset's intrinsic value. Such models can supply a point estimate of value that can be compared with the asset's market price. Present value models, the most important type of absolute equity valuation model, are regarded in academic finance theory as the fundamental approach to equity valuation. The logic of such models is that the value of an asset to an investor must be related to the returns that investor expects to receive from holding that asset. Loosely speaking, we can refer to those returns as the asset's cash flows, and such models are also referred to as discounted cash flow models.

A **present value model** or **discounted cash flow model** of equity valuation views the value of common stock as being the present or discounted value of its expected future cash flows. For common stock, one familiar type of cash flow is dividends, which are discretionary distributions to shareholders authorized by a corporation's board of directors. Dividends represent cash flows at the shareholder level in the sense that they are paid directly to shareholders. Present value models based on dividends are called **dividend discount models**. Rather than defining cash flows as dividends, analysts frequently define cash flows at the company level. Common shareholders in principle have an equity ownership claim on the balance of the cash flows generated by a company after payments have been made to claimants senior to common equity, such as bondholders and preferred stockholders (and the government as well, which takes taxes), whether or not such flows are distributed in the form of dividends.

The two main company-level definitions of cash flow in current use are free cash flow and residual income.[21] Free cash flow is based on cash flow from operations but takes into account the reinvestment in fixed assets and working capital necessary for a going concern; we will define free cash flow with more precision in later readings. Present value models based on a free cash flow concept include models known as the **free cash flow to equity model** and the **free cash flow to the firm model**. **Residual income models** are present value models of equity valuation based on accrual accounting earnings in excess of the opportunity cost of generating those earnings.

As discussed, an important group of equity valuation models is present value models. The present value approach is the familiar technique for valuing bonds,

---

[20] Liquidation value should be distinguished from what is sometimes called the **breakup value** or **private market value** of a company, which is the sum of the expected value of the company's parts if the parts were independent entities. In contrast to liquidation value, breakup value is a going-concern concept of value because in estimating a company's breakup value, the company's parts are usually valued individually as going concerns.

[21] To reiterate, we are using *cash flow* in a broad rather than technical accounting sense in this discussion.

and models such as the dividend discount model are often presented as straightforward applications of the bond valuation model to common stock. In practice, however, the application of present value models to common stock typically involves greater uncertainty than is the case with bonds; that uncertainty centers on two critical inputs for present value models—the cash flows and the discount rate(s). Bond valuation addresses a stream of cash payments specified in number and amount in a legal contract (the **bond indenture**). In contrast, in valuing a stock, an analyst must define the specific cash flow stream to be valued—dividends or free cash flow, for example. No cash flow stream is contractually owed to common stockholders. Evaluating business, financial, technological, and other risks, the analyst must then forecast the amounts of the chosen flows without reference to contractual targets. Substantial uncertainty often surrounds such forecasts. Furthermore, the forecasts must extend into the indefinite future because common stock has no maturity date. Establishing the appropriate discount rate or rates in equity valuation is also subject to greater uncertainty for a stock than for an option-free bond of an issuer with no credit risk (e.g., a U.S. government security) or a corporate issuer of high investment grade quality. The widespread availability, use, and acceptance of bond ratings—coupled with the more certain nature of cash flows described above for such bonds—mean that appropriate discount rates for different levels of risk can be at least inferred if not observed directly from yields in the bond market. No such ratings or certain cash flows exist for stocks, so the analyst is faced with a much more subjective and uncertain assessment of the appropriate discount rate for a given stock. (For some bonds, however, such as mortgage-backed securities, asset-backed securities, and structured notes, the appropriate discount rate as well as the bond's cash flows can pose challenges in estimation comparable to those for equity.) Finally, in addition to the uncertainty associated with cash flows and discount rates, the equity analyst may need to address other issues, such as the value of corporate control or the value of unutilized assets.

The present value approach applied to stock valuation, therefore, presents a high order of complexity. Present value models are ambitious in what they attempt—an estimate of intrinsic value—and offer concomitant challenges. Graham and Dodd (1934) suggested that the analyst consider stating a range of intrinsic values. To that end, in later readings we discuss the usefulness of sensitivity analysis in discounted cash flow valuation.

Although we present many of the equity valuation tools in wide professional use today, we cannot explore every specialist valuation tool the analyst may encounter. For example, a company may be valued on the basis of the market value of the assets or resources it controls. This approach is sometimes called **asset-based valuation** and also qualifies as a type of absolute valuation model. For appropriate companies, asset-based valuation can provide an independent estimate of value, and experienced analysts are always interested in alternative, independent estimates of value.

### EXAMPLE 7

#### Asset-Based Valuation

Analysts often apply asset-based valuation to natural resource companies. For example, a crude oil producer such as Petrobras (NYSE: PBR) might be valued on the basis of the market value of its current proven reserves in barrels of oil, minus a discount for estimated extraction costs. A forest industry company such as Weyerhauser (NYSE: WY) might be valued on the basis of the board meters (or board feet) of timber it controls. Today, however, fewer companies than in the past are involved only in natural resources extraction or production. For example, Occidental Petroleum (NYSE: OXY) features petroleum in its name but also has substantial chemical manufacturing operations. For such cases, the total company might be valued as the sum of its divisions, with the natural resource division valued on the basis of its proven resources.

### 3.4.3  Relative Valuation Models

Relative valuation models constitute the second chief type of going-concern valuation models. **Relative valuation models** specify an asset's value relative to that of another asset. The idea underlying relative valuation is that similar assets should sell at similar prices, and relative valuation is typically implemented using price multiples.

Perhaps the most familiar price multiple, reported in most newspaper stock quotation listings, is the price–earnings multiple (P/E), which is the ratio of a stock's market price to the company's earnings per share. A stock selling at a P/E that is low relative to the P/E of another closely comparable stock (in terms of anticipated earnings growth rates and risk, for example) is *relatively undervalued* (a good buy) relative to the comparison stock. For brevity, we might state simply *undervalued*, but we must realize that if the comparison stock is overvalued (in an absolute sense, in relation to intrinsic value), so might be the stock we are calling undervalued. Therefore, it is useful to maintain the verbal distinction between *undervalued* and *relatively undervalued*.[22] Frequently, relative valuation involves a group of comparison assets, such as an industry group, rather than a single comparison asset, and the comparison value of the P/E might be the mean or median value of the P/E for the group of assets. The approach of relative valuation as applied to equity valuation is often called the method of comparables (or just comparables).

---

**EXAMPLE 8**

**Relative Valuation Models**

While researching Smithson Genomics, Inc. (STHI),[23] in the Healthcare Information Services industry, you encounter a difference of opinions. One analyst's report claims that STHI is at least 15 percent *overvalued*, based on a comparison of its P/E with the median P/E of peer companies

---

[22] Only expectational arbitrage—investing on the basis of differential expectations—is possible whether a stock is absolutely or relatively mispriced. When two stocks are relatively mispriced, an investor might use the expectational arbitrage strategy known as pairs arbitrage to attempt to exploit the mispricing. Pairs arbitrage is a trade in two closely related stocks that involves buying the relatively undervalued stock and selling short the relatively overvalued stock.

[23] This company is fictional; as such, we do not identify a stock exchange or other marketplace before stating the (fictional) ticker symbol or acronym.

in the Healthcare Information Services industry and taking account of company and peer group fundamentals. A second analyst asserts that Smithson is *undervalued* by 10 percent, based on a comparison of STHI's P/E with the median P/E of the Russell 3000 Index, a broad-based U.S. equity index. Both analyses appear to be carefully executed and reported. Can both analysts be right?

Yes. The assertions of both analysts concern *relative* valuations. The first analyst claims that STHI is *relatively* overvalued compared with its peers (in the sense of the purchase cost of a unit of earnings, P/E). Suppose that the entire Healthcare Information Services industry is substantially undervalued in relation to the overall market as represented by the Russell 3000. STHI could then also be relatively undervalued relative to the Russell 3000. Both analysts can be right because they are making relative valuations. Analysts ultimately care about the investment implications of their information. If the second analyst believes that the market price of the Russell 3000 fairly represents that index's intrinsic value, then she might expect a positive alpha from investing in STHI, even if some other peer group companies possibly command higher expected alphas. In practice, the analyst may consider other factors such as market liquidity in relation to the intended position size. On the other hand, if the analyst thought that the overall market valuation was high, the analyst might anticipate a negative alpha from investing in STHI. Relative valuation is tied to relative performance. The analyst in many cases may want to supplement such information with estimates of intrinsic value.

The method of comparables is characterized by a wide range of possible implementation choices. Practitioners will often examine a number of price multiples for the complementary information they may provide. In summary, the method of comparables does not specify intrinsic value without making the further assumption that the comparison asset is fairly valued. The method of comparables has the advantages of being simple, related to market prices, and grounded in a sound economic principle (that similar assets should sell at similar prices). Price multiples are widely recognized by investors, and analysts can restate an absolute valuation in terms of a price multiple to communicate their analysis in a way that will be widely understood.

### 3.4.4 Issues in Model Selection and Interpretation

How do we select a valuation model? The broad criteria for model selection are that the valuation model be:

▶ consistent with the characteristics of the company being valued;

▶ appropriate given the availability and quality of data; and

▶ consistent with the purpose of valuation, including the analyst's ownership perspective.

We have argued that understanding the business is the first step in the valuation process. When we understand the company, we understand the nature of its assets and also how it uses those assets to create value. For example, a bank is composed largely of marketable or potentially marketable assets and securities, and a relative valuation based on assets (as recognized in accounting) has more relevance than a similar exercise for a service company with few marketable assets.

The availability and quality of data are limiting factors in making forecasts and sometimes in using specific financial performance measures. As a result, data availability and quality also bear on our choice of valuation model. Discounted cash flow models make intensive use of forecasts. As we shall see, the dividend discount model is the simplest such model, but if we do not have a record of dividends or other information to accurately assess a company's dividend policy, we may have more confidence applying an apparently more complex present value model. Similar considerations also apply in selecting a specific relative valuation approach. As an example, meaningful comparisons using P/E ratios may be hard to make for a company with highly volatile or persistently negative earnings.

The purpose or perspective of the analyst—for example, the ownership perspective—can also influence the choice of valuation approach. This point will become more apparent as we study concepts such as free cash flow and enterprise value later in this book. Related to purpose, the analyst is frequently a consumer as well as a producer of valuations and research reports. Analysts must consider potential biases when reading reports prepared by others: Why was this particular valuation method chosen? Are the valuation model and its inputs reasonable? Does the adopted approach make the security look better (or worse) than another standard valuation approach?

In addition to the preceding broad considerations in model selection, three other specific issues may affect the analyst's use and interpretation of valuation models: control premiums, marketability discounts, and liquidity discounts. A controlling ownership position in a company (e.g., more than 50 percent of outstanding shares) carries with it control of the board of directors and the valuable option of redeploying the company's assets. When control is at issue, the price of that company's stock will generally reflect a **control premium**. Most quantitative valuation expressions do not explicitly model such premiums. As we shall discuss later, however, certain models are more likely than others to yield valuations consistent with a control position. A second consideration generally not explicitly modeled is that investors require an extra return to compensate for lack of a public market or lack of marketability. The price of non-publicly traded stocks then generally reflects a **marketability discount**. There is also evidence that among publicly traded stocks, the price of shares with less depth to their markets (less liquidity) reflects a **liquidity discount**.[24]

As a final note to this introduction of model selection, it is important to recognize that professionals frequently use multiple valuation models or factors in common stock selection. According to the *Merrill Lynch Institutional Factor Survey* (2001), respondent institutional investors report using an average of approximately eight valuation factors in selecting stocks.[25] There are a variety of ways in which multiple factors can be used in stock selection. For example, analysts may rank each security in a given investment universe by relative attractiveness according to a particular valuation factor. They could then combine the rankings for a security into a single composite ranking by assigning weights to the individual factors. Analysts may use a quantitative model to assign those weights.

---

[24] See, for example, Amihud and Mendelson (1986).

[25] *Factors* include valuation models as well as variables such as return on equity; these surveys included 23 such factors and covered the period 1989–2001.

# PERFORMING VALUATIONS: THE ANALYST'S ROLE AND RESPONSIBILITIES

Whatever the setting in which they work, investment analysts are involved either directly or indirectly in valuation. Their activities are varied:

▶ Although sometimes focusing on organizing and analyzing corporate information, the publicly distributed research reports and services of independent vendors of financial information almost invariably offer valuation information and opinions.

▶ In investment management firms, trusts and bank trust departments, and similar institutions, an analyst may report valuation judgments to a portfolio manager or to an investment committee.[26] The analyst's valuation expertise is important not only in investment disciplines involving security selection based on detailed company analysis, but also in highly quantitative investment disciplines; quantitative analysts work in developing, testing, and updating security selection methodologies.[27]

▶ Analysts at corporations may perform some valuation tasks similar to those of analysts at money management firms (e.g., when the corporation manages in-house a sponsored pension plan). Both corporate analysts and investment bank analysts may also identify and value companies that could become acquisition targets.

▶ Analysts associated with investment firms' brokerage operations are perhaps the most visible group of analysts offering valuation judgments—their research reports are widely distributed to current and prospective retail and institutional brokerage clients.

In conducting their valuation activities, investment analysts play a critical role in collecting, organizing, analyzing, and communicating corporate information, and in recommending appropriate investment actions based on sound analysis. When they do those tasks well, analysts:

▶ help their clients achieve their investment objectives by enabling those clients to make better buy and sell decisions;

▶ contribute to the efficient functioning of capital markets. In providing analysis that leads to informed buy and sell decisions, analysts help make asset prices better reflections of underlying values. When asset prices accurately reflect underlying values, capital flows more easily to its highest-value uses; and

▶ benefit the suppliers of capital, including shareholders, by monitoring management's performance. Monitoring managers may inhibit those managers from exploiting corporate resources for their own benefit.[28]

---

[26] Such analysts are widely known as **buy-side analysts**, in contrast to analysts who work at brokerages, who are known as **sell-side analysts**. Brokerages provide or sell services to institutions such as investment management firms, explaining this terminology. **Brokerage** is the business of acting as agents for buyers or sellers, usually in return for commissions.

[27] Ranking stocks by some measure(s) of relative attractiveness (subject to a risk control discipline), as we will discuss in more detail later, forms one key part of quantitative equity investment disciplines.

[28] See Jensen and Meckling (1976) for a classic analysis of the costs of stockholder–manager conflicts.

## EXAMPLE 9

### What Are Analysts Expected to Do?

When analysts at brokerage firms recommend a stock to the public that later performs very poorly, or when they fail to uncover negative corporate activities, they can sometimes come under public scrutiny. Industry leaders may then be asked to respond to such criticism and to comment on expectations about the role and responsibilities of analysts. One such instance occurred in the United States as a consequence of the late 2001 collapse of Enron Corporation, an energy trading company. In testimony before the U.S. Senate (excerpted below), the President and CEO of AIMR offered a summary of the working conditions and responsibilities of brokerage analysts. In the following passage, **due diligence** refers to investigation and analysis in support of a recommendation; the failure to exercise due diligence may sometimes result in liability according to various securities laws. "Wall Street analysts" refers to analysts working in the U.S. brokerage industry (sell-side analysts).

What are Wall Street analysts expected to do? These analysts are assigned companies and industries to follow, are expected to research fully these companies and the industries in which they operate, and to forecast their future prospects. Based on this analysis, and using appropriate valuation models, they must then determine an appropriate fair price for the company's securities. After comparing this fair price to the current market price, the analyst is able to make a recommendation. If the analyst's "fair price" is significantly above the current market price, it would be expected that the stock be rated a "buy" or "market outperform."

How do Wall Street analysts get their information? Through hard work and due diligence. They must study and try to comprehend the information in numerous public disclosure documents, such as the annual report to shareholders and regulatory filings . . . and gather the necessary quantitative and qualitative inputs to their valuation models.

This due diligence isn't simply reading and analyzing annual reports. It also involves talking to company management, other company employees, competitors, and others, to get answers to questions that arise from their review of public documents. Talking to management must go beyond participation in regular conference calls. Not all questions can be voiced in those calls because of time constraints, for example, and because analysts, like journalists, rightly might not wish to "show their cards," and reveal the insights they have gotten through their hard work, by asking a particularly probing question in the presence of their competitors.

Wall Street analysts are also expected to understand the dynamics of the industry and general economic conditions before finalizing a research report and making a recommendation. Therefore, in order for their firm to justify their continued employment, Wall Street analysts must issue research reports on their assigned companies and must make recommendations based on their reports to clients who purchase their firm's research.[29]

---

[29] Thomas A. Bowman, CFA. Testimony to the Committee on Governmental Affairs (excerpted) U.S. Senate, 27 February 2002.

From the beginnings of the movement to organize financial analysis as a profession rather than as a commercial trade, one guiding principle has been that the analyst must hold himself accountable to both standards of competence and standards of conduct.[30]

Competence in investment analysis requires a high degree of training, experience, and discipline.[31] Additionally, the investment professional is in a position of trust, requiring ethical conduct towards the public, clients, prospects, employers, employees, and fellow analysts. For AIMR members, this position of trust is reflected in the Code of Ethics and Standards of Professional Conduct to which AIMR members subscribe, as well as in the Professional Conduct Statement that they submit annually. The Code and Standards guide the analyst to independent, well-researched, and well-documented analysis. Valuation is closely associated with analyst recommendations that often form the basis for investment action; ensuring that work product is consistent with the Code and Standards is therefore an overriding priority.

## 5  COMMUNICATING VALUATION RESULTS: THE RESEARCH REPORT

Writing is an important part of an analyst's job. Whether a research report is for review by an investment committee or a portfolio manager in an investment management firm, or for distribution to the retail or institutional clients of a brokerage firm, research reports share several common elements. In this section we discuss the content of an effective research report, one adaptable format for writing such a report, and the analyst's responsibilities in preparing a research report.

### 5.1  Contents of a Research Report

To understand what a research report should include, we need to ask what readers seek to gain from reading the report. One key focus is the investment recommendation. In evaluating how much attention and weight to give to a recommendation, the reader will look for persuasive supporting arguments. The relevance to this book, of course, is that a key element supporting a recommendation is the valuation of the security. Understanding the business is the first step in valuation. Therefore, the reader will want to understand the prospects for both the industry and the company. The quality of this industry and company analysis bears heavily on the quality of the valuation and recommendation. Some readers of research reports are also interested in background information, and some reports contain detailed historical descriptive statistics about the industry and company. To summarize, most research reports cover the following three broad areas:

▶ description (presentation of facts). This brings the reader up to date on the company's sales, earnings, new products, and the macroeconomic and industry contexts in which the company operates;

---

[30] See the Articles of Incorporation (1959) of the Institute of Chartered Financial Analysts, a predecessor organization of AIMR, as well as Hayes (1962) and Graham (1963).

[31] Competence in this sense is reflected in the examination and work experience requirements that are prerequisites for obtaining the CFA designation.

▶ analysis and forecasts for the industry and company; and

▶ valuation and recommendation.

How well the analyst executes the above tasks determines the usefulness of the report. Writing an effective research report is a challenging task. An effective research report:

▶ contains timely information;

▶ is written in clear, incisive language;

▶ is unbiased, objective, and well researched;

▶ contains analysis, forecasts, valuation, and a recommendation that are internally consistent;

▶ presents sufficient information that the reader can critique the valuation;

▶ states the risk factors present for an investment in the company; and

▶ discloses any potential conflicts of interests faced by the analyst.

Analysts, whose goal is to produce research of distinguished quality and usefulness, should keep the above points in mind when writing a research report.

Because our subject is valuation, we focus our remaining comments on the valuation information in research reports. Observers have sometimes criticized the valuation analysis in many research reports.[32] The analyst needs to maintain a conceptual distinction between a *good company* and a *good investment*. The expected alpha on a common stock purchase depends on the price paid for the stock, whatever the business prospects of the issuing company. The analyst who is overly enthusiastic about a company's prospects sometimes may be tempted to state a positive recommendation without substantial effort at valuation. Such a report might offer interesting background industry information, but the analysis would not be thorough.

The analyst can state his or her specific forecasts, convert those forecasts into an estimate of intrinsic value (describing the model), and compare intrinsic value with market price (or make a similarly careful relative valuation). Qualitative factors and other considerations may affect a recommendation and merit discussion. Superior research reports also contain a section on risk factors that objectively addresses the uncertainty associated with investing in the security. Research reports often state a target price for a stock. Readers can make little use of a target price for a stock unless the report describes the basis for computing the target, supplies a time frame for reaching the target, and conveys information on the uncertainty of reaching the target.

## EXAMPLE 10

### Research Reports

The following two passages are closely based on the valuation discussions of actual companies in two short research notes (for Passage A, a two-page report dated March 2002; for B, a single-page report issued July 2001). The company names used in the passages, however, are fictional.

---

[32] Cornell (2001) is one example, and comments in the financial press have appeared from time to time.

**A.** At a recent multiple of 6.5, our earnings per share multiple for 2002, the shares were at a discount to our projection of 14 percent growth for the period . . . MXI has two operating segments . . . In valuing the segments separately, employing relative acquisition multiples and peer mean values, we found fair value to be above recent market value. In addition, the shares trade at a discount to book value (0.76). Based on the value indicated by these two valuation metrics, we view the shares as worth holding. However, in light of a weaker economy over the near term, dampening demand for MXI's services, our enthusiasm is tempered. [*Elsewhere in the report, MXI receives the firm's highest numerical quantitative outlook evaluation.*]

**B.** Although TXI outperformed the overall stock market by 20 percent since the start of the year, it definitely looks undervalued as shown by its low multiples . . . [*the values of the P/E and another multiple are stated*]. According to our dividend discount model valuation, we get to a valuation of €3.08 implying an upside potential of 36.8 percent based on current prices. The market outperform recommendation is reiterated. [*In a parenthetical expression, the current dividend, assumed dividend growth rates and their time horizons are given. The analyst also briefly explains and calculates the discount rate. Elsewhere in the report the current price of TXI is given as €2.25.*]

Although some of the concepts mentioned in the two passages may not yet be familiar, we can begin to assess the above two reporting efforts.

Passage A communicates the analysis awkwardly. The meaning of "the shares were at a discount to our projection of 14 percent growth for the period" is not completely clear. Presumably the analyst is projecting the earnings growth rate for 2002 and stating that the P/E is low in relation to that expected growth rate. The analyst next discusses valuing MXI as the sum of its divisions. In describing the method as "employing relative acquisition multiples and peer mean values," the analyst does not convey a clear picture of what was done. It is probable that companies similar to each of MXI's divisions were identified; then the mean or average value of some unidentified multiple for those comparison companies was calculated and used as the basis for valuing MXI. The writer is vague, however, on the extent of MXI's undervaluation. The analyst states that MXI's price is below its book value (an accounting measure of shareholders' investment) but draws no comparison with the average price-to-book value ratio for stocks similar to MXI, for example. Finally, the verbal summation is feeble and hedged. Although filled with technical verbiage, Passage A does not communicate a coherent valuation of MXI.

In the second sentence of Passage B, by contrast, the analyst gives an explicit valuation of TXI and the information needed to critique it. The reader can also see that €3.08, which is elsewhere stated in the research note as the target price for TXI, implies the stated price appreciation potential for TXI (€3.08/€2.25 − 1, approximately 37 percent). In the first sentence in Passage B, the analyst gives information that might support the conclusion that TXI is undervalued, although the statement lacks strength because the analyst does not explain why the P/E is "low." The verbal summary is clear. Using much less space than the analyst in Passage A, the analyst in Passage B has done a superior job of communicating the results of his valuation.

## 5.2 Format of a Research Report

Equity research reports may be logically presented in several ways. The firm in which the analyst works sometimes specifies a fixed format for consistency and quality control purposes. Without claiming superiority to other ways to organize a report, we offer Table 3 as an adaptable format by which the analyst can communicate research and valuation findings in detail. (Shorter research reports and research notes obviously may employ a more compact format.)

**TABLE 3   A Format for Research Reports**

| Section | Purpose | Content | Comments |
|---|---|---|---|
| *Table of contents* | ▶ Show report's organization | ▶ Consistent with narrative in sequence and language | This is typically used in very long research reports only. |
| *Summary and investment conclusion* | ▶ Communicate the large picture | ▶ Capsule description of the company | An executive summary; may be called simply "Summary." |
| | ▶ Communicate major specific conclusions of the analysis | ▶ Major recent developments<br>▶ Earnings projections<br>▶ Other major conclusions | |
| | ▶ Recommend an investment course of action | ▶ Valuation summary<br>▶ Investment action | |
| *Business summary* | ▶ Present the company in more detail | ▶ Company description to the divisional level | Reflects the first and second steps of the valuation process. Financial forecasts should be explained adequately and reflect quality of earnings analysis. |
| | ▶ Communicate a detailed understanding of the company's economics and current situation | ▶ Industry analysis<br>▶ Competitive analysis<br>▶ Historical performance<br>▶ Financial forecasts | |
| | ▶ Provide and explain specific forecasts | | |
| *Risks* | ▶ Alert readers to the risk factors in investing in the security | ▶ Possible negative industry developments<br>▶ Possible negative regulatory and legal developments<br>▶ Possible negative company developments<br>▶ Risks in the forecasts<br>▶ Other risks | Readers should have enough information to determine how the analyst is defining and assessing the risks specific to investing in the security. |
| *Valuation* | ▶ Communicate a clear and careful valuation | ▶ Description of model(s) used<br>▶ Recapitulation of inputs<br>▶ Statement of conclusions | Readers should have enough information to critique the analysis. |
| *Historical and pro forma tables* | ▶ Organize and present data to support the analysis in the Business Summary | | This is generally a separate section in longer research reports only. Many reports fold all or some of this information into the Business Summary section. |

## 5.3 Research Reporting Responsibilities

All analysts have an obligation to provide substantive and meaningful content in a clear and comprehensive report format. Analysts who are AIMR members, however, have an additional and overriding responsibility to adhere to the Code of Ethics and the Standards of Professional Conduct in all activities pertaining to their research reports.[33] The AIMR Code of Ethics states:

> Members of the Association for Investment Management and Research shall use reasonable care and exercise independent professional judgment.

Going beyond this general statement of responsibility, some specific Standards of Professional Conduct particularly relevant to an analyst writing a research report are shown in Table 4.

**TABLE 4    Selected AIMR Standards of Professional Conduct Pertaining to Research Reports**

| Standard of Professional Conduct | Responsibility |
| --- | --- |
| II(C) | Members shall not copy or use, in substantially the same form as the original, material prepared by another without acknowledging and identifying the name of the author, publisher, or source of such material. Members may use, without acknowledgment, factual information published by recognized financial and statistical reporting services or similar sources. |
| IV(A)1(a) | Members shall exercise diligence and thoroughness in making investment recommendations or in taking investment actions. |
| IV(A)1(b) | Members shall have a reasonable and adequate basis, supported by appropriate research and investigation, for such recommendations or actions. |
| IV(A)1(c) | Members shall make reasonable and diligent efforts to avoid any material misrepresentation in any research report or investment recommendation. |
| IV(A)1(d) | Members shall maintain appropriate records to support the reasonableness of such recommendations or actions. |
| IV(A)2(a) | Members shall use reasonable judgment regarding the inclusion or exclusion of relevant factors in research reports. |
| IV(A)2(b) | Members shall distinguish between facts and opinions in research reports. |
| IV(A)2(c) | Members shall indicate the basic characteristics of the investment involved when preparing for public distribution a research report that is not directly related to a specific portfolio or client. |
| IV(A)3 | Members shall use reasonable care and judgment to achieve and maintain independence and objectivity in making investment recommendations or taking investment action. |

[33] AIMR changed its name to CFA Institute in 2004. The current Code and Standards are contained in Study Session 1.

# SUMMARY

In this reading, we have discussed the scope of equity valuation, outlined the valuation process, introduced valuation concepts and models, discussed the analyst's role and responsibilities in conducting valuation, and described the elements of an effective research report in which analysts communicate their valuation analysis.

▶ Valuation is the estimation of an asset's value based on variables perceived to be related to future investment returns, or based on comparisons with closely similar assets.

▶ Valuation is used for:
  ▶ stock selection;
  ▶ inferring (extracting) market expectations;
  ▶ evaluating corporate events;
  ▶ fairness opinions;
  ▶ evaluating business strategies and models;
  ▶ communication among management, shareholders, and analysts; and
  ▶ appraisal of private businesses.

▶ The three steps in the portfolio management process are planning, execution, and feedback. Valuation is most closely associated with the planning and execution steps.
  ▶ For active investment managers, plans concerning valuation models and criteria are part of the elaboration of an investment strategy.
  ▶ Skill in valuation plays a key role in the execution step (in selecting a portfolio, in particular).

▶ The valuation process has five steps:
  1. Understanding the business.
  2. Forecasting company performance.
  3. Selecting the appropriate valuation model.
  4. Converting forecasts to a valuation.
  5. Making the investment decision (recommendation).

▶ The tasks within "understanding the business" include evaluating industry prospects, competitive position, and corporate strategies. Because similar economic and technological factors typically affect all companies in an industry, and because companies compete with each other for sales, both industry knowledge and competitive analysis help analysts understand a company's economics and its environment. The analyst can then make more accurate forecasts.

▶ Two approaches to economic forecasting are top-down forecasting and bottom-up forecasting. In top-down forecasting, analysts use macroeconomic forecasts to develop industry forecasts and then make individual company and asset forecasts consistent with the industry forecasts. In bottom-up forecasting, individual company forecasts are aggregated to industry forecasts, which in turn may be aggregated to macroeconomic forecasts.

▶ Careful scrutiny and interpretation of financial statements, footnotes to financial statements, and other accounting disclosures are essential to a quality of earnings analysis. Quality of earnings analysis concerns the scrutiny of possible earnings management and balance sheet management.

▶ The intrinsic value of an asset is its value given a hypothetically complete understanding of the asset's investment characteristics.

▶ Alpha is an asset's excess risk-adjusted return. *Ex ante* alpha is expected holding-period return minus required return given risk. Historical alpha is actual holding-period return minus the contemporaneous required return.

▶ Active investing is consistent with rational efficient markets and the existence of trading costs and assets whose intrinsic value is difficult to determine.

▶ The going-concern assumption is the assumption that a company will continue operating for the foreseeable future. A company's going-concern value is its value under the going-concern assumption and is the general objective of most valuation models. In contrast, liquidation value is the company's value if it were dissolved and its assets sold individually.

▶ Fair value is the price at which an asset would change hands if neither buyer nor seller were under compulsion to buy/sell.

▶ Absolute valuation models specify an asset's intrinsic value, supplying a point estimate of value that can be compared with market price. Present value models of common stock (also called discounted cash flow models) are the most important type of absolute valuation model.

▶ Relative valuation models specify an asset's value relative to the value of another asset. As applied to equity valuation, relative valuation is known as the method of comparables: In applying the method of comparables, analysts compare a stock's price multiple to the price multiple of a similar stock or the average or median price multiple of some group of stocks.

▶ Relative equity valuation models do not address intrinsic value without the further assumption that the price of the comparison value accurately reflects its intrinsic value.

▶ The broad criteria for selecting a valuation approach are that the valuation approach be:
  ▶ consistent with the characteristics of the company being valued;
  ▶ appropriate given the availability and quality of the data; and
  ▶ consistent with the analyst's valuation purpose and perspective.

▶ Valuation may be affected by control premiums (premiums for a controlling interest in the company), marketability discounts (discounts reflecting the lack of a public market for the company's shares), and liquidity discounts (discounts reflecting the lack of a liquid market for the company's shares).

▶ Investment analysts play a critical role in collecting, organizing, analyzing, and communicating corporate information, as well as in recommending appropriate investment actions based on their analysis. In fulfilling this role, they help clients achieve their investment objectives and contribute to the efficient functioning of capital markets. Analysts can contribute to the welfare of shareholders through monitoring the actions of management.

▶ In performing valuations, analysts need to hold themselves accountable to both standards of competence and standards of conduct.

▶ An effective research report:
  ▶ contains timely information;
  ▶ is written in clear, incisive language;
  ▶ is unbiased, objective, and well researched;
  ▶ contains analysis, forecasts, valuation, and a recommendation that are internally consistent;

- ▶ presents sufficient information that the reader can critique the valuation;
- ▶ states the risk factors for an investment in the company; and
- ▶ discloses any potential conflicts of interests faced by the analyst.

▶ Analysts have an obligation to provide substantive and meaningful content. AIMR members have an additional overriding responsibility to adhere to the AIMR Code of Ethics and relevant specific Standards of Professional Conduct.

## PRACTICE PROBLEMS FOR READING 34

**1. A.** State four uses or purposes of valuation models.

   **B.** Which use of valuation models may be the most important to a working equity portfolio manager?

   **C.** Which uses would be particularly relevant to a corporate officer?

**2.** In Example 1 based on Cornell's (2001) study of Intel Corporation, in which Cornell valued Intel using a present value model of stock value, we wrote:

   "What future revenue growth rates were consistent with Intel's stock price of $61.50 just prior to the release, and $43.31 only five days later? Using a conservatively low discount rate, Cornell estimated that the price of $61.50 was consistent with a growth rate of 20 percent a year for the subsequent 10 years (and then 6 percent per year thereafter)."

   **A.** If Cornell had assumed a higher discount rate, would the resulting revenue growth rate estimate consistent with a price of $61.50 be higher or lower than 20 percent a year?

   **B.** Explain your answer to Part A.

**3. A.** Explain the role of valuation in the planning step of the portfolio management process.

   **B.** Explain the role of valuation in the execution step of the portfolio management process.

**4.** Explain why valuation models are important to active investors but not to investors trying to replicate a stock market index.

**5.** An analyst has been following Kerr-McGee Corporation (NYSE: KMG) for several years. He has consistently felt that the stock is undervalued and has always recommended a strong buy. Another analyst who has been following Nucor Corporation (NYSE: NUE) has been similarly bullish. The tables below summarize the prices, dividends, total returns, and estimates of the contemporaneous required returns for KMG and NUE from 1998 to 2001.

### Data for KMG

| Year | Price at Year-End | Dividends | Total Annual Return | Contemporaneous Required Return |
|------|-------------------|-----------|---------------------|--------------------------------|
| 1997 | $54.22 | | | |
| 1998 | 33.97 | $1.80 | −34.0% | 26.6% |
| 1999 | 54.38 | 1.80 | 65.4 | 19.6 |
| 2000 | 63.96 | 1.80 | 20.9 | −8.5 |
| 2001 | 53.93 | 1.80 | −12.9 | −11.0 |

| Data for NUE | | | | |
| --- | --- | --- | --- | --- |
| Year | Price at Year-End | Dividends | Total Annual Return | Contemporaneous Required Return |
| 1997 | $45.66 | | | |
| 1998 | 41.31 | $0.48 | −8.5% | 29.2% |
| 1999 | 52.93 | 0.52 | 29.4 | 21.5 |
| 2000 | 38.96 | 0.60 | −25.3 | −9.3 |
| 2001 | 52.80 | 0.68 | 37.3 | −12.1 |

The total return is the price appreciation and dividends for the year divided by the price at the end of the previous year. The contemporaneous required return is the average actual return for the year realized by stocks that were of the same risk as KMG or NUE, respectively.

**A.** Without reference to any numerical data, what can be said about each analyst's *ex ante* alpha for KMG and NUE, respectively?

**B.** Calculate the *ex post* alphas for each year 1998 through 2001 for KMG and for NUE.

**6.** On the last trading day of 2000 (29 December 2000), an analyst is reviewing his valuation of Wal-Mart Stores (NYSE: WMT). The analyst has the following information and assumptions:

▶ The current price is $53.12.

▶ The analyst's estimate of WMT's intrinsic value is $56.00.

▶ In addition to the full correction of the difference between WMT's current price and its intrinsic value, the analyst forecasts additional price appreciation of $4.87 and a cash dividend of $0.28 over the next year.

▶ The required rate of return for Wal-Mart is 9.2 percent.

**A.** What is the analyst's expected holding-period return on WMT?

**B.** What is WMT's *ex ante* alpha?

**C.** Calculate *ex post* alpha, given the following additional information:

▶ Over the next year, 29 December 2000 through 31 December 2001, Wal-Mart's actual rate of return was 8.9 percent.

▶ In 2001, the realized rate of return for stocks of similar risk was −10.4 percent.

**7.** The table below gives information on the expected and required rates of return based on the CAPM for three securities an analyst is valuing:

|  | **Expected Rate** | **CAPM Required Rate** |
|---|---|---|
| Security 1 | 0.20 | 0.21 |
| Security 2 | 0.18 | 0.08 |
| Security 3 | 0.11 | 0.10 |

   **A.** Define *ex ante* alpha.

   **B.** Calculate the expected alpha of Securities 1, 2, and 3 and rank them from most attractive to least attractive.

   **C.** Based on your answer to Part B, what risks attach to selecting among Securities 1, 2, and 3?

**8.** Benjamin Graham (1963) wrote that "[t]here is . . . a double function of the Financial Analyst, related in part to securities and in part to people."

   **A.** Explain the analyst's function related to people.

   **B.** How does the analyst's work contribute to the functioning of capital markets?

**9.** In a research note on the ordinary shares of the Mariella Burani Fashion Group (Milan Stock Exchange: MBFG.MI) dated early July 2001 when a recent price was €7.73 and projected annual dividends were €0.05, an analyst stated a target price of €9.20. The research note did not discuss how the target price was obtained or how it should be interpreted. Assume the target price represents the expected price of MBFG.MI. What further specific pieces of information would you need to form an opinion on whether MBFG.MI was fairly valued, overvalued, or undervalued?

**10.** You are researching XMI Corporation (XMI). XMI has shown steady earnings per share growth (18 percent a year during the last seven years) and trades at a very high multiple to earnings (its P/E ratio is currently 40 percent above the average P/E ratio for a group of the most comparable stocks). XMI has generally grown through acquisition, by using XMI stock to purchase other companies. These companies usually trade at lower P/E ratios than XMI.

   In investigating the financial disclosures of these acquired companies and in talking to industry contacts, you conclude that XMI has been forcing the companies it acquires to accelerate the payment of expenses before the acquisition deals are closed. Such acceleration drives down the acquired companies' last reported cash flow and earnings per share numbers. As one example, XMI asks acquired companies to immediately pay all pending accounts payable, whether or not they are due. Subsequent to the acquisition, XMI reinstitutes normal expense payment patterns. After it acquires a company, XMI appears to have a pattern of speeding up revenue recognition as well. For example, one overseas telecommunications subsidiary changed its accounting to recognize up front the expected revenue from sales of network capacity that spanned decades. The above policies and accounting facts do not appear to be have been adequately disclosed in XMI's shareholder communications.

   **A.** Characterize the effect of the XMI expensing policies with respect to acquisitions on XMI's post-acquisition earnings per share growth rate.

   **B.** Characterize the quality of XMI earnings based on its expensing and revenue-recognition policies with respect to acquisitions.

   **C.** In discussing the current price of XMI, the question states that XMI's "P/E ratio is currently 40 percent above the average P/E ratio for a group of the most comparable stocks." Characterize the type of valuation model implicit in such a statement.

   **D.** State two *risk factors* in investing in XMI, in the sense in which that term was used in the discussion of quality of earnings.

## The following information relates to Questions 11–16

Damon Houseman is a junior analyst with Alto Investment Advisors. Alto's portfolio managers have requested an analysis of equities of home healthcare providers. Wanda Kelty, CFA, a senior analyst with Alto, assigned the task to Houseman but is assisting him with the analysis. Kelty suggests that Houseman begin by preparing a top-down analysis of the four leading publicly-traded companies in the industry. Kelty also makes the following statements:

   Statement 1: "The valuation process is more critical for our actively managed portfolios than for our passively managed portfolios."

   Statement 2: "The valuation process should only consider quantitative factors so as to eliminate emotional biases."

Houseman completed his top-down valuation analysis using a present value model on the four companies. Care-RX, Homecare, and Leland Services are widely held and very liquid, while the majority of STR Home Health's shares are held by a small group of founding family members. Exhibit 1 contains Houseman's estimates of the expected and required rates of return for the four companies.

| EXHIBIT 1 | Expected and Required Rates of Return | |
|---|---|---|
| Company | Expected Rate of Return | CAPM Required Rate of Return |
| Care-Rx | 0.21 | 0.18 |
| Homecare | 0.16 | 0.18 |
| Leland Services | 0.09 | 0.15 |
| STR Home Health | 0.20 | 0.15 |

Houseman also decided to analyze the companies utilizing a second valuation model. Exhibit 2 shows his valuation of the four companies based on the S&P 500 Healthcare Index P/E ratio. Also shown is his estimation of each company's overvaluation relative to the expected price based on the index's P/E ratio.

| EXHIBIT 2 | Valuations of Four Healthcare Companies | | |
|---|---|---|---|
| Company | Current Price per Share | Expected Price Based on the S&P 500 Healthcare Index P/E | Percent Overvalued |
| Care-Rx | $52.50 | $51.00 | 2.85% |
| Homecare | $32.82 | $30.13 | 8.20% |
| Leland Services | $61.00 | $58.86 | 3.51% |
| STR Home Health | $17.74 | $16.52 | 6.88% |

Houseman notes that the two methodologies rank the securities differently and is concerned that his analyses might be incorrect. Houseman states, "One of the valuations must have been incorrectly applied because the outcomes are conflicting." Kelty reviews his analyses and confirms that both were completed correctly.

11. Which of the following *most accurately* reflects the *first* three steps, in order, of the top-down valuation approach?

   A. Understanding the business, forecasting company performance, selecting the appropriate valuation model.

   B. Selecting the appropriate valuation model, converting forecasts to a valuation, making the investment decision.

   C. Selecting the appropriate valuation model, forecasting company performance, converting forecasts to a valuation.

**12.** Are Kelty's statements *most likely* correct or incorrect with regard to valuation?

   **A.** Both statements are correct.

   **B.** The first statement is correct and the second statement is incorrect.

   **C.** The first statement is incorrect and the second statement is correct.

**13.** Based on Houseman's analysis, which company is *most likely* to offer the highest alpha?

   **A.** Care-Rx.

   **B.** Homecare.

   **C.** STR Home Health.

**14.** Houseman's second valuation analysis *most likely* makes use of a(n):

   **A.** relative valuation model.

   **B.** absolute valuation model.

   **C.** top-down valuation model.

**15.** Kelty has reviewed the analyses and suggests to Houseman that he adjust his analysis of STR Home Health to reflect its ownership structure. How is Houseman *most likely* to adjust his valuation of the stock?

   **A.** Increase.

   **B.** Decrease.

   **C.** No adjustment.

**16.** Houseman's statement that at least one of the analyses must have been incorrectly applied is *most likely*:

   **A.** correct because the analyses should produce the same outcome.

   **B.** incorrect because one analysis uses historical data and the other uses forecasted data.

   **C.** incorrect because one analysis uses relative valuation and the other uses absolute valuation.

$4\frac{5}{8}$  $4\frac{7}{16}$  $-\frac{5}{8}$

$5\frac{1}{2}$  $5\frac{1}{2}$  $-\frac{5}{8}$

$5\frac{1}{2}$  $21\frac{3}{16}$  $-1\frac{1}{16}$

$20\frac{5}{8}$  $21\frac{3}{16}$  $+\frac{7}{8}$

$17\frac{3}{8}$  $18\frac{1}{8}$  $+\frac{7}{8}$

$6\frac{1}{2}$  $6\frac{1}{2}$  $-\frac{1}{2}$

$7\frac{1}{4}$  $6\frac{1}{2}$  $-\frac{1}{2}$

$15\frac{1}{16}$  $3\frac{1}{32}$  $-\frac{1}{8}$

$9\frac{1}{16}$

$9\frac{1}{16}$  $\frac{9}{16}$

$15\frac{1}{32}$

$7\frac{5}{16}$  $7\frac{13}{16}$  $7\frac{15}{16}$

$2\frac{5}{8}$  $2\frac{11}{32}$  $2\frac{1}{2}$ $+$

$545$  $2\frac{5}{8}$  $2\frac{11}{32}$  $2\frac{1}{4}$

$327$  $2\frac{3}{4}$  $2\frac{1}{4}$  $2\frac{1}{4}$

$12\frac{1}{16}$  $11\frac{3}{8}$  $11\frac{3}{4}$ $+$

$6\frac{1}{8}$  $12\frac{1}{16}$  $11\frac{3}{8}$

$87$  $33\frac{3}{4}$  $33$  $33\frac{1}{8}$ $-$

$802$  $25\frac{5}{8}$  $24\frac{9}{16}$  $25\frac{3}{8}$ $+$

$833$  $12$  $11\frac{5}{8}$  $11\frac{5}{8}$ $+$

$16$  $10\frac{1}{2}$  $10\frac{1}{2}$  $10\frac{1}{2}$ $-$

$78$  $15\frac{7}{8}$  $15\frac{13}{16}$  $15\frac{7}{8}$ $-$

$4508$  $9\frac{1}{16}$  $8\frac{1}{4}$  $8\frac{1}{8}$ $+$

$430$  $11\frac{1}{4}$  $10\frac{1}{8}$  $10\frac{1}{8}$

# EQUITY: MARKETS AND INSTRUMENTS

by Bruno Solnik and Dennis McLeavey, CFA

## LEARNING OUTCOMES

| The candidate should be able to: | Mastery |
|---|:---:|
| **a.** explain the origins of different national market organizations; | ☐ |
| **b.** differentiate between an order-driven market and a price-driven market, and explain the risks and advantages of each; | ☐ |
| **c.** calculate the impact of different national taxes on the return of an international investment; | ☐ |
| **d.** discuss the various components of execution costs (i.e., commissions and fees, market impact, and opportunity cost) and explain ways to reduce execution costs, and discuss the advantages and disadvantages of each; | ☐ |
| **e.** describe an American Depositary Receipt (ADR), and differentiate among the various forms of ADRs in terms of trading and information supplied by the listed company; | ☐ |
| **f.** explain why firms choose to be listed abroad and calculate the cost tradeoff between buying shares listed abroad and buying ADRs; | ☐ |
| **g.** state the determinants of the value of a closed-end country fund; | ☐ |
| **h.** discuss the advantages of exchange-traded funds (ETFs) and explain the pricing of international ETFs in relation to their net asset value (NAV); | ☐ |
| **i.** discuss the advantages and disadvantages of the various alternatives to direct international investing. | ☐ |

This reading discusses equity markets worldwide and also presents facts and concepts relevant to executing trades in those markets. The financial specialist is often struck by the differences among stock market organizations across the world. Traditionally, national stock markets have not only different legal and

Jan R. Squires, CFA, and Philip J. Young, CFA, provided important suggestions for this reading.

physical organizations but also different transaction methodologies. The international investor must have a minimal familiarity with these technical differences because they influence the execution costs of every transaction. After reviewing some statistics on the market size, liquidity, and concentration, we discuss some practical aspects of international investing. These include taxes, market indexes, and the availability of information. A major practical aspect of international investing is the estimation of execution costs in each market. Understanding the determinants and magnitude of overall transaction costs is very important when implementing a global investment strategy. Getting best execution does not reduce to minimizing commissions and fees; market impact must also be estimated. Investment performance depends on the overall execution costs incurred in implementing a strategy. This reading concludes with a review of alternatives to direct international investing, which involve the purchase of foreign shares listed at home. These alternatives include American Depositary Receipts (ADRs), closed-end country funds, and open-end funds, especially exchange-traded funds (ETFs). Each of these investment vehicles has advantages and disadvantages relative to directly investing on foreign markets.

## 1  MARKET DIFFERENCES: A HISTORICAL PERSPECTIVE

Financial paper, in the form of debt obligations, has long been traded in Europe, whereas trading in company shares is relatively recent. The Amsterdam Bourse is usually considered the oldest stock market. The first common stock to be publicly traded in the Netherlands was the famous East Indies Trading Company (Verenigde Oost-Indische Compagnie) in the seventeenth century. But organized stock markets really started in the mid to late eighteenth century. In Paris, a stock market was started on a bridge (Pont au Change). In London, the stock market originated in a tavern; churches and open-air markets were also used as stock markets on the Continent. For example, the Amsterdam Bourse spent some time in the Oude-Kerk (Old Church) and later in the Nieuwe-Kerk (New Church). Most of these European exchanges became recognized as separate markets and were regulated around 1800. The same holds for the United States. However, stock exchanges in Japan and other countries in Asia and most of the Americas are more recent creations.

Historical and cultural differences explain most of the significant differences in stock-trading practices around the world. Rather than engage in a detailed analysis of each national market, this section looks at the major differences in terms of market structures and trading procedures. Many of these differences are being eliminated, but some historical perspective helps gain a better understanding of the current working of those stock markets.

### Historical Differences in Market Organization

Each stock exchange (bourse) has its own unique characteristics and legal organization, but broadly speaking, all exchanges have evolved from one of three market organization types.

### Private Bourses

Private stock exchange corporations are founded by private individuals and entities for the purpose of securities trading. Several private stock exchanges may compete within the same country, as in the United States, Japan, and Canada. In other countries, one leading exchange has emerged through either attrition or absorption of its competitors. Although these bourses are private, they are not free of public regulation, but the mix of self-regulation and government supervision is oriented more toward self-regulation than in the public bourses. Historically, these private bourses developed in the British sphere of influence.

### Public Bourses

The public bourse market structure has its origin in the legislative work of Napoleon I, the French emperor. He designed the *bourse* to be a public institution, with brokers appointed by the government and enjoying a monopoly over all transactions. Commissions are fixed by the state. Brokerage firms are private, but their number is fixed and new brokers are proposed to the state for nomination by the brokers' association. The Paris Bourse followed this model until 1990. Stock exchanges organized under the authority of the state were found in the sphere of influence of Napoleon I: Belgium, France, Spain, Italy, Greece, and some Latin American countries. Most have moved toward a private bourse model.

### Bankers' Bourses

In some countries, banks are the major, or even the only, securities traders. In Germany, the Banking Act granted a brokerage monopoly to banks. Bankers' bourses were found in the German sphere of influence: Austria, Switzerland, Scandinavia, and the Netherlands. Bankers' bourses may be either private or semipublic organizations, but their chief function is to provide a convenient place for banks to meet. Sometimes trading takes place directly between banks without involving the official bourse at all. Government regulation is imposed both on the bourse itself and directly on the banks. Bankers' bourses suffered from potential conflicts of interests, and more trading transparency was required by international investors. Most bankers' bourses moved to a private bourse model in the 1990s to allow foreign financial intermediaries to become brokers.

## Historical Differences in Trading Procedures

Apart from legal structure, numerous other historical differences are found in the operation of national stock markets. The most important differences are in the trading procedures.

### Cash versus Forward Markets

In most markets, stocks are traded on a cash basis, and transactions must be settled within a few days (typically three business days after the transaction). To allow more leveraged investment, margin trading is available on most cash markets. In *margin trading*, the investor borrows money (or shares) from a broker to finance a transaction. This is still a cash market transaction, and trade settlement takes place in three days; however, a third party steps in to lend money (shares) to the buyer (seller) to honor a cash transaction commitment.

In contrast, some stock markets were organized as a forward market. This was the case for London and Paris, as well as some markets in Latin America and Asia. In Paris, the settlement date was the end of the month for all transactions made during the month (London settled accounts every two weeks). To simplify the clearing operations, all transactions were settled at the end of the month on the settlement day. This is a periodic settlement system. Of course, a deposit is required to guarantee a position, as on most forward markets. Moreover, the transaction price is fixed at the time of the transaction and remains at this value even if the market price has changed substantially by the settlement time. Settling all accounts once a month greatly simplifies the security clearing system, but it also opens the door to short-term speculation and to frequent misconceptions on the part of foreign investors who are unfamiliar with the technique. Although most forward markets (including London and Paris) have moved to a cash market, they usually have institutionalized procedures to allow investors to trade forward, if desired.

### Price-Driven versus Order-Driven Markets

U.S. investors are accustomed to a *continuous* market, whereby transactions take place all day and *market makers* (also called *dealers*) ensure market liquidity at virtually any point in time. The market maker quotes both a *bid* price (the price at which the dealer offers to buy the security) and an *ask* price (the price at which the dealer offers to sell the security). The ask price is sometimes called the *offer price*. These quotes are firm commitments by the market maker to transact at those prices for a specified transaction size. The customer will turn to the market maker who provides the best quote. Of course, market makers adjust their quotes continuously to reflect supply and demand for the security as well as their own inventory. This type of market is often referred to as a *dealer market*. It is also known as a *price-driven* market (or *quote-driven* market), because market makers publicly post their bid–ask prices to induce orders. For example, NASDAQ is a dealer market.[1]

In many other markets and countries, however, active market makers do not exist, and the supply and demand for securities are matched directly in an *auction market*. Because the quantities demanded and supplied are a function of the transaction price, a price will exist that equilibrates demand and supply. In a traditional auction market, liquidity requires that an asset be traded only once or a few times per day. This is known as a *call auction* or *fixing* procedure, whereby orders are batched together in an order book until the auction when they are executed at a single price that equilibrates demand and supply. This auction price maximizes trade volume. In the past, many stock markets used an open *criée* (outcry) system in which brokers would negotiate loudly until a price was found that would equilibrate buy and sell orders (quietness is restored). All these stock markets have moved to computerized trading systems in which buy-and-sell orders are entered on the computer trading system, which matches them directly. An auction market is also known as an *order-driven market* because all traders publicly post their orders, and the transaction price is the result of the equilibrium of supply and demand. Although a single call auction provides

---

[1] The New York Stock Exchange (NYSE) has a unique system in which each stock is allocated to one specialist who acts both as a dealer and as an auctioneer. As a dealer, a specialist posts bid and ask quotes and uses his or her own capital to buy or sell securities (under strict regulations). As an auctioneer, a specialist maintains the order book of all orders that are submitted.

excellent liquidity at one point in time, it makes trading at other times difficult. Hence, the market-making function is being developed on all call auction markets (e.g., Paris, Tokyo, or Frankfurt) to allow the possibility of trading throughout the day.

## Automation on the Major Stock Exchanges

Trading on a floor where participants noisily meet is increasingly being replaced by computerized trading. Automation allows more efficient handling of orders, especially a large number of small orders. Competition across national stock exchanges and the increased volume of trading hastened the adoption of computerized systems, including price quotation, order routing, and automatic order matching. The design of the automated systems reflects the historical and cultural heritage of the national market. Automated trading systems have followed two different paths, depending on whether the traditional market organization was dominated by dealers making the market or by brokers acting as agents in an auction system.

### *Price-Driven and Order-Driven Systems*

The U.S. NASDAQ is a typical *price-driven* system. The automated system posts firm quotes by market makers. There is no centralized book of *limit orders*. When posting a quote, the market maker does not know what trades it will generate. In a price-driven system, a market maker is placing the equivalent of limit orders: a buy limit order representing his bid and a sell limit order representing his ask.

At the other extreme, auction markets, such as Paris, Frankfurt, or Tokyo (and most other markets), have put in place electronic order-driven systems. The computer stores all orders, which become public knowledge. All limit orders that have not been executed are stored in a central order book. A new order is immediately matched with the book of orders previously submitted (see Example 1). The central limit order book is the hub of these automated systems.

---

**EXAMPLE 1**

### Order-Driven Market

LVMH (Moët Hennesy Louis Vuitton) is a French firm listed on the Paris Bourse. You can access the central limit order book directly on the Internet and find the following information (the limit prices for sell orders are ask prices and those for buy orders are bid prices):

| Sell Orders | | Buy Orders | |
|---|---|---|---|
| Quantity | Limit | Limit | Quantity |
| 1,000 | 58 | 49 | 2,000 |
| 3,000 | 54 | 48 | 500 |
| 1,000 | 52 | 47 | 1,000 |
| 1,000 | 51 | 46 | 2,000 |
| 500 | 50 | 44 | 10,000 |

> You wish to buy 1,000 shares and enter a market order to buy those shares. A market order will be executed against the best matching order. At what price will you buy the shares?
>
> **Solution:** Unless a new sell order is entered at a price below 51 before your order is executed, you will buy 500 shares at 50 and 500 shares at 51.

Viewing all standing orders, a trader knows exactly what trades will be executed if she enters a new order. Market makers provide liquidity by entering limit buy-and-sell orders in the order book. The highest limit bid and the lowest limit offer act as the bid and ask prices in a price-driven market.

To improve liquidity, most order-driven markets have retained periodic call auctions. There is a fixing at the opening of the market, where all orders that arrived before opening are stored and the opening price is set through a call auction.[2] In Frankfurt, call auctions take place periodically throughout the day, at prespecified times other than opening and closing. At the time of the call auction, the continuous trading of the stock on XETRA is interrupted. (XETRA is a trading platform that includes all stocks on the Deutsche Boerse.) In a *pretrading* phase, traders can submit limit and market orders, which are accumulated in the order book. At auction time, orders are automatically crossed (matched) at a price that maximizes the volume of trading. In Tokyo, a call auction system, called *itayose*, is used to establish prices at the start of the morning and afternoon sessions (the market closes for lunch). During the sessions, a continuous auction is used for new orders. This auction system, called *zaraba*, is an order-matching method and does not require the intervention of a market maker.

The NYSE has developed a hybrid market that integrates traditional floor trading with electronic auction trading. The electronic system allows the order to find the best transaction price on the NYSE or elsewhere.

### Advantages and Risks of Each System

Automation brings many improvements in the speed and costs of trading. An order-driven system requires little human intervention and is therefore less costly to run. Cost considerations have pushed all markets in this direction. Only some U.S. stock markets have retained a price-driven model. Markets with lesser transaction volumes have found it more efficient to adopt order-driven electronic trading systems. For example, London had a price-driven market with competitive market makers. Cost-efficiency considerations caused it to move to an automated order-driven system called SETS (Stock Exchange Electronic Trading Service) at the end of the twentieth century.[3] Market makers enter their bid-and-ask quotes directly in the order book in the form of limit orders. Most emerging stock markets have adopted an order-driven electronic trading system.

The cost of running the trading system, however, is only one component of the transaction cost borne by investors. Investors try to get the best execution price for each trade. This raises the question: Which market structure provides the best liquidity and lowest execution costs? Theoretical and experimental

---

[2] On the NYSE, the opening price is determined through a call auction.

[3] Smaller and many foreign companies, however, are traded on an automated price-driven system called SEAQ (Stock Exchange Automated Quotation System).

research suggests that the market design affects trader behavior, transaction prices, and market efficiency. In real life, the answer depends on the market environment, and there is no clear-cut conclusion. An electronic auction market is cheaper to operate, but that could be at the expense of liquidity—hence, trading could be more costly because of overall execution costs, including price impact.[4] Domowitz (2001) suggests that the public dissemination of the electronic order book in order-driven markets allows traders to monitor liquidity and provide liquidity at a lower cost than in price-driven markets.

A drawback of electronic order-driven systems is their inability to execute large trades. In the absence of active market makers, trading a *block* (a large transaction) on an automated order-driven system is difficult. Because of the lack of depth in the market, it may take a long time before the block is traded. This will leave the trader who discloses the block on the system fully exposed to the risk that new information might hurt him unless he continuously updates the limit on the block order. This is the risk of being "picked off"—that is, having an order accepted at a price no longer desired by the trader at the time of the transaction. Blocks are generally traded away from the automated system. This is often called *upstairs trading*. Order-driven systems have developed in part because they are much cheaper to operate than traditional dealers' markets. However, market makers are still needed for trading large blocks.

Another drawback of a continuous order-driven system, in the absence of developed market making, is the danger in placing *market orders* (i.e., orders with no price limits). In the absence of competitive market makers providing liquidity, a sell market order will be immediately crossed with the highest buy limit order, which could be very far from the lowest sell limit order. The Tokyo Stock Exchange has a special procedure to limit this risk. Other markets are trying to implement rules protecting market orders. This is typically true for less active stocks, in which market making would help provide liquidity.

Any automated trading system exposes one party to transparency risk. It forces one side of the transaction to expose itself first and, therefore, run the risk of being picked off. In all cases, a limit order gives a free trading option to other market participants. In an order-driven market, the trader who submits the order implicitly gives the free option to the rest of the market. In a price-driven market, it is the dealer posting a firm quote who gives this free option, as shown in Example 2. Of course, the option holder depends on the dealer to deliver in a non-automated system, and "backing away" (reneging) can be a problem.

## EXAMPLE 2

### Exposition Risk in Two Types of Markets

LVMH is traded on the Paris Bourse, and the last transaction was at 50 euros per share. An investor entered on the French electronic trading system NSC (Nouveau Système Cotation) a limit order to sell LVMH shares at 51 euros while the market price was 50.

LVMH is also traded as an ADR on NASDAQ. One ADR represents one-fifth of an LVMH French share (so 5 ADRs equal 1 LVMH share). The exchange rate is one dollar per euro, and the ADR price is quoted

---

[4] Conrad, Johnson, and Wahal (2004) find some evidence that realized execution costs are lower on electronic trading systems for U.S. stocks. Using data up to 2000, Huang (2002) finds that electronic communication network quoted spreads are smaller than dealer spreads for NASDAQ stocks. However, the period of study was prior to the U.S. adoption of decimal quotations, which reduced spreads markedly.

by a market maker at 10–10.20. Assume that the exchange rate remains constant over time.

Suppose that favorable information suddenly arrives that justifies a higher price for LVMH—say, 55 euros. Who are the parties exposed to losses on the Paris Bourse and on NASDAQ if they do not react immediately?

**Solution:**

▶ On the Paris Bourse, informed market participants have an option worth four euros per share, and the investor who has a standing order in the electronic order book gets picked off (the informed participant can buy at 51 euros a share now worth 55 euros).

▶ On NASDAQ, the market maker posts a firm bid–ask quote for LVMH of 10–10.20 for the dollar ADR, which is equivalent for the French share of LVMH quoted in euros to a quote of 50–51. Under the same scenario, informed market participants suddenly get a free option worth 0.8 dollar per ADR or four euros per French share (they can buy at 10.2 dollars from the market maker a share now worth 11 dollars). In a price-driven market, dealers run the risk of being picked off.

The danger of automation is that market liquidity may be reduced because dealers (in a price-driven system) or public investors (in an order-driven system) may be less willing to publicly place limit orders.

### Electronic Communication Networks and Electronic Crossing Networks (ECNs)

Some electronic trading systems have developed alongside official exchanges. They tend to be privately owned and offer trading on stocks of one market or of a region. Electronic communication networks and electronic crossing networks are both often called ECNs, although they are quite different.

*Electronic communication networks* are order-driven systems, in which the limit order book plays a central role as previously described. Many of them coexist in the United States. Virt-x is a pan-European ECN specialized in blue chips.

*Electronic crossing networks* are different systems. These crossing systems anonymously match the buy and sell orders of a pool of participants, generally institutional investors and broker-dealers (see Example 3). Participants enter market orders,[5] which are crossed at prespecified times (once or a few times every day) at prices determined in the primary market for the security. The trade price is the mid-market quote, the midpoint between the bid and the ask, observed on the primary market at the prespecified time. POSIT is a major electronic crossing network in the United States, but there are many others in the United States, Asia, and Europe.

---

[5] Participants also can specify various constraints on their orders.

---

### EXAMPLE 3

#### Crossing

Market orders for LVMH have been entered on a crossing network for European shares. There is one order from Participant A to buy 100,000 shares, one order from Participant B to sell 50,000 shares, and one order from Participant C to sell 70,000 shares. Assume that orders were entered in that chronological order and that the network gives priority to the oldest orders. At the time specified for the crossing session, LVMH transacts at 51 euros on the Paris Bourse, its primary market.

1. What trades would take place on the crossing network?
2. Assume now that all the orders are AON (all or nothing), meaning that the whole block has to be traded at the same price. What trades would take place?

**Solution to 1:** A total of 100,000 shares would be exchanged at 51 euros. Participant A would buy 100,000. Participants B and C would sell 50,000. Participant B's order has priority, so Participant C's order would not be executed entirely (20,000 shares remain unsold).

**Solution to 2:** There is no way that the AON condition could be achieved for the three orders, so, no trade would take place.

---

Crossing networks present two advantages for large orders of institutional investors:

▶ *Low transaction costs*: The trade is executed at mid-market prices, so there is no market impact or bid–ask spread, even for large trades.

▶ *Anonymity*: The identity of the buyers and sellers, and the magnitude of their order, will not be revealed, so there is little exposure risk.

On the other hand, crossing networks have a distinct disadvantage:

▶ *No trading immediacy*: The trader must wait until the crossing session time to execute a trade, and the trade takes place only if there are offsetting orders entered by other participants. Only a small proportion of orders are executed at each crossing session. The order has to wait in the system or needs to be worked through other market mechanisms.

Basically, electronic crossing networks allow a substantial reduction in execution cost for large trades, to the detriment of immediacy.

### Cross-Border Alliances of Stock Exchanges

Fragmentation of national stock markets, especially the smaller ones, is a hindrance to international investors, who often think in terms of regions rather than individual countries. Periodically, plans for cross-border mergers of national stock exchanges are drafted. But most of these projects collapse, in part because the cultural heritage of different trading, legal, and regulatory systems make it very difficult to harmonize trading systems. The canceled merger between the London Stock Exchange and the Deutsche Boerse is a vivid example. As of 2007, Euronext was the only successful merger between Paris, Amsterdam, Brussels, and Lisbon. But the process of rapprochement between bourses accelerated in the mid 2000s. OMX progressively became the trading platform of most Nordic and Baltic exchanges. As of 2007, OMX includes the Copenhagen, Helsinki, Iceland, Stockholm, Tallinn, Riga, and Vilnius stock exchanges. Euronext and the NYSE merged in 2007; in the same year, Deutsche Boerse purchased 5 percent of the Bombay Stock Exchanges, and the Tokyo Stock Exchange announced alliances with the NYSE and the London Stock Exchange. The process of consolidation among stock exchanges is likely to continue. As we shall see later, stock markets also internationalize by listing shares of foreign companies.

A related hindrance is the fragmentation of settlement systems. The multiplicity of national settlement systems adds to the cost of international investing. But a consolidation of settlement systems is taking place, especially in Europe. A common depository and counterparty platform has been developed around Euronext and Euroclear, the international securities clearinghouse. So, trades in several European stock markets, as well as international bonds, use the same system, Clearnet. Another platform, Clearstream, has been created around the Deutsche Boerse from the former international securities clearinghouse, Cedel.

## 2    SOME STATISTICS

### Market Size

Relative national market capitalizations give some indication of the importance of each country for global investors. Market-capitalization weights are used in the commonly used global benchmarks; hence, market sizes guide global investment strategies.

Developed and emerging markets are usually classified in two different asset classes. Although they are somewhat arbitrary, and some countries have been moved from the status of emerging to developed in the recent past, these classifications are still widely used by investors. In the statistics given below, we adopt the widely used classification of Morgan Stanley Capital International.

### *Developed Markets*

The U.S. stock exchanges are the largest exchanges in the world. It is worth noting that the U.S. capital market is very large compared to the U.S. economy. The U.S. stock market capitalization (cap) is much larger than the annual U.S. gross domestic product (GDP). Britain also has a market cap almost double its GDP, but the corresponding figure for France or Germany is below 80 percent. This difference between the United States and continental Europe has several explanations. Most U.S. firms prefer to go public, whereas in France, as well as in the rest of Europe, tradition calls for maintaining private ownership as much as possible. In many European countries, corporations are undercapitalized and rely heavily on bank financing. Germany is a typical example because banks finance corporations extensively, thereby reducing the need for outside equity capital. In Europe, banks tend to provide corporations with all financial services, assisting them in both their commercial needs and their long-term debt and equity financing. In contrast to banks in the United States, it is common for European banks to own shares of their client companies. U.S. companies, especially small- and medium-sized ones, tend to go public and raise capital in the marketplace, thereby increasing the public stock market cap. In other countries, many large firms are still government-owned and therefore are not listed on the capital markets. In France, for example, portions of the telecommunication, arms manufacturing, banking, and transportation industries are partly owned by the government. Countries such as France, Italy, and Germany progressively evolve along the U.S. model, and their weights in a global index are likely to rise.

The size of the world stock market has grown dramatically since the 1970s, passing the $50 trillion mark at the end of 2000. It has multiplied by approximately 50 since the early 1970s. Developed markets had a total market cap of some $44 trillion at the end of 2006, while emerging markets cap reached $6.8 trillion. The market sizes of the largest developed stock markets (with market cap of $1 trillion or more in 2006) are given in Exhibit 1. Japan, the United Kingdom, and Euronext have the largest markets outside of the United States. Currency movements induce changes in the total size and geographical breakdown of the world market. A drop in the value of the dollar reduces the market share of U.S. stocks; the dollar value of non-U.S. stocks increases by the amount of the dollar depreciation, assuming that the stocks' values in domestic currency do not change and that the dollar value of U.S. stocks stays constant. The share of U.S. markets decreased from almost two-thirds of the world market cap in 1972 to only one-third by the early 1990s. It moved back up to over 50 percent after 2000, partly because of a big drop in Asian markets. At the end of 2006 it stood at 45 percent of developed market cap and 39 percent of total world market cap. Meanwhile, the shares of European and Asian markets in total world market cap are roughly equal at 30 percent.

| EXHIBIT 1 | Market Sizes of Developed Markets Billions of U.S. Dollars, End of 2006 |
|---|---|
| NYSE | 15,421 |
| Japan | 4,614 |
| NASDAQ | 3,865 |
| United Kingdom | 3,794 |
| Euronext | 3,708 |
| Hong Kong | 1,715 |
| Canada | 1,701 |
| Germany | 1,638 |
| Spain | 1,323 |
| Switzerland | 1,212 |
| OMX Nordic Exchange | 1,123 |
| Australia | 1,096 |
| Italy | 1,027 |
| Others | 1,636 |
| *Total* | **43,872** |

*Source*: World Federation of Exchanges.

The figure for Japan is somewhat inflated by the practice of cross-holding of stocks among publicly traded Japanese companies and financial institutions (*mochiai*). A similar feature can be found in South Korea, where companies within large conglomerates (*chaebols*) are linked with extensive equity cross-holding. Index providers are trying to adjust the market cap weights used in the index. This is part of the so-called free-float adjustment, which attempts to eliminate the effects of cross-holdings, as illustrated in Example 4.

### Emerging Markets

The 1980s saw the emergence and rapid growth of stock markets in many developing countries. In Africa, stock markets opened in Egypt, Morocco, and the Ivory Coast, but with limited growth. Growth has been somewhat faster in Latin America, especially in Brazil and Mexico. The most spectacular change, however, has been witnessed in Asia. Stock markets have grown rapidly in China, India, Indonesia, Malaysia, Thailand, South Korea, and Taiwan. The emerging market crisis of 1997 stopped that growth, but growth picked up again in 2002. We see in Exhibit 2 that the total capitalization of emerging markets represents over 13 percent of the world stock market cap at the end of 2006.

---

### EXAMPLE 4

**Example of Adjustment for Cross-Holding**

Three companies belong to a group and are listed on the stock exchange:

▶ Company A owns 30 percent of Company B.
▶ Company B owns 20 percent of Company C.
▶ Company C owns 10 percent of Company A.

Each company has a total market cap of 100 million.
    You wish to adjust for cross-holding to reflect the weights of these companies in a market cap–weighted index. What adjustment would you make to reflect the free float?

**Solution:** The apparent market cap of these three companies taken together is 300 million. But because of their cross-holding, there is some double counting. The usual free-float adjustment would be to retain only the portion that is not owned by other companies within the group. Hence, the adjusted market capitalization is:

$$90 + 70 + 80 = 240 \text{ million}$$

---

## Liquidity

Transaction volume gives indications on the liquidity of each market. In a liquid market, investors can be more active and design various arbitrage strategies. Some markets are large via their market cap, and hence their weight in a global index, but with little turnover. Illiquidity tends to imply higher transaction costs. Investors measuring performance relative to a global benchmark will tend to be more passive on such illiquid markets.

| EXHIBIT 2 | Sizes of Emerging Markets<br>*Billions of U.S. Dollars, End of 2006* | |
|---|---|---|
| China | 1,146 | Israel | 162 |
| Korea | 834 | Poland | 149 |
| India | 819 | Thailand | 140 |
| South Africa | 711 | Indonesia | 139 |
| Brazil | 710 | Egypt | 93 |
| Taiwan | 595 | Other Europe/Africa/ | |
| Mexico | 348 |    Middle East | 114 |
| Malaysia | 236 | Other Latin America | 150 |
| Chile | 174 | Other Asia | 81 |
| Turkey | 162 | *Total* | **6,763** |

*Source*: World Federation of Exchanges.

Exhibit 3 gives the turnover ratio of major markets computed as the ratio of the annual transaction volume to the market cap at year-end 2006. This is a simple indicator of the liquidity on each market. It is sometimes called *share turnover velocity*. Depending on market activity, these figures can vary widely from one year to the next, but it is apparent that some national markets are more active than others. The ranking of countries based on the volume of transactions differs slightly from that based on market cap.

In fact, the turnover ratio varies significantly over time. For example, the transaction volume in Japan soared in the late 1980s to surpass that of the NYSE, and the Japanese turnover ratio became a multiple of the U.S. ratio, but it dropped dramatically in the 1990s. Therefore, comparison of national market liquidity based on this variable could lead to different conclusions, depending on the years observed.

In addition, the transaction volume on some emerging markets is very large relative to their size. Transaction volumes in Korea or Taiwan are sometimes larger than that of any developed market except the United States. But this is not the case for many other emerging markets that are quite illiquid.

## Concentration

Another informative statistic is the degree of concentration of the market cap found in the major markets. It is important that investors know whether a national market is made up of a diversity of firms or concentrated in a few large firms. Institutional investors are reluctant to invest in small firms, fearing that they offer poor liquidity. Also, it is easier for the investor to track the performance of a market index, which is usually market cap–weighted, if it is dominated by a few large issues. On the other hand, a market dominated by a few large firms provides fewer opportunities for risk diversification and active portfolio strategies.

| EXHIBIT 3 | Annual Turnover on Major Stock Markets |

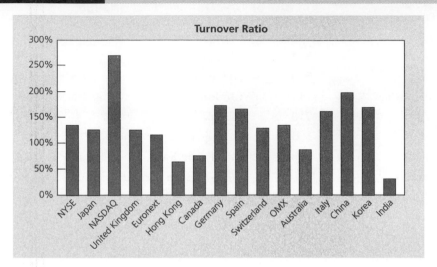

*Source*: World Federation of Exchanges.

| EXHIBIT 4 | Share of the Ten Largest Listed Companies in the National Market Capitalization |

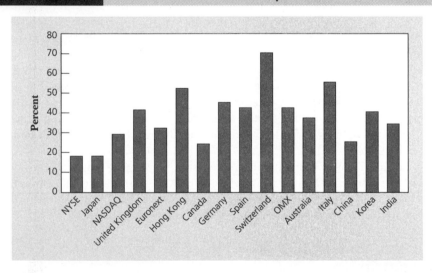

*Source*: World Federation of Exchanges.

As shown in Exhibit 4, the NYSE and Tokyo Stock Exchange are diverse markets in which the top ten firms represent less than 20 percent of total market cap. In the United States, the largest firm represents less than 3 percent of the capitalization for the NYSE. At the other end of the spectrum, the top ten Swiss multinational firms account for some 70 percent of the Swiss stock exchange. Nokia is larger than the sum of all other Finnish firms.

# SOME PRACTICAL ASPECTS     3

A few practical aspects must be taken into account when investing abroad.

## Tax Aspects

Taxes can add to the cost of international investment. Foreign investments may be taxed in two locations: the investor's country and the investment's country. Taxes are applied in any of three areas: transactions, capital gains, and income (dividends, etc.).

Some countries impose a tax on transactions. The United Kingdom has retained a stamp tax of 0.5 percent on purchases of domestic securities (but not on sales). Most countries have eliminated, or drastically reduced, such transaction taxes. In countries where brokers charge a commission rather than trade on net prices, a tax proportional to the commission is sometimes charged. For example, France levies a 19.6 percent value-added tax (VAT) on commissions (not on the transaction value), just as on any service. Market makers are usually exempted from these taxes when they trade for their own accounts.

Capital gains are normally taxed where the investor resides, regardless of the national origin of the investment. In other words, domestic and international investments are taxed the same way.

Income on foreign stocks is paid from the legal entity of one country to a resident of another country. This transaction often poses a conflict of jurisdiction, because both countries may want to impose a tax on that income. The international convention on taxing income is to make certain that taxes are paid by the investor in at least one country, which is why withholding taxes are levied on dividend payments. Because many investors are also taxed on income received in their country of residence, double taxation can result from this practice but is avoided through a network of international tax treaties. An investor receives a dividend net of withholding tax plus a tax credit from the foreign government. The investor's country of residence imposes its tax on the gross foreign dividends, but the amount of this tax is reduced by the withholding tax credit. In other words, the foreign tax credit is applied against the home taxes. Tax rules change frequently, but the typical withholding tax rate is 15 percent of dividends.

To a tax-free investor, such as a pension fund, this tax credit is worthless because the investor does not pay taxes at home. In this case, the investor can reclaim the tax withheld in the foreign country. Reclaiming a withholding tax is often a lengthy process requiring at least a few months and even up to a couple of years. In a few countries, part of the withholding tax is kept by the country of origin. In other countries, tax-free foreign investors, especially public pension funds, can apply for a direct exemption from tax withholding. Example 5 illustrates these fiscal aspects.

### EXAMPLE 5

#### Example of Tax Adjustments

A U.S. investor buys 100 shares of Heineken listed in Amsterdam for 40 euros. She goes through a U.S. broker, and the current exchange rate is 1 euro = 1.1 U.S. dollars. Her total cost is $4,400, or $44 per share of Heineken (40 × 1.1 $ per €). Three months later, a gross dividend of €2 is paid (15 percent withholding tax), and she decides to sell the Heineken shares. Each share is now worth 38 euros, and the current exchange rate is euro = 1.2 U.S. dollars because the euro has sharply risen against the dollar. The same exchange rate applied on the dividend payment date. What are the cash flows received in U.S. dollars?

**Solution:** The cash flows are as follows:

### Dividend Payment Minus Withholding Tax ($/€ = 1.2)

|  | Net Dividend | Tax Credit |
|---|---|---|
| In euros per share | 1.70 | 0.30 |
| In dollars per share | 2.04 | 0.36 |
| Net in dollars (100 shares) | 204 | 36 |

### Sale of Heineken Shares ($/€ = 1.2)

|  |  |
|---|---|
| In euros per share | 38 |
| In dollars per share | 45.6 |
| Net in dollars (100 shares) | 4560 |

Our investor has made a capital gain of $160 ($4,560 − $4,400), which will be taxed in the United States at the U.S. capital gains tax rate. She will also declare a total gross dividend of $240 as income, which will be taxed at her income tax rate. She can deduct from her income tax a tax credit of $36, however, thanks to the United States–Netherlands tax treaty.

## Stock Market Indexes

Stock market indexes allow us to measure the average performance of a national market. One or several market indexes may track a national market at any given time. Historically, country stock indexes were computed by the local stock market, but global organizations have started to provide indexes for national markets around the world, as well as a series of global indexes.

### Domestic Stock Indexes

Domestic investors usually prefer indexes that are calculated and published locally. Most of these are broadly based, market value–weighted indexes. Each company is assigned an index weight proportional to its market cap. Market value–weighted indexes are true market portfolio indexes in the sense that when the index portfolio is held by an investor, it truly represents movements in the market. This is not true of equal-weighted indexes, such as the U.S. Dow Jones 30 Industrial Average (DJIA) or the Japanese Nikkei 225 Stock Average. The DJIA adds up the stock price of 30 corporations. Each company is assigned an index weight proportional to its market price, when computing the index percentage price movement. For example, the return on a share with a price of $100 will have ten times more importance than the return on a share with a price of $10. So the weighting method is quite artificial. Not only is the DJIA narrowly based, but also its composition is somewhat arbitrary; for example, IBM was removed from the index in the 1970s because its price was too high compared with the other 29 corporations. Many stock exchanges have introduced indexes based on a small number of large stocks. There are two reasons for this trend toward narrow-based indexes. First, investors like to get instantaneous information and market movements by accessing Internet or information providers such as Reuters or Bloomberg. Meaningful market indicators must be computed using the most actively traded stocks, not those that trade infrequently. Second, exchanges have introduced *derivatives* (futures, options) on these stock indexes. Dealers in those derivative markets prefer to have an index that is based on a small number of actively traded stocks. Such an index makes it much easier to hedge their derivatives exposure in the cash stock market. Most stock indexes published do not include dividends, although some countries also report dividend-adjusted indexes.

Because some stocks are listed on several exchanges, some companies appear in different national indexes. For example, the S&P 500 used to include some very large non-U.S. companies.

### Global Stock Indexes

Morgan Stanley Capital International (MSCI) has published international market cap–weighted indexes since 1970. MSCI now publishes country indexes for all developed as well as numerous emerging markets, in addition to a variety of regional and global indexes. The World index includes only developed markets, while the All Country World index includes both developed and emerging markets. The MSCI index of non-U.S. stock markets has been extensively used as a benchmark of foreign equity portfolios by U.S. investors; it is called the *index EAFE* (for Europe, Australasia, Far East). Besides market cap–weighted indexes, MSCI also publishes indexes with various weighting schemes (e.g., GDP weights) and with full currency hedging. Global industry and style indexes are also available.

FTSE, created as a joint venture of the *Financial Times* and the London Stock Exchange, has published international indexes since 1987. The most important international indexes are the World index, the Europe index, the Pacific Basin index, and the Europe and Pacific index. Country indexes are provided for developed and emerging markets, as well as numerous industrial and regional indexes. Global industry indexes are available.

Other series of global indexes are also available. Dow Jones publishes, in collaboration with Wilshire Associates, a series of global indexes called the Dow Jones Wilshire Global Index that covers developed and emerging markets. The series includes country and industry indexes calculated daily. S&P publishes an S&P Global 1200 index of developed markets as well as various subindexes, including the S&P 350 Europe index, intended to be the European counterpart of the S&P 500.

The introduction of the euro has created intensive competition among index suppliers. They all try to provide a European index that will be used as a benchmark by global money managers. Besides the well-established indexes of MSCI and FTSE, Dow Jones has launched a series of European indexes in collaboration with the French, German, and Swiss stock exchanges, which are named DJ STOXX. The EURO DJ STOXX 50 is a widely used index of Eurozone blue chips (countries having adopted the euro). Other international blue-chip indexes are published by Dow Jones.

Emerging market indexes are available from the index providers mentioned previously/(MSCI, FTSE, Dow Jones, S&P). In the past the International Finance Corporation (IFC) of the World Bank published popular emerging market indexes. Standard and Poor's acquired its emerging market database and now performs the calculation of various S&P/IFC indexes. The Global index series (S&P/IFCG) is the broadest possible indicator of market movements, and the coverage exceeds 75 percent of local market capitalizations. Weights are adjusted for government and cross-holdings. The Investable index series (S&P/IFCI) is designed to represent the market that is legally and practically available to foreign investors. The Frontier index series tracks small and illiquid markets.

All these global indexes are widely used by international money managers for asset allocation decisions and performance measurements (benchmarks). They differ in terms of coverage and weights. Hence, these global indexes can have significant differences in performance. Besides deciding on which company and country should be included in the respective indexes, the provider must decide on the market-cap weights to be used. Because of cross-holding, government ownership, and/or regulations applying to foreign investors, the amount of market value available to foreign investors (the free float) can differ significantly from the market cap that can be obtained by multiplying the number of shares issued by their market price. Most indexes now perform an adjustment so that the weight of each security represents its free float.

Not all indexes are intended as investable benchmarks tracking an overall market. Specific European indexes have been launched, on which derivatives can be traded. They must comprise a small number of highly liquid stocks, so that market makers in the derivatives can easily hedge their exposure on the stock markets. The DJ Euro Stoxx 50 (50 leading Eurozone stocks) and the FTSE Eurotop 100 (100 leading European stocks) are European indexes on which futures, options, and ETFs are traded.

### Which Index to Use?

Local indexes are widely used by domestic investors. Private investors often prefer these indexes over country indexes of international providers, such as MSCI or FTSE, for several reasons:

▶ In most cases, the local indexes have been used for several decades.

▶ Local indexes are used for derivative contracts (futures, options) traded in that country.

▶ Local indexes are calculated immediately and are available at the same time as stock market quotations on all electronic price services.

▶ Local indexes are available every morning in all the newspapers throughout the world.

▶ The risk of error in prices and capital adjustment is possibly minimized in local indexes by the fact that all calculations are done locally, with excellent information available on the spot.

Institutional investors, on the other hand, prefer to use the MSCI, FTSE, or other international indexes for the following reasons:

▶ The institutional investors do not need up-to-the-minute indexes.

▶ The indexes on all stock markets are available in a central location, whereas local indexes must be drawn from several locations.

- ▶ All international indexes are calculated in a single consistent manner, allowing for direct comparisons between markets.
- ▶ MSCI and FTSE provide global or regional indexes (World, Europe, EAFE), which international money managers need to measure overall performance.
- ▶ They also provide indexes that include dividends.

The choice of index is important. In any given year, the performance between two indexes for the same stock market can differ by as much as several percentage points.

## Information

The information available from different countries and companies varies in quality. Accounting standards differ across countries (see the reading on equity: concepts and techniques), but most developed countries are now enforcing accounting standards of increased quality. Under the pressure of international investors, companies are learning that they must report accurate information on their accounts and prospects in a timely fashion. The situation can be worse for smaller firms in countries where there is less tradition of information transparency, and it can become worrisome in some emerging markets.

In some emerging countries, the earnings forecasts announced by companies that become publicly listed are totally unverifiable. A notable case is China. The rapid move from a centrally planned economy to a partly capitalistic system means that the notion of accounting at the firm level is a new concept. State-owned companies have been listed on Chinese or foreign stock exchanges but have no tradition of having separate accounts, and therefore they have problems trying to identify earnings to shareholders during a given time period. It is equally difficult to assess who is the legal owner of some of the assets of a Chinese firm; the state, the province, and the municipality all lay some claim on existing firms' assets, and legal property titles do not exist historically. Shanghai Petrochemical Co., for example, was the largest company to be introduced on the NYSE in 1993. Its value is clearly a function of its properties and equipment. A letter from America Appraisal Hong Kong Ltd., included in the 1993 listing prospectus, illustrates that reliable information on companies from emerging markets is sometimes difficult to get:

> We have relied to a considerable extent on information provided by you. . . . As all the properties are situated in the People's Republic of China, we have not searched the original documents to verify ownership. . . . All dimensions, measurements and areas are approximate. We have inspected the exterior and, when possible, the interior of all the properties valued. However, no structural survey has been made and we are therefore unable to report as to whether the properties are or not free of rot, infestation or any other structural defects.

Given the uncertainty about a company's information, it is not surprising that its valuation is a matter of highly subjective judgment. The uncertainty surrounding companies' information is damaging. Most emerging markets trade at low price–earnings ratios compared with developed markets with similar or lesser growth potential. Local authorities and the management of listed firms have come to realize that stricter standards must be applied to the timely release of reliable information. Many countries are adopting accounting standards that conform to the International Accounting Standards or U.S. *generally accepted accounting principles (GAAP)*, but progress in their implementation can only be slow.

## 4

# EXECUTION COSTS

The importance of execution costs, also referred to as *transaction costs*, is sometimes overlooked in portfolio management. These costs vary among countries and should be taken into account in active global investment strategies. Execution costs can reduce the expected return and diversification benefits of an international strategy. The difference in return between a paper portfolio and a managed portfolio can be significant. In theory, forecasted costs should be subtracted from expected return before implementing any active strategies. This is all the more important when investing in high-cost countries such as emerging countries. Portfolio managers must gain a good understanding of the determinants of execution costs and should develop some ability to measure them for trades worldwide.

A manager should try to get the best execution for each trade. *Best execution* refers to executing client transactions so that total cost is most favorable to the client under the particular circumstances at the time. Best execution is an objective even though it is difficult to quantify. Execution costs take many forms, some explicit and easily measurable, others implicit and more difficult to measure.

## Components of Execution Costs

Costs can be listed in decreasing reliability of estimation, as described in the following three sections.

### Commissions, Fees, and Taxes

Commissions paid to brokers are generally negotiated. They depend on the characteristics of the trade (market, liquidity of the stock, size of the order, etc.) and of the market mechanism used (see next section).

Some additional fees are generally paid to compensate for various services, including post-trade settlement costs. As discussed, some taxes are also levied in various countries.

The payment of commissions to brokers often allows access to the broker's research and other services. Therefore, some of the cost is an indirect way to obtain various services beyond direct trading execution. In theory, one should separate the direct dealing cost component and the cost of other services provided ("soft dollars").

All these costs are explicit and easily measurable, but getting the best execution is not equivalent to minimizing commissions and fees.

### Market Impact

Executing a transaction will generally have an impact on the price of the security traded. Market impact can be defined as the difference between the actual execution price and the market price that would have prevailed had the manager not sought to trade the security. For example, an order to buy that is large relative to the normal transaction volume in that security will move the price up, at least temporarily. So, one must estimate the market impact of any trade.

In a price-driven system, the bid–ask spread is a major component of the market impact.[6] However, a bid–ask spread is generally quoted for a maximum number of shares that the market maker is willing to trade and is adjusted upward for large transactions, so a large order will move quoted prices. When investing directly on an order-driven market, there is no bid–ask quote and the market impact has to be estimated from market data. Measuring the overall price impact is a difficult exercise because the price that would have prevailed if the transaction had not taken place, the benchmark price, is not observable. A traditional method to estimate this benchmark price is to compute the volume-weighted average price (VWAP) on the day of the transaction. The idea is that an average of the prices before and after the transaction is an unbiased estimate of the benchmark price. The VWAP method is further discussed below. Market impact is measured as the percentage difference between the execution price and this benchmark price. It must be stressed that the market impact is highly dependent on the order size, market liquidity for the security traded, and the speed of execution desired by the investor. Institutional investors often trade securities in order sizes which are a significant percentage, and even multiple, of the typical daily trading volume for that security. Hence, the market impact for institutional trades can be high, especially if the investor requires immediacy of trading.

### *Opportunity Cost*

The costs mentioned in the preceding section are incurred on an executed trade. But there is also an opportunity cost in case of nonexecution. This opportunity cost can be defined as the loss (or gain) incurred as the result of delay in completion of, or failure to complete in full, a transaction following an initial decision to trade. Opportunity costs can be significant for investors using crossing networks or order-driven systems, in which the risk of nonexecution or partial execution is significant. On any market, it could take hours or days to execute a large trade, and the opportunity cost can be significant in case of an adverse market movement over that period (for example, a price rise in the case of a buy order). Because of this opportunity cost, an active manager is reluctant to complete a trade over a long time period. The information on which the manager bases his trading decision could be quickly reflected in market prices, that is, before the trade is completed. Furthermore, there is a risk of information leakage, whereby the progressive price movement caused by the large order reveals that some trader possesses useful information; this can even be more pronounced if the trader's anonymity is not preserved. Anonymity is very important for large active fund managers. If it becomes known that a large active asset manager starts buying or selling some specific shares, other participants will immediately imitate on the assumption that the manager has some superior analysis or information or that the manager will continue buying or selling. The slower an order is completed, the higher the potential opportunity cost. But trading a large order with immediacy induces high market impact. So there is a trade-off between market impact and opportunity cost.

---

[6] This is also the case when transacting on an order-driven market but asking the broker for a firm bid–ask quotation.

## Estimation and Uses of Execution Costs

Deregulation and increased globalization of all stock markets has led to a global trend toward negotiated commissions. Market impact has also been reduced because of the improvement in trading mechanisms and liquidity on most markets. This does not alleviate the need for measurement of execution costs. Some surveys provide estimates of the average cost of a trade in various markets. Other methods, reviewed below, attempt to measure ex-post execution costs on a trade by trade basis. All these measures allow us to derive estimates of expected execution costs that can affect investment strategies.

### Global Surveys

Several global surveys of execution costs are available. These give market averages for a typical trade in each country. Various studies come up with different estimates. Exhibit 5 reports some cost estimates for trading in the shares on major developed and emerging stock markets obtained from Barclays Global Investors. Market impact is measured at half the bid–ask spread plus price impact for a typical small transaction; the impact would be larger for a large transaction. Trading in non-U.S. securities tends to be somewhat more expensive than trading in U.S. securities. But trading in some European markets, notably France, the Netherlands, Spain, and Germany, tends to be cheaper than in the United States. The execution cost on U.K. securities is large on the buy side (0.76%) because of the stamp tax levied on purchases; it is much lower on sales (0.26%). Trading on emerging markets incurs large execution costs, often close to 1 percent; these costs can significantly affect the return on a portfolio invested in emerging markets.

| EXHIBIT 5 | Execution Costs in Basis Points |
| --- | --- |

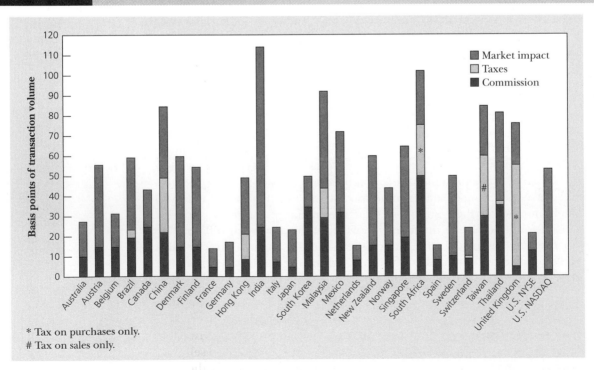

\* Tax on purchases only.
\# Tax on sales only.

*Source*: Barclays Global Investors, 2002.

Of course, the total execution cost is a function of the size of the transaction and the market depth. The average execution costs for buying a $10 million slice of an EAFE portfolio is estimated to be 0.36 percent by Barclays Global Investors (0.25% to sell). The same cost is 0.63 percent for a $1 billion slice (0.53% to sell). Execution costs for a large trade in a single stock can be considerably higher than the figures reported here for a diversified EAFE basket of stocks, for which the magnitude of a trade in each stock is rather small.

### Detailed Measures: VWAP

As mentioned above, a traditional method to estimate the ex-post execution costs for a trade is to compute the volume-weighted average price (VWAP) on the day of the transaction. The difference between the actual trade price and this benchmark price is an indication of execution costs. The idea is that an average of the prices before and after the transaction is an unbiased estimate of the benchmark price.

Unfortunately, this method tends to understate the true market price impact of a trade that represents a significant proportion of the day's trading volume. Another criticism is that this method fails to reflect another hidden cost, namely, opportunity cost. For example, suppose that a manager wishes to buy 100,000 shares of a stock in the belief that its price will rise in the near future. An immediate purchase will result in a transaction price that will be significantly higher than the daily VWAP. Spreading the trade over ten days would result in daily transaction prices which will be closer to their daily VWAP. However, if the expected price appreciation takes place very quickly, the manager will miss taking full advantage of the initial prediction. The opportunity cost is large and not reflected by the VWAP methodology.

The daily VWAP method has been adapted to measure the VWAP over longer time intervals to better reflect the impact of opportunity costs.

### Detailed Measures: Implementation Shortfall

A somewhat different approach to measure ex-post costs is the *implementation shortfall*. The implementation shortfall is the difference between the value of the executed portfolio (or share position) and the value of the same portfolio at the time the trading decision was made. This analysis does not require the use of market data on transaction prices and volumes over the period surrounding the executed transaction. The implementation shortfall measures the impact of the trade as well as the impact of intervening market events until the transaction is completed. While opportunity cost is captured, general market movements caused by other factors are also captured. This shortfall can be adjusted for general market movements by subtracting the return on some broad market index over the measurement period.

### Using Expected Execution Costs

Estimates of ex-post execution costs can be used to judge whether best execution has been achieved. They also allow us to formulate expectations for execution costs on various types of prospective trades. Indeed, some sophisticated execution cost models have been developed.

Active international strategies should factor forecasted execution costs into their expected return estimates. For example, a manager who desires to sell German stocks and replace them with French stocks should estimate whether the expected return overweighs the execution costs incurred in the buy-and-sell transactions. More generally, execution costs are a drag on returns. To see how execution costs should be taken into account to calculate net expected returns, let's consider a strategy with the following features:

▶ $E(R)$ is the annual expected return on a strategy before execution costs.

▶ Execution costs are measured (in percentage) as the average cost of a round trip trade (purchase and sale) on the portfolio.

▶ The annual turnover ratio is the percentage of the portfolio that is traded during the year; it is commonly measured as the lesser of purchases or sales for a year divided by the average market value of the portfolio during that year.

Then the annual expected return net of execution costs is measured as

Net expected return = $E(R)$ − Turnover ratio × Execution costs

The calculation is illustrated in Example 6. Clearly, the impact of execution costs on returns depends on the level of activity of the account and the markets in which the account is invested.

### EXAMPLE 6

**Example of the Impact of Execution Costs**

An asset manager follows an active international asset allocation strategy. The average execution cost for a buy or a sell order is forecasted at 0.5 percent. On average, the manager turns the portfolio over 1.5 times a year. The annual expected return before transaction costs is 10 percent. What is the annual expected return net of execution costs?

**Solution:** On the average, the portfolio is turned over 1.5 times. The average execution cost for a simultaneous purchase and sale of securities is 1 percent (0.5% for a buy and 0.5% for a sale). Hence, the net expected return is equal to

$E(R)$ − Turnover ratio × Execution costs = 10% − 1.5 × 1% = 8.5%

## Some Approaches to Reducing Execution Costs

International investment strategies can be costly, especially for large portfolios. Several approaches can be used to reduce execution costs. Let's take the example of a tactical asset allocation approach, whereby a fund manager decides to reduce the exposure to a country or a region. This would require the sale of a large number of stocks from that region. Rather than trading stock by stock, the manager could engage in *program trading*, in which the manager offers simultaneously a basket of securities for sale. The manager would require a quote from the broker for the whole basket. For the other counterparty, such large trades are often deemed as less risky than a large trade for a single stock because it is clear that they are not motivated by useful information on a specific company; hence, the bid–ask spread quoted could be smaller. There is less risk for the counterparty making a firm quote.

When engaging in a large trade—that is, a trade size that is beyond the normal trade size for which dealers give a standard bid–ask spread, or one that will result in significant market impact—a manager can try to get the best execution through a variety of trading techniques:

▶ *Internal crossing:* The manager will attempt to cross the order with an opposite order for another client of the firm.

  ▶ The *advantage* is that this is the trading method that minimizes costs.

  ▶ The *disadvantage* is that few managers can use this technique because having offsetting orders among clients is rare. There is also a problem in setting the transaction price. One must be sure to determine the price that would have been obtained in the marketplace and not privilege one client at the expense of another. Internal crossing is mostly applied by very large asset management firms specialized in passive strategies, such as index funds. For example, it could be the case that one client wants to reduce its exposure to European stocks, while another is in the process of building a global portfolio, including European stocks. Active managers would have a difficult time justifying selling shares of one company for a client, based on some forecast or model, and at the same time buying shares of the same company for another client.

▶ *External crossing:* The manager sends the order to an electronic crossing network, as described above.

  ▶ The *advantage* is that execution costs are very low and anonymity is assured.

  ▶ The *disadvantage* is that it can take a very long time before an opposite order is entered on the crossing network and the trade is executed. Often orders have to be redirected to another trading venue. A large block is less likely to be swiftly crossed than a small order, as it is unlikely that another party will happen to be interested in an opposite transaction of that magnitude. The speed of execution is a clear disadvantage of this technique, which is exposed to opportunity cost.

▶ *Principal trade:* The manager trades through a dealer who guarantees full execution at a specified discount/premium to the prevailing price. The dealer acts as a principal because she commits to taking the opposite side of the order at a firm price.

  ▶ The *advantage* is that trading immediacy is assured and opportunity cost minimized.

  ▶ The *disadvantage* is that the overall execution costs can be quite large. The principal broker commits some of its capital to complete the trade, often buying or selling shares on its own account. A principal dealer must maintain, and finance, an inventory of shares. Hence the dealer has to charge a "rent" for its capital, which increases execution costs. Anonymity cannot be assured, but this is not important as the trade is executed in full and immediately.

▶ *Agency trade:* The fund manager negotiates a competitive commission rate and selects a broker on the basis of his ability to reduce total execution costs. In turn the broker will "work" the order to try to get the best price for the manager. In a way, the search for best execution is delegated to the broker. The broker acts as an agent because he does not act as the counterparty on its own account but executes the order with another client.

  ▶ The *advantage* is that the fund manager expects to achieve best execution by relying on the quality of the broker, who is compensated by

a commission. This often leads to a compromise between opportunity
cost and market impact.

▶ The potential *disadvantage* is that the commission paid could be too large
for the quality of service provided. Also, anonymity cannot be assured.

▶ *Use of dealer "indications of interest" (IOI):* Some other party might have a wish
to engage in an opposite trade for a stock or basket of stocks. Polling IOIs
from various dealers helps to identify possible pools of liquidity.

▶ The *advantage* is that the fund manager can hope to achieve low
execution costs by finding some opposite trading interest.

▶ The *disadvantage* is that this search for liquidity among numerous dealers
reveals publicly an interest in the security. Even if the anonymity of the
investor is preserved, the trading interest is not.[7] It also slows trading
speed. This technique is best suited for informationless trading by
passive managers.

▶ *Use of futures:* There is an opportunity cost associated with the delay in
execution of a large trade. The fund manager could use futures to monitor
the position while the trade is progressively executed. For example, a
manager whose tactical asset allocation decision is to reduce the French
exposure on a large portfolio, because of the fear of a sudden drop in the
French stock market, could immediately sell futures on the CAC, the
French stock index. The manager will progressively sell the French stocks in
the portfolio with low execution costs, while simultaneously reducing his
position in futures.

▶ An *advantage* is the reduction in the opportunity cost component of
execution costs.

▶ A *disadvantage* is the additional source of risk if the price of the security
traded is not strongly correlated to that of the futures contract. Use of
futures is well suited for building positions in diversified portfolios of
stocks, with a high correlation between the price of the futures contract
and that of the portfolio traded. But it is not well suited for trading in a
single security, where the correlation with a stock index futures contract
is not so large. So adding a futures position does little to eliminate the
opportunity cost for that specific security while adding a new source of
risk (the futures price volatility).

Several services, and asset management firms, provide models of expected execution costs. These can also be used as a benchmark when executing a trade.
Looking at deviations from the forecasted cost model over a number of trades
allows one to review the quality of execution of a broker and of various trading
techniques. Choosing a venue to get best execution is basically searching for
liquidity. It is a difficult task that depends on the type of trade and implies trade-
offs that depend on several parameters, such as the following:

▶ *Desire for confidentiality:* An active manager looking for alphas (i.e., betting
on the misvaluation of some securities) will be very sensitive to the
confidentiality of trades, while a passive manager will be less sensitive.

---

[7] Investors can ask for IOI on a basket of securities to hide their interest in a specific security.

▶ *Desire for urgency:* An active manager looking for alphas will be very sensitive to the speed of transaction, while a passive manager will be a bit less sensitive.

▶ *Size of transaction:* The larger the transaction relative to the typical daily transaction volume, the higher the market impact.

Finally, fund managers often pay commissions to get additional services such as broker or third-party research (soft dollars). A detailed analysis of execution costs should unbundle these additional services, so that a broker charging a commission is not unduly penalized relative to other trading venues.

In the United Kingdom, the Myners report has prompted managers to focus on minimizing execution costs. A similar focus can be found in the United States. The need to invest in a sophisticated cost-reduction program[8] depends on the type of portfolio strategy followed. Passive index-linked strategies tend to incur lower execution costs than active stock-picking strategies because they trade on diversified baskets of securities. But execution cost is an important component of the performance of a manager attempting to closely track an index.[9] Saving a few basis points in execution costs is worth the effort, given the typical size of a passive portfolio. Also, index-linked basket trades are typically repetitive and more easily modeled.

On the other hand, in an active stock-picking strategy, trades are generally not repetitive. A pairwise trade, for example, buying an undervalued French oil company and selling an overvalued British one has unique characteristics. Such trades are not repetitive, and their costs are difficult to model ex ante. A focus on execution costs will usually mean finding the broker offering the best execution for this type of trade.

# INVESTING IN FOREIGN SHARES LISTED AT HOME

**5**

Investors need not go abroad to diversify internationally. We shall discuss several ways to accomplish this.

## Global Shares and American Depositary Receipts

Some companies are listed on several stock markets around the world. Multinational firms, such as Royal Dutch/Shell or BP, are traded on more than a dozen markets.

## Motivation for Multiple Listing

Foreign companies have a variety of reasons for being listed on several national stock markets, in spite of the additional costs involved:

▶ Multiple listing gives them more access to foreign ownership, allowing a better diversification of their capital and access to a larger amount of funds

---

[8] Such a program is quite costly in terms of human resources, data management, and modeling.

[9] This is true not only for a purely indexed strategy but also for any strategy that promises a small alpha while closely tracking a preassigned index (enhanced indexing).

than is available from smaller domestic equity markets. For example, numerous firms combine an initial listing on the NYSE with a public offering of new shares in their home market.

► Diversified ownership in turn reduces the risk of a domestic takeover.

► Foreign listing raises the profile of a firm in foreign markets, enabling it to raise financing more easily both on the national level and abroad, and is good advertising for its product brands.

► Some companies from emerging countries, especially from remote countries, find multiple listing particularly attractive. Listing abroad allows access to a wider capital base and increases the business visibility of the firm. Chinese companies provide a good illustration of this opportunity. Foreign listing is the way to raise new capital abroad. The advantage for non-Chinese investors is that it is easier, and sometimes cheaper, to buy shares on a well-known, developed market. The currency of quotation for shares listed in the United States is the dollar, dividends are paid in dollars, and information in English is provided.

A danger of foreign listing may be the increased volatility of the firm's stock due to a stronger response in foreign versus domestic markets to domestic economic news. Bad political and economic (domestic) news in the Scandinavian countries, for example, has frequently been followed by an immediate negative impact from shares cross-listed on foreign markets. Scandinavian shareholders display less volatile behavior than foreign investors for two reasons: They are not as shaken by bad domestic news, and they tend to keep their capital invested at home anyhow (home bias).

## Foreign Listing and ADRs

The procedure for admitting foreign stocks to a local market varies; in some markets, the regulations are quite lenient. For example, in 1986 the Quebec Securities Act allowed a foreign company to list in Montreal simply by meeting the same regulatory requirements as those in the foreign company's jurisdiction. In other markets, foreign companies must abide by the same rules as domestic companies. For instance, non-U.S. companies wanting to be listed on U.S. stock exchanges must satisfy the requirements of both the exchange and the U.S. Securities and Exchange Commission. Although this SEC regulation offers some protection to the U.S. investor, it imposes substantial dual-listing costs on non-U.S. companies, which must produce frequent reports in English.

In the United States and a few other countries, trading takes place in negotiable certificates representing ownership of shares of the foreign company. In the United States, trading is in *American Depositary Receipts (ADRs)*. Under this arrangement foreign shares are deposited with a U.S. bank, which in turn issues ADRs in the name of the foreign company. To avoid unusual share prices, ADRs may represent a combination of several foreign shares. For example, Japanese shares are often priced at only a few yen per share. They are therefore combined into lots of 100 or more so that their value is more like that of a typical U.S. share. Conversely, some ADRs represent a fraction of the original share. For example, the NASDAQ ADR of LVMH, the French luxury-goods firm, represents one-fifth of a French share.

The United States is the country of preference for foreign listing, with some 450 foreign companies traded on the NYSE and a similar number on the NASDAQ. The total turnover of foreign companies represents over 10 percent of the NYSE transaction volume. Foreign companies can be traded in several different ways in the United States.

An ADR program created without the company's involvement is usually called an *unsponsored* ADR. These over-the-counter (OTC) shares are traded through *pink sheets*, electronic bulletin boards, or an electronic trading system called PORTAL. An ADR program created with the assistance of the foreign company is called a *sponsored* ADR. Sponsored ADRs are often classified at three levels:

► *Level I*: The company does not comply with SEC registration and reporting requirements, and the shares can be traded only on the OTC market (but not NASDAQ).

► *Level II*: The company registers with the SEC and complies with its reporting requirements. The shares can be listed on an official U.S. stock exchange (NYSE, ASE) or NASDAQ.

► *Level III*: The company's ADRs are traded on a U.S. stock exchange or NASDAQ and the company may raise capital in the United States through a public offering of the ADRs.

A nonregistered (Level I) company can also raise capital in the United States, but it must be done through a private placement under rule 144A. A drawback of this type of private placement is that only certain private investors and qualified institutional buyers (QIBs) can participate. The retail sector is excluded. Furthermore, liquidity of ADRs on the OTC market is not good. The cost of being registered with the SEC (Levels II and III) is the public reporting that must be performed. The foreign company must file a Form 20-F annually. If domestic statements using national accounting standards are presented as primary statements on Form 20-F, the company must provide a reconciliation of earnings and shareholder equity under domestic and U.S. GAAP. This implies that the company must supply all information necessary to comply with U.S. GAAP. Furthermore, the stock exchanges require timely disclosure of various information, including quarterly accounting statements. Some national accounting practices can very easily be reconciled with U.S. practices. For example, the SEC considers that Canadian accounting practices are similar to U.S. practices and accepts Canadian statements; Canadian firms are not required to go through an ADR program; they can simply list their shares on a U.S. stock exchange. Many companies from Bermuda, the Cayman Islands, the Netherlands Antilles, Hong Kong, or Israel simply use the U.S. GAAP statements as their primary financial statements, so they do not even need to provide reconciliation data. At the other extreme, German and Swiss firms have been very reluctant to list shares in the United States because of the difficulty of reconciling U.S. and German or Swiss accounting practices and the detailed information that these firms are not accustomed to disclosing. German and Swiss have tended to smooth reported earnings by using various hidden reserves.

Some firms have issued Global Depositary Receipts (GDRs) that are simultaneously listed on several national markets. These GDRs give the firms access to a larger base to raise new capital. Several Japanese and Chinese firms have seized this opportunity.

When Daimler Benz merged with Chrysler, it decided to become listed on both the Deutsche Bourse and the NYSE. The *same* DaimlerChrysler share is traded on both exchanges, in euros in Frankfurt and in dollars in New York. This is exactly the same share, often called a "global share," that is traded on both exchanges (not an ADR), so an investor can buy shares in Frankfurt and sell them in New York. This would not be possible with an ADR that must go through a difficult conversion process. To make this dual trading possible, several legal and regulatory constraints have to be overcome, besides the accounting harmonization discussed previously. The Sarbanes-Oxley Act of 2002 introduced additional compliance requirements on foreign cross-listed companies. There is considerable discussion about whether the costs of compliance outweigh the benefits of cross-listing.

London is another market with trading of depositary receipts, as well as very active trading of foreign stocks. Foreign companies can list their shares, and the listings can be in all major currencies. The motivation for trading in London is to reduce transaction costs by avoiding some taxes or high commissions charged on the home market and to benefit from the liquidity provided by highly professional market makers based in London. Hong Kong has seen many initial public offerings by mainland Chinese companies. Their shares are referred to as H-shares.

## Valuation of ADRs

Multiple listing implies that the share values of a company are linked on several exchanges. One company should sell at the same share price all over the world, once adjustments for exchange rates and transactions costs have been made. Arbitrage among markets ensures that this is so. An important question is: What is the dominant force affecting the stock price of a multiple-listed company? In a dominant–satellite market relationship the home market is the dominant force, and the price in the foreign market (the satellite) simply adjusts to the home market price. This is clearly the case for many dual-listed stocks of which only a very small proportion of capitalization is traded abroad. For most ADRs, the price quoted by market makers is simply the home price of the share adjusted by the exchange rate. But, because the ADR market is less liquid, a large bid–ask spread is added. A fairly large discrepancy in prices between the home and foreign market can be observed because the arbitrage costs between the ADR and the original share can be sizable. The answer is less obvious, however, for a few large European, Chinese, and South American companies that have a very active market in other countries (especially the United States). The volume of trading of a few European multinationals is sometimes bigger in New York, Hong Kong, and London than on their home market. This situation also applies to a few Latin American firms and to many of the GDRs.

The influence of time zones should also be noted. Because stock trading takes place at different times around the world, U.S. stocks listed on the Paris Bourse are traded before the opening of the U.S. markets. Their French prices reflect not only the previous close in New York and the current exchange rate, but also anticipation about the current day's new price, based on new information released following the U.S. close.

## Advantages/Disadvantages

ADRs allow an easy and direct investment in some foreign firms. Although buying ADRs is an attractive alternative for retail investors, it is usually more costly than a direct purchase abroad for a large investor. On the other hand, some ADRs issued by companies from emerging countries tend to have larger trading volumes in New York than in their home markets, and the execution costs are lower in New York. Whereas the small investor may find it more convenient to trade in foreign shares listed on the home market, the large investor may often find the primary market of overseas companies to be more liquid and cheaper.

In all cases, price levels, transaction costs, taxes, and administrative costs should be major determinants of whichever market the investor chooses. This is illustrated in Example 7.

---

**EXAMPLE 7**

**Example of Price Arbitrage**

DaimlerChrysler shares are listed in Frankfurt (XETRA) and on the NYSE. You are a German investor with a large portfolio of German and international stocks. You just bought 10,000 shares in Frankfurt at 51 euros per share. In addition, your broker charges a 0.25 percent commission. At the same time, a U.S. broker quotes DaimlerChrysler traded on the NYSE at 44.70–44.90 dollars, net of commissions. The exchange rate quoted in dollar per euro is 0.8800–0.8820 net. So you can buy one euro for 0.8820 dollar and sell one euro for 0.8800 dollar. Would it have been better to buy the shares in New York rather than in Frankfurt, knowing that these are the same global shares?

**Solution:** Let's compute the euro purchase price of one share listed on the NYSE. You would buy the shares from the broker at 44.90 dollars. To pay for this purchase, you would need to exchange euros for dollars (sell euros, buy dollars) at the rate of 0.8800 dollar per euro. The net purchase cost per share in euros is

$$44.90/0.88 = 51.0227 \text{ euros}$$

The cost of purchasing shares directly in Frankfurt is the purchase price plus the 0.25 percent commission:

$$51 \times 1.0025 = 51.1275 \text{ euros}$$

You would have saved 0.1048 euro per share, or 1,048 euros for the 10,000 shares. Of course, you would end up with shares delivered in New York, but they could be held in custody with the rest of your U.S. stock portfolio.

---

Another disadvantage of ADRs is that only a limited number of companies have issued ADRs, and they represent only a small proportion of foreign market capitalization. They tend to be large companies in each country, so they do not offer full international diversification benefits.

## Closed-End Country Funds

*Closed-end country funds* have been created for many countries, especially emerging countries.

### Definition and Motivation

A *closed-end fund* is an investment vehicle that buys stocks in the market; in turn, shares of the closed-end fund are traded in the stock market at a price determined by supply and demand for that fund. The number of shares of the fund usually remains fixed, and shares cannot be redeemed but are only traded in the stock market. The fund's market price can differ from the value of the assets held in its portfolio, which is called the *net asset value (NAV)*. The *premium* on the fund is the difference between the fund market price and its NAV:

Fund market price = NAV + Premium

The premium is often expressed as a *percentage of the NAV* and is usually called a discount when negative. The situation is quite different for a portfolio directly entrusted to a portfolio manager or for an open-end fund, such as a mutual fund. There, the value of the portfolio or fund is, by definition, equal to the market value of the invested assets (the NAV). The advantage of a closed-end fund for the investment manager is that she does not have to worry about redemptions; once a closed-end fund is initially subscribed, the investment manager keeps the money under management. This vehicle is well suited to investing in emerging markets, because the manager does not face redemption demands and can invest in the long term without liquidity concerns. The disadvantage for the closed-end shareholder is the uncertainty in the premium, as will be discussed later.

A *country fund* (e.g., the Korea Fund) is a closed-end fund whose assets consist primarily of stocks of the country for which the fund is named (e.g., stocks of Korean companies). Numerous country funds are listed in the United States, the United Kingdom, and major stock markets.

The motivation for investing in those country funds is twofold. First, they offer a simple way to access the local market and benefit from international diversification. For example, country funds invested in Italy, Spain, Australia, the United Kingdom, or Germany can be purchased in the United States. These funds invested in developed markets are of interest primarily to private investors, who find an easy way to hold a diversified portfolio of that country. Country funds are simply managed portfolios specializing in stocks of a specific country. The case for country funds investing in emerging markets is more compelling, because the alternative of investing directly in emerging markets is a more difficult process. Furthermore, some countries (e.g., Brazil, India, Korea, and Taiwan) traditionally restricted foreign investment. Country funds, approved by the local government, are a way to overcome foreign investment restrictions. So, foreign investment restriction is a second motivation for the creation and use of some of these country funds. The International Finance Corporation (IFC) of the World Bank has been instrumental in the launching of country funds in small emerging markets.

### The Pricing of Country Funds

The price of a country fund is seldom equal to its NAV. Some funds trade at a substantial premium or discount from their NAV, posing problems for investors. The change in market price of a country fund is equal to the change in NAV plus the change in the premium (discount). If the premium decreases or the discount widens, the return on the fund will be less than the return on underlying assets making up the portfolio.

Some country funds provide a unique way to invest in emerging countries with foreign investment restrictions. When these foreign investment restrictions are binding, one would expect the country fund to sell at a premium over its NAV; see

Bonser-Neal et al. (1990) or Eun, Janakiramanan, and Senbet (1995). The premium should be equal to the amount that investors are willing to pay to circumvent the restriction. Indeed, funds invested in India, Korea, Taiwan, or Brazil have generally sold at a steep but volatile premium. Emerging countries are progressively liberalizing foreign access to their financial markets. When the lifting of a foreign investment restriction is announced, the premium on a local-country fund should drop, as local shares will be more widely available to foreign investors. This drop in premium is a risk associated with investing in these country funds. It can only be hoped that the local market will respond favorably to the prospect of attracting more foreign investors and that a rise in NAV will compensate for a drop in the fund's premium. The liberalization in Brazil and Korea has indeed led to large drops in the premium of closed-end funds invested in those countries.

---

### EXAMPLE 8

**Example of Movements in Premium**

Paf is an emerging country with severe foreign investment restrictions but an active stock market open mostly to local investors. The exchange rate of the pif, the local currency, with the U.S. dollar remains fixed at $\$:Pif = 1$. A closed-end country fund, called Paf Country Fund, has been approved by Paf. Its net asset value is 100 dollars. It trades in New York with a premium of 30 percent.

1. Give some intuitive explanations for this positive premium.
2. Paf unexpectedly announces that it will lift all foreign investment restrictions, which has two effects. First, stock prices in Paf go up by 20 percent because of the expectation of massive foreign investment attracted by the growth opportunities in Paf. Second, the premium on the Paf Country Fund drops to zero. Is this scenario reasonable? What would be your total gain (loss) on the shares of Paf Country Fund?

**Solution to 1:**  There is no alternative to investing in the closed-end fund for foreign investors. Foreign investors may find Paf shares so attractive from a risk–return viewpoint that they compete and bid up the price.

**Solution to 2:**  The scenario is reasonable. The net result can be calculated for 100 dollars of original NAV. Before the lifting of restrictions, the fund was worth 130 dollars for 100 dollars of NAV. After the lifting of restrictions, the NAV moves up to 120 dollars and the fund is now worth its NAV, or 120 dollars. The rate of return for the foreign investor is

$$\frac{120 - 130}{130} = -7.7\%$$

---

The volatility in the value of the premium can add volatility to that of the underlying assets. Historically, premiums on country funds have been very volatile. Johnson, Schneeweiss, and Dinning (1993) studied a sample of country funds listed in the United States and invested either in developed markets or in emerging markets. They measured the U.S. dollar volatilities of the fund, the fund's NAV, and the local underlying stock index (e.g., the Korean index for the

Korean Fund). For emerging-country funds, the volatility of the fund was about 30 percent more than that of its NAV, and 10 percent more than that of the local stock index. This additional volatility might be a necessary cost to bear when few other alternatives are open. Because these markets are becoming much more accessible, the attraction of country funds is reduced. For developed-country funds, Johnson et al. (1993) found that the volatility of a fund was almost twice as large as that of its NAV or of the local stock index. To avoid the additional volatility of closed-end country funds invested in developed markets, investors can buy open-end funds or buy a portfolio directly on the foreign market. These portfolios will always be valued at their NAV, without premium or discount. It can be argued that the large discount observed on many developed-country funds simply reflects large management fees[10] and the lack of liquidity of the market for the fund's shares.

Another interesting feature of the pricing of country closed-end funds listed in the United States is the fact that a fund's value is often strongly correlated with the U.S. stock market and reacts only slowly to changes in the fundamentals (i.e., changes in the NAV). Both phenomena are inconsistent with market efficiency. For example, a Korean fund is a portfolio of Korean stocks; its value should not be affected by movements in the U.S. stock market (beyond the normal correlation between Korea and the United States). Many behavioral finance explanations are provided, including over- and underreaction to news, investor demand, and investor "sentiment." Klibanoff, Lamont, and Wizman (1998) provide an interesting study that focuses on the "salience" of news. They show that, although the elasticity of the fund's price to news is less than one, it is much higher when the news appears on the front page of *The New York Times*. So, investors will react quickly only to salient news.

### *Advantages/Disadvantages*

Closed-end funds allow investors access to a portfolio invested in some foreign region. The portfolio is generally better diversified than a collection of a few ADRs of that region.

The previous discussion of costs and volatility suggests, however, that buying closed-end funds is an inferior substitute for direct investment in foreign stock markets, even for most emerging markets.

## Open-End Funds

An open-end mutual fund is publicly offered and its shares can be purchased and redeemed at the NAV of the assets owned by the fund. Although an *open-end fund* is attractive from the shareholders' viewpoint, it would be risky for the fund manager if investors could redeem shares at a known NAV (which the manager might not be able to realize if he needs to liquidate assets to meet redemptions). Typically investors must announce their decision to buy/redeem their shares before the NAV is calculated. For example, investors must notify their decision before noon, and the NAV is calculated at the end of the day. For open-end funds invested in foreign shares, the lag between notification and determination of the NAV that will be used to execute the transaction can be à couple of days. A large bid–ask spread on the fund's price can also be imposed. The efficiency improvements in many emerging markets have allowed managers to offer open-end funds on the most liquid mar-

---

[10] Indeed, Bekaert and Urias (1999) suggest that closed-end funds are not an attractive substitute for direct investment in foreign stock markets, even for most emerging markets.

kets. Open-end funds are now offered not only for individual countries but also for regions or international industries. Many of these funds take the form of index funds tracking an international index of developed or emerging market. Most new international open-end funds now take the form of ETFs.

## Exchange Traded Funds

*Exchange traded funds (ETFs)* trade on a stock market like shares of any individual company. They can be traded at any time during market hours and can be sold short or margined. But ETFs are shares of a portfolio, not of an individual company. ETFs are generally designed to closely track the performance of a specific index. ETFs on the indexes of several individual, developed stock markets, as well as on many international indexes, are listed on all major stock markets. ETFs on some emerging markets, or international emerging indexes, are also offered. So, they can be used for international diversification strategies. ETFs have been an exceptional commercial success in the early 2000s. ETFs are offered by the large asset management firms that specialize in indexing. Other financial institutions offer ETFs under their name by subcontracting with these specialists.

### *Definition and Motivation*

An ETF is an open-end fund with special characteristics (see Gastineau, 2001). ETFs have a management cost advantage over traditional mutual funds because there is no shareholder accounting at the fund level. ETFs are traded like common stocks. A major feature is the redemption in-kind process. Creation/redemption units are created in large multiples of individual ETF shares, for example, 50,000 shares. These units are available to exchange specialists (*authorized participants*) who will generally act as market makers for the individual shares. If an authorized participant decides to redeem ETF shares, it will do so by exchanging the redemption unit for a portfolio of stocks held by the fund and used to track the index. The fund publishes the portfolio that it is willing to accept for in-kind transactions. As opposed to traditional open-end funds, the in-kind redemption means that no capital gain will be realized in the fund's portfolio on redemption. If the redemption is in cash, a traditional fund may have to sell stocks held in the fund's portfolio. If their price has appreciated, the fund will realize a capital gain and the tax burden will have to be passed to all existing fund shareholders. This is not the case with ETFs. As in any open-end fund, though, individual ETF shareholders[11] can require in-cash redemption based on the NAV. Redemption in cash by individual ETF shareholders is discouraged in two ways:

▶ Redemption is based on the NAV computed one or a couple of days after the shareholder commits to redemption. So, the redemption value is unknown when the investor decides to redeem.

▶ A large fee is assessed on in-cash redemptions.

It is more advantageous for individual ETF shareholders to sell their shares on the market than to redeem them in cash. The sale can take place immediately based on observed share prices at a low cost. Arbitrage by authorized participants ensures that the listed price is close to the fund's NAV.[12] Authorized participants

---

[11] But authorized participants commit to redeem only in kind.

[12] The fund publishes an indicative intraday NAV every 15 seconds; it is available on major data providers, such as Bloomberg, Reuters, or Telekurs.

maintain a market in the ETF share by posting bid and ask prices with a narrow spread, or by entering buy-and-sell limit orders in an electronic order book. The transaction costs of ETFs can be estimated as the sum of the commission charged by the broker plus half this bid–ask spread.

International ETFs have distinguishing features. An ETF indexed on some less-liquid emerging market is bound to have high bid–ask spreads. Managing an ETF on a broad international index, such as EAFE, means holding stock from numerous countries with different custodial arrangements and time zones. Again, the bid–ask spreads are likely to be larger than for *plain-vanilla* ETFs. But the size of the ETF is an important factor influencing costs. The effect of non-overlapping time zones should be taken into account when comparing the ETF price with its NAV. Consider the example of an ETF on a Japanese stock index, traded in New York. During Wall Street opening hours, the Tokyo stock market is closed. The NAV available in the morning in the United States is based on the closing prices in Tokyo several hours before New York opens. Except for currency fluctuations, the NAV will remain unchanged as Tokyo is closed throughout the New York trading session. However, the ETF price will be affected by expectations about future stock prices in Tokyo, so it could differ significantly from the official NAV. This is not an inefficiency and there are no arbitrage opportunities, because the NAV is stale and does not correspond to current market pricing (see Example 9).

## EXAMPLE 9

### ETF Pricing

An ETF is indexed on a Japanese stock index and is listed in New York. Its NAV is computed based on closing prices in Tokyo. When it is 9 A.M. in New York, it is already 11 P.M. in Tokyo on the same day. The NAV based on Tokyo closing prices is 10,000 yen. The exchange rate at 9 A.M. EST is 1 dollar = 100 yen.

1. What is the dollar NAV of this ETF at the opening of trading in New York?

2. When New York closes at 4 P.M. EST, Tokyo is still closed (6 A.M. local time), but the exchange rate is now 99 yen per dollar. What is the dollar NAV at closing time?

3. Bad international news hit after the Tokyo closing. European and U.S. stock markets dropped by 5 percent. Should the ETF price have remained at its NAV? Assuming that the Tokyo market is strongly correlated with the U.S. market (at least for this type of international news), give an estimate of the ETF price at the New York closing.

**Solution to 1:** The dollar NAV is $100 (= 10,000/100).

**Solution to 2:** The closing dollar NAV is $101.01 (= 10,000/99)

**Solution to 3:** The price of the ETF should reflect expectations that the Tokyo stock index will drop in reaction to the news, so its price should be below the NAV computed on past closing prices in Tokyo. If the markets are strongly correlated, we could estimate that Tokyo will also drop by 5 percent. Hence, we should have an estimated market value for the dollar NAV equal to

$$10{,}000 \times (1 - 0.05)/99 = \$95.96$$

This is an estimate of the current price of the ETF. It will trade at a 5 percent discount from its "official" NAV.

## Advantages/Disadvantages

ETFs are attractive to individual investors because they offer the benefits of international diversification with excellent liquidity at a low cost. They are also designed to be tax efficient. ETFs are useful in an international portfolio strategy. They can be purchased in the home market while offering a diversified play on a foreign market or region. They are well designed to be used in active asset allocation. On the other hand, they usually are designed to match a benchmark and will not provide active return above that benchmark. To add active return, investors can combine them with the direct purchase of specific companies or ADRs.

For large institutional investors, the alternative is to invest directly in an indexed, or actively managed, international portfolio; the cost structure could be less and the tax situation equivalent or better.

# SUMMARY

▶ Stock exchanges throughout the world evolved from three models: private bourses, public bourses, and bankers' bourses.

▶ Trading procedures differ in order-driven and price-driven markets. In a price-driven market, market makers stand ready to buy or sell at posted prices (bid and ask prices). In an order-driven market, all buy-and-sell orders are entered in a central order book and a new order is immediately matched with the book of limit orders previously submitted. Each system presents advantages and risks for traders and customers.

▶ Electronic communication and crossing networks (ECNs) have developed alongside official stock exchanges. Electronic crossing networks match anonymously buy-and-sell orders submitted by institutional investors and broker-dealers at prespecified times and at prices determined in the primary market for the security. The trade is made at the midpoint between the bid and ask prices of the primary market, so there is no market impact or bid–ask spread even for large orders. But there is also no trading immediacy.

▶ The relative market capitalization of national equity markets has changed dramatically over time. The share of the U.S. equity markets moved from two-thirds of the world market in the early 1970s to only one-third by the early 1990s, when Japan had about the same market size as the United States. In 2007, U.S. equity markets represented some 40 percent of the world market cap, with Europe and Asia accounting for approximately 30 percent each.

▶ Numerous stock indexes are available to track country and regional markets and measure performance. They can be domestic stock indexes computed locally, such as the U.S. Dow Jones Industrial Average or the Japanese Nikkei 225 stocks average. They can be global stock indexes computed by a global organization, such as MSCI, FTSE, DJ, or S&P.

▶ Many practical aspects must be taken into account in global equity investing: market concentration, liquidity, tax aspects, and transaction costs.

▶ Asset managers should try to get the best execution for each trade. Execution costs include several components: commissions and fees, market impact, and opportunity cost. Although commissions and fees are easy to measure, this is less true for market impact and opportunity cost. A transaction has an impact on the price of the security traded, so market impact can be a significant component of execution cost.

▶ To optimize global asset management, one should forecast the execution cost of trading in the various markets. Several global surveys of execution costs are available, but the actual cost depends on the transaction size and the market depth for the specific trade. Various trading techniques allow reduction of execution costs.

► It is possible to get some of the benefits of international diversification by investing solely in securities or funds listed at home:

  ► Some companies have their shares traded on foreign exchanges; these are called ADRs in the United States. Unfortunately, the number of foreign-listed companies is small, and the price of these ADRs is sometimes unattractive. A few companies offer global shares listed and traded simultaneously in several stock markets.

  ► Some closed-end funds specialize in investing in foreign stock markets. The market price of these country funds often differs from their net asset value by a large premium (or discount). The uncertainty concerning this premium adds to investment risk.

  ► Exchange traded funds (ETFs) are special open-end funds that trade on a stock market like shares of individual companies. Their design has made them very successful. The most popular ETFs track some country or regional stock indexes.

## PRACTICE PROBLEMS FOR READING 35

1. Which of the following statements about stock markets is not true?

   I. Many of the stock markets are organized as private bourses.

   II. On most markets, stocks are traded on a cash basis, and transactions are settled within a two- to five-day period.

   III. The central electronic limit order book is the hub of those automated markets that are price-driven.

   IV. An auction market, such as the Paris Bourse, is also known as an order-driven market.

2. The central limit order book of Air Liquide, a French firm that trades on the Paris Bourse, is currently as follows:

| Sell Orders | | Buy Orders | |
| --- | --- | --- | --- |
| Quantity | Limit | Limit | Quantity |
| 500 | 151 | 145 | 500 |
| 2,000 | 150 | 143 | 2,000 |
| 1,000 | 149 | 142 | 1,000 |
| 500 | 147 | 141 | 2,000 |
| 500 | 146 | 140 | 1,000 |

   A. Vincent Jacquet wishes to buy 1,500 shares and enters a market order to buy those shares. At what price will Jacquet buy the shares?

   B. Suppose Vincent Jacquet had instead wanted to sell 1,000 shares of Air Liquide that he already had in his investment portfolio. At what price will he sell those shares?

3. *Business Objects* trades on the Paris Bourse as ordinary shares and on the NASDAQ as American Depositary Receipts (ADRs). One ADR of *Business Objects* corresponds to one share on the Paris Bourse. Suppose the last transaction of *Business Objects* on the Paris Bourse was at €25. An investor then entered on the French electronic trading system a limit order to purchase *Business Objects* shares at €24. The ADR price quoted by a NASDAQ dealer is $23.90–24.45. The exchange rate is $0.96/€. Suppose that some unfavorable information suddenly arrives that suggests that a lower price of *Business Objects* shares at €21 would be fair. Assuming that the exchange rate has not changed, discuss which parties stand to lose on the Paris Bourse and on NASDAQ?

4. It is often argued that automated order-driven trading systems must provide special arrangements for small trades (which are often market orders) as well as for block trades. Advance some explanations for this argument.

**5.** Which of the following statements about electronic communication and crossing networks (ECNs) is/are true?

   I. Electronic communication networks are order-driven systems, in which the limit order book plays a central role.

   II. Electronic crossing networks anonymously match buy-and-sell orders by a pool of participants, generally institutional investors and broker-dealers.

   III. In an ECN, a trade takes place only during a crossing session time and only if there are offsetting orders entered by other participants.

**6.** Consider a European electronic crossing network that runs six crosses daily, that is, the orders are matched six times a day. This network allows a participant to specify several constraints, such as price and minimum fill. Suppose that all the orders submitted to this network for the shares of Christian Dior are good for day (GFD); that is, any unfulfilled part of an order is automatically resubmitted to subsequent crossing sessions during the day.

   **A.** The following orders are on the network for the shares of Christian Dior at the time of the first crossing session of the day. The most recent trading price of Christian Dior at the Paris Bourse is €37.

   ▶ Participant A: a market order to buy 100,000 shares

   ▶ Participant B: a market order to sell 50,000 shares

   ▶ Participant C: a market order to sell 150,000 shares, with a minimum fill of 125,000 shares

   ▶ Participant D: an order to buy 20,000 shares at €36

   Discuss what trades would take place on the crossing network and what orders would remain unfulfilled.

   **B.** The following new orders are submitted to the next crossing session. The most recent trading price of Christian Dior at the Paris Bourse is €38.

   ▶ Participant E: a market order to buy 150,000 shares

   ▶ Participant F: a market order to sell 50,000 shares

   Discuss what trades would take place on the crossing network in this crossing session and what orders would remain unfulfilled.

**7.** The U.S. stock market capitalization is larger relative to U.S. GDP than is the case in most European countries for all the following reasons *except*:

   **A.** A greater proportion of firms in Europe is nationalized.

   **B.** European banks cannot own shares of stock of their client firms.

   **C.** Many European companies rely heavily on bank financing.

   **D.** Privately held companies are a tradition in Europe.

**8.** Standard & Poor's announced in 2001 that it was considering integrating free-float adjustments to its existing practices for the S&P Australian index. It said that it would use a measure called Investable Weight Factor (IWF) to reflect a company's free float. A full free-floated company will have an IWF of 100 percent. For others, the IWF will be adjusted downward by subtracting the percentage of shares that are not freely available for trade. Now consider three Australian manufacturing companies: Alpha, Beta, and Gamma. Alpha owns 5 percent each of Beta and Gamma. Gamma owns 15 percent of Beta. Taking into account the cross-holdings, what will be the IWF of each company?

9. Four companies belong to a group and are listed on a stock exchange. The cross-holdings of these companies are as follows:

 ► Company A owns 20 percent of Company B and 10 percent of Company C.

 ► Company B owns 15 percent of Company C.

 ► Company C owns 10 percent of Company A, 10 percent of Company B, and 5 percent of Company D.

 ► Company D has no ownership in any of the other three companies.

 Each company has a market capitalization of $50 million. You wish to adjust for cross-holding in determining the weights of these companies in a free-float market capitalization–weighted index.

 **A.** What are the market capitalizations of each company after adjustment to reflect free float?

 **B.** What would be the total adjusted market cap of the four companies?

10. The shares of Volkswagen trade on the Frankfurt stock exchange. A U.S. investor purchased 1,000 shares of Volkswagen at €56.91 each, when the exchange rate was €:$ = 0.9790–0.9795. Three months later, the investor received a dividend of €0.50 per share, and the investor decided to sell the shares at the then prevailing price of €61.10 per share. The exchange rate was €:$ = 0.9810–0.9815. The dividend withholding tax rate in Germany is 15% and there is a tax treaty between the United States and Germany to avoid double taxation.

 **A.** How much did the U.S. investor receive in dividends in dollars, net of tax?

 **B.** What were the capital gains from the purchase and sale of Volkswagen shares?

 **C.** How would the dividend income be declared by the investor on a U.S. tax return, and what tax credit would he receive?

11. The shares of Microsoft were trading on NASDAQ on January 1 at $41. A Swedish investor purchased 100 shares of Microsoft at that price. The Swedish kroner to dollar exchange rate then was $:Skr = 9.4173–9.4188. One year later, the investor received a dividend of $2 per share, and the investor then sold the shares at a price of $51 per share. The exchange rate at that time was $:Skr = 9.8710–9.8750. The dividend withholding tax rate in the United States is 15 percent and there is a tax treaty between the United States and Sweden that allows the U.S. withholding tax to be used as a tax credit in Sweden. Suppose the Swedish investor is taxed at 50 percent on income and 15 percent on capital gains, and ignore any commissions on purchase and sale of shares.

 **A.** What is the gross rate of return on the investment, in dollars?

 **B.** What is the gross rate of return on the investment, in kroners?

 **C.** What is the rate of return on the investment, in kroners, net of taxes?

**12.** Which of the following statements best characterizes the taxation of returns on international investments in an investor's country and the country where the investment is made?

   **A.** Capital gains normally are taxed only by the country where the investment is made.

   **B.** Tax-exempt investors normally must pay taxes to the country where the investment is made.

   **C.** Investors in non-domestic common stock normally avoid double taxation on dividend income by receiving a tax credit for taxes paid to the country where the investment is made.

   **D.** The investor's country normally withholds taxes on dividends payments.

**13.** A U.S. institutional investor would like to purchase 10,000 shares of Lafarge. Lafarge is a French firm that trades on the Paris Bourse, the London stock exchange, and the NYSE as an ADR. At the NYSE, one depositary receipt is equivalent to one-fourth of a Lafarge share. The U.S. investor asks its brokers to quote net prices, without any commissions, in the three trading venues. There is no stamp tax in London on foreign shares listed there. The stock quotes are as follows:

   | | |
   |---|---|
   | New York | $24.07–24.37 |
   | London | £66.31–67.17 |
   | Paris | €99.40–100.30 |

   The exchange rate quotes from banks are as follows:

   £:$ = 1.4575–1.4580

   €:$ = 0.9691–0.9695

   Compare the dollar costs of purchasing 10,000 shares, or its equivalent, in New York, London, and Paris.

**14.** The chief financial executive of a German firm is considering raising capital in the United States by cross-listing her firm on the NYSE as an ADR and having a public offering. However, she has some concerns about this. Discuss what you think some of these concerns might be.

**15.** A U.S. institutional investor would like to buy 10,000 shares of British Polythene Industries. This U.K. firm trades on the London stock exchange, but not on the NYSE or NASDAQ. A U.K.-based broker of the investor quotes the price as £3.45–3.60, with a commission of 0.10 percent of the transaction value. There is a 0.50 percent U.K. securities transaction tax on purchase. The exchange rate quoted by a bank is £:$ = 1.5005–1.5010. What would be the total cost in dollars?

**16.** A French institutional investor wishes to decrease its exposure to Taiwan. It is interested in selling 20,000 shares of a particular Taiwanese firm that is currently in its portfolio. This firm trades on the Taiwan Stock Exchange. A Taiwan-based broker quotes the Taiwan dollar (TW$) price of the shares of this firm as 150.35–150.75, with a commission of 0.10 percent of the transaction value. The Taiwan Stock Exchange charges a tax of 0.30 percent of the value traded from the seller. A bank is quoting the TW$ to € exchange rate as 32.8675–32.8800. How many euros will the French institutional investor receive on selling the shares?

**17.** Which of the following statements is/are true about stock indexes?

    I. Compared with the equal–weighted indexes, market value–weighted indexes are better representative of movements in the market.

    II. Many of the global indexes, such as those provided by MSCI and S&P, are widely used by international money managers for asset allocation decisions and performance measurements.

    III. It is possible that, in any given year, the performance between two indexes for the same stock market can differ significantly, by as much as several percentage points.

**18.** In 1996, a group of securities called the World Equity Benchmark Shares (WEBS) started trading on the American Stock Exchange. WEBS for a country is a passively managed ETF indexed on the MSCI country benchmark index for that country. All else equal, what do you think would be the effect of the launch of WEBS for a country on the premium or discount of the closed-end country fund for that country?

**19.** Consider a closed-end country fund that trades in the United States. Suppose that country decides to impose restrictions on investments by foreigners in that country. All other things constant, what do you think would be the effect of these international investment restrictions on the price–net asset value ratio of the closed-end fund for that country?

**20.** A U.S. institutional investor with a large portfolio of U.S. and international stocks wants to add 20,000 shares of DaimlerChrysler to its portfolio. DaimlerChrysler trades as the same global share on several exchanges in the world. A U.S. broker quotes the NYSE price of DaimlerChrysler as \$43.45–43.65, net of commissions. The institutional investor is also considering purchasing shares in Germany, where the offer price quoted for DaimlerChrysler's shares on the Frankfurt stock exchange (XETRA) is €44.95, with a 0.10 percent commission to be paid on the transaction value. Which of the two alternatives is better for the investor? How much would be the total saving by using the better of the two alternatives? The exchange rate is €:\$ 0.9705–0.9710.

**21.** Consider a U.K. index fund that trades on a U.S. exchange. This fund is indexed on a British stock index based on several stocks that trade on the London stock exchange. The different time zones of the U.K. and the U.S. markets result in four distinct time periods in a 24-hour period: (a) a 6-hour time period prior to the U.S. open, when the market in London is open but the market in the United States is not; (b) a 2-hour period between 9:30 A.M. and 11:30 A.M. in New York, when both London and New York markets are open; (c) a 4.5-hour time period between 11:30 A.M. and 4:00 P.M. in New York, when the New York market is open but the London market is not; (d) the subsequent period when both markets are closed. For each of these time periods, discuss how British pound NAV and the U.S. dollar price of the fund would fluctuate.

# RETURN CONCEPTS

by John D. Stowe, CFA, Thomas R. Robinson, CFA, Jerald E. Pinto, CFA, and Dennis W. McLeavey, CFA

## LEARNING OUTCOMES

| The candidate should be able to: | Mastery |
|---|:---:|
| **a.** distinguish among the following return concepts: holding period return, realized return and expected return, required return, discount rate, the return from convergence of price to intrinsic value (given that price does not equal value), and internal rate of return; | ☐ |
| **b.** explain the equity risk premium and its use in required return determination, and demonstrate the use of historical and forward-looking estimation approaches; | ☐ |
| **c.** discuss the strengths and weaknesses of the major methods of estimating the equity risk premium; | ☐ |
| **d.** explain and demonstrate the use of the capital asset pricing model (CAPM), Fama–French model (FFM), the Pastor–Stambaugh model (PSM), macroeconomic multifactor models, and the build-up method (including bond yield plus risk premium method) for estimating the required return on an equity investment; | ☐ |
| **e.** discuss beta estimation for public companies, thinly traded public companies, and nonpublic companies; | ☐ |
| **f.** analyze the strengths and weaknesses of the major methods of estimating the required return on an equity investment; | ☐ |
| **g.** discuss international considerations in required return estimation; | ☐ |
| **h.** explain and calculate the weighted average cost of capital for a company; | ☐ |
| **i.** explain the appropriateness of using a particular rate of return as a discount rate, given a description of the cash flow to be discounted and other relevant facts. | ☐ |

www.cfainstitute.org/toolkit—Your online preparation resource

# 1    INTRODUCTION

The return on an investment is a fundamental element in evaluating an investment:

▶ Investors evaluate an investment in terms of the return they expect to earn on it compared to a level of return viewed as fair given everything they know about the investment, including its risk.

▶ Analysts need to specify the appropriate rate or rates with which to discount expected future cash flows when using present value models of stock value.

This reading presents and illustrates key return measures relevant to valuation and is organized as follows. Section 2 provides an overview of return concepts. Section 3 presents the chief approaches to estimating the equity risk premium, a key input in determining the required rate of return on equity in several important models. With a means to estimate the equity risk premium in hand, Section 4 discusses and illustrates the major models for estimating the required return on equity. Section 5 presents the weighted average cost of capital, a discount rate used when finding the present value of cash flows to all providers of capital. Section 6 presents certain facts concerning discount rate selection. A summary and practice problems conclude the reading.

# 2    RETURN CONCEPTS

A sound investment decision depends critically on the correct use and evaluation of rate of return measures. The following sections explain the major return concepts most relevant to valuation.[1]

## 2.1  Holding Period Return

The holding period rate of return (for short, the **holding period return**)[2] is the return earned from investing in an asset over a specified time period. The specified time period is the holding period under examination, whether it is one day, two weeks, four years, or any other length of time. To use a hypothetical return figure of 0.8 percent for a one-day holding period, we would say that "the one-day holding period return is 0.8 percent" (or equivalently, "the one-day return is 0.8 percent" or "the return is 0.8 percent over one day"). Such returns can be separated into investment income and price appreciation components. If the asset is a share purchased now (at $t = 0$, with $t$ denoting time) and sold at $t = H$, the holding period is $t = 0$ to $t = H$ and the holding period return is

---

[1] This is by no means an exhaustive list of return concepts. In particular, other areas of finance such as performance evaluation make use of return concepts not covered here (e.g., time-weighted rate of return).

[2] References to *return* in this reading refer to *rate of return*, not a money amount of return.

$$r = \frac{D_H + P_H}{P_0} - 1 = \frac{D_H}{P_0} + \frac{P_H - P_0}{P_0} = \text{Dividend yield} \quad \text{(36-1)}$$
$$+ \text{Price appreciation return}$$

where $D_t$ and $P_t$ are per-share dividends and share price at time $t$. Equation 36-1 shows that the holding period return is the sum of two components: dividend yield $(D_H/P_0)$ and price appreciation return $([P_H - P_0]/P_0)$, also known as the capital gains yield.

Equation 36-1 assumes, for simplicity, that any dividend is received at the end of the holding period. More generally, the holding period return would be calculated based on reinvesting any dividend received between $t = 0$ and $t = H$ in additional shares on the date the dividend was received at the price then available. Holding period returns are sometimes annualized—e.g., the return for a specific holding period may be converted to an annualized return, usually based on compounding at the holding period rate. For example, $(1.008)^{365} - 1 = 17.3271$ or 1,732.71 percent, is one way to annualize a one-day 0.80 percent return. As the example shows, however, annualizing holding period returns, when the holding period is a fraction of a year, is unrealistic when the reinvestment rate is not an actual, available reinvestment rate.

## 2.2 Realized and Expected (Holding Period) Return

In the expression for the holding period return, the selling price, $P_H$, and in general, the dividend, $D_H$, are not known as of $t = 0$. For a holding period in the past, the selling price and the dividend are known, and the return is called a realized holding period return, or more simply, a realized return. For example, with a beginning price of €50.00, an ending or selling price of €52.00 six months later, and a dividend equal to €1.00 (all amounts referring to the past), the realized return is €1.00/€50.00 + (€52.00 − €50.00)/€50.00 = 0.02 + 0.04 = 0.06 or 6 percent over 6 months. In forward-looking contexts, holding-period returns are random variables because future selling prices and dividends may both take on a range of values. Nevertheless, an investor can form an expectation concerning the dividend and selling price and thereby have an **expected holding-period return**, or simply expected return, for the stock that consists of the expected dividend yield and the expected price appreciation return.

Although professional investors often formulate expected returns based on explicit valuation models, a return expectation does not have to be based on a model or on specific valuation knowledge. Any investor can have a personal viewpoint on the future returns on an asset. In fact, because investors formulate expectations in varying ways and on the basis of different information, different investors generally have different expected returns for an asset. The comparison point for interpreting the investment implication of the expected return for an asset is its required return, the subject of the next section.

## 2.3 Required Return

A **required rate of return** (for short, required return) is the minimum level of expected return that an investor requires in order to invest in the asset over a specified time period, given the asset's riskiness. It represents the opportunity cost for investing in the asset—the highest level of expected return available elsewhere from investments of similar risk. As the opportunity cost for investing in the asset, the required return represents a threshold value for being fairly compensated for the risk of the asset. If the investor's expected return exceeds the required return, the asset will appear to be undervalued because it is expected to return more-than-fair compensation for the asset's risk. By contrast, if the expected return on the asset falls short of the required rate of return, the asset will appear to be overvalued.

The valuation examples presented in these readings will illustrate the use of required return estimates grounded in market data (such as observed asset returns) and explicit models for required return. We will refer to any such estimate of the required return used in an example as *the* required return on the asset for the sake of simplicity, although other estimates are usually defensible. For example, using the capital asset pricing model (discussed in more detail later), the required return for an asset is equal to the risk-free rate of return plus a premium (or discount) related to the asset's sensitivity to market returns. That sensitivity can be estimated based on returns for an observed market portfolio and the asset. That is one example of a required return estimate grounded in a formal model based on marketplace variables (rather than a single investor's return requirements). Market variables should contain information about investors' asset risk perceptions and their level of risk aversion, both of which are important in determining fair compensation for risk.

In this reading, we use the notation $r$ for the required rate of return on the asset being discussed. The required rate of return on common stock and debt are also known as the **cost of equity** and **cost of debt**, respectively, taking the perspective of the issuer. To raise new capital, the issuer would have to price the security to offer a level of expected return that is competitive with the expected returns being offered by similarly risky securities. The required return on a security is therefore the issuer's marginal cost for raising additional capital of the same type.

The difference between the expected return and the required rate of return on an asset is the asset's expected alpha (or *ex ante* alpha) or expected abnormal return:

$$\text{Expected alpha} = \text{Expected return} - \text{Required return} \qquad \textbf{(36-2a)}$$

When an asset is efficiently priced (its price equals its intrinsic value), expected return should equal required return and the expected alpha is zero. In investment decision-making and valuation, the focus is on expected alpha. However, to evaluate the actual results of an investment discipline, the analyst would examine realized alpha. Realized alpha (or *ex post* alpha) over a given holding period is

$$\begin{aligned}\text{Realized alpha} = \ &\text{Actual holding-period return} \\ &- \text{Contemporaneous required return}\end{aligned} \qquad \textbf{(36-2b)}$$

Estimates of required returns are essential for using present value models of value. Present value models require the analyst to establish appropriate discount rates for determining the present values of expected future cash flows.

*Expected return* and *required rate of return* are sometimes used interchangeably in conversation and writing.[3] As discussed, that is not necessarily correct. When

---

[3] Some financial models—such as the standard capital asset pricing model discussed later—assume that investors have the same expectations about the parameters of assets' return distributions and derive the level of required return for risky assets that clears the market for those assets. In the context of such a model with homogenous expectations, the required return is also *the* expected return for the asset. In discussions of such models, therefore, *expected return* and *required return* are used interchangeably.

current price equals perceived value, expected return should be the same as the required rate of return. However, when price is below (above) the perceived value, expected return will exceed (be less than) the required return as long as the investor expects price to converge to value over his or her time horizon.

Given an investor's expected holding-period return, we defined expected alpha in relation to a required return estimate. In the next section, we show the conversion of a value estimate into an estimate of expected-holding period return.

## 2.4 Expected Return Estimates from Intrinsic Value Estimates

When an asset is mispriced, one of several outcomes is possible. Take the case of an asset that an investor believes is 25 percent undervalued in the marketplace. Over the investment time horizon, the mispricing may:

▶ increase (the asset may become more undervalued),

▶ stay the same (the asset may remain 25 percent undervalued),

▶ be partially corrected (e.g., the asset may become undervalued by 15 percent),

▶ be corrected (price changes to exactly reflect value), or

▶ reverse, or be overcorrected (the asset may become overvalued).

Generally, convergence of price to value is the equilibrium and anticipated outcome when the investor's value estimate is more accurate than the market's, as reflected in the market price. In that case, the investor's expected rate of return has two components: the required return (earned on the asset's current market price) and a return from convergence of price to value.

We can illustrate how expected return may be estimated when an investor's value estimate, $V_0$, is different from the market price. Suppose the investor expects price to fully converge to value over $\tau$ years. $(V_0 - P_0)/P_0$ is an estimate of the return from convergence over the period of that length, essentially the expected alpha for the asset stated on a per-period basis. With $r_\tau$ being the required return on a periodic (not annualized) basis and $E(R_\tau)$ the expected holding-period return on the same basis, then:

$$E(R_\tau) \approx r_\tau + \frac{V_0 - P_0}{P_0}$$

Although only an approximation, the expression does illustrate that an expected return can be viewed as the sum of two returns: the required return and a return from convergence of price to intrinsic value.[4]

To illustrate, as of the end of the first quarter of 2007, one estimate of the required return for Proctor & Gamble (NYSE: PG) shares was 7.6 percent. At a time when PG's market price was \$63.16, a research report estimated PG's

---

[4] The expression assumes that the required rate of return and intrinsic value are static over the holding period and that convergence happens smoothly over the holding period (or all at once at its end). We conduct the analysis on a periodic (holding period) basis because one cannot assume reinvestment at a rate incorporating a return from convergence is feasible. For example, a 12.4 percent return from convergence earned over a month would be over 300 percent annualized, which is not meaningful as a performance expectation.

intrinsic value at $71.00 share. Thus, in the report author's view, PG was under-valued by $V_0 - P_0 = \$71 - \$63.16 = \$7.84$, or 12.4 percent as a fraction of the market price ($7.84/$63.16). If price were expected to converge to value in exactly one year, an investor would earn 7.6% + 12.4% = 20%. The expected alpha of Proctor & Gamble is 12.4 percent per annum. But if the investor expected the undervaluation to disappear by the end of nine months, then the investor might anticipate achieving a return of about 18 percent over the 9-month period. The required return on a nine-month basis ($\tau = 9/12 = 0.75$) is $(1.076)^{0.75} - 1 = 0.0565$ or 5.65 percent, so the total expected return is

$$E(R_\tau) \approx r_\tau + \frac{V_0 - P_0}{P_0}$$

$$= 5.65\% + 12.4\%$$

$$= 18.05 \text{ percent.}$$

In this case, expected alpha is 12.4 percent on a nine-month basis which, when added to the required return of 5.65 percent on a nine-month basis, gives an estimate of the nine-month holding period return of 18.05 percent. Another possibility is that price converges to value in two years. The expected two-year expected holding period return would be 15.78% + 12.4% = 28.18%, in which the required return component is calculated as $(1.076)^2 - 1 = 0.1578$. This expected return based on two-year convergence could be compared to the expected return based on one-year convergence of 20 percent by annualizing it: $(1.2818)^{1/2} - 1 = 0.1322$ or 13.22 percent per year.

Active investors essentially "second-guess" the market price. The risks of that activity include the risks that (1) their value estimates are not more accurate than the market price, and that, (2) even if they are more accurate, the value discrepancy may not narrow over the investors' time horizon. Clearly, the convergence component of expected return can be quite risky.

### EXAMPLE 1

#### An Analyst Case Study (1): The Required Return on Microsoft Shares

Thomas Weeramantry and Françoise Delacour are co-managers of a U.S.-based diversified global equity portfolio. They are researching Microsoft Corporation (NASDAQ-GS: MSFT),[5] the largest U.S.-headquartered technology sector company. Weeramantry gathered a number of research reports on MSFT and began his analysis of the company in late August 2007, when the current price for MSFT was $28.27. In one research report, the analyst offered the following facts, opinions, and estimates concerning MSFT:

▶ The most recent quarterly dividend was $0.10 per share. Over the coming year, two more quarterly dividends of $0.10 are expected, followed by two quarterly dividends of $0.11 per share.

▶ MSFT's required return on equity is 9.5 percent.

▶ A one-year target price for MSFT is $32.00.

---

[5] NASDAQ-GS: The Global Select Market tier of NASDAQ.

An analyst's target price is the price at which the analyst believes the security should sell at a stated future point in time. Based only on the information given, answer the following questions concerning MSFT. For both questions, ignore returns from reinvesting the quarterly dividends.

1. What is the analyst's one-year expected return?
2. What is a target price that is *most* consistent with MSFT being fairly valued?

**Solution to 1:** Over one year, the analyst expects MSFT to pay $0.10 + $0.10 + $0.11 + $0.11 = $0.42 in dividends. Using the target price of $32.00 and dividends of $0.42, the analyst's expected return is ($0.42/$28.27) + ($32.00 − $28.27)/$28.27 = 0.015 + 0.132 = 0.147 or 14.7 percent.

**Solution to 2:** If MSFT is fairly valued, it should return its cost of equity (required return), which is 9.5 percent. Under that assumption, Target price = Current price × (1 + Required return) − Dividend = $28.27(1.095) − $0.42 = $30.54; the dividend is subtracted to isolate the return from price appreciation. Another solution approach involves subtracting the dividend yield from the required return to isolate the anticipated price appreciation return: 9.5% − 1.5% = 8%. Thus, (1.08)($28.27) = $30.53 (the one cent difference from this approach's answer comes from rounding the dividend yield to 1.5 percent).

## 2.5 Discount Rate

**Discount rate** is a general term for any rate used in finding the present value of a future cash flow. A discount rate reflects the compensation required by investors for delaying consumption—generally assumed to equal the risk-free rate—and their required compensation for the risk of the cash flow. Generally, the discount rate used to determine intrinsic value depends on the characteristics of the investment rather than on the characteristics of the purchaser. That is, *for the purposes of estimating intrinsic value,* a required return based on marketplace variables is used rather than a personal required return influenced by such factors as whether the investor is diversified in his or her personal portfolio. On the other hand, some investors will make judgmental adjustments to such required return estimates, knowing the limitations of the finance models used to estimate such returns.

In principle, because of varying expected future inflation rates and the possibly varying risk of expected future cash flows, a distinct discount rate could be applicable to each distinct expected future cash flow. In practice, a single required return is generally used to discount all expected future cash flows.[6]

Sometimes an internal rate of return is used as a required return estimate, as discussed in the next section.

---

[6] When analysts sort expected future cash flows into multiple groups and each group has a different assumed growth rate, analysts sometimes apply different required returns to the different groups in discounting expected cash flows.

## 2.6 Internal Rate of Return

The **internal rate of return** (IRR) on an investment is the discount rate that equates the present value of the asset's expected future cash flows to the asset's price—i.e., the amount of money needed today to purchase a right to those cash flows.

In a model that views the intrinsic value of a common equity share as the present value of expected future cash flows, if price is equal to current intrinsic value—the condition of market informational efficiency—then, generally, a discount rate can be found, usually by iteration, which equates that present value to the market price. An IRR computed under the assumption of market efficiency has been used to estimate the required return on equity. An example is the historical practice of many U.S. state regulators of estimating the cost of equity for regulated utilities using the model illustrated in Equation 36-3b below.[7] (The issue of cost of equity arises because regulators set prices sufficient for utilities to earn their cost of capital.)[8]

To illustrate, the simplest version of a present value model results from defining cash flows as dividends and assuming a stable dividend growth rate for the indefinite future. The stable growth rate assumption reduces the sum of results in a very simple expression for intrinsic value:[9]

$$\text{Intrinsic value} = \frac{\text{Year-ahead dividend}}{\text{Required return} - \text{Expected dividend growth rate}}$$

**(36-3a)**

If the asset is correctly valued now (market price = intrinsic value), given consensus estimates of the year-ahead dividend and future dividend growth rate (which are estimates of the dividend expectations built in price), we can solve for a required return—an IRR implied by the market price:

$$\text{Required return estimate} = \frac{\text{Year-ahead dividend}}{\text{Market price}}$$
$$+ \text{Expected dividend growth rate} \quad \textbf{(36-3b)}$$

The use of such an IRR as a required return estimate assumes not only market efficiency, but also the correctness of the particular present value model (in the above example, the stable growth rate assumption is critical) and the estimated inputs to the selected model. In Equation 36-3b and similar cases, although the asset's risk is incorporated indirectly into the required return estimate via the market price, the adjustment for risk is not explicit as it is in many competing models that will be presented.

Finally, obtaining an IRR from a present value model should not be confused with the somewhat similar-looking exercise that involves inferring what the market price implies about future growth rates of cash flows, given an independent estimate of required return: that exercise has the purpose of assessing the reasonableness of the market price.

---

[7] See Cornell (1999), p. 103, or Brealey, Myers, and Allen (2006) for an introduction to this use.

[8] To avoid circularity, analysts must avoid using such an estimate as the discount rate in the same or closely similar present value model solved for intrinsic value.

[9] This will be discussed in more detail in the reading on discounted dividend valuation.

# THE EQUITY RISK PREMIUM

The equity risk premium is the incremental return (*premium*) that investors require for holding equities rather than a risk-free asset. Thus, it is the difference between the required return on equities and a specified expected risk-free rate of return. The equity risk premium, like the required return, depends strictly on expectations for the future because the investor's returns depend only on the investment's future cash flows. Possibly confusingly, *equity risk premium* is also commonly used to refer to the realized excess return of stocks over a risk-free asset over a given past time period. The realized excess return could be very different from the premium that, based on available information, was contemporaneously being expected by investors.[10]

Using the equity risk premium, the required return on the broad equity market or an average-systematic-risk equity security is

$$\text{Required return on equity} = \text{Current expected risk-free return} \\ + \text{Equity risk premium}$$

where, for consistency, the definition of risk-free asset (e.g., government bills or government bonds) used in estimating the equity risk premium should correspond to the one used in specifying the current expected risk-free return.

The importance of the equity risk premium in valuation is that, in perhaps a majority of cases in practice, analysts estimate the required return on a common equity issue as either

$$\text{Required return on share } i = \text{Current expected risk-free return} \\ + \beta_i(\text{Equity risk premium}) \qquad \textbf{(36-4)}$$

or

$$\text{Required return on share } i = \text{Current expected risk-free return} + \text{Equity} \\ \text{risk premium} \\ \pm \text{ Other risk premia/discounts} \\ \text{appropriate for } i \qquad \textbf{(36-5)}$$

▶ Equation 36-4 adjusts the equity risk premium for the share's particular level of systematic risk as measured by beta ($\beta_i$)—an average systematic risk security has a beta of 1, whereas beta values above and below 1 indicate greater-than-average and smaller-than-average systematic risk. Equation 36-4 will be explained in Section 4.1 as the capital asset pricing model (CAPM).

▶ Equation 36-5 does not make a beta adjustment to the equity risk premium but adds premia/discounts required to develop an overall equity risk adjustment. Equation 36-5 will be explained in Section 4.3 as the build-up method for estimating the required return. It is primarily used in the valuation of private businesses.

Typically, analysts estimate the equity risk premium for the national equity market of the issues being analyzed (but if a global CAPM is being used, a world equity premium is estimated that takes into account the totality of equity markets).

---

[10] Bernstein and Arnott (2002) underscore and discuss this topic at length.

Even for the longest established developed markets, the magnitude of the equity risk premium is difficult to estimate and can be a reason for differing investment conclusions among analysts. Therefore, we will introduce the topic of estimation in some detail. Whatever estimates analysts decide to use, when an equity risk premium estimate enters into a valuation, analysts should be sensitive to how their value conclusions could be affected by estimation error.

Two broad approaches are available for estimating the equity risk premium. One is based on historical average differences between equity market returns and government debt returns, and the other is based on current expectational data. These are presented in the following sections.

## 3.1 Historical Estimates

The mean value of the differences between broad-based equity-market-index returns and government debt returns over some selected sample period is a historical estimate of the equity risk premium. When reliable long-term records of equity returns are available, historical estimates have been a familiar and popular choice. If investors do not make systematic errors in forming expectations, then, over the long term, average returns should be an unbiased estimate of what investors expected. The fact that historical estimates are grounded in data also gives them an objective quality.

In using a historical estimate to represent the equity risk premium going forward, the analyst is assuming that returns are stationary—that is, the parameters that describe the return-generating process are unchanged over the past and into the future.

That assumption points to the analyst's first decision: the specification of the length of the sample period. Dividing a data period of a given length into smaller subperiods does not increase precision in estimating the mean—only extending the length of the data set can increase precision.[11] Thus a common choice is to use the longest reliable returns series available. Countering that advantage to increasing series length, the assumption of stationarity is usually more difficult to maintain as the series starting point is extended to the distant past. The specifics of the type of nonstationarity are also important. For a number of equity markets, research has brought forth abundant evidence of non-constant underlying return volatility. However, the underlying mean return is of more concern. Nonstationarity in which the equity risk premium has fluctuated in the short-term, but around a central value, is a less serious impediment to using a long data series than the case in which the risk premium has shifted to a permanently different level.[12] Empirically, the expected equity risk premium is countercyclical in the United States—that is, the expected premium is high during bad times but low during good times.[13] This property leads to some interesting challenges: For example, when a series of strong market returns has increased enthusiasm for equities and historical mean equity risk premium estimates, the forward-looking equity risk premium may have actually declined.

Apart from selection of the equity index series and time period, for practitioners taking a historical approach to equity premium estimation there are four major methodological choices: two choices for computing the mean and two broad choices for the proxy for the risk-free asset.

---

[11] See Merton (1980). This result contrasts with the estimation of variance and covariance in which higher frequency of estimation for a given time span does increase the precision in estimating variance and covariance.

[12] See Cornell (1999).

[13] Fama and French (1989) and Ferson and Harvey (1991).

The mean return of a historical set of annual return differences between equities and government debt securities can be calculated using a geometric mean or an arithmetic mean:

▶ A geometric mean equity risk premium estimate—equal to the compound annual excess return of equities over the risk-free asset, or

▶ An arithmetic mean equity risk premium estimate—equal to the sum of the annual return differences divided by the number of observations in the sample.

The risk-free rate can also be represented in two ways:

▶ As a long-term government bond return, or

▶ As a short-term government debt instrument (Treasury bill) return.

Dimson, Marsh, and Staunton (2006) presented authoritative evidence on realized excess returns ("historical risk premia") using survivorship-bias free return datasets for 17 developed markets for the 106 years extending from 1900 through 2005. Exhibit 1 excerpts their findings. In the table, *standard deviation* is the standard deviation of the annual excess return series (Equity market return − Risk-free rate) and *minimum value* and *maximum value* are, respectively, the smallest and largest observed values of that series.

| EXHIBIT 1 | Historical Equity Risk Premia: Seventeen Major Markets, 1900–2005 |

**Panel A: Historical Equity Risk Premia Relative to Bonds, 1900–2005**

| Country | Geometric Mean | Arithmetic Mean | Standard Deviation | Minimum Value | Maximum Value |
|---|---|---|---|---|---|
| Australia | 6.2% | 7.8% | 18.8% | −30.6% | 66.3% |
| Belgium | 2.6 | 4.4 | 20.1 | −36.2 | 79.8 |
| Canada | 4.2 | 5.7 | 17.9 | −36.8 | 56.6 |
| Denmark | 2.1 | 3.3 | 16.2 | −29.8 | 74.9 |
| France | 3.9 | 6.0 | 22.3 | −37.7 | 84.3 |
| Germany* | 5.3 | 8.3 | 27.4 | −27.4 | 116.6 |
| Ireland | 3.6 | 5.2 | 18.4 | −36.7 | 83.2 |
| Italy | 4.3 | 7.7 | 29.7 | −39.6 | 152.2 |
| Japan | 5.9 | 10.0 | 33.1 | −43.3 | 193.0 |
| Netherlands | 3.9 | 5.9 | 21.6 | −43.9 | 107.6 |
| Norway | 2.6 | 5.3 | 27.4 | −45.1 | 192.1 |
| South Africa | 5.4 | 7.0 | 19.3 | −29.2 | 70.9 |
| Spain | 2.3 | 4.2 | 20.2 | −34.0 | 69.1 |
| Sweden | 5.2 | 7.5 | 22.3 | −42.0 | 88.1 |
| Switzerland | 1.8 | 3.3 | 17.5 | −35.1 | 52.2 |
| United Kingdom | 4.1 | 5.3 | 16.6 | −38.0 | 80.8 |
| United States | 4.5 | 6.5 | 20.2 | −40.8 | 57.7 |
| World | 4.0 | 5.1 | 15.0 | −32.7 | 38.4 |

*(Exhibit continued on next page . . .)*

| EXHIBIT 1 | (continued) |
|---|---|

**Panel B: Historical Equity Risk Premia Relative to Bills, 1900–2005**

| Country | Geometric Mean | Arithmetic Mean | Standard Deviation | Minimum Value | Maximum Value |
|---|---|---|---|---|---|
| Australia | 7.1% | 8.5% | 17.0% | –30.2% | 49.2% |
| Belgium | 2.8 | 5.0 | 23.1 | –35.6 | 120.6 |
| Canada | 4.5 | 5.9 | 16.7 | –34.7 | 49.1 |
| Denmark | 2.9 | 4.5 | 19.8 | –32.0 | 95.3 |
| France | 6.8 | 9.3 | 24.2 | –34.3 | 85.7 |
| Germany* | 3.8 | 9.1 | 33.5 | –88.6 | 131.4 |
| Ireland | 4.1 | 6.0 | 20.3 | –49.8 | 72.0 |
| Italy | 6.6 | 10.5 | 32.1 | –48.6 | 150.3 |
| Japan | 6.7 | 9.8 | 27.8 | –48.3 | 108.6 |
| Netherlands | 4.5 | 6.6 | 22.4 | –35.0 | 126.7 |
| Norway | 3.1 | 5.7 | 25.9 | –49.7 | 157.1 |
| South Africa | 6.2 | 8.3 | 22.1 | –33.9 | 106.2 |
| Spain | 3.4 | 5.5 | 21.4 | –38.6 | 98.1 |
| Sweden | 5.7 | 8.0 | 22.1 | –38.6 | 85.1 |
| Switzerland | 3.6 | 5.3 | 18.8 | –37.0 | 54.8 |
| United Kingdom | 4.4 | 6.1 | 19.8 | –54.6 | 121.8 |
| United States | 5.5 | 7.4 | 19.6 | –44.5 | 57.1 |
| World | 4.7 | 6.1 | 16.6 | –41.4 | 70.3 |

*German data based on 104 years, excluding 1922–1923.

*Note:* "World" represents a simple arithmetic average of country results.

*Source:* Dimson, Marsh, and Staunton (2006), Tables 10, 11.

The excerpt from Exhibit 1 presented below presents a comparison of historical equity risk premium estimates for the United States and Japan. This comparison highlights some of the issues that can arise in using historical estimates. As background to the discussion, note that as a mathematical fact, the geometric mean is always less than (or equal to) the arithmetic mean and that the yield curve is typically upward sloping (long-term bond yields are typically higher than short-term yields).

| EXHIBIT 1 | Historical Equity Risk Premia: 1900–2005 (Excerpted) |
|---|---|

| | United States | | Japan | |
|---|---|---|---|---|
| | Geometric Mean | Arithmetic Mean | Geometric Mean | Arithmetic Mean |
| Premium relative to bills | 5.5% | 7.4% | 6.7% | 9.8% |
| Premium relative to bonds | 4.5 | 6.5 | 5.9 | 10.0 |

For the United States, estimates of the equity risk premium relative to long-term government bonds runs from 4.5 percent (geometric mean) to 6.5 (arithmetic mean). The United States also illustrates the typical case in which realized values relative to bills, for any definition of mean, are higher than those relative to bonds.

The premium estimates for Japan are notably higher than for the United States. The promised yield on long-term bonds is usually higher than that on short-term bills, so the higher arithmetic mean premium relative to bonds compared to bills in the case of Japan is atypical and an appropriate subject for investigation before being carried over as a forecast for the future. In virtually all markets, the geometric mean premium relative to long-term bonds gives the smallest risk premium estimate (the exception is Germany). Note that:

▶ For each market, the variation in year-to-year results is very large as shown by standard deviations and ranges (maximum − minimum values). As a result, the sample mean estimates the true mean with potentially very substantial error. To explain, the standard deviation of the sample mean in estimating the underlying mean (the standard error) is given by sample standard deviation ÷ square root of the number of observations, for example, 20.2 percent ÷ $\sqrt{106} \approx 2$ percent for the United States relative to bonds.[14] So a two standard deviation interval for the underlying mean (an interval within which the underlying mean is expected to lie with a 0.95 probability) is a wide 2.5 percent to 10.5 percent (i.e., 6.5% ± 4%) even with 106 years of data. This problem of sampling error becomes more acute, the shorter the series on which the mean estimate is based.

▶ The country-by-country variation in experience is substantial. Referring to Panel A of Exhibit 1, the histogram in Exhibit 2, focusing on the geometric mean, shows a roughly equal distribution of values in one-percentage-point intervals from 2 percent to 6 percent with one observation outside this range on both the low and the high end; as Exhibit 1, Panel A shows, the mean ("World") value is 4 percent.

| EXHIBIT 2 | Distribution of Geometric Mean Realized Premium Relative to Bonds |
|---|---|

**Interval for Realized Premium x (in Percent):**

| | | 1 ≤ x < 2 | 2 ≤ x < 3 | 3 ≤ x < 4 | 4 ≤ x < 5 | 5 ≤ x < 6 | 6 ≤ x ≤ 7 |
|---|---|---|---|---|---|---|---|
| No. of | 5 | | | | | | |
| Markets | 4 | | | | | | |
| | 3 | | | | | | |
| | 2 | | | | | | |
| | 1 | | | | | | |

The next two sections discuss choices related to the calculation of a historical equity risk premium estimate.

[14] The statement can be made by appealing to the central limit theorem which states, informally, that the sample mean is approximately normally distributed for large samples. The calculation shown assumes that returns are serially uncorrelated and provides a lower limit for the standard error of the mean. In the case where returns are serially correlated, the standard error is larger.

### 3.1.1 Arithmetic Mean or Geometric Mean

A decision with an important impact on the risk premium estimate is the choice between an arithmetic mean and a geometric mean: the geometric mean is smaller by an amount equal to about one half the variance of returns, so it is always smaller than the arithmetic mean given any variability in returns (the geometric mean is equal to the arithmetic mean when the returns for all periods are equal).

In actual professional practice, both means have been used in equity risk premium estimation.

The arithmetic mean return as the average one-period return best represents the mean return in a single period. There are two traditional arguments in favor of using the arithmetic mean in equity risk premium estimation, one relating to the type of model in which the estimates are used and the second relating to a statistical property. The major finance models for estimating required return—in particular the CAPM and multifactor models—are single-period models; so the arithmetic mean, with its focus on single period returns, appears to be a model-consistent choice. A statistical argument has also been made for the arithmetic mean: With serially uncorrelated returns and a *known* underlying arithmetic mean, the unbiased estimate of the expected terminal value of an investment is found by compounding forward at the arithmetic mean. For example, if the arithmetic mean is 8 percent, an unbiased estimate of the expected terminal value of a €1 million investment in 5 years is €1(1.08)$^5$ = €1.47 million. In practice, however, the underlying mean is not known. It has been established that compounding forward using the *sample* arithmetic mean, whether or not returns are serially uncorrelated, overestimates the expected terminal value of wealth.[15] In the example, if 8 percent is merely the sample arithmetic mean (used as an estimate of the unknown underlying mean), we would expect terminal wealth to be less than €1.47 million. Practically, only the first traditional argument still has force.

The geometric mean return of a sample represents the compound rate of growth that equates the beginning value to the ending value of one unit of money initially invested in an asset. Present value models involve the discounting over multiple time periods. Discounting is just the reverse side of compounding in terms of finding amounts of equivalent worth at different points in time; because the geometric mean is a compound growth rate, it appears to be a logical choice for estimating a required return in a multiperiod context, even when using a single-period required return model. In contrast to the sample arithmetic mean, using the sample geometric mean does not introduce bias in the calculated expected terminal value of an investment.[16] Equity risk premium estimates based on the geometric mean have tended to be closer to supply-side and demand-side estimates from economic theory than arithmetic mean estimates.[17] For the above reasons, the geometric mean is increasingly preferred for use in historical estimates of the equity risk premium.

---

[15] See Hughson, Stutzer, and Yung (2006) for a proof. Even when returns are not serially uncorrelated, using the arithmetic mean (even a known value) tends to overestimate the expected value of terminal wealth. Returns that revert to the mean are one example of serial correlation of practical concern.

[16] See Hughson, Stutzer, and Yung (2006).

[17] The relatively large size of the historical U.S. equity premium relative to that predicted by demand-side theory is known as the "equity premium puzzle" (Mehra and Prescott 1985). Cornell (1999) provides an accessible summary of the research.

### 3.1.2 Long-Term Government Bonds or Short-Term Government Bills

The choices for the risk-free rate are a short-term government debt rate, such as a 30-day T-bill rate, or a long-term government bond yield to maturity (YTM). Government bonds are preferred to even the highest rated corporate bonds as they typically have less (near zero) default and equity market risk.

A bond-based equity risk premium estimate in almost all cases is smaller than a bill-based estimate (see Exhibit 1). But a normal upward-sloping yield curve tends to offset the effect of the risk-free rate choice on a required return estimate, because the current expected risk-free rate based on a bond will be larger than the expectation based on a bill. However, with an inverted yield curve, the short-term yields exceed long-term yields and the required return estimate based on using a risk-free rate based on a bill can be much higher.

Industry practice has tended to favor use of a long-term government bond rate in premium estimates despite the fact that such estimates are often used in one-period models such as the CAPM. A risk premium based on a bill rate may produce a better estimate of the required rate of return for discounting a one-year-ahead cash flow, but a premium relative to bonds should produce a more plausible required return/discount rate in a multiperiod context of valuation.[18]

To illustrate a reason for the preference, take the case of bill-relative and bond-relative premia estimates of 5.5 percent and 4.5 percent, respectively, for a given market. Assume the yield curve is inverted: The current bill rate is 9 percent and the bond rate is 6 percent, respectively. The required return on average-risk equity based on bills is 14.5 percent (9% + 5.5%) compared with 10.5 percent based on bonds (6% + 4.5%). That 14.5 percent rate may be appropriate for discounting a one-year-ahead cash flow in a current high interest and inflation environment. The inverted yield curve, however, predicts a downward path for short-rates and inflation. Most of the cash flows lie in the future and the premium for expected average inflation rates built into the long-bond rate is more plausible. A practical principle is that for the purpose of valuation, the analyst should try to match the duration of the risk-free-rate measure to the duration of the asset being valued.[19] If the analyst has adopted a short-term risk-free rate definition, nevertheless, a practical approach to dealing with the situation just presented would be to use an expected average short-term bill rate rather than the current 9 percent rate. Advocates of using short-term rates point out that long-term government bonds are subject to risks, such as interest rate risk, that complicate their interpretation.

In practice, many analysts use the current YTM on a long-term government bond as an approximation for the expected return on it. The analyst needs to be clear that he or she is using a current yield observation, reflecting current inflation expectations. The yield on a recently issued ("on the run") bond mitigates distortions related to liquidity and discounts/premiums relative to face value. The available maturities of liquid government bonds change over time and differ among national markets. If a 20-year maturity is available and trades in a liquid market, however, its yield is a reasonable choice as an estimate of the risk-free rate for equity valuation.[20] In many international markets, only bonds of shorter maturity are available or have a liquid market. A 10-year government bond yield is another common choice.

---

[18] The argument is also made by Arzac (2005).

[19] **Duration** is a measure of the price sensitivity of an asset (or liability) to interest-rate changes. See Fabozzi (2004) for details.

[20] The Ibbotson U.S. long-term government bond yield is based on a portfolio of 20-year average maturity T-bonds. We use that series in the suggested historical estimate of the U.S. equity risk premium.

Valuation requires definite estimates of required returns. The data in Exhibit 1 provide one practical starting point for an estimate of equity risk premium for the markets given. As discussed, one mainstream choice among alternative estimates of the historical equity risk premium is the geometric mean historical equity risk premium relative to government bonds.

### 3.1.3 Adjusted Historical Estimates

A historical risk premium estimate may be adjusted in several ways to neutralize the effect of biases that may be present in the underlying equity market return series. One type of adjustment is made to offset the effect of biases in the data series being used to estimate the equity risk premium. A second type of adjustment is made to take account of an independent estimate of the equity risk premium. In both cases the adjustment could be upward or downward.

One issue is **survivorship bias** in equity market data series. The bias arises when poorly performing or defunct companies are removed from membership in an index, so that only relative winners remain. Survivorship bias tends to inflate historical estimates of the equity risk premium. For many developed markets, equity returns series are now available that are free or nearly free of survivorship bias (see Exhibit 1). When using a series that has such bias, however, the historical risk premium estimate should be adjusted downward. Guidance for such adjustment based on research is sometimes available.[21]

A conceptually related issue with historical estimates can arise when a market has experienced a string of unexpectedly positive or negative events and the surprises do not balance out over the period of sampled data. For example, a string of positive inflation and productivity surprises may result in a series of high returns that increase the historical mean estimate of the equity risk premium. In such cases, a forward-looking model estimate may suggest a much lower value of the equity risk premium. To mitigate that concern, the analyst may adjust the historical estimate downward based on an independent forward-looking estimate (or upward, in the case of a string of negative surprises). Many experts believe that the historical record for various major world markets has benefited from a majority of favorable circumstances that cannot be expected to be duplicated in the future; their recommended adjustments to historical mean estimates is downward. Dimson, Marsh, and Staunton (2002) have argued that historical returns have been advantaged by re-pricings as increasing scope for diversification has lead to a lower level of market risk. In the case of the United States, Ibbotson and Chen (2001) recommended a 1.25 percentage point downward adjustment to the Morningstar (Ibbotson) historical mean U.S. equity risk premium estimate based on a lower estimate from a supply-side analysis of the equity risk premium.

Example 2 illustrates difficulties in historical data that could lead to a preference for an adjusted historical or forward-looking estimate.

---

[21] Copeland, Koller, and Murrin (2000) recommend a downward adjustment of 1.5 percent to 2.0 percent for survivorship bias in the S&P 500 Index, using arithmetic mean estimates. Dimson et al. (2006), the source for Exhibit 1, took care to correct for survivorship bias. See also Dimson, Marsh, and Staunton (2002), which explains survivorship bias in greater detail.

**EXAMPLE 2**

### The Indian Equity Risk Premium: Historical Estimates of the Equity Risk Premium in a Developing Market[22]

Historical estimates of the equity risk premium in developing markets are often attended by a range of concerns. The case of India can serve as an example. A number of equity indexes are available and each has possible limitations. Although not as broad-based as the alternatives, the Bombay Stock Exchange Sensex 30, a market-capitalization weighted index of the shares of 30 leading companies, has the longest available record: Compiled since 1986, returns go back to 1979. Note the following facts concerning this index and other issues relevant to estimating the equity risk premium:

► The backfilled returns from 1979 to 1985 are based on the initial 30 issues selected in 1986, which were among the largest market-cap as of 1986.

► The Sensex is a price index; a total return version of the index incorporating dividends is available from 1997 forward.

► Interest rates were suppressed by regulation prior to 1991 and moved higher thereafter. The post-regulation period appears to be associated with higher stock market volatility.

► Objective estimates of the extent of any bias can be developed.

Based only on the information given, address the following.

1. What factors could bias an unadjusted historical risk premium estimate upward?
2. What factors could bias an unadjusted historical risk premium estimate downward?
3. State and explain two indications that the historical time series is nonstationary.
4. Recommend and justify a preference for a historical or an adjusted historical equity risk premium estimate.

**Solution to 1:** The backfilling of returns from 1979 to 1985 based on companies selected in 1986 could upward bias the estimate because of survivorship bias. The companies that were selected in 1986 are likely to have been among the most successful of the companies on the exchange as of 1979. Another but less clear factor is the suppression of interest rates prior to 1991. An artificially low risk-free rate would bias the equity risk premium estimate upward unless the required return on equity was smaller by an equal amount.

**Solution to 2:** The failure to incorporate the return from dividends biases the equity risk premium estimate downward.

---

[22] Jayanth R. Varma and Samir K. Barua, "A First Cut Estimate of the Equity Risk Premium in India," Indian Institute of Management Ahmedabad, Working Paper No. 2006-06-04, June 2006, is the source for most of the institutional background used in this example.

**Solution to 3:** The different levels of interest rates before and after the lifting of regulation in 1991 is one indication that the equity risk premium pre- and post-1991 could be different and that the overall series is nonstationary. A second is the higher level of stock market volatility pre- and postregulation.

**Solution to 4:** Given that objective estimates of the extent of biases can be developed, an adjusted historical estimate would be preferred because such an estimate is more likely to be unbiased and accurate.

In Example 2, one criticism that could be raised relative to any historical estimate is the shortness of the period in the data set—the post-1991 reform period—that is definitely relevant to the present. Sampling error in any mean estimate—even one based on clean data—would be a major concern for this data set. The analyst might address specific concerns through an adjusted historical estimate. The analyst may also decide to investigate one or more forward-looking estimates. Forward-looking estimates are the subject of the next section. A later section on international issues will have more information on equity risk premium estimation for emerging markets such as India.

## 3.2 Forward-Looking Estimates

Because the equity risk premium is based only on expectations for economic and financial variables from the present going forward, it is logical to estimate the premium directly based on current information and expectations concerning such variables. Such estimates are often called forward-looking or *ex ante* estimates. In principle, such estimates may agree with, be higher, or be lower than historical equity risk premium estimates.[23] *Ex ante* estimates are likely to be less subject to an issue such as nonstationarity or data biases than historical estimates. However, such estimates are often subject to other potential errors related to financial and economic models and potential behavioral biases in forecasting.

### 3.2.1 Gordon Growth Model Estimates

Probably the most frequently encountered forward-looking estimate of the equity risk premium is based on a very simple form of a present value model called the constant growth dividend discount model or Gordon growth model, already shown as Equation 36-3a. For mature developed equity markets such as Eurozone, the United Kingdom, and North American markets, the assumptions of this model are often met, at least approximately. Broad-based equity indices are nearly always associated with a dividend yield, and year-ahead dividend payment may be fairly predictable. The expected dividend growth rate may be inferred based on published analyst or economic expectations, such as consensus analyst expectations of the earnings growth rate for an equity market index (which may be based on forecasts for the constituent companies or a top-down

---

[23] Fama and French (2001) found that prior to 1950, the historical and Gordon growth model estimates for the U.S. equity risk premium agree, but from 1950–99, the Gordon growth model estimate averages less than half the historical estimate. They attribute the difference to the effect of positive earnings surprises relative to expectations on realized returns.

forecast). Specifically, the Gordon growth model (GGM) equity risk premium estimate is:[24]

> GGM equity risk premium estimate
> = Dividend yield on the index based on year-ahead aggregate forecasted dividends and aggregate market value
> + Consensus long-term earnings growth rate
> − Current long-term government bond yield                    **(36-6)**

We can illustrate with the case of the United States. As of September 2007, the dividend yield on the S&P 500 as defined in Equation 36-6 was approximately 1.9 percent based on a price level of the S&P 500 of 1,471. The consensus analyst view was that earnings on the S&P 500 would grow from a trailing amount of $86.38 to $95.18 over the next year, a 10.2 percent growth rate. However, at a five-year horizon (the longest analyst forecast horizon commonly available), a consensus growth estimate was close to the 7 percent long-term average growth rate.[25] We will use the 7 percent long-term average growth rate as the long-term earnings growth forecast. Dividend growth should track earnings growth over the long term. The 20-year U.S. government bond yield was 5.0 percent. Therefore, according to Equation 36-6, the Gordon growth model estimate of the U.S. equity risk premium was 1.9% + 7.0% − 5% or 3.9%. Like historical estimates, Gordon growth model estimates generally change through time. For example, the risk premium estimate of 3.9 percent just given compares with a GGM estimate of 2.4 percent (computed as 1.2% + 7% − 5.8%) made in the last edition of this reading, as of the end of 2001.

Equation 36-6 is based on an assumption of earnings growth at a stable rate. An assumption of multiple earnings growth stages is more appropriate for very rapidly growing economies. Taking an equity index in such an economy, the analyst may forecast a fast growth stage for the aggregate of companies included in the index, followed by a transition stage in which growth rates decline and a mature growth stage characterized by growth at a moderate, sustainable rate. The discount rate $r$ that equates the sum of the present values of the expected cash flows of the three stages to the current market price of the equity index defines an IRR. Letting PVFastGrowthStage($r$) stand for the present value of the cash flows of the fast earnings growth stage with the present value shown as a function of the discount rate $r$, and using a self-explanatory notation for the present values of the other phases, the equation for IRR is as follows:

$$\text{Equity index price} = \text{PVFastGrowthStage}(r) + \text{PVTransition}(r) + \text{PVMatureGrowthStage}(r)$$

The IRR is computable using a spreadsheet's IRR function. Using the IRR as an estimate of the required return on equities (as described in Section 2.6), subtracting a government bond yield gives an equity risk premium estimate.

A consequence of the model underlying Equation 36-6, making assumptions of a constant dividend payout ratio and efficient markets, is that earnings,

---

[24] Recent examples of the application of this model (to U.S. markets) are Jagannathan, McGrattan, and Scherbina (2000) and Fama and French (2001). The GGM estimate has also been used in institutional research for international markets (Stux 1994). Most analysts forecast the earnings growth rate rather than the dividend growth rate, which is technically specified in theory, so we use the earnings growth rate in the expression. Given a constant dividend payout ratio, a reasonable approximation for broad equity indexes, the two growth rates should be equal.

[25] www.standardandpoors.com.

dividends, and prices are expected to grow at dividend growth rate, so that the P/E ratio is constant. The analyst may believe, however, that the P/E ratio will expand or contract. Some analysts make an adjustment to the estimate in Equation 36-6 to reflect P/E multiple expansion or contraction. From a given starting market level associated with a given level of earnings and a given P/E ratio, the return from capital appreciation cannot be greater than the earnings grown rate unless the P/E multiple expands. P/E multiple expansion can result from an increase in the earnings growth rate and/or a decrease in risk.

### 3.2.2 Macroeconomic Model Estimates

Using relationships between macroeconomic variables and the financial variables that figure in equity valuation models, analysts can develop equity risk premium estimates. Such models may be more reliable when public equities represent a relatively large share of the economy, as in many developed markets. Many such analyses focus on the supply-side variables that fuel gross domestic product (GDP) growth (and are thus known as supply-side estimates). The Gordon growth model estimate, when based on a top-down economic analysis rather than using consensus analyst estimates, can be viewed as a supply-side estimate.[26]

To illustrate a supply-side analysis, the total return to equity can be analyzed into four components as explained by Ibbotson and Chen:[27]

▶ Expected inflation: EINFL,

▶ Expected growth rate in real earnings per share: EGREPS,

▶ Expected growth rate in the P/E ratio (the ratio of share price to earnings per share): EGPE, and

▶ Expected income component (including return from reinvestment of income): EINC.

The growth in P/E arises as a factor from a decomposition of the capital appreciation portion of returns.[28] So,

$$
\begin{aligned}
\text{Equity risk premium} = \{[(1 + \text{EINFL})(1 + \text{EGREPS})(1 + \text{EGPE}) \\
- 1.0] + \text{EINC}\} - \text{Expected risk-free} \\
\text{return}
\end{aligned}
\qquad \textbf{(36-7)}
$$

In the following we illustrate this type of analysis using data for U.S. equity markets as represented by the S&P 500.

▶ *Expected inflation.* A market forecast is available from the U.S. treasury and U.S. treasury inflation protected securities (TIPS) yield curve:

$$
\begin{aligned}
\text{Implicit inflation forecast} &\approx \frac{1 + \text{YTM of 20-year maturity T-bonds}}{1 + \text{YTM of 20-year maturity TIPS}} - 1 \\
&= \frac{1.05}{1.026} - 1 \\
&= 0.023 \text{ or } 2.3 \text{ percent.}
\end{aligned}
$$

---

[26] Demand-side models estimate the equity risk premium based on estimates of investors' average risk aversion and the correlation of asset returns with changes in consumption. Such models are rarely encountered in professional practice, however.

[27] This is based on Ibbotson and Chen's (2003) method 3, the earnings method.

[28] That is, $(P_t/P_{t-1}) - 1.0 = [(P_t/E_t)/(P_{t-1}/E_{t-1})](E_t/E_{t-1}) - 1.0 = (1 + \text{EGPE})(1 + \text{EGREPS}) - 1.0$.

We will use an estimate of 2.5 percent per year, consistent with the TIPS analysis and other long-term forecasts. So, 1 + EINFL = 1.025.

▶ *Expected growth in real earnings per share.* This quantity should approximately track the real GDP growth rate. An adjustment upward or downward to the real GDP growth rate can be made for any expected differential growth between the companies represented in the equity index being used to represent the stock market and the overall economy.

According to economic theory, the real GDP growth rate should equal the sum of labor productivity growth and the labor supply growth rate (which can be estimated as the sum of the population growth rate and the increase in the labor force participation rate). A forecasted 2 percent per year U.S. labor productivity growth rate and 1 percent per year labor supply growth rate produces a 3 percent overall real GDP growth rate estimate of 3 percent. So, 1 + EGREPS = 1.03.

▶ *Expected growth in the P/E ratio.* The baseline value for this factor is zero, reflecting an efficient markets view. When the analyst views a current P/E level as reflecting overvaluation or undervaluation, however, a negative or positive value, respectively, can be used, reflecting the analyst's investment time horizon. So, without presenting a case for misevaluation, 1+ EGPE = 1.

▶ *Expected income component.* Historically, for U.S. markets the long-term value has been close to 4.5 percent (including reinvestment return of 20 bps).[29] However, the current S&P 500 dividend yield is below the long-term average. A forward looking estimate based on the forward expected dividend yield of 2.1 percent and 10 bps reinvestment return is 2.2 percent. So, EINC = 0.022.

Using the Ibbotson–Chen format and a risk-free rate of 5 percent, an estimate of the U.S. equity risk premium estimate is

$$\{[(1.025)(1.03)(1) - 1.0] + 0.022)\} - 0.05 = 0.078 - 0.05 = 2.8\%$$

The supply side estimate of 2.8 percent is smaller than the historical geometric mean estimate of 4.5 percent, although the difference is within one standard error (2 percentage points) of the latter forecast.[30]

### 3.2.3 Survey Estimates

One way to gauge expectations is to ask people what they expect. Survey estimates of the equity risk premium involve asking a sample of people—frequently, experts—about their expectations for it, or for capital market expectations from which the premium can be inferred.

For example, a 2002 survey of global bond investors by Schroder Salomon Smith Barney found an average equity risk premium in the range of 2–2.5 percent, while a Goldman Sachs survey of global clients recorded a mean long-run equity risk premium of 3.9 percent.[31]

---

[29] See Ibbotson and Chen (2003), p. 90.

[30] Strictly speaking, standard errors apply only to the arithmetic mean; but as an approximate guide to "closeness," they have also been applied to the geometric mean. See Dimson, Marsh, and Staunton (2002), p. 168.

[31] See Ilmanen, Byrne, Gunasekera, and Minikin (2002) and O'Neill, Wilson, and Masih (2002).

## 4 THE REQUIRED RETURN ON EQUITY

With means to estimate the equity risk premium in hand, the analyst can estimate the required return on the equity of a particular issuer. The choices include the following:

► the CAPM,

► a multifactor model such as the Fama–French or related models, and

► a build-up method, such as the bond yield plus risk premium method.

### 4.1 The Capital Asset Pricing Model

The CAPM is an equation for required return that should hold in **equilibrium** (the condition in which supply equals demand) if the model's assumptions are met; among the key assumptions are that investors are risk averse and that they make investment decisions based on the mean return and variance of returns of their total portfolio. The chief insight of the model is that investors evaluate the risk of an asset in terms of the asset's contribution to the systematic risk of their total portfolio (systematic risk is risk that cannot be shed by portfolio diversification). Because the CAPM provides an economically grounded and relatively objective procedure for required return estimation, it has been widely used in valuation.

The expression for the CAPM that is used in practice was given earlier as Equation 36-4:[32]

$$\text{Required return on share } i = \text{Current expected risk-free return} \\ + \beta_i \text{ (Equity risk premium)}$$

For example, if the current expected risk-free return is 5 percent, the asset's beta is 1.20, and the equity risk premium is 4.5 percent, then the asset's required return is

$$\text{Required return on share } i = 0.05 + 1.20(0.045) = 0.104 \text{ or } 10.4 \text{ percent}$$

The asset's beta measures its market or systematic risk, which in theory is the sensitivity of its returns to the returns on the "market portfolio" of risky assets. Concretely, beta equals the covariance of returns with the returns on the market portfolio divided by the market portfolio's variance of returns. In typical practice for equity valuation, the market portfolio is represented by a broad value-weighted equity market index. The asset's beta is estimated by a least squares regression of the asset's returns on the index's returns and is available also from many vendors. In effect, in Equation 4 the analyst is adjusting the equity risk premium up or down for the asset's level of systematic risk by multiplying it by the asset's beta, adding that asset-specific risk premium to the current expected risk-free return to obtain a required return estimate.

---

[32] Formally, the CAPM is $E(R_i) = R_F + \beta_i[E(R_M) - R_F]$ where $E(R_i)$ is asset $i$'s expected return in equilibrium given its beta, equal to its required return, $R_F$ is the risk-free rate of return, and $E(R_M)$ is the expected return on the market portfolio. In theory, the market portfolio is defined to include all risky assets held according to their market value weights. In typical practice when applying the CAPM to value equities, a broad equity index is used to represent the market portfolio and an estimate of the equity risk premium is used for $E(R_M) - R_F$.

In the typical case in which the equity risk premium is based on a national equity market index and estimated beta is based on sensitivity to that index, the assumption is being made implicitly that equity prices are largely determined by *local* investors. When equities markets are *segmented* in that sense (i.e., local market prices are largely determined by local investors rather than by investors worldwide), two issues with the same risk characteristics can have different required returns if they trade in different markets.

The opposite assumption is that all investors worldwide participate equally in setting prices (perfectly integrated markets). That assumption results in the international CAPM (or world CAPM) in which the risk premium is relative to a world market portfolio. Taking an equity view of the market portfolio, the world equity risk premium can be estimated historically based on the MSCI World index (returns available from 1970), for example, or indirectly as the (U.S. equity risk premium estimate)/(beta of U.S. stocks relative to MSCI World) = 4.5%/0.9218 = 4.9%. Computing beta relative to MSCI World and using a national risk-free interest rate, the analyst can obtain international CAPM estimates of required return. In practice, the international CAPM is not commonly relied on for required return on equity estimation.[33]

### 4.1.1 Beta Estimation for a Public Company

The simplest estimate of beta results from an ordinary least squares regression of the return on the stock on the return on the market. The result is often called an unadjusted or "raw" historical beta. The actual values of beta estimates are influenced by several choices:

▶ *The choice of the index used to represent the market portfolio.* For a number of markets there are traditional choices. For U.S. equities, the S&P 500 (vendors include Morningstar/Ibbotson, Merrill Lynch, Compustat) and NYSE Composite (vendors include Value Line) have been traditional choices.

▶ *The length of data period and the frequency of observations.* The most common choice is five years of monthly data, yielding 60 observations (Morningstar/Ibbotson, Merrill Lynch, Compustat make that choice). Value Line uses five years of weekly observations. The Bloomberg default is two years of weekly observations, which can be changed at the user's option. One study of U.S. stocks found support for five years of monthly data over alternatives.[34] An argument can be made that the Bloomberg default can be especially appropriate in fast growing markets.

The beta value in a future period has been found to be on average closer to the mean value of 1.0, the beta of an average-systematic-risk security, than to the value of the raw beta. Because valuation is forward looking, it is logical to adjust the raw beta so it more accurately predicts a future beta. The most commonly used adjustment was introduced by Blume (1971):

$$\text{Adjusted beta} = (2/3)(\text{Unadjusted beta}) + (1/3)(1.0) \qquad \textbf{(36-8)}$$

---

[33] Other methods appear to give more plausible estimates in practice. See Morningstar (2007), pp. 177–179, 184. One variation on the international CAPM, called the Singer–Terhaar method, that does find use in professional practice, particularly for asset classes, is discussed in Calverley, Meder, Singer, and Staub (2007); this approach involves taking a weighted average of domestic and international CAPM estimates.

[34] Bartholdy and Peare (2004).

For example, if the beta from a regression of an asset's returns on the market return is 1.30, adjusted beta is $(2/3)(1.30) + (1/3)(1.0) = 1.20$. Vendors of financial information often report raw and adjusted beta estimates together. Although most vendors use the Blume adjustment, some do not. For example, Morningstar (Ibbotson) adjusts raw beta toward the peer mean value (rather than toward the overall mean value of 1.0). The analyst of course needs to understand the basis behind the presentation of any data that he or she uses.

The following examples apply the CAPM to estimate the required return on equity.

### EXAMPLE 3

**An Analyst Case Study (2): The Required Return on Larsen & Toubro Shares**

While Weeramantry has been researching Microsoft, his colleague Delacour has been investigating the required return on Larsen & Toubro Ltd shares (BSE: 500510, NSE: LT).[35] Larsen & Toubro Ltd. is the largest India-based engineering and construction company. Calling up the beta function for LT on her Bloomberg terminal on 5 September 2007, Delacour sees the screen shown in Exhibit 3.

Delacour notes that Bloomberg has chosen the BSE Sensex 30 as the equity index for estimating beta. Delacour changes the Bloomberg default for time period/frequency to the specification shown in the exhibit for consistency with her other estimation work; in doing so, she notes approvingly that the beta estimate is approximately the same at both horizons.

Raw beta, 1.157, is the slope of the regression line running through the scatterplot of 60 points denoting the return on LT ($y$-axis) for different returns on the Sensex ($x$-axis); a bar graph of the distribution of returns in local currency terms is superimposed over the $x$-axis.

Noting from $R^2$ that beta explains more than 56 percent of variation in LT returns—an exceptionally good fit—Delacour also decides to use the CAPM to estimate LT stock's required return.[36] Delacour has decided to use her own adjusted historical estimate of 7 percent for the Indian equity risk premium and the 10-year Indian government bond yield of 7.9 percent as the risk-free rate.[37] Delacour notes that a 7.9 percent yield is shown on the Bloomberg cost of capital screen for LT (as the "bond rate") and that the same screen shows an estimate of the Indian equity risk premium ("country premium") of 7.46 percent—close to her own estimate of 7 percent.

[35] BSE: Bombay Stock Exchange; NSE: National Stock Exchange. The Bloomberg reference for the company is LT IN whereas the Reuters reference is LART.BO.

[36] The Bloomberg screen interprets $R^2$ as "correlation." More precisely, in a univariate regression as here, it is equivalent to the squared correlation between the dependent (stock return) and independent (market return) variables. It is interpreted as the fraction of the variation in the dependent variable explained by the independent variable.

[37] Varma and Barua (2006) estimated a historical geometric mean equity risk premium of 8.75 percent for Indian equities using their own database. This was adjusted downward by 1.7 percentage points based on a supply-side analysis. Some estimates of the Indian equity risk premium, e.g., country risk rating estimates, are much higher.

| EXHIBIT 3 | A Bloomberg Screen for Beta Larsen & Toubro Ltd. |
|-----------|---------------------------------------------------|

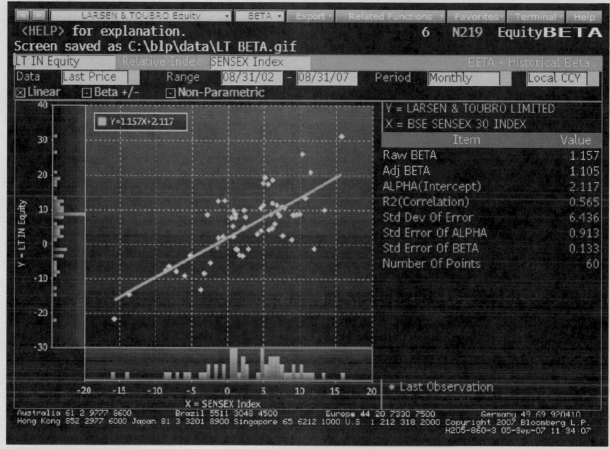

Based only on the information given, address the following:

1. Demonstrate the calculation of adjusted beta using the Blume method.
2. Estimate the required return on LT using the CAPM with an adjusted beta.
3. Explain one fact from the Bloomberg screen as evidence that beta has been estimated with accuracy.

**Solution to 1:** The calculation for adjusted beta is $(2/3)(1.157) + (1/3)(1.0) = 1.105$.

**Solution to 2:** $r = 7.9\% + 1.105(7\%) = 15.6$ percent.

**Solution to 3:** The standard error of beta at 0.133 is relatively small in relation to the magnitude of the raw estimate, 1.157.

## EXAMPLE 4

### Calculating the Required Return on Equity Using the CAPM (1)

Exxon Mobil Corporation, BP p.l.c., and Total S.A. are three "super major" integrated oil and gas companies headquartered, respectively, in the United States, the United Kingdom, and France. An analyst estimates that the equity risk premium in the United States, the United Kingdom, and the Eurozone are, respectively, 4.5 percent, 4.1 percent, and 4.0 percent. Other information is summarized in Exhibit 4.

| EXHIBIT 4 | Exxon Mobile, BP, and Total | | |
| --- | --- | --- | --- |
| Company | Beta | Estimated Equity Risk Premium | Risk-Free Rate |
| Exxon Mobil Corp (NYSE: XOM) | 0.74 | 4.5% | 4.9% |
| BP p.l.c. (LSE SETS: BP, NYSE: BP) | 1.00 | 4.1 | 5.0 |
| Total S.A. (Euronext: FR0000120271, NYSE: TOT) | 1.07 | 4.0 | 4.75 |

*Sources:* Standard & Poor's, Reuters.

Using the capital asset pricing model, calculate the required return on equity for

1. Exxon Mobil.
2. BP p.l.c.
3. Total.

**Solution to 1:** The required return on Exxon Mobil according to the CAPM is 4.9% + 0.74(4.5%) = 8.23 percent.

**Solution to 2:** The required return on BP according to the CAPM is 5.0% + 1.00(4.1%) = 9.10 percent.

**Solution to 3:** The required return on Total stock according to the CAPM is 4.75 + 1.07(4.0) = 9.03 percent.

## EXAMPLE 5

### Calculating the Required Return on Equity Using the CAPM (2): Non-Traded Asset Case

Jill Adams is an analyst at a hedge fund that has been offered an equity stake in a privately held U.S. property and liability insurer. Adams identifies Alleghany Corporation (NYSE: Y) as a publicly traded comparable company, and intends to use information about Alleghany in evaluating the offer. One sell-side analyst that Adams contacts puts Alleghany's required return on equity at 10.0 percent. Researching the required return herself, Adams determines that Alleghany has the historical betas shown in Exhibit 5 as of late August 2007:

| EXHIBIT 5 | Alleghany Corporation: Historical Betas |
| --- | --- |
| **5-Year Beta** | **10-Year Beta** |
| 0.30 | 0.21 |

*Source*: Bloomberg LLC.

The estimated U.S. equity risk premium (relative to bonds) is 4.5 percent. The YTM for:

▶ 30 day U.S. Treasury bills is 3.9 percent.
▶ 20-year U.S. government bonds is 4.9 percent.

Adams follows the most common industry practices concerning time period for estimating beta and adjustments to beta.

1. Estimate Alleghany Corporation's adjusted beta and required return based on the CAPM.
2. Is the sell-side analyst's estimate of 10 percent for Alleghany's cost of equity *most* consistent with Alleghany shares having above-average or below-average systematic risk?

**Solution to 1:** Adjusted beta = $(2/3)(0.30) + (1/3) = 0.533$ or 0.53. Using a five-year horizon for calculating beta is the most common practice. Consistent with the definition of the equity risk premium, a long-bond yield is used in the CAPM: $4.9\% + 0.53(4.5) = 7.29\%$ or 7.3 percent, approximately.

**Solution to 2:** The analyst's estimate implies above-average systematic risk. A beta of 1 by definition represents the beta of the market and so shares of average systematic risk. A beta of 1 implies a required return of $4.9\% + 1.0(4.5\%) = 9.4\%$.

When a share issue trades infrequently, the most recent transaction price may be stale and not reflect underlying changes in value. If beta is estimated based on, for example, a monthly data series in which missing values are filled with the most recent transaction price, the estimated beta will be too small and the required return on equity will be underestimated. There are several econometric techniques that can be used to estimate the beta of infrequently traded securities.[38] A practical alternative is to base the beta estimate on the beta of a comparable security.

### 4.1.2  Beta Estimation for Thinly Traded Stocks and Nonpublic Companies

Analysts do not have access to a series of market price observations for nonpublic companies with which to calculate a regression estimate of beta. However, using an industry classification system such as the MSCI/Standard & Poor's Global Industry Classification Standard (GICS) or the Dow Jones/FTSE Industry Classification Benchmark (ICB) to identify publicly traded peer companies, the analyst can estimate indirectly the beta of the nonpublic company on the basis of the public peer's beta.

The procedure must take into account the effect on beta of differences in financial leverage between the nonpublic company and the benchmark. First, the benchmark beta is unlevered to estimate the beta of the benchmark's assets—reflecting just the systematic risk arising from the economics of the industry. Then, the asset beta is re-levered to reflect the financial leverage of the nonpublic company.

Let $\beta_E$ be the equity beta before removing the effects of leverage, if any. This is the benchmark beta. If the debt of the benchmark is high quality (so an assumption that the debt's beta is zero should be approximately true), analysts can use the following expression for unleveraging the beta:[39]

$$\beta_U \approx \left[\frac{1}{1 + (D/E)}\right]\beta_E. \tag{36-9a}$$

Then, if the subject company has debt and equity levels $D'$ and $E'$, respectively, and assuming the subject company's debt is high grade, the subject company's equity beta, $\beta'_E$, is estimated as follows:

$$\beta'_E \approx [1 + (D'/E')]\beta_U \tag{36-9b}$$

Expressions 36-9a and 36-9b hold under the assumption that the level of debt adjusts to the target capital structure weight as total firm value changes, consistent with the definition for the weighted average cost of capital that will be presented later.[40] Exhibit 6 summarizes the steps.

---

[38] See Elton, Gruber, Brown, and Goetzmann (2005) for a summary of the methods of Scholes and Williams (1977) and Dimson (1979).

[39] Equation 36-9a comes from the expression $\beta_U \approx [1 + (D/E)]^{-1}[\beta_E + (D/E)\beta_D]$, making the assumption that $\beta_D = 0$. The expression in this footnote can be used when the debt's beta is known to be definitely non-zero.

[40] See Miles and Ezzell (1985). Another expression (the one usually presented by textbooks) is appropriate under the typically less plausible assumption that the level of debt is constant from period to period: Still assuming the beta of debt is zero, the correct expression to unlever is then $\beta_U = [1 + (1 - t)(D/E)]^{-1}\beta_E$ and re-leveraging is done using $\beta_E = [1 + (1 - t)(D/E)]^{-1}\beta_U$ as shown by Hamada (1972). See Arzac (2005) for a more detailed presentation.

| EXHIBIT 6 | Estimating a Beta for a Non-Traded Company |

Step 1
Select the benchmark (comparable)
▼
Step 2
Estimate benchmark's beta
▼
Step 3
Unlever the benchmark's beta
▼
Step 4
Lever the beta to reflect the
subject company's financial leverage

To illustrate, suppose that a benchmark company is identified (Step 1) that is 40 percent funded by debt. By contrast, the weight of debt in the subject company's capital structure is only 20 percent. The benchmark's beta is estimated at 1.2 (Step 2). The 40 percent weight of debt in the benchmark implies that the weight of equity is $100\% - 40\% = 60$ percent. Unlevering the benchmark beta (Step 3):

$$\beta_U \approx \left[ \frac{1}{1 + (D/E)} \right]\beta_E = \left[ \frac{1}{1 + (40/60)} \right]1.2 = 0.6 \times 1.2 = 0.72$$

Next, the unlevered beta of 0.72 is re-levered according to the financial leverage of the subject company, which uses 20 percent debt and 80 percent equity:

$$\beta_E' \approx [1 + (D'/E')]\beta_U = [1 + (20/80)]0.72 = 1.25 \times 0.72 = 0.90$$

Sometimes, instead of using an individual company as a benchmark, the required return will be benchmarked on a median or average industry beta. A process of unlevering and re-levering can be applied to such a beta based on the median or average industry capital structure.

## EXAMPLE 6

### Calculating the Required Return on Equity Using the CAPM (3)

Adams turns to determining a beta for use in evaluating the offer of an equity stake in a private insurer and rounds her beta estimate of Alleghany, the public comparable, to 0.5. As of the valuation date, Alleghany Corporation has no debt in its capital structure. The private insurer is 20 percent funded by debt.

If a beta of 0.50 is assumed for the comparable, what is the estimated beta of the private insurer?

**Solution:** Because Alleghany does not use debt, its beta does not have to be unlevered. For the private insurer, if debt is 20 percent of capital then equity is 80 percent of capital and $D'/E' = 20/80 = 0.25$. Therefore, the estimate of the private insurer's equity beta is $(1.25)(0.50) = 0.625$ or 0.63.

The CAPM is a simple, widely accepted, theory-based method of estimating the cost of equity. Beta, its measure of risk, is readily obtainable for a wide range of securities from a variety of sources and can be estimated easily when not available from a vendor. In portfolios, the idiosyncratic risk of individual securities tends to offset against each other leaving largely beta (market) risk. For individual securities, idiosyncratic risk can overwhelm market risk and, in that case, beta may be a poor predictor of future average return. Thus the analyst needs to have multiple tools available.

## 4.2 Multifactor Models

A substantial amount of evidence has accumulated that the CAPM beta describes risk incompletely. In practice, coefficients of determination ($R$-squared) for individual stocks' beta regressions may range from 2 percent to 40 percent, with many under 10 percent. For many markets, evidence suggests that multiple factors drive returns. At the cost of greater complexity and expense, the analyst can consider a model for required return based on multiple factors. Greater complexity does not ensure greater explanatory power, however, and any selected multifactor model should be examined for the value it is adding.

Whereas the CAPM adds a single risk premium to the risk-free rate, arbitrage pricing theory (APT) models add a set of risk premia. APT models are based on a multifactor representation of the drivers of return. Formally, APT models express the required return on an asset as follows:

$$r = R_F + (\text{Risk premium})_1 + (\text{Risk premium})_2 + ... \\ + (\text{Risk premium})_K$$

**(36-10)**

where $(\text{Risk premium})_i = (\text{Factor sensitivity})_i \times (\text{Factor risk premium})_i$. **Factor sensitivity** or **factor beta** is the asset's sensitivity to a particular factor (holding all other factors constant). In general, the **factor risk premium** for factor $i$ is the expected return in excess of the risk-free rate accruing to an asset with unit sensitivity to factor $i$ and zero sensitivity to all other factors.[41]

One of the best known models based on multiple factors expands upon the CAPM with two additional factors. That model, the Fama–French model, is discussed next.

### 4.2.1 The Fama–French Model

By the end of the 1980s, empirical evidence had accumulated that, at least over certain long time periods, in the U.S. and several other equity markets, investment strategies biased toward small-market capitalization securities and/or value might generate higher returns over the long-run than the CAPM predicts.[42]

In 1993, researchers Eugene Fama and Kenneth French addressed these perceived weaknesses of the CAPM in a model with three factors, known as the Fama–French model (FFM). The FFM is among the most widely known non-proprietary multifactor models. The factors are:

---

[41] In the case of the Fama–French model, however, the premiums of two factors are not stated as quantities in excess of the risk-free rate.

[42] For example, Fama and French (1993) and Strong and Xu (1997) documented size and book-to-market premiums for the United States and the United Kingdom, respectively. Capaul, Rowley, and Sharpe (1993) and Chen and Zhang (1998) documented a value premium in developed markets internationally.

▶ RMRF, standing for $R_M - R_F$, the return on a market value-weighted equity index in excess of the one-month T-bill rate—this is one way the equity risk premium can be represented and is the factor shared with the CAPM.

▶ SMB (small minus big), a size (market capitalization) factor. SMB is the average return on three small-cap portfolios minus the average return on three large-cap portfolios. Thus SMB represents a small-cap return premium.

▶ HML (high minus low), the average return on two high book-to-market portfolios minus the average return on two low book-to-market portfolios.[43] With high book-to-market (equivalently, low price-to-book) shares representing a value bias and low book-to-market representing a growth bias, in general, HML represents a value return premium.

Each of the factors can be viewed as the mean return to a zero-net investment, long–short portfolio. SMB represents the mean return to shorting large-cap shares and investing the proceeds in small-cap shares; HML is the mean return from shorting low book-to-market (high P/B) shares and investing the proceeds in high book-to-market shares. The FFM estimate of the required return is:

$$r_i = R_F + \beta_i^{mkt}RMRF + \beta_i^{size}SMB + \beta_i^{value}HML. \tag{36-11}$$

Historical data on the factors are publicly available for at least 24 countries.[44] The historical approach is frequently used in estimating the risk premia of this model. The definitions of RMRF, SMB, and HML have a specificity that lends itself to such estimation. Nevertheless, the range of estimation approaches discussed earlier could also be applied to estimating the FFM factors. Note the definition of RMRF in terms of a short-term rate; available historical series are in terms of a premium over a short-term government debt rate. In using Equation 36-11, we would take a current short-term risk-free rate. Note as well that because other factors besides the market factor are included in Equation 36-11, the beta on the market in Equation 36-11 is generally not exactly the same value as the CAPM beta for a given stock.

We can illustrate the FFM using the case of the U.S. equity market. A current short-term interest rate is 4.1 percent. We take RMRF to be 5.5 percent based on Panel B of Exhibit 1. The historical size premium is 2.7 percent based on Fama–French data from 1926. However, over the last quarter century approximately (1980 to 2006) the realized SML premium has averaged about one-half of that. Therefore, the historical estimate is adjusted downward to 2.0 percent. The realized value premium has had wide swings, but absent the case for a secular decline as for the size premium, we take the historical value of 4.3 percent based on Fama–French data. Thus, one estimate of the FFM for the U.S. market as of 2007 is:

$$r_i = 0.041 + \beta_i^{mkt}0.055 + \beta_i^{size}0.02 + \beta_i^{value}0.043$$

---

[43] See http://mba.tuck.dartmouth.edu/pages/faculty/ken.french/ for more information on the Fama–French model and factor data information.

[44] The countries include Australia, Austria, Belgium, Canada, Denmark, Finland, France, Germany, Hong Kong, Ireland, Italy, Japan, Malaysia, Netherlands, New Zealand, Norway, Singapore, Spain, Sweden, Switzerland, the United Kingdom, and the United States. See http://mba.tuck.dartmouth.edu/pages/faculty/ken.french/ for more information on the Fama–French model and factor data information.

Consider the case of a small-cap issue with value characteristics and above-average market risk—assume the FFM market beta is 1.20. If the issue's market capitalization is small we expect it to have a positive size beta; for example, $\beta_i^{size} = 0.05$. If the shares sell cheaply in relation to book equity (i.e., they have a high book-to-market ratio) the value beta is also expected to be positive; for example, $\beta_i^{value} = 0.8$. For both the size and value betas, zero is the neutral value, in contrast with the market beta, where the neutral value is 1. Thus, according to the FFM, the shares' required return is slightly over 15 percent:

$$r_i = 0.041 + 1.20(0.055) + 0.5(0.02) + 0.8(0.043) = 0.151$$

The FFM market beta of 1.2 could be above or below the CAPM beta, but for this comparison, suppose it is 1.20. The CAPM estimate would be $0.041 + 1.20(0.055) = 0.107$ or less by about $15.1 - 10.7$ or 4.4 percentage points. In this case, positive size and value exposures help account for the different estimates in the two models.

Returning to the specification of the FFM to discuss its interpretation, note that the FFM factors are of two types:

▶ an equity market factor, which is identified with systematic risk as in the CAPM, and

▶ two factors related to company characteristics and valuation, size (SMB) and value (HML).

The FFM views the size and value factors as representing ("proxying for") a set of underlying risk factors. For example, small market-cap companies may be subject to risk factors such as less ready access to private and public credit markets and competitive disadvantages. High book-to-market may represent shares with depressed prices because of exposure to financial distress. The FFM views the return premiums to small size and value as compensation for bearing types of systematic risk. Many practitioners and researchers believe, however, that those return premiums arise from market inefficiencies rather than compensation for systematic risk.[45]

---

**EXAMPLE 7**

### An Analyst Case Study (3): The Required Return on Microsoft Shares

Weeramantry's next task in researching Microsoft shares is to estimate a required return on equity (which is also a required return on total capital because Microsoft has no long-term debt). Weeramantry uses an equally weighted average of the CAPM and FFM estimates unless one method appears to be superior as judged by more than a five point difference in adjusted $R^2$; in that case, only the estimate with superior explanatory power is used. Exhibit 7 shows the cost of equity information for Microsoft Corporation. All the beta estimates in Exhibit 7 are significant at the 5 percent level.

---

[45] Lakonishok, Shleifer, and Vishny (1994) and La Porta, Lakonishok, Shleifer, and Vishny (1997).

| EXHIBIT 7 | CAPM and FFM Required Return Estimates, Microsoft Corporation | |
|---|---|---|
| | **Model A** | **Model B** |
| (1) Current risk-free rate | 4.7% | 4.7% |
| (2) Beta | 1.04 | 1.14 |
| (3) Market (equity) risk premium | 5.5% | 5.5% |
| *Premium for stock: (2) × (3) =* | *5.72%* | *6.27%* |
| (4) Size beta | — | −0.222 |
| (5) Size Premium (SMB) | — | 2.7% |
| *Premium for stock: (4) × (5) =* | — | *−0.60%* |
| (6) Value beta | — | −0.328 |
| (7) Value Premium | — | 4.3% |
| *Premium for stock: (6) × (7) =* | — | *−1.41%* |
| $R^2$ | 0.34 | 0.35 |
| Adjusted $R^2$ | 0.33 | 0.32 |

*Sources*: http://mba.tuck.dartmouth.edu/pages/faculty/ken.french/data_library.html for size and value historical premia data (1926–2006) and Morningstar Ibbotson, The Cost of Capital Resources (March 2007 report for Microsoft) for CAPM and FFM betas and $R^2$.

Weeramantry's and Delacour's fund holds positions for 4 years on average. Weeramantry and his colleague Delacour are apprised that their firm's economic unit expects that the marketplace will favor growth-oriented equities over the coming year. Reviewing all the information, Delacour makes the following statements:

▶ "Microsoft's cost of equity benefits from the company's above average market capitalization, which offsets the stock's above average premium for market risk."

▶ "If our economic unit's analysis is correct, growth-oriented portfolios are expected to outperform value-oriented portfolios over the next year. As a consequence, we should favor the CAPM required return estimate over the Fama–French estimate."

Using only the above information, address the following.

1. Estimate Microsoft's cost of equity using the
   A. CAPM.
   B. Fama–French model.
2. Judge whether Delacour's first statement, concerning Microsoft's cost of equity, is accurate.

**3.** Judge whether Delacour's second statement, concerning the expected relative performance of growth-oriented portfolios and the use of the CAPM and FFM required return estimates, is correct.

**Solution to 1:**

**A.** The required return according to the CAPM is 4.7% + 1.04(5.5%) = 4.7% + 5.72% = 10.42%.

**B.** The required return according to the FFM is 4.7% + 1.14(5.5%) + (−0.222)(2.7%) + (−0.328)(4.3%) = 4.7% + 6.27% + (−0.60%) + (−1.41%) = 8.96 percent.

**Solution to 2:** The statement is accurate. Because the SMB premium is positive and Microsoft has negative exposure to it (size beta is −0.222), the effect of size on Microsoft's required return is to reduce it, offsetting the opposite effect on the required return of Microsoft's above average market risk (Microsoft's market beta is above 1.0).

**Solution to 3:** The statement is incorrect. It suggests that computing a required return using a positive value premium is questionable when the investor short-term forecast is for growth to outperform value. Required return estimates should reflect the expected or long-run compensation for risk. The positive value of the value premium in the FFM reflects expected compensation for bearing risk over the long run, consistent with the company's cash flows extending out to the indefinite future. The economic unit's prediction for a short-term time horizon does invalidate the use of a positive value premium for the Fama–French model.

The regression fit statistics for both the CAPM and FFM in Example 7 were high. There is more to learn about the relative merits of the CAPM and FFM in practice, but the FFM appears to have the potential for being a practical addition to the analyst's toolkit. One study contrasting the CAPM and FFM for U.S. markets found that whereas differences in the CAPM beta explained on average 3 percent of the cross-sectional differences in returns of the stocks over the next year, the FFM betas explained on average 5 percent of the differences.[46] Neither performance appears to be impressive, but keep in mind that equity returns are subject to a very high degree of randomness over short horizons.

### 4.2.2 Extensions to the Fama–French Model

The thought process behind the FFM of extending the CAPM to capture observed patterns in equity returns that differences in the CAPM beta appear not to explain has been extended by other researchers. One well-established relationship is that investors demand a return premium for assets that are relatively illiquid—assets that cannot be quickly sold in quantity without high explicit or implicit transaction costs. Pastor and Stambaugh (2003) extended the FFM to encompass compensation for the degree of liquidity of an equity investment.

[46] Bartholdy and Peare (2004).

This model has been applied to public security investment as well as certain private security investments.[47] The Pastor–Stambaugh model (PSM) adds to the FFM a fourth factor, LIQ, representing the excess returns to a portfolio that invests the proceeds from shorting high-liquidity stocks in a portfolio of low-liquidity stocks:

$$r_i = R_F + \beta_i^{mkt}RMRF + \beta_i^{size}SMB + \beta_i^{value}HML + \beta_i^{liq}LIQ \qquad \textbf{(36-12)}$$

An estimate of the liquidity premium for U.S. equity markets is 4.5 percent.[48] An estimate of the PSM model for U.S. markets is:

$$r_i = 0.041 + \beta_i^{mkt} 0.055 + \beta_i^{size} 0.02 + \beta_i^{value} 0.043 + \beta_i^{liq} 0.045$$

An average-liquidity equity should have a liquidity beta of 0, with no impact on required return. But below-average liquidity (positive liquidity beta) and above-average liquidity (negative liquidity beta) will tend to increase and decrease required return, respectively.

### EXAMPLE 8

**The Required Return for a Common Stock Investment**

A common stock has the following characteristics:

| | |
|---|---|
| Market beta | 1.50 |
| Size beta | 0.15 |
| Value beta | −0.52 |
| Liquidity beta | 0.20 |

Based only on the information given, infer the style characteristics of the above common stock issue.

**Solution:** The issue appears to be small-cap and have a growth orientation. The positive size beta indicates sensitivity to small-cap returns as would characterize small-cap stocks. (A positive liquidity beta, as shown, would also be typical for small-cap stocks because they usually trade in less liquid markets than do large-cap stocks.) The negative value beta indicates a growth orientation.

The concept of liquidity may be distinguished from marketability. With reference to equities, liquidity relates to the ease and potential price impact of the sale of an equity interest into the market. Liquidity is a function of several factors including the size of the interest and the depth and breadth of the market and its ability to absorb a block (i.e., a large position) without an adverse price impact. In the strictest sense, marketability relates to the right to sell an asset.

---

[47] See Metrick (2007).

[48] Metrick (2007), pp. 77–78, applied the PSM to venture capital fund investment.

Barring securities law or other contractual restrictions, all equity interests are potentially marketable, i.e., they can be potentially marketed for sale in the sense of the existence of a market into which the security can be sold. However, in private business valuation, the two terms are often used interchangeably.[49] The typical treatment in that context is to take a discount for lack of marketability (liquidity) from the value estimate, where justified,[50] rather than incorporate the effect in the discount rate, as in the PSM.

### 4.2.3 Macroeconomic and Statistical Multifactor Models

The FFM and PSM are examples of one type of a range of models for required return that are based on multiple fundamental factors (factors that are attributes of the stocks or companies themselves, e.g., the price-to-earnings ratio for a share or the company's financial leverage); the group includes several proprietary models as well. Models for required return have also been based on macroeconomic and statistical factors.

► In macroeconomic factor models the factors are economic variables that affect the expected future cash flows of companies and/or the discount rate that is appropriate to determining their present values.

► In statistical factor models, statistical methods are applied to historical returns to determine portfolios of securities (serving as factors) that explain those returns in various senses.

A specific example of macroeconomic factor models is the five-factor BIRR model, presented in Burmeister, Roll, and Ross (1994), with factor definitions as follows:

1. Confidence risk: the unanticipated change in the return difference between risky corporate bonds and government bonds, both with maturities of 20 years. To explain the factor's name, when their confidence is high, investors are willing to accept a smaller reward for bearing the added risk of corporate bonds.

2. Time horizon risk: the unanticipated change in the return difference between 20-year government bonds and 30-day Treasury bills. This factor reflects investors' willingness to invest for the long term.

3. Inflation risk: the unexpected change in the inflation rate. Nearly all stocks have negative exposure to this factor, as their returns decline with positive surprises in inflation.

4. Business cycle risk: the unexpected change in the level of real business activity. A positive surprise or unanticipated change indicates that the expected growth rate of the economy, measured in constant dollars, has increased.

5. Market timing risk: The portion of the total return of an equity market proxy (e.g., the S&P 500 for the United States) that remains unexplained by the first four risk factors. Almost all stocks have positive sensitivity to this factor.

---

[49] Hitchner (2006), p. 390.

[50] See Hitchner (2006), pp. 390–391.

The fifth factor acknowledges the uncertainty surrounding the correct set of underlying variables for asset pricing; this factor captures influences on the returns to the market proxy not explained by the first four factors. For example, using such a model, the required return for a security could have the form

$r_i =$ T-bill rate + (Sensitivity to confidence risk × 2.59%) − (Sensitivity to time horizon risk × 0.66%) − (Sensitivity to inflation risk × 4.32%) + (Sensitivity to business-cycle risk × 1.49%) + (Sensitivity to market-timing risk × 3.61%)

where the risk premia estimates are developed using econometric techniques referenced in Burmeister, et al. (1994). Similar to models based on fundamental factors, models based on macroeconomic and statistical factors have various proprietary implementations.

## 4.3 Build-Up Method Estimates of the Required Return on Equity

Widely used by valuators of closely held businesses, the build-up method estimates the required return on an equity investment as the sum of the risk-free rate and a set of risk premia:

$r_i =$ Risk-free rate + Equity risk premium ± One or more premia
(discounts)

The build-up method parallels the risk premium approach embodied in multi-factor models with the difference that specific beta adjustments are not applied to factor risk premiums.

### 4.3.1 Build-Up Approaches for Private Business Valuation

The need for estimates of the required return on the equity of a private business arises when present value models—known in such contexts as income models—are used in the process of valuing business interests. Because the valuation of such interests takes place not only for completely private investment purposes but where courts and tax authorities may play a role—e.g., in the valuation of a business included in an estate or the valuation of an equity interest for a legal dispute—the valuator may need to research which methods such authorities have found to be acceptable.

Standard approaches to estimating the required return on equity for publicly traded companies, such as the CAPM and the FFM, are adaptable for estimating the required rate of return for non-publicly traded companies. However, valuators often use an approach to valuation that relies on building up the required rate of return as a set of premia added to the risk-free rate. The premia include the equity risk premium and one or more additional premia, often based on factors such as size and perceived company-specific risk, depending on the facts of the exercise and the valuator's analysis of them. An expression for the build-up approach was presented in Equation 36-5. A traditional specific implementation is as follows:[51]

$$r_i = \text{Risk-free rate} + \text{Equity risk premium} + \text{Size premium}_i + \text{Specific-company premium}_i$$

Exhibit 8 explains the logic for a typical case. The equity risk premium is often estimated with reference to equity indices of publicly traded companies. The market's largest market-capitalization companies typically constitute a large fraction of such indices' value. With a beta of 1.0 implicitly multiplying the equity risk premium, the sum of the risk-free rate and equity risk premium is effectively the required return on an average-systematic-risk large-cap public equity issue. In the great majority of cases, private business valuation concerns companies much smaller in size than public large-cap issues. Valuators often add a premium related to the excess returns of small stocks over large stocks reflecting an incremental return for small size. (The premium is typically after adjustment for the differences in the betas of small- and large-cap stocks to isolate the effect of size—a beta-adjusted size premium.) The level of the size premium is typically assumed to be inversely related to the size of the company being valued. When the size premium estimate is appropriately based on the lowest market-cap decile—frequently the case because many private businesses are small relative to publicly traded companies—the result corresponds to the return on an average-systematic-risk micro-cap public equity issue. An analysis of risk factors that are incremental to those captured by the previously included premia may lead the valuator to add a specific company premium. This risk premium sometimes includes a premium for unsystematic risk of the subject company under the premise that such risk related to a privately-held company may be less easily diversified away.

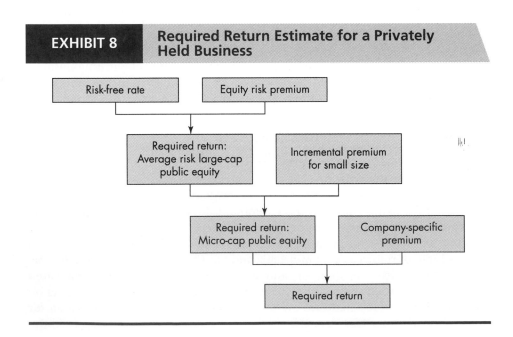

**EXHIBIT 8    Required Return Estimate for a Privately Held Business**

---

[51] See Hitchner (2006), p. 173.

Two additional issues related to required return estimation for private companies include 1) consideration of the relative values of controlling versus minority interests in share value and 2) the effect on share value of the lack of ready marketability for a small equity interest in a private company. Lack of marketability is the inability to immediately sell shares due to lack of access to public equity markets because the shares are not registered for public trading. (Marketability may also be restricted by contractual or other reasons.)

With respect to the potential adjustment for the relative control associated with an equity interest in a private company, any adjustments related to the type of interest (controlling or minority) are traditionally not made in the required return but, if appropriate, directly to the preliminary value estimate. The issues involved in such adjustments are complex with some diversity of viewpoints among practitioners. Given these considerations, a detailed discussion is outside the scope of this reading.[52] Similarly, adjustments for lack of marketability are traditionally taken as an adjustment to the estimated value for an equity interest after any adjustment for the degree of control of the equity interest.

To illustrate, suppose an analyst is valuing a private integrated document management solutions company. The risk-free rate is 5 percent, the analyst's estimate of the equity risk premium is 4.5 percent, and based on assets and revenues the company appears to correspond to the top half of the 10th decile of U.S. public companies, which is decile 10a in Exhibit 9 with market capitalizations of equity ranging from about $174 million to about $314 million.

| EXHIBIT 9 | Estimates of U.S. Beta Adjusted Size Premia | |
| --- | --- | --- |
| Market Cap Decile | Market Cap Range (Millions) | Size Premium |
| 6 | $1,379.267 to $1,946.588 | 1.67% |
| 7 | $977.912 to $1,378.476 | 1.62 |
| 8 | $627.017 to $976.624 | 2.28 |
| 9 | $314.912 to $626.955 | 2.70 |
| 10 | $2.247 to $314.433 | 6.27 |
| | Breakdown of the 10th Decile | |
| 10a | $173.664 to $314.433 | 4.35% |
| 10b | $2.247 to $173.439 | 9.68 |

*Source*: Ibbotson (2007), p. 262.

Thus, ignoring any appropriate specific-company premium, an estimate of the required return on equity is 5% + 4.5% + 4.35% = 13.85%. A caution is that the size premium for the smallest decile (and especially the 10b component) may reflect not only the premium for healthy small-cap companies, but former large-cap companies that are in financial distress. If that is the case, the historical estimate may not be applicable without a downward adjustment for estimating the required return for a small but financially healthy private company.

---

[52] For more information on adjustments for relative control, see Hitchner (2006), ch. 8, and Bruner (2004), ch.15.

A so-called modified CAPM formulation would seek to capture departures from average systematic risk. For example, if the analyst estimated that the company would have a beta of 1.2 if publicly traded, based on its publicly traded peer group, the required return estimate would be

Risk-free rate + Beta × Equity risk premium + Size premium

or 5% + 1.2 × 4.5% + 4.35% = 14.75%. This result could be reconciled to a simple build-up estimate by including a differential return of (1.2 − 1.0)(4.5%) = 0.9% in the specific-company premium.

### 4.3.2 Bond Yield Plus Risk Premium

For companies with publicly traded debt, the **bond yield plus risk premium method** provides a quick estimate of the cost of equity.[53] The estimate is

$$\text{BYPRP cost of equity} = \text{YTM on the company's long-term debt} \\ + \text{Risk premium} \qquad \text{(36-13)}$$

The YTM on the company's long-term debt includes

▶ a real interest rate and a premium for expected inflation, which are also factors embodied in a government bond yield, and

▶ a default risk premium.

The default risk premium captures factors such as profitability, the sensitivity of profitability to the business cycle, and leverage (operating and financial) that also affect the returns to equity. The risk premium in Equation 36-13 is the premium that compensates for the additional risk of the equity issue compared with the debt issue (recognizing that debt has a prior claim on the cash flows of the company). In U.S. markets, the typical risk premium added is 3–4 percent, based on experience.

In the first edition of the book from which this reading was taken, IBM's required return was estimated as 12.9 percent using the CAPM; the inputs used were an equity risk premium estimate of 5.7 percent, a beta of 1.24, and a risk-free rate of 5.8. Based on the YTM of 6.238 percent for the IBM 8.375s of 2019, a bond yield plus risk premium estimate was 9.2 percent.

---

### EXAMPLE 9

**The Cost of Equity of IBM from Two Perspectives**

You are valuing the stock of International Business Machines Corporation (NYSE: IBM) as of early September 2007, and you have gathered the following information:

| | |
|---|---|
| 20-year T-bond YTM: | 5.0% |
| IBM 8.375s of 2019 YTM: | 5.632% |

---

[53] Although simple, the method has been used in serious contexts. For example, the Board of Regents of the University of California in a retirement plan asset/liability study (July 2000) used the 20-year T-bond rate plus 3.3 percent as the single estimate of the equity risk premium.

The IBM bonds, you note, are investment grade (rated A1 by Standard & Poor's, A+ by Moody's Investors Service, and A by Fitch). The beta on IBM stock is 1.72. In prior valuations you have used a risk premium of 3 percent in the bond yield plus risk premium approach. However, the estimated beta of IBM has increased by more than one third over the past five years. As a matter of judgment, you have decided as a consequence to use a risk premium of 3.5 percent in the bond yield plus risk premium approach.

1. Calculate the cost of equity using the CAPM. Assume that the equity risk premium is 4.5 percent.

2. Calculate the cost of equity using the bond yield plus risk premium approach, with a risk premium of 3.5 percent.

3. Suppose you found that IBM stock, which closed at 117.43 on 4 September 2007, was slightly undervalued based on a DCF valuation using the CAPM cost of equity from Question 1. Does the alternative estimate of the cost of equity from Question 2 support the conclusion based on Question 1?

**Solution to 1:** $5\% + 1.72(4.5\%) = 12.7\%$.

**Solution to 2:** Add 3.5 percent to the IBM bond YTM: $5.632\% + 3.5\% = 9.132\%$, or 9.1 percent. Note that the difference between the IBM bond YTM and T-bond YTM is 0.632 percent, or 63 basis points. This amount plus 3.5 percent is the total estimated risk premium versus Treasury debt.

**Solution to 3:** *Undervalued* means that the value of a security is greater than market price. All else equal, the lower the discount rate, the higher the estimate of value. The inverse relationship between discount rate and value, holding all else constant, is a basic relationship in valuation. If IBM appears to be undervalued using the CAPM cost of equity estimate of 12.7 percent, it will appear to be even more undervalued using a 9.1 percent cost of equity based on the bond yield plus risk premium method.

Thus, updating Example 9 to 2007 shows that a lower equity risk premium estimate is offset by IBM's higher current beta, leaving the required return on equity almost unchanged according to the CAPM. With IBM's credit rating unchanged, the lower level of interest rates in 2007 would have lowered the bond yield plus risk premium estimate, all else equal. Because a lower level of interest rates is consistent with lower opportunity costs for investors, that result would have been logical. Because IBM's systematic risk had increased, a risk premium increase was justified and the cost of equity estimate was essentially unchanged.

The bond yield plus risk premium method can be viewed as a build-up method applying to companies with publicly traded debt. The estimate provided can be a useful check when the explanatory power of more rigorous models is low. Given that a company's shares have positive systematic risk, the yield on its long-term debt is revealing as a check on cost of equity estimate. For example, Abitibi-Consolidated Inc.'s 7.5 debentures (rated by Moody's and Standard &

Poor's as B3 and B, respectively) mature in 2028 and were priced to yield approximately 11 percent as of mid August 2007, so required return estimates for its stock (NYSE: ABY) not greater than 11 percent would be suspect.

## 4.4 The Required Return on Equity: International Issues

Among the issues that concern analysts estimating the required return of equities in a global context are

▶ Exchange rates and

▶ Data and model issues in emerging markets.

An investor is ultimately concerned with returns and volatility stated in terms of his or her own currency. Historical returns are often available or can be constructed in local currency and home currency terms. Equity risk premium estimates in home currency terms can be higher or lower than estimates in local currency terms because exchange rate gains and losses from the equity component are generally not exactly offset by gains and losses from the government security component of the equity risk premium. For example, the arithmetic mean U.K. premium over 1970 to 2005 was 6.58 percent in pound sterling terms but for a U.S. investor it was 5.54 percent.[54] The U.S. dollar estimate more accurately reflects a U.S. investor's historical experience. A sound approach for any investor is to focus on the local currency record, incorporating any exchange rate forecasts.

The difficulty of required return and risk premium estimation in emerging markets has been previously mentioned. Of the numerous approaches that have been proposed to supplement or replace traditional historical and forward looking methods, we can mention two.

▶ The country spread model for the equity risk premium. For an emerging equity market, this states that

$$\text{Equity risk premium estimate} = \text{Equity risk premium for a developed market} + \text{Country premium}$$

The country premium represents a premium associated with the expected greater risk of the emerging market compared to the benchmark developed market. Typically, analysts hope that a sovereign bond yield spread is adequate for approximating this premium. Thus, the country premium is often estimated as the yield on emerging market bonds (denominated in the currency of the developed market) minus the yield on developed market government bonds.

To illustrate, taking the approximate 13 percent yield differential between U.S. dollar denominated government of Russia bonds ("Brady bonds") and U.S. Treasury bonds as the Russian country premium and using an estimate of 4.5 percent for the U.S. equity risk premium, the Russian equity risk premium equals 4.5% + 13% = 17.5%.

▶ The country risk rating model[55] provides a regression-based estimate of the equity risk premium based on the empirical relationship between

---

[54] Morningstar (2007), p. 176.

[55] Erb, Claude, Campbell R. Harvey, and Tadas Viskanta, "Country Credit Risk and Global Portfolio Selection," *Journal of Portfolio Management*, Winter 1995: 74–83.

developed equity market returns and Institutional Investor's semi-annual risk ratings for those markets. The estimated regression equation is then used with the risk ratings for less developed markets to predict the required return for those markets. This model has been recommended by Morningstar (Ibbotson).

# THE WEIGHTED AVERAGE COST OF CAPITAL  **5**

The overall required rate of return of a company's suppliers of capital is usually referred to as the company's cost of capital. The cost of capital is most commonly estimated using the company's after-tax weighted average cost of capital, or weighted average cost of capital (WACC) for short: a weighted average of required rates of return for the component sources of capital.

The cost of capital is relevant to equity valuation when an analyst takes an indirect, total firm value approach using a present value model. Using the cost of capital to discount expected future cash flows available to debt and equity, the total value of these claims is estimated. The balance of this value after subtracting off the market value of debt is the estimate of the value of equity.

In many jurisdictions, corporations may deduct net interest expense from income in calculating taxes owed, but they cannot deduct payments to shareholders, such as dividends. The following discussion reflects that base case.

If the suppliers of capital are creditors and common stockholders, the expression for WACC is

$$\text{WACC} = \frac{\text{MVD}}{\text{MVD} + \text{MVCE}} r_d (1 - \text{Tax rate}) + \frac{\text{MVE}}{\text{MVD} + \text{MVCE}} r \qquad \textbf{(36-14)}$$

where MVD and MVCE are the current market values of debt and (common) equity, not their book or accounting values. Dividing MVD or MVCE by the total market value of the firm, which is MVD + MVCE, gives the proportions of the company's total capital from debt or equity, respectively. These weights will sum to 1.0. The expression for WACC multiplies the weights of debt and equity in the company's financing by, respectively, the after-tax required rates of return for the company's debt and equity under current market conditions. "After-tax," it is important to note, refers to just corporate taxes in this discussion. Multiplying the before-tax required return on debt ($r_d$) by 1 minus the marginal corporate tax rate (1 − Tax rate) adjusts the pretax rate $r_d$ downward to reflect the tax deductibility of corporate interest payments that is being assumed. Because distributions to equity are assumed not to be deductible by the corporations, a corporation's before and after-tax costs of equity are the same; no adjustment to $r$ involving the corporate tax rate is appropriate. Generally speaking, it is appropriate to use a company's marginal tax rate rather than its current effective tax rate (reported taxes divided by pretax income) because the effective tax rate can reflect nonrecurring items. A cost of capital based on the marginal tax rate usually better reflects a company's future costs in raising funds.

Because the company's capital structure (the proportions of debt and equity financing) can change over time, WACC may also change over time. In addition, the company's current capital structure may also differ substantially from what it will be in future years. For these reasons, analysts often use *target* weights instead of the current market-value weights when calculating WACC. These target weights incorporate both the analyst's and investors' expectations about the target capital structure that the company will tend to use over time. Target weights provide a good approximation of the WACC for cases in which the current weights misrepresent the company's normal capital structure.[56]

The before-tax required return on debt is typically estimated using the expected YTM of the company's debt based on current market values. Analysts can choose from any of the methods presented in this reading for estimating the required return on equity, $r$. No tax adjustment is appropriate for the cost of equity assuming payments to shareholders such as dividends are not tax deductible by companies.

---

### EXAMPLE 10

**The Weighted Average Cost of Capital for IBM**

Taking an indirect, total firm value approach to valuing equity, suppose you have the inputs for estimating the cost of capital shown in Exhibit 10. Based only on the information given, estimate IBM's WACC.

| EXHIBIT 10 | Cost of Capital Data: IBM |
|---|---|

| Panel A: Capital Structure | Value |
|---|---|
| Long-term debt as a percent of total capital, at market value | 35% |
| Tax rate | 29% |

| Panel B: Component Costs of Capital | |
|---|---|
| Cost of equity: CAPM estimate | 12.7% |
| YTM of IBM long bond | 5.6% |

*Source:* Estimates based on company reports; Standard & Poor's.

**Solution:** Long-term debt as a percent of total capital stated at market value is the weight to be applied to IBM's after-tax cost of debt in the WACC calculation. Therefore, IBM's WACC is approximately 9.65 percent, calculated as follows:

$$\text{WACC} = 0.35(5.6\%)(1 - 0.29) + 0.65(12.7\%)$$
$$= 1.392\% + 8.255\% = 9.647 \text{ percent}$$

---

[56] See a modern corporate finance textbook, such as Brealey, Myers, and Allen (2006), for a review of capital structure theory.

# DISCOUNT RATE SELECTION IN RELATION TO CASH FLOWS

When used as discount rates in valuation, required returns need to be defined appropriately relative to the cash flows to be discounted.

A cash flow after more senior claims (e.g., promised payments on debt and taxes) have been fulfilled is a cash flow to equity. When a cash flow to equity is discounted, the required return on equity is an appropriate discount rate. When a cash flow is available to meet the claims of all of a company's capital providers—usually called a cash flow to the firm— the firm's cost of capital is the appropriate discount rate.

Cash flows may be stated in nominal or real terms. When cash flows are stated in real terms, amounts reflect offsets made for actual or anticipated changes in the purchasing power of money. Nominal discount rates must be used with nominal cash flows and real discount rates must be used with real cash flows. In valuing equity, we will use only nominal cash flows and therefore we will make use of nominal discount rates. Because the tax rates applying to corporate earnings are generally stated in nominal money terms—such and such tax rates applying at stated levels of nominal pretax earnings—using nominal quantities is an exact approach because it reflects taxes accurately.

Equation 36-14 presents an after-tax weighted average cost of capital using the after-tax cost of debt. In later readings, we will present cash flow to the firm definitions for which it is appropriate to use that definition of the cost of capital as the discount rate (i.e., rather than a pretax cost of capital reflecting a pretax cost of debt). The exploration of the topic is outside the scope of this reading because the definitions of cash flows have not been introduced and explained.[57]

In short, in later readings we will be able to illustrate present value models of stock value using only two discount rates: the nominal required return on equity when the cash flows are those available to common shareholders, and the nominal after-tax weighted average cost of capital when the cash flows are those available to all the company's capital providers.

---

[57] Technically, in discounting a cash flow to the company, the definitions of the cash flow and cost of capital should be coordinated so the value of the tax saving associated with the deductibility of interest expense is not counted twice (i.e., in the cash flow and the discount rate).

# SUMMARY

In this reading we introduced several important return concepts. Required returns are important because they are used as discount rates in determining the present value of expected future cash flows. When an investor's intrinsic value estimate for an asset differs from its market price, the investor generally expects to earn the required return plus a return from the convergence of price to value. When an asset's intrinsic value equals price, however, the investor only expects to earn the required return.

For two important approaches to estimating a company's required return, the CAPM and the build-up model, the analyst needs an estimate of the equity risk premium. This reading examined realized equity risk premia for a group of major world equity markets and also explained forward-looking estimation methods. For determining the required return on equity, the analyst may choose from the CAPM and various multifactor models such as the Fama–French model and its extensions, examining regression fit statistics to assess the reliability of these methods. For private companies, the analyst can adapt public equity valuation models for required return using public company comparables, or use a build-up model, which starts with the risk-free rate and the estimated equity risk premium and adds additional appropriate risk premia.

When the analyst approaches the valuation of equity indirectly, by first valuing the total firm as the present value of expected future cash flows to all sources of capital, the appropriate discount rate is a weighted average cost of capital based on all sources of capital. Discount rates must be on a nominal (real) basis if cash flows are on a nominal (real) basis.

Among the reading's major points are the following:

▶ The return from investing in an asset over a specified time period is called the *holding period return*. *Realized return* refers to a return achieved in the past, and *expected return* refers to an anticipated return over a future time period. A *required return* is the minimum level of expected return that an investor requires to invest in the asset over a specified time period, given the asset's riskiness. The (*market*) *required return*, a required rate of return on an asset that is inferred using market prices or returns, is typically used as the *discount rate* in finding the present values of expected future cash flows. If an asset is perceived (is not perceived) as fairly priced in the marketplace, the required return should (should not) equal the investor's expected return. When an asset is believed to be mispriced, investors should earn a *return from convergence of price to intrinsic value*.

▶ An estimate of the equity risk premium—the incremental return that investors require for holding equities rather than a risk-free asset— is used in the CAPM and in the build-up approach to required return estimation.

▶ Approaches to equity risk premium estimation include historical, adjusted historical, and forward-looking approaches.

▶ In historical estimation, the analyst must decide whether to use a short-term or a long-term government bond rate to represent the risk-free rate and whether to calculate a geometric or arithmetic mean for the equity risk premium estimate. Forward-looking estimates include Gordon growth model estimates, supply-side models, and survey estimates. Adjusted historical estimates can involve an adjustment for biases in data series and an adjustment to incorporate an independent estimate of the equity risk premium.

▶ The CAPM is a widely used model for required return estimation that uses beta relative to a market portfolio proxy to adjust for risk. The Fama–French model (FFM) is a three factor model that incorporates the market factor, a size factor, and a value factor. The Pastor-Stambaugh extension to the FFM adds a liquidity factor. The bond yield plus risk premium approach finds a required return estimate as the sum of the YTM of the subject company's debt plus a subjective risk premium (often 3 percent to 4 percent).

▶ When a stock is thinly traded or not publicly traded, its beta may be estimated on the basis of a peer company's beta. The procedure involves unlevering the peer company's beta and then re-levering it to reflect the subject company's use of financial leverage. The procedure adjusts for the effect of differences of financial leverage between the peer and subject company.

▶ Emerging markets pose special challenges to required return estimation. The country spread model estimates the equity risk premium as the equity risk premium for a developed market plus a country premium. The country risk rating model approach uses risk ratings for developed markets to infer risk ratings and equity risk premiums for emerging markets.

▶ The weighted average cost of capital is used when valuing the total firm and is generally understood as the nominal after-tax weighted average cost of capital, which is used in discounting nominal cash flows to the firm in later readings. The nominal required return on equity is used in discounting cash flows to equity.

## PRACTICE PROBLEMS FOR READING 36

1. A Canada-based investor buys shares of Toronto-Dominion Bank (Toronto: TD.TO) for C$72.08 on 15 October 2007 with the intent of holding them for a year. The dividend rate was C$2.11 per year. The investor actually sells the shares on 5 November 2007 for C$69.52. The investor notes the following additional facts:

   ▶ No dividends were paid between 15 October and 5 November.

   ▶ The required return on TD.TO equity was 8.7 percent on an annual basis and 0.161 percent on a weekly basis.

   A. State the lengths of the expected and actual holding-periods.

   B. Given that TD.TO was fairly priced, calculate the price appreciation return (capital gains yield) anticipated by the investor given his initial expectations and initial expected holding period.

   C. Calculate the investor's realized return.

   D. Calculate the realized alpha.

2. The estimated betas for AOL Time Warner (NYSE: AOL), J.P. Morgan Chase & Company (NYSE: JPM), and The Boeing Company (NYSE: BA) are 2.50, 1.50, and 0.80, respectively. The risk-free rate of return is 4.35 percent and the equity risk premium is 8.04 percent. Calculate the required rates of return for these three stocks using the CAPM.

3. The estimated factor sensitivities of TerraNova Energy to Fama–French factors and the risk premia associated with those factors are given in the table below:

| | Factor Sensitivity | Risk Premium (%) |
|---|---|---|
| Market factor | 1.20 | 4.5 |
| Size factor | −0.50 | 2.7 |
| Value factor | −0.15 | 4.3 |

   A. Based on the Fama–French model, calculate the required return for TerraNova Energy using these estimates. Assume that the Treasury bill rate is 4.7 percent.

   B. Describe the expected style characteristics of TerraNova based on its factor sensitivities.

4. Newmont Mining (NYSE: NEM) has an estimated beta of −0.2. The risk-free rate of return is 4.5 percent, and the equity risk premium is estimated to be 7.5 percent. Using the CAPM, calculate the required rate of return for investors in NEM.

5. An analyst wants to account for financial distress and market-capitalization as well as market risk in his cost of equity estimate for a particular traded company. Which of the following models is *most appropriate* for achieving that objective?

   A. The capital asset pricing model (CAPM).

   B. The Fama–French model.

   C. A macroeconomic factor model.

**6.** The following facts describe Larsen & Toubro Ltd's component costs of capital and capital structure. Based on the information given, calculate Larsen & Toubro's WACC.

### Component Costs of Capital

| | |
|---|---|
| Cost of equity based on the CAPM: | 15.6% |
| Pretax cost of debt: | 8.28% |
| Tax rate: | 30% |
| Target weight in capital structure: | Equity 80%, Debt 20% |

## Use the following information to answer Questions 7–12

An equity index is established in 2001 for a country that has relatively recently established a market economy. The index vendor constructed returns for the five years prior to 2001 based on the initial group of companies constituting the index in 2001. Over 2004 to 2006 a series of military confrontations concerning a disputed border disrupted the economy and financial markets. The dispute is conclusively arbitrated at the end of 2006. In total, ten years of equity market return history is available as of the beginning of 2007. The geometric mean return relative to 10-year government bond returns over 10 years is 2 percent per year. The forward dividend yield on the index is 1 percent. Stock returns over 2004 to 2006 reflect the setbacks but economists predict the country will be on a path of a 4 percent real GDP growth rate by 2009. Earnings in the public corporate sector are expected to grow at a 5 percent per year real growth rate. Consistent with that, the market P/E ratio is expected to grow at 1 percent per year. Although inflation is currently high at 6 percent per year, the long-term forecast is for an inflation rate of 4 percent per year. Although the yield curve has usually been upward sloping, currently the government yield curve is inverted; at the short-end, yields are 9 percent and at 10-year maturities, yields are 7 percent.

**7.** The inclusion of index returns prior to 2001 would be expected to

   **A.** bias the historical equity risk premium estimate upwards.

   **B.** bias the historical equity risk premium estimate downwards.

   **C.** have no effect on the historical equity risk premium estimate.

**8.** The events of 2004 to 2006 would be expected to

   **A.** bias the historical equity risk premium estimate upwards.

   **B.** bias the historical equity risk premium estimate downwards.

   **C.** have no effect on the historical equity risk premium estimate.

**9.** In the current interest rate environment, using a required return estimate based on the short-term government bond rate and a historical equity risk premium defined in terms of a short-term government bond rate would be expected to

   **A.** bias long-term required return on equity estimates upwards.

   **B.** bias long-term required return on equity estimates downwards.

   **C.** have no effect on long-term required return on equity estimates.

**10.** A supply side estimate of the equity risk premium as presented by the Ibbotson–Chen earnings model is *closest* to

    **A.** 3.2 percent.

    **B.** 4.0 percent.

    **C.** 4.3 percent.

**11.** Common stock issues in the above market with average systematic risk are *most likely* to have required rates of return

    **A.** between 2 percent and 7 percent.

    **B.** between 7 and 9 percent.

    **C.** 9 percent or greater.

**12.** Which of the following statements is *most accurate?* If two equity issues have the same market risk but the first issue has higher leverage, greater liquidity, and a higher required return, the higher required return is most likely the result of the first issue's

    **A.** greater liquidity.

    **B.** higher leverage.

    **C.** higher leverage and greater liquidity.

# STUDY SESSION 11
## EQUITY INVESTMENTS:
## Industry and Company Analysis in a Global Context

This study session provides insights on issues that affect security valuation internationally. Analyzing industries in a global context and evaluating competitive forces that will affect returns provide a foundation for security valuation decisions. Discounted dividend models are examined in detail.

## READING ASSIGNMENTS

**Reading 37**    Equity: Concepts and Techniques
*Global Investments,* Sixth Edition, by Bruno Solnik and Dennis McLeavey, CFA

**Reading 38**    The Five Competitive Forces that Shape Strategy
*Harvard Business Review*

**Reading 39**    Industry Analysis
*Security Analysis on Wall Street: A Comprehensive Guide to Today's Valuation Methods,* by Jeffrey C. Hooke

**Reading 40**    Valuation in Emerging Markets
*Valuation: Measuring and Managing the Value of Companies,* Fourth Edition, by Tim Koller, Marc Goedhart, and David Wessels

**Reading 41**    Discounted Dividend Valuation
*Analysis of Equity Investments: Valuation,* by John D. Stowe, CFA, Thomas R. Robinson, CFA, Jerald E. Pinto, CFA, and Dennis W. McLeavey, CFA

23⅜ 24

4⅝ 4¹¹⁄₁₆ ⅜

5½ 5½ — ⅜

5½ 5½ — ¹⁄₁₆

20⅝ 21¹³⁄₁₆ — ⅛

18⅛ + ⅞

17⅜ 18⅛ +

6½ 6½ — ½

7¼ 6½ 6½ — ⅛

31⁄₃₂ — ⅛

15⁄₁₆

9⁄₁₆

9⁄₁₆

7¹⁵⁄₁₆ 7¹³⁄₁₆ 7¹⁵⁄₁₆

2⅝ 2¹¹⁄₃₂ 2½ +

2¾ 2¼ 2¼

121⁄₁₆ 11⅜ 11¾ +

87 33¾ 33 33¼ —

802 25⅝ 24⁹⁄₁₆ 25⅝ +

833 12 11⅝ 11⅞ +

16 10½ 10½ 10⅛ —

78 15⅞ 15¹³⁄₁₆ 15⅛ —

9¹⁄₁₆ 8¼ 8⅝ +

11¼ 10⅛

# EQUITY: CONCEPTS AND TECHNIQUES

by Bruno Solnik and Dennis McLeavey, CFA

## LEARNING OUTCOMES

| The candidate should be able to: | Mastery |
|---|---|
| **a.** discuss the most important issues, such as the information problem, that arise when investing internationally; | ☐ |
| **b.** demonstrate the various steps involved in global industry analysis, including country analysis; | ☐ |
| **c.** distinguish between country analysis and industry analysis and compare and evaluate key concepts of industry analysis such as demand analysis, industry life cycle analysis, and competition structure analysis as well as risk elements inherent in industry analysis; | ☐ |
| **d.** demonstrate how to conduct a global industry analysis by analyzing the return potential and risk characteristics of a prospective investment in a global context; | ☐ |
| **e.** evaluate two common approaches of equity analysis (ratio analysis and discounted cash flow models including the franchise value model) and demonstrate how to find attractively priced stocks by using either of these methods; | ☐ |
| **f.** analyze the effects of inflation on asset valuation; | ☐ |
| **g.** discuss multifactor models as applied in a global context. | ☐ |

Investing in foreign stocks poses at least two types of problems: First, the portfolio manager must gain sufficient familiarity with the operations, trading mechanisms, costs, and constraints of foreign markets. This issue was addressed in the reading on equity markets and instruments. Second, the portfolio manager's investment approach must be global; that is, his method of analyzing and selecting stocks should be part of an optimal worldwide investment strategy. The conceptual and technical aspects of this analysis are discussed in this reading.

Thomas R. Robinson, CPA, CFA, made significant contributions to the accounting material in this chapter.

*Global Investments*, Sixth Edition, by Bruno Solnik and Dennis McLeavey, CFA. Copyright © 2009 by Pearson Education. Reprinted with permission of Pearson Education, publishing as Pearson Addison Wesley.

145

To structure their analysis of expected return and risk of stocks, investors must start from a view of the world. What are the worldwide factors affecting stock prices? In an open-economy world, companies should be valued relative to their global competitors; hence, global industry analysis is of primary importance. Before conducting such an analysis, it is important to understand the differences in national accounting standards that affect the raw information used. Then the important aspects of global industry analysis can be studied with data adjusted for comparability across countries. Global industry analysis of expected returns and risks leads naturally to a discussion of risk factor models used to structure global portfolios and manage their risk.

# 1    APPROACHING INTERNATIONAL ANALYSIS

There is nothing unique to financial analysis in an international context. Analysts must already take foreign variables into account in evaluating domestic firms. After all, product markets in which many domestic industrial companies compete are international.

Large domestic firms tend to export extensively and head a network of foreign subsidiaries. These companies must be analyzed as global firms, not purely domestic ones. In many sectors, the competition is fully global. The methods and data required to analyze international manufacturers are quite similar. In brief, research on a company should produce two pieces of information:

▶ *Expected return*: The *expected return* on an investment can be measured by a rate of return, including potential price appreciation, over some time period, or by some other quantified form of buy-or-sell recommendation.

▶ *Risk exposure*: Risk sensitivity, or risk exposure, measures how much a company's value responds to certain key factors, such as economic activity, energy costs, interest rates, currency volatility, and general market conditions. Risk analysis enables a manager or investment policy committee to simulate the performance of an investment in different scenarios. It also helps the manager design more diversified portfolios.

The overall purpose of analysis is to find securities with superior expected returns, given current (or foreseeable) domestic and international risks.

Quantifying the analysis facilitates a consistent global approach to international investment. This is all the more desirable when the parameters that must be considered are numerous and their interrelationships are complex. Although qualitative analysis seems easier to conduct in some institutions than in others, it must be carefully structured so that it is consistent for every security, and provides an estimation of the reaction of security prices to various risk factors.

## The Information Problem

Information on foreign firms is often difficult to obtain; once obtained, it is often difficult to interpret and analyze using domestic methods. It is no wonder, then, that comparisons of similar figures for foreign firms are often misleading.

In the United States, companies publish their quarterly earnings, which are publicly available within just a couple of weeks after the close of the quarter. The 10-K reports are particularly useful for trend analysis and intercompany comparisons. Moreover, these reports are available on computerized databases. In contrast, certain European and Asian firms publish their earnings only once a year and with a considerable reporting time lag. French companies, for example, follow this pattern and don't actually publish their official earnings until two to six months after the end of their fiscal years. As a result, official earnings figures are outdated before they become public. To remedy this lack of information, most corporations with significant foreign ownership have begun announcing quarterly or semiannual earnings estimates a short time after the close of the quarter. This is true worldwide for large international corporations. These corporations also follow the U.S. practice of issuing "warnings" as soon as some bad news is likely to affect earnings. The format and reliability of these announcements vary from firm to firm, but overall, they help investors get better financial information more quickly. As do U.S. firms, British firms publish detailed financial information frequently. Similarly, Japanese firms have begun publishing U.S.-style financial statements, though sometimes only once a year.

Other problems arise from the language and presentation of the financial reports. Many reports are available only in a company's domestic language. Whereas multinational firms tend to publish both in their domestic language and in English, many smaller but nevertheless attractive firms do not. In general, financial reports vary widely from country to country in format, degree of detail, and reliability of the information disclosed. Therefore, additional information must sometimes be obtained directly from the company. Differences in national accounting standards are discussed later in this reading.

As international investment has grown, brokers, banks, and information services have, fortunately, started to provide more financial data to meet investors' needs. In fact, today, many large global brokerage houses and banks provide analysts' guides covering companies from a large number of countries. The guides include information ranging from summary balance sheet and income statement information to growth forecasts, expected returns on equity investments, and risk measures, such as betas, which are discussed later. The reports are usually available in both the domestic language and English. Similarly, several data services, such as Bloomberg, Reuters, Thomson Financial, Factset, and Moody's, are extending their international coverage on companies and currently feature summary financial information on an increasing number of international corporations. Some financial firms, such as Thomson First Call, have specialized in collecting earnings forecasts from financial analysts worldwide. They provide a service giving the individual analyst's forecast for most large companies listed on the major stock exchanges of the world. They also calculate a consensus forecast, as well as various other global statistics.

Despite these developments, to get the most timely information possible, financial analysts may have to visit international corporations. This, of course, is a time-consuming and expensive process. Moreover, the information obtained is often not homogeneous across companies and countries. The next section reviews differences in international accounting standards.

## A Vision of the World

A major challenge faced by all investment organizations is structuring their international research efforts. Their choice of method depends on what they believe are the major factors influencing stock returns. The objective of security analysis is to detect relative misvaluation, that is, investments that are preferable to other *comparable* investments. That is why sectoral analysis is so important. A financial analyst should be assigned the study of securities that belong to the same sector, that is, that are influenced by the *same* common factors and that can therefore be directly compared. The first task, though, is defining these sectors, or common factors. For example, one can reasonably claim that all oil companies belong to the same sector. Another sector would be French common stocks, which are all influenced by national factors. An alternative would be all high-technology companies across the world, which should be influenced by similar worldwide industrial factors. In a homogeneous sector, research should detect securities that are underpriced or overpriced relative to the others.

A first step for an organization to structure its global equity investment requires that it adhere to some vision of the world regarding the dominant factors affecting stock returns. Traditionally, investment organizations use one of three major approaches to international research, depending on their vision of the world:

► If a portfolio manager believes that the value of companies worldwide is affected primarily by global industrial factors, her research effort should be structured according to industrial sectors. This means that companies are valued relative to others within the same industry, for example, the chemical industry. Naturally, financial analysts who use this approach are specialists in particular industrial sectors.

► If a portfolio manager believes that all securities in a national stock market are influenced primarily by domestic factors, her research effort should be structured on a country-by-country or region-by-region basis. The most important investment decision in this approach is how to allocate assets among countries or regions. Thereafter, securities are given a relative valuation within each national market.

► If a portfolio manager believes that some particular attributes of firms are valued worldwide, she will engage in *style investing*. For example, *value stocks* (corporations with a low stock market price compared with their book value) could be preferred to *growth stocks* (corporations with a high stock market price compared with their book value).

In general, an organization must structure its investment process based on some vision of the major common factors influencing stock returns worldwide.

## 2    DIFFERENCES IN NATIONAL ACCOUNTING STANDARDS

In this reading, we develop a top-down approach to global equity investing. We examine country and industry analysis before moving to equity security analysis. Global industry financial analysis examines each company in the industry against the industry average. Plots of one financial ratio against another can show the relative location of individual companies within the industry. To carry out such analysis, we must first know something about the differences in national accounting standards so that we can adjust ratios to make them comparable. For example, discounted cash flow analysis (DCF) and compound annual growth rates (CAGR) in cash flows must be based on comparable data to be meaningful.

In global industry financial analysis, the pattern is to contrast the financial ratios of individual firms against the same ratios for industry averages. The analyst will encounter and possibly need to adjust such ratios as enterprise value (EV) to earnings before interest, taxes, depreciation, and amortization (EBIDTA), return on equity (ROE), and the book value multiple of price to book value per share (BV). In practice, one also sees such ratios as price to net asset value (NAV), EV to capital employed (CE), return on capital employed (ROCE), and value added margin. *Capital employed* is usually defined as equity plus long-term debt.[1] *Net asset value* is usually defined on a per-share basis as equity minus goodwill. *Value added margin* is ROCE minus the weighted average cost of capital (WACC). Such ratios are detailed later.

With an understanding of differences in national accounting standards, the analyst will be prepared to evaluate companies from around the world within the context of global industry. After discussing these differences, we will return to global industry analysis.

Today all companies compete globally. Capital markets of developed countries are well integrated, and international capital flows react quickly to any perceived mispricing. Hence, companies tend to be priced relative to their global competitors, and it is for this reason that this reading focuses on global industry analysis.

Companies and investors have become more global. Mergers and acquisitions often occur on a global basis. Further, it is not unusual for a company to have its shares listed on multiple exchanges. Similarly, investors often seek to diversify their holdings and take advantage of opportunities across national borders. This globalization of financial markets creates challenges for investors, creditors, and other users of financial statements. Comparing financial statements of companies located in different countries can be a difficult task. Different countries may employ different accounting principles, and even where the same accounting methods are used, currency, cultural, institutional, political, and tax differences can make between-country comparisons of accounting numbers hazardous and misleading.

For example, the treatment of depreciation and extraordinary items varies greatly among countries, so that net income of a company located in one country might be different from that of a similarly performing company located in another country, even after adjustment for differences in currency. This disparity is partly the result of different national tax incentives and the creation of *secret* or *hidden reserves* (provisions) in certain countries. German and Swiss firms (among others), for example, have been known to stretch the definition of a liability; that is, they tend to overestimate contingent liabilities and future uncertainties when compared with other firms. The provisions for these liabilities reduce income in the current year, but increase income in later years when the provisions are reduced. This practice can have a smoothing impact on earnings and mask the underlying variability or riskiness of business operations.

Similarly, German and Swiss firms allow goodwill resulting from acquisitions to be deducted from equity immediately, bypassing the income statement and resulting in reporting the balance sheet based on book value, not on actual transaction prices. Similar idiosyncrasies often make comparisons of Japanese and U.S. earnings figures or accounting ratios meaningless. As a result, many large Japanese companies publish secondary financial statements in English that conform to the U.S. generally accepted accounting principles (GAAP). But even when we examine these statements, we find that financial ratios differ markedly

---

[1] See Temple (2002) for definitions.

between the two countries. For example, financial *leverage* is high in Japan compared with the United States, and coverage ratios are poor. But this does not necessarily mean that Japanese firms are more risky than their U.S. counterparts, only that the relationship between banks and their client corporations is different than in the United States.

With increasing globalization there has been a movement toward convergence of accounting standards internationally. In spite of this movement, there are still differences in existing accounting standards that must be considered by investors.

## Historical Setting

Each country follows a set of accounting principles that are usually prepared by the accounting profession and the national authorities. These sets of accounting principles are sometimes called national GAAP. Two distinct models can describe the preparation of these national accounting principles:

▶ In the Anglo-American model, accounting rules have historically been set in standards prepared by a well-established, influential accounting profession.

▶ In the Continental model, used by countries in Continental Europe and Japan, accounting rules have been set in a codified law system; governmental bodies write the law, and the accounting profession is less influential than in the Anglo-American model.

Anglo-American countries typically report financial statements intended to give a true and fair view of the firm's financial position. Hence, there can be large differences between accounting statements, the intent of which is to give a fair representation of the firm's financial position, and tax statements, the intent of which is to reflect the various tax provisions used to calculate the amount of income tax owed. Many other countries (France, Germany, Italy, and Japan, for example) have a tradition that the reported financial statements and earnings conform to the method used to determine taxable income. This implies that financial statements were geared to satisfy legal and tax provisions and may not give a true and fair view of the firm. This confusion between tax and financial reporting is slowly disappearing under the pressure of international harmonization, as noted in the next section.

## International Harmonization of Accounting Practices

Investors, creditors, and other users of financial statements have exerted pressure to harmonize national accounting principles. The International Accounting Standards Committee (IASC) was set up in 1973 by leading professional accounting organizations in nine countries: Australia, Canada, France, Germany, Japan, Mexico, the Netherlands, the United Kingdom and Ireland, and the United States. Over time, additional countries became members of the IASC. In 1974 the IASC issued its first international accounting standard (IAS), the Disclosure of Accounting Policies. In 2001, the IASC was renamed the International Accounting Standards Board (IASB), and we will use this name hereafter.

The IASB publishes both International Accounting Standards (IAS) and International Financial Reporting Standards (IFRS). The twenty-nine standards IAS adopted in 2001 form the body of the accounting standard and are periodically updated. Since 2002, new standards published by the IASB have taken the form of IFRS. Detailed interpretations of some of these IFRS are published by the International Financial Reporting Standards Interpretation Committee (IFRIC) of the IASB. A list of these standards, as of early 2007, is given in Exhibit 1. Given the numerous appellations (IAS, IFR, IFRIC), the set of standards edicted by the IASB is usually simply referred to as IFRS, as we will do here. Although the IASB is able to propose international accounting standards, it does not have the authority to require companies to follow these standards. Without a mechanism to compel companies to use IFRS and enforce the standards, harmonization is not easily achievable. In 2000, the International Organization of Securities Commissions (IOSCO) endorsed the existing IAS. IOSCO is an important organization whose members are the agencies regulating securities markets in all countries. IOSCO's objectives are to promote high standards of regulation in order to maintain just, efficient, and sound markets. In 2005 IOSCO encouraged its members to accept financial statements prepared under the IFRS in filings for cross-border listings and new offerings, with additional reconciliation or disclosure as necessary to meet national standards.

These two international organizations, one representative of the accounting profession (private sector) and the other of government regulators, play an important role in moving toward global harmonization of disclosure requirements and accounting practices. This goal is all the more important for multinational corporations that wish to raise capital globally. They need to be able to present their accounts in a single format wherever they want to be listed or raise capital. Of particular importance is the attitude of the United States toward international accounting standards. Convergence of the U.S. GAAP and IFRS is a desirable but difficult goal. A topic under discussion is to allow foreign firms listed on a U.S. stock exchange to publish accounts according to IFRS rather than asking them to provide earnings statements calculated according to the U.S. GAAP.

The IASB also received the support of the *World Bank*. A large number of emerging countries have adopted the IFRS as a basis for their accounting standards. In some cases national standards are virtually word-for-word IFRS, while in some others there are slight differences. Australia, Hong Kong and New Zealand have basically adopted the IFRS. In 2006, Canada decided to incorporate IRFS into Canadian GAAP within five years. Other developed countries are taking convergence steps. In 2005, the Accounting Standards Board of Japan decided to work on the convergence of Japanese GAAP with IFRS. In countries where national accounting standards are still different from IFRS, many corporations voluntarily use IFRS in their financial reporting. For example, most of the leading industrial companies in Switzerland voluntarily report their accounts according to international accounting standards.

A major step toward the worldwide acceptance of IFRS has been the decision by the European Union (*EU*) to adopt them. In countries where accounting rules are governed by law, specific legislation is required to allow for the use of other accounting standards. The harmonization of European accounting principles has come mostly through *Directives* published by the EU. These EU Directives are drafted by the EU Commission, and member states' parliaments must adapt the national law to conform to these Directives. The EU also issues *Regulations*, which have the force of law without requiring formal transposition into national legislation. In 2002, the EU issued a Regulation requiring listed companies to prepare their consolidated financial statements in accordance with IAS from 2005 onward. Endorsement and implementation of the IFRS by all members of the EU can be a lengthy process that requires translation into all national laws or regulations. But by March 2007, the EU Commission had voted

| EXHIBIT 1 | List of IFRS and IAS as of March 2007 |
| --- | --- |

**IFRS**

| IFRS 1 | First-time Adoption of International Financial Reporting Standards |
| --- | --- |
| IFRS 2 | Share-based Payment |
| IFRS 3 | Business Combinations |
| IFRS 4 | Insurance Contracts |
| IFRS 5 | Non-current Assets Held for Sale and Discontinued Operations |
| IFRS 6 | Exploration for and Evaluation of Mineral Resources |
| IFRS 7 | Financial Instruments: Disclosures |
| IFRS 8 | Operating Segments |

**IAS**

| IAS 1 | Presentation of Financial Statements |
| --- | --- |
| IAS 2 | Inventories |
| IAS 7 | Cash Flow Statements |
| IAS 8 | Accounting Policies, Changes in Accounting Estimates and Errors |
| IAS 10 | Events After the Balance Sheet Date |
| IAS 11 | Construction Contracts |
| IAS 12 | Income Taxes |
| IAS 16 | Property, Plant and Equipment |
| IAS 17 | Leases |
| IAS 18 | Revenue |
| IAS 19 | Employee Benefits |
| IAS 20 | Accounting for Government Grants and Disclosure of Government Assistance |
| IAS 21 | The Effects of Changes in Foreign Exchange Rates |
| IAS 23 | Borrowing Costs |
| IAS 24 | Related Party Disclosures |
| IAS 26 | Accounting and Reporting by Retirement Benefit Plans |
| IAS 27 | Consolidated and Separate Financial Statements |
| IAS 28 | Investments in Associates |
| IAS 29 | Financial Reporting in Hyperinflationary Economies |
| IAS 31 | Interests in Joint Ventures |
| IAS 32 | Financial Instruments: Presentation |
| IAS 33 | Earnings per Share |
| IAS 34 | Interim Financial Reporting |
| IAS 36 | Impairment of Assets |
| IAS 37 | Provisions, Contingent Liabilities and Contingent Assets |
| IAS 38 | Intangible Assets |
| IAS 39 | Financial Instruments: Recognition and Measurement |
| IAS 40 | Investment Property |
| IAS 41 | Agriculture |

to endorse all IAS and IFRS published to date, with one carve-out from IAS 39, Financial Instruments: Recognition and Measurement, relevant only for financial institutions. As of 2007, IFRS applies to the 27 EU members, plus members of the European Economic Area (Iceland, Liechtenstein, and Norway). EU listed companies are now required to perform their financial reporting according to IFRS, but this is not yet the case for unlisted companies, although most countries now permit IFRS for consolidated statements. In most Continental European countries, the national GAAP is codified in a law with a tax focus. But the trend is clearly to separate the financial reporting objective from the tax calculation objective.

While most countries are adopting IFRS, the United States retains the U.S. GAAP. The U.S. Securities and Exchange Commission (SEC) requests that all foreign firms listed on a public stock exchange in the United States, including NASDAQ, provide financial reports according to the U.S. GAAP (10-K reports) or provide all necessary reconciliation information (20-F reports). Strong efforts are devoted by financial reporting standard setters on both sides to achieve convergence of the two sets of standards. The U.S. GAAP are prepared by the U.S. Financial Accounting Standards Board (FASB) in consultations with various bodies, including the SEC. In October 2002, the FASB and the IASB formalized their commitment to the convergence of their standards by issuing a memorandum of understanding (commonly referred to as the *Norwalk agreement*). The two boards pledged to use their best efforts to

► make their existing financial reporting standards fully compatible as soon as is practicable, and

► coordinate their future work programs to ensure that once achieved, compatibility is maintained.

*Compatible* does not mean word-for-word identical standards; rather, it means that there are no significant differences between the two sets of standards. In February 2006, the IASB and the FASB released a "road map" that identified short- and long-term convergence projects. The objective is to remove the need for IFRS reconciliation requirements by 2009.

The road to global cooperation is never easy, and it will take time before full harmonization of financial reporting is achieved, especially between the United States and other countries.

## Differences in Global Standards

Financial reporting standards are evolving rapidly, at least for listed companies. Historical financial information for these companies, or that available for unlisted companies, is based on national GAAP that can differ markedly from IFRS. In many countries adopting the IFRS there were huge differences between the existing national GAAP and the new IFRS. For example, generous provisions could be taken in Germany and Switzerland for all types of general risks. In good times, German firms build provisions to reduce earnings growth; in bad times, they draw on these provisions to boost reported earnings. Adoption of IFRS by listed companies greatly reduces the leeway for provisioning.

But the major differences that remain are between IFRS and U.S. GAAP, and we will focus on those. A complete presentation of accounting standards is beyond the scope of this reading. The full text of standards can be obtained from the

International Accounting Standards Board and the Financial Accounting Standards Board.[2] Many of the differences in reporting are progressively eliminated.

The differences can be highlighted by looking at the reconciliation statements (20-F reports) that are provided by foreign firms listed in the United States. Ernst & Young surveyed 130 major foreign firms in 2006.[3] IFRS are new standards with transitional provisions for first-time adoption, that is, when a company adopts IFRS for the first time. A considerable number of reconciling differences may arise as a result of the first-time adoption rules in IFRS 1, First-time Adoption of International Financial Reporting Standards. A company preparing an IFRS-to-U.S. GAAP reconciliation is required to apply U.S. standards as if it had always applied those standards. Conversely, IFRS 1 provides first-time adopters with a number of exemptions from full retrospective application. In some cases these rules permit a first-time adopter to base IFRS information on measurements under its previous GAAP. Hence, some of the reconciling items may reflect differences between a first-time adopter's previous GAAP and U.S. GAAP rather than differences between IFRS and U.S. GAAP. The impact of IFRS 1 will decline over time as companies accumulate years of reporting under IFRS. In 2006, the major differences that needed reconciliation were in the following areas:

▶ Consolidation methods

▶ Business combinations

▶ Foreign currency translation

▶ Intangible assets

▶ Impairment

▶ Capitalization of borrowing costs

▶ Financial instruments—recognition and measurement

▶ Financial instruments—shareholders' equity

▶ Financial instruments—derivatives and hedge accounting

▶ Leasing

▶ Provisions and contingencies

▶ Revenue recognition

▶ Share-based payments

▶ Pensions and post-retirement benefits

A technical discussion of these differences is beyond the scope of this reading. Furthermore, the IASB and FASB are working on convergence of the reporting standards, and most differences will disappear in financial statements by 2010. A few illustrations of major points in mid-2000 are nevertheless useful:

▶ Consolidation under IFRS and U.S. GAAP can lead to some differences. IFRS bases the consolidation of subsidiaries in terms of "control," either through voting rights or through power to govern. U.S. GAAP distinguishes between a *voting interest* model and a *variable interest* model. There can be significant differences for minority interest and joint ventures. The Enron collapse, for example, illustrated the importance of accounting for *special purpose entities* (*SPEs*), sometimes referred to as off-balance-sheet

---

[2] See www.iasb.org and www.fasb.org. Detailed information and comparisons of various standards are also provided by the Web sites of major accounting firms, for example, www.iasplus.com.

[3] "Towards Convergence: A Survey of IFRS to US GAAP Differences," Ernst & Young, 2006.

**CONCEPTS IN ACTION    Rules Set for Big Change**

### Millions of Dollars of Debt Could Be Brought Back on to Companies' Balance Sheets

Among the many consequences of the collapse of Enron has been a new focus by regulators on how companies account for off-balance-sheet transactions.

Enron's swift demise raised questions over its complex web of off-balance-sheet transactions, leading the U.S.'s Financial Standards Accounting Board to consider new rules governing special purpose entities (SPEs). The changes could result in millions of dollars of debt being brought back on to corporate balance sheets, and represent a significant challenge for the rapidly developing structured finance market. SPEs are used for a wide range of financial transactions because they isolate assets from the financial fortunes of companies that own them.

SPEs can be organized in a variety of forms, such as trusts or corporations, but usually have no full-time employees or operating business. They can be used for different activities, including acquiring financial assets, property or equipment, and as a vehicle for raising funds from investors by issuing stock or other securities.

Depending on the type of SPE, its assets and liabilities may not appear in the financial statements of the entity that created it. . . .

*Source*: Jenny Wiggins, "Special Purpose Entities," *Financial Times*, October 7, 2002, p. 4. From *Financial Times*. Copyright © 2002 Financial Times. All Rights Reserved.

arrangements. The ability of firms to avoid consolidation of SPE has often enabled them to keep large amounts of liabilities off the balance sheet, to the detriment of investors and creditors alike. Under IAS 27, SPEs are consolidated if controlled. In the United States, pre-Enron accounting standards did not provide an accurate picture of the relationships between the parent companies and their SPEs, leaving plenty of leeway to avoid consolidation. In December 2003, the FASB issued a revised interpretation known as FIN 46(R), Consolidation of Variable Interest Entities, which enlarges the scope of SPE consolidation. There are still cases, however, where a SPE would be consolidated under IFRS but not under U.S. GAAP. Further convergence is planned.

▶ Under U.S. GAAP, investments are reported at historical cost (acquisition cost less depreciation and impairment), except for some financial instruments revalued to fair value. Under IFRS, intangible assets, property plant and equipment (PPE), and investment property may be revalued to *fair value*. Derivatives, biological assets, and some financial securities must be fair valued.

▶ Share-based payments have been the object of heated debate in the United States. *Employee stock options* represent potential earnings dilution to existing shareholders. As a form of employee compensation, these stock options should be treated as expenses from an economic perspective. Under IFRS 2, Share-based Payment, the fair value of employee share offers (stock options) are recorded immediately in personnel costs, with an adjustment to equity. So share options are treated as expenses. Under U.S. GAAP, many companies were accounting for share-based payments under the intrinsic value method in accordance with APB 25, Accounting for Stock Issued to Employees. The *intrinsic value* of an option is simply the difference between the market value of the share minus the *strike price* or *exercise price* indicated in the option. If the stock price is below the exercise price when the option is granted, the intrinsic value is nil. In December 2004, the FASB published FAS 123(R), Accounting for Stock-Based Compensation, which supersedes APB 25. It requires the application of a fair value option pricing model to determine the value of the option to be expensed. As of 2007, there are still some slight technical differences between IFRS and U.S. GAAP in terms of timing principles, namely, the valuation of options that are granted but not yet vested (i.e., they cannot yet be exercised by the employee). There exist different option pricing models that can be used (mainly the *Black-Scholes model* and the binomial model) and different calculation assumptions can lead to very different fair values. Hence, the expense reported by a company can be more or less conservative. An illustration of option expensing is given in Example 1.

---

### EXAMPLE 1

**Employee Stock Options**

A company has 100,000 shares outstanding at $100 per share. To its senior management, the company granted employee stock options on 5,000 shares. The options can be exercised at a price of $105 any time during the next five years. For five years, the employees thus have the right but not the obligation to purchase shares at the $105 price, regardless of the prevailing market price of the stock. Using price volatility estimates for the stock, a standard Black-Scholes valuation model gives an estimated value of $20 per share option. Without expensing the options, the company's pretax earnings per share are reported as $1 million/100,000 = $10 per share. What would they have been if they had been expensed?

**Solution:**

The expense is 5000 × $20 = $100,000.
The pretax income per share would be ($1,000,000 − $100,000)/100,000 = $9 per share.

---

## The Effects of Accounting Principles on Earnings and Stock Prices

The same company using different national accounting standards could report different earnings. Some accounting standards are more conservative than others, in the sense that they lead to smaller reported earnings. Several comparative studies have attempted to measure the relative conservativeness of national standards. For example, Radebaugh and Gray (1997) conclude that U.S. accounting principles are significantly more conservative than U.K. accounting principles but significantly less conservative than Japanese and Continental European accounting principles. If the United States' earnings are arbitrarily scaled at 100, Japanese earnings would scale at 66, German earnings at 87, French earnings at 97, and British earnings at 125. These national accounting principles also affect the reported book value of equity. Now that most countries are adopting IFRS for listed companies, the differences are going to be much smaller. The reconciliation statements (Form 20-F) that are provided by foreign firms listed in the United States still show some differences in reported net profit and book value between IFRS and U.S. GAAP. Part of these differences are caused by first-time adoption of IFRS by some of these firms, but significant discrepancies in reported numbers are caused by existing differences between the two reporting systems.

*Price-earnings (P/E) ratios* are of great interest to international investors, who tend to compare the P/E ratios of companies in the same industrial sector across the world. The P/E ratio divides the market price of a share by its current or estimated annual earnings. Japanese companies have traditionally traded at high P/E ratios in comparison with U.S. companies. For comparison purposes, these P/E ratios should be adjusted because of the accounting differences in reporting earnings. They also should be adjusted to reflect the fact that Japanese firms tend to report nonconsolidated statements despite the extent of cross-holding. For example, if Company A owns 20 percent of the shares of Company B, it will include in its own earnings only the dividend paid by Company B, not a proportion of Company B's earnings. In the P/E ratio of Company A, the stock price reflects the value of the holding of shares of Company B, but the earnings do not reflect the earnings of Company B. For all these reasons, French and Poterba (1991) claim that the average 1989 Japanese P/E ratio should be adjusted from 53.7 to 32.6. Again, these differences are likely to be reduced in the near future as Japanese GAAP evolves toward IFRS in requiring consolidation of controlled subsidiaries.

All investment managers regard accounting harmonization as a good thing.[4] But they stress the importance of the quality and timeliness of the information disclosed. Indeed, the quality and speed of information disclosure are of paramount importance to investors. Restating the same information in a different accounting standard does not address the issue of the quality of the information disclosed or the firm's future prospects. Investment managers deciding to include a specific stock in a portfolio need to do more than simply look at past accounting data.

# GLOBAL INDUSTRY ANALYSIS 3

The valuation of a common stock is usually conducted in several steps. A company belongs to a global industry and is based in a country; hence, country and industry analysis are necessary. Companies compete against global players within their industry, so studying a company within its global industry is the primary approach to stock valuation.

With the knowledge that financial ratios from different international companies are difficult to compare, the analyst still faces the task of looking forward. What conditions in the industry prevail, and how are companies likely to compete in the future?

Within the framework of industrial organization, this section outlines the most important elements that should be looked at when conducting a company analysis in a global setting. We begin with a general introduction to country analysis to provide a starting point for the analysis of the company and industry.

---

[4] See a survey of European fund managers conducted by PriceWaterhouseCoopers/Ipsos MORI: *IFRS—The European Investors' View*, February 2006.

## Country Analysis

Companies tend to favor some countries in their business activities: They target some countries for their sales and base their production in only a few countries. Hence, country analysis is of importance in studying a company. In each country, economists try to monitor a large number of economic, social, and political variables, such as the following:

► Anticipated real growth
► Monetary policy
► Fiscal policy (including fiscal incentives for investments)
► Wage and employment rigidities
► Competitiveness
► Social and political situations
► Investment climate

In the long run, real economic growth is probably the major influence on a national stock market. Economists focus on economic growth at two horizons:

► Business cycle
► Long-term sustainable growth

What are favorable country conditions for equity investment? There can be favorable business cycle conditions as well as favorable long-term sustainable growth conditions. If the favorable conditions are a consensus view, however, they will already be priced in the equity markets. The analyst must find a way of discerning these conditions before others do.

A high long-term sustainable growth rate in gross domestic product (GDP) is favorable, because this translates into high long-term profits and stock returns. In creating GDP and productivity growth rate expectations, the analyst will undoubtedly examine the country's savings rate, investment rate, and total factor productivity (TFP). TFP measures the efficiency with which the economy converts capital and labor into goods and services. Increased investment rates due to technical progress will increase rates of return, but the savings and investment rates themselves must be closely analyzed. A country's investments reflect replacement and capacity expansion and influence future productivity gains. If the ratio of investment to GDP is low, then the investments are largely replacement investments; whereas a high rate suggests that capacity expansion is under way.[5] Further, a positive correlation between investment rates and subsequent GDP growth rates cannot be taken for granted because there are other factors to consider.

The main factors that interact with the country's investment rate to affect GDP growth are the rate of growth in employment, work hours, educational levels, technological improvement, business climate, political stability, and the public or private nature of the investment. A higher long-term growth in the work force will lead to higher GDP growth just as a reduction in work hours will lead to less GDP growth. Increasing skills in the work force complement technological advances as they will both lead to higher GDP growth. A business climate of more privatization and reduced regulation is conducive to more investment.

---

[5] See Calverley (2003), p. 11.

Attractive investment opportunities will also lead to more investment, although an increased propensity to invest can depress rates of return. Political stability will reduce the risk and hence increase the attractiveness of investments. Finally, private investments are more likely to be made with maximal return on equity as the objective and hence lead to higher GDP growth.

In the short term, business cycle conditions can be favorable for investments, but business cycle turning points are so difficult to predict that such predictions should cause the analyst to make investment recommendations to only slightly adjust portfolio. Business cycles represent a complex control system with many causes and interacting private and governmental decisions. For example, companies invest in plant and equipment and build inventories based on expected demand but face the reality that actual demand does not continuously meet expectations. Although an investor would benefit from buying stocks at the trough of a business cycle and bonds at the peak, such perfect market timing is virtually impossible, and one might better take the approach of ignoring the country's business cycle and concentrate rather on its long-term sustainable growth rate in GDP. Nevertheless, even limited prescient ability can lead to informed adjustments to portfolio holdings. Calverley (2003, pp. 15–19) classifies the business cycle stages and attractive investment opportunities as follows:

▶ *Recovery*: The economy picks up from its slowdown or recession. Good investments to have are the country's cyclical stocks and commodities, followed by riskier assets as the recovery takes hold.

▶ *Early upswing*: Confidence is up and the economy is gaining some momentum. Good investments to have are the country's stocks and also commercial and residential property.

▶ *Late upswing*: Boom mentality has taken hold. This is not usually a good time to buy the country's stocks. The country's commodity and property prices will also be peaking. This is the time to purchase the country's bonds (yields are high) and interest-rate-sensitive stocks.

▶ *Economy slows or goes into recession*: The economy is declining. Good investments to have are the country's bonds, which will rally (because of a drop in market interest rates), and its interest-rate-sensitive stocks.

▶ *Recession*: Monetary policy will be eased but there will be a lag before recovery. Particularly toward the end of the recession, good investments to make are the country's stocks and commodities.

Inflation is generally associated with the late upswing, and deflation is possible in a recession. Inflation effects on equity valuation are analyzed later in this reading.

### Business Cycle Synchronization

Stock market performance is clearly related to the business cycle and economic growth.[6] National business cycles are not fully synchronized. This lack of synchronization makes country analysis all the more important. For example, the United States witnessed a strong economic recovery in 1992, Britain started to enjoy strong economic growth in 1993, and the European continent only started to recover in 1995, but Japan's economy was still stagnant.

---

[6] See Canova and De Nicolo (1995). An analysis of the business cycle is provided in Reilly and Brown (2006).

However, economies are becoming increasingly integrated. Growth of major economies is, in part, exported abroad. For example, growth in the United States can sustain the activity of an exporting European firm even if demand by European consumers is stagnant. But rigidities in a national economy can prevent it from quickly joining growth in a world business cycle. Studies of rigidities are important here.

What are the business cycle synchronization implications for equity valuation? Although national economies are becoming increasingly integrated with a world economy, there are so many economic variables involved that the chances of full synchronization are extremely remote. For example, within the European Union, tensions arise because governments are not free to pursue domestic and fiscal economic policies to deal with their own domestic business cycles. The experience of the 1990s and early 2000s is that the economies of Continental Europe, Japan, the United Kingdom, and the United States had markedly different GDP growth rates and entered various stages of the business cycle at different times. Recalling that any correlation less than unity supports diversification benefits, the lack of perfect business cycle synchronization is an a priori argument in favor of international diversification. If long-term GDP growth and business cycles were perfectly synchronized among countries, then one would expect a high degree of correlation between markets, especially in periods of crisis. In making investment asset-allocation decisions, one must always consider long-term expected returns, variances, and correlations. In the long term, international diversification will always be advantageous until national economies are expected to be perfectly synchronized around the world. It is difficult to imagine such a possibility. Expected returns and expected standard deviations will differ among countries with unsynchronized short-term business cycles and long-term GDP growth rates, even though investors may follow the crowd in their short-term reactions to crises.

Further considerations in the divergence between countries come from a consideration of growth clubs. Baumol (1986) examined three convergence growth clubs (clubs of countries converging to a similar steady state in terms of income per capita): western industrialized countries, centrally planned economies, and less developed countries. Regardless of the number of growth clubs, one can expect within-group convergence but intergroup divergence in TFP and income per capita. The degree of business cycle synchronicity also varies over time depending on the pattern of regional shocks and changes in economies' propagation mechanisms.

### Growth Theory

Growth theory is a branch of economics that examines the role of countries in value creation. The output of a country is measured by gross domestic product (GDP), and growth theory attempts to explain the rate of GDP growth in different countries. For two countries with equal risk, portfolio managers will want to overweight the country with sustainable expected long-term GDP growth. The inputs considered are labor, capital, and productivity. In addition to labor and capital, there are also human capital and natural resources. Increases in educational levels can lead to an increase in labor skills, and discoveries of natural resources can lead to resource-based growth. Two competing economic theories attempt to shed light on the sustainable long-term growth rate of a nation.

*Neoclassical growth theory* assumes that the marginal productivity of capital declines as more capital is added. This is the traditional case in economics with diminishing marginal returns to input factors. *Endogenous growth theory* assumes that the marginal productivity of capital does not necessarily decline as capital is added. Technological advances and improved education of the labor force can lead to efficiency gains. Any one firm faces diminishing returns, but endogenous growth theory assumes that externalities arise when a firm develops a new technology. Thus, one firm's technical breakthrough begets another's breakthrough, perhaps through imitation. In this case, the marginal product of capital does not decline with increasing capital per capita.

In growth theory, *steady state* is defined as the condition of no change in capital per capita. This comes about when the savings rate times GDP per capita just matches the investment required to maintain the amount of capital per capita. The rate of growth in the population plus the yearly depreciation in equipment gives a replacement rate to be multiplied by the amount of capital per capita, and this multiplication yields the investment required to maintain the amount of capital per capita.

Neoclassical growth theory predicts that the long-term level of GDP depends on the country's savings rate, but the long-term growth rate in GDP does not depend on the savings rate. This is because a steady state is reached, and this steady state is reached because additions to the capital stock provide smaller and smaller increases to GDP and consequently to savings (the savings rate times GDP). In the context of endogenous growth theory, steady state may never be reached because the ability to avoid a decline in the marginal product of capital means there is no necessary decline in savings as capital is increased. Thus, endogenous growth theory predicts that the long-term growth rate in GDP depends on the savings rate.

Neoclassical growth theory suggests that countries above steady state will slow to steady state and countries below steady state will have their growth speed up. Thus, there will be convergence in the case of countries that have similar steady states. Endogenous growth theory, however, maintains that technological progress is not exogenous but rather depends on research and development and the generation of ideas. Essentially, the productivity term in the production function does not grow exogenously at a constant rate as specified in neoclassical growth theory. Rather, the rate of change in the productivity term depends on the stock of innovations to date and the number of researchers at work on innovations.

Equity valuation implications are different for countries experiencing neoclassical versus endogenous growth. If a country is experiencing neoclassical growth and its savings rate increases, there would be an increase in dividends as the new level of GDP is reached, but not an increase in the dividend growth rate. For a country experiencing endogenous growth with cascading breakthroughs, however, there would be an increase in both dividends and the dividend growth rate.

In an open world economy, it is important to ascertain whether growth is caused by an increased mobilization of inputs or by efficiency gains. Input-driven growth is necessarily limited. For example, many developing countries have witnessed high growth rates because of capital flows from abroad, but they face diminishing returns in the absence of productivity gains. National sustainable growth rates require careful examination.

### The Limitation of the Country Concept in Financial Analysis

The distinction between countries and companies is misleading in some respects. Both types of economic entities produce and market a portfolio of products. Indeed, some companies are bigger in economic size than some countries.

Many companies compete globally. The national location of their headquarters is not a determinant variable. Many multinational corporations realize most of their sales and profits in foreign countries. So, an analysis of the economic situation of the country of their headquarters is not of great importance. In the reading on equity concepts and techniques, we showed that many national stock markets are dominated by a few multinationals. For example, Nokia market capitalization is larger than the sum of that of all other Finnish firms. The top ten Swiss multinational firms account for more than 70 percent of the Swiss stock exchange. But these companies do most of their business outside of their home country, so their valuation should be based on the global competition they face in their industry, not on the state of their home economy.

## Industry Analysis: Return Expectation Elements

To achieve excess equity returns on a risk-adjusted basis, an investor must find companies that can earn return on equity (ROE) above the required rate of return and do this on a sustained basis. For this reason, global industry analysis centers on an examination of sources of growth and sustainability of competitive advantage. Growth must be distinguished from level. A high profit level may yield high current cash flows for valuation purposes, but there is also the question of how these cash flows will grow. Continued reinvestment opportunities in positive net present value investment opportunities will create growth. Curtailment of research and development expenditures may yield high current cash flows at the expense of future growth.

An analyst valuing a company within its global industry should study several key elements. Following are some important conceptual issues.

### Demand Analysis

Value analysis begins with an examination of demand conditions. The concepts of complements and substitutes help, but demand analysis is quite complex. Usually, surveys of demand as well as explanatory regressions are used to try to estimate demand. Demand is the target for all capacity, location, inventory, and production decisions. Often, the analyst tries to find a leading indicator to help give some forecast of demand.

In the global context, *demand* means *worldwide demand*. One cannot simply define the automobile market as a domestic market. A starting point, then, is a set of forecasts of global and country-specific GDP figures. The analyst will want to estimate the sensitivity of sales to global and national GDP changes.

Country analysis is important for demand analysis because most companies tend to focus on specific regions. Many European car manufacturers tend to sell and produce outside of Europe, but the European car market is their primary market. An increase in demand for cars in Europe will affect these companies more than it will affect Japanese car producers.

### Value Creation

Sources of value come from using inputs to produce outputs in the value chain. The *value chain* is the set of transformations in moving from raw materials to product or service delivery. This chain can involve many companies and countries, some providing raw materials, some producing intermediate goods, some producing finished consumer goods, and some delivering finished goods to the consumer. From the point of view of an intermediate goods producer, basic raw materials are considered to be *upstream* in the value chain, and transformations closer to the consumer are considered *downstream*.

Within the value chain, each transformation adds value. Value chain analysis can be used to determine how much value is added at each step. Indeed, some countries have a value-added tax (VAT). The value added at each transformation stage is partly a function of four major factors:

▶ *The learning (experience) curve*: As companies produce more output, they gain experience, so that the cost per unit produced declines.

▶ *Economies of scale*: As a company expands, its fixed costs may be spread over a larger output, and average costs decline over a range of output.

▶ *Economies of scope*: As a company produces related products, experience and reputation with one product may spill over to another product.

▶ *Network externalities*: Some products and services gain value as more consumers use them, so that they are able to share something popular.

Equity valuation implications come from an analysis of the industry's value chain and each company's strategy to exploit current and future profit opportunities within the chain. For company managers, Christensen, Raynor, and Verlinden (2001) recommend a strategy of predicting profit migration within the industry's value chain. For example, they break the computer industry down into value chain stages: equipment, materials, components, product design, assembly, operating system, application software, sales and distribution, and field service. In the early days of the computer industry, vertically integrated manufacturers delivered the entire value chain. The advent of the personal computer led to specialization within each stage, and profits migrated to stages such as components and operating systems. For the analyst also, the strategy of predicting dividends and dividend growth rates must be based on profit migration in the value chain. The risk can be gauged from the degree of competition within the stage—the more the competition, the more the risk. The ability of companies to compete at each stage will be enhanced by their learning curve progress, economies of scale or scope, and network externalities.

Christensen et al. also point out that industries often evolve from vertical integration to disintegration. If an industry becomes too fragmented, however, consolidation pressures will come from resource bottlenecks as well as the continuing search for economies of scale. During the industry's life cycle, tension between disintegration and consolidation will require the company and the analyst to constantly monitor company positions in the profit migration cycle.

### Industry Life Cycle

Traditionally, the industry life cycle is broken down into stages from pioneering development to decline. Of course, one must be careful in industry definition. If railroads were defined as an *industry*, we would see a global industry life cycle. Defining the industry as transportation provides a different picture. In any case, industry life cycles are normally categorized by rates of growth in sales. The stages of growth can clearly vary in length:

1. Pioneering development is the first stage, and has a low but slowly increasing industry sales growth rate. Substantial development costs and acceptance by only early adopters can lead to low profit margins.

2. Rapid accelerating growth is the second stage, and the industry sales growth rate is still modest but is rapidly increasing. High profit margins are

possible because firms from outside the new industry may face barriers to entering the newly established markets.

3. Mature growth is the third stage and has a high but more modestly increasing industry sales growth rate. The entry of competitors lowers profit margins, but the return on equity is high.

One would expect that somewhere in stage 2 or 3 the industry sales growth rate would move above the GDP growth rate in the economy.

4. Stabilization and market maturity is the fourth stage and has a high but only slowly increasing sales growth rate. The sales growth rate has not yet begun to decline, but increasing capacity and competition may cause returns on equity to decline to the level of average returns on equity in the economy.

5. Deceleration of growth and decline is the fifth stage, with a decreasing sales growth rate. At this stage, the industry may experience overcapacity, and profit margins may be completely eroded.

One would expect that somewhere in stage 5, the industry sales growth rate would fall back to the GDP growth rate and then decline below it. (This cannot happen in stage 4, where the sales growth is still increasing.) The position of an industry in its life cycle should be judged on a global basis.

### *Competition Structure*

One of the first steps in analyzing an industry is the determination of the amount of industry concentration. If the industry is fragmented, many firms compete, and the theories of competition and product differentiation are most applicable. With more concentration and fewer firms in the industry, oligopolistic competition and game theories become more important. Finally, the case of one firm is the case in which the theory of monopoly applies.

In analyzing industry concentration, two methods are normally used. One method is the $N$ firm concentration ratio: the combined market share of the largest $N$ firms in the industry. For example, a market in which the three largest firms have a combined share of 80 percent would indicate largely oligopolistic competition. A related but more precise measure is the *Herfindahl index (H)*, the sum of the squared market shares of the firms in the industry. Letting $M_i$ be the market share of an individual firm, the index is $H = M_1^2 + M_2^2 + \ldots + M_N^2$.

If two firms have a 15 percent market share each and one has a 70 percent market share, $H = 0.15^2 + 0.15^2 + 0.7^2 = 0.535$.

The Herfindahl index has a value that is always smaller than one. A small index indicates a competitive industry with no dominant players. If all firms have an equal share, $H = N(1/N^2) = 1/N$, and the reciprocal of the index shows the number of firms in the industry. When the firms have unequal shares, the reciprocal of the index indicates the "equivalent" number of firms in the industry. Using our example above, we find that the market structure is equivalent to having 1.87 firms of the same size:

$$\frac{1}{H} = \frac{1}{(0.15^2 + 0.15^2 + 0.70^2)} = \frac{1}{0.535} = 1.87$$

One can classify the competition structure of the industry according to this ratio.

In practice, the equity analyst will see both the N firm concentration ratio and the Herfindahl index. The analyst is searching for indicators of the likely degree of cooperation versus competition within the industry. Although the balance between cooperation and competition is dynamic and changing, the higher the N firm concentration ratio and the higher the Herfindahl index, the less likely it is that there is cut-throat competition and the more likely it is that companies will cooperate.

The advantage of the N firm concentration ratio is that it provides an intuitive sense of industry competition. If the analyst knows that the seven largest firms have a combined share of less than 15 percent, he or she immediately knows that the industry is extremely fragmented and thus more risky because of competitive pressures and the likely lack of cooperation.

The Hefindahl index has the advantage of greater discrimination because it reflects all firms in the industry and it gives greater weight to the companies with larger market shares. An H below 0.1 indicates an unconcentrated industry, an H of 0.1 to 0.18 indicates moderate concentration, and an H above 0.18 indicates high concentration. A high Herfindahl index can also indicate the presence of a market leader with a higher share than others, another indication of likely coordination as the leader might impose discipline on the industry.

Suppose the analyst is comparing two industries:

| Market Shares in Industry A | Market Shares in Industry B |
| --- | --- |
| One firm has 45% | Four firms have 15% each |
| Three firms have 5% each | Four firms have 10% each |
| Ten firms have 4% each | |
| Four firm concentration ratio is 60% | Four firm concentration ratio is 60% |
| Herfindahl index is 0.23 | Herfindahl index is 0.13 |

Even though the four firm concentration ratios are the same for both industries, the Herfindahl index indicates that industry A is highly concentrated, but industry B is only moderately concentrated.

## Competitive Advantage

In his book *The Competitive Advantage of Nations,*[7] Michael Porter used the notions of economic geography that different locations have different competitive advantages. Some national factors can lead to a competitive advantage:

► Factor conditions such as human capital, perhaps measured by years of schooling

► Demand conditions such as the size and growth of the domestic market

► Related supplier and support industries such as the computer software industry to support the hardware industry

► Strategy, structure, and rivalry such as the corporate governance, management practices, and the financial climate

[7] Porter (1998b).

## Competitive Strategies

A competitive strategy is a set of actions that a firm is taking to optimize its future competitive position. In *Competitive Advantage*, Porter distinguishes three generic competitive strategies:[8]

▶ *Cost leadership*: The firm seeks to be the low-cost producer in its industry.

▶ *Differentiation*: The firm seeks to provide product benefits that other firms do not provide.

▶ *Focus*: The firm targets a niche with either a cost or a benefit (differentiation) focus.

Equity valuation analysis in large part is analysis of the probability of success of company strategies. Analysts will consider the company's commitment to a strategy as well as the likely responses of its competitors. Is the company a tough competitor that is likely to survive a war of attrition? Is it likely that a Nash equilibrium will hold, in which each company adopts a strategy to leave itself with the best outcome regardless of the competitor's strategy and, by doing this, causes a reduction in the size of the total reward to both?

## Co-opetition and the Value Net

*Co-opetition* refers to cooperation along the value chain and is an application of game theory. Brandenberger and Nalebuff developed the concept of the value net as the set of participants involved in producing value along the value chain: the suppliers, customers, competitors, and firms producing complementary goods and services.[9] Although these participants compete with each other, they can also cooperate to produce mutually beneficial outcomes. In this respect, co-opetition is an application of cooperative game theory.

In the context of equity valuation, co-opetition analysis is an important element of risk analysis. Cooperating participants in a good economy may become staunch competitors in a poor economy. If a company's abnormal profits depend on co-opetition, those profits are riskier than if they are the result of a purely competitive environment. In a good economy, a company may outsource some of its production to cooperating value net participants who may build capabilities based on lucrative long-term contracts. In a poor economy, however, no new contracts may be forthcoming.

## Sector Rotation

Many commercial providers sell reports on the relative performance of industries or sectors over the business cycle, and sector rotation is a popular investment-timing strategy. Some investors put more weight on industries entering a profitable portion of their role in the business cycle. Certainly industries behave differently over the business cycle. Because consumer cyclical industries (durables and nondurables) correlate highly with the economy as a whole, these industries do well in the early and middle growth portion of the business cycle. Defensive consumer staples (necessities) maintain their profitability during recessions. Nevertheless, a successful sector rotation strategy depends on an intensive

---

[8] Porter (1998a).

[9] Brandenberger and Nalebuff (1996).

analysis of the industry and faces many pitfalls. An upturn in the economy and the demand for industry products does not automatically mean an increase in profits, because factors such as the status of industry capacity, the competitive structure, the lead time to increase capacity, and the general supply/demand conditions in the industry also have an impact on profits.

Indicators of the various stages of the business cycle are complex. We have already seen that different sectors—for example, cyclical sectors—will do well at various stages of the business cycle. Again, the five stages are

▶ *Recovery*: The economy picks up from its slowdown or recession.

▶ *Early upswing*: Confidence is up and the economy is gaining some momentum.

▶ *Late upswing*: Boom mentality has taken hold.

▶ *Economy slows or goes into recession*: The economy is declining.

▶ *Recession*: Monetary policy will be eased but there will be a lag before recovery.

## Industry Analysis: Risk Elements

To achieve excess equity returns on a risk-adjusted basis, investors must be able to distinguish sources of risk in the investments they make. For example, an increase in ROE may be attributable solely to an increase in leverage (gearing). This increased leverage raises the financial risk and hence the required rate of return; the increased ROE then does not yield an excess risk-adjusted return. Although return expectations can be established by evaluating firm strategies within the industry, the analyst must always examine the risk that the strategy may be flawed or that assumptions about competition and co-opetition may hold only in a good economic environment. What seems to be an attractive strategy in good times can turn into a very dangerous one in bad times. The risks can differ widely, not only between firms in the same industry but also across industries. Some industries are more sensitive to technological change and the business cycle than are others. So, the outlined growth factors that affect return expectations should also be taken into account to assess industry risk.

Ultimately, firms that follow high-risk strategies in an industry that is also risky will have a higher ex ante stock market risk, and this fact should be incorporated in expected risk measures. Ex post, this stock market risk will eventually be measured by looking at volatility and covariance measures.

### *Market Competition*

Microeconomics[10] examines the various types of competition in markets. The question is always to look at price versus average cost. Particularly with oligopolies and monopolies, game theory helps to discern the likely success or failure of corporate strategies. Preservation of competitive position and competitive advantage often involves entry-deterring or exit-promoting strategies. *Limit pricing* is pricing below average cost to deter entry. Similarly, *holding excess capacity* can deter entry. *Predatory pricing* is pricing below average cost to drive others out of the industry. Any valuation of an individual company must examine the strategy

---

[10] See Besanko, Dranove, and Shanley (2007).

contest in which companies in the industry are engaged. Risks are always present that the company's strategy will not sustain its competitive advantage.

### Value Chain Competition

In producing goods and services of value, companies compete not just in markets, but also along the value chain. Suppliers can choose to compete rather than simply cooperate with the intermediate company. Labor, for example, may want some of the profit that a company is earning. In lean times labor may make concessions, but in good times labor may want a larger share of the profits. Buyers may organize to wrest some of the profit from the company.

A major issue in value chain analysis is whether labor is unionized. Japanese automobile companies producing in the United States face lower production costs because of their ability to employ non-unionized workers. Union relations are a major factor in valuing airline companies worldwide.

Suppliers of commodity raw materials have less ability to squeeze profits out of a downstream company than do suppliers of differentiated intermediate products. Companies may manage their value chain competition by vertically integrating (buying upstream or downstream) or, for example, by including labor in their ownership structure.

Co-opetition risks are presented by the possibility that the company's supply may be held up or that its distributors may find other sources of products and services. Suppose a firm acts as a broker between producers and distributors and outsources its distribution services by selling long-term distribution contracts to producers, thus also keeping distributors happy. Because of the low fixed costs involved in brokering, this business strategy should make the firm less sensitive to recession than a distribution company with heavy fixed costs. But what if producers are unwilling to enter long-term distribution contracts during a recession?

In his book, Porter (1998a) discussed five industry forces, as well as the generic competitive strategies mentioned earlier. Porter's so-called five forces analysis can be seen as an examination of the risks involved in the value chain. Oster (1999) provides a useful analysis of the five forces, and we show her insights as bulleted points below. In some cases, we slightly modify or extend them.

### Rivalry Intensity

This is the degree of competition among companies in the industry. For example, airline competition is more intense now with more carriers and open skies agreements between countries than in the days of heavier regulation with fewer carriers limited to domestic companies. Coordination can make rivalry much less intense. The analyst must be alert for possible changes in coordination and rivalry intensity that are not yet reflected in equity prices.

- ► Intense rivalry among firms in an industry reduces average profitability.
- ► In an industry in which coordination yields excess profits (prices exceed marginal costs), there are market share incentives for individual companies to "shade" (slightly cut) prices as they weigh the benefits and costs of coordination versus shading.
- ► Large numbers of companies in a market reduce coordination opportunities.
- ► Rivalry is generally more intense when the major companies are all similarly sized and no one large company can impose discipline on the industry.

▶ Generally, coordination is easier if companies in the market are similar. All gravitate to a mutually agreeable focal point, the solution that similar companies will naturally discern.

▶ Industries that have substantial specific assets (which cannot be used for other purposes) exhibit high barriers to exit and intensified rivalry.

▶ Variability in demand creates more rivalry within an industry. For example, high fixed costs and cyclical demand create capacity mismatches and price cutting from excess capacity.

### Substitutes

This is the threat of products or services that are substitutes for the products or services of the industry. For example, teleconferencing is a substitute for travel. The analyst must be alert for possible changes in substitutes that are not yet reflected in equity prices.

▶ Substitute products constrain the ability of firms in the industry to raise their prices substantially.

▶ Industries without excess capacity or intense rivalry can present attractive investment opportunities; but substitute products can reduce the attraction by constraining the ability of firms in the industry to substantially raise their prices.

### Buyer Power

This is the bargaining power of buyers of the producer's products or services. For example, car rental agencies have more bargaining power with automobile manufacturers than have individual consumers. The analyst must be alert for possible changes in buyer power that are not yet reflected in equity prices.

▶ The larger the number of buyers and the smaller their individual purchases, the less the bargaining power.

▶ Standardization of products increases buyer power because consumers can easily switch between suppliers.

▶ If buyers can integrate backwards, they can increase their bargaining power because they would cut out the supplier if they choose to integrate.

▶ Greater buyer power makes an equity investment in the producer less attractive because of lower profit margins.

### Supplier Power

This is the bargaining power of suppliers to the producers. For example, traditional aircraft manufacturers lost supplier power when niche players entered the market and began producing short-haul jets. The analyst must be alert for possible changes in supplier power that are not yet reflected in equity prices.

▶ The more suppliers there are for the industry, the less is the supplier power.

▶ Standardized raw materials (commodities) reduce supplier power because the supplier has no differentiation or quality advantage.

▶ If buyers can integrate backwards, this reduces supplier power because the buyer would cut out the supplier if it chooses to integrate.

▶ Greater supplier power makes an equity investment in the producer less attractive because of the possibility of a squeeze on profits.

### New Entrants

This is the threat of new entrants into the industry. For example, a European consortium entered the aircraft manufacturing industry and has become a major company now competing globally. In addition, a Brazilian and a Canadian company have entered the short-haul aircraft market. The analyst must be alert for possible changes in new entrant threats that are not yet reflected in equity prices.

▶ The higher the payoffs, the more likely will be the entry, all else equal.

▶ Barriers to entry are industry characteristics which reduce the rate of entry below that needed to remove excess profits.

▶ Expectations of incumbent reactions influence entry.

▶ Exit costs influence the rate of entry.

▶ All else equal, the larger the volume needed to reach minimal unit costs, the greater the difference between pre- and post-entry price (the increase in industry capacity would drive down prices), and thus the less likely entry is to occur.

▶ The steeper the cost curve, the less likely is entry at a smaller volume than the minimal unit cost volume.

▶ Long-term survival at a smaller than minimal unit cost volume requires an offsetting factor to permit a company to charge a price premium. Product differentiation and a monopoly in location are two possible offsets.

▶ Excess capacity deters entry by increasing the credibility of price-cutting as an entry response by incumbents.

▶ Occasional actions that are unprofitable in the short run can increase a company's credibility for price cutting to deter entry, giving an entry-deterring reputation as a tough incumbent.

▶ An incumbent contract to meet the price of any responsible rival can deter entry.

▶ Patents and licenses can prevent free entry from eliminating excess profits in an industry. They deter entry.

▶ Learning curve effects can deter entry unless new entrants can appropriate the experience of the incumbents. For example, Boeing learned about metal fatigue from the British experience of accidents with the Comet, the first commercial jet airliner.

▶ Pioneering brands can dominate the industry and deter entry when network externalities exist and when consumers find it costly to make product mistakes.

▶ High exit costs discourage entry. A primary determinant of high exit costs is asset specificity and the irreversibility of capital investments.

After presenting the insights above, Oster follows up with an excellent presentation of many related topics: strategic groups within industries, competition in global markets, issues of organizational structure and design, competitive advantage, corporate diversification, and the effect of rival behavior. Indeed, industry analysis is a complex subject as the analyst attempts to deduce the valuation implications of corporate strategies.

### Government Participation

Governments' subsidies to companies can seed companies in the early stages and can also give companies an unfair advantage in steady state. There is extra uncertainty for a company competing head to head with one subsidized by its home country. Governments also participate by supporting their domestic country stock prices in one way or another. This creates uncertainty about future policy in addition to the normal risk associated with cash flows.

Governments participate indirectly by their involvement in the social contract. In the United States, automobile companies bear the costs of defined benefit pension funds. Japanese automobile companies do not bear these costs because of government-sponsored pension schemes. Some European governments dealt with the possibility of increased unemployment by shortening the work week to keep employment spread out. Such government policy may make a European company less competitive.

Governments control competition. Open-skies laws allow foreign airlines to operate between domestic cities. Closed-skies laws in the past prevented Canadian carriers from operating between U.S. cities. Closed-skies laws have also been a factor in the Eurozone. Risks are presented by the uncertainty involved in trying to predict government policy.

### Risks and Covariance

Investors care about stock market risk, that is, the uncertainty about future stock prices. Risk is usually viewed at two levels. The total risk of a company or an industry is the first level of risk, and it is usually measured by the *standard deviation of return* (that is, stock returns) of that company or industry. But part of this risk can be diversified away in a portfolio. So, the second level of risk is measured by the covariance with the aggregate economy, which tells how the returns of a company vary with global market indexes. Although this risk is usually measured by the beta from regressions of company returns against market returns, it is useful to note those beta changes over time as a function of business cycle conditions and shifting competition within the industry.

When analyzing an industry, the analyst is faced with a continuing challenge of determining diversifiable versus nondiversifiable risk. Because future cash flow and return covariance must be predicted in order to estimate the firm and industry's beta, simple reliance on past regressions is not sufficient. Part of the risk from a strategy failure or a change from co-opetition to competition may be firm-specific and diversifiable. At the same time, part of the risk may be nondiversifiable, because it involves fundamental shifts in industry structure.

In order to manage a global equity portfolio, the risk of a company is usually summarized by its exposure to various risk factors. The last section of this reading is devoted to global risk factor models.

## EQUITY ANALYSIS     4

Because it should be forward looking, equity analysis needs to be carried out within the context of the country and the industry. Reasonable prediction of cash flows and risk is required to provide useful inputs to the valuation process.

### *Industry Valuation or Country Valuation*

A frequently asked question is whether a company should primarily be valued relative to the global industry to which it belongs or relative to other national companies listed on its home stock market. Indeed, many corporations are now very active abroad and, even at home, face worldwide competition. So, there are really two aspects to this question:

▶ Should the *financial analysis* of a company be conducted within its global industry?

▶ Do the stock prices of companies within the same global industry move together worldwide, so that the *relative valuation* of a company's equity should be conducted within the global industry rather than within its home stock market?

The answer to the first question is a clear yes. Prospective earnings of a company should be estimated taking into account the competition it is facing. In most cases, this competition is international as well as domestic. Most large corporations derive a significant amount of their cash flows from foreign sales and operations, so their competition is truly global.

The answer to the second question raised is less obvious. At a given point in time, different industries face different growth prospects, and that is true worldwide. Furthermore, different industries exhibit different sensitivities to unexpected changes in worldwide economic conditions. This implies that the stock market valuation should differ across industries. Some industries, such as electronic components or health care, have large P/E and P/BV ratios while other industries, such as energy and materials, have low P/E and P/BV ratios. The major question related to the importance of industry factors in stock prices, however, is whether a company has more in common with other companies in the same global industry than with other companies in the same country. By "more in common," we mean that its stock price tends to move together with that of other companies, and to be influenced by similar events. Before presenting some empirical evidence on the relative importance of country and industry factor in stock pricing, let's stress some caveats:

▶ Any industry classification is open to questions. MSCI, S&P, FTSE, and Dow Jones produce global industry indexes with different industry classification systems. The number of industry groups identified differs. It is not easy to assign each company to a single industry group. Some industry activities are clearly identified (e.g., producing automobiles), but others are not so clear-cut. It is not unusual to see the same company assigned to different industry groups by different classification systems. Some large corporations have diversified activities that cut across industry groups. Standard and Poor's and MSCI have recently designed a common Global Industry Classification Standard (GICS). The GICS system consists of four levels of detail: 10 sectors, 23 industry groupings, 59 industries, and 122 subindustries. At the most specific level of detail, an individual company is assigned to a single GICS subindustry, according to the definition of its principal business activity determined by S&P and MSCI. The hierarchical nature of the GICS structure will automatically assign the company's industry, industry group, and sector. There are currently over 25,000 companies globally that have been classified.

▶ The answer could be industry-specific. Some industries are truly global (e.g., oil companies), while others are less so (e.g., leisure and tourism). However, competition is becoming global in most, if not all, industries. For example, travel agencies have become regional, if not global, through a wave of mergers and acquisitions. Supermarket chains now cover many continents, and many retailers capitalize on their brand names globally.

▶ The answer could be period-specific. There could be periods in which global industry factors dominate, and other periods in which national factors are more important (desynchronized business cycles).

▶ The answer could be company-specific. Some companies in an industry group have truly international activities with extensive global competition, while others are mostly domestic in all respects. Small Swiss commercial banks with offices located only in one province (canton) of Switzerland have little in common with large global banks (even Crédit Suisse or UBS).

▶ Even if industry factors dominate, two opposing forces could be at play.[11] A worldwide growth in the demand for goods produced could benefit all players within the industry. However, competition also means that if one major player is highly successful, it will be at the expense of other major players in the industry. For example, Japanese car manufacturers could grow by extensively exporting to the United States, but it will be at the expense of U.S. car manufacturers. The stock price of Nissan would therefore be negatively correlated with that of GM or Ford.

Despite these caveats, all empirical studies find that industry factors have grown in importance in stock price valuation.[12] Global industry factors tend now to dominate country factors, but country factors are still significant. Companies should be valued relative to their industry, but country factors should not be neglected, particularly when conducting a risk analysis.

Two industry valuation approaches are traditionally used: ratio analysis and discounted cash flow models.

### Global Financial Ratio Analysis

As already mentioned, global industry financial analysis examines each company in the industry against the industry average. One well-accepted approach to this type of analysis is the DuPont model. (It may be better to think of this as an *approach* of decomposing return ratios, but this approach is usually called the DuPont model.) The basic technique of the DuPont model is to explain ROE or return on assets (ROA) in terms of its contributing elements. For example, we will see that ROA can be explained in terms of net profit margin and asset turnover. The analysis begins with five contributing elements, and these elements appear in several variations, depending on what most interests the analyst. The five elements reflect the financial and operating portions of the income statement as linked to the assets on the balance sheet and the equity supporting those assets. In the analysis here, past performance is being examined. Because income is a flow earned over a period of time, but the balance sheet reflects a balance (stock) at only one point in time, economists would calculate the flow (e.g., net income) over an average (e.g., the average of beginning and ending assets). The typical decomposition of ROE is given by

$$\frac{NI}{EBT} \times \frac{EBT}{EBIT} \times \frac{EBIT}{Sales} \times \frac{Sales}{Assets} \times \frac{Assets}{Equity} = \frac{NI}{Equity}$$

---

[11] See Griffin and Stulz (2001).

[12] See, for example, Cavaglia, Brightman, and Aked (2000) and Hopkins and Miller (2001).

where

NI is net income

EBT is earnings before taxes

NI/EBT is 1 minus the tax rate, or the tax retention rate with a maximum value of 1.0 if there were no taxes (lower values imply higher tax burden)

EBIT is earnings before interest and taxes, or operating income

EBT/EBIT is interest burden, with a maximum value of 1.0 if there are no interest payments (lower values imply greater debt burden)

EBIT/Sales is operating margin

Sales/Assets is asset turnover ratio (a measure of efficiency in the use of assets)

Assets/Equity is leverage (higher values imply greater use of debt)

NI/Equity is return on equity (ROE)

The analyst would then compare each firm ratio with the comparable ratio for the industry. Does the firm have a higher operating margin than the industry's? If the company has a higher ROE than the industry ROE, is this higher-than-average ROE due to leverage, or is it due to more operations management-oriented ratios, such as operating margin or asset turnover?

Depending on the analyst's focus, the ratios can be combined in different ways. What is essential in DuPont analysis is the specification of the question of interest rather than the question of whether the model has five, three, or two factors.

We can collapse the first three ratios into the net profit margin (NI/sales) to leave

$$\text{ROE} = \text{Net profit margin} \times \text{Asset turnover} \times \text{Leverage}$$

We could also combine the first three ratios and include the fourth ratio to yield a return on assets breakdown:

$$\text{ROA} = \frac{\text{NI}}{\text{Assets}} = \text{Net profit margin} \times \text{Asset turnover}$$

Without combining the first three ratios, we could also have a four-ratio ROA breakdown (Tax retention rate × Interest burden × Operating margin × Asset turnover). Also, we could explore a two-ratio ROE explanation by using ROA × Leverage.

In all of this analysis, a global comparison of ratios of different companies in the same industry should take into account national valuation specificities. Due to national accounting differences detailed previously, earnings figures should sometimes be reconciled to make comparisons meaningful.

In addition to understanding how the financial statements are decomposed for DuPont analysis, it is important to maintain some context of what the analyst is trying to accomplish. The DuPont model was developed in 1919 to dissect (analyze) performance as due to such factors as operating efficiency and asset utilization. Of course, this dissection depends on the financial statements, so the link to underlying economics is not direct. Nevertheless, a comparison of companies within an industry and companies across time can serve as a starting point for the analyst to ask more questions.

Because simple DuPont analysis is surely reflected in security prices, the analyst invariably digs deeper into the questions raised by the analysis and maintains a focus on the future. Beyond its service as a starting point for asking questions, DuPont analysis also serves as a framework for making forecasts. But

Soliman (2004) refers to the lack of forecasting ability available in the standard forecasting models. These models assume that DuPont ratios revert to the economy-wide mean. He proposes and successfully tests an approach assuming reversion to an industry-wide rather than economy-wide mean for profit margin and asset turnover ratios, using the time series for each of these. Example 2 illustrates an application of DuPont analysis.

---

### EXAMPLE 2

#### DuPont Analysis Comparison of Two Companies

Consider two representative companies in an industry. The return on equity for the two companies, A and B, is 15 percent and 7 percent, respectively. Company B has a superior net profit margin but inferior ROE. Despite Company A's advantages in operating margin (16%) and tax rate (40%), Company B's much lower interest burden (30%) translates into a distinct advantage in net profit margin (4%).

| Ratio | DuPont Analysis | A | B |
|-------|-----------------|-----|-----|
| 1 | NI/EBT = One minus tax rate | 0.60 | 0.50 |
| 2 | EBT/EBIT = One minus interest burden | 0.19 | 0.70 |
| 3 | EBIT/Sales = Operating margin | 0.16 | 0.12 |
| 4 | Net profit margin = 1 × 2 × 3 | 0.02 | 0.04 |
| 5 | Sales/Assets = Asset turnover = Efficiency | 0.60 | 0.70 |
| 6 | Assets/Equity = Leverage | 14.00 | 2.50 |
| 7 | ROE = 4 × 5 × 6 | 0.15 | 0.07 |

Nevertheless, a raw comparison of ROE is dramatically in favor of Company A (15%), although Company B has the advantage in net profit margin (4%) and efficiency (0.70). Company A's interest burden of 81 percent tells the story of more leverage with a 14 to 1 ratio of assets to equity. Leverage means volatility and a question of the required return on equity. Which company will have the higher beta?

**Solution:** Company A should have a much larger beta. Company A is highly leveraged so its return on equity is likely to be much more volatile than that of Company B. Its return on equity will be higher than that of Company B in good times, but will be much lower in bad times.

---

### The Role of Market Efficiency in Individual Stock Valuation

The notion of an efficient market is central to finance theory and is important for valuing securities. Generally, the question in company analysis is whether a security is priced correctly, and if it is not, for how long will it be mispriced. In an efficient market, any new information would be immediately and fully reflected in prices. Because all current information is already impounded in the asset price, only news (unanticipated information) could cause a change in price in the future.

An efficient financial market quickly, if not instantaneously, discounts all available information. Any new information will immediately be used by some privileged investors, who will take positions to capitalize on it, thereby making the asset price adjust (almost) instantaneously to this piece of information. For example, a new balance of payments statistic would immediately be used by foreign exchange traders to buy or sell a currency until the foreign exchange rate reached a level considered consistent with the new information. Similarly, investors might use surprise information about a company, such as a new contract or changes in forecasted income, to reap a profit until the stock price reached a level consistent with the news. The adjustment in price would be so rapid it would not pay to buy information that has already been available to other investors. Hundreds of thousands of expert financial analysts and professional investors throughout the world search for information and make the world markets close to fully efficient.

In a perfectly efficient market, the typical investor could consider an asset price to reflect its true *fundamental value* at all times. The notion of fundamental value is somewhat philosophical; it means that at each point in time, each asset has an intrinsic value that all investors try to discover. Nevertheless, the analyst tries to find mispriced securities by choosing from a variety of valuation models and by carefully researching the inputs for the model. In this research, forecasting cash flows and risk is critical.

## Valuation Models

Investors often rely on some form of a discounted cash flow analysis (DCF) for estimating the intrinsic value of a stock investment. This is simply a *present value* model, where the intrinsic value of an asset at time zero, $P_0$, is determined by the stream of cash flows it generates for the investor. This price is also called the *justified price* because it is the value that is "justified" by the forecasted cash flows. In a dividend discount model (DDM), the stock market price is set equal to the stream of forecasted dividends $D$ discounted at the required rate of return $r$:

$$P_0 = \frac{D_1}{1+r} + \frac{D_2}{(1+r)^2} + \frac{D_3}{(1+r)^3} \cdots \qquad \text{(37-1)}$$

Financial analysts take great care in forecasting future earnings and hence, dividends.

A simple version of the DDM assumes that dividends will grow indefinitely at a constant compounded annual growth rate (CAGR), $g$. Hence, Equation 37-1 becomes

$$P_0 = \frac{D_1}{1+r} + \frac{D_1(1+g)}{(1+r)^2} + \frac{D_1(1+g)^2}{(1+r)^3} \cdots$$

or

$$P_0 = \frac{D_1}{r-g} \qquad \text{(37-2)}$$

Analysts forecast earnings, and a payout ratio is applied to transform earnings into dividends. Under the assumption of a constant earnings payout ratio, we find

$$P_0 = \frac{E_1(1-b)}{r-g} \qquad \text{(37-3)}$$

where

$P_0$ is the justified or intrinsic price at time 0 (now)

$E_1$ is next year's earnings

$b$ is the earnings retention ratio

$1 - b$ is the earnings payout ratio

$r$ is the required rate of return on the stock

$g$ is the growth rate of earnings

Note that Equation 37-3 requires that the growth rate $g$ remain constant indefinitely and that it must be less than the required rate of return $r$. Take the example of a German corporation whose next annual earnings are expected to be €20 per share, with a constant growth rate of 5 percent per year, and with a 50 percent payout ratio. Hence, the next-year dividend is expected to be €10. Let's further assume that the required rate of return for an investment in such a corporation is 10 percent, which can be decomposed into a 6 percent risk-free rate plus a 4 percent risk premium. Then the firm's value is equal to

$$P_0 = \frac{10}{0.10 - 0.05} - €200$$

The intrinsic price-to-earnings (P/E) ratio is defined as $P_0/E_1$. The intrinsic P/E of this corporation, using prospective earnings, is equal to

$$P/E = \frac{1 - b}{r - g} = \frac{0.50}{0.10 - 0.05} = 10$$

A drop in the risk-free interest rate would lead to an increase in the P/E and in the stock price. For example, if the risk-free rate drops to 5 percent and everything else remains unchanged, a direct application of the formula indicates that the P/E will move up to 12.5 and the stock price to €250.

A more realistic DDM approach is to decompose the future in three phases. In the near future (e.g., the next two years), earnings are forecasted individually. In the second phase (e.g., years 3 to 5), a general growth rate of the company's earnings is estimated. In the final stage, the growth rate in earnings is assumed to revert to some sustainable growth rate.[13]

A final step required by this approach is to estimate the normal rate of return required on such an investment. This rate is equal to the risk-free interest rate plus a risk premium that reflects the relevant risks of this investment. Relevant risks refer to risks that should be priced by the market.

## Franchise Value and the Growth Process

Given the risk of the company's forecasted cash flows, a key determinant of value is the growth rate in cash flows. The growth rate depends on relevant country GDP growth rates, the industry growth rates, and the company's sustainable competitive advantage within the industry. Regardless of the valuation model used, some analysis of the growth-rate input is useful. Using the DDM as a representative model, Leibowitz and Kogelman (2000) developed the *franchise value* method and separated the intrinsic P/E value of a corporation into a tangible P/E value (the no-growth or zero-earnings retention P/E value of existing business) and the franchise P/E value (derived from prospective new investments). The franchise P/E value is related to the *present value of growth opportunities* (PVGO) in the traditional breakdown of intrinsic value into the no-growth value per share and the present value of growth opportunities. In that breakdown, the

---

[13] A detailed analysis of the use of DDM in companies' valuation is provided in Stowe et al. (2002).

no-growth value per share is the value of the company if it were to distribute all its earnings in dividends, creating a perpetuity valued at $E_1/r$, where $E_1$ is next year's earnings and $r$ is the required rate of return on the company's equity. Using the DDM and the company's actual payout ratio to generate an intrinsic value per share, $P_0$, the present value of growth opportunities must be the difference between intrinsic value and the no-growth value per share, $P_0 - E_1/r$.

The franchise value approach focuses on the intrinsic P/E rather than on the intrinsic value $P_0$; thus, the franchise value P/E is $PVGO/E_1$. In the franchise value approach, however, the franchise value P/E is further broken down into the *franchise factor* and the *growth factor*. The growth factor captures the present value of the opportunities for productive new investments, and the franchise factor is meant to capture the return levels associated with those new investments. The *sales-driven franchise value* has been developed to deal with multinational corporations that do business globally (see Leibowitz, 1997, 1998).

The separation of franchise P/E value into a franchise factor and a growth factor permits a direct examination of the response of the intrinsic P/E to ROE.[14] This factor helps an investor determine the response of the P/E to the ROE expected to be achieved by the company. It focuses on the sustainable growth rate of earnings per share. Earnings per share will grow from one period to the next because reinvested earnings will earn the rate of ROE. So the company's sustainable growth rate is equal to the retention rate $b$ multiplied by ROE: $g = b \times$ ROE. Substituting into Equation 37-3 the sustainable growth rate calculation for $g$, we get the intrinsic price:

$$P_0 = \frac{E_1(1 - b)}{r - b \times \text{ROE}}$$

and converting to an intrinsic P/E ratio,

$$\frac{P_0}{E_1} = \frac{(1 - b)}{r - b \times \text{ROE}}$$

Now, multiplying through by $r/r$ yields

$$\frac{P_0}{E_1} = \frac{1}{r}\left[\frac{r(1 - b)}{r - b \times \text{ROE}}\right]$$
$$= \frac{1}{r}\left[\frac{r - r \times b}{r - \text{ROE} \times b}\right]$$

and arbitrarily adding and subtracting ROE $\times b$ in the numerator,

$$\frac{P_0}{E_1} = \frac{1}{r}\left[\frac{r - r \times b + \text{ROE} \times b - \text{ROE} \times b}{r - \text{ROE} \times b}\right]$$
$$= \frac{1}{r}\left[\frac{r - \text{ROE} \times b + \text{ROE} \times b - r \times b}{r - \text{ROE} \times b}\right]$$

or

$$\frac{P_0}{E_1} = \frac{1}{r}\left[1 + \frac{b(\text{ROE} - r)}{r - \text{ROE} \times b}\right] \tag{37-4}$$

This $P_0/E_1$ equation[15] is extremely useful because we can use it to examine the effects of different values of $b$ and of the difference between ROE and $r$, that is,

---

[14] The model is derived here under the assumptions of a constant growth rate $g$, a constant earnings retention rate $b$, and a constant ROE. It can accommodate more complex assumptions about the pattern of growth.

[15] Note that in all equations, $E_1$ refers to estimated (future) earnings, not past earnings. This is also the case in derivations in Leibowitz and Kogelman (2000).

ROE − $r$. Two interesting results can be found. First, if ROE $= r$, the intrinsic $P_0/E_1$ equals $1/r$ regardless of $b$, the earnings retention ratio. Second, if $b = 0$, the intrinsic $P_0/E_1$ equals $1/r$ regardless of whether ROE is greater than $r$. These two results have an intuitive explanation:

► When the return on equity is exactly equal to the required rate of return (ROE $= r$), there is no *added* value in retaining earnings for additional investments rather than distributing them to shareholders. A company with ROE $= r$ has no franchise value potential because its return on equity is just what the market requires, but no more.

► An earnings retention ratio of zero ($b = 0$) means that the company distributes all its earnings, so equity per share stays constant. There is no growth of equity, and the stream of future earnings will be a perpetuity because the rate of return on equity (ROE) remains constant. The value of a share is given by discounting a perpetuity of $E_1$ at a rate $r$; hence the $P_0/E_1 = 1/r$ result. Of course, the total equity of the company could grow by issuing new shares, but there will be no growth of earnings per existing share. There is potential franchise value in the company with ROE $> r$, but because the company does not reinvest earnings at this superior rate of return, existing shareholders do not capture this potential.

In general, there is a franchise value created for existing shareholders if the company can reinvest past earnings ($b > 0$) at a rate of return (ROE) higher than the market-required rate $r$.

Examining Equation 37-4 further, we return to the intrinsic value version. We can transform Equation 37-4 by multiplying and dividing by ROE and replacing $b \times$ ROE by $g$:

$$\frac{P_0}{E_1} = \frac{1}{r}\left[1 + \frac{\text{ROE} \times b \times (\text{ROE} - r)}{\text{ROE} \times (r - \text{ROE} \times b)}\right] = \frac{1}{r} + \frac{g \times (\text{ROE} - r)}{r \times \text{ROE} \times (r - g)}$$

and simplify it as

$$\frac{P_0}{E_1} = \frac{1}{r} + \left(\frac{\text{ROE} - r}{\text{ROE} \times r}\right)\left(\frac{g}{r - g}\right)$$

$$\frac{P_0}{E_1} = \frac{1}{r} + \text{FF} \times \text{G} \tag{37-5}$$

where the franchise factor is FF $=$ (ROE $- r)/($ROE $\times r)$ or $1/r - 1/$ROE and the growth factor is G $= g/(r - g)$.

The growth factor is the ratio of the present value of future increases in the book value (BV) of equity to the current BV of equity. If the current BV of equity is $B_0$, then next year's increment to BV is $gB_0$. With a constant growth rate in BV increments, these increments can be treated as a growing perpetuity with a present value of $gB_0/(r - g)$. Because the present value of the BV increments is to be given as a ratio to the most recent BV, the growth factor is then given as $g/(r - g)$.

The franchise factor stems from the fact that a firm has a competitive advantage allowing it to generate a rate of return (ROE) greater than the rate of return normally required by investors for this type of risk, $r$. If the franchise factor is positive, it gives the rate of response of the intrinsic $P_0/E_1$ ratio to the growth factor. The growth factor G will be high if the firm can sustain a growth rate that is high relative to $r$.

Consider a pharmaceutical firm with some attractive new drugs with large commercial interest. Its ROE will be high relative to the rate of return required by investors for pharmaceutical stocks. Hence, it has a large positive franchise factor FF. If it continues to make productive new investments (G positive), such a firm can continue to generate a return on equity well above the rate of return required by the stock market, and thus it has a large positive franchise value. On the other hand, if the pharmaceutical company's sustainable growth rate is small because of a low earnings retention rate $b$, then G will be small and so will the franchise value, even though the franchise factor is large. For a firm with less franchise potential and ROE possibilities only equal to the company's required rate of return ($r$ = ROE), the franchise factor is zero and the intrinsic $P_0/E_1$ is simply $1/r$, regardless of the earnings retention ratio. Example 3 illustrates the calculation of the franchise value.

### EXAMPLE 3

#### Franchise Value

A company can generate an ROE of 15 percent and has an earnings retention ratio of 0.60. Next year's earnings are projected at $100 million. If the required rate of return for the company is 12 percent, what are the company's tangible P/E value, franchise factor, growth factor, and franchise P/E value?

#### Solution:
The company's tangible P/E value is $1/r = 1/0.12 = 8.33$.

The company's franchise factor is $1/r - 1/\text{ROE} = 1/0.12 - 1/0.15 = 1.67$.

Because the company's sustainable growth rate is $0.6 \times 0.15 = 0.09$, the company's growth factor is $g/(r - g) = 0.09/(0.12 - 0.09) = 3$.

The company's franchise P/E value is the franchise factor times the growth factor, $1.67 \times 3 = 5.01$.

Because its tangible P/E value is 8.33 and its franchise P/E value is 5.01, the company's intrinsic P/E is 13.34. Note that the intrinsic P/E calculated directly is $\text{P/E} = (1 - b)/(r - g) = 0.4/(0.12 - 0.09) = 13.33$. Thus, the franchise value method breaks this P/E into its basic components.

### The Effects of Inflation on Stock Prices

Because inflation rates vary around the world and over time, it is important to consider the effects of inflation on stock prices. To do this, we begin at the obvious place—earnings. After examining the effects of inflation on reported earnings, we discuss an inflation flow-through model.[16]

Because historical costs are used in accounting, inflation has a distorting effect on reported earnings. These effects show up primarily in replacement, inventories, and borrowing costs. Replacement must be made at inflated costs, but depreciation is recorded at historical cost—hence, reported earnings based on depreciation as an estimate of replacement costs gives an overstatement of

---

[16] For example, see Leibowitz and Kogelman (2000).

earnings. Similarly, a first-in, first-out (FIFO) inventory accounting system leads to an understatement of inventory costs and an overstatement of reported earnings. Unlike replacement and inventory distortions, borrowing costs at historical rates cause an understatement of reported earnings. Inflation causes borrowing costs to increase, but nominal interest costs do not reflect the increase. Finally, capital gains taxes reflect an inflation tax because the base for the capital gains tax is historical cost.

To analyze the effects of inflation on the valuation process, analysts try to determine what part of inflation flows through to a firm's earnings. A full-flow-through firm has earnings that fully reflect inflation. Thus, any inflation cost increases must be getting passed along to consumers.

In an inflationary environment, consider a firm that would otherwise have no growth in earnings, a zero earnings retention ratio, and full-inflation flow-through. So, earnings only grow because of the inflation rate $I$, assumed constant over time. For example, we have

$$E_1 = E_0 \times (1 + I)$$

By discounting this stream of inflation-growing earnings at the required rate $r$, we find that the intrinsic value of such a firm would then be

$$P_0 = \frac{E_1}{r - I} = E_0\left(\frac{1 + I}{r - I}\right) \qquad \textbf{(37-6)}$$

where
 $P_0$ is the intrinsic value
 $E_0$ is the initial earnings level
 $I$ is the annual inflation rate
 $r$ is the nominal required rate of return

Let's now consider a company with a partial inflation flow-through of $\lambda$ percent, so that earnings are only inflated at a rate $\lambda I$:

$$E_1 = E_0(1 + \lambda I)$$

By discounting this stream of earnings at the nominal required rate $r$, we find

$$P_0 = E_0 \times \frac{1 + \lambda I}{r - \lambda I} \qquad \textbf{(37-7)}$$

If we introduce the real required rate of return $\rho = r - I$, we get

$$P_0 = E_0 \times \frac{1 + \lambda I}{\rho + (1 - \lambda)I} = \frac{E_1}{\rho + (1 - \lambda)I}$$

The intrinsic P/E using prospective earnings is now equal to

$$P_0/E_1 = \frac{1}{\rho + (1 - \lambda)I} \qquad \textbf{(37-8)}$$

From Equation 37-8 we can see that the higher the inflation flow-through rate, the higher the price of the company. Indeed, a company that cannot pass inflation through its earnings is penalized. Thus, the P/E ratio ranges from a high of $1/\rho$ to a low of $1/r$. For example, assume a real required rate of return of 6 percent and an inflation rate of 4 percent. Exhibit 2 shows the P/E of the company with different flow-through rates. With a full-flow-through rate ($\lambda = 100\%$), the P/E is equal to $1/\rho = 1/0.06 = 16.67$. The ratio drops to 12.5 if the company can pass only 50 percent of inflation through its earnings. If the company cannot pass through any inflation ($\lambda = 0$), its earnings remain constant, and the P/E ratio is equal to $1/(\rho + I) = 1/r = 10$. The higher the inflation rate, the more negative the influence on the stock price if full inflation pass-through cannot be achieved. Example 4 illustrates the influence of inflation on the P/E of two companies.

This observation is important if we compare similar companies in different countries experiencing different inflation rates. A company operating in a high-inflation environment will be penalized if it cannot pass through inflation.

### The Inflation-Like Effects of Currency Movements on Stock Prices

A currency movement is a monetary variable that affects stock valuation in a fashion similar to the inflation variable. Just as some companies cannot fully pass inflation through their earnings, they cannot fully pass exchange rate movements either. Consider an importing firm faced with a sudden depreciation of the home currency. The products it imports suddenly become more expensive in terms of the home currency. If this price increase can be passed through to customers, earnings will not suffer from the currency adjustment. But this is often not the case. First, the price increase will tend to reduce demand for these imported products. Second, locally produced goods will become more attractive than imported goods, and some substitution will take place.

The currency exposure of individual companies is discussed in the reading on international asset pricing. Currency exposure depends on such factors as each particular company's production cycle, the competitive structure of its product market, and the company's financing structure.

| EXHIBIT 2 | Inflation Effects on P/E |
| --- | --- |

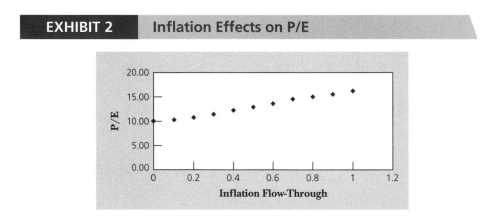

## EXAMPLE 4

### Inflation

Consider two companies in the same line of business, but with mostly domestic operations. Company A is based in a country with no inflation. Company B is based in a country with a 4 percent inflation rate. There is no real growth in earnings for both companies. The real rate of return required by global investors for this type of stock investment is 6 percent. Company B can pass only 80 percent of inflation through its earnings. What should be the P/E of the two companies?

**Solution:** The nominal required rate of return for Company A is equal to the real rate because there is no inflation: $r = \rho = 6$ percent. Earnings are constant, and the P/E is equal to

$$P/E(A) = 1/\rho = 1/0.06 = 16.67$$

There is a 4 percent inflation rate in the country of Company B. Its earnings will be inflated only at a rate of $\lambda\, I = 80$ percent $\times$ 4 percent = 3.2 percent. The P/E of company B will be

$$P/E(B) = \frac{1}{6\% + (20\%) \times 4\%} = \frac{1}{6.8\%} = 14.71$$

In the inflationary environment, Company B's earnings cannot grow as fast as inflation. Penalized by inflation and its inability to pass along inflation, Company B's P/E ratio is below that of Company A.

# GLOBAL RISK FACTORS IN SECURITY RETURNS

**5**

The analysis of an individual company can require a detailed review of various strategic risk elements that are difficult to quantify precisely. However, a portfolio manager needs to summarize the information on a large number of securities into a few statistics that help construct a portfolio and manage its risk. To structure a portfolio properly, a manager must have a clear understanding of the main factors influencing the return on a security and of the risk exposures of each security.

Global equilibrium pricing is discussed in the reading on international asset pricing. We show that the risk premium of a security should be proportional to the covariance (or beta) of the security's return with the world market return; this is the world market risk of a security. However, the world market risk of a security is the result of the exposure to many sources of risk that can be detailed in factor models. Factor models allow a better understanding of the risks that affect stock returns in the short run and allow the risk management of a portfolio.

## Risk-Factor Model: Industry and Country Factors

A factor model, where $R$ is the rate of return on the security, may be written mathematically as

$$R = \alpha + \beta_1 f_1 + \beta_2 f_2 + \cdots + \beta_k f_k + \epsilon \qquad (37\text{-}9)$$

where
  $R$ is the rate of return on a security
  $\alpha$ is a constant
  $f_1 \cdots f_k$ are the $k$ factors common to all securities
  $\beta_1 \cdots \beta_k$ represent the sensitivity, or risk exposure, of this security to each factor
  $\epsilon$ is a random term specific to this security

The $\epsilon$ is the source of idiosyncratic or diversifiable risk for the security, and $\beta_1 \ldots \beta_k$ represent the risk exposure of this security to each factor. The betas vary among securities. Some stocks may be highly sensitive to certain factors and much less sensitive to others, and vice versa.

A global risk-factor model would use industry and country as factors. The degree of granularity can be adapted; for example, one could use global sector factors, global industry factors, or regional industry factors. The geographical factors could be a list of regions (e.g., Europe) or of individual countries.

The factors are measured as the return on some index portfolio representative of the factor ("mimicking portfolios"). For example, the oil industry factor could be proxied by the return on a global stock index of oil firms. Various statistical techniques can be used to optimize the factor structure.

The determination of the risk-factor exposures can follow one of two techniques or a combination of the two:

▶ The exposure can be assessed a priori by using information on the company studied. This usually leads to a 0/1 exposure. For example, the oil company Total would have a unitary exposure to the oil industry factor and zero exposures to all other industry factors, because it is an oil company.

▶ The exposure can be estimated using a multiple regression approach. The exposures would then be the estimated betas in a time-series regression.

The question of currency should be addressed. A global risk-factor model can be written in some arbitrary currency (e.g., the U.S. dollar). It also can be written in currency-hedged terms. If companies are reacting differently to currency movements, currencies could be added as risk factors. For example, an exporting firm could be influenced negatively by an appreciation of its currency, while the reverse would be true for an importing firm. These currency exposures could be cancelled if the company adopts a currency-hedging policy in its business operations.

## Other Risk Factors: Styles

Other factors influence the stock price behavior of companies worldwide. As mentioned, many researchers believe that the future performance of a stock also depends on other attributes of a company that have not been discussed so far. Among many others, three attributes have been researched extensively:

▶ *Value* stocks do not behave like *growth* stocks. A value stock is a company whose stock price is "cheap" in relation to its book value, or in relation to the cash flows it generates (low stock price compared with its earnings, cash flows, or dividends). A growth stock has the opposite attribute, implying that the stock price capitalizes growth in future earnings. This is known as the *value effect*.

▶ *Small* firms do not exhibit the same stock price behavior as *large* firms. The size of a firm is measured by its stock market capitalization. This is known as the *size effect*.

▶ In the short run, winners tend to repeat. In other words, stocks that have performed well (or badly) in the recent past, say in the past six months, will tend to be winners (or losers) in the next six months. This is known as the *momentum, success*, or *relative strength effect*.

The observation of these effects, or factors, has led to the development of *style investing*, in which portfolios are structured to favor some of these attributes (e.g., value stocks).

Risk-factor models often incorporate style factors in which the factors are proxied by some mimicking portfolio (e.g., long in value stocks and short in growth stocks). A security's exposure is either measured a priori by using some information on the company, by a regression technique, or by a combination of the two techniques.

Although this style approach has been extensively used in the United States, there is some practical difficulty in applying it in a global setting. This is best illustrated by looking at the size factor. An Austrian company that is regarded as "large" in Austria would be regarded as medium-sized in Europe and probably as small according to U.S. standards. To construct a global size factor, one must make assumptions on how to measure relative size. Different risk-factor models use different criteria.

## Other Risk Factors: Macroeconomic

Factors are postulated a priori as sources of risk that are common to all companies. This clearly leads us to some macroeconomic variables that affect the economics of all firms, as well as the behavior of stock market participants who price those firms.

Selecting a set of *macroeconomic factors* is as much an art as a science. These factors must be logical choices, easy to interpret, robust over time, and able to explain a significant percentage of variation in stock returns. Some macroeconomic variables are logical candidates as factors but suffer from serious measurement error or long publication lags. For example, the evolution in industrial production is a logical candidate, but it is difficult to get timely, good-quality, reliable data. The technique is to use as factor proxies the returns on mimicking portfolios that are most strongly correlated with the economic variable.

Burmeister, Roll, and Ross (1994) propose a set of five factors.[17] These five factors, listed here, apply to domestic U.S. stocks:

▶ *Confidence factor* ($f_1$): This factor is measured by the difference in return on risky corporate bonds and on government bonds. The *default risk* premium

---

[17] Earlier, Chen, Roll, and Ross (1986) had identified four factors for the U.S. equity market as (a) growth rate in industrial production, (b) unexpected inflation, (c) slope of the yield curve (the difference between long- and short-term interest rates), and (d) changes in the attitude toward risk as proxied by changes in the pricing of default risk implicit in the difference between yields on Aaa and Baa corporate bonds.

required by the market to compensate for the risk of default on corporate bonds is measured as the spread between the yields on risky corporate bonds and government bonds. A decrease in the default-risk spread will give a higher return on corporate bonds and implies an improvement in the investors' confidence level. Hence, confidence risk focuses on the willingness of investors to undertake risky investments. Most stocks have a positive exposure to the confidence factor ($\beta_1 > 0$), so their prices tend to rise when the confidence factor is positive ($f_1 > 0$). The underlying idea is that in periods when investors are becoming more sensitive to risks (less confident with $f_1 < 0$), they require a higher premium on risky corporate bonds, compared with government bonds. They also require a higher risk premium on risky stocks and will bid their prices down, inducing a negative stock-price movement.

▶ *Time horizon factor* ($f_2$): This factor is measured as the difference between the return on a 20-year government bond and a 1-month Treasury bill. A positive difference in return is caused by a decrease in the term spread (long minus short interest rates). This is a signal that investors require a lesser premium to hold long-term investments. Growth stocks are more exposed (higher $\beta_2$) to time horizon risk than income stocks. The underlying idea is to view the stock price as the discounted stream of its future cash flows. The present value of growth stocks is determined by the long-term prospects of growing earnings while current earnings are relatively weak (high P/E ratio). An increase in the market-required discount rate will penalize the price of growth stocks more than the price of value stocks.

▶ *Inflation factor* ($f_3$): This factor is measured as the difference between the actual inflation for a month and its expected value, computed the month before, using an econometric inflation model. An unexpected increase in inflation tends to be bad for most stocks ($\beta_3 < 0$), so they have a negative exposure to this inflation surprise ($f_3 > 0$). Luxury goods stocks tend to be most sensitive to inflation risk, whereas firms in the sectors of foods, cosmetics, or tires are less sensitive to inflation risk. Real estate holdings typically benefit from increased inflation.

▶ *Business cycle factor* ($f_4$): This factor is measured by the monthly variation in a business activity index. Business cycle risk comes from unanticipated changes in the level of real activity. The business cycle factor is positive ($f_4 > 0$) when the expected real growth rate of the economy has increased. Most firms have a positive exposure to business cycle risk ($\beta_4 > 0$). Retail stores are more exposed to business cycle risk than are utility companies because their business activity (sales) is much more sensitive to recession or expansion.

▶ *Market-timing factor* ($f_5$): This factor is measured by the part of the S&P 500 total return that is not explained by the first four factors. It captures the global movements in the market that are not explained by the four macroeconomic factors. The inclusion of this market-timing factor makes the capital asset pricing model (CAPM) a special case of this approach. If all relevant macroeconomic factors had been included, it would not be necessary to add this market-timing factor.

A common criticism of this approach is that the risk exposures (betas) have to be estimated statistically from past data and may not be stable over time. Even the factor proxies (mimicking portfolios) have to be constructed using statistical optimization, and the procedure could yield unstable proxies.

## Practical Use of Factor Models

Risk-factor models are used in risk management and in selecting stocks. A major application is the analysis of the risk profile of portfolios. The exposure of the portfolio to the various factors is the weighted average of the exposures of the stocks making up the portfolio. A manager can estimate the risks taken and the exposure of the portfolio to the various sources of risk. If some specific stock index is assigned as a benchmark to measure performance, the manager can analyze the risks of deviations from the benchmark. This helps the manager identify and quantify the bets and risks that are taken in the portfolio.

Managers can also use factor models to tilt the portfolio along some factor bets. Assume, for example, that a manager believes that the economy is going to grow at a faster rate than generally forecasted, leading to some inflationary pressure. The manager will tend to increase the portfolio exposure to business risk but reduce its exposure to inflation risk. This could also lead the manager to take some industry bets and invest in small companies.

We have seen that companies operate globally and compete within an industry. As background to the following concept in action, it is useful to look at key financial ratios and beta for General Motors (http://finance.yahoo.com/q/ks?s=GM) and Toyota (http://finance.yahoo.com/q/ks?s=TM).

---

### CONCEPTS IN ACTION   Detroit Begins Spring in a Fog

#### Housing, Gas Prices Crimp Big Three's March Sales; Toyota Reaches a Record

Detroit's Big Three auto makers face worsening economic headwinds as they head into the crucial spring selling season, threatening their efforts to stem sales declines.

General Motors Corp., Ford Motor Co. and DaimlerChrysler AG's Chrysler Group have suffered year-over-year sales drops as they work to restructure and wean themselves off lower-margin sales to daily rental fleets. Yesterday, the Big Three posted sales declines for March, while Toyota Motor Corp.'s sales rose 11.7%, making it the Japanese auto maker's best sales month ever.

Now, auto makers must contend with a run-up in fuel prices and a weakening housing market. Both could undermine sales and force cash-sapping production cuts and incentives. GM cut its second-quarter production forecast by 15,000 vehicles, to 1.16 million, and several auto makers indicated incentives like low interest rates and rebates on many vehicles would remain.

Auto makers sold 1.5 million cars and trucks last month, translating into an annual sales rate of 16.3 million, according to Autodata Corp. Auto makers are hoping the industry will end the year selling around 16.5 million, roughly flat with last year.

GM's sales declined 4% to 345,418 vehicles in March from a year earlier, according to Autodata. Truck sales fell 8%. But GM said declines in fleet sales overshadowed relatively strong retail sales, with the new Chevrolet Silverado pickup, GMC Sierra and Acadia, and Saturn Outlook exceeding expectations.

"We're very content with sales for the month," said Paul Ballew, GM's top sales analyst, adding that GM had "a terrific first quarter on full-size pickups." Sales of those pickup trucks rose 8.2% in the first quarter, he said. Even so, March Silverado sales were off 5.2% from February, according to Autodata, a hiccup as GM ramps up introduction of the new truck.

Ford's sales dropped 9% to 263,441 vehicles, a trend the company's top sales analyst, George Pipas, has warned will continue as the auto maker restructures and recalibrates its mix of cars and trucks.

---

Ford has adjusted its business close to a 50–50 split between trucks and passenger cars, Mr. Pipas said, whereas just three years ago it tilted toward 70% trucks. Ford trumpeted a 37% increase from February in sales of its new Edge—a sport-utility vehicle known as a crossover because it is built on a car platform—but sales of the auto maker's best-selling F-Series pickups dropped 15%. Mr. Pipas said Ford may consider a production increase during this year's second half, depending on economic conditions.

DaimlerChrysler's sales dipped 4% to 228,077 vehicles in March. A 4.6% drop at the unprofitable Chrysler Group, which many investors want DaimlerChrysler to sell, offset a 1% gain at Mercedes-Benz.

GM said incentive spending rose slightly from last year, while Ford said its spending remained steady. A March truck incentive that offered a free Hemi engine upgrade helped Chrysler's Dodge pickup sales. In April, Chrysler will launch a nationwide minivan incentive that includes offers of a free DVD system on top of consumer cash as high as $4,000. Chrysler is sticking it out in the minivan segment while its domestic rivals retrench.

Toyota's sales totaled 242,675 vehicles, boosted by robust sales of hybrid gasoline-electric vehicles. Toyota has been offering discounts on the Prius hybrid and is expected to roll out new discount offers for April.

The average retail price of gasoline in the U.S. climbed to $2.70 a gallon as of Monday, according to the Energy Department, 12 cents higher than the same time last year. That's bad news for GM, Ford and Chrysler, whose best-selling vehicles are fuel-thirsty pickup trucks and SUVs.

Still, Ford's Mr. Pipas said he is less worried that rising gasoline prices will substantially change what consumers want. Now, he worries about the effect on auto sales generally, as more pain at the pump saps consumers' spending power. "The more money they're spending on [gasoline], the less they have for other things," Mr. Pipas said in an interview. "I really think that's the biggest factor."

Moreover, softness in the housing market threatens future sales. Depreciating homes deprive consumers of equity to finance car purchases, and economists worry the rise in subprime-mortgage defaults could spill to other parts of the economy, perhaps causing auto lenders to tighten standards, which would make it harder for consumers to buy new cars. So far, a noticeable spillover hasn't occurred.

Overall, the largest auto markets continue to present challenges. Retail sales—considered the best gauge of consumer demand—dropped 17% in California and 11% in Florida through the first 10 weeks of the year, according to CNW Marketing Research. U.S. car makers suffered declines amid slower conditions in those markets while sales for Toyota and Honda were closer to flat.

---

*Source:* Mike Spector, Terry Kosdrosky, and John D. Stoll, *The Wall Street Journal*, April 4, 2007, p. A3. Reproduced with permission from *The Wall Street Journal* via Copyright Clearance Center.

# SUMMARY

► Differences in national accounting standards used to be significant. But most countries, except the United States, are moving toward adopting the International Financial Reporting Standards (IFRS).

► U.S. GAAP and IFRS are converging, but they can yield somewhat different values for the reported earnings and book equity of specific companies.

► From an economic perspective, employee stock option compensation should be treated as an expense, with the options valued by an option-pricing model.

► Neoclassical growth theory predicts that the long-term level of GDP depends on the country's savings rate, but the long-term growth rate in GDP does not depend on the savings rate. Endogenous growth theory predicts that the long-term growth rate in GDP depends on the savings rate.

► A global industry analysis should examine return potential evidenced by demand analysis, value creation, industry life cycle, competition structure, competitive advantage, competitive strategies, co-opetition and the value net, and sector rotation. The analysis also should examine risk elements evidenced by market competition, value chain competition, government participation, and cash flow covariance.

► Global financial analysis involves comparing company ratios with global industry averages. In this context, DuPont analysis uses various combinations of the tax retention, debt burden, operating margin, asset turnover, and leverage ratios.

► The role of market efficiency in individual asset valuation is to equate fundamental value with asset valuation so that the analyst searches for mispricing or market inefficiency.

► Franchise value is the present value of growth opportunities divided by next year's earnings. The intrinsic $P_0/E_1$ ratio equals $1/r$ plus the franchise value, where $r$ is the nominal required return on the stock. The franchise value is further divided into a franchise factor (FF) and a growth factor (G) to give $P_0/E_1 = 1/r + \text{FF} \times \text{G}$.

► To analyze the effects of inflation for valuation purposes, the analyst must recognize the distorting effects of historical inventory and borrowing costs on reported earnings, as well as recognize the inflation tax reflected in capital gains taxes. Further, the analyst must estimate the degree of inflation flow-through, $\lambda$.

► With earnings that are constant except for inflation, $I$ as the inflation rate, $r$ as the required nominal return on the stock, and $\rho$ as the required real return on the stock, the P/E ratio can be estimated as $P_0/E_1 = 1/(\rho + (1 - \lambda)I)$.

► Multifactor models can be used in the analysis of the risk profile of portfolios. The exposure of a portfolio to the various factors is the weighted average of the exposures of the stocks making up the portfolio.

## PRACTICE PROBLEMS FOR READING 37

1. Explain why a corporation can have a stock market price well above its accounting book value.

2. The accounting and fiscal standards of countries allow corporations to build general provisions (or "hidden reserves") in anticipation of foreseen or unpredictable expenses. How would this practice affect the book value of a corporation and its ratio of market price to book value?

3. Discuss some of the reasons the earnings of German firms tend to be understated compared with the earnings of U.S. firms.

4. Consider a firm that has given stock options on 20,000 shares to its senior executives. These call options can be exercised at a price of $22 anytime during the next three years. The firm has a total of 500,000 shares outstanding, and the current price is $20 per share. The firm's net income before taxes is $2 million.

   A. What would be the firm's pretax earnings per share if the options are not expensed?

   B. Under certain assumptions, the Black-Scholes model valued the options given by the firm to its executives at $4 per share option. What would be the firm's pretax earnings per share if the options are expensed accordingly?

   C. Under somewhat different assumptions, the Black-Scholes model valued the options at $5.25 per share option. What would be the firm's pretax earnings per share if the options are expensed based on this valuation?

5. Japanese companies tend to belong to groups (*keiretsu*) and to hold shares of one another. Because these cross-holdings are minority interest, they tend not to be consolidated in published financial statements. To study the impact of this tradition on published earnings, consider the following simplified example:

   Company A owns 10 percent of Company B; the initial investment was 10 million yen. Company B owns 20 percent of Company A; the initial investment was also 10 million yen. Both companies value their minority interests at historical cost. The annual net income of Company A was 10 million yen. The annual net income of Company B was 30 million yen. Assume that the two companies do not pay any dividends. The current stock market values are 200 million yen for Company A and 450 million yen for Company B.

   A. Restate the earnings of the two companies, using the equity method of consolidation. Remember that the share of the minority-interest earning is consolidated on a one-line basis, proportionate to the share of equity owned by the parent.

   B. Calculate the P/E ratios, based on nonconsolidated and consolidated earnings. How does the nonconsolidation of earnings affect the P/E ratios?

**6.** The annual revenues (in billion dollars) in financial year 2001 for the top five players in the global media and entertainment industry are given in the following table. The top five corporations in this industry include three U.S.-based corporations (AOL Time Warner, Walt Disney, and Viacom), one French corporation (Vivendi Universal), and one Australian corporation (News Corporation). The revenue indicated for Vivendi Universal does not include the revenue from its environmental business. Assume that the total worldwide revenue of all firms in this industry was $250 billion.

| Company | Revenue |
|---|---|
| AOL Time Warner | 38 |
| Walt Disney | 25 |
| Vivendi Universal | 25 |
| Viacom | 23 |
| News Corporation | 13 |

  **A.** Compute the three-firm and five-firm concentration ratios.

  **B.** Compute the three-firm and five-firm Herfindahl indexes.

  **C.** Make a simplistic assumption that in addition to the five corporations mentioned in the table, there are 40 other companies in this industry with an equal share of the remaining market. Compute the Herfindahl index for the overall industry.

  **D.** Suppose there were not 40, but only 10 other companies in the industry with an equal share of the remaining market. Compute the Herfindahl index for the overall industry.

  **E.** Interpret your answers to parts C and D in terms of the competition structure of the industry.

**7.** News Corporation is headquartered in Australia, and its main activities include television entertainment, films, cable, and publishing.

  **A.** Collect any relevant information that you may need, and discuss whether an analyst should do the valuation of News Corporation primarily relative to the global media and entertainment industry or relative to other companies based in Australia.

  **B.** One of the competitors of News Corporation is Vivendi Universal, a firm headquartered in France. Should an analyst be concerned in comparing financial ratios of News Corporation with those of Vivendi Universal?

**8.** You are given the following data about Walt Disney and News Corporation, two of the major corporations in the media and entertainment industry. The data are for the end of the financial year 1999, and are in US$ millions. Though News Corporation is based in Australia, it also trades on the NYSE, and its data in the following table, like those for Walt Disney, are according to the U.S. GAAP.

|        | Walt Disney | News Corporation |
|--------|-------------|------------------|
| Sales  | 23,402      | 14,395           |
| EBIT   | 3,035       | 1,819            |
| EBT    | 2,314       | 1,212            |
| NI     | 1,300       | 719              |
| Assets | 43,679      | 35,681           |
| Equity | 20,975      | 16,374           |

**A.** Compute the ROE for Walt Disney and News Corporation.

**B.** Use the DuPont model to analyze the difference in ROE between the two companies, identifying the elements that primarily cause this difference.

**9.** In the past 20 years, the best-performing stock markets have been found in countries with the highest economic growth rates. Should the current growth rate guide you in choosing stock markets if the world capital market is efficient?

**10.** Consider a French company that pays out 70 percent of its earnings. Its next annual earnings are expected to be €4 per share. The required return for the company is 12 percent. In the past, the company's compound annual growth rate (CAGR) has been 1.25 times the world's GDP growth rate. It is expected that the world's GDP growth rate will be 2.8 percent p.a. in the future. Assuming that the firm's earnings will continue to grow forever at 1.25 times the world's projected growth rate, compute the intrinsic value of the company's stock and its intrinsic P/E ratio.

**11.** Consider a company that pays out all its earnings. The required return for the firm is 13 percent.

**A.** Compute the intrinsic P/E value of the company if its ROE is 15 percent.

**B.** Compute the intrinsic P/E value of the company if its ROE is 20 percent.

**C.** Discuss why your answers to parts A and B differ or do not differ from one another.

**D.** Suppose that the company's ROE is 13 percent. Compute its intrinsic P/E value.

**E.** Would the answer to part D change if the company retained half of its earnings instead of paying all of them out? Discuss why or why not.

**12.** Consider a firm with a ROE of 12 percent. The earnings next year are projected at $50 million, and the firm's earnings retention ratio is 0.70. The required return for the firm is 10 percent. Compute the following for the firm:

   i.  Franchise factor
   ii.  Growth factor
   iii.  Franchise P/E value
   iv.  Tangible P/E value
   v.  Intrinsic P/E value

**13.** Consider a firm for which the nominal required rate of return is 8 percent. The rate of inflation is 3 percent. Compute the P/E ratio of the firm under the following situations:

   i.  The firm has a full inflation flow-through.
   ii.  The firm can pass only 40 percent of inflation through its earnings.
   iii.  The firm cannot pass any inflation through its earnings.

   What pattern do you observe from your answers to items i through iii?

**14.** Company B and Company U are in the same line of business. Company B is based in Brazil, where inflation during the past few years has averaged about 9 percent. Company U is based in the United States, where the inflation during the past few years has averaged about 2.5 percent. The real rate of return required by global investors for investing in stocks such as B and U is 8 percent. Neither B nor U has any real growth in earnings, and both of them can pass only 60 percent of inflation through their earnings. What should be the P/E of the two companies? What can you say based on a comparison of the P/E for the two companies?

**15.** Omega, Inc., is based in Brazil, and most of its operations are domestic. During the period 1995–99, the firm has not had any real growth in earnings. The annual inflation in Brazil during this period is given in the following table:

| Year | Inflation (%) |
| --- | --- |
| 1995 | 22.0 |
| 1996 | 9.1 |
| 1997 | 4.3 |
| 1998 | 2.5 |
| 1999 | 8.4 |

*Source:* International Monetary Fund.

The real rate of return required by global investors for investing in stocks such as Omega, Inc., is 7 percent.

   **A.**  Compute the P/E for Omega in each of the years if it can completely pass inflation through its earnings.

   **B.**  Compute the P/E for Omega in each of the years if it can pass only 50 percent of inflation through its earnings.

   **C.**  What conclusion can you draw about the effect of inflation on the stock price?

**16.** Consider a French company that exports French goods to the United States. What effect will a sudden appreciation of the euro relative to the dollar have on the P/E ratio of the French company? Discuss the effect under both the possibilities—the company being able to completely pass through the euro appreciation to its customers and the company being unable to completely pass through the euro appreciation to its customers.

**17.** Using the five macroeconomic factors described in the text, you outline the factor exposures of two stocks as follows:

| Factor | Stock A | Stock B |
|---|---|---|
| Confidence | 0.2 | 0.6 |
| Time horizon | 0.6 | 0.8 |
| Inflation | −0.1 | −0.5 |
| Business cycle | 4.0 | 2.0 |
| Market timing | 1.0 | 0.7 |

  **A.** What would be the factor exposures of a portfolio invested half in stock A and half in stock B?

  **B.** Contrary to general forecasts, you expect strong economic growth with a slight increase in inflation. Which stock should you overweigh in your portfolio?

**18.** Here is some return information on firms of various sizes and their price-to-book (value) ratios. Based on this information, what can you tell about the *size* and *value* style factors?

| Stock | Size | P/BV | Return (%) |
|---|---|---|---|
| A | Huge | High | 4 |
| B | Huge | Low | 6 |
| C | Medium | High | 9 |
| D | Medium | Low | 12 |
| E | Small | High | 13 |
| F | Small | Low | 15 |

**19.** You are analyzing whether the difference in returns on stocks of a particular country can be explained by two common factors, with a linear-factor model. Your candidates for the two factors are changes in interest rates and changes in the approval rating of the country's president, as measured by polls. The following table gives the interest rate, the percentage of people approving the president's performance, and the prices of three stocks (A, B, and C) for the past 10 periods.

| Period | Interest Rate (%) | Approval (%) | Price of Stock A | B | C |
|---|---|---|---|---|---|
| 1 | 7.3 | 47 | 22.57 | 24.43 | 25.02 |
| 2 | 5.2 | 52 | 19.90 | 12.53 | 13.81 |
| 3 | 5.5 | 51 | 15.46 | 17.42 | 19.17 |
| 4 | 7.2 | 49 | 21.62 | 24.70 | 23.24 |
| 5 | 5.4 | 68 | 14.51 | 16.43 | 18.79 |
| 6 | 5.2 | 49 | 12.16 | 11.56 | 14.66 |
| 7 | 7.5 | 72 | 25.54 | 24.73 | 28.68 |
| 8 | 7.6 | 45 | 25.83 | 28.12 | 21.47 |
| 9 | 5.3 | 47 | 13.04 | 14.71 | 16.43 |
| 10 | 5.1 | 67 | 11.18 | 12.44 | 12.50 |

Try to assess whether the two factors have an influence on stock returns. To do so, estimate the factor exposures for each of the three stocks by doing a time-series regression for the return on each stock against the changes in the two factors.

**20.** You are a U.S. investor considering investing in Switzerland. The world market risk premium is estimated at 5 percent, the Swiss franc offers a 1 percent risk premium, and the current risk-free rates are equal to 4 percent in dollars and 3 percent in francs. In other words, you expect the Swiss franc to appreciate against the dollar by an amount equal to the interest rate differential plus the currency risk premium, or a total of 2 percent. You believe that the following equilibrium model (ICAPM) is appropriate for your investment analysis:

$$E(R_i) = R_f + \beta_1 \times RP_w + \beta_2 \times RP_{SFr}$$

where all returns are measured in dollars, $RP_w$ is the risk premium on the world index, and $RP_{SFr}$ is the risk premium on the Swiss franc. Your broker provides you with the following estimates and forecasted returns.

|                                     | Stock A | Stock B | Stock C | Stock D |
|-------------------------------------|---------|---------|---------|---------|
| Forecasted return (in francs)       | 0.08    | 0.09    | 0.11    | 0.07    |
| World beta ($\beta_1$)              | 1       | 1       | 1.2     | 1.4     |
| Dollar currency exposure ($\beta_2$)| 1       | 0       | 0.5     | –0.5    |

**A.** What should be the expected dollar returns on the four stocks, according to the ICAPM?

**B.** Which stocks would you recommend buying or selling?

# THE FIVE COMPETITIVE FORCES
# THAT SHAPE STRATEGY

by Michael E. Porter

## LEARNING OUTCOMES

| The candidate should be able to: | Mastery |
|---|:---:|
| **a.** distinguish among the five competitive forces that drive industry profitability in the medium and long run; | ☐ |
| **b.** illustrate how the competitive forces drive industry profitability; | ☐ |
| **c.** describe why industry growth rate, technology and innovation, government, and complementary products and services are fleeting factors rather than forces shaping industry structure; | ☐ |
| **d.** indicate why eliminating rivals is a risky strategy; | ☐ |
| **e.** show how positioning a company, exploiting industry change, and the ability to shape industry structure are creative strategies for achieving a competitive advantage. | ☐ |

*Awareness of the five forces can help a company understand the structure of its industry and stake out a position that is more profitable and less vulnerable to attack.*

Michael E. Porter is the Bishop William Lawrence University Professor at Harvard University, based at Harvard Business School in Boston. He is a six-time McKinsey Award winner, including for his most recent HBR article, "Strategy and Society," coauthored with Mark R. Kramer (December 2006).

**Editor's Note:** In 1979, *Harvard Business Review* published "How Competitive Forces Shape Strategy" by a young economist and associate professor, Michael E. Porter. It was his first HBR article, and it started a revolution in the strategy field. In subsequent decades, Porter has brought his signature economic rigor to the study of competitive strategy for corporations, regions, nations, and, more recently, health care and philanthropy. "Porter's five forces" have shaped a generation of academic research and business practice. With prodding and assistance from Harvard Business School Professor Jan Rivkin and longtime colleague Joan Magretta, Porter here reaffirms, updates, and extends the classic work. He also addresses common misunderstandings, provides practical guidance for users of the framework, and offers a deeper view of implications for strategy today.

# THE FIVE COMPETITIVE FORCES THAT SHAPE STRATEGY

## The Idea in Brief

You know that to sustain long-term profitability you must respond strategically to competition. And you naturally keep tabs on your **established rivals**. But as you scan the competitive arena, are you also looking *beyond* your direct competitors? As Porter explains in this update of his revolutionary 1979 HBR article, four additional competitive forces can hurt your prospective profits:

▶ Savvy **customers** can force down prices by playing you and your rivals against one another.

▶ Powerful **suppliers** may constrain your profits if they charge higher prices.

▶ Aspiring **entrants**, armed with new capacity and hungry for market share, can ratchet up the investment required for you to stay in the game.

▶ **Substitute offerings** can lure customers away.

Consider commercial aviation: It's one of the least profitable industries because all five forces are strong. **Established rivals** compete intensely on price. **Customers** are fickle, searching for the best deal regardless of carrier. **Suppliers**—plane and engine manufacturers, along with unionized labor forces—bargain away the lion's share of airlines' profits. **New players** enter the industry in a constant stream. And **substitutes** are readily available—such as train or car travel.

By analyzing all five competitive forces, you gain a complete picture of what's influencing profitability in your industry. You identify game-changing trends early, so you can swiftly exploit them. And you spot ways to work around constraints on profitability—or even reshape the forces in your favor.

## The Idea in Practice

By understanding how the five competitive forces influence profitability in your industry, you can develop a strategy for enhancing your company's long-term profits. Porter suggests the following:

*Position Your Company where the Forces Are Weakest*

▶ Example:
In the heavy-truck industry, many buyers operate large fleets and are highly motivated to drive down truck prices. Trucks are built to regulated standards and offer similar features, so price competition is stiff; unions exercise considerable supplier power; and buyers can use substitutes such as cargo delivery by rail.

To create and sustain long-term profitability within this industry, heavy-truck maker Paccar chose to focus on one customer group where competitive forces are weakest: individual drivers who own their trucks and contract directly with suppliers. These operators have limited clout as buyers and are less price sensitive because of their emotional ties to and economic dependence on their own trucks.

For these customers, Paccar has developed such features as luxurious sleeper cabins, plush leather seats, and sleek exterior styling. Buyers can select from thousands of options to put their personal signature on these built-to-order trucks.

Customers pay Paccar a 10% premium, and the company has been profitable for 68 straight years and earned a long-run return on equity above 20%.

### Exploit Changes in the Forces

▶ Example:
With the advent of the Internet and digital distribution of music, unauthorized downloading created an illegal but potent substitute for record companies' services. The record companies tried to develop technical platforms for digital distribution themselves, but major labels didn't want to sell their music through a platform owned by a rival.

Into this vacuum stepped Apple, with its iTunes music store supporting its iPod music player. The birth of this powerful new gatekeeper has whittled down the number of major labels from six in 1997 to four today.

### Reshape the Forces in Your Favor

Use tactics designed specifically to reduce the share of profits leaking to other players. For example:

▶ To neutralize **supplier power**, standardize specifications for parts so your company can switch more easily among vendors.
▶ To counter **customer power**, expand your services so it's harder for customers to leave you for a rival.
▶ To temper price wars initiated by **established rivals**, invest more heavily in products that differ significantly from competitors' offerings.
▶ To scare off **new entrants**, elevate the fixed costs of competing; for instance, by escalating your R&D expenditures.
▶ To limit the threat of **substitutes**, offer better value through wider product accessibility. Soft-drink producers did this by introducing vending machines and convenience store channels, which dramatically improved the availability of soft drinks relative to other beverages.

**1**

# INTRODUCTION

In essence, the job of the strategist is to understand and cope with competition. Often, however, managers define competition too narrowly, as if it occurred only among today's direct competitors. Yet competition for profits goes beyond established industry rivals to include four other competitive forces as well: customers, suppliers, potential entrants, and substitute products. The extended rivalry that results from all five forces defines an industry's structure and shapes the nature of competitive interaction within an industry.

As different from one another as industries might appear on the surface, the underlying drivers of profitability are the same. The global auto industry, for instance, appears to have nothing in common with the worldwide market for art masterpieces or the heavily regulated health-care delivery industry in Europe. But to understand industry competition and profitability in each of those three cases, one must analyze the industry's underlying structure in terms of the five forces. (See Exhibit 1, "The Five Forces that Shape Industry Competition.")

If the forces are intense, as they are in such industries as airlines, textiles, and hotels, almost no company earns attractive returns on investment. If the forces are benign, as they are in industries such as software, soft drinks, and toiletries, many companies are profitable. Industry structure drives competition and profitability, not whether an industry produces a product or service, is emerging or mature, high tech or low tech, regulated or unregulated. While a myriad of factors can affect industry profitability in the short run—including the weather and the

| EXHIBIT 1 | The Five Forces that Shape Industry Competition |

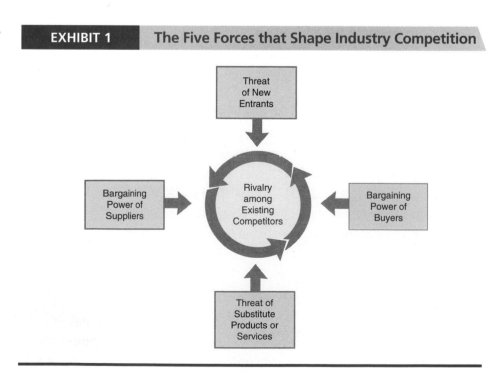

| **EXHIBIT 2** | **Differences in Industry Profitability** |
|---|---|

The average return on invested capital varies markedly from industry to industry. Between 1992 and 2006, for example, average return on invested capital in U.S. industries ranged as low as zero or even negative to more than 50%. At the high end are industries like soft drinks and prepackaged software, which have been almost six times more profitable than the airline industry over the period.

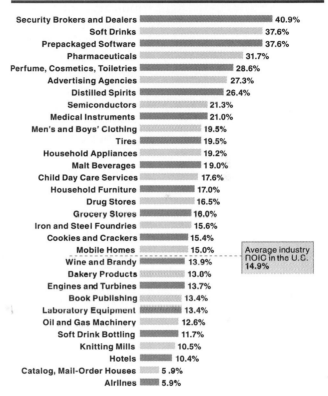

**FIGURE 1    Average Return on Invested Capital in U.S. Industries, 1992–2006**

**FIGURE 2    Profitability of Selected U.S. Industries**
Average ROIC, 1992–2006

| Industry | Average ROIC |
|---|---|
| Security Brokers and Dealers | 40.9% |
| Soft Drinks | 37.6% |
| Prepackaged Software | 37.6% |
| Pharmaceuticals | 31.7% |
| Perfume, Cosmetics, Toiletries | 28.6% |
| Advertising Agencies | 27.3% |
| Distilled Spirits | 26.4% |
| Semiconductors | 21.3% |
| Medical Instruments | 21.0% |
| Men's and Boys' Clothing | 19.5% |
| Tires | 19.5% |
| Household Appliances | 19.2% |
| Malt Beverages | 19.0% |
| Child Day Care Services | 17.6% |
| Household Furniture | 17.0% |
| Drug Stores | 16.5% |
| Grocery Stores | 16.0% |
| Iron and Steel Foundries | 15.6% |
| Cookies and Crackers | 15.4% |
| Mobile Homes | 15.0% |
| Wine and Brandy | 13.9% |
| Bakery Products | 13.0% |
| Engines and Turbines | 13.7% |
| Book Publishing | 13.4% |
| Laboratory Equipment | 13.4% |
| Oil and Gas Machinery | 12.6% |
| Soft Drink Bottling | 11.7% |
| Knitting Mills | 10.5% |
| Hotels | 10.4% |
| Catalog, Mail-Order Houses | 5.9% |
| Airlines | 5.9% |

Average industry ROIC in the U.S. 14.9%

**Return on invested capital (ROIC)** is the appropriate measure of profitability for strategy formulation, not to mention for equity investors. Return on sales or the growth rate of profits fail to account for the capital required to compete in the industry. Here, we utilize earnings before interest and taxes divided by average invested capital less excess cash as the measure of ROIC. This measure controls for idiosyncratic differences in capital structure and tax rates across companies and industries.

*Sources:* Standard & Poor's, Compustat, and author's calculations.

business cycle—industry structure, manifested in the competitive forces, sets industry profitability in the medium and long run. (See Exhibit 2, "Differences in Industry Profitability.")

Understanding the competitive forces, and their underlying causes, reveals the roots of an industry's current profitability while providing a framework for anticipating and influencing competition (and profitability) over time. A healthy industry structure should be as much a competitive concern to strategists as their company's own position. Understanding industry structure is also essential to effective strategic positioning. As we will see, defending against the competitive forces and shaping them in a company's favor are crucial to strategy.

## 2  FORCES THAT SHAPE COMPETITION

The configuration of the five forces differs by industry. In the market for commercial aircraft, fierce rivalry between dominant producers Airbus and Boeing and the bargaining power of the airlines that place huge orders for aircraft are strong, while the threat of entry, the threat of substitutes, and the power of suppliers are more benign. In the movie theater industry, the proliferation of substitute forms of entertainment and the power of the movie producers and distributors who supply movies, the critical input, are important.

The strongest competitive force or forces determine the profitability of an industry and become the most important to strategy formulation. The most salient force, however, is not always obvious.

For example, even though rivalry is often fierce in commodity industries, it may not be the factor limiting profitability. Low returns in the photographic film industry, for instance, are the result of a superior substitute product—as Kodak and Fuji, the world's leading producers of photographic film, learned with the advent of digital photography. In such a situation, coping with the substitute product becomes the number one strategic priority.

Industry structure grows out of a set of economic and technical characteristics that determine the strength of each competitive force. We will examine these drivers in the pages that follow, taking the perspective of an incumbent, or a company already present in the industry. The analysis can be readily extended to understand the challenges facing a potential entrant.

**Threat of Entry**    New entrants to an industry bring new capacity and a desire to gain market share that puts pressure on prices, costs, and the rate of investment necessary to compete. Particularly when new entrants are diversifying from other markets, they can leverage existing capabilities and cash flows to shake up competition, as Pepsi did when it entered the bottled water industry, Microsoft did when it began to offer internet browsers, and Apple did when it entered the music distribution business.

The threat of entry, therefore, puts a cap on the profit potential of an industry. When the threat is high, incumbents must hold down their prices or boost investment to deter new competitors. In specialty coffee retailing, for example, relatively low entry barriers mean that Starbucks must invest aggressively in modernizing stores and menus.

The threat of entry in an industry depends on the height of entry barriers that are present and on the reaction entrants can expect from incumbents. If entry barriers are low and newcomers expect little retaliation from the entrenched competitors, the threat of entry is high and industry profitability is moderated. It is the *threat* of entry, not whether entry actually occurs, that holds down profitability.

*Barriers to entry.* Entry barriers are advantages that incumbents have relative to new entrants. There are seven major sources:

1. *Supply-side economies of scale.* These economies arise when firms that produce at larger volumes enjoy lower costs per unit because they can spread fixed costs over more units, employ more efficient technology, or command better terms from suppliers. Supply-side scale economies deter entry by forcing the aspiring entrant either to come into the industry on a large scale, which requires dislodging entrenched competitors, or to accept a cost disadvantage.

Scale economies can be found in virtually every activity in the value chain; which ones are most important varies by industry.[1] In microprocessors, incumbents such as Intel are protected by scale economies in research, chip fabrication, and consumer marketing. For lawn care companies like Scotts Miracle-Gro, the most important scale economies are found in the supply chain and media advertising. In small-package delivery, economies of scale arise in national logistical systems and information technology.

2. *Demand-side benefits of scale.* These benefits, also known as network effects, arise in industries where a buyer's willingness to pay for a company's product increases with the number of other buyers who also patronize the company. Buyers may trust larger companies more for a crucial product: Recall the old adage that no one ever got fired for buying from IBM (when it was the dominant computer maker). Buyers may also value being in a "network" with a larger number of fellow customers. For instance, online auction participants are attracted to eBay because it offers the most potential trading partners. Demand-side benefits of scale discourage entry by limiting the willingness of customers to buy from a newcomer and by reducing the price the newcomer can command until it builds up a large base of customers.

3. *Customer switching costs.* Switching costs are fixed costs that buyers face when they change suppliers. Such costs may arise because a buyer who switches vendors must, for example, alter product specifications, retrain employees to use a new product, or modify processes or information systems. The larger the switching costs, the harder it will be for an entrant to gain customers. Enterprise resource planning (ERP) software is an example of a product with very high switching costs. Once a company has installed SAP's ERP system, for example, the costs of moving to a new vendor are astronomical because of embedded data, the fact that internal processes have been adapted to SAP, major retraining needs, and the mission-critical nature of the applications.

4. *Capital requirements.* The need to invest large financial resources in order to compete can deter new entrants. Capital may be necessary not only for fixed facilities but also to extend customer credit, build inventories, and fund start-up losses. The barrier is particularly great if the capital is required for unrecoverable and therefore harder-to-finance expenditures, such as up-front advertising or research and development. While major corporations have the financial resources to invade almost any industry, the huge capital requirements in certain fields limit the pool of likely entrants. Conversely, in such fields as tax preparation services or short-haul trucking, capital requirements are minimal and potential entrants plentiful.

It is important not to overstate the degree to which capital requirements alone deter entry. If industry returns are attractive and are expected to remain so, and if capital markets are efficient, investors will provide entrants with the funds they need. For aspiring air carriers, for instance, financing is available to purchase expensive aircraft because of their high resale value, one reason why there have been numerous new airlines in almost every region.

---

[1] For a discussion of the value chain framework, see Michael E. Porter, *Competitive Advantage: Creating and Sustaining Superior Performance* (The Free Press, 1998).

5. *Incumbency advantages independent of size.* No matter what their size, incumbents may have cost or quality advantages not available to potential rivals. These advantages can stem from such sources as proprietary technology, preferential access to the best raw material sources, preemption of the most favorable geographic locations, established brand identities, or cumulative experience that has allowed incumbents to learn how to produce more efficiently. Entrants try to bypass such advantages. Upstart discounters such as Target and Wal-Mart, for example, have located stores in free-standing sites rather than regional shopping centers where established department stores were well entrenched.

6. *Unequal access to distribution channels.* The new entrant must, of course, secure distribution of its product or service. A new food item, for example, must displace others from the supermarket shelf via price breaks, promotions, intense selling efforts, or some other means. The more limited the wholesale or retail channels are and the more that existing competitors have tied them up, the tougher entry into an industry will be. Sometimes access to distribution is so high a barrier that new entrants must bypass distribution channels altogether or create their own. Thus, upstart low-cost airlines have avoided distribution through travel agents (who tend to favor established higher-fare carriers) and have encouraged passengers to book their own flights on the internet.

7. *Restrictive government policy.* Government policy can hinder or aid new entry directly, as well as amplify (or nullify) the other entry barriers. Government directly limits or even forecloses entry into industries through, for instance, licensing requirements and restrictions on foreign investment. Regulated industries like liquor retailing, taxi services, and airlines are visible examples. Government policy can heighten other entry barriers through such means as expansive patenting rules that protect proprietary technology from imitation or environmental or safety regulations that raise scale economies facing newcomers. Of course, government policies may also make entry easier—directly through subsidies, for instance, or indirectly by funding basic research and making it available to all firms, new and old, reducing scale economies.

Entry barriers should be assessed relative to the capabilities of potential entrants, which may be start-ups, foreign firms, or companies in related industries. And, as some of our examples illustrate, the strategist must be mindful of the creative ways newcomers might find to circumvent apparent barriers.

*Expected retaliation.* How potential entrants believe incumbents may react will also influence their decision to enter or stay out of an industry. If reaction is vigorous and protracted enough, the profit potential of participating in the industry can fall below the cost of capital. Incumbents often use public statements and responses to one entrant to send a message to other prospective entrants about their commitment to defending market share.

Newcomers are likely to fear expected retaliation if:

▶ Incumbents have previously responded vigorously to new entrants.

▶ Incumbents possess substantial resources to fight back, including excess cash and unused borrowing power, available productive capacity, or clout with distribution channels and customers.

▶ Incumbents seem likely to cut prices because they are committed to retaining market share at all costs or because the industry has high fixed costs, which create a strong motivation to drop prices to fill excess capacity.

## BOX 1   INDUSTRY ANALYSIS IN PRACTICE

**Good industry analysis looks rigorously at the structural underpinnings of profitability. A first step is to understand the appropriate time horizon.** One of the essential tasks in industry analysis is to distinguish temporary or cyclical changes from structural changes. A good guideline for the appropriate time horizon is the full business cycle for the particular industry. For most industries, a three-to-five-year horizon is appropriate, although in some industries with long lead times, such as mining, the appropriate horizon might be a decade or more. It is average profitability over this period, not profitability in any particular year, that should be the focus of analysis.

**The point of industry analysis is not to declare the industry attractive or unattractive but to understand the underpinnings of competition and the root causes of profitability.** As much as possible, analysts should look at industry structure quantitatively, rather than be satisfied with lists of qualitative factors. Many elements of the five forces can be quantified: the percentage of the buyer's total cost accounted for by the industry's product (to understand buyer price sensitivity); the percentage of industry sales required to fill a plant or operate a logistical network of efficient scale (to help assess barriers to entry); the buyer's switching cost (determining the inducement an entrant or rival must offer customers).

**The strength of the competitive forces affects prices, costs, and the investment required to compete; thus the forces are directly tied to the income statements and balance sheets of industry participants.** Industry structure defines the gap between revenues and costs. For example, intense rivalry drives down prices or elevates the costs of marketing, R&D, or customer service, reducing margins. How much? Strong suppliers drive up input costs. How much? Buyer power lowers prices or elevates the costs of meeting buyers' demands, such as the requirement to hold more inventory or provide financing. How much? Low barriers to entry or close substitutes limit the level of sustainable prices. How much? It is these economic relationships that sharpen the strategist's understanding of industry competition.

**Finally, good industry analysis does not just list pluses and minuses but sees an industry in overall, systemic terms.** Which forces are underpinning (or constraining) today's profitability? How might shifts in one competitive force trigger reactions in others? Answering such questions is often the source of true strategic insights.

▶ Industry growth is slow so newcomers can gain volume only by taking it from incumbents.

An analysis of barriers to entry and expected retaliation is obviously crucial for any company contemplating entry into a new industry. The challenge is to find ways to surmount the entry barriers without nullifying, through heavy investment, the profitability of participating in the industry.

**The Power of Suppliers**   Powerful suppliers capture more of the value for themselves by charging higher prices, limiting quality or services, or shifting costs to industry participants. Powerful suppliers, including suppliers of labor, can squeeze profitability out of an industry that is unable to pass on cost increases in its own prices. Microsoft, for instance, has contributed to the erosion of profitability among personal computer makers by raising prices on operating systems. PC makers, competing fiercely for customers who can easily switch among them, have limited freedom to raise their prices accordingly.

Companies depend on a wide range of different supplier groups for inputs. A supplier group is powerful if:

▶ It is more concentrated than the industry it sells to. Microsoft's near monopoly in operating systems, coupled with the fragmentation of PC assemblers, exemplifies this situation.

▶ The supplier group does not depend heavily on the industry for its revenues. Suppliers serving many industries will not hesitate to extract maximum profits from each one. If a particular industry accounts for a large portion of a supplier group's volume or profit, however, suppliers will want to protect the industry through reasonable pricing and assist in activities such as R&D and lobbying.

▶ Industry participants face switching costs in changing suppliers. For example, shifting suppliers is difficult if companies have invested heavily in specialized ancillary equipment or in learning how to operate a supplier's equipment (as with Bloomberg terminals used by financial professionals). Or firms may have located their production lines adjacent to a supplier's manufacturing facilities (as in the case of some beverage companies and container manufacturers). When switching costs are high, industry participants find it hard to play suppliers off against one another. (Note that suppliers may have switching costs as well. This limits their power.)

▶ Suppliers offer products that are differentiated. Pharmaceutical companies that offer patented drugs with distinctive medical benefits have more power over hospitals, health maintenance organizations, and other drug buyers, for example, than drug companies offering me-too or generic products.

▶ There is no substitute for what the supplier group provides. Pilots' unions, for example, exercise considerable supplier power over airlines partly because there is no good alternative to a well-trained pilot in the cockpit.

▶ The supplier group can credibly threaten to integrate forward into the industry. In that case, if industry participants make too much money relative to suppliers, they will induce suppliers to enter the market.

**The Power of Buyers** Powerful customers—the flip side of powerful suppliers—can capture more value by forcing down prices, demanding better quality or more service (thereby driving up costs), and generally playing industry participants off against one another, all at the expense of industry profitability. Buyers are powerful if they have negotiating leverage relative to industry participants, especially if they are price sensitive, using their clout primarily to pressure price reductions.

As with suppliers, there may be distinct groups of customers who differ in bargaining power. A customer group has negotiating leverage if:

▶ There are few buyers, or each one purchases in volumes that are large relative to the size of a single vendor. Large-volume buyers are particularly powerful in industries with high fixed costs, such as telecommunications equipment, offshore drilling, and bulk chemicals. High fixed costs and low marginal costs amplify the pressure on rivals to keep capacity filled through discounting.

▶ The industry's products are standardized or undifferentiated. If buyers believe they can always find an equivalent product, they tend to play one vendor against another.

▶ Buyers face few switching costs in changing vendors.

▶ Buyers can credibly threaten to integrate backward and produce the industry's product themselves if vendors are too profitable. Producers of soft drinks and beer have long controlled the power of packaging manufacturers by threatening to make, and at times actually making, packaging materials themselves.

A buyer group is price sensitive if:

▶ The product it purchases from the industry represents a significant fraction of its cost structure or procurement budget. Here buyers are likely to shop around and bargain hard, as consumers do for home mortgages. Where the product sold by an industry is a small fraction of buyers' costs or expenditures, buyers are usually less price sensitive.

▶ The buyer group earns low profits, is strapped for cash, or is otherwise under pressure to trim its purchasing costs. Highly profitable or cash-rich customers, in contrast, are generally less price sensitive (that is, of course, if the item does not represent a large fraction of their costs).

▶ The quality of buyers' products or services is little affected by the industry's product. Where quality is very much affected by the industry's product, buyers are generally less price sensitive. When purchasing or renting production quality cameras, for instance, makers of major motion pictures opt for highly reliable equipment with the latest features. They pay limited attention to price.

▶ The industry's product has little effect on the buyer's other costs. Here, buyers focus on price. Conversely, where an industry's product or service can pay for itself many times over by improving performance or reducing labor, material, or other costs, buyers are usually more interested in quality than in price. Examples include products and services like tax accounting or well logging (which measures below-ground conditions of oil wells) that can save or even make the buyer money. Similarly, buyers tend not to be price sensitive in services such as investment banking, where poor performance can be costly and embarrassing.

Most sources of buyer power apply equally to consumers and to business-to-business customers. Like industrial customers, consumers tend to be more price sensitive if they are purchasing products that are undifferentiated, expensive relative to their incomes, and of a sort where product performance has limited consequences. The major difference with consumers is that their needs can be more intangible and harder to quantify.

Intermediate customers, or customers who purchase the product but are not the end user (such as assemblers or distribution channels), can be analyzed the same way as other buyers, with one important addition. Intermediate customers gain significant bargaining power when they can influence the purchasing decisions of customers downstream. Consumer electronics retailers, jewelry retailers, and agricultural-equipment distributors are examples of distribution channels that exert a strong influence on end customers.

Producers often attempt to diminish channel clout through exclusive arrangements with particular distributors or retailers or by marketing directly to end users. Component manufacturers seek to develop power over assemblers by creating preferences for their components with downstream customers. Such is the case with bicycle parts and with sweeteners. DuPont has created enormous clout by advertising its Stainmaster brand of carpet fibers not only to the carpet manufacturers that actually buy them but also to downstream consumers. Many consumers request Stainmaster carpet even though DuPont is not a carpet manufacturer.

**The Threat of Substitutes**    A substitute performs the same or a similar function as an industry's product by a different means. Video-conferencing is a substitute for travel. Plastic is a substitute for aluminum. E-mail is a substitute for express mail. Sometimes, the threat of substitution is downstream or indirect, when a substitute replaces a buyer industry's product. For example, lawn-care products and services are threatened when multifamily homes in urban areas substitute for single-family homes in the suburbs. Software sold to agents is threatened when airline and travel websites substitute for travel agents.

Substitutes are always present, but they are easy to overlook because they may appear to be very different from the industry's product: To someone searching for a Father's Day gift, neckties and power tools may be substitutes. It is a substitute to do without, to purchase a used product rather than a new one, or to do it yourself (bring the service or product in-house).

When the threat of substitutes is high, industry profitability suffers. Substitute products or services limit an industry's profit potential by placing a ceiling on prices. If an industry does not distance itself from substitutes through product performance, marketing, or other means, it will suffer in terms of profitability—and often growth potential.

Substitutes not only limit profits in normal times, they also reduce the bonanza an industry can reap in good times. In emerging economies, for example, the surge in demand for wired telephone lines has been capped as many consumers opt to make a mobile telephone their first and only phone line.

The threat of a substitute is high if:

▶ It offers an attractive price-performance trade-off to the industry's product. The better the relative value of the substitute, the tighter is the lid on an industry's profit potential. For example, conventional providers of long-distance telephone service have suffered from the advent of inexpensive internet-based phone services such as Vonage and Skype. Similarly, video rental outlets are struggling with the emergence of cable and satellite video-on-demand services, online video rental services such as Netflix, and the rise of internet video sites like Google's YouTube.

▶ The buyer's cost of switching to the substitute is low. Switching from a proprietary, branded drug to a generic drug usually involves minimal costs, for example, which is why the shift to generics (and the fall in prices) is so substantial and rapid.

Strategists should be particularly alert to changes in other industries that may make them attractive substitutes when they were not before. Improvements in plastic materials, for example, allowed them to substitute for steel in many automobile components. In this way, technological changes or competitive discontinuities in seemingly unrelated businesses can have major impacts on industry profitability. Of course the substitution threat can also shift in favor of an industry, which bodes well for its future profitability and growth potential.

**Rivalry among Existing Competitors**    Rivalry among existing competitors takes many familiar forms, including price discounting, new product introductions, advertising campaigns, and service improvements. High rivalry limits the profitability of an industry. The degree to which rivalry drives down an industry's profit potential depends, first, on the *intensity* with which companies compete and, second, on the *basis* on which they compete.

The intensity of rivalry is greatest if:

▶ Competitors are numerous or are roughly equal in size and power. In such situations, rivals find it hard to avoid poaching business. Without an industry leader, practices desirable for the industry as a whole go unenforced.

▶ Industry growth is slow. Slow growth precipitates fights for market share.

▶ Exit barriers are high. Exit barriers, the flip side of entry barriers, arise because of such things as highly specialized assets or management's devotion to a particular business. These barriers keep companies in the market even though they may be earning low or negative returns. Excess capacity remains in use, and the profitability of healthy competitors suffers as the sick ones hang on.

▶ Rivals are highly committed to the business and have aspirations for leadership, especially if they have goals that go beyond economic performance in the particular industry. High commitment to a business arises for a variety of reasons. For example, state-owned competitors may have goals that include employment or prestige. Units of larger companies may participate in an industry for image reasons or to offer a full line. Clashes of personality and ego have sometimes exaggerated rivalry to the detriment of profitability in fields such as the media and high technology.

▶ Firms cannot read each other's signals well because of lack of familiarity with one another, diverse approaches to competing, or differing goals.

The strength of rivalry reflects not just the intensity of competition but also the basis of competition. The *dimensions* on which competition takes place, and whether rivals converge to compete on the *same dimensions,* have a major influence on profitability.

Rivalry is especially destructive to profitability if it gravitates solely to price because price competition transfers profits directly from an industry to its customers. Price cuts are usually easy for competitors to see and match, making successive rounds of retaliation likely. Sustained price competition also trains customers to pay less attention to product features and service.

Price competition is most liable to occur if:

▶ Products or services of rivals are nearly identical and there are few switching costs for buyers. This encourages competitors to cut prices to win new customers. Years of airline price wars reflect these circumstances in that industry.

▶ Fixed costs are high and marginal costs are low. This creates intense pressure for competitors to cut prices below their average costs, even close to their marginal costs, to steal incremental customers while still making some contribution to covering fixed costs. Many basic-materials businesses, such as paper and aluminum, suffer from this problem, especially if demand is not growing. So do delivery companies with fixed networks of routes that must be served regardless of volume.

▶ Capacity must be expanded in large increments to be efficient. The need for large capacity expansions, as in the polyvinyl chloride business, disrupts the industry's supply-demand balance and often leads to long and recurring periods of overcapacity and price cutting.

▶ The product is perishable. Perishability creates a strong temptation to cut prices and sell a product while it still has value. More products and services are perishable than is commonly thought. Just as tomatoes are perishable because they rot, models of computers are perishable because they soon become obsolete, and information may be perishable if it diffuses rapidly or becomes outdated, thereby losing its value. Services such as hotel accommodations are perishable in the sense that unused capacity can never be recovered.

Competition on dimensions other than price—on product features, support services, delivery time, or brand image, for instance—is less likely to erode profitability because it improves customer value and can support higher prices. Also, rivalry focused on such dimensions can improve value relative to substitutes or raise the barriers facing new entrants. While nonprice rivalry sometimes escalates to levels that undermine industry profitability, this is less likely to occur than it is with price rivalry.

As important as the dimensions of rivalry is whether rivals compete on the *same* dimensions. When all or many competitors aim to meet the same needs or compete on the same attributes, the result is zero-sum competition. Here, one firm's gain is often another's loss, driving down profitability. While price competition runs a stronger risk than nonprice competition of becoming zero sum, this may not happen if companies take care to segment their markets, targeting their low-price offerings to different customers.

Rivalry can be positive sum, or actually increase the average profitability of an industry, when each competitor aims to serve the needs of different customer segments, with different mixes of price, products, services, features, or brand identities. Such competition can not only support higher average profitability but also expand the industry, as the needs of more customer groups are better met. The opportunity for positive-sum competition will be greater in industries serving diverse customer groups. With a clear understanding of the structural underpinnings of rivalry, strategists can sometimes take steps to shift the nature of competition in a more positive direction.

## 3    FACTORS, NOT FORCES

Industry structure, as manifested in the strength of the five competitive forces, determines the industry's long-run profit potential because it determines how the economic value created by the industry is divided—how much is retained by companies in the industry versus bargained away by customers and suppliers, limited by substitutes, or constrained by potential new entrants. By considering all five forces, a strategist keeps overall structure in mind instead of gravitating to any one element. In addition, the strategist's attention remains focused on structural conditions rather than on fleeting factors.

It is especially important to avoid the common pitfall of mistaking certain visible attributes of an industry for its underlying structure. Consider the following:

**Industry Growth Rate**    A common mistake is to assume that fast-growing industries are always attractive. Growth does tend to mute rivalry, because an expanding pie offers opportunities for all competitors. But fast growth can put suppliers in a powerful position, and high growth with low entry barriers will draw in entrants. Even without new entrants, a high growth rate will not guarantee profitability if customers are powerful or substitutes are attractive. Indeed, some fast-growth businesses, such as personal computers, have been among the least profitable industries in recent years. A narrow focus on growth is one of the major causes of bad strategy decisions.

**Technology and Innovation**    Advanced technology or innovations are not by themselves enough to make an industry structurally attractive (or unattractive). Mundane, low-technology industries with price-insensitive buyers, high switching costs, or high entry barriers arising from scale economies are often far more profitable than sexy industries, such as software and internet technologies, that attract competitors.[2]

**Government**    Government is not best understood as a sixth force because government involvement is neither inherently good nor bad for industry profitability. The best way to understand the influence of government on competition is to analyze how specific government policies affect the five competitive forces. For instance, patents raise barriers to entry, boosting industry profit potential. Conversely, government policies favoring unions may raise supplier power and diminish profit potential. Bankruptcy rules that allow failing companies to reorganize rather than exit can lead to excess capacity and intense rivalry. Government operates at multiple levels and through many different policies, each of which will affect structure in different ways.

**Complementary Products and Services**    Complements are products or services used together with an industry's product. Complements arise when the customer benefit of two products combined is greater than the sum of each product's value in isolation. Computer hardware and software, for instance, are valuable together and worthless when separated.

In recent years, strategy researchers have highlighted the role of complements, especially in high-technology industries where they are most obvious.[3] By no means, however, do complements appear only there. The value of a car, for example, is greater when the driver also has access to gasoline stations, roadside assistance, and auto insurance.

Complements can be important when they affect the overall demand for an industry's product. However, like government policy, complements are not a sixth force determining industry profitability since the presence of strong complements is not necessarily bad (or good) for industry profitability. Complements affect profitability through the way they influence the five forces.

The strategist must trace the positive or negative influence of complements on all five forces to ascertain their impact on profitability. The presence of complements can raise or lower barriers to entry. In application software, for example, barriers to entry were lowered when producers of complementary operating system software, notably Microsoft, provided tool sets making it easier to write applications. Conversely, the need to attract producers of complements can raise barriers to entry, as it does in video game hardware.

The presence of complements can also affect the threat of substitutes. For instance, the need for appropriate fueling stations makes it difficult for cars using alternative fuels to substitute for conventional vehicles. But complements can also make substitution easier. For example, Apple's iTunes hastened the substitution from CDs to digital music.

---

[2] For a discussion of how internet technology improves the attractiveness of some industries while eroding the profitability of others, see Michael E. Porter, "Strategy and the Internet" (HBR, March 2001).

[3] See, for instance, Adam M. Brandenburger and Barry J. Nalebuff, *Co-opetition* (Currency Doubleday, 1996).

Complements can factor into industry rivalry either positively (as when they raise switching costs) or negatively (as when they neutralize product differentiation). Similar analyses can be done for buyer and supplier power. Sometimes companies compete by altering conditions in complementary industries in their favor, such as when videocassette-recorder producer JVC persuaded movie studios to favor its standard in issuing prerecorded tapes even though rival Sony's standard was probably superior from a technical standpoint.

Identifying complements is part of the analyst's work. As with government policies or important technologies, the strategic significance of complements will be best understood through the lens of the five forces.

## 4    CHANGES IN INDUSTRY STRUCTURE

So far, we have discussed the competitive forces at a single point in time. Industry structure proves to be relatively stable, and industry profitability differences are remarkably persistent over time in practice. However, industry structure is constantly undergoing modest adjustment—and occasionally it can change abruptly.

Shifts in structure may emanate from outside an industry or from within. They can boost the industry's profit potential or reduce it. They may be caused by changes in technology, changes in customer needs, or other events. The five competitive forces provide a framework for identifying the most important industry developments and for anticipating their impact on industry attractiveness.

**Shifting Threat of New Entry**   Changes to any of the seven barriers described above can raise or lower the threat of new entry. The expiration of a patent, for instance, may unleash new entrants. On the day that Merck's patents for the cholesterol reducer Zocor expired, three pharmaceutical makers entered the market for the drug. Conversely, the proliferation of products in the ice cream industry has gradually filled up the limited freezer space in grocery stores, making it harder for new ice cream makers to gain access to distribution in North America and Europe.

Strategic decisions of leading competitors often have a major impact on the threat of entry. Starting in the 1970s, for example, retailers such as Wal-Mart, Kmart, and Toys "R" Us began to adopt new procurement, distribution, and inventory control technologies with large fixed costs, including automated distribution centers, bar coding, and point-of-sale terminals. These investments increased the economies of scale and made it more difficult for small retailers to enter the business (and for existing small players to survive).

**Changing Supplier or Buyer Power**   As the factors underlying the power of suppliers and buyers change with time, their clout rises or declines. In the global appliance industry, for instance, competitors including Electrolux, General Electric, and Whirlpool have been squeezed by the consolidation of retail channels (the decline of appliance specialty stores, for instance, and the rise of big-box retailers like Best Buy and Home Depot in the United States). Another example is travel agents, who depend on airlines as a key supplier. When the internet allowed airlines to sell tickets directly to customers, this significantly increased their power to bargain down agents' commissions.

**Shifting Threat of Substitution**   The most common reason substitutes become more or less threatening over time is that advances in technology create new substitutes or shift price-performance comparisons in one direction or the other. The earliest microwave ovens, for example, were large and priced above $2,000, making them poor substitutes for conventional ovens. With technological advances, they became serious substitutes. Flash computer memory has improved enough recently to become a meaningful substitute for low-capacity hard-disk drives. Trends in the availability or performance of complementary producers also shift the threat of substitutes.

**New Bases of Rivalry**   Rivalry often intensifies naturally over time. As an industry matures, growth slows. Competitors become more alike as industry conventions emerge, technology diffuses, and consumer tastes converge. Industry profitability falls, and weaker competitors are driven from the business. This story has played out in industry after industry; televisions, snowmobiles, and telecommunications equipment are just a few examples.

A trend toward intensifying price competition and other forms of rivalry, however, is by no means inevitable. For example, there has been enormous competitive activity in the U.S. casino industry in recent decades, but most of it has been positive-sum competition directed toward new niches and geographic segments (such as riverboats, trophy properties, Native American reservations, international expansion, and novel customer groups like families). Head-to-head rivalry that lowers prices or boosts the payouts to winners has been limited.

The nature of rivalry in an industry is altered by mergers and acquisitions that introduce new capabilities and ways of competing. Or, technological innovation can reshape rivalry. In the retail brokerage industry, the advent of the internet lowered marginal costs and reduced differentiation, triggering far more intense competition on commissions and fees than in the past.

In some industries, companies turn to mergers and consolidation not to improve cost and quality but to attempt to stop intense competition. Eliminating rivals is a risky strategy, however. The five competitive forces tell us that a profit windfall from removing today's competitors often attracts new competitors and backlash from customers and suppliers. In New York banking, for example, the 1980s and 1990s saw escalating consolidations of commercial and savings banks, including Manufacturers Hanover, Chemical, Chase, and Dime Savings. But today the retail-banking landscape of Manhattan is as diverse as ever, as new entrants such as Wachovia, Bank of America, and Washington Mutual have entered the market.

# IMPLICATIONS FOR STRATEGY          5

Understanding the forces that shape industry competition is the starting point for developing strategy. Every company should already know what the average profitability of its industry is and how that has been changing over time. The five forces reveal *why* industry profitability is what it is. Only then can a company incorporate industry conditions into strategy.

The forces reveal the most significant aspects of the competitive environment. They also provide a baseline for sizing up a company's strengths and weaknesses: Where does the company stand versus buyers, suppliers, entrants, rivals, and substitutes? Most importantly, an understanding of industry structure guides managers toward fruitful possibilities for strategic action, which may include any or all of the following: positioning the company to better cope with the current competitive forces; anticipating and exploiting shifts in the forces; and shaping the balance of forces to create a new industry structure that is more favorable to the company. The best strategies exploit more than one of these possibilities.

**Positioning the Company**     Strategy can be viewed as building defenses against the competitive forces or finding a position in the industry where the forces are weakest. Consider, for instance, the position of Paccar in the market for heavy trucks. The heavy-truck industry is structurally challenging. Many buyers operate large fleets or are large leasing companies, with both the leverage and the motivation to drive down the price of one of their largest purchases. Most trucks are built to regulated standards and offer similar features, so price competition is rampant. Capital intensity causes rivalry to be fierce, especially during the recurring cyclical downturns. Unions exercise considerable supplier power. Though there are few direct substitutes for an 18-wheeler, truck buyers face important substitutes for their services, such as cargo delivery by rail.

In this setting, Paccar, a Bellevue, Washington–based company with about 20% of the North American heavy-truck market, has chosen to focus on one group of customers: owner-operators—drivers who own their trucks and contract directly with shippers or serve as subcontractors to larger trucking companies. Such small operators have limited clout as truck buyers. They are also less price sensitive because of their strong emotional ties to and economic dependence on the product. They take great pride in their trucks, in which they spend most of their time.

Paccar has invested heavily to develop an array of features with owner-operators in mind: luxurious sleeper cabins, plush leather seats, noise-insulated cabins, sleek exterior styling, and so on. At the company's extensive network of dealers, prospective buyers use software to select among thousands of options to put their personal signature on their trucks. These customized trucks are built to order, not to stock, and delivered in six to eight weeks. Paccar's trucks also have aerodynamic designs that reduce fuel consumption, and they maintain their resale value better than other trucks. Paccar's roadside assistance program and IT-supported system for distributing spare parts reduce the time a truck is out of service. All these are crucial considerations for an owner-operator. Customers pay Paccar a 10% premium, and its Kenworth and Peterbilt brands are considered status symbols at truck stops.

Paccar illustrates the principles of positioning a company within a given industry structure. The firm has found a portion of its industry where the competitive forces are weaker—where it can avoid buyer power and price-based rivalry. And it has tailored every single part of the value chain to cope well with the forces in its segment. As a result, Paccar has been profitable for 68 years straight and has earned a long-run return on equity above 20%.

In addition to revealing positioning opportunities within an existing industry, the five forces framework allows companies to rigorously analyze entry and exit. Both depend on answering the difficult question: "What is the potential of this business?" Exit is indicated when industry structure is poor or declining and the company has no prospect of a superior positioning. In considering entry into a new industry, creative strategists can use the framework to spot an industry with a good future before this good future is reflected in the prices of acquisition candidates. Five forces analysis may also reveal industries that are not necessarily attractive for the average entrant but in which a company has good reason to believe it can surmount entry barriers at lower cost than most firms or has a unique ability to cope with the industry's competitive forces.

**Exploiting Industry Change**     Industry changes bring the opportunity to spot and claim promising new strategic positions if the strategist has a sophisticated understanding of the competitive forces and their underpinnings. Consider, for instance, the evolution of the music industry during the past decade. With the advent of the internet and the digital distribution of music, some analysts predicted the birth of thousands of music labels (that is, record companies that develop artists and bring their music to market). This, the analysts argued, would break a pattern that had held since Edison invented the phonograph: Between three and six major record companies had always dominated the industry. The internet would, they predicted, remove distribution as a barrier to entry, unleashing a flood of new players into the music industry.

A careful analysis, however, would have revealed that physical distribution was not the crucial barrier to entry. Rather, entry was barred by other benefits that large music labels enjoyed. Large labels could pool the risks of developing new artists over many bets, cushioning the impact of inevitable failures. Even more important, they had advantages in breaking through the clutter and getting their new artists heard. To do so, they could promise radio stations and record stores access to well-known artists in exchange for promotion of new artists. New labels would find this nearly impossible to match. The major labels stayed the course, and new music labels have been rare.

This is not to say that the music industry is structurally unchanged by digital distribution. Unauthorized downloading created an illegal but potent substitute. The labels tried for years to develop technical platforms for digital distribution themselves, but major companies hesitated to sell their music through a platform owned by a rival. Into this vacuum stepped Apple with its iTunes music store, launched in 2003 to support its iPod music player. By permitting the creation of a powerful new gatekeeper, the major labels allowed industry structure to shift against them. The number of major record companies has actually declined—from six in 1997 to four today—as companies struggled to cope with the digital phenomenon.

When industry structure is in flux, new and promising competitive positions may appear. Structural changes open up new needs and new ways to serve existing needs. Established leaders may overlook these or be constrained by past strategies from pursuing them. Smaller competitors in the industry can capitalize on such changes, or the void may well be filled by new entrants.

**Shaping Industry Structure**   When a company exploits structural change, it is recognizing, and reacting to, the inevitable. However, companies also have the ability to shape industry structure. A firm can lead its industry toward new ways of competing that alter the five forces for the better. In reshaping structure, a company wants its competitors to follow so that the entire industry will be transformed. While many industry participants may benefit in the process, the innovator can benefit most if it can shift competition in directions where it can excel.

An industry's structure can be reshaped in two ways: by redividing profitability in favor of incumbents or by expanding the overall profit pool. Redividing the industry pie aims to increase the share of profits to industry competitors instead of to suppliers, buyers, substitutes, and keeping out potential entrants. Expanding the profit pool involves increasing the overall pool of economic value generated by the industry in which rivals, buyers, and suppliers can all share.

*Redividing profitability.* To capture more profits for industry rivals, the starting point is to determine which force or forces are currently constraining industry profitability and address them. A company can potentially influence all of the competitive forces. The strategist's goal here is to reduce the share of profits that leak to suppliers, buyers, and substitutes or are sacrificed to deter entrants.

To neutralize supplier power, for example, a firm can standardize specifications for parts to make it easier to switch among suppliers. It can cultivate additional vendors, or alter technology to avoid a powerful supplier group altogether. To counter customer power, companies may expand services that raise buyers' switching costs or find alternative means of reaching customers to neutralize powerful channels. To temper profit-eroding price rivalry, companies can invest more heavily in unique products, as pharmaceutical firms have done, or expand support services to customers. To scare off entrants, incumbents can elevate the fixed cost of competing—for instance, by escalating their R&D or marketing expenditures. To limit the threat of substitutes, companies can offer better value through new features or wider product accessibility. When soft-drink producers introduced vending machines and convenience store channels, for example, they dramatically improved the availability of soft drinks relative to other beverages.

Sysco, the largest food-service distributor in North America, offers a revealing example of how an industry leader can change the structure of an industry for the better. Food-service distributors purchase food and related items from farmers and food processors. They then warehouse and deliver these items to restaurants, hospitals, employer cafeterias, schools, and other food-service institutions. Given low barriers to entry, the food-service distribution industry has historically been highly fragmented, with numerous local competitors. While rivals try to cultivate customer relationships, buyers are price sensitive because food represents a large share of their costs. Buyers can also choose the substitute approaches of purchasing directly from manufacturers or using retail sources, avoiding distributors altogether. Suppliers wield bargaining power: They are often large companies with strong brand names that food preparers and consumers recognize. Average profitability in the industry has been modest.

Sysco recognized that, given its size and national reach, it might change this state of affairs. It led the move to introduce private-label distributor brands with specifications tailored to the food-service market, moderating supplier power. Sysco emphasized value-added services to buyers such as credit, menu planning, and inventory management to shift the basis of competition away from just price. These moves, together with stepped-up investments in information technology and regional distribution centers, substantially raised the bar for new entrants while making the substitutes less attractive. Not surprisingly, the industry has been consolidating, and industry profitability appears to be rising.

Industry leaders have a special responsibility for improving industry structure. Doing so often requires resources that only large players possess. Moreover, an improved industry structure is a public good because it benefits every firm in the industry, not just the company that initiated the improvement. Often, it is more in the interests of an industry leader than any other participant to invest for the common good because leaders will usually benefit the most. Indeed, improving the industry may be a leader's most profitable strategic opportunity, in part because attempts to gain further market share can trigger strong reactions from rivals, customers, and even suppliers.

There is a dark side to shaping industry structure that is equally important to understand. Ill-advised changes in competitive positioning and operating practices can *undermine* industry structure. Faced with pressures to gain market share or enamored with innovation for its own sake, managers may trigger new kinds of competition that no incumbent can win. When taking actions to improve their own company's competitive advantage, then, strategists should ask whether they are setting in motion dynamics that will undermine industry structure in the long run. In the early days of the personal computer industry, for instance, IBM tried to make up for its late entry by offering an open architecture that would set industry standards and attract complementary makers of application software and peripherals. In the process, it ceded ownership of the critical components of the PC—the operating system and the microprocessor—to Microsoft and Intel. By standardizing PCs, it encouraged price-based rivalry and shifted power to suppliers. Consequently, IBM became the temporarily dominant firm in an industry with an enduringly unattractive structure.

*Expanding the profit pool.* When overall demand grows, the industry's quality level rises, intrinsic costs are reduced, or waste is eliminated, the pie expands. The total pool of value available to competitors, suppliers, and buyers grows. The total profit pool expands, for example, when channels become more competitive or when an industry discovers latent buyers for its product that are not currently being served. When soft-drink producers rationalized their independent bottler networks to make them more efficient and effective, both the soft-drink companies and the bottlers benefited. Overall value can also expand when firms work collaboratively with suppliers to improve coordination and limit unnecessary costs incurred in the supply chain. This lowers the inherent cost structure of the industry, allowing higher profit, greater demand through lower prices, or both. Or, agreeing on quality standards can bring up industrywide quality and service levels, and hence prices, benefiting rivals, suppliers, and customers.

Expanding the overall profit pool creates win-win opportunities for multiple industry participants. It can also reduce the risk of destructive rivalry that arises when incumbents attempt to shift bargaining power or capture more market share. However, expanding the pie does not reduce the importance of industry structure. How the expanded pie is divided will ultimately be determined by the five forces. The most successful companies are those that expand the industry profit pool in ways that allow them to share disproportionately in the benefits.

**Defining the Industry**   The five competitive forces also hold the key to defining the relevant industry (or industries) in which a company competes. Drawing industry boundaries correctly, around the arena in which competition actually takes place, will clarify the causes of profitability and the appropriate unit for setting strategy. A company needs a separate strategy for each distinct industry. Mistakes in industry definition made by competitors present opportunities for staking out superior strategic positions. (See Box 2, "Defining the Relevant Industry.")

# COMPETITION AND VALUE                        6

The competitive forces reveal the drivers of industry competition. A company strategist who understands that competition extends well beyond existing rivals will detect wider competitive threats and be better equipped to address them. At the same time, thinking comprehensively about an industry's structure can uncover opportunities: differences in customers, suppliers, substitutes, potential entrants, and rivals that can become the basis for distinct strategies yielding superior performance. In a world of more open competition and relentless change, it is more important than ever to think structurally about competition.

Understanding industry structure is equally important for investors as for managers. The five competitive forces reveal whether an industry is truly attractive, and they help investors anticipate positive or negative shifts in industry structure before they are obvious. The five forces distinguish short-term blips from structural changes and allow investors to take advantage of undue pessimism or optimism. Those companies whose strategies have industry-transforming potential become far clearer. This deeper thinking about competition is a more powerful way to achieve genuine investment success than the financial projections and trend extrapolation that dominate today's investment analysis.

## BOX 2   DEFINING THE RELEVANT INDUSTRY

Defining the industry in which competition actually takes place is important for good industry analysis, not to mention for developing strategy and setting business unit boundaries. Many strategy errors emanate from mistaking the relevant industry, defining it too broadly or too narrowly. Defining the industry too broadly obscures differences among products, customers, or geographic regions that are important to competition, strategic positioning, and profitability. Defining the industry too narrowly overlooks commonalities and linkages across related products or geographic markets that are crucial to competitive advantage. Also, strategists must be sensitive to the possibility that industry boundaries can shift.

The boundaries of an industry consist of two primary dimensions. First is the *scope of products or services*. For example, is motor oil used in cars part of the same industry as motor oil used in heavy trucks and stationary engines, or are these different industries? The second dimension is *geographic scope*. Most industries are present in many parts of the world. However, is competition contained within each state, or is it national? Does competition take place within regions such as Europe or North America, or is there a single global industry?

The five forces are the basic tool to resolve these questions. If industry structure for two products is the same or very similar (that is, if they have the same buyers, suppliers, barriers to entry, and so forth), then the products are best treated as being part of the same industry. If industry structure differs markedly, however, the two products may be best understood as separate industries.

In lubricants, the oil used in cars is similar or even identical to the oil used in trucks, but the similarity largely ends there. Automotive motor oil is sold to fragmented, generally unsophisticated customers through numerous and often powerful channels, using extensive advertising. Products are packaged in small containers and logistical costs are high, necessitating local production. Truck and power generation lubricants are sold to entirely different buyers in entirely different ways using a separate supply chain. Industry structure (buyer power, barriers to entry, and so forth) is substantially different. Automotive oil is thus a distinct industry from oil for truck and stationary engine uses. Industry profitability will differ in these two cases, and a lubricant company will need a separate strategy for competing in each area.

Differences in the five competitive forces also reveal the geographic scope of competition. If an industry has a similar structure in every country (rivals, buyers, and so on), the presumption is that competition is global, and the five forces analyzed from a global perspective will set average profitability. A single global strategy is needed. If an industry has quite different structures in different geographic regions, however, each region may well be a distinct industry. Otherwise, competition would have leveled the differences. The five forces analyzed for each region will set profitability there.

The extent of differences in the five forces for related products or across geographic areas is a matter of degree, making industry definition often a matter of judgment. A rule of thumb is that where the differences in any one force are large, and where the differences involve more than one force, distinct industries may well be present.

Fortunately, however, even if industry boundaries are drawn incorrectly, careful five forces analysis should reveal important competitive threats. A closely related product omitted from the industry definition will show up as a substitute, for example, or competitors overlooked as rivals will be recognized as potential entrants. At the same time, the five forces analysis should reveal major differences within overly broad industries that will indicate the need to adjust industry boundaries or strategies.

## BOX 3    TYPICAL STEPS IN INDUSTRY ANALYSIS

Define the relevant industry:

▶ What products are in it? Which ones are part of another distinct industry?

▶ What is the geographic scope of competition?

Identify the participants and segment them into groups, if appropriate:
Who are

▶ the buyers and buyer groups?

▶ the suppliers and supplier groups?

▶ the competitors?

▶ the substitutes?

▶ the potential entrants?

Assess the underlying drivers of each competitive force to determine which forces are strong and which are weak and why.

Determine overall industry structure, and test the analysis for consistency:

▶ *Why* is the level of profitability what it is?

▶ Which are the *controlling* forces for profitability?

▶ Is the industry analysis consistent with actual long-run profitability?

▶ Are more-profitable players better positioned in relation to the five forces?

Analyze recent and likely future changes in each force, both positive and negative

Identify aspects of industry structure that might be influenced by competitors, by new entrants, or by your company

## BOX 4    COMMON PITFALLS

In conducting the analysis avoid the following common mistakes:

▶ Defining the industry too broadly or too narrowly.

▶ Making lists instead of engaging in rigorous analysis.

▶ Paying equal attention to all of the forces rather than digging deeply into the most important ones.

▶ Confusing effect (price sensitivity) with cause (buyer economics).

▶ Using static analysis that ignores industry trends.

▶ Confusing cyclical or transient changes with true structural changes.

▶ Using the framework to declare an industry attractive or unattractive rather than using it to guide strategic choices.

If both executives and investors looked at competition this way, capital markets would be a far more effective force for company success and economic prosperity. Executives and investors would both be focused on the same fundamentals that drive sustained profitability. The conversation between investors and executives would focus on the structural, not the transient. Imagine the improvement in company performance—and in the economy as a whole—if all the energy expended in "pleasing the Street" were redirected toward the factors that create true economic value.

## Duvalier Securities
Maxim Duvalier, CFA

**International/Switzerland**
**Manufacturers**
**6 March 2006**

## JQC Industries (JQC)

| | |
|---|---|
| Price – Local/ADR: | CHF36.05/$27.87 |
| 12-Month Price Target: | CHF42.50/$32.90 |

Only Time Will Tell?        **Accumulate**

### Overview

We are upgrading our rating on JQC to "Accumulate" from "Hold" and increasing our price target to CHF42.50/$32.90 from CHF39.10/$30.25. JQC is a manufacturer of fine watches headquartered in Geneva, Switzerland. Our change in rating is based on four factors: JQC's development of a new product line, its expansion into China and India, strong growth in exports of Swiss watches, and consolidation occurring within the Swiss watch making industry. We estimate a long-term EPS growth rate of 10 percent annually. This reflects our expectation of 4 to 7 percent unit growth and operating margin improvement of 40–60 basis points.

### Swiss Watch Industry

Swiss watchmakers' most serious competitors are Chinese and Hong Kong producers. The Swiss enjoy a worldwide reputation for quality and style. Although 80 percent of the approximately 500 million watches sold worldwide are made in China and Hong Kong, more than 50 percent of the sales value is generated by the Swiss watch industry.

In 2005, the watch industry was Switzerland's third largest exporter after the machine and chemical industries. Swiss watch exports are distributed mainly in three continents: Asia (43 percent), Europe (34 percent), and North America (21 percent). Sales and earnings have followed the overall economic growth of these primary export markets. Industry profits benefit from economic upturns but suffer in downturns. Assuming a 3.5 percent average real GDP growth and an inflation rate of 2.5 percent in their primary export markets, Duvalier Securities forecasts that sales will grow by 6 percent in 2006 in the industry's three primary export markets.

Based on an analysis of the underlying economic and technical characteristics of the Swiss watch making industry, we believe the primary determinant of industry profitability is high barriers to entry. In 1992, Switzerland passed a law regulating the use of the term "Swiss made" for watches. This law requires that the assembly work on the watch and its movement, as well as the final testing of the movement, be carried out in Switzerland. It also requires that at least 50 percent of the components of the movement be manufactured in Switzerland. As a result, the "Swiss made" designation enjoys a solid reputation throughout the world and globalization of trade has not diminished its importance.

### JQC's Industry Position

Three years ago, JQC hired renowned designer Luigi Gastón to be its president and chief executive officer because of his successful career in fashion design and extensive marketing experience. Gastón has implemented a differentiation strategy and concentrated the company's manufacturing and marketing efforts. At the same time, he has expanded and rejuvenated JQC's product line. Gastón's philosophy is that "a watch has to be more than just technically brilliant to sell; it has to be desirable, modern, and glamorous." As a result, he has launched fashionable new lines for both men and women. Both lines consist of watches targeted at the high-end, standard, and entry-level segments of the market.

**1.** Based on Duvalier's description, the Swiss watch making industry can *best* be described in terms of its industrial life cycle and business cycle reaction, respectively, as:

|    | Industrial Life Cycle | Business Cycle Reaction |
|----|-----------------------|-------------------------|
| **A.** | Growth | Cyclical |
| **B.** | Mature | Defensive |
| **C.** | Mature | Cyclical |

**2.** Duvalier's conclusion about the primary determinant of industry profitability in the Swiss watch making industry is *least likely* to be based on:

   **A.** brand identity.

   **B.** switching costs.

   **C.** supplier concentration.

**3.** The value implied by the premium prices of Swiss watches is *most likely* to be:

   **A.** appropriated by suppliers.

   **B.** dissipated by competition among Swiss watch makers.

   **C.** kept by companies in the industry in the form of higher profits.

**4.** The structure of the Swiss watch industry could *most likely* influence the industry's balance between supply and demand by:

   **A.** reducing the likelihood of new entrants and lower prices.

   **B.** increasing the likelihood that existing companies will expand capacity.

   **C.** reducing the likelihood of prolonged periods of excess capacity as a result of companies leaving the industry.

**5.** Which of the following is a risk that is *most likely* associated with JQC's competitive strategy?

   **A.** Cost proximity is lost.

   **B.** Segmentation declines.

   **C.** Proximity in differentiation is lost.

**6.** The factors that have contributed *most* to the Swiss watch industry's profitability are:

   **A.** government intervention and product segmentation.

   **B.** technological developments and product segmentation.

   **C.** technological developments and a high degree of industry concentration.

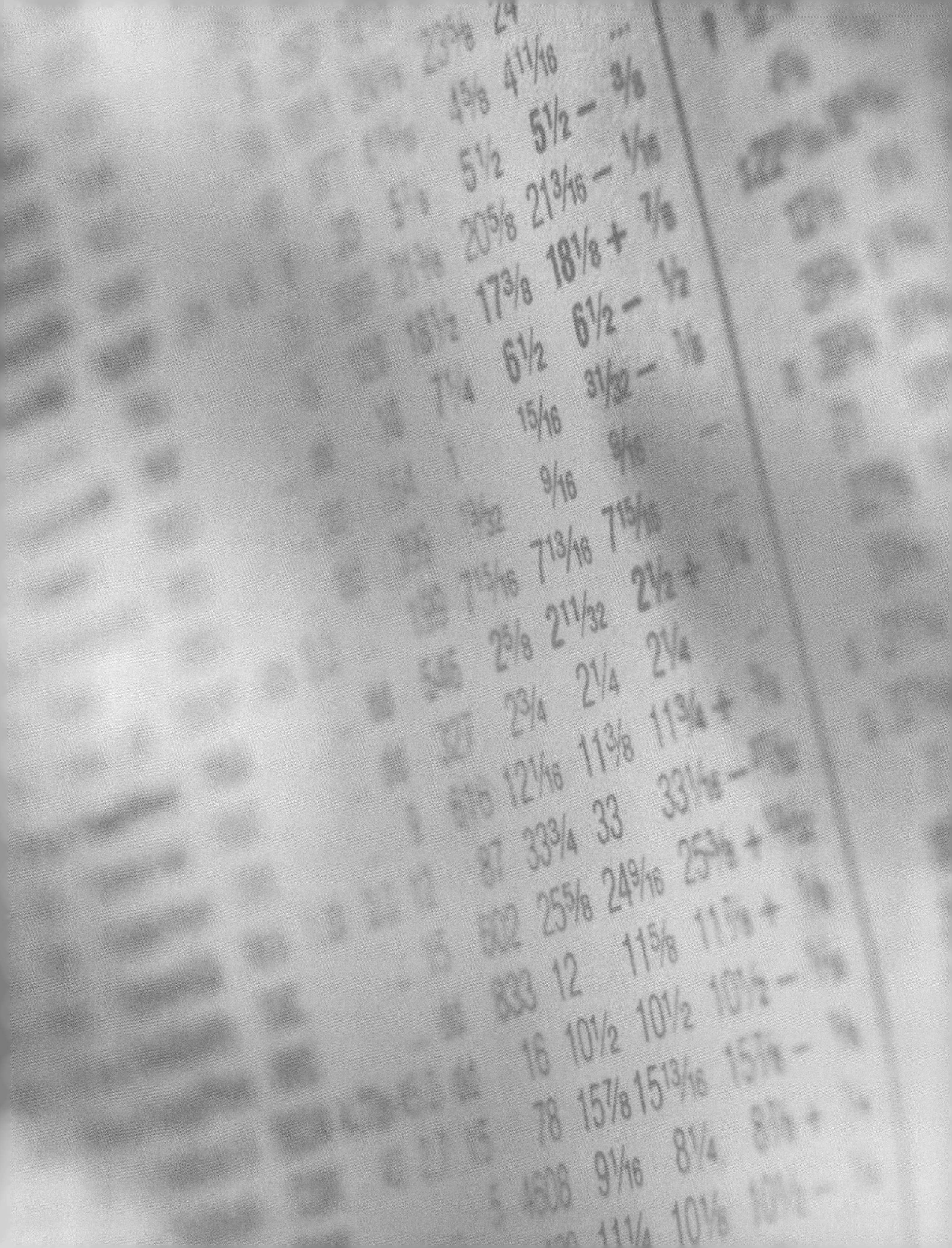

23⅜  24

4⅝  4¹¹/₁₆  ...  
5½  5½  −  ⅜  
5½  5½  2¹³/₁₆  −  ¹/₁₆  
20⅝  21¹³/₁₆  −  ⅞  
17⅜  18⅛  +  ⅞  
18½  17⅜  18⅛  +  ⅞  
6½  6½  −  ½  
7¼  6½  6½  −  ½  
15/16  31/32  −  ⅛  
9/16  9/16  
¹¹/₃₂  9/16  9/16  
7¹³/₁₆  7¹⁵/₁₆  
7¹⁵/₁₆  7¹³/₁₆  7¹⁵/₁₆  
2⅝  2¹¹/₃₂  2½  +  
2¾  2¼  2¼  
6⅛  2¾  2¼  2¼  
12¹/₁₆  11⅜  11¾  +  
33¾  33  33¹/₁₆  −  
87  33¾  33  33¹/₁₆  −  
25⅝  24⁹/₁₆  25⅜  +  
602  25⅝  24⁹/₁₆  25⅜  +  
12  11⅝  11⅝  +  
833  12  11⅝  11⅝  +  
16  10½  10½  10½  −  
78  15⅝  15¹³/₁₆  15⅞  −  
9¹/₁₆  8¼  8⅛  +  
508  9¹/₁₆  8¼  
11¼  10⅛

# INDUSTRY ANALYSIS

by Jeffrey C. Hooke

## LEARNING OUTCOMES

| The candidate should be able to: | Mastery |
|---|:---:|
| **a.** discuss the key components that should be included in an industry analysis model; | ☐ |
| **b.** illustrate the life cycle of a typical industry; | ☐ |
| **c.** analyze the effects of business cycles on industry classification (i.e., growth, defensive, cyclical); | ☐ |
| **d.** analyze the impact of external factors (e.g., technology, government, foreign influences, demography, and social changes) on industries; | ☐ |
| **e.** illustrate the inputs and methods used in preparing an industry demand-and-supply analysis; | ☐ |
| **f.** explain factors that affect industry pricing practices. | ☐ |

*The industry analysis is an important part of the research report. The proper organization of this analysis, the five principal themes of such a study and the common pitfalls of an industry evaluation are discussed herein.*

In developing investment recommendations, the typical analyst begins serious research at the industry level. The analyst receives "top-down" economic and capital market forecasts from others. The initial responsibility is tying these macro parameters into an industry outlook, thus laying the groundwork for judging the prospects of selected participants. The fortunes of an individual company are closely intertwined with those of the industry in which it operates. An in-depth industry study is thus a prerequisite for a proper security analysis. A thorough understanding of the industry facilitates the evaluation process, and for this reason, many practitioners limit themselves to one or two industries. This reading

**223**

reviews preparing an industry analysis, which is covered under Section 4 of the model research report (Exhibit 1).

## 1　BACKGROUND

Whatever outlook an analyst develops for a particular industry, not all companies have prospects mirroring the broader view. Some perform better than the general expectation; others worse. Consider the waste disposal industry in December 1996. The principal companies were mired in the industry's image of operating problems, poor economics in recycling, and a glut of landfill space. As a result, their P/E ratios suffered. Meanwhile, three young enterprises carried premium P/E ratios, as the market showed interest in their strong acquisition programs (see Exhibit 2).

The dual track status of waste disposal firms is duplicated in other industries. Wal-Mart, for example, has enjoyed far higher valuation ratios than other general merchandise retailers, such as Sears, although many of these competitors make money. The big difference has been Wal-Mart's higher growth rate.

| EXHIBIT 2 | Snapshot of the Waste Disposal Industry |
|---|---|

| Established Companies | P/E Ratio |
|---|---|
| Laidlaw | 23 |
| WMX Technologies | 25 |
| Browning-Ferris | 18 |

| New Acquisitive Players | |
|---|---|
| Allied Waste | 56 |
| USA Waste Services | 26 |
| Republic Industries | 72 |

As a general rule, institutional investors want analysts to stick to industries with a positive outlook. Even the best buggy whip manufacturer was a poor bet at the turn of the 20th century. Similarly, the most attractive CB radio producer turned out to be a loser in the 1980s. The chosen industries don't have to be stellar performers; they just require a reasonable justification for investment.

## Broad Industry Trends

While the competent analyst has a broad knowledge of the industry he covers, his research reports have a narrow focus, limiting reviews of industry trends to those that affect a specific company's future performance. Contributing to the reader's understanding of the industry requires comparisons. For example, analysts covering the early years of the VCR compared it with the introduction of the television. Original themes are important. Rehashing widely available data is of little use to the reader, unless it sets the stage for company-specific projections. These forecasts appear toward the end of the research report, after a groundwork has been laid.

As the subject company grows larger, the industry analysis becomes complicated. Major corporations today have multiple lines, many of which are not comparable. General Electric has 13 separate divisions producing products as dissimilar as gas turbines and home appliances. For those firms with disparate businesses, the industry analysis evolves into an *industries* analysis, as each distinct segment is valued separately as a part of a larger whole.

## Contrary Opinions

Of particular interest to investors are contrarian opinions. Research analysts are reluctant to stick their necks out. They follow the herd, and as a result, their reports are disappointingly similar. For the most part, analysts work around the edges of the consensus view on an industry's prospects and a company's forecasts. When a practitioner reaches a strikingly different conclusion from that of everyone else, he tends to couch it in vague terms. Then, if he ends up wrong, his error is less obvious. The depressing outcome of this environment is that many analysts, particularly those on the sell side, are reduced to arguing about a company's next quarterly earnings report. Will earnings be 46 cents per share or 45 cents? When a respected analyst goes against the grain and replies that earnings will be 15 cents instead of 45 cents, institutional investors sit up and take notice.

Few analysts predict reversals of trends that have been long accepted on Wall Street, despite the frequency of such occurrences, so a fresh look at the status quo is real news. One important industry reversal happened in June 1996. After years of raising prices for their brand-name products, Kellogg Co., General Mills, and Ralcorp.—the three principal U.S. cereal makers—cut prices by 20 percent in response to declining demand for their products. In a few days, cereal prices dropped to the levels of the late 1980s. Some observers had noticed increasing consumer resistance to high cereal prices, but few analysts predicted this change, which caused cereal company share prices to decline as earnings projections fell.

# ORGANIZING AN INDUSTRY ANALYSIS                    2

An industry analysis can take various forms, but the outline set forth in Exhibit 3 is customary. The industry analysis begins with positioning the specific industry within its life cycle. Defining a sector in this way is important on Wall Street. Investors place

| EXHIBIT 3 | Model of an Industry Analysis |
|-----------|-------------------------------|

Industry classification
  Life cycle position
  Business cycle

External factors
  Technology
  Government
  Social
  Demographic
  Foreign

Demand analysis
  End users
  Real and nominal growth
  Trends and cyclical variation around trends

Supply analysis
  Degree of concentration
  Ease of entry
  Industry capacity

Profitability
  Supply/demand analysis
  Cost factors
  Pricing
  International competition and markets

*Source:* Association for Investment Management and Research. Note how the industry analysis is broken down into its key components.

a premium on simple investment themes. Thus, the faster the analyst pigeonholes an industry into the "life cycle" chart, the better.

## 3    INDUSTRY CLASSIFICATION

### Classification by Industrial Life Cycle

In general conversation, industries are described by the product they produce or the service they provide. Hospital chains, HMOs, and physician health groups are "medical service" industries. Newspaper firms, magazine publishers, and book companies fall in the "publishing" category. Sporting goods manufacturers, recorded music distributors, and toy producers are lumped into the "recreation" sector. Security analysis uses these descriptions, while further classifying industries by certain economic characteristics.

The most popular segmentation tool is the industrial life cycle, which reflects the vitality of an industry over time. A staple of business textbooks and management consulting firms, the life cycle theory outlines four phases that

| | | |
|---|---|---|
| **EXHIBIT 4** | **Industry Classification:** **The Industrial Life Cycle** | |

| Life Cycle Phase | Description |
|---|---|
| Pioneer | Product acceptance is questionable and implementation of business strategy is unclear. There is high risk and many failures. |
| Growth | Product acceptance is established. Roll-out begins and growth accelerates in sales and earnings. Proper execution of strategy remains an issue. |
| Mature | Industry trend line corresponds to the general economy. Participants compete for share in a stable industry. |
| Decline | Shifting tastes or technologies have overtaken the industry, and demand for its products steadily decreases. |

mark the beginning to end of an industry: the *pioneer, growth, mature,* and *decline* phases (see Exhibit 4).

As its name implies, the pioneer phase is the riskiest point of corporate life. The industry is struggling to establish a market for its products. Cash needs for working capital and fixed assets are substantial, yet the industry is losing money or is marginally profitable. Its potential for success attracts equity investors, who are prepared to take a total loss on their investment and know that. Seven out of 10 start-up businesses fail to survive. During overheated stock markets, speculative ventures often go public and become fodder for the security analyst community.

The second stage is the growth phase. Here, practitioners acknowledge the industry's product acceptance and have a brief historical framework for estimating future demand. The big questions are: How far, and how fast? So-called growth industries occupy a large amount of analysts' time, because they sometimes provide excellent returns. Of particular interest to analysts is identifying a growth industry at the ground floor, before everyone jumps on the bandwagon and boosts the stock price.

A classic growth industry spurs demand for a product that the consumer (or the industrial client) didn't know he needed. The best example is a new technology; cellular advances, for example, sparked a demand for car phones, which few people realized they needed beforehand. Another growth story is the better mousetrap. Before Office Depot, few people realized they needed an office supply superstore; most shopped at local stationers and department stores for these items. The total market for office supplies is stagnant, but office superstores represent a legitimate growth industry within the larger market. Growth companies prosper independent of the business cycle.

Besides experiencing rapidly increasing sales, growth industries frequently enjoy fat profit margins. This happy situation continues until new competitors, attracted to the high returns, enter the industry. As competition stabilizes and market penetration reaches practical limits, the industry progresses to the mature phase.

If growth industries have above-average increases in sales and earnings, mature industries produce "average" results. Unit sales gains follow economic growth. Thus, if the economy improves by 3 percent in one year, an analyst expects a mature industry's unit sales to rise by 3 percent. Adding a 5 percent inflation factor means the industry's sales increase by 8 percent annually. Mature industries usually provide a staple product or service. Examples include the food, auto, and furniture industries.

Within a mature industry may be one or more *growth companies*. Typically, such firms achieve above-average growth in one of two ways. First, they gain market share by offering an improved quality or service (i.e., the better mousetrap). American Greetings' market share in the mature greeting card industry has increased from 33 to 35 percent over the past five years. Consumers like its products better than those of the competition. Alternatively, a company grows in a mature industry by gobbling up others. Since 1991, Service Corporation International has increased its market share in the funeral business from 5 to 10 percent, by acquiring over 200 competitors. Sales in its industry advanced 8 percent annually over that time, but Service Corporation's gains averaged 31 percent each year.

The last stage in the life cycle is the decline phase. Demand for the industry's products decreases and the remaining participants fight over shares of a smaller market. With no new capacity needs and diminished profit margins, the industry attracts little capital and established firms begin to exit the sector. As demand dries up, companies fail and the remaining participants consolidate. The better-managed survivors anticipate this fate and avoid it by using cash flow to diversify into promising industries. Westinghouse's takeover of CBS exemplified such diversification.

## Classification by Business Cycle Reaction

In addition to the industry life cycle, Wall Street characterizes industries by the way in which they react to the business cycle. Market economies do not grow in a straight line. They expand, go into a recession where growth slows or stops, and then enter a recovery, which leads into the next expansion (see Exhibit 5). The duration of a U.S. business cycle can be 5 to 10 years. Certain industries

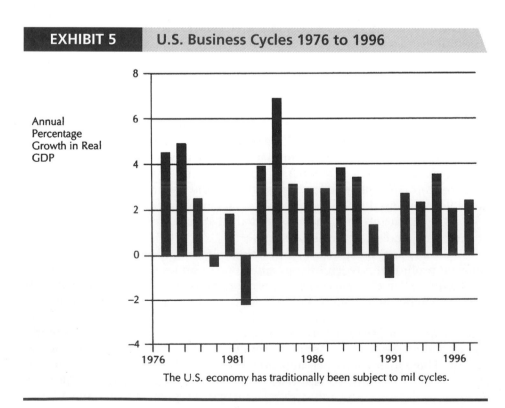

| EXHIBIT 5 | U.S. Business Cycles 1976 to 1996 |
| --- | --- |

Annual Percentage Growth in Real GDP

The U.S. economy has traditionally been subject to mil cycles.

| EXHIBIT 6 | Industry Classification by Business Cycle Behavior | |
|-----------|---------------------------------------------------|---|

| Behavior Pattern | Description |
|------------------|-------------|
| Growth | Above-normal expansion in sales and profits occurs independent of the business cycle. |
| Defensive | Stable performance during both ups and downs of business cycle. |
| Cyclical | Profitability tracks the business cycle, often in an exaggerated manner. |

prosper more than others during different phases of the business cycle. Industry's behavior places it into one of three categories: *growth, defensive,* or *cyclical* (see Exhibit 6).

A growth industry achieves an above-normal rate of expansion, independent of the business cycle. Even if the economy is in a recession, the growth industry's sales and earnings rise. New technology and products are the hallmarks of a growth industry. The computer software industry sailed through the 1990–1991 recession with higher revenues.

Defensive industries exhibit stable performance through the business cycle. Sales and earnings proceed in an upward direction. Strong growth is apparent during an economic upturn, but there is a slight dip in profitability during recession years. Defensive industries usually fall into the mature category. Examples include (1) electric and gas utilities since people require heat and light in their homes regardless of economic conditions; (2) food, cigarette, and beer companies since demand for their products remains inelastic (although consumers may shift to lower-priced brands); and (3) government contractors since governments tend to spend whether or not the economy expands.

Cyclical industries are those whose earnings track the cycle. Their profits benefit from economic upturns, but suffer in a downturn. The earnings movement is exaggerated. Boom times are followed by "bust times." Thus, when economic growth rates only move a few percentage points, cyclicals go from substantial losses to huge profits. General Motors' operating loss in 1991 was $2.8 billion; its 1996 operating profit topped $4 billion, representing a huge swing in profitability.

Classic cyclical businesses produce discretionary products, the consumption of which is dependent on economic optimism. The auto industry is cyclical, because consumers defer large purchases until they are confident of the economy's positive direction. Heavy equipment and machine tool producers are cyclical businesses. Their customers, capital-intensive concerns, defer investment during recessions and increase spending during recoveries.

Exhibits 7 and 8 provide examples of three firms and how their earnings changed over the preceding business cycle.

Certain cyclical firms experience earnings patterns that do not correlate well against the general economy, but trend against other economic variables. Brokerage firms, for example, show cyclicality based on stock prices. Agricultural firms exhibit earnings tied to the crop price cycle. These firms are lumped into the cyclical category.

The characterization of an industry through the life cycle or business cycle techniques colors the follow-up analysis. Practitioners compare those industries with similar designations and draw inferences about future revenue, earnings

| EXHIBIT 7 | Business Cycle Earnings Comparison Gross National Product (GNP) versus Earnings per Share (EPS) |
|---|---|

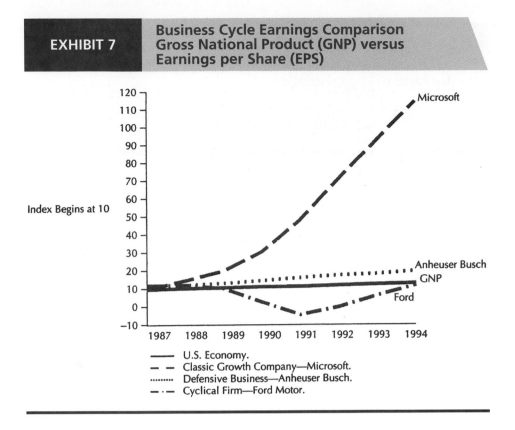

Index Begins at 10

- —— U.S. Economy.
- – – Classic Growth Company—Microsoft.
- ·········· Defensive Business—Anheuser Busch.
- – · – Cyclical Firm—Ford Motor.

| EXHIBIT 8 | Business Cycle Earnings Comparison GNP Changes versus EPS Changes |
|---|---|

|  |  | 1987 | 1988 | 1989 | 1990 | 1991 | 1992 | 1993 | 1994 |
|---|---|---|---|---|---|---|---|---|---|
| Real GDP | % Chg | 2.9 | 3.8 | 3.4 | 1.3 | −1.0 | 2.7 | 2.3 | 3.5 |
| Growth company— Microsoft | EPS | 0.16 | 0.25 | 0.34 | 0.52 | 0.82 | 1.21 | 1.58 | 1.98 |
|  | % Chg | 77.8 | 56.3 | 36.0 | 52.9 | 57.7 | 47.6 | 30.6 | 25.3 |
| Defensive business— Anheuser Busch | EPS | 1.02 | 1.23 | 1.34 | 1.48 | 1.63 | 1.73 | 1.78 | 1.94 |
|  | % Chg | 20.0 | 20.6 | 8.9 | 10.4 | 10.1 | 6.1 | 2.9 | 9.0 |
| Cyclical firm— Ford Motor | EPS | 4.53 | 5.48 | 4.57 | 0.93 | −2.40 | −0.73 | 2.28 | 4.97 |
|  | % Chg | 47.1 | 21.0 | −16.6 | −79.6 | Neg. | Neg. | — | 218.0 |

*Note:* The recession began in 1990 and extended through 1991. The cyclical behavior of Ford Motor is evident.

performance, and valuation. In such side-by-side evaluations, industry-specific nuances are ignored in favor of the broader theme.

A second problem associated with industry classification is self-deception. Once an analyst labels an industry as a growth industry, he (and his audience) is tempted to place subsequent facts that come to light within the growth framework. Pigeonholing an industry helps in telling the investment story, but the experienced analyst doesn't let labels prejudge developments that don't fit the model.

As one illustration, consider the Internet service industry in 1996. Many early investors compared this industry with cable TV in the late 1970s. Both Internet and cable TV were hooked into the home by wire and both required monthly subscription charges. As analysts monitored the Internet services industry more closely, however, they noticed a significant difference. Internet service was not a quasi monopoly like cable TV, and customers switched suppliers more frequently than cable TV subscribers. The Internet industry fell into the growth classification, but practitioners needed a fresh look at its economics. Internet stock prices dropped accordingly in late 1996.

Likewise, the bagel chain industry attracts comparisons with the formerly fast food business. Dennis Lombardi, who heads a restaurant consulting practice, repeated a familiar premise, "There's an awful lot of room for more bagel shops. All you have to do is contrast it to the hamburger chains." With 11,000 restaurants, McDonald's has several times the total number of bagel shops, but the differences are compelling. Hamburgers are viewed as all-American lunch and dinner food. In contrast, bagels occupy the breakfast segment and have an ethnic tradition.

A common error with industry classification occurs when the analyst paints all industry participants with the same brush. Inevitably, not all companies in a *mature* industry are *mature* companies. Beer brewing is a mature industry, yet small microbrewers are considered growth companies. Steel is a cyclical industry, but Nucor's stability defies this classification.

The process of placing an industry into its life cycle and business cycle categories involves performing the work outlined in Exhibit 3. By studying the industry's external influences, demand trends, supply factors, profitability and competition, an analyst forms opinions about its prospects and suitability for investment.

# EXTERNAL FACTORS                    ◢ 4 ◣

No industry operates in a vacuum. Each is subject to numerous outside influences that significantly impact sales and earnings. The first stage of the top-down analysis considers the economic variables that affect industry performance, and the life cycle and business cycle techniques provide direction in this regard. As the industry study unfolds, however, the practitioner examines external factors that aren't purely economic (see Exhibit 9).

External issues fall into five broad categories: technology, government, social changes, demographics, and foreign influences. For each of these categories, there are "big picture" themes that affect a particular industry, and the analyst's job is twofold. One, he avoids the temptation to fall into the role of futuristic visionary. Instead, he concentrates on trends that can demonstrably affect the industry over a three- to five-year period. Two, he addresses the impact of these trends in quantifiable form. It is not enough to say "advances in satellite technology and capacity will fuel the global pager business"; investors want to know the percentage gains in industry sales from these factors. A numerical forecast is better than a vague pronouncement.

| EXHIBIT 9 | Industry Analysis—External Factors Affecting Sales and Profitability |
|---|---|
| Technology | For established industries, the question is: Does the industry face obsolescence from competing technologies? (Typewriters were quickly replaced by word processors in the early 1980s). Infant industries introducing new technologies pose a different question: Will the market accept innovation? |
| Government | Government plays a large role in many industries. New regulations, or changes to old laws, can impact an industry's sales and earnings. In certain cases, government policies create new industries (e.g., the automobile protective safety bag industry). |
| Social changes | Changes in lifestyle spark many industries. The rise of two-earner families fueled growth in the convenience food and restaurant industries. Concern over animal rights hurt the fur retailing industry. |
| Demographics | Demographic shifts are watched by analysts. The "greying" of America supports nursing home stocks. It is also a factor in the rebound of the golf equipment industry, as baby boomers reduce strenuous activity in their later years. |
| Foreign influences | The United States is the largest economy, but its industries are subject to foreign influences. Overseas textile firms decimated the U.S. textile industry. Higher income levels in developing nations, meanwhile, contributed to huge overseas demand for U.S. movies and musical recordings. |

In the majority of research reports, the basic assumption regarding the industry's external environment is that history will repeat itself. Past trends continue into the future, and thus, most industry sales projections are based on time series analysis. Projecting the sales of new industries is more tricky, but 99 percent of public companies are beyond the start-up stage, so analysts extrapolate brief historical results into a forecast. Unless there is a firm basis for a contrary opinion, this rearview-mirror approach is reasonable. As noted earlier, this method encourages complacency, and the analyst relying on it can miss important reversals. Nonetheless, a historical grounding in an industry is a prerequisite for an evaluation of external influences. Exhibit 10 provides an example of the effects of external factors on an industry.

## Technology

The initial analysis of technology focuses on *survival*. Will the industry's product offerings fend off perceived substitutes derived from newer technology?

| EXHIBIT 10 | Sample External Factors Affecting Health Care Industry Sales |
|---|---|

The *"Big Picture"*

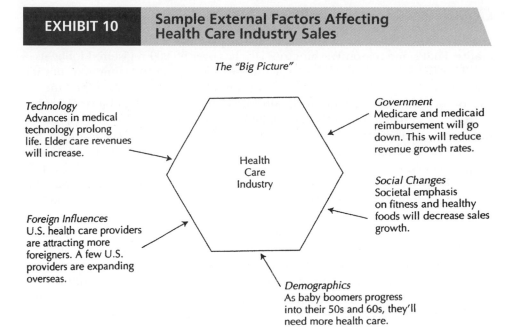

*Technology*
Advances in medical technology prolong life. Elder care revenues will increase.

*Foreign Influences*
U.S. health care providers are attracting more foreigners. A few U.S. providers are expanding overseas.

Health Care Industry

*Government*
Medicare and medicaid reimbursement will go down. This will reduce revenue growth rates.

*Social Changes*
Societal emphasis on fitness and healthy foods will decrease sales growth.

*Demographics*
As baby boomers progress into their 50s and 60s, they'll need more health care.

The eyeglass industry, for example, has prospered for years against several contact lens technologies. The record player industry, in contrast, became obsolete with the introduction of the CD player.

In many cases, an outside technological idea enhances an industry. Gains in the biotechnology area were eventually transferred to the agricultural industry, where they contributed to higher crop yields. Improvements in civil aviation technology led directly to a travel boom, which lifted tourist industry revenues. VCRs represented 100 percent of electric appliance sales growth in the mid-1980s. Current pundits believe digital technology will spur growth in digital TV sales.

Sometimes, a new technology is a blessing and a curse. Nuclear power originated in the defense industry. Transferred to electric utilities, nuclear power was quickly accepted in the 1970s because its variable costs were lower than conventional technologies, such as coal and oil generation. Unforeseen problems in safety and the environment tainted nuclear power in the 1980s, and the related expenses crippled many utilities.

In the case of a new competing technology, the established industry usually has several years to prepare a defense. A common strategic response is either:

1. Copy the competition, as Wal-Mart did in the wholesale club industry with Sam's Wholesale Club (a virtual clone of Price Club).

2. Buy the competition, as IBM's software division did when it acquired Lotus Development Corporation.

Competent managements recognize technological trends and adjust their companies accordingly.

## Government

Government taxes, laws, and regulations impact every industry in the United States. That's one reason Washington, DC, has over 50,000 registered lobbyists.

The federal tax code serves a legitimate revenue raising function, but it's loaded with loopholes designed to serve special interests. For example, the oil exploration industry has depreciation allowances that are far more favorable than those available to the average manufacturing industry. Federal quotas on imported goods provide certain industries with extra benefits. For example, the quota levied on Japanese auto imports protects the sales and earnings of domestic producers. A negative shift in the political fortunes of either the oil exploration industry or the auto industry could result in unfavorable government actions, leading to lower earnings. The analyst's projections would be modified accordingly.

Business organizations complain about regulation, but regulations play a valuable role in promoting worker safety, consumer protection, and fair play. Government influence cuts both ways. Some government agencies practice regulatory overkill that harms industry unnecessarily, but it is a fact that multiple businesses were founded on new government initiatives or rely on government regulation to prosper. If you're a business, what better way to avoid risk than to have the government require a minimum price for your products, set up barriers to foreign imports, or allow you to merge with the competition? Regulation "creep" has continued in Republican and Democratic administrations, and the analysts of the 1990s monitor government developments much more closely than did their 1960s' counterparts.

A recent example of a negative external influence is the government assault on the tobacco industry. By declaring tobacco a drug and placing it under FDA jurisdiction, the government clearly seeks to diminish the industry's prospects. Alternatively, the federal emphasis on environment enforcement is a boon to the environmental services sector. One relatively new industry that received a huge leg up from the government was the cellular phone industry. Rather than sell cellular monopolies to the highest bidder, the government gave the rights away via lottery in the 1980s, saving the operators billions of dollars. State deregulation is sweeping through the electric utilities, and this turning point means dramatic changes for this staid industry.

Consider Paxson Communications Corp., a network of 46 UHF stations that run half-hour informercials most of the day. Faced with limited capacity, many cable TV systems declined to carry these broadcasts, but in March 1997 the U.S. Supreme Court upheld the government's "must carry" rules, requiring cable companies to show any and all local broadcast channels, even Paxson's low-rent UHF programs. On the day of the ruling, the company's share price jumped 30 percent, illustrating the effect of government.

Federal, state, and local government spending accounts for 35 percent of gross national product. Any shifts in the spending patterns of these organizations influence the affected industries. Declines in the defense budget during the 1990s prompted a wave of consolidations among defense contractors. At the local level, the privatization of municipal waste services contributed to revenue gains among waste management firms. Imagine the shift in dollars if the government privatized just a small portion of the public education system!

External factors relating to government play a significant role in the analysis of foreign stocks. Most countries have more restrictive trade regimes than the United States, and local producers get complacent after years of protection. A dramatic liberalization in tariff policy can destroy a local industry that is uncompetitive with the global multinationals. Similarly, nations set up artificial barriers to protect favored industries (and companies) from outside threats. Japan, for example, has a maze of bizarre regulations that limit U.S. agricultural imports, thereby assisting Japanese farmers. Brazil's "local content" rules forestall the importation of cars and ensure the survival of the inefficient local auto industry. Argentina has a special tax on cola drinks, designed to punish Coke and Pepsi bottlers in favor of local fruit drink producers.

## Social Changes

Social factors boil down to lifestyle and fashion changes. In either case, the analyst is ready to evaluate their impacts on the relevant industry.

Of the two social influences, fashion is the more unpredictable, and this complicates the job of researching fashion-oriented industries. The women's fashion cycle, for example, is quite short, and a hot clothing item may only have a shelf life of one, maybe two years, before it is replaced by another style. Baseline sales for the industry trend upward, but fashion changes impact short-term projections. Similar phenomena occur in the toy, recreation, and film industries.

Analysts can mistake a short-term fashion cycle for a long-term trend. In one of my financings, an analyst projected a steady upward move in leather coat sales, despite evidence that demand for such garments historically went through up and down cycles. Three years after the transaction, leather coat sales had dropped by over 20 percent.

Lifestyle changes, in contrast, take place over long periods of time. An increase in health consciousness, for example, resulted in a per capita decline in hard liquor consumption. Given fair warning, several spirits producers, such as Seagram's, responded by diversifying into the production of wine, which increased in popularity over the same time span. The gradual shift of women into the workforce, from 41 percent in 1965 to 58 percent in 1995, and the increasing suburbanization of society, acutely affected the auto industry. Besides spawning a need for two cars per family, these changes prompted the minivan boom, as suburban parents juggled responsibilities for ferrying children to after-school activities.

## Demographics

Demography is the science that studies the vital statistics of population, such as distribution, age, and income. By observing trends in these statistics, analysts develop investment themes regarding various industries. In the United States for example, the age shift of the baby boomers into their 40s and 50s has sparked a strong interest in retirement planning. The result has been higher revenues for money management firms as the boomers put savings into stocks and bonds. In Malaysia, about 50 percent of the population is under the age of 21, and analysts tout local brewing stocks, in anticipation of a large increase in the beer-drinking population. In Indonesia, rising per capita incomes push a demand for electric appliances, giving analysts reason to be optimistic about the future growth of local utilities.

Demographic trends unfold over long periods of time, and they are thus easier to identify and track than other external factors. This circumstance doesn't lead to absolute certainty. Analysts frequently agree on the existence of a trend (e.g., the rising percentage of single-parent families) but disagreement occurs in sizing up its impact on relevant industries.

## Foreign Influences

As global trade expands, industries become sensitive to foreign influences. For example, the U.S. economy's health is heavily dependent on imported oil. Overseas disruptions in the supply/demand dynamic of this resource ripple through several industries, including the oil, chemical, and leisure sectors. Other U.S. industries are under assault from foreign competitors: automobile parts, apparel, and electronics are three of the more popular targets. At the same time, U.S. exports have never been stronger, reflecting the economic liberalization of nations previously keeping out U.S. products.

Reflecting this liberalization theme, analysts evaluate selected industries on a global basis. Demand projections are aggregated by country, and the external influences referred to herein are considered from a global perspective. This approach is appropriate for worldwide commodity businesses such as oil, metals, and agricultural products, although it is applied at times to categories such as defense, semiconductors, and airlines.

## Keeping Your Focus

Big-picture trends are interesting to study, but undisciplined research does little to advance an equity evaluation. Isolating the critical elements in an external analysis is difficult and most research reports fail in this regard. The reports often present outside factors that resemble a jumble of competing influences, and the identifiable opportunities for an industry seem canceled out by the emerging threats. The end result: analysts extrapolate the past into the future, and fail to uncover compelling changes that can move an industry's sales off historical trends. As noted earlier, this rearview-mirror method is appropriate for many industries, but an incisive effort is required either to unlock an industry's potential or to spot its incumbent weakness.

Two external reviews are set forth in the following case studies.

---

### CASE STUDY

#### Cable TV Industry

The cable TV industry is a latter stage growth business. It is a defensive industry in terms of the business cycle, with growth aspects. Most U.S. homes have been wired for cable TV, but the industry is still grabbing advertising dollars away from the broadcast networks. Cable TV is fundamentally a regulated monopoly, and regulators generally allow monthly subscriber charges to track inflation.

December 1996 research reports emphasized the influence of technology and government in the industry's future, as shown in Exhibit 11.

The external factors were largely positive in 1996, and analysts concluded that the cable TV industry's above-average revenue growth rate would continue. Higher pay-TV revenues and increased channel availability would enable the industry to garner a growing share of ad revenues, while docile regulators would rubber-stamp inflation-driven subscriber rates. Direct broadcast satellite service, an obvious cable TV substitute was a minor threat. It had just a 3 percent market share in TV homes and its premium service (and rates) were acceptable to only high-end consumers.

---

| EXHIBIT 11 | Cable TV Industry External Factors and Related Threats |
|---|---|

## Technology

*Opportunities*

Improved pay TV technology increases revenues.

More compression means more channels *and* more revenues.

New technology permits phone service over cable lines.

*Threats*

Improved technology enhances the direct broadcast satellite (DBS) industry's ability to attract customers.

Technology may be available for phone companies to send TV programming through telephone wires.

## Government

*Opportunities*

There is no political will to cut the industry's monthly subscriber rates.

Liberal regulatory policies expand cable merger options to phone companies and software providers.

After new telecommunications law passed, U.S. West (5th largest telephone company) agreed to merge with Continental Cablevision (third largest cable TV company).

*Threats*

Regulators can change their minds on subscriber fees.

New law allows phone companies to compete in cable TV. These companies are larger and have more resources than most cable firms.

## Social Changes

*Opportunities*

No significant opportunities were gleaned from existing social trends.

*Threats*

American television viewing on a per capita basis is up 5% from 1990 to 1995, but it may be reaching a saturation point at 4.3 hours per day.

## Demographics

No significant opportunities or threats are apparent from underlying demographic changes.

## Foreign Influences

The industry's customers and principal suppliers are located in the United States. Foreign influences are practically nil.

## CASE STUDY

### Trucking Industry

The trucking industry is divided into two sectors, the long-haul business, whereby a full truckload is shipped long distances over several days; and the short-haul business, which consists primarily of less than full loads shipped within a 200-mile radius. Trucking is a cyclical industry, and its volumes are directly correlated to industrial production. The industry also follows a capacity cycle. The industry over-expands during good times, and new trucks may be running half empty when the economy is prospering. Labor costs are 60 percent of sales and qualified drivers are hard to find. This capacity problem and labor issue can lead to rate cuts in good economic times and lower profits. The primary competitors are railroads in the long-haul segment and air freight companies in the short-haul business. Exhibit 12 lists external factors affecting the trucking industry.

No external factors threaten the industry's survival. Trucking is going to be with us for a long time, but serious issues involve new competition and a driver shortage, with few counterbalancing opportunities. External factors contribute to the consensus belief that trucking industry revenues will grow slower than the general economy. Future profitability will be below average.

| EXHIBIT 12 | Trucking Industry External Factors and Related Threats |
|---|---|

**Technology**

*Opportunities*

Growing use of on-board computers and satellite tracking improve delivery times for truckers.

Just-in-time-inventory acceptance is helping truckers vis-à-vis railroads.

*Threats*

Railroads' introduction of *Roadrailer* (a trailer equipped with highway and rail wheels) and the *Iron Highway* (a flexible train that facilitates truck trailer hauling) brings new competitive threats to the short-haul market.

**Government**

*Opportunities*
No significance.

*Threats*

The federal government is permitting large railroad mergers, which will increase pressure on the long-haul segment.

New safety regulations tighten the driver licensing process, acerbating a shortage of drivers.

Government is cutting back its loan program to truck driving schools, thus contributing to the driver shortage.

*(Exhibit continued on next page . . .)*

## EXHIBIT 12 (continued)

### Social Changes

| *Opportunities* | *Threats* |
|---|---|
| Increasing acceptance of women and minorities as truck drivers could relieve driver shortage. | Desire to spend more time at home reduces pool of applicants, as people choose alternative professions. |

### Demographics

| *Opportunities* | *Threats* |
|---|---|
| No special issues. | Truck driving is a younger person's profession. The baby boom years (1946–1964) were followed by a birth decline, so there's a smaller pool of eligible drivers. |

### Foreign Influences

The trucking industry's customers and principal suppliers are located in the United States, except for oil, which is 50% imported. Gasoline costs account for 15% to 20% of revenues, but gas prices are reasonably stable.

# DEMAND ANALYSIS                5

The ultimate purpose of preparing an economic analysis, industry life cycle placement, and external factor review is an assessment of future demand for the industry's products. Applying such study to numerical forecasts is accomplished differently, as discussed below:

1. *Top-down economic analysis.* We look for specific macroeconomic variables that affect an industry's sales. An ideal situation is when revenues correlate strongly to one economic statistic, thus reducing the need for multiple forecast inputs. Cement demand growth in Mexico, for example, is historically $1.7 \times$ GNP growth. Analysts, as a result, rely on GNP forecasts to project cement unit volume.

2. *Industry life cycle.* Categorizing the industry within its life cycle position (or its business cycle sensitivity) provides a framework for demand forecasts. The U.S. food industry is "mature," so unit sales should track GNP and population growth. The Internet industry is "growing," and this characterization provides a guide to above-normal sales increases.

**3.** *External factors.* Many outside factors are fairly stable, and their impact on an industry are easily predictable. Others are highly variable, and thus bring an element of uncertainty into the analysis. Including these items, items into a sales forecast is a qualitative exercise, requiring judgment.

By considering the preceding three major themes, the analyst establishes a future sales line for the industry. Most times, this sales trend turns out to be an extrapolation of past history, as suggested by the trend line for the established industry in Exhibit 13, but not always. Sometimes, careful study reveals the likelihood of a turning point that affects the industry's fortunes dramatically. Even an extrapolation result provides useful insights. For example, the water service industry has shown a 7 percent growth rate. Suppose your analysis indicates a continuation of the trend, but only at 5 percent. The 2 percent difference leads you to believe the industry's prospects are overblown, and you sell your shareholdings while prices are still high. In Exhibit 13, a mild decrease in the growth rate produces 10 percent lower sales in the future.

Once a trend has been forecast, the analyst's next step is studying the industry's customers. Where does the demand originate? Who's buying and why?

## Customer Study

A forecast of aggregate demand is helpful, but a full understanding of what drives an industry's revenue is achieved through learning the customers. Since a typical industry serves thousands of clients, evaluating them individually is impossible. Segmenting the customers into submarkets, on the other hand, enables the analyst to study a smaller number of factors that contribute to demand. As he sequentially studies each submarket, he builds an aggregate demand profile, submarket by submarket.

For example, the demand forecast for the Mexican cement market relied heavily on GNP trends. As a backup to this methodology, I subdivided the market into five segments and considered demand in each segment to verify the accu-

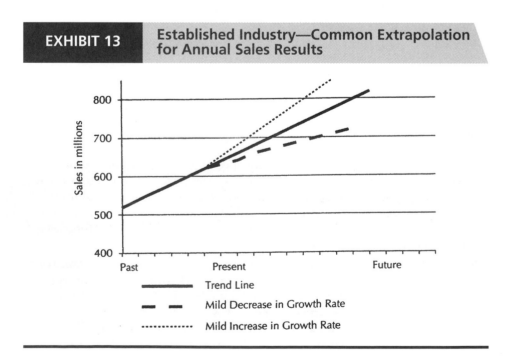

**EXHIBIT 13**    **Established Industry—Common Extrapolation for Annual Sales Results**

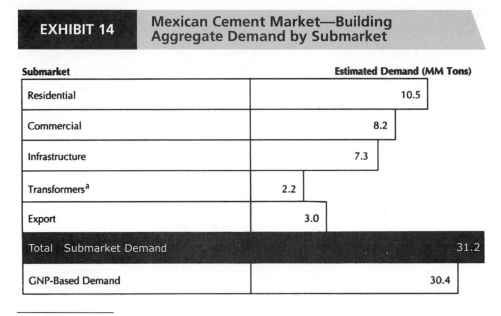

| EXHIBIT 14 | Mexican Cement Market—Building Aggregate Demand by Submarket |
|------------|-------------------------------------------------------------|

| Submarket | Estimated Demand (MM Tons) |
|-----------|----------------------------|
| Residential | 10.5 |
| Commercial | 8.2 |
| Infrastructure | 7.3 |
| Transformers[a] | 2.2 |
| Export | 3.0 |
| **Total   Submarket Demand** | **31.2** |
| GNP-Based Demand | 30.4 |

[a] Manufacturing of concrete block, concrete pipe, and so on.

racy of the GNP multiplier. Both methods revealed a likely demand around 31 million tons, including exports (see Exhibit 14).

In Exhibit 14, I categorized the submarkets by usage: homebuilding, infrastructure projects, and commercial construction. But demand segments can be classified by different definitions. David Aaker, a noted business strategist, divides segments between customer characteristics and product-related approaches. Exhibit 15 shows samples from the U.S. market.

A careful analyst studies demand on the basis of several submarket classifications. Following Dr. Aaker's advice, I examined Mexican cement forecasts on a geographic basis. I divided Mexico into five regions and looked at individual market need (see Exhibit 16). In this instance, the GNP, usage, and geographic methods delivered aggregate forecasts that were highly correlated. Utilizing multiple approaches is a good double check for any sales forecast.

**Established Industries**   For established industries, the analyst should contact long-time customers to figure what drives demand in each submarket. What guides the customer's buying decisions? How does it differ by submarket? What changes are occurring in the customer's motivation? What implication will they have on industry revenues? Discussions with customers and a study of buying habits indicate whether prior trends continue.

For example, VCRs captured 70 percent of the U.S. housing market after ten years. Unit growth dropped in the 1990s. Personal computers represent a newer appliance. They appear in 32 percent of U.S. homes but are concentrated in the higher income households. This low penetration (relative to VCRs) promotes a high growth rate until computer saturation occurs in all income segments (see Exhibit 17).

**Growth Industries**   A growth industry has yet to penetrate all its future submarkets. In addition to researching the existing customer base, the analyst considers new outlets for the industry's products. The pager business, for example, was

| EXHIBIT 15 | Approaches to Defining Demand Segments |
|---|---|

| Customer Characteristics | Demand Segment |
|---|---|
| Geographic | Southern region as a market for trendy clothing versus the West Coast |
| Type of business | Computer needs of restaurants versus manufacturing firms versus banks versus retailers |
| Size of firm | Large hospital versus midsize versus small |
| Lifestyle | Tendency of Jaguar buyers to be more adventurous, less conservative than buyers of Mercedes-Benz |
| Sex | The Virginia Slims cigarettes for women |
| Age | Cereals for children versus adults |
| Occupation | The paper copier needs of lawyers versus dentists |

| Product-Related Approaches | Demand Segment |
|---|---|
| User type | Appliance buyer—home builder, homeowner, small business |
| Usage | The heavy potato users—the fast-food outlets |
| Benefits sought | Dessert eaters—those who are calorie-conscious versus those who are more concerned with convenience |
| Price sensitivity | Price-sensitive Honda Civic buyer versus the luxury Mercedes-Benz buyer |
| Competitor | Those computer users now committed to IBM |
| Application | Professional users of chain saws versus the homeowner |
| Brand loyalty | Those committed to IBM versus others |

*Source: Developing Business Strategies*, by David Aaker (New York: John Wiley & Sons, Inc., 1995).

confined to businesspeople. In recent years, it has expanded to personal use. Fast-food chains were selling to the lunch and dinner market. In the 1980s, they attracted the breakfast segment. Identifying a new use or user group is important to confirming a growth industry's upward movement.

**Untested Industries**   Some publicly-traded companies furnish a truly new product or service. Given a minimal level of product acceptance, these firms have little or no track record from which the analyst can build a sales forecast. Although the risk profile of these stocks is higher than most, the decision process is not entirely speculative.

## EXHIBIT 16 — Mexican Cement Market: Building Aggregate Demand by Submarket Geographic Basis

| Geographic Market | Estimated Demand (MM Tons) |
|---|---|
| Central Mexico | 11.2 |
| Northern Gulf | 5.9 |
| South Mexico | 5.2 |
| Central Pacific | 3.2 |
| North Pacific | 2.2 |
| Export | 3.0 |
| **Total Geographic Market Demand** | **30.7** |
| Submarket Based Demand | 31.2 |
| GNP-Based Demand | 30.4 |

A first step is determining whether the new industry fulfills a need that (1) exists, and (2) isn't being met by another industry. The managed care industry was founded in response to the urgent need of corporations to cut employee medical costs. Assuming a need is verified, analysts typically forecast new industry sales based on the experience of a similar industry.

One illustration is the office products superstore industry, as typified by Office Depot and Staples. No sooner did these two companies go public than analysts settled into a comparison with discount warehouse clubs, such as Price Club and Costco. Market share and saturation levels for Office Depot and Staples were calculated on models similar to the warehouse club experience. For every 250,000 people in a metropolitan market, for example, analysts figured one warehouse club could succeed. After some observation, they used similar logic in quantifying 25,000 white collar workers and 100,000 people per office products superstore.

## EXHIBIT 17 — Comparable Household Penetration: Two Electronic Products

| | 1980 | 1985 | 1990 |
|---|---|---|---|
| VCR | 2% | 37% | 70% |

| | 1985 | 1990 | 1995 |
|---|---|---|---|
| Personal computers | 10% | 23% | 32% |

| EXHIBIT 18 | Demand Analysis Model for the Hotel Furniture Market |
| --- | --- |

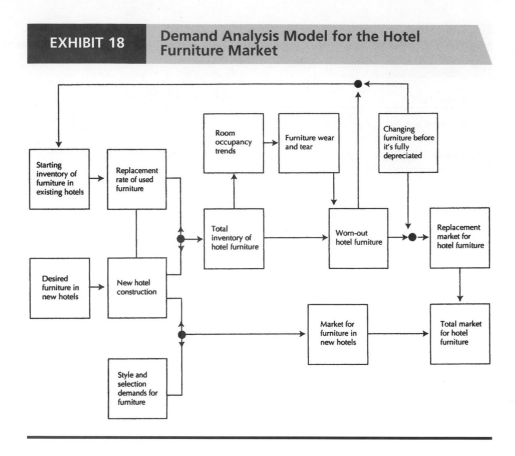

## Input/Output and Industry Demand Forecasts

Input-output analysis observes the flow of goods and services through the production process, including intermediate steps as the goods proceed raw-material to finished product. A rising consumption of the finished product boosts demand for industries supplying the intermediate steps. For example, the personal computer boom elevates the demand for the semiconductor, an important PC component.

If one industry is a major customer of another, an analyst uses input-output analysis to derive partial demand for the latter's products. Alternatively, the higher consumption of one industry's offerings sparks demand for complementary products. The wide-scale introduction of the VCR boosted the video rental business. In the 1980s, analysts calculated video demand through algebraic formulas based on VCR purchases. A typical formula was that one VCR purchase meant three video rentals per month. The demand models can be complex and contain many variables. Exhibit 18 shows one rendition for the hotel furniture market.

## 6    SUPPLY ANALYSIS IN THE INDUSTRY STUDY

In reviewing industries, analysts spend most of their time studying *demand* trends. They usually assume the supply side of the equation takes care of itself. If industry revenues are rising, more investment pours in. If revenues are declining, existing capacity services the falling demand. This model is valid in the long term, but its applicability over the short to intermediate term varies by industry.

The temporary help industry fits the classic model well. With its emphasis on low-skilled workers, the industry can find new employees quickly, thus ramping up capacity in a short time. In contrast, supply that is dependent on capital intensive producers is a different story. Steel and packaging require three- to five-year periods to build plants that add capacity. Industries that use highly skilled workers, such as software, can face short-term capacity constraints as they wait for training programs to provide new employees.

## Projecting Supply Availability

Supply is a function of unused capacity and the ability to bring on new capacity. Interpreting these variables well enough to make a reasonable forecast is complicated. That's why few analysts attempt the job. Ideally, a supply forecast dovetails with a demand forecast, and the analyst has an idea about future market equilibrium. If future supply and demand are out of balance, prices for the industry's products will be affected unless the suppliers change their behavior in time. The ideal research report has a supply/demand graph like the one shown in Exhibit 19. In this case, the graph predicts a future capacity problem.

The supply projection is easiest when the industry has only a few competitors, generating output at a discrete number of sizable facilities. It also helps if the industry's economics make imports prohibitively expensive, so the analyst can ignore foreign capacity. The cement industry is a good example of this model. First, only large plants, with long construction lead times, make cement. Second, the low value per ton makes transportation uneconomical beyond a 250-mile radius from the plant. Thus, it's a simple matter to forecast available supply: An analyst counts nearby capacity and adds expansions planned for the next three to five years.

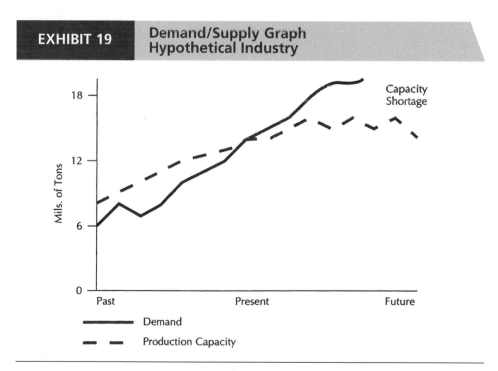

**EXHIBIT 19**    **Demand/Supply Graph Hypothetical Industry**

*Note:* There's a capacity shortage in the future. This could mean higher product prices.

| EXHIBIT 20 | 1996 Mexican Cement Market Availability of Supply Calculation (Millions of Tons per Year) | | | |
|---|---|---|---|---|
|  | **1996** | **1997** | **1998** | **1999** |
| 1996 capacity | 36.0 | 36.0 | 36.0 | 36.0 |
| 1997 additions, net | — | 1.0 | 1.0 | 1.0 |
| 1998 additions, net | — | — | 3.7 | 3.7 |
| 1999 additions, net | — | — | — | 1.3 |
| Total estimated capacity | 36.0 | 37.0 | 40.7 | 42.0 |

*Note:* Additions are net of closures.

| EXHIBIT 21 | 1996 Supply/Demand Forecast Mexican Cement Industry | | | |
|---|---|---|---|---|
|  | **1996** | **1997** | **1998** | **1999** |
| Available capacity | 36.0 | 37.0 | 40.7 | 42.0 |
| Expected demand | 31.0 | 33.0 | 35.5 | 38.0 |
| Capacity utilization | 86% | 89% | 87% | 90.5% |

In Mexico, for example, this process is straightforward. The cement market is dominated by two companies operating just 29 plants, and their expansion plans are public knowledge. All plants have ample reserves of raw materials. An illustrative calculation for supply appears in Exhibit 20.

The forecast demand for cement is matched against the supply trend, as shown in Exhibit 21. The chart shows capacity utilization rates exceeding 88 percent from 1996 to 1999, which is considered *high* for the industry. The projection suggests that additional capacity be initiated.

## 7 PROFITABILITY, PRICING, AND THE INDUSTRY STUDY

A security analyst wants to select profitable industries. What's the point of investing in growth industries if sales go up, but profits go down? A supply/demand forecast gives an indication of future profitability. If supply appears to be in line with demand, industry earnings will probably stay on their trend line. Indeed, profitability is vital for industries to make the investment needed to increase supply. A projected oversupply will retard investment since it augurs lower prices. A 1997 study by Lehman Brothers predicted sharply lower prices for copper (from 110¢/lb. to 60¢/lb.), resulting from prospective increases in mining capacity.

Factors contributing to *pricing* include:

► Product segmentation.
► Degree of industry concentration.
► Ease of industry entry.
► Price changes in key supply inputs.

To begin, most industries effectively segment their product offerings by brand name, reputation, or service, even when the products are quite similar. Over-the-counter medicines are one example. The ingredients of the store brand and the name-brand are typically identical, yet the name-brand product has a 40 percent price premium.

An industry with a high degree of concentration inhibits price movements. Assuming that demand and supply are in reasonable balance, the major players have an incentive to engage in monopolistic behavior. Artificially high prices can be sustained by price signaling, confidential agreements, and other means. Outsiders have problems breaking into the inner circle to learn what's going on. In Mexico's cement market, for example, the two major producers control 85 percent of the market, and they barely hide the fact that collusion exists. In several U.S. industries, similar behavior occurs, but it's kept behind closed doors.

Monopolies promote artificial pricing, and an industry's ease of entry is a key variable in holding prices to the free market model. Semiconductor production poses an obvious problem; the entry ticket—a new plant—costs $1 billion. The specialty retailing industry, in contrast, is wide-open. An entrepreneur can rent store space, lease fixtures, and stock inventory for less than $75,000.

Certain industries rely heavily on one or two inputs. Price changes in these inputs affect products costs and profitability. Sometimes, the industry can pass through increased costs in the form of higher prices. At other times, competitive pressures stand in the way. In 1996, for example, the price of corn, a key chicken feed, reached historical highs. Poultry producers, such as Tyson Foods and WLR Corp., were unable to raise prices enough to compensate and their profitability fell.

## Industry Profitability Is Important

Supply/demand analysis, cost factors, and pricing flexibility are critical elements in determining future industry profitability. Without earnings, an industry can't finance the commitment to personnel, plant, and research and development that is needed to prosper. An industry with a poor profit outlook is an unlikely investment candidate indeed.

# INTERNATIONAL COMPETITION AND MARKETS
8

## Competition

Competitive analysis is the topic of many books. Michael Porter of the Harvard Business School, is a leader in the field, and approaches competition from multiple directions, as set forth in Exhibit 22. Security analysis synthesizes the work of experts like Dr. Porter, and this section provides a brief treatment of the subject.

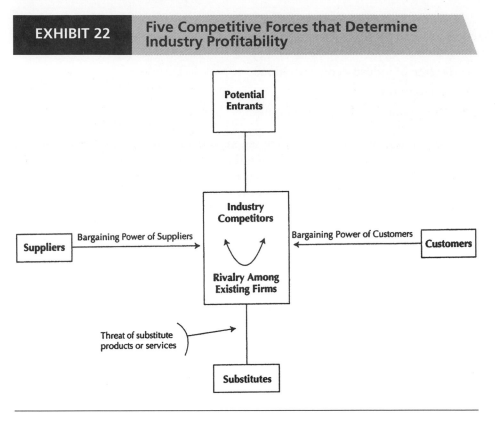

| EXHIBIT 22 | Five Competitive Forces that Determine Industry Profitability |

*Source: Competitive Advantage*, by Michael E. Porter (New York: The Free Press, 1985).

A first step in the competitive analysis is defining the industry. While this task was discussed earlier, it is helpful to remember that some analysts cover the chemical industry; some follow the chemical fertilizer industry; and still others research the specialty chemical industry. Industries are segmented into smaller industries. *Institutional Investor* magazine divides the computer industry into seven subindustries: computer services, data networking, the Internet, PC hardware, PC software, server and enterprise hardware, and server and enterprise software. Placing your company into its subindustry and identifying its competitors becomes the second step in your competitive analysis.

For each competitor, the analyst develops an appreciation of its business strategy and its effects on the company under study. For example, in the managed care business, Aetna pursues a national program. Physician Health Services focuses on the Southeast region. Managed Care Solutions sticks to Medicaid managed care. If Aetna shifted to Medicaid contracts, it would harm Managed Care Solutions' prospects.

Finally, the analyst is advised to outline the strengths and weaknesses of industry participants. Exhibit 23 illustrates many of the items considered in such an outline. Financial track record and balance sheet strength are priorities for analysts, but a review of other factors reveals whether better results can be achieved by the competition, perhaps at the expense of the subject company. Similarly, if the subject company's strengths dominate areas where the competition is weak, a higher degree of confidence is gained for your forecasts.

Each industry has a few dominant success factors that can be drawn from Exhibit 23. Analysts (and corporate strategists) inventory these items and the relative positions of competitors. Exhibit 24 presents this comparative analysis in tabular form.

| EXHIBIT 23 | Competitive Analysis: Analysis of Strengths and Weaknesses of Each Industry Participant |
|---|---|

| **Innovation** | **Management** |
|---|---|
| Technical product or service superiority | Quality of top and middle management |
| New product capability | Knowledge of business |
| Research & development | Culture |
| Technologies | Strategic goals and plans |
| Patents | Entrepreneurial thrust |
| | Planning/operation system |
| | Loyalty—turnover |
| | Quality of strategic decision making |

| **Manufacturing** | **Marketing** |
|---|---|
| Cost structure | Product quality reputation |
| Flexible production operations | Product characteristics/differentiation |
| Equipment | Brand-name recognition |
| Access to raw material | Breadth of product line—systems capability |
| Vertical integration | Customer orientation |
| Workforce attitude and motivation | Segmentation/focus |
| Capacity | Distribution |
| | Retailer relationship |
| | Advertising/promotion skills |
| | Sales force |
| | Customer service/product support |

| **Finance—Access to Capital** | **Customer Base** |
|---|---|
| From operations | Size and loyalty |
| From cash on hand | Market share |
| Ability to use debt and equity financing | Growth of segments served |

*Source: Developing Business Strategies*, by David Aaker (New York: John Wiley & Sons, Inc., 1995).

A firm's ability to sustain its sales and earnings is highly dependent on the status of the competition. Does the subject company have the ability to be aggressive—take the offense? Or, does it have to protect market share and husband financial resources—play defense? The competitor profile facilitates game theory for the practitioner.

| EXHIBIT 24 | Sample Competitor Analysis for a Research Report | | | |
|---|---|---|---|---|
| | **Major Competitors** | | | |
| **Competition Indicators** | **A** | **B** | **C** | **D** |
| Market position | Vulnerable | Prevalent | Strong | Vulnerable |
| Profitability | Low | Average | Average | Average |
| Financial strength | Low | High | Unknown | Low |
| Product mix | Narrow | Broad | Narrow | Narrow |
| Technological capability | Average | Strong | Average | Weak |
| Product quality | Minimum | Good | Satisfactory | Minimum |

Source: *Management Policy, Strategy and Plans,* by Milton Leontiades (New York: Little, Brown & Company, 1982).

## International Competition

The world is becoming a smaller place and industries increasingly reflect a globalization theme. This characterization is most advanced with commodity industries such as oil, metals, and basic foodstuffs, but it also dominates intermediate sectors such as textiles, semiconductors, and chemicals. Indeed, about 40 percent of the S&P 500's earnings are connected to international activities.

The United States is the leading economy, has the greatest number of publicly traded securities, and operates the most developed financial markets. For these reasons, the security analysis profession has made great strides here. The downside of this situation has been a nearsightedness on the part of many United States practitioners. Even though industries extend globally, Wall Street research often stops at the U.S. border, and analysts frequently give short shrift to corporate foreign operations and international trends. As institutions emphasize global research, more work will be dedicated to this important area.

# SUMMARY

The industry analysis is a continuation of the top-down approach. By studying the industry, its external environment, demand and supply balance, likely profitability and competitive situation, the security analyst confirms whether the industry is appropriate for investment. The written research report only presents a limited amount of information and practitioners highlight a few key factors in reviewing an industry. Frequently, their audience prefers a one-word summary in the industry review, such as *growth, mature,* or *decline.* With a knowledge of the industry terrain, the analyst proceeds to a specific stock selection. Which of the participants are the winners? Which are the losers?

$4\frac{5}{8}$

$5\frac{1}{2}$ $5\frac{1}{2}$ $-$

$5\frac{1}{2}$ $5\frac{1}{2}$ $-\frac{1}{16}$

$20\frac{5}{8}$ $21\frac{13}{16}$ $-\frac{1}{4}$

$17\frac{3}{8}$ $18\frac{1}{8}$ $+$ $\frac{7}{8}$

$18\frac{1}{2}$ $6\frac{1}{2}$ $6\frac{1}{2}$ $-$ $\frac{1}{2}$

$7\frac{1}{4}$ $6\frac{1}{2}$ $3\frac{1}{32}$ $-$ $\frac{1}{8}$

$15\frac{1}{16}$

$9\frac{1}{16}$ $\frac{9}{16}$

$\frac{9}{32}$ $9\frac{1}{16}$ $7\frac{15}{16}$

$7\frac{15}{16}$ $7\frac{13}{16}$

$2\frac{5}{8}$ $2\frac{11}{32}$ $2\frac{1}{2}$ $+$

$2\frac{3}{4}$ $2\frac{1}{4}$ $2\frac{1}{4}$

$6\frac{1}{8}$ $12\frac{1}{16}$ $11\frac{3}{8}$ $11\frac{1}{4}$ $+$

$87$ $33\frac{3}{4}$ $33$ $33\frac{1}{8}$ $-$

$602$ $25\frac{5}{8}$ $24\frac{9}{16}$ $25\frac{3}{8}$ $+$

$833$ $12$ $11\frac{5}{8}$ $11\frac{7}{8}$ $+$

$16$ $10\frac{1}{2}$ $10\frac{1}{2}$ $10\frac{1}{2}$ $-$

$78$ $15\frac{5}{8}$ $15\frac{13}{16}$ $15\frac{1}{8}$ $-$

$4508$ $9\frac{1}{16}$ $8\frac{1}{4}$ $8\frac{1}{8}$ $+$

$430$ $11\frac{1}{4}$ $10\frac{1}{8}$ $10\frac{1}{8}$

$5$ $4\frac{1}{8}$

# VALUATION IN EMERGING MARKETS

by Tim Koller, Marc Goedhart, and David Wessels

## LEARNING OUTCOMES

| The candidate should be able to: | Mastery |
|---|---|
| **a.** describe how inflation affects the estimation of cash flows for a company domiciled in an emerging market; | ☐ |
| **b.** calculate nominal and real-term financial projections in order to prepare a discounted cash flow valuation of an emerging market company; | ☐ |
| **c.** discuss the arguments for adjusting cash flows, rather than adjusting the discount rate, to account for emerging market risks (e.g., inflation, macroeconomic volatility, capital control, and political risk) in a scenario analysis; | ☐ |
| **d.** estimate the cost of capital for emerging market companies, and calculate and interpret a country risk premium. | ☐ |

The emerging economies in Asia and South America will experience strong growth over the next decades; many analysts see China and India moving into the ranks of the world's largest economies.[1] This sometimes spectacular economic development will produce many situations requiring sound analysis and valuation. In the rising number of privatizations, joint ventures, mergers and acquisitions, local financial parties such as banks and capital markets will display growing sophistication. Institutional investors will also continue to diversify their portfolios, adding international holdings in emerging-market stocks.

In this reading we focus on issues that arise in financial analysis and valuation of businesses in emerging markets. Valuation is much more difficult in these

---

Special thanks to our colleagues William Jones and Gustavo Wigman, who contributed to this reading.

[1] See, for example, D. Wilson and R. Purushothaman, "Dreaming with BRICs: The Path to 2050" (Global Economics paper no. 99, Goldman Sachs & Co., October 2003).

environments because of risks and obstacles to businesses, including great macroeconomic uncertainty, illiquid capital markets, controls on the flow of capital into and out of the country, less-rigorous accounting standards and disclosure levels, and high levels of political risk. Academics, investment bankers, and industry practitioners have yet to agree on how to address these challenges. Methods vary considerably and practitioners often make arbitrary adjustments based on intuition and limited empirical evidence.

With agreement lacking and emerging-market valuations so complex, we recommend a triangulation approach—comparing estimates of the value from three methods. First, we use discounted cash flows with probability-weighted scenarios that explicitly model the risks the business faces. Then we compare the value obtained from this approach with the results of two secondary approaches: a DCF approach with a country risk premium built into the cost of capital, and a valuation based on comparable trading and transaction multiples.

The basics of estimating a DCF value are the same in emerging markets as elsewhere. Therefore, we focus on complications specific to emerging-market valuations:

> ▶ handling foreign exchange rates, inflation, and interest rate gaps with developed markets consistently when making financial projections
> ▶ factoring inflation into historical financial analysis and cash flow projections
> ▶ incorporating special emerging-market risks consistently in the valuation
> ▶ estimating the cost of capital in emerging markets
> ▶ using market-based references such as trading multiples and transaction multiples when interpreting and calibrating valuation results

We will apply our valuation approach in this reading to ConsuCo, a leading Brazilian manufacturer of consumer goods.[2]

## 1    EXCHANGE RATES, INFLATION, AND INTEREST RATE GAPS

Because exchange rates, inflation, and interest rates can fluctuate wildly from year to year in emerging markets, assumptions underlying estimates of future financial results in domestic or foreign currency and cost of capital must be consistent. Some fundamental monetary assumptions should be defined consistently to avoid any biases in the valuation results. This becomes even more important when you value companies in emerging markets.

The components of the cash flows of emerging-market companies are often denominated in several currencies. Consider an oil exporter. Its revenues are determined by the dollar price of oil, while many of its costs (labor and domestic

---

[2] This case illustration is a disguised example.

purchases) are determined by the domestic currency. If foreign-exchange rates would perfectly reflect inflation differentials—so that purchasing power parity would hold—the company's operating margins and cash flows in real terms would be unaffected. In that case, changes in exchange rates would be irrelevant for valuation purposes.

However, at least in the short run, this does not always hold, because in emerging markets, exchange rates move far and fast. For example, in Argentina at the end of 2001, the exchange rate rose from 1.0 peso per U.S. dollar to nearly 1.9 pesos per U.S. dollar in 15 days, and to 3.1 in less than 4 months. During a period of just a couple of weeks in 1999, Brazil's currency, the Real, weakened by more than 50 percent relative to the U.S. dollar.

When estimating the impact of exchange rate movements on cash flow forecasts, keep in mind that evidence shows that, over the long run, purchasing power parity does hold,[3] even between emerging and developed economies. In other words, exchange rates ultimately do adjust for differences in inflation between countries. For example, if you held $100 million of Brazilian currency in 1964, by 2004 it would have been practically worthless in U.S. dollars. Yet, if we adjust for purchasing power, the value of the currency didn't change very much, as Exhibit 1 shows. In other words, suppose that, instead of holding $100 million of Brazilian currency, you held $100 million of assets in Brazil whose value increased with inflation. In 2004, your assets would have been worth about $90 million (in real terms). Therefore, when you perform valuations, your best assumption is that purchasing power parity holds in the long term; any other approach implies taking a bet on future real exchange rate movements.

Nevertheless, as Exhibit 1 also shows, exchange rates can deviate from purchasing power parity (PPP) by as much as 20 percent to 30 percent for several years (keeping in mind that PPP-adjusted exchange rates are difficult to

**EXHIBIT 1      Brazilian PPP-Adjusted Dollar Exchange Rates**

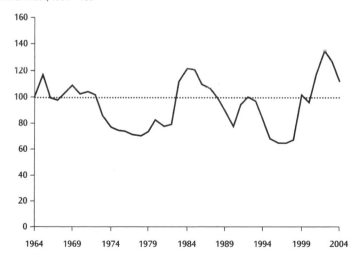

Reais per U.S. dollar index, 1964 = 100

*Source:* MCM Consultants, IMF International Financial Statistics.

---

[3] For a recent overview, see Alan M. Taylor and Mark Peter Taylor, "The Purchasing Power Parity Debate" (CEPR discussion paper no. 4495, 2004).

estimate). Therefore, before making financial projections, assess whether the current exchange rate is over- or undervalued on a PPP basis and, if so, by how much. Then model the convergence of currency rates to purchasing power parity, and reflect its impact on the company's profitability in your long-term financial projections. Because it is hard to predict how long the current PPP deviation will persist, you could conduct a sensitivity analysis to assess the valuation impact of the timing of the return to purchasing power parity. As you develop your forecasts, remember your overall perspective about the economics of the business. The long-term sustainable operating profit margin and ROIC should not be affected by any short-term deviations from PPP. Relying on a set of fundamental monetary assumptions keeps your projections consistent with your cost of capital whether you project in domestic, foreign, real, or nominal currency.

Regardless of any short- or long-term economic exposure to varying exchange rates, your valuation results should be independent of the currency or mix of currencies in which you forecast the company's cash flows. Use actual or synthetic forward exchange rates to convert any future cash flow into another currency. In many emerging economies, the forward-exchange market is nonexistent or illiquid, so actual forward rates provide little guidance on likely future exchange rate movements or inflation differentials. In that case, estimate a synthetic forward rate from your assumptions about future inflation and interest rates for the currencies concerned.

## 2    FACTORING INFLATION INTO HISTORICAL ANALYSIS AND FORECASTS

Even with consistent assumptions about inflation, interest rates, and foreign exchange rates, sound analysis and forecasting of the financial performance of emerging-market companies remains challenging. Inflation distorts the financial statements, so it is hard to make year-to-year historical comparisons, perform ratio analysis, or forecast performance.

For companies operating in high-inflation environments, historical analysis and forecasting should be carried out in both nominal and real (constant currency) terms whenever possible. As we will explain, nominal indicators are sometimes not meaningful (e.g., for capital turnover), and in other cases, real indicators are problematic (e.g., to determine corporate income taxes). Proper valuation requires insights from both nominal- and real-terms historical analyses. Financial projections can be made in real or nominal terms or both; properly done projections should yield an identical value.

### Historical Analysis

Accounting conventions in emerging markets often differ substantially from those of developed markets, so a company's economics may be difficult to understand. Furthermore, in many countries, complicated tax credits and adjustments make cash taxes harder to estimate than in developed markets. For example, Brazil has made large and frequent changes to its tax code. Brazil eliminated inflation accounting and reduced the corporate tax rate to 30.5 percent in 1996, and in 1997 disallowed the deductibility of the social contribution tax, effectively increasing the tax rate to 33 percent. To make up for the loss of the tax shields that inflation accounting had generated, Brazil's government allowed companies to deduct deemed interest on equity net of a withholding tax of 15 percent.

Large accounting and tax differences are frequently eliminated when the income statement and the balance sheet are brought together in the cash flow calculation. Still, before starting a valuation, you need to understand these differences. Unfortunately, the differences across emerging markets are too complex and varied for a detailed discussion in this reading. Instead, we highlight the most common issues involving the impact of high inflation on your historical analysis.

In countries experiencing extreme inflation (more than 25 percent per year), companies often report in year-end currency. In the income statement, items such as revenues and costs that were booked throughout the year are restated at year-end purchasing power. Otherwise, the addition of these items would not be meaningful. The balance sheet usually has adjustments to fixed assets, inventory, and equity; the accounts payable and receivable are already in year-end terms.

In most countries, however, financial statements are not adjusted to reflect the effects of inflation. If inflation is high, this leads to distortions in the balance sheet and income statement. In the balance sheet, so-called nonmonetary assets, such as inventories and property, plant, and equipment, are shown at values far below current replacement value if they are long-lived assets. In the income statement, depreciation charges are too low relative to current replacement costs. Sales and costs in December and January of the same year are typically added as if they represent the same purchasing power.

As a result, many financial indicators typically used in historical analyses can be distorted when calculated directly from the financial statements. In emerging markets, companies often index their internal management accounts to overcome these issues. If they do not, or if you are doing an outside-in analysis, at least correct for the following distortions:

▶ Growth is overstated in times of inflation, so restate it in real terms by deflating with an annual inflation index if sales are evenly spread across the year. If sales are not spread evenly, use quarterly or monthly inflation indexes to deflate the sales in each corresponding interval.

▶ Capital turnover is typically overstated because operating assets are carried at historical costs. You can approximate the current costs of long-lived assets by adjusting their reported value with an inflation index for their estimated average lifetime. Or consider developing ratios of real sales relative to physical capacity indicators appropriate for the sector—for example, sales per square meter in consumer retail. Inventory levels also need restating if turnover is low and inflation is very high.

▶ Operating margins (operating profit over sales) can be overstated because of too-low depreciation and large holding gains on slow-moving inventories. Corrections for depreciation charges follow from adjustments to property, plant, and equipment. You can estimate cash operating expenses at current-cost basis by inflating the reported costs for the average time held in inventory. Alternatively, use historical EBITDA-to-sales ratios to assess the company's performance relative to peers; these ratios at least do not suffer from any depreciation-induced bias.

▶ Use caution in interpreting credit ratios and other indicators of capital structure health. Distortions are especially significant in solvency ratios such as debt to equity or total assets, because long-lived assets are understated relative to replacement costs, and floating-rate debt is at current currency units. Use coverage ratios such as EBITDA to interest expense.[4] These are

---

[4] Distortions occur in the ratio of EBITA to interest coverage if operating profit is overstated due to low depreciation charges and low costs of procured materials.

less exposed to accounting distortions because depreciation has no impact and debt financing in emerging markets is mostly at floating interest rates or in foreign currency.

## Financial Projections in Real and Nominal Terms

When you make financial projections of income statements and balance sheets under high inflation for a valuation, keep in mind that accounting adjustments cannot affect free cash flow. Thus, for valuation purposes, we project financial statements without any accounting adjustments for inflation. The projections can be made in nominal or real terms. Exhibit 2 summarizes the major advantages and shortcomings of each approach.

Neither approach is perfect, so use elements of both to prepare consistent financial projections. Specifically, when projecting in real terms, it is often difficult to calculate taxes correctly, as taxes are often calculated based on nominal financial statements. Furthermore, you need to explicitly project the cash flow effects of working capital changes because these do not automatically follow from the annual change in working capital. The main downside of using nominal cash flows is that future capital expenditures are difficult to project because the typically stable relationship between revenues and fixed assets does not hold under high inflation. As a result, depreciation charges and EBITA also are difficult to project.

| EXHIBIT 2 | Combining Real and Nominal Approaches to Financial Modeling |

| Estimates | Modeling approach | | Preferred application |
|---|---|---|---|
| | Real | Nominal | |
| **Operational performance** | | | |
| Sales | ✓ | ✓ | |
| EBITDA | ✓ | ✓ | |
| EBITA | ✓ | – | |
| Capital expenditures | ✓ | – | |
| Investments in working capital | ✓ a | ✓ | |
| **Income taxes** | – | ✓ | |
| **Financial statements** | ✓ b | ✓ | |
| **Continuing value** | ✓ a | ✓ | |

a If inflation impact on investments in working capital is explicitly included.
b If inflation corrections are separately modeled and included in income statement and balance sheet.

## Five-Step Approach to Combined Nominal and Real-Terms Financial Projections

We illustrate below how to combine both nominal and real forecasts in a DCF valuation. In this example, the company's revenues grow at 2 percent in real terms, and the annual inflation rate is 20 percent in the first forecasted year and 10 percent thereafter (see Exhibit 3). To simplify, we assumed that all cash flows

| EXHIBIT 3 | DCF under Inflation: Key Assumptions |
|-----------|-------------------------------------|

| | | Forecasts | | | | |
|---|---|---|---|---|---|---|
| **Operations** | Year 1 | 2 | 3 | 4 | 5 | 25 |
| Real growth rate (percent) | 2 | 2 | 2 | 2 | 2 | |
| Real revenues | 1,000 | 1,020 | 1,040 | 1,061 | 1,082 | 1,608 |
| Real EBITDA | 300 | 306 | 312 | 318 | 325 | 483 |
| Net working capital/revenues (percent) | 20 | 20 | 20 | 20 | 20 | 20 |
| Real net PPE/real revenues (percent) | 40 | 40 | 40 | 40 | 40 | 40 |
| Lifetime of net PPE | 5 | | | | | |
| | | | | | | |
| **Other** | | | | | | |
| Inflation rate (percent) | | 20 | 10 | 10 | 10 | 10 |
| Inflation index | 1.00 | 1.20 | 1.32 | 1.45 | 1.60 | 10.75 |
| Tax rate (percent) | 35 | 35 | 35 | 35 | 35 | 35 |
| Real WACC (percent) | | 8.0 | 8.0 | 8.0 | 8.0 | 8.0 |
| Nominal WACC (percent) | | 29.6 | 18.8 | 18.8 | 18.8 | 18.8 |

*Note:* Adjusted formula for real-terms continuing value.

occur at the end of the year. Under extreme inflation levels, this assumption could distort financial projections because the cash flows that accumulate throughout the year are subject to different inflation rates. In that case, split the year into quarterly or even monthly intervals, project cash flows for each interval, and discount the cash flows at the appropriate discount rate for that interval.

In practice, many more issues around financial projections arise in emerging-market valuations than in this simplified example. Nevertheless, it shows how to address some key issues when developing a cash flow forecast under high inflation, by means of the following step-by-step approach, leading to the real and nominal valuation results shown in Exhibit 4.

**Step 1: Forecast Operating Performance in Real Terms** To the extent possible, convert historical nominal balance sheets and income statements into real terms (usually at the current year's currency value). At a minimum, make a real-terms approximation of the historical development of the key value drivers: growth and return on capital and the underlying capital turnover and EBITA margin, so you can understand the true economics of the business. With these approximations, forecast the operating performance of the business in real terms:

▶ Project future revenues and cash expenses to obtain EBITDA forecasts.[5]

▶ Estimate property, plant, and equipment (PPE) and capital expenditures from your assumptions on real-terms capital turnover.

▶ Working capital follows from projected revenues and assumptions on days of working capital required.

▶ From projected net PPE and assumptions on the lifetime of the assets, derive the annual depreciation to estimate real-terms EBITA.

---

[5] This step assumes that all expenses included in EBITDA are cash costs.

## EXHIBIT 4 DCF under Inflation: Real and Nominal Models

| | Real projections | | | | | | Nominal projections | | | | | |
|---|---|---|---|---|---|---|---|---|---|---|---|---|
| | Year 1 | 2 | 3 | 4 | 5 | 25 | Year 1 | 2 | 3 | 4 | 5 | 25 |
| **NOPLAT** | | | | | | | | | | | | |
| Revenues | 1,000 | 1,020 | 1,040 | 1,061 | 1,082 | 1,608 | 1,000 | 1,224 | 1,373 | 1,541 | 1,729 | 17,283 |
| EBITDA | 300 | 306 | 312 | 318 | 325 | 483 | 300 | 367 | 412 | 462 | 519 | 5,185 |
| Depreciation | (80) | (80) | (82) | (83) | (85) | (126) | (80) | (80) | (85) | (92) | (100) | (926) |
| EBITA | 220 | 226 | 231 | 235 | 240 | 356 | 220 | 287 | 327 | 370 | 419 | 4,259 |
| Taxes | (77) | (84) | (87) | (89) | (92) | (139) | (77) | (101) | (114) | (130) | (147) | (1,491) |
| NOPLAT | 143 | 142 | 144 | 146 | 148 | 218 | 143 | 187 | 212 | 241 | 272 | 2,768 |
| **Free cash flow** | | | | | | | | | | | | |
| NOPLAT | 143 | 142 | 144 | 146 | 148 | 218 | 143 | 187 | 212 | 241 | 272 | 2,768 |
| Depreciation | 80 | 80 | 82 | 83 | 85 | 126 | 80 | 80 | 85 | 92 | 100 | 926 |
| Capital expenditures | (80) | (88) | (90) | (92) | (93) | (139) | (80) | (106) | (118) | (133) | (149) | (1,491) |
| Investment in net working capital | | (37) | (23) | (23) | (24) | (35) | | (45) | (30) | (34) | (38) | (376) |
| Free cash flow | | 97 | 113 | 114 | 116 | 170 | | 116 | 149 | 166 | 185 | 1,827 |
| **Invested capital** | | | | | | | | | | | | |
| Net PPE (beginning of year) | 400 | 400 | 408 | 416 | 424 | 631 | 400 | 400 | 426 | 459 | 500 | 4,631 |
| Depreciation | (80) | (80) | (82) | (83) | (85) | (126) | (80) | (80) | (85) | (92) | (100) | (926) |
| Capital expenditures | 80 | 88 | 90 | 92 | 93 | 139 | 80 | 106 | 118 | 133 | 149 | 1,491 |
| Net PPE (end of year) | 400 | 408 | 416 | 424 | 433 | 643 | 400 | 426 | 459 | 500 | 549 | 5,196 |
| Net working capital | 200 | 204 | 208 | 212 | 216 | 322 | 200 | 245 | 275 | 308 | 346 | 3,457 |
| Invested capital | 600 | 612 | 624 | 637 | 649 | 965 | 600 | 670 | 734 | 808 | 895 | 8,653 |
| **Ratios** (percent) | | | | | | | | | | | | |
| Net PPE/revenues | 40 | 40 | 40 | 40 | 40 | 40 | 40 | 35 | 33 | 32 | 32 | 30 |
| Net working capital/revenues | 20 | 20 | 20 | 20 | 20 | 20 | 20 | 20 | 20 | 20 | 20 | 20 |
| ROIC | 24 | 24 | 24 | 23 | 23 | 23 | 24 | 31 | 32 | 33 | 34 | 36 |
| Free cash flow growth rate | | | 17 | 1 | 1 | 2 | | | 28 | 11 | 12 | 12 |
| **DCF valuation** | | | | | | | | | | | | |
| Free cash flow | | 97 | 113 | 114 | 116 | 170 | | 116 | 149 | 166 | 185 | 1,827 |
| Continuing value (value driver formula)[a] | | | | | | 2,891 | | | | | | 31,063 |
| Continuing value (cash flow perpetuity formula) | | | | | | 2,891 | | | | | | 31,064 |
| Present value factor | | 0.93 | 0.86 | 0.79 | 0.74 | 0.16 | | 0.77 | 0.65 | 0.55 | 0.46 | 0.01 |
| DCF value | 1,795 | | | | | | 1,795 | | | | | |

[a] Adjusted formula for real-terms continuing value.

**Step 2: Build Financial Statements in Nominal Terms** Nominal projections can be readily derived by converting the real operating projections into nominal terms (note that these projections do not include any monetary adjustments as under, for example, inflation accounting):

▶ Project nominal revenues, cash expenses, EBITDA, and capital expenditures by multiplying their real-terms equivalents by the inflation index for the year.

▶ Estimate net property, plant, and equipment on a year-by-year basis from the prior-year balance plus nominal capital expenditures minus nominal depreciation (which is estimated as a percentage of net PPE according to the estimated lifetime).

▶ Working capital follows from revenues and days of working capital required.

▶ Subtract the depreciation charges from EBITDA to obtain nominal EBITA.

▶ Calculate income taxes on nominal EBITA without inflation corrections. (Always check the local tax rules for the reasonableness of this assumption.)

In contrast to the real-terms projections, the capital turnover is now increasing over time because nominal net PPE grows slower than revenues in a high-inflation environment. In this example, we did not build a complete balance sheet and income statement. That would require the following additional steps:

▶ Forecast interest expense and other nonoperating income statement items in nominal terms (based on the prior year's balance sheet).

▶ Equity should equal last year's equity plus earnings, less dividends, plus or minus any share issues or repurchases.

▶ Finally, balance the balance sheet with debt or marketable securities.[6]

**Step 3: Build Financial Statements in Real Terms** Most of the operating items for the real-terms income statement and balance sheet were already estimated in step 1. Now also include the real-terms taxes on EBITA by deflating the nominal taxes as estimated in step 2. For full financial statements, use the inflation index to convert debt, marketable securities, interest expense, income taxes, and nonoperating terms from the nominal statements into real terms. The real-terms equity account is a plug to balance the balance sheet. To make sure you have done this correctly, be sure the real equity account equals last year's equity plus earnings, less dividends, plus or minus share issues or repurchases, and plus or minus inflationary gains or losses on the monetary assets (such as cash, receivables, payables, and debt).

**Step 4: Forecast the Future Free Cash Flows in Real and Nominal Terms from the Projected Income Statements and Balance Sheets** The real-terms investment

---

[6] As noted, these projections are made for valuation purposes and not necessarily in accordance with local or international accounting standards prescribing any inflation or monetary corrections for particular groups of assets and liabilities. Free cash flows are not affected by such adjustments.

in net working capital (NWC$^R$) is equal to the increase in working capital plus a monetary loss due to inflation:[7]

$$\text{Investment in NWC}_t = \text{Increase in NWC}_t^R + \text{NWC}_{t-1}^R\left[1 - \frac{\text{IX}_{t-1}}{\text{IX}_t}\right]$$

where IX$_t$ is the inflation index for the year $t$.

To check for consistency, use the inflation index to convert the free cash flows from the nominal projections to real terms. These should equal the free cash flows from the real-terms projections in each year.

**Step 5: Estimate DCF Value in Real and Nominal Terms**   When discounting real and nominal cash flows under high inflation, you must address three key issues:

1. Ensure that the WACC estimates in real terms (WACC$^R$) and nominal terms (WACC$^N$) are defined consistently with the inflation assumptions in each year:

$$(1 + \text{WACC}_t^N) = (1 + \text{WACC}_t^R) \times (1 + \text{Inflation}_t)$$

   Later in this reading, we will discuss how to estimate WACC for companies in emerging markets.

2. The value-driver formula should be adjusted when estimating continuing value in real terms. The returns on capital in real-terms projections overestimate the economic returns in the case of positive net working capital. The free cash flow in real terms differs from the cash flow implied by the value driver formula by an amount equal to the annual monetary loss on net working capital:

$$\text{FCF}_t^R = \left(1 - \frac{g_t^R}{\text{ROIC}_t^R}\right) \times \text{NOPLAT}_t^R - \text{NWC}_{t-1}^R\left(1 - \frac{\text{IX}_{t-1}}{\text{IX}_t}\right)$$

   The real-terms value driver formula is adjusted for this monetary loss, reflecting the perpetuity assumptions for inflation ($i$) and the ratio of net working capital to invested capital (NWC$^R$/IC$^R$):

$$\text{CV}^R = \frac{\left(1 - \dfrac{G^R}{\text{ROIC}^R}\right)\text{NOPLAT}^R}{\text{WACC}^R - g^R}$$

   where

$$G^R = g^R - \left[\frac{\text{NWC}^R}{\text{IC}^R} \times \left(\frac{i}{1 + i}\right)\right]$$

---

[7] Even for assets held at constant levels in real-terms balance sheets, replacement investments are required at increasing prices in an inflationary environment. These replacement investments represent a cash outflow, also in real terms, but do not show up from real-terms balance sheet differences from year to year. In contrast, the nominal investment cash flow does follow from the nominal balance sheet differences from year to year.

The resulting continuing-value estimate is the same as that obtained from a free cash flow perpetuity formula. After indexing for inflation, it also equals the continuing-value estimates derived from nominal projections.

3. When using the continuing-value formulas, make sure the explicit forecast period is long enough for the model to reach a steady state with constant growth rates of free cash flow. Because of the way inflation affects capital expenditures and depreciation, you need a much longer horizon than for valuations with no or low inflation.

## ConsuCo Case Example: Inflation Adjustments

Let's explore how to handle inflation and accounting issues in the financial analysis and valuation of ConsuCo.

**Historical Analysis**   In analyzing ConsuCo's historical financial statements, we made adjustments in two areas. First, we rearranged the balance sheet and the income statements to get the statements for NOPLAT, invested capital, and free cash flow. The ConsuCo statements follow Brazilian GAAP, so we had to make some additional adjustments. Most of these were relatively minor. The largest involved the consolidation of a securitization vehicle, for which only the net asset position is shown under Brazilian GAAP.

Second, we estimated some key financial ratios on an approximate real-terms basis. Although annual inflation in Brazil has been moderate since 1997 at levels between 5 and 10 percent, ratios such as operating margin and capital turnover are likely to be biased when directly calculated from the financial statements. Therefore, we looked at trends in cash operating margins (EBITDA over sales). In addition, we estimated the sales revenues in real terms per unit of production capacity over time to better understand the development of real-terms capital turnover.

The results are reflected in Exhibit 5. Between 1998 and 2003, ConsuCo's sales grew significantly in real terms at around 15 percent per year, largely driven by acquisitions. But growth has slowed considerably since 2000. Cash operating margins improved significantly, from 5.7 percent in 1998 to 9.2 percent in 2003. In real terms, annual sales per unit of production capacity have been fairly stable

## EXHIBIT 5    ConsuCo: Key Historical Financial Indicators

percent

| Nominal indicators | 1998 | 1999 | 2000 | 2001 | 2002 | 2003 |
|---|---|---|---|---|---|---|
| Sales growth | 41 | 32 | 31 | 6 | 17 | 14 |
| Adjusted EBITA/sales | 3.5 | 4.6 | 5.7 | 5.3 | 5.3 | 6.9 |
| NOPLAT/sales | 2.9 | 3.3 | 4.8 | 4.5 | 3.9 | 5.3 |
| Invested capital (excluding goodwill)/sales | 35.2 | 34.8 | 57.0 | 64.9 | 62.4 | 64.5 |
| Invested capital (including goodwill)/sales | 42.3 | 40.3 | 61.9 | 74.7 | 71.7 | 72.9 |
| ROIC (excluding goodwill) | 8.3 | 9.5 | 8.4 | 6.9 | 6.2 | 8.2 |
| ROIC (including goodwill) | 6.9 | 8.2 | 7.7 | 6.0 | 5.4 | 7.3 |
| | | | | | | |
| **Approximate real indicators** | | | | | | |
| Sales growth (inflation-adjusted) | 32 | 24 | 23 | (2) | 9 | 5 |
| EBITDA/sales | 5.7 | 6.7 | 7.2 | 7.6 | 7.5 | 9.2 |
| Sales/capacity[a] | 8.7 | 7.9 | 7.0 | 6.4 | 6.3 | 6.2 |

[a]In inflation-adjusted Reais million per capacity unit.

since 2000 at around 6.0 to 6.5 million Reais, as have nominal turnover levels for invested capital (excluding goodwill).

**Financial projections**    Based on the findings from the historical analysis and analyst consensus forecasts as of July 2004, we made the operating and financial forecasts summarized in Exhibit 6 in real and nominal terms. We assumed that no major economic crisis will materialize in Brazil.

ConsuCo is investing heavily for future growth. Real-terms sales growth is projected to peak at 8 percent in 2005 and then gradually decline over the next four years to around 3 percent, close to Brazil's long-term expected real GDP growth. Cash margins will continue to rise to 9.7 percent in 2005 and stay at that level in perpetuity. Tougher competition will create downward pressure on margins, but the company's improvements in selling, general and administrative expenses compensate for this.

Capacity requirements are derived from sales forecasts in real terms, assuming sales productivity of 6.2 million Reais per unit of capacity. Capital expenditures for maintenance are estimated in real terms as a percentage of projected total capacity and expenditures for capacity expansion are projected at around 2.3 million Reais per unit. The future development of net PPE in real terms is derived from the capital expenditure projections.

The resulting ROIC (excluding goodwill) in real terms for ConsuCo decreases from its current value of around 7.6 percent to around 6.6 percent in the continuing value period. In contrast, the ROIC in nominal terms increases from 8.4 to around 10.1 percent because of the inflation impact on capital turnover.

| EXHIBIT 6 | ConsuCo: Summary Financial Projections, Base Case |
|---|---|

Reais million, percent

| | 2004 | 2005 | 2006 | 2007 | 2008 | 2009 | 2014 | 2019 |
|---|---|---|---|---|---|---|---|---|
| **Operating projections** | | | | | | | | |
| Sales growth (real, percent) | 7.0 | 8.0 | 7.0 | 6.0 | 5.0 | 3.0 | 3.0 | 3.0 |
| EBITDA/sales (percent) | 9.5 | 9.7 | 9.7 | 9.7 | 9.7 | 9.7 | 9.7 | 9.7 |
| EBITDA (real terms, percent) | 2,201 | 2,427 | 2,597 | 2,753 | 2,890 | 2,977 | 3,451 | 4,001 |
| Sales/capacity[a] | 6.2 | 6.2 | 6.2 | 6.2 | 6.2 | 6.2 | 6.2 | 6.2 |
| Capacity units | 3,757 | 4,058 | 4,342 | 4,602 | 4,832 | 4,977 | 5,770 | 6,689 |
| Capital expenditures (expansion)[b] | 558 | 682 | 645 | 591 | 522 | 329 | 382 | 442 |
| Capital expenditures (maintenance)[b] | 663 | 709 | 766 | 819 | 869 | 912 | 1,057 | 1,226 |
| | | | | | | | | |
| **Real projections** | | | | | | | | |
| Sales | 23,126 | 24,976 | 26,724 | 28,327 | 29,744 | 30,636 | 35,516 | 41,172 |
| Adjusted EBITA/sales (percent) | 7.2 | 7.4 | 7.5 | 7.5 | 7.6 | 7.6 | 7.7 | 7.8 |
| NOPLAT/sales (percent) | 4.8 | 4.8 | 4.7 | 4.6 | 4.5 | 4.4 | 4.2 | 4.1 |
| Invested capital (excluding goodwill)/ sales (percent) | 70.2 | 69.3 | 68.6 | 68.0 | 67.6 | 67.2 | 65.9 | 65.0 |
| ROIC (excluding goodwill, percent) | 7.6 | 7.6 | 7.4 | 7.3 | 7.2 | 7.0 | 6.7 | 6.6 |
| | | | | | | | | |
| **Nominal projections** | | | | | | | | |
| Sales | 24,778 | 28,258 | 31,721 | 35,164 | 38,558 | 41,474 | 59,717 | 85,984 |
| Adjusted EBITA/sales (percent) | 6.9 | 7.0 | 7.0 | 7.0 | 6.9 | 6.9 | 6.8 | 6.8 |
| NOPLAT/sales (percent) | 5.0 | 5.2 | 5.2 | 5.2 | 5.2 | 5.1 | 5.1 | 5.1 |
| Invested capital (excluding goodwill)/ sales (percent) | 60.0 | 58.3 | 57.2 | 56.3 | 55.5 | 54.7 | 52.2 | 51.0 |
| ROIC (excluding goodwill, percent) | 8.4 | 8.9 | 9.0 | 9.2 | 9.3 | 9.3 | 9.8 | 10.1 |

[a] In inflation-adjusted Reais million per capacity unit.
[b] In inflation-adjusted Reais million.

# INCORPORATING EMERGING-MARKET RISKS IN THE VALUATION

## 3

The major distinction between valuing companies in developed markets and emerging markets is the increased level of risk. Not only must you account for risks related to the company's strategy, market position, and industry dynamics, as you would in a developed market, you must also deal with the risks caused by greater volatility in the capital markets and in the macroeconomic and political environments.

There is no consensus on how to reflect this higher level of risk in a DCF valuation. The most common approach is to add a country risk premium to the discount rate. The alternative is to model risks explicitly in the cash flow projections in what we call the *scenario DCF approach*. Both methodologies, if correctly and consistently applied, lead to the same result. We show this in the following example of an investment in two identical production plants, one in Europe and the other in an emerging economy (see Exhibit 7). However, the scenario DCF approach is analytically more robust and better shows the impact of emerging-market risks on value.

## Scenario DCF Approach

The scenario DCF approach simulates alternative trajectories for future cash flows. At a minimum, model two scenarios: One should assume that cash flow develops according to conditions reflecting business as usual (i.e., without major economic distress). The second should reflect cash flows assuming that any emerging-market risks materialize.

In the example, the cash flows for the European plant grow steadily at 3 percent per year into perpetuity. For the plant in the emerging market, the cash flow growth is the same under a business-as-usual scenario, but there is a 25 percent probability of economic distress resulting in a cash flow that is 55 percent lower into perpetuity. The emerging-market risk is taken into account, not in the cost of capital, but in the lower expected value of future cash flows from weighting both scenarios at the assumed probabilities. The resulting value of the emerging-market plant (€1,017) is clearly below the value of its European sister plant (€2,222), using a WACC of 7.5 percent.

We assumed for simplicity that if adverse economic conditions develop in the emerging market, they will do so in the first year of the plant's operation. In reality, of course, the investment will face a probability of domestic economic distress in each year of its lifetime. Modeling risk over time would require more complex calculations yet would not change the basic results. We also assumed that in a local crisis, the emerging-market business would face significantly lower cash flows but not wind up entirely worthless.

## Country Risk Premium DCF Approach

The second approach is to add a country risk premium to the cost of capital for comparable investments in developed markets. We then apply the resulting discount rate to the cash flow projections following a business-as-usual scenario. The key drawback is that there is no objective way to establish the country risk premium. For our two-plant example, we can derive in hindsight what the premium should be to obtain the same result as under the scenario DCF approach. For us to arrive at a value of €1,917 for the emerging-market plant, the

## EXHIBIT 7   Scenario DCF versus Country Risk Premium DCF

**Net present value for identical facilities in ...**

### Scenario approach

**... a European market**

Cash flows in perpetuity[a]

| Probability | | Year 1 | 2 | 3 | 4... |
|---|---|---|---|---|---|
| 100% | "As usual" | 100 | 103 | 106 | 109 |
| 0% | "Distressed" | | | | |
| | Expected cash flows | 100 | 103 | 106 | 109 |

Cost of capital   7.5%

Net present value   **2,222**

**... an emerging market**

Cash flows in perpetuity[b]

| Probability | | Year 1 | 2 | 3 | 4... |
|---|---|---|---|---|---|
| 75% | "As usual" | 100 | 103 | 106 | 109 |
| 25% | "Distressed" | 45 | 46 | 48 | 49 |
| | Expected cash flows | 86 | 89 | 92 | 94 |

Cost of capital   7.5%

Net present value   **1,917**   **86% of European NPV**

### Country risk premium approach

Cash flows in perpetuity[a]

| | Year 1 | 2 | 3 | 4... |
|---|---|---|---|---|
| "As usual" | 100 | 103 | 106 | 109 |

Cost of capital   7.5%

Net present value   **2,222**

Cash flows in perpetuity[b]

| | Year 1 | 2 | 3 | 4... |
|---|---|---|---|---|
| "As usual" | 100 | 103 | 106 | 109 |

Cost of capital   7.5%

Country risk premium   0.7%

Adjusted cost of capital   8.2%

Net present value   **1,917**   **86% of European NPV**

[a] Assuming perpetuity cash flow growth of 3%.

[b] Assuming perpetuity cash flow growth of 3% and recovery under distress of 45% of cash flows "as usual."

discount rate for the business-as-usual projections would have to be 8.2 percent, which translates to a country risk premium of 0.7 percent.

On occasion, practitioners make the mistake of adding the country risk premium to the cost of capital to discount the *expected* value of future cash flows rather than to the "promised" cash flows of a business-as-usual scenario. The resulting value is too low because the probability of a crisis is accounted for twice.[8]

## Scenario DCF as Prime Valuation Approach

Some surveys show that managers generally adjust for emerging-market risks by adding a risk premium to the discount rate.[9] Nonetheless, we recommend the scenario DCF approach. It provides a more solid analytical foundation and a more robust understanding of the value than incorporating country risks in the discount rate.

One reason is that most country risks, including expropriation, devaluation, and war, are largely diversifiable (though not entirely, as the economic crisis in 1998 demonstrated). Consider the international consumer goods player illustrated in Exhibit 8. Its returns on capital were highly volatile for individual emerging markets, but taken together, these markets were hardly more volatile than developed markets; the corporate portfolio diversified away most of the risks. Finance theory clearly indicates that the cost of capital should not reflect risk that can be diversified. This does not mean that diversifiable risk is irrelevant for a valuation: the possibility of adverse future events will affect the level of

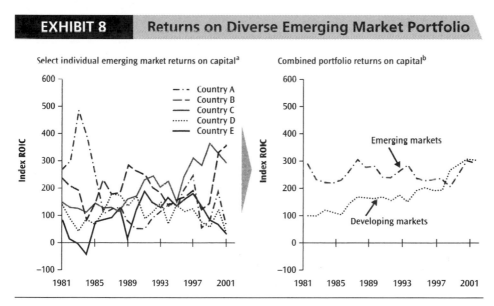

**EXHIBIT 8**      **Returns on Diverse Emerging Market Portfolio**

[a] In stable currency and adjusted for local accounting differences.
[b] Combined portfolio included additional countries not reflected here.

*Source:* Company information.

---

[8] This is analogous to the error made by discounting the expected coupon and principal payments on a corporate bond at the promised yield (i.e., the yield to maturity) instead of the expected yield (i.e., the cost of debt).

[9] T. Keck, E. Levengood, and A. Longfield, "Using Discounted Cash Flow Analysis in an International Setting: A Survey of Issues in Modeling the Cost of Capital," *Journal of Applied Corporate Finance,* 11(3) (1998).

expected cash flows, as in the example in Exhibit 7. But once this has been incorporated in the forecast for cash flows, there is no need for an additional markup of the cost of capital if the risk is diversifiable.

Another argument against a country risk premium is that many country risks apply unequally to companies in a given country. For example, banks are more likely to be affected than retailers. Some companies (raw-materials exporters) might benefit from a currency devaluation, while others (raw-materials importers) will be damaged. For the consumer goods company in Exhibit 8, economic crises had only a short-term impact on sales and profit as measured in stable currency. In most cases, after a year or two, sales and profits roughly regained their original growth trajectories. Applying the same risk premium to all companies in an emerging market could overstate the risk for some businesses and understate it for others.

Furthermore, there is no systematic method to calculate a country risk premium. In our example, we could reengineer this premium because the true value of the plant was already known from the scenario approach. In practice, the country risk premium is sometimes set at the spread of the local government debt rate[10] denominated in U.S. dollars and a U.S. government bond of similar maturity. However, that is reasonable only if the returns on local government debt are highly correlated with returns on corporate investments.

Finally, when managers have to discuss emerging-market risks and their effect on cash flow in scenarios, they gain more insights than they would get from a "black box" addition to the discount rate. By identifying specific factors with a large impact on value, managers can plan to mitigate these risks. Furthermore, managers easily underestimate the impact of even a small country risk premium in the discount rate: In the example of Exhibit 8, setting a country risk premium to 3 percent would be equivalent to assuming a 70 percent probability of economic distress.

## Constructing Cash Flow Scenarios and Probabilities

To use the scenario DCF approach, construct at least two scenarios. The base case, or business-as-usual scenario, describes how the business will perform if no major crises occur. The downside scenario describes the financial results if a major crisis does occur.

For both scenarios, start by projecting the macroeconomic environment because this influences industry and company performance. The major macroeconomic variables to forecast are GDP growth, inflation rates, foreign-exchange rates, and interest rates. These items must be linked in a way that reflects economic realities and should be included in the basic set of monetary assumptions underlying your valuation. For instance, when constructing a downside scenario with high inflation, make sure that the same inflation rates underlie the financial projections and cost of capital estimates for the company to be valued. Foreign exchange rates should also reflect this inflation in the long run because of purchasing power parity.

Given the assumptions for macroeconomic performance, construct the industry scenarios basically in the same way as in developed markets. The major difference is in the greater uncertainty involved in modeling outcomes under severe crises for which there may be no precedent.

---

[10] This is also a promised yield rather than an expected yield on government bonds, further underlining the point that the cost of capital based on country risk premium should not be applied to expected cash flows, but to "promised" cash flows (those following a business-as-usual scenario in which no country risk materializes).

While estimating probabilities for the cash flow scenarios is ultimately a matter of management judgment, there are indicators of reasonable probabilities. Historical data on previous crises can give some indication of frequency and severity of country risk and the time required for recovery. Analyzing the changes in GDP of 20 emerging economies over the past 20 years, we found that these economies had experienced economic distress about once every five years (a real-terms GDP decline of more than 5 percent). This would suggest a 20 percent probability for a downside scenario.

Another source of information for estimating probabilities is prospective data from current government bond prices.[11] Recent academic research suggests that government default probabilities five years into the future in emerging markets such as Argentina, were around 30 percent in nondistress years.[12]

## ConsuCo Case Example: Cash Flow Scenarios and Probabilities

Returning to the ConsuCo example, we already constructed a business-as-usual scenario in the previous section. For a downward scenario, we analyzed ConsuCo's performance under more adverse economic conditions in the past. Brazil has experienced several severe economic and monetary downturns, including an inflation rate that surpassed 2,000 percent in 1993. Judging by its key financial indicators, such as EBITDA to sales and real-terms sales growth, the impact on ConsuCo's business performance was significant. ConsuCo's cash operating margin was negative for four years, at around $-10$ to $-5$ percent, and then recovered to its normal levels. In the same period, sales in real terms declined by 10 to 15 percent per year but grew sharply after the crisis. For the downside scenario projections, we assumed similar negative cash margins and real-terms sales decline for up to five years, followed by a gradual return to the long-term margins and growth assumed under the business-as-usual scenario. Exhibit 9 compares the nominal and real returns on invested capital under both scenarios: In the downside scenario, the returns plummet and then increase as the recovery starts. After 2010, the nominal returns even surpass those in the base case as the extreme inflation levels push up the capital turnovers. Of course, the nominal returns are artificially high, as a comparison with the real returns shows. The DCF value under the downside scenario will turn out to be only half of the base-case value. We estimated the probability of this downside scenario at 25 to 35 percent.

## ESTIMATING COST OF CAPITAL IN EMERGING MARKETS

**4**

Calculating the cost of capital in any country can be challenging, but for emerging markets, the challenge is an order of magnitude higher. In this section, we provide our fundamental assumptions, background on the important issues, and a practical way to estimate the components of the cost of capital.

---

[11] See, for example, D. Duffie and K. Singleton, "Modeling Term Structures of Defaultable Bonds," *Review of Financial Studies* 12 (1999): 687–720; and R. Merton, "On the Pricing of Corporate Debt: The Risk Structure of Interest Rates," *Journal of Finance*, 29(2) (1974): 449–470.

[12] See J. Merrick, "Crisis Dynamics of Implied Default Recovery Ratios: Evidence from Russia and Argentina," *Journal of Banking and Finance*, 25(10) (2001): 1921–1939.

| EXHIBIT 9 | ConsuCo: ROIC in Downside Scenario versus Base Case |

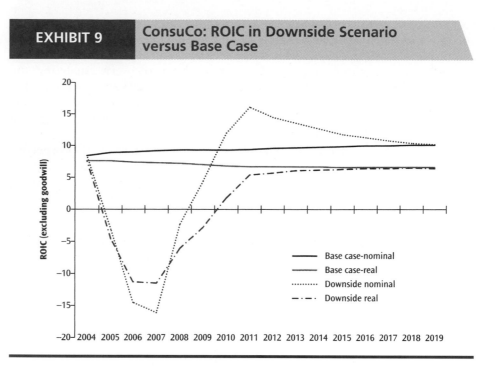

## Fundamental Assumptions

Our analysis adopts the perspective of a global investor—either a multinational company or an international investor with a diversified portfolio. Of course, many emerging markets are not well integrated with the global market, and local investors may face barriers to investing outside their home market. As a result, local investors cannot always hold well-diversified portfolios, and their cost of capital may be considerably different from that of a global investor. Unfortunately, there is no established framework for estimating the capital cost for local investors. Furthermore, as long as international investors have access to local investment opportunities, local prices will be based on an international cost of capital. Finally, according to empirical research, emerging markets have become increasingly integrated into global capital markets.[13] We believe that this trend will continue and that most countries will gradually reduce foreign-investment restrictions for local investors in the long run.

Another assumption is that most country risks are diversifiable from the perspective of the global investor. We therefore need no additional risk premiums in the cost of capital for the risks encountered in emerging markets when discounting expected cash flows. Of course, if you choose to discount the cash flow from the business-as-usual scenario only, you should add a country risk premium.

Given these assumptions, the cost of capital in emerging markets should generally be close to a global cost of capital adjusted for local inflation and capital structure. It is also useful to keep some general guidelines in mind:

▶ *Use the CAPM to estimate the cost of equity in emerging markets.* The CAPM may be a less robust model for the less-integrated emerging markets, but there is no better alternative model today. Furthermore, we believe it will become a better predictor of equity returns world-wide as markets continue to become more integrated.

---

[13] See, for example, C. Harvey, "The Drivers of Expected Returns in International Markets," *Emerging Markets Quarterly* (Fall 2000): 1–17.

▶ *There is no one "right" answer, so be pragmatic.* In emerging markets, there are often significant information and data gaps (e.g., for estimating betas or the risk-free rate in local currency). Be flexible as you assemble the available information piece by piece to build the cost of capital, and triangulate your results with country risk premium approaches and multiples.

▶ *Be sure monetary assumptions are consistent.* Ground your model in a common set of monetary assumptions to ensure that the cash flow forecasts and discount rate are consistent. If you are using local nominal cash flows, the cost of capital must reflect the local inflation rate that is embedded in the cash flows. For real-terms cash flows, subtract inflation from the nominal cost of capital.

▶ *Allow for changes in cost of capital.* The cost of capital in an emerging-market valuation may change, based on evolving inflation expectations, changes in a company's capital structure and cost of debt, or foreseeable reforms in the tax system. For example, for valuations in Argentina during the economic and monetary crisis of 2002, the short-term inflation rate of 30 percent could not be considered a reasonable basis for a long-term cost of capital estimate because such a crisis could not be expected to last forever.[14] In such cases, estimate the cost of capital on a year-by-year basis, following the underlying set of basic monetary assumptions.

▶ *Don't mix approaches.* Use the cost of capital to discount the cash flows in a probability-weighted scenario approach. Do not add any risk premium, because you would be double-counting risk. If you are discounting only future cash flows in a business-as-usual scenario, add a risk premium to the discount rate.

## Estimating the Cost of Equity

To estimate the components of the cost of equity, use the standard CAPM model.

**Risk-Free Rate**    In emerging markets, the risk-free rate is harder to estimate from government bonds than in developed markets. Three main problems arise. First, most of the government debt in emerging markets is not, in fact, risk free: The ratings on much of this debt are often well below investment grade. Second, it is difficult to find long-term government bonds that are actively traded with sufficient liquidity. Finally, the long-term debt that is traded is often in U.S. dollars, a European currency, or the Japanese yen, so it is not appropriate for discounting local nominal cash flows.

Our recommendation is to follow a very straightforward approach. Start with a risk-free rate based on the 10-year U.S. government bond yield, as in developed markets. Add to this the projected difference over time between U.S. and local inflation to develop a nominal risk-free rate in local currency.[15] Sometimes you can derive this inflation differential from the spread between local government bond yields denominated in local currency versus U.S. dollars.[16]

**Beta**    Sometimes practitioners calculate beta relative to the local market index. This is not only inconsistent from the perspective of a global investor, but also

---

[14] Annual consumer price inflation came down to around 5 percent in Argentina in 2004.

[15] In this way, we do not model the U.S. term structure of interest rates. Technically, this should be included as well, but it will not make a large difference in the valuation.

[16] Technically, this is correct only if the emerging-market bonds are relatively low risk, as for example for Chile and South Korea.

potentially distorted by the fact that the index in an emerging market will rarely be representative of a diversified economy. Instead, estimate industry betas relative to a well-diversified or global market index as recommended in the reading on the mortgage-backed sector of the bond market. Since equity markets in emerging economies are often small, with liquidity concentrated in a few stocks, it may be hard to find a representative sample of publicly traded local companies to estimate an industry beta. In that case, derive an industry beta from international comparables that operate in the same or a similar sector. The implicit assumption is that the fundamental drivers of systematic risk will be similar in emerging and developed markets.

For ConsuCo, we used three sources for estimates of beta in an international peer group: Bloomberg betas calculated against the FT World Index, Barra betas, and betas adjusted for the high-tech boom. Note that the unlevered beta estimates are similar for industry peers, with some exceptions, as shown in Exhibit 10. Overall, our estimate for the unlevered industry beta is 0.55, translating into an equity beta for ConsuCo of 0.8 (given a debt-to-capital target weight of 0.3, as discussed later).

**Market Risk Premium**    Excess returns of local equity markets over local bond returns are not a good proxy for the market risk premium. This holds even more so for emerging markets given the lack of diversification in the local equity market. Furthermore, the quality and length of available data on equity and bond market returns are usually unsuitable for making long-term estimates. To use a market risk premium that is consistent with the perspective of a global investor, use a global estimate of 4.5 to 5.5 percent.

In Exhibit 11, we summarize the nominal cost of equity calculation for ConsuCo. In the base case, we have assumed a decreasing rate of inflation for the Brazilian economy from 7.1 percent in 2004 to 4.4 percent in 2008 and beyond. This is also reflected in the cost of capital estimates going forward. For the downside scenario, inflation projections follow a different trajectory, and the cost of capital for this scenario is adjusted accordingly.

| EXHIBIT 10 | ConsuCo: Estimating Beta |
| --- | --- |

| Peers | Unlevered betas | | | |
| --- | --- | --- | --- | --- |
| | Bloomberg[a] | Barra | Adjusted[b] | Average |
| ConsuCo | 0.733 | 1.343 | 0.748 | 1.038 |
| PeerCo 1 | 0.664 | 0.712 | 0.782 | 0.688 |
| PeerCo 2 | 0.589 | 0.407 | 0.846 | 0.498 |
| PeerCo 3 | 0.795 | 0.693 | 1.232 | 0.744 |
| PeerCo 4 | 0.492 | 0.236 | 0.346 | 0.364 |
| PeerCo 5 | 0.475 | 0.749 | 0.439 | 0.612 |
| PeerCo 6 | 0.480 | 0.231 | 0.381 | 0.356 |
| PeerCo 7 | 0.294 | 0.198 | 0.271 | 0.246 |
| PeerCo 8 | 0.278 | 0.361 | 0.386 | 0.319 |
| PeerCo 9 | 0.418 | 0.384 | 0.641 | 0.401 |
| PeerCo 10 | 0.820 | 0.635 | 0.803 | 0.728 |
| PeerCo 11 | 0.649 | 0.688 | 0.625 | 0.669 |
| **Average** | **0.557** | **0.553** | **0.625** | **0.555** |
| **Median** | **0.541** | **0.521** | **0.633** | **0.531** |

[a] Against FT World Index on a weekly basis over past two years.
[b] Adjusted for the high-tech boom.

*Source:* Bloomberg, Barra, Datastream, McKinsey analysis.

| EXHIBIT 11 | ConsuCo: Estimating the Nominal Cost of Equity | | | | | | | |
|---|---|---|---|---|---|---|---|---|

| | 2004 | 2005 | 2006 | 2007 | 2008 | 2009 | 2014 | 2019 |
|---|---|---|---|---|---|---|---|---|
| **United States** | | | | | | | | |
| Inflation (percent) | 2.0 | 2.0 | 2.0 | 2.0 | 2.0 | 2.0 | 2.0 | 2.0 |
| Risk-free interest rate (percent) | 4.6 | 4.6 | 4.6 | 4.6 | 4.6 | 4.6 | 4.6 | 4.6 |
| **Brazil** | | | | | | | | |
| Inflation (IPCA, percent) | 7.1 | 5.6 | 4.9 | 4.6 | 4.4 | 4.4 | 4.4 | 4.4 |
| Risk-free interest rate (percent)[a] | 9.8 | 8.2 | 7.5 | 7.2 | 7.0 | 7.0 | 7.0 | 7.0 |
| Relevered beta | 0.8 | 0.8 | 0.8 | 0.8 | 0.8 | 0.8 | 0.8 | 0.8 |
| Market risk premium (percent) | 5.0 | 5.0 | 5.0 | 5.0 | 5.0 | 5.0 | 5.0 | 5.0 |
| Cost of equity (percent) | 14.0 | 12.4 | 11.7 | 11.3 | 11.1 | 11.1 | 11.1 | 11.1 |

[a] Brazilian risk-free rate estimated as: $(1 + \text{U.S. risk free rate}) \times (1 + \text{Brazilian inflation}) \div (1 + \text{U.S. inflation}) - 1$.

*Sources:* Banco Central do Brasil, Bloomberg, EIU Viewswire, McKinsey analysis.

## Estimating the After-Tax Cost of Debt

In most emerging economies, there are no liquid markets for corporate bonds, so little or no market information is available to estimate the cost of debt. However, from an international investor's perspective, the cost of debt in local currency should simply equal the sum of the dollar (or euro) risk-free rate, the systematic part of the credit spread, and the inflation differential between local currency and dollars (or euros). Most of the country risk can be diversified away in a global bond portfolio. Therefore, the systematic part of the default risk is probably no larger than that of companies in international markets, and the cost of debt should not include a separate country risk premium. This explains why the funding costs of multinationals with extensive emerging-market portfolios, companies including Coca-Cola and Colgate-Palmolive, have a cost of debt no higher than their mainly U.S.-focused competitors.

Returning to the ConsuCo example, we calculated the cost of debt in Brazilian Reais. ConsuCo does not have its own credit rating, but based on its EBITDA coverage ratios versus rated peers, we estimated that ConsuCo would probably have a B to B+ rating. ConsuCo's cost of debt can be estimated as the sum of the risk-free rate in Brazilian Reais plus the systematic credit spread for a U.S. corporate bond rated B+ versus the U.S. government bond yield as shown in Exhibit 12. Of course, the inflation assumptions underlying the estimates for cost of debt should be consistent with those for the base-case and downside scenarios.

Remember that ConsuCo's cost of debt is significantly lower than the interest rate it is currently paying because the latter represents the promised yield, not the expected yield.

The marginal tax rate in emerging markets can be very different from the effective tax rate, which often includes investment tax credits, export tax credits, taxes, equity or dividend credits, and operating loss credits. Many of these do not provide a tax shield on interest expense. Only taxes that apply to interest expense should be used in the WACC estimate. Other taxes or credits should be modeled directly in the cash flows. For ConsuCo, we used the Brazilian corporate income tax rate of 25 percent plus social contribution tax of 9 percent.

| EXHIBIT 12 | ConsuCo: Estimating the Nominal Cost of Debt |
|---|---|

percent

|  | 2004 | 2005 | 2006 | 2007 | 2008 | 2009 | 2014 | 2019 |
|---|---|---|---|---|---|---|---|---|
| Risk-free interest rate | 9.8 | 8.2 | 7.5 | 7.2 | 7.0 | 7.0 | 7.0 | 7.0 |
| BBB credit spread | 1.2 | 1.2 | 1.2 | 1.2 | 1.2 | 1.2 | 1.2 | 1.2 |
| Systematic credit spread for B+ | 0.5 | 0.5 | 0.5 | 0.5 | 0.5 | 0.5 | 0.5 | 0.5 |
| Cost of debt | 11.5 | 9.9 | 9.2 | 8.9 | 8.8 | 8.8 | 8.8 | 8.8 |
|  |  |  |  |  |  |  |  |  |
| Tax rate | 34 | 34 | 34 | 34 | 34 | 34 | 34 | 34 |
| After-tax cost of debt | 7.6 | 6.6 | 6.1 | 5.9 | 5.8 | 5.8 | 5.8 | 5.8 |

*Source:* Standard & Poor's, McKinsey analysis.

## Estimating WACC

Given the estimates for cost of equity and after-tax cost of debt, we need debt and equity weights to derive an estimate of the weighted average cost of capital. In emerging markets, many companies have unusual capital structures compared with their international peers. One reason is, of course, the country risk. The possibility of macroeconomic distress makes companies more conservative in setting their leverage. Another reason could be anomalies in the local debt or equity markets. In the long run, when the anomalies are corrected, the companies should expect to converge to a capital structure similar to that of their global competitors. You could forecast explicitly how the company evolves to a capital structure that is more similar to global standards. In that case, you should consider using the APV approach.

For the ConsuCo case, we kept the capital structure going forward at its long-term historical levels, with leverage somewhat below the peer group average at a ratio of debt to enterprise value of 0.3. Exhibit 13 summarizes the WACC estimates for both the base case and downside scenario in nominal terms. Note how the extreme inflation assumption underlying the downside scenario leads to a radically higher cost of capital in the crisis years until 2009.

## Estimating the Country Risk Premium

If you are discounting business-as-usual cash flows instead of expected cash flows, you should add a country risk premium to the WACC. There is no agreed-upon approach to estimating this premium, but we have some advice.

**Do Not Simply Use the Sovereign Risk Premium**    The long-term sovereign risk premium equals the difference between a long-term (e.g., 10-year) U.S. government bond yield and a dollar-denominated local bond's stripped yield[17] with the same maturity. This difference will reasonably approximate the country risk premium only if the cash flows of the corporation being valued move closely in line with the payments on government bonds. This is not necessarily the case. In the consumer goods or raw-materials sector, for example, cash flows have low correlation with local government bond payments and lower volatility.

---

[17] Some emerging markets' country debt is partially guaranteed by international institutions or backed by U.S. Treasury bonds. For these bonds, you need to estimate the yield on the nonguaranteed part of the bond, the "stripped" yield. Stripped yields are available from bond data suppliers.

| EXHIBIT 13 | ConsuCo: Estimating Nominal WACC for ConsuCo |
|---|---|

|  | 2004 | 2005 | 2006 | 2007 | 2008 | 2009 | 2014 | 2019 |
|---|---|---|---|---|---|---|---|---|
| **Base case** | | | | | | | | |
| After-tax cost of debt (percent) | 7.6 | 6.6 | 6.1 | 5.9 | 5.8 | 5.8 | 5.8 | 5.8 |
| Cost of equity (percent) | 14.0 | 12.4 | 11.7 | 11.3 | 11.1 | 11.1 | 11.1 | 11.1 |
| Debt/enterprise value | 0.3 | 0.3 | 0.3 | 0.3 | 0.3 | 0.3 | 0.3 | 0.3 |
| WACC (percent) | 12.0 | 10.5 | 9.9 | 9.5 | 9.4 | 9.4 | 9.4 | 9.4 |
| | | | | | | | | |
| **Downside** | | | | | | | | |
| After-tax cost of debt (percent) | 7.6 | 37.1 | 105.9 | 37.1 | 19.9 | 6.2 | 5.8 | 5.8 |
| Cost of equity (percent) | 14.0 | 59.6 | 166.0 | 59.6 | 33.0 | 11.7 | 11.1 | 11.1 |
| Debt/enterprise value | 0.3 | 0.3 | 0.3 | 0.3 | 0.3 | 0.3 | 0.3 | 0.3 |
| WACC (percent) | 12.0 | 52.3 | 146.5 | 52.3 | 28.8 | 9.9 | 9.4 | 9.4 |

**Understand Estimates from Different Sources**    Estimates for country risk premiums from different sources usually fall in a very wide range because analysts use different methods.[18] But they frequently compensate for high estimates of country risk premiums by making aggressive estimates for growth and return forecasts.

An example is the valuation of a large Brazilian chemicals company that we undertook in 2002. Using a local WACC of 10 percent, we reached an enterprise value of 4.0 to 4.5 times EBITDA. A second advisor was also asked to value the company and came to a very similar valuation result—an EBITDA multiple of around 4.5—in spite of using a very high country risk premium of 11 percent on top of the WACC. The result was similar because the second advisor made performance assumptions that were extremely aggressive: real sales growth of almost 10 percent per year and a ROIC increasing to 46 percent in the long term. Such long-term performance assumptions are unrealistic for a commodity-based, competitive industry such as chemicals.

**Be Careful to Avoid Setting the Country Risk Premium Too High**    Make sure you understand the economic implications of a high country risk premium. We believe that a country risk premium for Brazil is far below the premiums of 5 percent and higher that analysts typically use.

One reason is that current valuations in the stock market do not support the discount rates implied by higher risk premiums. We estimated the trading multiples of enterprise value to the 2004 forecasted EBITA for the 30 largest Brazilian companies in terms of market capitalization. The median value for the multiple was 7.4 in October 2004. We estimated the implied WACC by means of a DCF valuation. We set the future long-term return on invested capital at 11 percent, approximately equal to the median historical ROIC for these companies over the past five or six years (a period after Brazil brought inflation under control, so it is indicative of a business-as-usual scenario). Assuming future long-term inflation at 4.4 percent and real growth at 3.0 percent for the Brazilian economy as a whole, the WACC for the Brazilian market implied by the EBITA multiple of 7.4 is around 10.3 percent. The WACC estimated with the CAPM method previously described is around 9.8 percent.[19] This would imply a country risk

---

[18] For an overview, see, for example, L. Pereiro, *Valuation of Companies in Emerging Markets: A Practical Approach* (New York: Wiley, 2002), 118.

[19] Based on a real risk-free rate of 2 percent, long-term inflation of 4.4 percent, a market risk premium of 5.0 percent, cost of debt of 7.6 percent, and a debt-to-capital ratio of 0.25.

premium for Brazil of around 0.5 percent. Of course, this is not a precise estimate; as the Brazilian market goes up and down, the implied WACC and country risk premium would change as well. But it does suggest a country risk premium that is far below the 5 percent that many analysts currently use.

The other reason for such a low country risk premium is that historical returns in the Brazilian stock market do not support a high premium. The average real-terms return on the Brazilian stock market over the past 10 years is 3.8 percent per year. Let's take this period as a proxy for a business-as-usual scenario: real GPD grew by around 2 percent per year on average, and inflation was moderate at around 9 percent annually. At a country risk premium of 5 percent, the expected return on a stock with a beta equal to one under a business-as-usual scenario should be around 12 percent in real terms,[20] which is far above these historical returns.

## 5     CALCULATING AND INTERPRETING RESULTS

Given the estimates for cash flow and the cost of capital, we can discount the free cash flows for ConsuCo under the base-case and downside scenarios. The resulting present values of operations are shown in Exhibit 14. Under each scenario, the valuation results are exactly the same for the nominal and real projections. The next step is to weight the valuation results by the scenario probabilities and derive the present value of operations. Finally, add the market value of the nonoperating assets and subtract the financial claims to get at the estimated equity value. The estimated value obtained for ConsuCo is 188 to 206 Reais per share, given a probability of economic distress of 25 to 35 percent.

ConsuCo's share price, like the Brazilian stock market in general, has been extremely volatile over recent years, as shown in Exhibit 15 on page 278. Thus, you need to be careful in comparing the valuation outcome of 188 to 206 Reais per share with the current (December 2004) share price of 230 Reais. Just four months earlier, the price was 150 Reais. At the beginning of that year it traded for 270 Reais.

Of course, in emerging markets share prices are not always reliable references for intrinsic value, for several reasons. First, free float is often limited, with large equity stakes in the hands of a small group of owners, leaving public shareholders with little or no influence. As a result, the share price in the market could well be below intrinsic value, as estimated from a DCF analysis. Also, liquidity in emerging-markets stocks is often much lower than in developed markets. Share prices may not fully reflect intrinsic value because not all information is incorporated in the market value. Finally, share prices in emerging markets are often much more volatile than in developed markets. The share price on any particular day could therefore be off from intrinsic value.

ConsuCo has a primary listing on the Brazilian stock exchange. Turnover in the stock, as measured by the number of days to trade the free float, is around 130 days, not too far above typical levels of around 100 days in the United States and Europe. Still, because of the share price volatility, triangulation of the DCF results with multiples and a country risk premium approach is important.

---

[20] Assuming a real risk-free rate of 2 percent and a market risk premium of 5 percent.

## EXHIBIT 14 ConsuCo: Scenario DCF Valuation

Reais million, percent

| | 2004 | 2005 | 2006 | 2007 | 2008 | 2009 | 2014 | 2019 |
|---|---|---|---|---|---|---|---|---|
| **Base case** | | | | | | | | |
| *Nominal projections* | | | | | | | | |
| Free cash flow | 331 | (161) | (14) | 166 | 379 | 833 | 1,065 | 1,491 |
| WACC (percent) | 12.0 | 10.5 | 9.9 | 9.5 | 9.4 | 9.4 | 9.4 | 9.4 |
| *Real projections* | | | | | | | | |
| Free cash flow | 309 | (143) | (12) | 134 | 293 | 615 | 633 | 714 |
| WACC (percent) | 4.5 | 4.6 | 4.7 | 4.7 | 4.7 | 4.7 | 4.7 | 4.7 |
| **Downside** | | | | | | | | |
| *Nominal projections* | | | | | | | | |
| Free cash flow | 135 | (2,817) | (11,192) | (11,205) | (10,491) | (4,039) | (3,851) | 8,004 |
| WACC (percent) | 12.0 | 52.3 | 146.5 | 52.3 | 28.8 | 9.9 | 9.4 | 9.4 |
| *Real projections* | | | | | | | | |
| Free cash flow | 126 | (1,753) | (2,786) | (1,859) | (1,392) | (511) | (392) | 656 |
| WACC (percent) | 4.5 | 1.5 | (1.4) | 1.5 | 3.0 | 4.7 | 4.7 | 4.7 |

**Base case**

| **DCF value** | **24,459** |
|---|---|
| Nonoperating assets | 3,010 |
| Debt and debt equivalents | (11,097) |
| **Equity value** | **16,372** |
| **Value per share (Reais)** | 253 |

1 – p^a = 75%
(65%)

**Downside**

| **DCF value** | **12,427** |
|---|---|
| Nonoperating assets | 3,010 |
| Debt and debt equivalents | (11,097) |
| **Equity value** | **4,340** |
| **Value per share (Reais)** | 67 |

p^a = 25%
(35%)

Value per share (Reais)
**206**
**(188)**

a p = probability of economic distress.

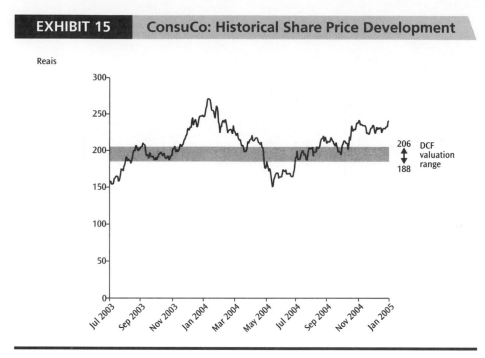

**EXHIBIT 15    ConsuCo: Historical Share Price Development**

## Triangulating with Multiples and Country Risk Premium Approach

For triangulation with multiples, do a best-practice multiples analysis to check valuation results. For the ConsuCo example, we compared the implied multiples of enterprise value over EBITDA with those of peer companies across the world. All multiples are forward-looking multiples over EBITDA as expected for 2005, based on analyst consensus forecasts. As Exhibit 16 illustrates, the implied multiple from our ConsuCo valuation is quite similar to most of its peers, at around seven times EBITDA. Apparently, the fact that ConsuCo is domiciled in Brazil does not matter much for the relative pricing of its stock. This is another indication that any country risk premium for ConsuCo should be very small. Using the average multiple for the peer group of 8.3, the value of ConsuCo would end up at 228 Reais, as shown in Exhibit 17. Note that this is probably an aggressive estimate, given that there are some outliers in the peer group with extremely high multiples. Using the median multiple of 7.1 would lead to a valuation estimate of 176 Reais per share.

The last part of the triangulation consists of a valuation of ConsuCo using a country risk premium approach. We estimated the country risk premium for Brazil at around 0.5 percent earlier in this reading. Discounting the business-as-usual scenario at the cost of capital plus this country risk premium leads to a value per share of 167 Reais, below the result obtained in the scenario DCF approach.

Note that a risk premium of 5 percent (as typically used in Brazil) would either result in unrealistically low valuations relative to current share price and peer group multiples, or require an unrealistic, bullish forecast of future performance with returns on capital of at least 15 percent and real growth rates of at least 6 percent for many years. Given long-term returns and growth in its industry and the historical performance of ConsuCo, even taking just the good years into account, such forecasts are unreasonable.

| EXHIBIT 16 | ConsuCo: Multiples Analysis versus Peers |
|---|---|

EV/EBITDA 05

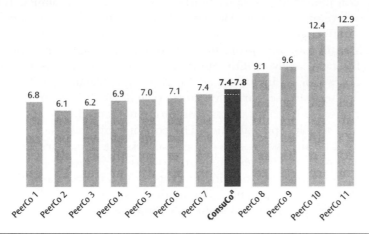

[a] Multiple of EV/EBITDA implied by DCF valuation range.

| EXHIBIT 17 | ConsuCo: Valuation Summary |
|---|---|

Reais, million

| | Scenario DCF valuation[a] low | Scenario DCF valuation[a] high | Average multiple valuation | Median multiple valuation | Country risk premium DCF valuation |
|---|---|---|---|---|---|
| EBITDA multiple | | | 8.3 | 7.1 | |
| EBITDA 2005 | | | 2,746 | 2,746 | |
| | | | | | |
| DCF value | 20,248 | 21,451 | 22,841 | 19,496 | 18,933 |
| Nonoperating assets | 3,010 | 3,010 | 3,010 | 3,010 | 3,010 |
| Debt and debt equivalents | (11,097) | (11,097) | (11,097) | (11,097) | (11,097) |
| Equity value | 12,161 | 13,364 | 14,754 | 11,409 | 10,846 |
| | | | | | |
| Number of shares (million) | 65 | 65 | 65 | 65 | 65 |
| Value per share | 188 | 206 | 228 | 176 | 167 |

[a] Shown are the probability-weighted values.

Given the inherent uncertainty in valuing emerging-market companies, it is best to use an explicit value range instead of a point estimate. For ConsuCo, we summarize the valuation findings in Exhibit 17. Based on the DCF valuation and multiples comparison, we end up with a range of about 175 to 205 Reais per share, depending on the exact scenario and probability assumptions, compared with a 12-month share price range of 150 to 270 Reais per share.

## SUMMARY

To value companies in emerging markets, we use concepts similar to the ones applied to developed markets. However, the application of these concepts can be somewhat different. Inflation, which is often high in emerging markets, is factored into the cash flow projections by combining insights from both real and nominal financial analyses. Emerging market risks such as macroeconomic or political crises can be incorporated following the scenario DCF approach by developing alternative scenarios for future cash flows, discounting the cash flows at the cost of capital without country risk premium, and then weighting the DCF values by the scenario probabilities. The cost of capital estimates for emerging markets build on the assumption of a global risk-free rate, market risk premium and beta, following guidelines similar to those used for developed markets. Since the value of companies in emerging markets is often more volatile than in developed markets, we recommend triangulating the scenario DCF results with a country risk premium DCF and a multiples-based valuation.

# DISCOUNTED DIVIDEND VALUATION

by John D. Stowe, CFA, Thomas R. Robinson, CFA, Jerald E. Pinto, CFA, and Dennis W. McLeavey, CFA

## LEARNING OUTCOMES

| The candidate should be able to: | Mastery |
|---|---|
| **a.** compare and contrast dividends, free cash flow, and residual income as measures of cash flow in discounted cash flow valuation, and identify the investment situations for which each measure is suitable; | ☐ |
| **b.** determine whether a dividend discount model (DDM) is appropriate for valuing a stock; | ☐ |
| **c.** calculate the value of a common stock using the DDM for one-, two-, and multiple-period holding periods; | ☐ |
| **d.** calculate the value of a common stock using the Gordon growth model and explain the model's underlying assumptions; | ☐ |
| **e.** calculate the implied growth rate of dividends using the Gordon growth model and current stock price; | ☐ |
| **f.** calculate and interpret the present value of growth opportunities (PVGO) and the component of the leading price-to-earnings (P/E) related to PVGO, given no-growth earnings per share, earnings per share, the required rate of return, and the market price of the stock (or value of the stock); | ☐ |
| **g.** calculate the justified leading and trailing P/Es based on fundamentals using the Gordon growth model; | ☐ |
| **h.** calculate the value of noncallable fixed-rate perpetual preferred stock given the stock's annual dividend and the discount rate; | ☐ |
| **i.** explain the strengths and limitations of the Gordon growth model and justify the selection of the Gordon growth model to value a company's common shares, given the characteristics of the company being valued; | ☐ |
| **j.** explain the assumptions and justify the selection of the two-stage DDM, the H-model, the three-stage DDM, or spreadsheet modeling to value a company's common shares, given the characteristics of the company being valued; | ☐ |

www.cfainstitute.org/toolkit—Your online preparation resource

| **k.** explain the growth phase, transitional phase, and maturity phase of a business; | ☐ |
| **l.** explain terminal value and discuss alternative approaches to determining the terminal value in a discounted dividend model; | ☐ |
| **m.** calculate the value of common shares using the two-stage DDM, the H-model, and the three-stage DDM; | ☐ |
| **n.** explain how to estimate a required return based on any DDM, and calculate that return using the Gordon growth model and the H-model; | ☐ |
| **o.** define, calculate, and interpret the sustainable growth rate of a company, explain the calculation's underlying assumptions, and demonstrate the use of the DuPont analysis of return on equity in conjunction with the sustainable growth rate expression; | ☐ |
| **p.** illustrate the use of spreadsheet modeling to forecast dividends and value common shares. | ☐ |

# 1 INTRODUCTION

Common stock represents an ownership interest in a business. A business in its operations generates a stream of cash flows, and as owners of the business, common stockholders have an equity ownership claim on those future cash flows. Beginning with John Burr Williams (1938), analysts have developed this insight into a group of valuation models known as discounted cash flow (DCF) valuation models. DCF models—which view the intrinsic value of common stock as the present value of its expected future cash flows—are a fundamental tool in both investment management and investment research. This reading is the first of three that describe DCF models and address how to apply those models in practice.

Although the principles behind discounted cash flow valuation are simple, applying the theory to equity valuation can be challenging. Four broad steps in applying DCF analysis to equity valuation are

► choosing the class of DCF model—equivalently, selecting a specific definition of cash flow;
► forecasting the cash flows;
► choosing a discount rate methodology; and
► estimating the discount rate.

In this reading, we take the perspective that dividends—distributions to shareholders authorized by a corporation's board of directors—are an appropriate definition of cash flows. The class of models based on this idea is called dividend discount models, or DDMs. The basic objective of any DDM is to value a stock: The variety of implementations corresponds to different ways to model a company's future stream of dividend payments. The steps of choosing a discount rate methodology and estimating the discount rate involve the same considerations for all DCF models and so have been presented separately in a reading on return concepts.

The reading is organized as follows: Section 2 provides an overview of present value models. A general statement of the dividend discount model follows in Section 3. Forecasting dividends, individually and in detail, into the indefinite future is not generally practicable, so we usually simplify the dividend-forecasting problem. One approach is to assign dividends to a stylized growth pattern. The simplest pattern—dividends growing at a constant rate forever—is the constant growth (or Gordon growth) model, discussed in Section 4. For some companies, it is more appropriate to view earnings and dividends as having multiple stages of growth; we present multistage dividend discount models in Section 5. We present spreadsheet modeling in Section 5 as well. Section 6 lays out the determinants of dividend growth rates, and we conclude with a summary of the reading.

# PRESENT VALUE MODELS 2

Present value models as a group constitute a demanding and rigorous approach for valuing assets. In this section, we discuss the economic rationale for valuing an asset as the present value of its expected future cash flows. We also discuss alternative definitions of cash flows and present the major alternative methods for estimating the discount rate.

## 2.1 Valuation Based on the Present Value of Future Cash Flows

The value of an asset must be related to the benefits or returns we expect to receive from holding it. We call those returns the asset's future cash flows (we will define *cash flow* more concretely and technically later). We also need to recognize that a given amount of money received in the future is worth less than the same amount of money received today. Money received today gives us the option of immediately spending and consuming it, so money has a time value. Therefore, when valuing an asset, before adding up the estimated future cash flows, we must **discount** each cash flow back to the present: We reduce the cash flow's value with respect to how far away it is in time. The two elements of discounted cash flow valuation—estimating the cash flows and discounting the cash flows to account for the time value of money—provide the economic rationale for discounted cash flow valuation. In the simplest case, in which the timing and amounts of future cash flows are known with certainty, if we invest an amount equal to the present value of future cash flows at the given discount rate, that investment will replicate all of the asset's cash flows (with no money left over).

For some assets, such as government debt, cash flows may be essentially known with certainty—that is, they are default-risk-free. The appropriate discount rate for such a risk-free cash flow is a risk-free rate of interest. For example, if an asset has a single, certain cash flow of $100 to be received in two years, and the risk-free interest rate is 5 percent a year, the value of the asset is the present value of $100 discounted at the risk-free rate, $100/(1.05)2 = $90.70.

In contrast to risk-free debt, future cash flows for equity investments are not known with certainty—they are risky. Introducing risk makes applying the present value approach much more challenging. The most common approach to dealing with risky cash flows involves two adjustments relative to the risk-free case. First, we discount the *expected* value of the cash flows, viewing the cash flows as random variables.[1] Second, we adjust the discount rate to reflect the risk of the cash flows.

The following equation expresses the concept that an asset's value is the present value of its (expected) future cash flows:

$$V_0 = \sum_{t=1}^{n} \frac{CF_t}{(1 + r)^t}$$

(41-1)

where

$V_0$ = the value of the asset at time $t = 0$ (today)

$n$ = number of cash flows in the life of the asset ($n$ is set equal to $\infty$ for equities)

$CF_t$ = the cash flow (or the expected cash flow, for risky cash flows) at time $t$

$r$ = the discount rate or required rate of return

For simplicity, we represent the discount rate in Equation 41-1 as the same for all time periods (i.e., we assume a flat term structure of discount rates). The analyst has the latitude in this model, however, to apply different discount rates to different cash flows.[2]

Equation 41-1 gives an asset's value from the perspective of today ($t = 0$). Likewise, an asset's value at some point in the future equals the value of all subsequent cash flows discounted back to that point in time. Example 1 illustrates these points.

## EXAMPLE 1

**Value as the Present Value of Future Cash Flows**

We expect an asset to generate cash flows of $100 in one year, $150 in two years, and $200 in three years. The value of this asset today, using a 10 percent discount rate, is

$$V_0 = \frac{100}{(1.10)^1} + \frac{150}{(1.10)^2} + \frac{200}{(1.10)^3}$$

$$= 90.909 + 123.967 + 150.263 = \$365.14$$

The value at $t = 0$ is $365.14. We use this same logic to value an asset at a future date. The value of the asset at $t = 1$ is the present value, discounted back to $t = 1$, of all cash flows after this point. This value, $V_1$, is

$$V_1 = \frac{150}{(1.10)^1} + \frac{200}{(1.10)^2}$$

$$= 136.364 + 165.289 = \$301.65$$

---

[1] The expected value of a random quantity is the mean or average value of its possible outcomes, in which each outcome's weight in the average is its probability of occurrence. See DeFusco, McLeavey, Pinto, and Runkle (2004) for all statistical concepts used in this reading.

[2] Different discount rates could reflect different degrees of cash flow riskiness or different risk-free rates at different time horizons. Differences in cash flow riskiness may be caused by differences in business risk, operating risk (use of fixed assets in production), or financial risk or leverage (use of debt in the capital structure). The simple expression given is adequate for the discussion, however.

At any point in time, the asset's value is the value of future cash flows (CF) discounted back to that point. Because $V_1$ represents the value of $CF_2$ and $CF_3$ at $t = 1$, the value of the asset at $t = 0$ is also the present value of $CF_1$ and $V_1$:

$$V_0 = \frac{100}{(1.10)^1} + \frac{301.653}{(1.10)^1}$$

$$= 90.909 + 274.23 = \$365.14$$

Finding $V_0$ as the present value of $CF_1$, $CF_2$, and $CF_3$ is logically equivalent to finding $V_0$ as the present value of $CF_1$ and $V_1$.

In the next section, we present an overview of three alternative definitions of cash flow. The selected cash flow concept defines the type of DCF model we can use: the dividend discount model, the free cash flow model, or the residual income model. We also broadly characterize the types of valuation problems for which analysts often choose a particular model. (We supply further details when each model is discussed individually.)

## 2.2 Streams of Expected Cash Flows

In present value models of stock valuation, the three most widely used definitions of returns are dividends, free cash flow, and residual income. We discuss each definition in turn.

The dividend discount model defines cash flows as dividends. The basic argument for using this definition of cash flow is that an investor who buys and holds a share of stock generally receives cash returns only in the form of dividends.[3] In practice, analysts usually view investment value as driven by earnings. Does the definition of cash flow as dividends ignore earnings not distributed to shareholders as dividends? Reinvested earnings should provide the basis for increased future dividends. Therefore, the DDM accounts for reinvested earnings when it takes all future dividends into account. Because dividends are less volatile than earnings and other return concepts, the relative stability of dividends may make DDM values less sensitive to short-run fluctuations in underlying value than alternative DCF models. Analysts often view DDM values as reflecting long-run intrinsic value.

A stock either pays dividends or does not pay dividends. A company might not pay dividends on its stock because the company is not profitable and has no cash to distribute. Also, a company might not pay dividends for the opposite reason: because it is very profitable. For example, a company may reinvest all earnings—paying no dividends—to take advantage of profitable growth opportunities. As that company matures and faces fewer attractive investment opportunities, it may initiate dividends.

There are international differences in dividend policy. As one contrast, more than 90 percent of the FTSE Eurofirst 300 stocks pay dividends, compared with approximately 70 percent of the stocks in the S&P 500 as of the beginning of 2002.[4] Wanger (2007) has noted a much higher propensity for Europe- and

---

[3] Corporations can also effectively distribute cash to stockholders through stock repurchases (also called buybacks). This fact does not affect the argument, however.

[4] *Financial Times of London,* January 28, 2002.

Asia-based small-cap companies to be dividend-payers. Nevertheless, in the United States, the majority of all companies with publicly traded shares do not pay dividends, and the fraction of dividend-paying companies has been declining. According to Fama and French (2001), 20.8 percent of U.S. stocks paid dividends in 1999, compared with 66.5 percent in 1978. This decline was caused by a reduced propensity to pay dividends over time as well as an increase in the population of smaller publicly traded companies with low profitability and large growth opportunities.[5] Can we apply the DDM to non-dividend paying companies? In theory we can, as we will illustrate later, but in practice we generally do not.

Predicting the timing of dividend initiation and the magnitude of future dividends without any prior dividend data or specifics about dividend policy to guide the analysis is generally not practical. For a non-dividend-paying company, analysts usually prefer a model that defines returns at the company level (as free cash flow or residual income—we define these concepts shortly) rather than at the stockholder level (as dividends). Another consideration in the choice of models relates to ownership perspective. An investor purchasing a small ownership share does not have the ability to meaningfully influence the timing or magnitude of the distribution of the company's cash to shareholders. That perspective is the one taken in applying a dividend discount model. The only access to the company's value is through the receipt of dividends, and dividend policy is taken as a given. If dividends do not bear an understandable relation to value creation in the company, applying the DDM to value the stock is prone to error.

Generally, the definition of returns as dividends, and the DDM, is most suitable when

▶ the company is dividend-paying (i.e., the analyst has a dividend record to analyze);

▶ the board of directors has established a dividend policy that bears an understandable and consistent relationship to the company's profitability; and

▶ the investor takes a non-control perspective.

Often, companies with established dividends are seasoned companies, profitable but operating outside the economy's fastest-growing subsectors. Professional analysts often apply a dividend discount model to value the common stock of such companies.

---

### EXAMPLE 2

#### Coca-Cola Bottling Company and Hormel Foods: Is the DDM an Appropriate Choice?

As director of equity research at a brokerage, you have final responsibility in the choice of valuation models. An analyst covering consumer/noncyclicals has approached you on the use of a dividend discount model for valuing the equity of two companies: Coca-Cola Bottling Company Consolidated (NASDAQ: COKE) and Hormel Foods (NYSE: HRL). Exhibit 1 gives the most recent 15 years of data. (In the table, EPS is earnings per share, DPS is dividends per share, and payout ratio is DPS divided by EPS.)

---

[5] Even controlling for profitability and growth opportunities, the propensity of companies to pay dividends has been declining in the U.S. markets, according to Fama and French (2001).

| EXHIBIT 1 | | | COKE and HRL: The Earnings and Dividends Record | | | |
|---|---|---|---|---|---|---|
| | **COKE** | | | **HRL** | | |
| Year | EPS ($) | DPS ($) | Payout Ratio (%) | EPS ($) | DPS ($) | Payout Ratio (%) |
| 2006 | 2.55 | 1.00 | 39 | 2.05 | 0.56 | 27 |
| 2005 | 2.53 | 1.00 | 40 | 1.82 | 0.52 | 29 |
| 2004 | 2.41 | 1.00 | 41 | 1.65 | 0.45 | 27 |
| 2003 | 3.40 | 1.00 | 29 | 1.33 | 0.42 | 32 |
| 2002 | 2.56 | 1.00 | 39 | 1.35 | 0.39 | 29 |
| 2001 | 1.07 | 1.00 | 93 | 1.30 | 0.37 | 28 |
| 2000 | 0.71 | 1.00 | 141 | 1.20 | 0.35 | 29 |
| 1999 | 0.37 | 1.00 | 270 | 1.11 | 0.33 | 30 |
| 1998 | 1.75 | 1.00 | 57 | 0.93 | 0.32 | 34 |
| 1997 | 1.79 | 1.00 | 56 | 0.72 | 0.39 | 54 |
| 1996 | 1.73 | 1.00 | 58 | 0.52 | 0.30 | 58 |
| 1995 | 1.67 | 1.00 | 60 | 0.79 | 0.29 | 37 |
| 1994 | 1.52 | 1.00 | 66 | 0.77 | 0.25 | 32 |
| 1993 | 1.60 | 0.88 | 55 | 0.66 | 0.22 | 33 |
| 1992 | (0.23) | 0.88 | NM* | 0.62 | 0.18 | 29 |

*NM = Not meaningful

*Source*: Standard & Poor's Stock Reports, www.sec.edgar-online.com.

Answer the following questions based on the information in Exhibit 1:

1. State whether a dividend discount model is an appropriate choice for valuing COKE. Explain your answer.

2. State whether a dividend discount model is an appropriate choice for valuing HRL. Explain your answer.

**Solution to 1:** Based only on the data given in Exhibit 1, a DDM does not appear to be an appropriate choice for valuing COKE. COKE's dividends have been $1.00 per share since 1994. In 1994, COKE's EPS was $1.52 and EPS grew through 1997. After a steep decline in the period 1999 through 2001, COKE's earnings have re-established themselves at a level above $2.40 per share from 2002 on. In short, over a twelve year period 1994–2006, COKE achieved compound annual growth of 4.4 percent with considerable variability while DPS were flat. Just based on the record presented, it is hard to discern an understandable and consistent relationship of dividends to earnings. Because dividends do not appear to adjust to reflect changes in profitability, applying a DDM to COKE is probably inappropriate. Valuing COKE on another basis, such as company-level definition of cash flows, appears to be more appropriate.

**Solution to 2:** The historical earnings of HRL show a long-term upward trend, with the exception of 1996, 1997, and 2003. Although you might want to research those divergent payout ratios, HRL's

> dividends have generally followed its growth in earnings. Earnings per share and dividends per share grew at comparable compound annual growth rates of 8.9 percent and 8.4 percent over the entire period. Over the most recent five year period, EPS and DPS also grew at comparable rates, reflecting a dividend payout ratio varying only between 29 percent and 32 percent. In summary, because HRL is dividend-paying and dividends bear an understandable and consistent relationship to earnings, using a DDM to value HRL is appropriate.
>
> Valuation is a forward-looking exercise. In practice, the analyst would check for public disclosures concerning changes in dividend policy going forward.

A second definition of returns is free cash flow. The term *cash flow* has been given many meanings in different contexts. Above, we have used the term informally, referring to returns to ownership (equity). We now want to give it a more technical meaning, related to accounting usage. Over a given period of time, a company can add to cash (or use up cash) by selling goods and services. This money is cash flow from operations (for that time period). Cash flow from operations is the critical cash flow concept addressing a business's underlying economics. Companies can also generate (or use up) cash in two other ways. First, a company affects cash through buying and selling assets, including investment and disinvestment in plant and equipment. Second, a company can add to or reduce cash through its financing activities. Financing includes debt and equity. For example, issuing bonds increases cash, and buying back stock decreases cash (all else equal).[6]

Assets supporting current sales may need replacement because of obsolescence or wear and tear, and the company may need new assets to take advantage of profitable growth opportunities. The concept of free cash flow responds to the reality that, for a going concern, some of the cash flow from operations is not "free" but rather needs to be committed to reinvestment and new investment in assets. **Free cash flow to the firm** (FCFF) is cash flow from operations minus capital expenditures. Capital expenditures—reinvestment in new assets, including working capital—are needed to maintain the company as a going concern, so only that part of cash flow from operations remaining after such reinvestment is "free." (This definition is conceptual; a later reading defines free cash flow concepts in detail.) FCFF is the part of the cash flow generated by the company's operations that can be withdrawn by bondholders and stockholders without economically impairing the company. Conceptually, the value of common equity is the present value of expected future FCFF—the total value of the company—minus the market value of outstanding debt.

Another approach to valuing equity works with free cash flow to equity. **Free cash flow to equity** (FCFE) is cash flow from operations minus capital expenditures, or FCFF, from which we net all payments to debtholders (interest and principal repayments net of new debt issues). Debt has a claim on the cash of the

---

[6] Internationally, accounting definitions may not be fully consistent with the above concepts in distinguishing between types of sources and uses of cash. Although the implementation details are not the focus here, an example can be given. U.S. generally accepted accounting principles (GAAP) include a financing item, net interest payments, in *cash flow from operating activities*, so careful analysts working with U.S. accounting data often add back after-tax net interest payments to cash flow from operating activities when calculating cash flow from operations. Under International Accounting Standards, companies may or may not include interest expense as an operating cash flow.

company that must be satisfied before any money can be paid to stockholders, so money paid on debt is not available to common stockholders. Conceptually, common equity can be valued as the present value of expected FCFE. FCFF is a pre-debt free cash flow concept; FCFE is a post-debt free cash flow concept. The FCFE model is the baseline free cash flow valuation model for equity, but the FCFF model may be easier to apply in several cases, such as when the company's leverage (debt in its capital structure) is expected to change significantly over time.

Valuation using a free cash flow concept is popular in current investment practice. We can calculate free cash flow (FCFF or FCFE) for any company. We can examine the record of free cash flows even for a non-dividend-paying company. FCFE can be viewed as measuring what a company can afford to pay out in dividends. Even for dividend-paying companies, a free cash flow model valuation may be preferred when dividends exceed or fall short of FCFE by significant amounts.[7] FCFE also represents cash flow that can be redeployed outside the company without affecting the company's capital investments. A controlling equity interest can effect such redeployment. As a result, free cash flow valuation is appropriate for investors who want to take a control perspective. (Even a small shareholder may want to take such a perspective when there is potential for the company to be acquired, because stock price should reflect the price an acquirer would pay.)

Just as there are cases in which an analyst would find it impractical to apply the DDM, applying the free cash flow approach is a problem in some cases. Some companies have intense capital demands and, as a result, have negative expected free cash flows far into the future. As one example, a retailer may be constantly constructing new outlets and be far from saturating even its domestic market. Even if the retailer is currently very profitable, free cash flow may be negative indefinitely because of the level of capital expenditures. The present value of a series of negative free cash flows is a negative number: The use of a free cash flow model may entail a long forecast horizon to capture the point at which expected free cash flow turns positive. The uncertainty associated with distant forecasts may be considerable. In such cases, the analyst may have more confidence using another approach, such as residual income valuation.

Generally, defining returns as free cash flow and using the FCFE (and FCFF) models are most suitable when

▶ the company is not dividend-paying;

▶ the company is dividend-paying but dividends significantly exceed or fall short of free cash flow to equity;

▶ the company's free cash flows align with the company's profitability within a forecast horizon with which the analyst is comfortable; and

▶ the investor takes a control perspective.

The third and final definition of returns that we will discuss in this overview is residual income. Conceptually, **residual income** for a given time period is the earnings for that period in excess of the investors' required return on beginning-of-period investment (common stockholders' equity). Suppose shareholders' initial investment is $200 million, and the required rate of return on the stock is 8 percent. The required rate of return is investors' **opportunity cost** for investing

---

[7] In theory, when period-by-period dividends equal FCFE, the DDM and FCFE models should value stock identically, if all other assumptions are consistent. See Miller and Modigliani (1961), a classic reference for the mathematics and theory of present value models of stock value.

in the stock: the highest expected return available from other equally risky investments which is the return that investors forgo when investing in the stock. The company earns $18 million in the course of a year. How much value has the company added for shareholders? A return of $0.08 \times \$200$ million = $16 million just meets the amount investors could have earned in an equivalent-risk investment (by the definition of opportunity cost). Only the residual or excess amount of $18 million − $16 million = $2 million represents value added, or an economic gain, to shareholders. So, $2 million is the company's residual income for the period. The residual income approach attempts to match profits to the time period in which they are earned (but not necessarily realized as cash). In contrast to accounting net income (which has the same matching objective in principle), however, residual income attempts to measure the value added in excess of opportunity costs.

The residual income model states that a stock's value is book value per share plus the present value of expected future residual earnings. (Book value per share is common stockholders' equity divided by the number of common shares outstanding.) In contrast to the dividend and free cash flow models, the residual income model introduces a stock concept, book value per share, into the present value expression. Nevertheless, the residual income model can be viewed as a restatement of the dividend discount model, using a company-level return concept. Dividends are paid out of earnings and are related to earnings and book value through a simple expression.[8] The residual income model is a useful addition to an analyst's toolbox. Because we can always calculate the record of residual income, we may use a residual income model for both dividend-paying and non-dividend-paying stocks. Analysts may choose a residual income approach for companies with negative expected free cash flows within their comfortable forecast horizon. In such cases, a residual income valuation often brings the recognition of value closer to the present as compared with a free cash flow valuation, producing higher value estimates.

The residual income model has an attractive focus on profitability in relation to opportunity costs.[9] Knowledgeable application of the residual income model requires a detailed knowledge of accrual accounting; consequently, in cases for which the dividend discount model is suitable, analysts may prefer it as the simpler choice. Management sometimes exercises its discretion within allowable accounting practices to distort the accuracy of its financials as a reflection of economic performance. If the quality of accounting disclosure is good, the analyst may be able to calculate residual income by making appropriate adjustments (to reported net income and book value, in particular). In some cases, the degree of distortion and the quality of accounting disclosure can be such that the application of the residual income model is error-prone.

Generally, the definition of returns as residual income, and the residual income model, is most suitable when

---

[8] Book value of equity at $t$ = (Book value of equity at $t − 1$) + (Earnings over $t − 1$ to $t$) − (Dividends paid at $t$), so long as anything that goes through the balance sheet (affecting book value) first goes through the income statement (reflected in earnings), apart from ownership transactions. The condition that all changes in the book value of equity other than transactions with owners are reflected in income is known as **clean surplus accounting**. U.S. and international accounting standards do not always follow clean surplus accounting; the analyst, therefore, in using this expression, must critically evaluate whether accounting-based results conform to clean surplus accounting and, if they do not, adjust them appropriately.

[9] Executive compensation schemes are sometimes based on a residual income concept, including branded variations such as Economic Value Added (EVA®) from Stern Stewart & Co.

▶ the company is not dividend-paying, as an alternative to a free cash flow model; or

▶ the company's expected free cash flows are negative within the analyst's comfortable forecast horizon.

In summary, the three most widely used definitions of returns to investors are dividends, free cash flow, and residual income. Although claims are often made that one cash flow definition is inherently superior to the rest—often following changing fashions in investment practice—a more flexible viewpoint is practical. The analyst may find that one model is more suitable to a particular valuation problem. The analyst may also develop more expertise in applying one type of model. In practice, skill in application—in particular, the quality of forecasts—is frequently decisive for the usefulness of the analyst's work.

In the next section, we present the general form of the dividend discount model as a prelude to discussing the particular implementations of the model that are suitable for different sets of attributes of the company being valued.

# THE DIVIDEND DISCOUNT MODEL                3

Investment analysts use a wide range of models and techniques to estimate the value of common stock, including present value models. In Section 2.2, we discussed three common definitions of returns for use in present value analysis: dividends, free cash flow, and residual income. In this section, we develop the most general form of the dividend discount model.

The DDM is the simplest and oldest present value approach to valuing stock. In a survey of CFA Institute[10] members by Block (1999), 42 percent of respondents viewed the DDM as "very important" or "moderately important" for determining the value of individual stocks. Beginning in 1989, the *Merrill Lynch Institutional Factor Survey* has assessed the popularity of 23 valuation factors and methods among a group of institutional investors. The highest recorded usage level of the DDM was in the first survey in 1989, when just over 50 percent of respondents reported using the DDM. Although DDMs have had five years of popularity increases since 1989 (with a notable rebound to 39 percent usage in 2002), the long term trend has been one of decline, with usage at just over 20 percent in 2006—still a significant presence. Besides its continuing significant position in practice, the DDM has an important place in both academic and practitioner equity research. The DDM is, for all these reasons, a basic tool in equity valuation.

## 3.1 The Expression for a Single Holding Period

From the perspective of a shareholder who buys and holds a share of stock, the cash flows he or she will obtain are the dividends paid on it and the market price of the share when he or she sells it. The future selling price should in turn reflect expectations about dividends subsequent to the sale. In this section, we will see how this argument leads to the most general form of the dividend discount model. In addition, the general expression we develop for a finite holding period corresponds to one practical approach to DDM valuation; in that

---

[10] Then called and referred to in the Block (1999) paper as the Association for Investment Management and Research. The name was changed to CFA Institute in 2004.

approach, the analyst forecasts dividends over a finite horizon, as well as the terminal sales price.

If an investor wishes to buy a share of stock and hold it for one year, the value of that share of stock today is the present value of the expected dividend to be received on the stock plus the present value of the expected selling price in one year:

$$V_0 = \frac{D_1}{(1 + r)^1} + \frac{P_1}{(1 + r)^1} = \frac{D_1 + P_1}{(1 + r)^1} \tag{41-2}$$

where

$V_0$ = the value of a share of stock today, at $t = 0$
$P_1$ = the expected price per share at $t = 1$
$D_1$ = the expected dividend per share for Year 1, assumed to be paid at the end of the year at $t = 1$
$r$ = the required rate of return on the stock

Equation 41-2 applies to a single holding period the principle that an asset's value is the present value of its future cash flows. In this case, the expected cash flows are the dividend in one year (for simplicity, assumed to be received as one payment at the end of the year)[11] and the price of the stock in one year.

---

### EXAMPLE 3

**DDM Value with a Single Holding Period**

Suppose that you expect Carrefour SA (NYSE Euronext Paris: CA) to pay a €1.10 dividend next year. You expect the price of CA stock to be €53.55 in one year. The required rate of return for CA stock is 9 percent. What is your estimate of the value of CA stock?

Discounting the expected dividend of €1.10 and the expected sales price of €53.55 at the required return on equity of 9 percent, we obtain

$$V_0 = \frac{D_1 + P_1}{(1 + r)^1} = \frac{1.10 + 53.55}{(1 + 0.09)^1} = \frac{54.65}{1.09} = 50.14$$

---

## 3.2 The Expression for Multiple Holding Periods

If an investor plans to hold a stock for two years, the value of the stock is the present value of the expected dividend in Year 1, plus the present value of the expected dividend in Year 2, plus the present value of the expected selling price at the end of Year 2.

$$V_0 = \frac{D_1}{(1 + r)^1} + \frac{D_2}{(1 + r)^2} + \frac{P_2}{(1 + r)^2} = \frac{D_1}{(1 + r)^1} + \frac{D_2 + P_2}{(1 + r)^2} \tag{41-3}$$

The expression for the DDM value of a share of stock for any finite holding period is a straightforward extension of the expressions for one-year and two-

---

[11] Throughout the discussion of the DDM, we assume that dividends for a period are paid in one sum at the end of the period.

year holding periods. For an $n$-period model, the value of a stock is the present value of the expected dividends for the $n$ periods plus the present value of the expected price in $n$ periods (at $t = n$).

$$V_0 = \frac{D_1}{(1 + r)^1} + \Lambda + \frac{D_n}{(1 + r)^n} + \frac{P_n}{(1 + r)^n} \qquad \text{(41-4)}$$

If we use summation notation to represent the present value of the first $n$ expected dividends, the general expression for an $n$-period holding period or investment horizon can be written as

$$V_0 = \sum_{t=1}^{n} \frac{D_t}{(1 + r)^t} + \frac{P_n}{(1 + r)^n} \qquad \text{(41-5)}$$

Equation 41-5 is significant in DDM application, because analysts may make individual forecasts of dividends over some finite horizon (often two to five years), and then estimate the terminal price, $P_n$, based on one of a number of approaches. (We will discuss valuation using a finite forecasting horizon later, under the heading of spreadsheet modeling.) Example 4 reviews the mechanics of this calculation.

## EXAMPLE 4

### Finding the Stock Price for a Five-Year Forecast Horizon

For the next five years, the annual dividends of a stock are expected to be $2.00, $2.10, $2.20, $3.50, and $3.75. In addition, the stock price is expected to be $40.00 in five years. If the required return on equity is 10 percent, what is the value of this stock?

The present values of the expected future cash flows can be written out as

$$V_0 = \frac{2.00}{(1.10)^1} + \frac{2.10}{(1.10)^2} + \frac{2.20}{(1.10)^3} + \frac{3.50}{(1.10)^4}$$

$$+ \frac{3.75}{(1.10)^5} + \frac{40.00}{(1.10)^5}$$

Calculating and summing these present values gives a stock value of $V_0 = 1.818 + 1.736 + 1.653 + 2.391 + 2.328 + 24.837 = \$34.76$.

The five dividends have a total present value of $9.926 and the terminal stock value has a present value of $24.837, for a total stock value of $34.76.

With a finite holding period, whether one, two, five, or some other number of years, the dividend discount model finds the value of stock as the sum of (1) the present values of the expected dividends over the holding period, and (2) the present value of the expected stock price at the end of the holding period. As we increase the holding period by one year, we have an extra expected dividend term. In the limit (i.e., if we let the holding period extend into the indefinite future), the stock's value is the present value of all expected future dividends.

$$V_0 = \frac{D_1}{(1 + r)^1} + \dots + \frac{D_n}{(1 + r)^n} + \dots \qquad \text{(41-6)}$$

This value can be expressed with summation notation as

$$V_0 = \sum_{t=1}^{\infty} \frac{D_t}{(1 + r)^t} \qquad \text{(41-7)}$$

Equation 41-7 is the general form of the dividend discount model, first presented by John Burr Williams (1938). Even from the perspective of an investor with a finite investment horizon, the value of stock depends on all future dividends. For that investor, stock value today depends *directly* on the dividends the investor expects to receive before the stock is sold and *indirectly* on the expected dividends after the stock is sold, because those future dividends determine the expected selling price.

Equation 41-7, expressing the value of stock as the present value of expected dividends into the indefinite future, presents a daunting forecasting challenge. In practice, of course, we cannot make detailed, individual forecasts of an infinite number of dividends. To use the DDM, we must simplify the forecasting problem. There are two broad approaches, each of which has several variations:

1. We can forecast future dividends by assigning the stream of future dividends to one of several stylized growth patterns. The most commonly used patterns are
   ▶ constant growth forever (the Gordon growth model),
   ▶ two distinct stages of growth (the two-stage growth model and the H-model), and
   ▶ three distinct stages of growth (the three-stage growth model).

   The DDM value of the stock is then found by discounting the dividend streams back to the present. We present the Gordon growth model in Section 4. We present the two-stage, H-model, and three-stage growth models in Section 5.

2. We can forecast a finite number of dividends individually up to a terminal point, using pro forma financial statement analysis, for example. Typically, such forecasts extend from three to ten years into the future. Although some analysts apply the same horizon to all companies under analysis, the horizon selected often depends on the perceived predictability (sometimes called the **visibility**) of the company's earnings. We can then forecast either
   ▶ the remaining dividends from the terminal point forward by assigning those dividends to a stylized growth pattern, or
   ▶ the share price at the terminal point of our dividend forecasts (**terminal share price**), using some method (such as taking a multiple of forecasted book value or earnings per share as of that point, based on one of several methods for estimating such multiples).

   The stock's DDM value is then found by discounting the dividends (and forecasted price, if any) back to the present.

Spreadsheets are particularly convenient tools for implementing a DDM with individual dividend forecasts, but are useful in all cases. We address spreadsheet modeling in Section 5.

Whether we are using dividends or some other definition of cash flow, we generally use one of the above forecasting approaches when we value stock. The challenge in practice is to choose an appropriate model for a stock's future dividends and to develop quality inputs to that model.

# THE GORDON GROWTH MODEL                     **4**

The Gordon growth model, developed by Gordon and Shapiro (1956) and Gordon (1962), assumes that dividends grow indefinitely at a constant rate. This assumption, applied to the general dividend discount model (Equation 41-7), leads to a simple and elegant valuation formula that has been influential in investment practice. This section explores the development of the Gordon growth model and illustrates its uses.

## 4.1 The Gordon Growth Model Equation

The simplest pattern we can assume in forecasting future dividends is growth at a constant rate. In mathematical terms, we can state this assumption as

$$D_t = D_{t-1}(1 + g)$$

where $g$ is the expected constant growth rate in dividends and $D_t$ is the expected dividend payable at time $t$. Suppose, for example, that the most recent dividend, $D_0$, was €10. Then, if we forecast a 5 percent dividend growth rate, we have for the expected dividend at $t = 1$, $D_1 = D_0(1 + g) = €10 \times 1.05 = €10.5$. For any time $t$, $D_t$ also equals the $t = 0$ dividend, compounded at $g$ for $t$ periods:

$$D_t = D_0(1 + g)^t$$                    **(41-8)**

To continue the example, at the end of five years the expected dividend is $D_5 = D_0(1 + g)^5 = €10 \times (1.05)^5 = €10 \times 1.276282 = €12.76$. If $D_0(1 + g)^t$ is substituted into Equation 41-7 for $D_t$, we obtain the Gordon growth model. If all of the terms are written out, they are

$$V_0 = \frac{D_0(1 + g)}{(1 + r)} + \frac{D_0(1 + g)^2}{(1 + r)^2} + \ldots + \frac{D_0(1 + g)^n}{(1 + r)^n} + \ldots$$    **(41-9)**

Equation 41-9 is a geometric series; that is, each term in the expression is equal to the previous term times a constant, which in this case is $(1 + g)/(1 + r)$. This equation can be simplified algebraically into a much more compact equation:[12]

$$V_0 = \frac{D_0(1 + g)}{r - g}, \text{ or } V_0 = \frac{D_1}{r - g}$$    **(41-10)**

Both equations are equivalent because $D_1 = D_0(1 + g)$. In Equation 41-10 we must specify that the required return on equity must be greater than the

---

[12] The simplification involves the expression for the sum of an infinite geometric progression with first term equal to $a$ and growth factor equal to $m$ with $|m| < 1$ (i.e., the sum of $a + am + am^2 + \ldots$ is $a/(1 - m)$). Setting $a = D_1/(1 + r)$ and $m = (1 + g)/(1 + r)$, we obtain the Gordon growth model.

expected growth rate: $r > g$. If $r = g$ or $r < g$, Equation 41-10 as a compact formula for value assuming constant growth is not valid. If $r = g$, dividends grow at the same rate at which they are discounted, so the value of the stock (as the undiscounted sum of all expected future dividends) is infinite. If $r < g$, dividends grow faster than they are discounted, so the value of the stock is infinite. Of course, infinite values do not make economic sense; so constant growth with $r = g$ or $r < g$ does not make sense.

To illustrate the calculation, suppose that an annual dividend of €5 has just been paid ($D_0 = $ €5). The expected long-term growth rate is 5 percent and the required return on equity is 8 percent. The Gordon growth model value per share is $D_0(1 + g)/(r - g) = ($ €5 $\times$ 1.05$)/(0.08 - 0.05) = $ €5.25$/0.03 = $ €175. When calculating the model value, be careful to use $D_1$ and not $D_0$ in the numerator.

The Gordon growth model (Equation 41-10) is one of the most widely recognized equations in the field of security analysis. Because the model is based on indefinitely extending future dividends, the model's required rate of return and growth rate should reflect long-term expectations. Further, model values are very sensitive to both the required rate of return, $r$, and the expected dividend growth rate, $g$. In this and other valuation models, it is helpful to perform a sensitivity analysis on the inputs, particularly when we are not confident about the proper values.

Earlier we stated that analysts typically apply DDMs to dividend-paying stocks when dividends bear an understandable and consistent relation to the company's profitability. The same qualifications hold for the Gordon growth model. In addition, the Gordon growth model form of the DDM is most appropriate for companies with earnings expected to grow at a rate comparable to or lower than the economy's nominal growth rate. Businesses growing at much higher rates than the economy often grow at lower rates in maturity, and our horizon in using the Gordon growth model is the entire future stream of dividends.

To determine whether the company's growth rate qualifies it as a candidate for the Gordon growth model, we need an estimate of the economy's nominal growth rate. This is usually measured by the growth in **gross domestic product** (GDP). (GDP is a money measure of the goods and services produced within a country's borders.) National government agencies as well as the World Bank (www.worldbank.org) publish GDP data, which are also available from several secondary sources. Exhibit 2 shows the recent real GDP growth record for a number of major developed markets.

| EXHIBIT 2 | Average Annual Real GDP Growth Rates: 1980–2006 (in Percent) | | |
|---|---|---|---|
| | **Time Period** | | |
| **Country** | **1980–89** | **1990–99** | **2000–06** |
| Australia | 3.4% | 3.3% | 3.1% |
| Canada | 3.0 | 2.4 | 3.0 |
| Denmark | 2.2 | 2.3 | 2.0 |
| France | 2.1 | 1.8 | 2.0 |
| Germany | 1.9 | 1.3 | 1.3 |
| Italy | 2.4 | 1.5 | 1.3 |

*(Exhibit continued on next page . . .)*

| EXHIBIT 2 | (continued) | | |
|---|---|---|---|

| | Time Period | | |
|---|---|---|---|
| **Country** | **1980–89** | **1990–99** | **2000–06** |
| Japan | 3.9 | 1.7 | 1.6 |
| Netherlands | 2.0 | 3.0 | 1.9 |
| Sweden | 2.4 | 1.8 | 2.9 |
| Switzerland | 1.8 | 1.1 | 1.9 |
| United Kingdom | 2.4 | 2.1 | 2.7 |
| United States | 3.1 | 3.1 | 2.6 |

*Source*: OECD, Datastream, Bloomberg.

Based on historical and/or forward-looking information, nominal GDP growth can be estimated as the sum of the estimated real growth rate in GDP plus the expected long-run inflation rate. For example, an estimate of the underlying real growth rate of the Canadian economy is 3 percent as of early 2007. Using the Bank of Canada's inflation target of 2 percent as the expected inflation rate, an estimate of the Canadian economy's nominal annual growth rate is 3% + 2% = 5 percent. Publicly traded companies constitute varying amounts of the total corporate sector, but always less than 100 percent. As a result, the overall growth rate of the public corporate sector can diverge from the nominal GDP growth rate over a long horizon; furthermore, within the public corporate sector, some subsectors may experience persistent growth rate differentials. Nevertheless, an earnings growth rate far above the nominal GDP growth rate is not sustainable in perpetuity.

When forecasting an earnings growth rate far above the economy's nominal growth rate, analysts should use a multistage DDM in which the final-stage growth rate reflects a growth rate that is more plausible relative to the economy's nominal growth rate, rather than using the Gordon growth model.

## EXAMPLE 5

### Valuation Using the Gordon Growth Model (1)

Joel Williams follows Sonoco Products Company (NYSE: SON), a manufacturer of paper and plastic packaging for both consumer and industrial use. SON appears to have a dividend policy of recognizing sustainable increases in the level of earnings with increases in dividends, keeping the dividend payout ratio within a range of 40 percent to 60 percent. Williams also notes:

▶ SON's most recent quarterly dividend (ex-dividend date: 15 August 2007) was $0.26, consistent with a current annual dividend of 4 × $0.26 = $1.04 per year.

▶ Williams forecasts dividend growth rate of 6.0 percent per year.

► With a beta ($\beta_i$) of 1.13, given an equity risk premium (expected excess return of equities over the risk-free rate, $E(R_M) - R_F$) of 4.5 percent and risk-free rate ($R_F$) of 5 percent, SON's required return on equity is $r = R_F + \beta_i[E(R_M) - R_F] = 5.0 + 1.13(4.5) = 10.1$ percent, using the CAPM.

Williams believes the Gordon growth model may be an appropriate model for valuing SON.

**1.** Calculate the Gordon growth model value for SON stock.

**2.** The current market price of SON stock is $30.18. Using your answer to Question 1, judge whether SON stock is fairly valued, undervalued, or overvalued.

**Solution to 1:** Using Equation 41-10,

$$V_0 = \frac{D_0(1 + g)}{r - g} = \frac{\$1.04 \times 1.06}{0.101 - 0.06} = \frac{\$1.10}{0.041} = \$26.89$$

**Solution to 2:** The market price of $30.18 is $3.29 or approximately 12 percent above the Gordon growth model intrinsic value estimate of $26.89. SON appears to be overvalued, based on the Gordon growth model estimate.

The next example illustrates a Gordon growth model valuation introducing some problems the analyst might face in practice. The example refers to adjusted beta; the most common calculation adjusts raw historical beta toward the overall mean value of 1 for beta.

## EXAMPLE 6

### Valuation Using the Gordon Growth Model (2)

As an analyst for a U.S. domestic equity–income mutual fund, Roberta Kim is evaluating Middlesex Water Company (NASDAQ: MSEX), a publicly traded water utility, for possible inclusion in the approved list of investments. Kim is conducting the analysis in early 2007.

Not all countries have traded water utility stocks. In the United States, about 85 percent of the population gets its water from government entities. A group of investor-owned water utilities, however, also supplies water to the public. With a market capitalization of about $250 million as of late 2007, MSEX is among the ten largest publicly traded U.S. water utilities. MSEX's historical base is the Middlesex System, serving residential, industrial, and commercial customers in a well-developed area of central New Jersey. Through various subsidiaries, MSEX also provides water and wastewater collection and treatment services to areas of southern New Jersey and Delaware.

Net income growth over the past five years has been 7 percent, in line with the long-term growth rate of nominal U.S. GDP. Over the last five years, MSEX's return on equity averaged 9 percent with relatively little variation, slightly below the 10 percent level targeted by some faster growing peer companies. Because MSEX obtains most of its revenue from the regulated business providing an important staple, water, to a relatively stable population, Kim feels confident in forecasting future earnings and dividend growth. MSEX appears to have a policy of small annual increases in the dividend rate, maintaining a dividend payout ratio of at least 80 percent. Other facts and forecasts include the following:

▶ MSEX's per-share dividends for 2006 ($D_0$) were \$0.68.

▶ Kim forecasts a long-term earnings growth rate of 6 percent per year, somewhat below the 8 percent consensus 3-to-5-year earnings growth rate forecast reported by Zacks Investment Research (based on two analysts).

▶ MSEX's raw beta and adjusted beta are, respectively, 0.717 and 0.811 based on 60 monthly returns. However, the $R^2$ associated with beta is under 10 percent.

▶ Kim estimates that MSEX's pretax cost of debt is 6.9 percent based on Standard & Poor's issuer rating for MSEX of A– and the current corporate yield curve.

▶ Kim's estimate of MSEX's required return on equity is 9.25 percent.

▶ MSEX's current market price is \$18.39.

**1.** Calculate the Gordon growth model estimate of value for MSEX using Kim's required return on equity estimate.

**2.** State whether MSEX appears to be overvalued, fairly valued, or undervalued based on the Gordon growth model estimate of value.

**3.** Justify the selection of the Gordon growth model for valuing MSEX.

**4.** Calculate the CAPM estimate of the required return on equity for MSEX under the assumption that beta regresses to the mean. (Assume an equity risk premium of 4.5 percent and a risk-free rate of 5 percent as of the price quotation date.)

**5.** Calculate the Gordon growth estimate of value (A) using the required return on equity from your answer to Question 4, and (B) using a bond-yield-plus-risk-premium approach using a risk premium of 3 percent.

**6.** Evaluate the effect of uncertainty in MSEX's required return on equity on the valuation conclusion in Question 2.

**Solution to 1:** From Equation 41-10,

$$V_0 = \frac{D_0(1 + g)}{r - g} = \frac{\$0.68(1.06)}{0.0925 - 0.06} = \$22.18$$

**Solution to 2:** Because the Gordon growth model estimate of \$22.18 is \$3.79 or about 21 percent higher than the market price of \$18.39, MSEX appears to be undervalued.

**Solution to 3:** The Gordon growth model, which assumes that dividends grow at a stable rate in perpetuity, is a realistic model for MSEX for the following reasons:

▶ MSEX profitability is stable as reflected in its return on equity. This reflects predictable demand and regulated prices for its product, water.

▶ Dividends bear an understandable and consistent relationship to earnings, as evidenced here by the company's policy of annual increases and predictable dividend payout ratios.

▶ Historical earnings growth, at 7 percent a year, is in line with long-term nominal annual GDP growth for the United States and is plausibly sustainable long term.

▶ Forecasted earnings growth is also in line with a plausible nominal GDP growth and does not include a period of forecasted very high or very low growth.

**Solution to 4:** The assumption of regression to the mean is characteristic of adjusted historical beta. The required return on equity as given by the CAPM is $5\% + 0.811(4.5\%) = 8.6$ percent using adjusted beta, which assumes reversion to the mean of 1.0.

**Solution to 5A:** The Gordon growth value of MSEX using a required return on equity of 8.6 percent is

$$V_0 = \frac{D_0(1 + g)}{r - g} = \frac{\$0.68(1.06)}{0.086 - 0.06} = \$27.72$$

**Solution to 5B:** The bond-yield-plus-risk premium estimate of the required return on equity is $6.9\% + 3\% = 9.9$ percent.

$$V_0 = \frac{D_0(1 + g)}{r - g} = \frac{\$0.68(1.06)}{0.099 - 0.06} = \$18.48$$

**Solution to 6:** Using the CAPM estimate of the required return on equity (Question 5A), MSEX appears to be definitely undervalued. However, beta explains less than 10 percent of the variation in MSEX's returns, according to the fact given concerning $R^2$. Using a bond-yield-plus-risk-premium approach, MSEX appears to be approximately fairly valued ($18.48 exceeds the market price of $18.39 by less than 1 percent). However, no specific evidence supports the particular value of the risk premium selected in the bond yield plus risk premium approach. In this case, because of the uncertainty in the required return on equity estimate, one has less confidence that MSEX is undervalued. In particular, the analyst may view MSEX as approximately fairly valued.

As mentioned earlier, we need to be aware that Gordon growth model values can be very sensitive to small changes in the values of the required rate of return and expected dividend growth rate. Example 7 illustrates a format for a sensitivity analysis.

## EXAMPLE 7

### Valuation Using the Gordon Growth Model (3)

In Example 6, the Gordon growth model value for MSEX was estimated as $22.18 based on a current dividend of $0.68, an expected dividend growth rate of 6 percent, and a required return on equity of 9.25 percent. What if our estimates of $r$ and $g$ can each vary by 25 basis points? How sensitive is the model value to changes in our estimates of $r$ and $g$? Exhibit 3 provides information on this sensitivity.

| EXHIBIT 3 | Estimated Price Given Uncertain Inputs | | |
|---|---|---|---|
|  | $g = 5.75\%$ | $g = 6.00\%$ | $g = 6.25\%$ |
| $r = 9.00\%$ | $22.13 | $24.03 | $26.27 |
| $r = 9.25\%$ | $20.55 | **$22.18** | $24.08 |
| $r = 9.50\%$ | $19.18 | $20.59 | $22.23 |

A point of interest following from the mathematics of the Gordon growth model is that when the spread between $r$ and $g$ is widest ($r = 9.50$ percent and $g = 5.75$ percent) the Gordon growth model value is smallest ($19.18), and when the spread is narrowest ($r = 9.00$ percent and $g = 6.25$ percent) the model value is largest ($26.27). As the spread goes to zero, in fact, the model value increases without bound. The largest value in Exhibit 3, $26.27, is 37 percent larger than the smallest value, $19.18. The values in Exhibit 3 all exceed MSEX's current market price of $18.39, tending to support the conclusion that MSEX is undervalued. In summary, our best estimate of the value of MSEX given our assumptions is $22.18, bolded in Exhibit 3, but the estimate is quite sensitive to rather small changes in inputs.

Examples 6 and 7 illustrate the application of the Gordon growth model to a utility, a traditional source for such illustrations because of the stability afforded by providing an essential service in a regulated environment. Before applying any valuation model, however, we need to know much more about a company than industry membership. For example, another water utility, Aqua America Inc. (NYSE: WTR) is expected to be on an above-10-percent per year growth path for a substantial period as a result of an aggressive acquisition program. Furthermore, many utility holding companies in the United States have major, non-regulated business subsidiaries so the traditional picture of steady and slow growth often does not hold.

In addition to individual stocks, analysts have often used the Gordon growth model to value broad equity market indexes, especially in developed markets. Because the value of publicly traded issues typically represents a large fraction of the overall corporate sector in developed markets, such indexes reflect average economic growth rates. Furthermore, in such economies, a sustainable trend value of growth may be identifiable.

We can also use the Gordon growth model to value the noncallable form of a traditional type of preferred stock, **fixed-rate perpetual preferred stock** (stock with a specified dividend rate that has a claim on earnings senior to the claim of common stock, and no maturity date). Perpetual preferred stock has been used particularly by financial institutions such as banks to obtain permanent equity capital while diluting the interests of common equity. Generally, such issues have been callable after a certain period by the issuer, so valuation must take account of the issuer's call option. However, valuation of the noncallable form is straightforward.

If the dividend on such preferred stock is $D$, because payments extend into the indefinite future, we have a **perpetuity** (a stream of level payments extending to infinity) in the constant amount of $D$. With $g = 0$, which is true because dividends are fixed for such preferred stock, the Gordon growth model becomes

$$V_0 = \frac{D}{r}$$

(41-11)

The discount rate, $r$, capitalizes the amount $D$, and for that reason is often called a **capitalization rate** in this and any other expression for the value of a perpetuity.

### EXAMPLE 8

**Valuing Noncallable Fixed-Rate Perpetual Preferred Stock**

Kansas City Southern Preferred 4% (NYSE: KSU.PR), issued 2 January 1963, has a par value of $25 per share. Thus, a share pays 0.04($25) = $1.00 in annual dividends. The required return on this security is estimated at 9 percent. Estimate the value of this issue.

**Solution:** According to the model in Equation 41-11, KSU.PR preferred stock is worth $D/r = 1.00/0.09 = \$11.11$.

A perpetual preferred stock has a level dividend, thus a dividend growth rate of zero. Another case is a declining dividend—a negative growth rate. The Gordon growth model also accommodates this possibility, as illustrated in Example 9.

### EXAMPLE 9

**Gordon Growth Model with Negative Growth**

Afton Mines is a profitable company that is expected to pay a $4.25 dividend next year. Because it is depleting its mining properties, the best estimate is that dividends will decline forever at a 10 percent rate. The required rate of return on Afton stock is 12 percent. What is the value of Afton shares?

**Solution:** For Afton, the value of the stock is

$$V_0 = \frac{4.25}{0.12 - (-0.10)}$$

$$= \frac{4.25}{0.22} = \$19.32$$

The negative growth results in a $19.32 valuation for the stock.

## 4.2 The Links among Dividend Growth, Earnings Growth, and Value Appreciation in the Gordon Growth Model

The Gordon growth model implies a set of relationships for the growth rates of dividends, earnings, and stock value. With dividends growing at a constant rate $g$, stock value also grows at $g$ as well. The current stock value is $V_0 = D_1/(r - g)$. Multiplying both sides by $(1 + g)$, we have $V_0(1 + g) = D_1(1 + g)/(r - g)$, which is $V_1 = D_2/(r - g)$: Both dividends and value have grown at a rate of $g$ (holding $r$ constant).[13] Given a constant payout ratio—a constant, proportional relationship between earnings and dividends—dividends and earnings grow at $g$.

To summarize, $g$ in the Gordon growth model is the rate of value or capital appreciation (sometimes also called the capital gains yield). Some textbooks state that $g$ is the rate of price appreciation. If prices are efficient (price equals value), price is indeed expected to grow at a rate of $g$. If there is mispricing, however (price is different from value), the actual rate of capital appreciation depends on the nature of the mispricing and how fast it is corrected, if at all. This topic is discussed in the reading on return concepts.

Another characteristic of the constant growth model is that the components of total return (dividend yield and capital gains yield) will also stay constant over time, given that price tracks value exactly. The dividend yield, which is $D_1/P_0$ at $t = 0$, will stay unchanged because both the dividend and the price are expected to grow at the same rate, leaving the dividend yield unchanged over time. For example, consider a stock selling for €50.00 with a forward dividend yield (a dividend yield based on the anticipated dividend over the next 12 months) of 2 percent based on an expected dividend of €1. The estimate of $g$ is 5.50 percent per year. The dividend yield of 2 percent, the capital gains yield of 5.50 percent, and the total return of 7.50 percent are expected to be the same at $t = 0$ and at any future point in time.

## 4.3 Share Repurchases

An issue of increasing importance in many developed markets is share repurchases. Companies can distribute free cash flow to shareholders in the form of share repurchases (also called buybacks) as well as dividends. In the United States currently, more than half of dividend-paying firms also make regular share repurchases.[14] Clearly, analysts using DDMs need to understand share repurchases. Share repurchases and cash dividends have several distinctive features:

▶ Share repurchases involve a reduction in the number of shares outstanding, all else equal. Selling shareholders see their relative ownership position reduced compared to non-selling shareholders.

▶ Whereas many corporations with established cash dividends are reluctant to reduce or omit cash dividends, corporations generally do not view themselves as committed to maintain share repurchases at any specified level.

---

[13] More formally, the fact that the value grows at a rate equal to $g$ is demonstrated as follows:

$$\frac{V_{t+1} - V_t}{V_t} = \frac{D_{t+2}/(r - g) - D_{t+1}/(r - g)}{D_{t+1}/(r - g)} = \frac{D_{t+2} - D_{t+1}}{D_{t+1}} = 1 + g - 1 = g$$

[14] See Skinner (2007), who also finds evidence that this group of companies increasingly has tended to distribute earnings increases via share repurchases rather than cash dividends.

▶ Cash dividends tend to be more predictable in money terms and more predictable as to timing.[15] Although evidence from the United States suggests that, for companies with active repurchase programs, the amount of repurchases over two-year intervals bears a relationship to earnings, companies appear to be opportunistic in timing exactly when to repurchase.[16] Thus share repurchases are generally harder to forecast than the cash dividends of companies with an identifiable dividend policy.

▶ As a baseline case, share repurchases are neutral in their impact on the wealth of ongoing shareholders if the repurchases are accomplished at market prices.

The analyst could account for share repurchases directly by forecasting the total earnings, total distributions to shareholders (via either cash dividends or share repurchases), and shares outstanding. Experience and familiarity with such models is much less than for DDMs. However, DDMs, focusing on cash dividends, supply accurate valuations consistent with such an approach if the analyst takes account of the effect of expected repurchases on the per-share growth rates of dividends. Correctly applied, the DDM is a valid approach to common stock valuation even when the company being analyzed engages in share repurchases.

## 4.4 The Implied Dividend Growth Rate

Because the dividend growth rate affects the estimated value of a stock using the Gordon growth model, differences between estimated values of a stock and its actual market value might be explained by different growth rate assumptions. Given price, the expected next-period dividend, and an estimate of the required rate of return, we can infer the dividend growth rate reflected in price assuming the Gordon growth model. (Actually, it is possible to infer the market-price-implied dividend growth based on other DDMs as well.) An analyst can then judge whether the implied dividend growth rate is reasonable, high, or low, based on what he or she knows about the company. In effect, the calculation of the implied dividend growth rate provides an alternative perspective on the valuation of the stock (fairly valued, overvalued, or undervalued). Example 10 shows how the Gordon growth model can be used to infer the market's implied growth rate for a stock.

---

### EXAMPLE 10

**The Growth Rate Implied by the Current Stock Price**

Suppose a company has a beta of 1.1. The risk-free rate is 5.6 percent and the equity risk premium is 6 percent. The current dividend of $2.00 is expected to grow at 5 percent indefinitely. The price of the stock is $40.

1. Estimate the value of the company's stock.
2. Determine the dividend growth rate that would be required to justify the market price of $40.

---

[15] As discussed by Wanger (2007).

[16] See Skinner (2007).

**Solution to 1:** The required rate of return is 5.6% + 1.1(6%) = 12.2 percent. The value of one share, using the Gordon growth model, is

$$V_0 = \frac{D_1}{r - g}$$

$$= \frac{2.00(1.05)}{0.122 - 0.05}$$

$$= \frac{2.10}{0.072} = \$29.17$$

**Solution to 2:** The valuation estimate of the model ($29.17) is less than the market value of $40.00, thus the market price must be forecasting a growth rate above the assumed 5 percent. Assuming that the model and the required return assumption are appropriate, the growth rate in dividends required to justify the $40 stock price can be calculated by substituting all known values into the Gordon growth model equation except for $g$:

$$40 = \frac{2.00(1 + g)}{0.122 - g}$$

$$4.88 - 40g = 2 + 2g$$
$$42g = 2.88$$
$$g = 0.0686$$

An expected dividend growth rate of 6.86 percent is required for the stock price to be correctly valued at the market price of $40.

## 4.5 The Present Value of Growth Opportunities

The value of a stock can be analyzed as the sum of 1) the value of the company if it had no opportunities to profitably reinvest earnings, and 2) the **present value of growth opportunities** (PVGO). PVGO, also known as the **value of growth**, sums the expected value today of opportunities to profitably reinvest future earnings. In this section, we present an expression for analyzing the total value of a stock into these two components.

Earnings growth can be positive, neutral, or negative for shareholder wealth depending on whether the growth results from earning returns in excess of, equal to, or less than the opportunity cost of funds. Consider a company with a required return on equity of 10 percent that has earned €1 per share. The company is deciding whether to pay out current earnings as a dividend or to reinvest them at 10 percent and distribute the ending value as a dividend in 1 year. If it reinvests, the present value of investment is €1.10/1.10 = €1.00, equaling its cost, so the decision to reinvest has a net present value (NPV) of zero. If the company were able to earn more than 10 percent (had "a growth opportunity"), reinvesting would have a positive NPV, increasing shareholder wealth. Suppose the company could reinvest earnings at 25 percent for one year: The per-share NPV of the growth opportunity would be €1.25/1.10 − €1 = €0.14, approximately. Note that any reinvestment at a positive rate below 10 percent, although increasing EPS, is not in shareholders' interests. Increases in shareholder wealth occur only when reinvested earnings earn more than the opportunity cost of the funds needed to undertake them (positive net present value projects).[17] Thus, investors actively assess whether and to what degree companies will have the opportunity to invest in profitable projects in the future. In principle, companies without any positive NPV projects should distribute most or all earnings to shareholders as dividends so the shareholders can redirect capital to more attractive areas.

We define a company without positive expected NPV projects as a **no-growth company** (a term for a company without opportunities for *profitable* growth). When a company distributes all its earnings in dividends (appropriate for a no-growth company), earnings will be flat in perpetuity, assuming a constant return on equity $\overline{ROE}$. This flatness occurs because earnings equal $\overline{ROE} \times$ Equity, and equity is constant because retained earnings are not added to it. The present value of a perpetuity in the amount of $E_1$ is $E_1/r$ where $r$ is the required return on equity. $E_1$ is $t = 1$ earnings, which is the constant level of earnings or the average earnings of a no-growth company if we view ROE as varying about the level $\overline{ROE}$. The capitalization rate $r$ is the required return on equity of the company. We define the **no-growth value per share** as $E_1/r$. For any company, the difference between the actual value per share and the no-growth value per share must be the present value of growth opportunities (PVGO). We can also interpret this as the value of assets in place because of the assumption that we are making no new investments because none is profitable.

$$V_0 = \frac{E_1}{r} + \text{PVGO}$$

(41-12)

If prices reflect value ($P_0 = V_0$), PVGO gives the market's estimate of the value of the company's growth. In Example 6, suppose that MSEX would have average EPS of $0.79 were it to distribute all earnings as dividends. With its required return of 9.2 percent and a current price of $19.10, we have $19.10 = ($0.79/0.092) + PVGO, $19.10 = $8.59 + PVGO, so PVGO = $19.10 − $8.59 = $10.51. The market assigns 55 percent of the company's value to the value of growth ($10.51/$19.10 = 0.55). A related expression can be shown analyzing the familiar P/E ratio based on forecasted earnings:

$$\frac{V_0}{E_1} \text{ or } \frac{P_0}{E_1} \text{ or P/E} = \frac{1}{r} + \frac{\text{PVGO}}{E_1}$$

(41-13)

The first term, $1/r$, is the value of the P/E ratio for a no-growth company. The second term is the component of the P/E value that relates to growth opportunities. For MSEX, the P/E is $19.10/$0.79 = 24.2. The no-growth P/E is $1/0.092 = 10.87$ and is what the company should sell at if it has no growth opportunities. The growth component of $10.51/$0.79 = 13.30 reflects anticipated growth opportunities. Leibowitz and Kogelman (1990) and Leibowitz (1997) have provided elaborate analyses of the drivers of the growth component of P/E as a franchise-value approach.

---

[17] We can interpret this condition of profitability as ROE > $r$ with ROE calculated with the *market* value of equity (rather than the book value of equity) in the denominator. Book value based on historical cost accounting can present a distorted picture of the value of shareholders' investment in the company.

As analysts, we may be interested in this assignment because the value of growth and the value in hand (no-growth value, based on existing assets) may have different risk characteristics. Whenever we calculate a stock's value, $V_0$, whether using the Gordon growth or any other valuation model, we can calculate the value of growth, based on the value estimate, using the above equation.

## 4.6 Gordon Growth Model and the Price–Earnings Ratio

The price–earnings ratio (P/E) is perhaps the most widely recognized valuation indicator, familiar to readers of both newspaper financial tables and institutional research reports. Using the Gordon growth model, we can develop an expression for P/E in terms of the fundamentals. This expression has two uses:

▶ When used with forecasts of the inputs to the model, the analyst obtains a **justified (fundamental) P/E**—the P/E that is fair, warranted, or justified on the basis of fundamentals (given that the valuation model is appropriate). The analyst can then state his or her view of value in terms not of the Gordon growth model value but of the justified P/E. Because P/E is so widely recognized, this method may be an effective way to communicate the analysis.

▶ The analyst may also use the expression for P/E to weigh whether the forecasts of earnings growth built into the current stock price are reasonable. What expected earnings growth rate is implied by the actual market P/E? Is that growth rate plausible?

We can state the expression for P/E in terms of the current (or trailing) P/E (today's market price per share divided by trailing 12 months' earnings per share) or in terms of the leading (or forward) P/E (today's market price per share divided by a forecast of the next 12 months' earnings per share, or sometimes the next fiscal year's earnings per share).

Leading and trailing justified P/E expressions can be developed from the Gordon growth model. Assuming that the model can be applied for a particular stock's valuation, the dividend payout ratio is considered fixed. Define $b$ as the retention rate, the fraction of earnings reinvested in the company rather than paid out in dividends. The dividend payout ratio is then, by definition, $(1 - b) =$ Dividend per share/Earnings per share $= D_t/E_t$. If we divide $P_0 = D_1/(r - g)$ by next year's earnings per share, $E_1$, we have

$$\frac{P_0}{E_1} = \frac{D_1/E_1}{r - g} = \frac{1 - b}{r - g} \qquad \textbf{(41-14)}$$

This represents a leading P/E, current price divided by next year's earnings. Alternatively, if we divide $P_0 = D_0(1 + g)/(r - g)$ by the current year's earnings per share, $E_0$, we have

$$\frac{P_0}{E_0} = \frac{D_0(1 + g)/E_0}{r - g} = \frac{(1 - b)(1 + g)}{r - g} \qquad \textbf{(41-15)}$$

This is a trailing P/E, current price divided by trailing (current-year) earnings.

**EXAMPLE 11**

**The Justified P/E Based on the Gordon Growth Model**

Harry Trice wants to use the Gordon growth model to find a justified P/E for the French company Carrefour SA (NYSE Euronext: CA), a global food retailer specializing in hypermarkets and supermarkets. Trice has assembled the following information:

▶ Current stock price = €47.46
▶ Trailing annual earnings per share = €3.22
▶ Current level of annual dividends = €1.03
▶ Dividend growth rate = 7%
▶ Risk-free rate = 4.4%
▶ Equity risk premium = 6.39%
▶ Beta versus the CAC index = 0.72

1. Calculate the justified trailing and leading P/Es based on the Gordon growth model.
2. Based on the justified trailing P/E and the actual P/E, judge whether CA is fairly valued, overvalued, or undervalued.

**Solution to 1:** For CA, the required rate of return using the CAPM is

$$r_i = 4.4\% + 0.72(6.39\%)$$
$$= 9.0\%$$

The dividend payout ratio is

$$(1 - b) = D_0/E_0$$
$$= 1.03/3.22$$
$$= 0.32$$

The justified leading P/E (based on next year's earnings) is

$$\frac{P_0}{E_1} = \frac{1 - b}{r - g} = \frac{0.32}{0.09 - 0.07} = 16.0$$

The justified trailing P/E (based on trailing earnings) is

$$\frac{P_0}{E_0} = \frac{(1 - b)(1 + g)}{r - g} = \frac{0.32(1.07)}{0.09 - 0.07} = 17.1$$

**Solution to 2:** Based on a current price of €47.46 and trailing earnings of €3.22, the trailing P/E is €47.46/€3.22 = 14.7. Because the actual P/E of 14.7 is smaller than the justified trailing P/E of 17.1, we conclude that CA appears to be undervalued. We can also express the apparent mispricing in terms of the Gordon growth model. Using Trice's assumptions, the Gordon growth model assigns a value of 1.03(1.07)/(0.09 − 0.07) = €55.11, which is above the current market value of €47.46. The Gordon growth model approach gives a higher stock value than the market price and a higher justified P/E than the current market P/E.

Later in the reading, we will present multistage DDMs. We can also develop expressions for the P/E in terms of the variables of multistage DDMs, but the usefulness of these expressions is not commensurate with their complexity. For multistage models, the simple way to calculate a justified leading P/E is to divide the model value directly by the first year's expected earnings. In all cases, the P/E is explained in terms of the required return on equity, expected dividend growth rate(s), and the dividend payout ratio(s). All else equal, higher prices are associated with higher anticipated dividend growth rates.

## 4.7 Estimating a Required Return Using the Gordon Growth Model

Under the assumption of efficient prices, the Gordon growth model has been used to estimate a stock's required rate of return, or equivalently, the market-price-implied expected return. The Gordon growth model solved for $r$ is

$$r = \frac{D_0(1 + g)}{P_0} + g = \frac{D_1}{P_0} + g \qquad \text{(41-16)}$$

As explained in the reading on return concepts, $r$ in Equation 41-16 is technically an internal rate of return (IRR). The rate $r$ is composed of two parts; the dividend yield $(D_1/P_0)$ and the capital gains (or appreciation) yield $(g)$.

### EXAMPLE 12

**Finding the Expected Rate of Return with the Gordon Growth Model**

Bob Inguigiatto, CFA, has been given the task of developing mean return estimates for a list of stocks as preparation for a portfolio optimization. On his list is FPL Group, Inc. (NYSE: FPL). On analysis, he decides that it is appropriate to model FPL using the Gordon growth model, and he takes prices as reflecting value. The company paid dividends of $2.24 during the past year, and the current stock price is $56.60. The growth rates of dividends and earnings per share have been 4.01 percent and 5.30 percent, respectively, for the past five years. Analysts' consensus estimate of the five-year earnings growth rate is 7.0 percent. Based on his own analysis, Inguigiatto has decided to use 5.50 percent as his best estimate of the long-term earnings and dividend growth rate. Next year's projected dividend, $D_1$, should be $2.24(1.055) = $2.363. Using the Gordon growth model, FPL's expected rate of return should be

$$r = \frac{D_1}{P_0} + g$$

$$= \frac{2.363}{56.60} + 0.055$$

$$= 0.0417 + 0.055$$

$$= 0.0967 = 9.67\%$$

FPL's expected rate of return is 9.67 percent. The total return can be broken into two components, the dividend yield $(D_1/P_0 = 4.17$ percent$)$ and the capital gains yield $(g = 5.50$ percent$)$.

## 4.8 The Gordon Growth Model: Concluding Remarks

The Gordon growth model is the simplest practical implementation of discounted dividend valuation. The Gordon growth model is appropriate for valuing the equity of dividend-paying companies when its key assumption of a stable future dividend and earnings growth rate is expected to be satisfied. Broad equity market indices of developed markets frequently satisfy the conditions of the model fairly well; as a result, analysts have used it to judge whether an equity market is fairly valued or not and for estimating the equity risk premium associated with the current market level. In the multistage models discussed in the next section, the Gordon growth model has often been used to model the last growth stage, when a previously high growth company matures and the growth rate drops to a long-term sustainable level. In any case in which the model is applied, the analyst must be aware that the output of the model is typically sensitive to small changes in the assumed growth rate and required rate of return.

The Gordon growth model is a single-stage DDM because all future periods are grouped into one stage characterized by single growth rate. For many or even the majority of companies, however, future growth can be expected to consist of multiple stages. Multistage DDMs are the subject of the next section.

## 5    MULTISTAGE DIVIDEND DISCOUNT MODELS

Earlier, we noted that the basic expression for the DDM (Equation 41-7) is too general for investment analysts to use in practice, as one cannot forecast individually more than a relatively small number of dividends. The strongest simplifying assumption—a stable dividend growth rate from now into the indefinite future, leading to the Gordon growth model—is not realistic for many or even most companies. For many publicly traded companies, practitioners assume growth falls into three stages (see Sharpe, Alexander, and Bailey, 1999):

▶ **Growth phase.** A company in its growth phase typically enjoys rapidly expanding markets, high profit margins, and an abnormally high growth rate in earnings per share (**supernormal growth**). Companies in this phase often have negative free cash flow to equity, because the company invests heavily in expanding operations. Given high prospective returns on equity, the dividend payout ratios of growth-phase companies are often low, or even zero. As the company's markets mature or as unusual growth opportunities attract competitors, earnings growth rates eventually decline.

▶ **Transition phase.** In this phase, which is a transition to maturity, earnings growth slows as competition puts pressure on prices and profit margins, or as sales growth slows because of market saturation. In this phase, earnings growth rates may be above average but declining towards the growth rate for the overall economy. Capital requirements typically decline in this phase, often resulting in positive free cash flow and increasing dividend payout ratios (or the initiation of dividends).

▶ **Mature phase.** In maturity, the company reaches an equilibrium in which investment opportunities on average just earn their opportunity cost of capital. Return on equity approaches the required return on equity, and earnings growth, the dividend payout ratio, and the return on equity stabilize at levels that can be sustained long term. We call the dividend and earnings growth rate of this phase the **mature growth rate**. This phase, in fact, reflects the stage in which a company can properly be valued using the

Gordon growth model, and that model is one tool for valuing this phase of a currently high-growth company's future.

A company may attempt and succeed in restarting the growth phase by changing its strategic focuses and business mix. Technological advances may alter a company's growth prospects for better or worse with surprising rapidity. Nevertheless, this growth-phase picture of a company is a useful approximation. The growth-phase concept provides the intuition for multistage discounted cash flow (DCF) models of all types, including multistage dividend discount models. Multistage models are a staple valuation discipline of investment management companies using DCF valuation models.

In the following sections, we present three popular multistage DDMs: the two-stage DDM, the H-model (a type of two-stage model), and the three-stage DDM. Keep in mind that all these models represent stylized patterns of growth; we are attempting to identify the pattern that most accurately approximates our view of the company's future growth.

## 5.1 Two-Stage Dividend Discount Model

Two common versions of the two-stage DDM exist. Both versions assume constant growth at a mature growth rate (for example, 7 percent) in Stage 2. In the first version ("the general two-stage model"), the whole of Stage 1 represents a period of abnormal growth—for example, growth at 15 percent. The transition to mature growth in Stage 2 is generally abrupt. In the second version, called the H-model, the dividend growth rate is assumed to decline from an abnormal rate to the mature growth rate over the course of Stage 1. For example, the growth rate could begin at 15 percent and decline continuously in Stage 1 until it reaches 7 percent. This second model will be presented after the general two-stage model.

The first two-stage DDM provides for a high growth rate for the initial period, followed by a sustainable and usually lower growth rate thereafter. The two-stage DDM is based on the multiple-period model

$$V_0 = \sum_{t=1}^{n} \frac{D_t}{(1+r)^t} + \frac{V_n}{(1+r)^n} \qquad \text{(41-17)}$$

where we use $V_n$ as an estimate of $P_n$. The two-stage model assumes that the first $n$ dividends grow at an extraordinary short-term rate, $g_S$:

$$D_t = D_0(1+g_S)^t$$

After time $n$, the annual dividend growth rate changes to a normal long-term rate, $g_L$. The dividend at time $n+1$ is $D_{n+1} = D_n(1+g_L) = D_0(1+g_S)^n(1+g_L)$, and this dividend continues to grow at $g_L$. Using $D_{n+1}$, we can use the Gordon growth model to find $V_n$:

$$V_n = \frac{D_0(1+g_S)^n(1+g_L)}{r-g_L} \qquad \text{(41-18)}$$

To find the value at $t = 0$, $V_0$, we simply find the present value of the first $n$ dividends and the present value of the projected value at time $n$

$$V_0 = \sum_{t=1}^{n} \frac{D_0(1+g_S)^t}{(1+r)^t} + \frac{D_0(1+g_S)^n(1+g_L)}{(1+r)^n(r-g_L)} \qquad \text{(41-19)}$$

## EXAMPLE 13

### Valuing a Stock Using the Two-Stage Dividend Discount Model

Carl Zeiss Meditec AG (Deutsche Börse XETRA: AFX), 65 percent owned by the Carl Zeiss Group, provides screening, diagnostic, and therapeutic systems for the treatment of ophthalmologic (vision) problems. Reviewing the issue as of the beginning of October 2007 when it is trading for €19.10, Hans Mattern, a buy-side analyst covering Meditec, forecasts that the current dividend of €0.14 will grow by 15 percent per year over the next 10 years. Thereafter, Mattern believes that the growth rate will decline to 8 percent and remain at that level indefinitely.

Mattern estimates Meditec's required return on equity as 9.7 percent based on a beta of 0.89 against the DAX, a 4.5 percent risk-free rate, and his equity risk premium estimate of 5.8 percent.

Exhibit 4 shows the calculations of the first ten dividends and their present values discounted at 9.7 percent. The terminal stock value at $t = 10$ is

$$V_{10} = \frac{D_0(1 + g_S)^n(1 + g_L)}{r - g_L}$$

$$= \frac{0.14(1.15)^{10}(1.08)}{0.097 - 0.08}$$

$$= 35.9817$$

The terminal stock value and its present value are also given.

| EXHIBIT 4 | | Carl Zeiss Meditec AG | | |

| Time | Value | Calculation | $D_t$ or $V_t$ | Present Values $D_t/(1.097)^t$ or $V_t/(1.097)^t$ |
|------|-------|-------------|----------------|---------------------------------------------------|
| 1 | $D_1$ | €0.14(1.15) | €0.1610 | €0.1468 |
| 2 | $D_2$ | $0.14(1.15)^2$ | 0.1852 | 0.1539 |
| 3 | $D_3$ | $0.14(1.15)^3$ | 0.2129 | 0.1613 |
| 4 | $D_4$ | $0.14(1.15)^4$ | 0.2449 | 0.1691 |
| 5 | $D_5$ | $0.14(1.15)^5$ | 0.2816 | 0.1772 |
| 6 | $D_6$ | $0.14(1.15)^6$ | 0.3238 | 0.1858 |
| 7 | $D_7$ | $0.14(1.15)^7$ | 0.3724 | 0.1948 |
| 8 | $D_8$ | $0.14(1.15)^8$ | 0.4283 | 0.2042 |
| 9 | $D_9$ | $0.14(1.15)^9$ | 0.4925 | 0.2141 |
| 10 | $D_{10}$ | $0.14(1.15)^{10}$ | 0.5664 | 0.2244 |
| 10 | $V_{10}$ | $0.14(1.15)^{10}(1.08)/$ $(0.097 - 0.08)$ | 35.9817 | 14.2566 |
| Total | | | | €16.0882 |

In this two-stage model, we forecast the dividends during the first stage and then calculate their present values. We use the Gordon growth model to derive the terminal value (the value of the dividends in the second stage as of the beginning of that stage). As shown in Exhibit 4, the terminal value is $V_{10} = D_{11}/(r - g_L)$. Ignoring rounding errors, the Period 11 dividend is €0.6117 (= $D_{10} \times 1.08$ = €0.5664 × 1.08). Using the standard Gordon growth model, $V_{10}$ = €35.98 = €0.6117/(0.097 − 0.08). The present value of the terminal value is €14.26 = €35.9817/$1.097^{10}$. The total estimated value of Meditec is €16.09 using this model. Notice that approximately 89 percent of this value, €14.26, is the present value of $V_{10}$, and the balance, €16.09 − €14.26 = €1.83, is the present value of the first ten dividends. Recalling our discussion of the sensitivity of the Gordon growth model to changes in the inputs, we might calculate an interval for the intrinsic value of Meditec by varying the mature growth rate over the range of plausible values.

The two-stage DDM is useful because many scenarios exist in which a company can achieve a supernormal growth rate for a few years, after which time the growth rate falls to a more sustainable level. For example, a company may achieve supernormal growth through possession of a patent, first-mover advantage, or another factor that provides a temporary lead in a specific marketplace. Subsequently, earnings will quite likely descend to a level that is more consistent with competition and the growth in the overall economy. Accordingly, that is why in the two-stage model, extraordinary growth is often forecast for a few years and normal growth is forecast thereafter. A possible limitation of the two-stage model is that the transition between the initial abnormal growth period and the final steady-state growth period is abrupt.

The accurate estimation of $V_n$, the **terminal value of the stock** (also known as its **continuing value**) is an important part of the correct use of DDMs. In practice, analysts estimate the terminal value either by applying a multiple to a projected terminal value of a fundamental, such as earnings per share or book value per share, or they estimate $V_n$ using the Gordon growth model. In the reading on market multiples, we will discuss using price–earnings multiples in this context.

In our examples, we use a single discount rate, $r$, for all phases, reflecting both a desire for simplicity and lack of a clear objective basis for adjusting the discount rate for different phases. Some analysts, however, use different discount rates for different growth phases.

The following example values E. I. DuPont de Nemours and Company by combining the dividend discount model and a P/E valuation model.

## EXAMPLE 14

### Combining a DDM and P/E Model to Value a Stock

An analyst is reviewing the valuation of DuPont (NYSE: DD) as of the beginning of October 2007 when DD is selling for $50. Over the previous year, DuPont paid a $1.48 dividend that the analyst expects to grow at a rate of 10 percent annually for the next four years. At the end of Year 4, the analyst expects the dividend to equal 40 percent of earnings per share and the trailing P/E for DD to be 14. If the required return on DD common stock is 10.5 percent, calculate the per-share value of DD common stock.

Exhibit 5 summarizes the relevant calculations. When the dividends are growing at 10 percent, the expected dividends and the present value of each (discounted at 10.5 percent) are shown. The terminal stock price, $V_4$, deserves some explanation. As shown in the table, the Year 4 dividend is $1.48(1.10)^4 = 2.1669$. Because dividends at that time are assumed to be 40 percent of earnings, the EPS projection for Year 4 is $EPS_4 = D_4/0.40 = 2.1669/0.40 = 5.4172$. With a trailing P/E of 14.0, the value of DD at the end of Year 4 should be $14.0(5.4172) = \$75.84$. Discounted at 10.5 percent for four years, the present value of $V_4$ is $50.87.

| EXHIBIT 5 | | Value of DuPont Common Stock | | |
|---|---|---|---|---|
| Time | Value | Calculation | $D_t$ or $V_t$ | Present Values $D_t/(1.105)^t$ or $V_t/(1.105)^t$ |
| 1 | $D_1$ | $1.48(1.10)^1$ | 1.6280 | 1.4733 |
| 2 | $D_2$ | $1.48(1.10)^2$ | 1.7908 | 1.4666 |
| 3 | $D_3$ | $1.48(1.10)^3$ | 1.9699 | 1.4600 |
| 4 | $D_4$ | $1.48(1.10)^4$ | 2.1669 | 1.4534 |
| 4 | $V_4$ | $14 \times [1.48(1.10)^4/0.40]$ $= 14 \times [2.1669/0.40]$ $= 14 \times 5.4172$ | 75.8404 | 50.8688 |
| Total | | | | 56.72 |

The present values of the dividends for Years 1 through 4 sum to $5.85. The present value of the terminal value of $75.84 is $50.87. The estimated total value of DD is the sum of these, or $56.72 per share.

## 5.2 Valuing a Non-Dividend-Paying Company

The fact that a stock is currently paying no dividends does not mean that the principles of the dividend discount model do not apply. Even though $D_0$ and/or $D_1$ may be zero, and the company may not begin paying dividends for some time, the present value of future dividends may still capture the value of the company. Of course, if a company pays no dividends and will never be able to distribute cash to shareholders, the stock is worthless.

To value a non-dividend-paying company using a DDM, we generally can use a multistage DDM model in which the first-stage dividend equals zero. Example 15 illustrates the approach.

**EXAMPLE 15**

### Valuing a Non-Dividend-Paying Stock

Assume that a company is currently paying no dividend and will not pay one for several years. If the company begins paying a dividend of $1.00 five years from now, and the dividend is expected to grow at 5 percent thereafter, we can discount this future dividend stream back to find the value of the company. This company's required rate of return is 11 percent. Because the expression

$$V_n = \frac{D_{n+1}}{r - g}$$

values a stock at period $n$ using the next period's dividend, the $t = 5$ dividend is used to find the value at $t = 4$:

$$V_4 = \frac{D_5}{r - g} = \frac{1.00}{0.11 - 0.05} = \$16.67$$

To find the value of the stock today, we simply discount $V_4$ back for four years:

$$V_0 = \frac{V_4}{(1 + r)^4} = \frac{16.67}{(1.11)^4} - \$10.98$$

The value of this stock, even though it will not pay a dividend until Year 5, is $10.98.

If a company is not paying a dividend but is very profitable, an analyst might be willing to forecast its future dividends. Of course, for non-dividend-paying, unprofitable companies, such a forecast would be very difficult. Furthermore, as discussed in Section 2.2 (Streams of Expected Cash Flows), it is usually difficult for the analyst to estimate the timing of the initiation of dividends and the dividend policy that will then be established by the company. Thus, the analyst may prefer a free cash flow or residual income model for valuing such companies.

## 5.3 The H-Model

The basic two-stage model assumes a constant, extraordinary rate for the supernormal growth period that is followed by a constant, normal growth rate thereafter. The difference in growth rates may be substantial. For instance, in Example 13, the growth rate for Carl Zeiss Meditec was 15 percent annually for 10 years, followed by a drop to 8 percent growth in Year 11 and thereafter. In some cases, a smoother transition to the mature phase growth rate would be more realistic. Fuller and Hsia (1984) developed a variant of the two-stage model in which growth begins at a high rate and declines linearly throughout the supernormal growth period until it reaches a normal rate at the end. The value of the dividend stream in the H-model is

$$V_0 = \frac{D_0(1 + g_L)}{r - g_L} + \frac{D_0 H(g_S - g_L)}{r - g_L} \tag{41-20}$$

or

$$V_0 = \frac{D_0(1 + g_L) + D_0 H(g_S - g_L)}{r - g_L}$$

where

$V_0$ = value per share at $t = 0$

$D_0$ = current dividend

$r$ = required rate of return on equity

$H$ = half-life in years of the high-growth period (i.e., high-growth period = $2H$ years)

$g_S$ = initial short-term dividend growth rate

$g_L$ = normal long-term dividend growth rate after Year $2H$

The first term on the right-hand side of Equation 41-20 is the present value of the company's dividend stream if it were to grow at $g_L$ forever. The second term is an approximation to the extra value (assuming $g_S > g_L$) accruing to the stock because of its supernormal growth for Years 1 through $2H$ (see Fuller and Hsia for technical details).[18] Logically, the longer the supernormal growth period (i.e., the larger the value of $H$, which is one-half the length of the supernormal growth period) and the larger the extra growth rate in the supernormal growth period (measured by $g_S$ minus $g_L$), the higher the share value, all else equal. To illustrate the expression, if the analyst in Example 13 had forecast a linear decline of the growth rate from 15 percent to 8 percent over the next 10 years, his estimate of value using the H-model would have been €11.78 (rather than €16.09 as in Example 13):

$$
\begin{aligned}
V_0 &= \frac{D_0(1 + g_L) + D_0 H(g_S - g_L)}{r - g_L} \\
&= \frac{0.14(1.08) + 0.14(5)(0.15 - 0.08)}{0.097 - 0.08} \\
&= \frac{0.1512 + 0.0490}{0.017} \\
&= 11.78
\end{aligned}
$$

Note that an $H$ of 5 corresponds to the 10-year high-growth period of Example 13. Example 16 provides another illustration of the H-model.

### EXAMPLE 16

**Valuing a Stock with the H-Model**

Françoise Delacour, a portfolio manager of a U.S.-based diversified global equity portfolio, is researching the valuation of Vinci SA (NYSE Euronext: DG). Vinci is the world's largest construction company, oper-

---

[18] We can provide some intuition on the expression, however. On average, the expected excess growth rate in the supernormal period will be $(g_S - g_L)/2$. Over $2H$ periods, we expect a total excess amount of dividends (compared with the level given $g_L$) of $2HD_0(g_S - g_L)/2 = D_0 H(g_S - g_L)$. This term is the H-model upward adjustment to the first dividend term, reflecting the extra expected dividends as growth declines from $g_S$ to $g_L$ over the first period. Note, however, that the timing of the individual dividends in the first period is not reflected by individually discounting them; the expression is thus an approximation.

ating chiefly in France (approximately two-thirds of revenue) and the rest of Europe (approximately one quarter of revenue). Through 2003, DG paid a single regular cash dividend per fiscal year. Since 2004 it has paid two dividends per (fiscal) year, an interim dividend in December and a final dividend in May. Although over the past five years total annual dividends grew at 26 percent per year, Delacour foresees less rapid future growth.

Having decided to compute the H-model value estimate for DG, Delacour gathers the following facts and forecasts:

▶ The price as of mid-August 2007 was €57.

▶ The current dividend is €1.37.

▶ The initial dividend growth rate is 24 percent, declining linearly over a 12-year period to a final and perpetual growth rate of 6 percent.

▶ Delacour estimates DG's required rate of return on equity as 10 percent.

1. Using the H-model and the information given, estimate the per-share value of DG.

2. Estimate the value of DG shares if its normal growth period began immediately.

3. Evaluate whether DG shares appear to be fairly valued, overvalued, or undervalued.

**Solution to 1:** Using the H-model expression, we obtain

$$V_0 = \frac{D_0(1 + g_L)}{r - g_L} + \frac{D_0 H(g_S - g_L)}{r - g_L}$$

$$= \frac{1.37(1.06)}{0.10 - 0.06} + \frac{1.37(6)(0.24 - 0.06)}{0.10 - 0.06}$$

$$= 36.31 + 36.99 = €73.30$$

**Solution to 2:** If DG experienced normal growth starting now, its estimated value would be the first component of the H-model estimate, €36.31. Note that extraordinary growth adds €36.99 to its value, resulting in an estimate of €73.30 for the value of a DG share.

**Solution to 3:** €73.30 is approximately 30 percent greater than DG's current market price. Thus DG appears to be undervalued.

The H-model is an approximation model, which estimates the valuation that would result from discounting all of the future dividends individually. In many circumstances, this approximation is very close. For a long extraordinary growth period (a high $H$) or for a large difference in growth rates (the difference between $g_S$ and $g_L$), however, the analyst might abandon the approximation model for the more exact model. Fortunately, the many tedious calculations of the exact model are made fairly easy using a spreadsheet program.

## 5.4 Three-Stage Dividend Discount Models

There are two popular versions of the three-stage DDM, distinguished by the modeling of the second stage. In the first version ("the general three-stage model"), the company is assumed to have three distinct stages of growth and the growth rate of the second stage is typically constant. For example, Stage 1 could assume 20 percent growth for three years, Stage 2 could have 10 percent growth for four years, and Stage 3 could have 5 percent growth thereafter. In the second version, in the middle (second) stage, the growth rate is assumed to decline linearly to the mature growth rate: essentially, the second and third stages are treated as an H-model.

The example below shows how the first type of three-stage model can be used to value a stock, in this case IBM.

### EXAMPLE 17

**The Three-Stage DDM with Three Distinct Stages**

IBM currently (2007) pays a dividend of $1.60 per year. A current price is $118.36. An analyst makes the following estimates:

▶ the current required return on equity for IBM is 12 percent

▶ dividends will grow at 14 percent for the next two years, 12 percent for the following five years, and 10.2 percent thereafter.

Based only on the information given, estimate the value of IBM using a three-stage DDM approach.

**Solution:** Exhibit 6 gives the calculations:

### EXHIBIT 6     Estimated Value of IBM

| Time | Value | Calculation | $D_t$ or $V_t$ | Present Values $D_t/(1.12)^t$ or $V_t/(1.12)^t$ |
|------|-------|-------------|----------------|---------------------------------------------------|
| 1 | $D_1$ | $1.60(1.14)$ | 1.8240 | 1.6286 |
| 2 | $D_2$ | $1.60(1.14)^2$ | 2.0794 | 1.6577 |
| 3 | $D_3$ | $1.60(1.14)^2(1.12)$ | 2.3289 | 1.6577 |
| 4 | $D_4$ | $1.60(1.14)^2(1.12)^2$ | 2.6083 | 1.6577 |
| 5 | $D_5$ | $1.60(1.14)^2(1.12)^3$ | 2.9214 | 1.6577 |
| 6 | $D_6$ | $1.60(1.14)^2(1.12)^4$ | 3.2719 | 1.6577 |
| 7 | $D_7$ | $1.60(1.14)^2(1.12)^5$ | 3.6645 | 1.6577 |
| 7 | $V_7$ | $1.60(1.14)^2(1.12)^5(1.102)/$ $(0.12 - 0.102)$ | 224.3515 | 101.4852 |
| Total | | | | 113.0600 |

> Given these assumptions, the three-stage model indicates that a fair price should be $113.06, which is very close to the current market price. Characteristically, the terminal value of $101.49 constitutes the overwhelming portion (here, about 90 percent) of total estimated value.

A second version of the three-stage DDM has a middle stage similar to the first stage in the H-model. In the first stage, dividends grow at a high, constant (supernormal) rate for the whole period. In the second stage, dividends decline linearly as they do in the H-model. Finally, in Stage 3, dividends grow at a sustainable, constant growth rate. The process of using this model involves four steps:

► Gather the required inputs:
  ► The current dividend
  ► The lengths of the first, second, and third stages
  ► The expected growth rates for the first and third stages
  ► An estimate of the required return on equity
► Compute the expected dividends in the first stage and find the sum of their present values.
► Apply the H-model expression to the second and third stages to obtain an estimate of their value as of the beginning of the second stage. Then find the present value of this H-value as of today ($t = 0$).
► Sum the values obtained in the second and third steps.

In the first step, analysts often investigate the company more deeply, making explicit, individual earnings and dividend forecasts for the near future (often three, five, or ten years), rather than applying a growth rate to the current level of dividends.

## EXAMPLE 18

### The Three-Stage DDM with Declining Growth Rates in Stage 2

Elaine Bouvier is evaluating Energen (NYSE: EGN) for possible inclusion in a small-cap growth oriented portfolio. Headquartered in Alabama, EGN is a diversified energy company involved in oil and gas exploration through its subsidiary, Energen Resources, and in natural gas distribution through its Alabama Gas Corporation subsidiary. In light of EGN's aggressive program of purchasing producing oil and gas properties, Bouvier expects above average growth for the next five years. Bouvier establishes the following facts and forecasts (as of the beginning of October 2007):

► The current market price is $57.77.
► The current dividend is $0.46.
► Bouvier forecasts an initial 5-year period of 12 percent per year earnings and dividend growth.

▶ Bouvier anticipates that EGN can grow 7.5 percent per year as a mature company, and allows 10 years for the transition to the mature growth period.

▶ To estimate the required return on equity using the CAPM, Bouvier uses an adjusted beta of 1.11 based on 2 years of weekly observations, an estimated equity risk premium of 4.5 percent, and a risk-free rate based on the 20-year Treasury bond yield of 5 percent.

▶ Bouvier considers any security trading within a band of ± 20 percent of her estimate of intrinsic value to be within a "fair value range."

1. Estimate the required return on EGN using the CAPM. (Use only one decimal place in stating the result.)

2. Estimate the value of EGN using a three-stage dividend discount model with a linearly declining dividend growth rate in Stage 2.

3. Calculate the percentages of the total value that each of the three stages represents.

4. Judge whether EGN is undervalued or overvalued according to Bouvier's perspective.

5. Some analysts are forecasting essentially flat EPS and dividends in the second year. Estimate the value of EGN making the assumption that EPS is flat in the second year and that 12 percent growth resumes in the third year.

**Solution to 1:** The required return on equity is $r = 5\% + 1.11(4.5\%) = 10$ percent.

**Solution to 2:** The first step is to compute the five dividends in Stage 1 and find their present values at 10 percent. The dividends in Stages 2 and 3 can be valued with the H-model, which estimates their value at the beginning of Stage 2. This value is then discounted back to find the dividends' present value at $t = 0$.

The calculation of the five dividends in Stage 1 and their present values are given in Exhibit 7 below. The H-model for calculating the value of the Stage 2 and Stage 3 dividends at the beginning of Stage 2 ($t = 5$) would be

$$V_5 = \frac{D_5(1 + g_L)}{r - g_L} + \frac{D_5 H(g_S - g_L)}{r - g_L}$$

where
$D_5 = D_0(1 + g_S)^5 = 0.46(1.12)^5 = \$0.8107$
$g_S = 12.0\%$
$g_L = 7.5\%$
$r = 10.0\%$
$H = 5$ (the second stage lasts $2H = 10$ years)

Substituting these values into the equation for the H-model gives us $V_5$:

$$V_5 = \frac{0.8107(1.075)}{0.10 - 0.075} + \frac{0.8107(5)(0.12 - 0.075)}{0.10 - 0.075}$$

$$= 34.8601 + 7.2963$$

$$= \$42.1564$$

The present value of $V_5$ is $\$42.1564/(1.10)^5 = \$26.1758$.

| EXHIBIT 7 | | Energen | | |
|---|---|---|---|---|
| Time | $D_t$ or $V_t$ | Explanation of $D_t$ or $V_t$ | Value of $D_t$ or $V_t$ | PV at 10% |
| 1 | $D_1$ | $0.46(1.12)^1$ | 0.5152 | 0.4684 |
| 2 | $D_2$ | $0.46(1.12)^2$ | 0.5770 | 0.4769 |
| 3 | $D_3$ | $0.46(1.12)^3$ | 0.6463 | 0.4855 |
| 4 | $D_4$ | $0.46(1.12)^4$ | 0.7238 | 0.4944 |
| 5 | $D_5$ | $0.46(1.12)^5$ | 0.8107 | 0.5034 |
| 5 | $V_5$ | H-model explained above | 42.1564 | 26.1758 |
| | Total | | | 28.6044 |

According to this three-stage DDM model, the total value of EGN is $28.60.

**Solution to 3:** The first stage represents $2.4286/$28.6044 = 8.5 percent of total value. To supply similar information for Stages 2 and 3 we have to find the present value of the second stage piece of $7.2963 and the third stage piece $34.8601. These are $4.5304 and $21.6454, respectively. So the second stage represents $4.5304/$28.6044 = 15.8 percent and the third stage represents $21.6454/$28.6044 = 75.7 percent.

**Solution to 4:** The band Bouvier is looking at is $28.60 ± 0.20($28.60) which runs from $28.60 + $5.72 = $34.32 on the upside to $28.60 − $5.72 = $22.88 on the downside. Because $57.77 is above $34.32, Bouvier would consider EGN to be overvalued.

**Solution to 5:** The estimated value becomes $25.59 with no growth in Year 2 as shown in Exhibit 8. The value of the second and third stages are given by

$$V_5 = \frac{0.7238(1.075)}{0.10 - 0.075} + \frac{0.7238(5)(0.12 - 0.075)}{0.10 - 0.075}$$

$$= \$37.6376$$

| | | EXHIBIT 8 | Energen with No Growth in Year 2 | | |
|---|---|---|---|---|---|
| Time | $D_t$ or $V_t$ | Explanation of $D_t$ or $V_t$ | | Value of $D_t$ or $V_t$ | PV at 10% |
| 1 | $D_1$ | $0.46(1.12)^1$ | | 0.5152 | 0.4684 |
| 2 | $D_2$ | No growth in Year 2 | | 0.5152 | 0.4258 |
| 3 | $D_3$ | $0.46(1.12)^2$ | | 0.5770 | 0.4335 |
| 4 | $D_4$ | $0.46(1.12)^3$ | | 0.6463 | 0.4414 |
| 5 | $D_5$ | $0.46(1.12)^4$ | | 0.7238 | 0.4494 |
| 5 | $V_5$ | H-model explained above | | 37.6376 | 23.3700 |
| | Total | | | | 25.5885 |

In Problem 5 of the above example, the analyst examined the consequences of 12 percent growth in Year 1 and no growth in Year 2, with 12 percent growth resuming in Years 3, 4, and 5. In the first stage, analysts may forecast earnings and dividends individually for a certain number of years.

The three-stage DDM with declining growth in Stage 2 has been widely used among companies using a DDM approach to valuation. An example is the DDM adopted by Bloomberg L.P., a financial services company that provides "Bloomberg terminals" to professional investors and analysts. The Bloomberg DDM is a model that provides an estimated value for any stock that the user selects. The DDM is a three-stage model with declining growth in Stage 2. The model uses fundamentals about the company for assumed Stage 1 and Stage 3 growth rates, and then assumes that the Stage 2 rate is a linearly declining rate between the Stage 1 and Stage 3 rates. The model also makes estimates of the required rate of return and the lengths of the three stages, assigning higher growth companies shorter growth periods (i.e., first stages) and longer transition periods, and slower growth companies longer growth periods and shorter transition periods. Fixing the total length of the growth and transition phases together at 17 years, the growth stage/transition stage durations for Bloomberg's four growth classifications are 3 years/14 years for "explosive growth" equities, 5 years/12 years for "high growth" equities, 7 years/10 years for "average growth" equities, and 9 years/8 years for "slow/mature growth" equities. Analysts, by tailoring stage specifications to their understanding of the specific company being valued, should be able to improve on the accuracy of valuations compared to a fixed specification.

## 5.5 Spreadsheet (General) Modeling

DDMs such as the Gordon growth model and the multistage models presented earlier assume stylized patterns of dividend growth. With the computational power of personal computers, calculators, and personal digital assistants, however, *any* assumed dividend pattern is easily valued.

Spreadsheets allow the analyst to build complicated models that would be very cumbersome to describe using algebra. Furthermore, built-in spreadsheet functions (such as those to find rates of return) use algorithms to get a numerical answer when a mathematical solution would be impossible or extremely challenging. Because of spreadsheets' widespread use, several analysts can work together or exchange information through the sharing of their spreadsheet models. The example below presents the results of using a spreadsheet to value a stock with dividends changing substantially through time.

### EXAMPLE 19

**Finding the Value of a Stock Using a Spreadsheet Model**

Yang Co. is expected to pay a \$21.00 dividend next year. The dividend will decline by 10 percent annually for the following three years. In Year 5, Yang will sell off assets worth \$100 per share. The Year 5 dividend, which includes a distribution of some of the proceeds of the asset sale, is expected to be \$60. In Year 6, we expect the dividend to decrease to \$40. We expect that this dividend will be maintained at \$40 for one additional year. It is then expected to grow by 5 percent annually thereafter. If the required rate of return is 12 percent, what is the value of one share of Yang?

**Solution:** The value is shown in Exhibit 9. Each dividend, its present value discounted at 12 percent, and an explanation are included in the table. The final row treats the dividends from $t = 8$ forward as a Gordon growth model because after Year 7, the dividend grows at a constant 5 percent annually. $V_7$ is the value of these dividends at $t = 7$.

### EXHIBIT 9    Value of Yang Co. Stock

| Year | $D_t$ or $V_t$ | Value of $D_t$ or $V_t$ | Present Value at 12% | Explanation of $D_t$ or $V_t$ |
|------|------|------|------|------|
| 1 | $D_1$ | 21.00 | 18.75 | Dividend set at \$21 |
| 2 | $D_2$ | 18.90 | 15.07 | Previous dividend × 0.90 |
| 3 | $D_3$ | 17.01 | 12.11 | Previous dividend × 0.90 |
| 4 | $D_4$ | 15.31 | 9.73 | Previous dividend × 0.90 |
| 5 | $D_5$ | 60.00 | 34.05 | Set at \$60 |
| 6 | $D_6$ | 40.00 | 20.27 | Set at \$40 |
| 7 | $D_7$ | 40.00 | 18.09 | Set at \$40 |
| 7 | $V_7$ | 600.00 | 271.41 | $V_7 = D_8/(r - g)$ |
|  |  |  |  | $V_7 = (40.00 \times 1.05)/$ $(0.12 - 0.05)$ |
| Total |  |  | 399.48 |  |

As the table shows, the total present value of Yang Co.'s dividends is $399.48. In this example, the terminal value of the company ($V_n$) at the end of the first stage was found using the Gordon growth model using a mature growth rate of 5 percent. Several alternative approaches to estimating $g$ are available in this context:

▶ Use the formula $g = (b$ in the mature phase$) \times ($ROE in the mature phase$)$. We will discuss the expression $g = b \times$ ROE in Section 6. Analysts estimate mature-phase ROE in several ways, such as:

▶ The DuPont decomposition of ROE based on forecasts for the components of the DuPont expression.

▶ Setting ROE $= r$, the required rate of return on equity, based on the assumption that in the mature phase companies can do no more than earn investors' opportunity cost of capital.

▶ Setting ROE in the mature phase equal to the median industry ROE.

▶ The analyst may estimate the growth rate $g$ with other models relating the mature growth rate to macroeconomic, including industry, growth projections.

When the analyst uses the sustainable growth expression, the earnings retention ratio, $b$, may be empirically based. For example, Bloomberg L.P.'s model assumes that $b = 0.55$ in the mature phase, equivalent to a dividend payout ratio of 45 percent, a long-run average payout ratio for mature dividend-paying companies in the United States. In addition, sometimes analysts project the dividend payout ratio for the company individually.

---

**EXAMPLE 20**

**A Sustainable Growth Rate Calculation**

In Example 17, the analyst estimated the dividend growth rate of IBM in the final stage of a three stage model as 10.2 percent. This was based on the expression

$$g = (b \text{ in the mature phase}) \times (\text{ROE in the mature phase})$$

Using the typical retention ratio of 85 percent for mature technology companies and assuming that in the final stage IBM achieves a ROE equal to its estimated required return on equity of 12 percent, the calculation is:

$$g = 0.85(12\%) = 10.2 \text{ percent}$$

---

## 5.6 Estimating a Required Return Using Any DDM

This reading has focused on finding the value of a security using assumptions for dividends, required rates of return, and expected growth rates. Given current price and all inputs to a DDM except for the required return, we can calculate an IRR. Such an IRR has been used as a required return estimate (although re-using it in a DDM is not appropriate as it risks circularity). It can also be interpreted as the expected return on the issue implied by the market price—essentially, an efficient markets expected return. In the following discussion, keep in mind that if price does not equal intrinsic value, the expected return will need to be adjusted to reflect the additional component of return that accrues when the mispricing is corrected, as discussed earlier.

In some cases, it is very easy to find the IRR. In the Gordon growth model, $r = D_1/P_0 + g$. The required return estimate is the dividend yield plus the expected dividend growth rate. For a security with a current price of $10, an expected dividend of $0.50, and expected growth of 8 percent, the required return estimate is 13 percent.

For the H-model, the expected rate of return can be derived as[19]

$$r = \left(\frac{D_0}{P_0}\right)[(1 + g_L) + H(g_S - g_L)] + g_L \qquad \text{(41-21)}$$

When the short- and long-term growth rates are the same, this model reduces to the Gordon growth model. For a security with a current dividend of $1, a current price of $20, and an expected short-term growth rate of 10 percent declining over 10 years ($H = 5$) to 6 percent, the expected rate of return would be

$$r = \left(\frac{\$1}{\$20}\right)[(1 + 0.06) + 5(0.10 - 0.06)] + 0.06 = 12.3\%$$

For multistage models and spreadsheet models, it can be more difficult to find a single equation for the rate of return. The process generally used is similar to that of finding the internal rate of return for a series of varying cash flows. Using a computer or trial and error, the analyst must find the rate of return such that the present value of future expected dividends equals the current stock price.

## EXAMPLE 21

### Finding the Expected Rate of Return for Varying Expected Dividends

An analyst expects JNJ's (Johnson & Johnson) current dividend of $1.66 to grow by 9 percent for six years and then grow by 7 percent into perpetuity. A recent price for JNJ as of mid-October 2007 is $66.19. What is the internal rate of return on an investment in JNJ's stock?

In performing trial and error with the two-stage model to estimate the expected rate of return, it is important to have a good initial guess. We can use the expected rate of return formula from the Gordon growth model and JNJ's long-term growth rate to find a first approximation: $r = (\$1.66 \times 1.07)/\$66.19 + 0.07 = 9.68\%$. Because we know that the growth rate in the first six years is more than the long-term growth rate of 7 percent, the estimated rate of return must be above 9.68 percent. Exhibit 10 shows the value estimate of JNJ for two discount rates, 9.68% and 10%.

---

[19] Fuller and Hsia (1984).

| EXHIBIT 10 | | Johnson & Johnson | |
| --- | --- | --- | --- |
| Time | $D_t$ | Present Value of $D_t$ and $V_6$ at $r = 9.68\%$ | Present Value of $D_t$ and $V_6$ at $r = 10\%$ |
| 1 | $1.8094 | $1.6497 | $1.6449 |
| 2 | $1.9722 | $1.6394 | $1.6300 |
| 3 | $2.1497 | $1.6293 | $1.6151 |
| 4 | $2.3432 | $1.6192 | $1.6005 |
| 5 | $2.5541 | $1.6092 | $1.5859 |
| 6 | $2.7840 | $1.5992 | $1.5715 |
| 7 | $2.9789 | | |
| Subtotal 1 ($t = 1$ to 6) | | $ 9.75 | $ 9.65 |
| Subtotal 2 ($t = 7$ to $\infty$) | | $63.85 | $56.05 |
| Total | | $73.60 | $65.70 |
| Market Price | | $66.19 | $66.19 |

In the exhibit, the first subtotal is the present value of the expected dividends for years 1 through 6. The second subtotal is the present value of the terminal value, $V_6/(1 + r)^6 = [D_7/(r - g)]/(1 + r)^6$. For $r = 9.68$ percent, that present value is $[2.9789/(0.0968-0.07)]/(1.0968)^6 = $63.85$. The present value for other values of $r$ is found similarly.

Using 9.68 percent as the discount rate, we see that the value estimate for JNJ is $73.60, which is larger than JNJ's market price. That indicates that the IRR is greater than 9.68 percent. With a 10 percent discount rate, the present value of $65.70 is just slightly under the market price. Thus the IRR is slightly less than 10 percent. The IRR can be determined to be 9.98 percent, using a calculator or spreadsheet.

## 5.7 Multistage DDM: Concluding Remarks

The multistage dividend discount models can accommodate a variety of patterns of future streams of expected dividends.

In general, multistage DDMs make stylized assumptions about growth based on a lifecycle view of business. The first stage of a multistage DDM frequently incorporates analysts' individual earnings and dividend forecasts for the next two to five years (sometimes longer). The final stage is often modeled using the Gordon growth model based on an assumption of the firm's long-run sustainable growth rate. In the case of the H-model, the transition to the mature growth phase happens smoothly over the first stage. In the case of the standard two-stage model, the growth rate typically transitions immediately to mature growth rate in the second period. In three-stage models, the middle stage is a stage of transition. Using a spreadsheet, an analyst can model an almost limitless variety of cash flow patterns.

Multistage DDMs have several limitations. Often, the present value of the terminal stage represents more than three-quarters of the total value of shares. Terminal value can be very sensitive to the growth and required return assumptions. Furthermore, technological innovation can make the lifecycle model a crude representation.

# THE FINANCIAL DETERMINANTS OF GROWTH RATES

**6**

In a number of examples earlier in this reading, we have implicitly used the relationship that the dividend growth rate ($g$) equals the earning retention ratio ($b$) times the return on equity (ROE). In this section, we explain this relationship and show how we can combine it with a method of analyzing return on equity, called DuPont analysis, as a simple tool for forecasting dividend growth rates.

## 6.1 Sustainable Growth Rate

We define the **sustainable growth rate** as the rate of dividend (and earnings) growth that can be sustained for a given level of return on equity, assuming that the capital structure is constant over time and that additional common stock is not issued. The reason to study this concept is that it can help us estimate the stable growth rate in a Gordon growth model valuation, or the mature growth rate in a multistage DDM in which we use the Gordon growth formula for the terminal value of the stock.

The expression to calculate the sustainable growth rate is

$$g = b \times \text{ROE} \tag{41-22}$$

where

$g$     = dividend growth rate
$b$     = earnings retention rate ($1 -$ Dividend payout ratio)
ROE = return on equity

More precisely, in Equation 41-22 the retention rate should be multiplied by the rate of return expected to be earned on new investment. Analysts commonly assume that that rate is well approximated by the return on equity, as shown in Equation 41-22; however, whether that is actually the case should be investigated by the analyst on a case-by-case basis.

Example 22 is an illustration of the fact that growth in shareholders' equity is driven by reinvested earnings alone (no new issues of equity, and debt growing at the rate $g$).[20]

---

[20] With debt growing at the rate $g$, the capital structure is constant. If the capital structure is not constant, ROE would not be constant in general because ROE depends on leverage.

### EXAMPLE 22

#### Example Showing $g = b \times$ ROE

Suppose that a company's ROE is 25 percent and its retention rate is 60 percent. According to the expression for the sustainable growth rate, the dividends should grow at $g = b \times$ ROE $= 0.60 \times 25\% = 15\%$.

To demonstrate the working of the expression, let us suppose that, in the year just ended, a company began with shareholders' equity of $1,000,000, earned $250,000 net income, and paid dividends of $100,000. The company begins the next year with $1,000,000 + 0.60($250,000) = $1,000,000 + $150,000 = $1,150,000 of shareholders' equity. There are no additions to equity from the sale of additional shares.

If the company again earns 25 percent on equity, net income will be $0.25 \times \$1,150,000 = \$287,500$, which is a $287,500 − $250,000 = $37,500 or a $37,500/$250,000 = 0.15 percent increase from the prior year level. The company retains 60 percent of earnings, 60% × $287,500 = $172,500, and pays out the other 40 percent, 40% × $287,500 = $115,000 as dividends. Dividends for the company grew from $100,000 to $115,000, which is exactly a 15 percent growth rate. With the company continuing to earn 25 percent each year on the $0.40 of earnings that is reinvested in the company, dividends would continue to grow at 15 percent.

Equation 41-22 implies that the higher the return on equity, the higher the dividend growth rate, all else constant. That relation appears to be reliable. Another implication of the expression is that the lower (higher) the earnings retention ratio, the lower (higher) the growth rate in dividends, holding all else constant; this has been called *the dividend displacement of earnings.*[21] Of course, all else may not be equal—the return on reinvested earnings may not be constant at different levels of investment, or companies with changing future growth prospects may change their dividend policy. Arnott and Asness (2003) and Zhou and Ruland (2006), in providing U.S.-based evidence that dividend-paying companies had higher future growth rates over the period studied, indicate that caution is appropriate in assuming that dividends displace earnings.

A practical logic for defining *sustainable* in terms of growth through internally generated funds (retained earnings) is that external equity (secondary issues of stock) is considerably more costly than internal equity (reinvested earnings), for several reasons including the investment banker fees associated with secondary equity issues. Continuous issuance of new stock is not a practical fund-

---

[21] ROE is a variable that reflects underlying profitability as well as the use of leverage or debt. The retention ratio or dividend policy, in contrast, is not a fundamental variable in the same sense as ROE. A higher dividend growth rate through a higher retention ratio (lower dividend payout ratio) is neutral for share value in and of itself. Holding investment policy (capital projects) constant, the positive effect on value from an increase in $g$ will just be offset by the negative effect from a decrease in dividend payouts in the expression for the value of the stock in any DDM. Sharpe, Alexander, and Bailey (1999) discuss this concept in more detail.

ing alternative for companies, in general.[22] Growth of capital through issuance of new debt can sometimes be sustained for considerable periods, however. Further, if a company manages its capital structure to a target percentage of debt to total capital (debt and common stock), it will need to issue debt to maintain that percentage as equity grows through reinvested earnings. (This approach is one of a variety of observed capital structure policies.) In addition, the earnings retention ratio nearly always shows year-to-year variation in actual companies. For example, earnings may have transitory components that management does not want to reflect in dividends. The analyst may thus observe actual dividend growth rates straying from the growth rates predicted by Equation 41-22 because of these effects, even when his input estimates are unbiased. Nevertheless, the equation can be useful as a simple expression for approximating the average rate at which dividends can grow over a long horizon.

## 6.2 Dividend Growth Rate, Retention Rate, and ROE Analysis

Thus far we have seen that a company's sustainable growth, as defined above, is a function of its ability to generate return on equity (which depends on investment opportunities) and its retention rate. We now expand this model by examining what drives ROE. Remember that ROE is the return (net income) generated on the equity invested in the company:

$$\text{ROE} = \frac{\text{Net income}}{\text{Shareholders' equity}} \tag{41-23}$$

If a company has a ROE of 15 percent, it generates $15 of net income for every $100 invested in stockholders' equity. For purposes of analyzing ROE, we can relate it to several other financial ratios. For example, ROE can be seen as related to return on assets (ROA) and the extent of financial leverage (equity multiplier):

$$\text{ROE} = \frac{\text{Net income}}{\text{Total assets}} \times \frac{\text{Total assets}}{\text{Shareholders' equity}} \tag{41-24}$$

Therefore, a company can increase its ROE either by increasing ROA or the use of leverage (assuming the company can borrow at a rate lower than that it earns on its assets).

We can further expand this model by breaking ROA into two components, profit margin and turnover (efficiency):

$$\text{ROE} = \frac{\text{Net income}}{\text{Sales}} \times \frac{\text{Sales}}{\text{Total assets}} \times \frac{\text{Total assets}}{\text{Shareholders' equity}} \tag{41-25}$$

---

[22] As a long-term average, about 2 percent of U.S. publicly traded companies issue new equity in a given year, which corresponds to a secondary equity issue once every 50 years, on average. Businesses may be rationed in their access to secondary issues of equity because of the costs associated with informational asymmetries between management and the public. Because management has more information on the future cash flows of the company than the general public, and equity is an ownership claim to those cash flows, the public may react to additional equity issuance as possibly motivated by an intent to "share (future) misery" rather than "share (future) wealth."

The first term is the company's profit margin. A higher profit margin will result in a higher ROE. The second term measures total asset turnover, which is the company's efficiency. A turnover of 1 indicates that a company generates $1 in sales for every $1 invested in assets. A higher turnover will result in higher ROE. The last term is the equity multiplier, which measures the extent of leverage, as noted earlier. This relationship is widely known as the DuPont model or analysis of ROE. Although ROE can be analyzed further using a five-way analysis, the three-way analysis will provide us with insight into the determinants of ROE that are pertinent to our understanding of the growth rate. Combining Equations 41-22 and 41-25, we find that the dividend growth rate is equal to the retention rate multiplied by ROE:

$$g = \frac{\text{Net income} - \text{Dividends}}{\text{Net income}} \times \frac{\text{Net income}}{\text{Sales}} \times \frac{\text{Sales}}{\text{Total assets}}$$

$$\times \frac{\text{Total assets}}{\text{Shareholders' equity}} \qquad \textbf{(41-26)}$$

This expansion of the sustainable growth expression has been called the PRAT model (Higgins 2001). Growth is a function of profit margin (P), retention rate (R), asset turnover (A), and financial leverage (T). The profit margin and the asset turnover determine ROA. The other two factors, the retention rate and financial leverage, reflect the company's financial policies. So, the growth rate in dividends can be viewed as determined by the company's ROA and financial policies. Analysts may use Equation 41-26 to forecast a company's dividend growth rate in the mature growth phase.

Theoretically, the sustainable growth rate expression and this expansion of it based on the DuPont decomposition of ROE hold exactly only when ROE is calculated using beginning-of-period shareholders' equity, as illustrated in Example 22. Such calculation assumes that retained earnings are not available for reinvestment until the end of the period. Analysts and financial databases more frequently prefer to use average total assets in calculating ROE and, practically, DuPont analysis is frequently performed using that definition.[23] The example below illustrates the logic behind this equation.

## EXAMPLE 23

### ROA, Financial Policies, and the Dividend Growth Rate

Baggai Enterprises has an ROA of 10 percent, retains 30 percent of earnings, and has an equity multiplier of 1.25. Mondale Enterprises also has an ROA of 10 percent, but it retains two-thirds of earnings and has an equity multiplier of 2.00.

1. What are the sustainable dividend growth rates for (A) Baggai Enterprises and (B) Mondale Enterprises?
2. Identify the drivers of the difference in the sustainable growth rates of Baggai Enterprises and Mondale Enterprises.

---

[23] See Robinson, van Greuning, Henry, and Broihahn, "Financial Analysis Techniques" (CFA Institute, 2006).

> **Solution to 1:.**
>
> **A.** Baggai's dividend growth rate should be $g = 0.30 \times 10\% \times 1.25 = 3.75\%$
>
> **B.** Mondale's dividend growth rate should be $g = (2/3) \times 10\% \times 2.00 = 13.33\%$
>
> **Solution to 2:** Because Mondale has the higher retention rate and higher financial leverage, its dividend growth rate is much higher.

If we are forecasting growth for the next five years, we should use our expectations of the four factors driving growth over this five-year period. If we are forecasting growth into perpetuity, we should use our very long-term forecasts for these variables.

To illustrate the calculation and implications of the sustainable growth rate using the expression for ROE given by the DuPont formula, assume the growth rate is $g = b \times \text{ROE} = 0.60\,(15\%) = 9\%$. The ROE of 15 percent was based on a profit margin of 5 percent, an asset turnover of 2.0, and an equity multiplier of 1.5. Given fixed ratios of sales-to-assets and assets-to-equity, sales, assets, and debt will also be growing at 9 percent. Because dividends are fixed at 40 percent of income, dividends will grow at the same rate as income, or 9 percent. If the company increases dividends faster than 9 percent, this growth rate would not be sustainable using internally generated funds. Earning retentions would be reduced, and the company would not be able to finance the assets required for sales growth without external financing.

The analyst should be careful in projecting historical financial ratios into the future in using this analysis. Although a company may have grown at 25 percent a year for the last five years, this rate of growth is probably not sustainable indefinitely. Abnormally high ROEs, which may have driven that growth, are unlikely to persist indefinitely because of competitive forces and possibly other reasons such as adverse changes in technology or demand. In the following example, an above average terminal growth rate is plausibly forecasted because the company has positioned itself in businesses that may have relatively high margins on an ongoing basis.

## EXAMPLE 24

### Forecasting Growth with the PRAT Formula

International Business Machines (NYSE: IBM), which currently pays a dividend of $1.60 per share, has been the subject of two other examples in this reading. In one example, an analyst estimated IBM's mature phase growth rate at 10.2 percent, based on its mature phase ROE exactly equaling its estimated required return on equity of 12 percent. Another estimate can be made using the DuPont decomposition of ROE.

An analysis of IBM's ROE for the past four years is shown in Exhibit 11. Over the period shown, EPS grew at a compound annual rate of 11.8 percent. IBM's retention ratio is 0.85.

| EXHIBIT 11 | | IBM Corporation | | |
|---|---|---|---|---|
| Year | ROE (%) | Profit Margin (%) | Asset Turnover | Financial Leverage |
| 2006 | 30.6 = | 10.30 | × 0.821 | × 3.62 |
| 2005 | 24.7 = | 8.77 | × 0.880 | × 3.20 |
| 2004 | 29.3 = | 8.77 | × 0.910 | × 3.67 |
| 2003 | 30.1 = | 8.54 | × 0.940 | × 3.75 |

IBM achieved relatively high ROEs in this most recent period, both compared to the historical median ROE of U.S. businesses of 12.2 percent and compared to variously defined comparison groups. Take IBM's formal Global Industry Classification System (GICS) peer group, "computer hardware − large system vendors." Making a pretax comparison to avoid the factor of differing tax effective rates, IBM's pretax profit margin at 14.6 percent for 2006 exceeded the GICS peer group mean of about 7 percent.[24] Suppose the analyst accepts IBM's asset turnover and financial leverage performance as shown in Exhibit 11 as relevant to IBM's performance in its mature phase, but believes that IBM's recent superiority in profit margin in comparison to peers will be much reduced in the mature phase. The analyst forecasts a peer mean pretax profit margin of 6 percent during IBM's mature phase. With its strategy of searching for high-margined growth and its strong ability to compete in integrated hardware–software solutions for businesses, the analyst forecasts a long-run pretax profit margin of 6.5 percent for IBM, equal to a profit margin (after tax) of about 4.6 percent based on an effective tax rate of about 30 percent. Based on an asset turnover ratio of 0.8 and financial leverage of 3.6 (close to the mean values in Exhibit 11), but using a profit margin estimate of 4.6, a forecast of ROE in the maturity phase is $(4.6\%)(0.8)(3.6) = 13.2$ percent. Therefore, based on this analysis, the estimate of the sustainable growth rate for IBM would be $g = (0.85)(13.2\%) = 11.2$ percent.

## 6.3 Financial Models and Dividends

Analysts can also forecast dividends by building more-complex models of the company's total operating and financial environment. Because there can be so many aspects to such a model, a spreadsheet is used to build pro forma income statements and balance sheets. The company's ability to pay dividends in the future can be predicted using one of these models. The example below shows the dividends that a highly profitable and rapidly growing company can pay when its growth rates and profit margins decline because of increasing competition over time.

---

[24] Based on the Standard & Poor's Stock Report of 6 October 2007.

**A Spreadsheet Model for Forecasting Dividends**

An analyst is preparing a forecast of dividends for Hoshino Distributors for the next five years. He uses a spreadsheet model with the following assumptions:

▶ Sales are $100 million in Year 1. They grow by 20 percent in Year 2, 15 percent in Year 3, and 10 percent in Years 4 and 5.

▶ Operating profits (EBIT = earnings before interest and taxes) are 20 percent of sales in Years 1 and 2, 18 percent of sales in Year 3, and 16 percent of sales in Years 4 and 5.

▶ Interest expenses are 10 percent of total debt for the current year.

▶ The income tax rate is 40 percent.

▶ Hoshino pays out 20 percent of earnings in dividends in Years 1 and 2, 30 percent in Year 3, 40 percent in Year 4, and 50 percent in Year 5.

▶ Retained earnings are added to equity in the next year.

▶ Total assets are 80 percent of the current year's sales in all years.

▶ In Year 1, debt is $40 million and shareholders' equity is $40 million. Debt equals total assets minus shareholders' equity. Shareholders' equity will equal the previous year's shareholders' equity plus the addition to retained earnings from the previous year.

▶ Hoshino has 4 million shares outstanding.

▶ The required return on equity is 15 percent.

▶ The value of the company at the end of Year 5 is expected to be 10.0 times earnings.

The analyst wishes to estimate the current value per share of Hoshino. Exhibit 12 adheres to the modeling assumptions above. Total dividends and earnings are found at the bottom of the income statement.

| **EXHIBIT 12** | **Hoshino Distributors Pro Forma Financial Statements (in Millions)** | | | | |
|---|---|---|---|---|---|
| | **Year 1** | **Year 2** | **Year 3** | **Year 4** | **Year 5** |
| Income statement | | | | | |
| Sales | $100.00 | $120.00 | $138.00 | $151.80 | $166.98 |
| EBIT | $20.00 | $24.00 | $24.84 | $24.29 | $26.72 |
| Interest | $4.00 | $4.83 | $5.35 | $5.64 | $6.18 |
| EBT | $16.00 | $19.17 | $19.49 | $18.65 | $20.54 |
| Taxes | $6.40 | $7.67 | $7.80 | $7.46 | $8.22 |
| Net income | $9.60 | $11.50 | $11.69 | $11.19 | $12.32 |
| Dividends | $1.92 | $2.30 | $3.51 | $4.48 | $6.16 |

*(Exhibit continued on next page . . .)*

| EXHIBIT 12 | | (continued) | | | |
|---|---|---|---|---|---|
| | **Year 1** | **Year 2** | **Year 3** | **Year 4** | **Year 5** |
| Balance sheet | | | | | |
| Total assets | $80.00 | $96.00 | $110.40 | $121.44 | $133.58 |
| Total debt | $40.00 | $48.32 | $53.52 | $56.38 | $61.81 |
| Equity | $40.00 | $47.68 | $56.88 | $65.06 | $71.77 |

Dividing the total dividends by the number of outstanding shares gives the dividend per share for each year shown below. The present value of each dividend, discounted at 15 percent, is also shown.

| | **Year 1** | **Year 2** | **Year 3** | **Year 4** | **Year 5** | **Total PV** |
|---|---|---|---|---|---|---|
| DPS | $0.480 | $0.575 | $0.877 | $1.120 | $1.540 | $4.59 |
| PV | $0.417 | $0.435 | $0.577 | $0.640 | $0.766 | $2.84 |

The earnings per share in Year 5 are $12.32 million divided by 4 million shares, or $3.08 per share. Given a P/E of 10, the market price in Year 5 is predicted to be $30.80. Discounted at 15 percent, the required return on equity noted above, the present value of this price is $15.31. Adding the present values of the five dividends, which sum to $2.84, gives a total stock value today of $18.15 per share.

# SUMMARY

This reading provided an overview of DCF models of valuation, discussed the estimation of a stock's required rate of return, and presented in detail the dividend discount model.

▶ In DCF models, the value of any asset is the present value of its (expected) future cash flows

$$V_0 = \sum_{t=1}^{n} \frac{CF_t}{(1 + r)^t}$$

where $V_0$ is the value of the asset as of $t = 0$ (today), $CF_t$ is the (expected) cash flow at time $t$, and $r$ is the discount rate or required rate of return. For infinitely lived assets such as common stocks, $n$ runs to infinity.

▶ Several alternative streams of expected cash flows can be used to value equities, including dividends, free cash flow, and residual income. A discounted dividend approach is most suitable for dividend-paying stocks, where the company has a discernible dividend policy that has an understandable relationship to the company's profitability, and the investor has a non-control (minority ownership) perspective.

▶ The free cash flow approach (FCFF or FCFE) might be appropriate when the company does not pay dividends, dividends differ substantially from FCFE, free cash flows align with profitability, or the investor takes a control (majority ownership) perspective.

▶ The residual income approach can be useful when the company does not pay dividends (as an alternative to a FCF approach), or free cash flow is negative.

▶ The DDM with a single holding period gives stock value as

$$V_0 = \frac{D_1}{(1 + r)^1} + \frac{P_1}{(1 + r)^1} = \frac{D_1 + P_1}{(1 + r)^1}$$

where $D_t$ is the expected dividend at time $t$ (here $t = 1$) and $V_t$ is the stock's (expected) value at time $t$. Assuming that $V_0$ is equal to today's market price, $P_0$, the expected holding-period return is

$$r = \frac{D_1 + P_1}{P_0} - 1 = \frac{D_1}{P_0} + \frac{P_1 - P_0}{P_0}$$

▶ The expression for the DDM for any given finite holding period $n$ and the general expression for the DDM are, respectively,

$$V_0 = \sum_{t=1}^{n} \frac{D_t}{(1 + r)^t} + \frac{P_n}{(1 + r)^n} \text{ and } V_0 = \sum_{t=1}^{\infty} \frac{D_t}{(1 + r)^t}$$

▶ There are two main approaches to the problem of forecasting dividends: First, we can assign the entire stream of expected future dividends to one of several stylized growth patterns. Second, we can forecast a finite number of dividends individually up to a terminal point, valuing the remaining dividends by assigning them to a stylized growth pattern, or forecasting share price as of the terminal point of our dividend forecasts.

▶ The Gordon growth model assumes that dividends grow at a constant rate $g$ forever, so that $D_t = D_{t-1}(1 + g)$. The dividend stream in the Gordon growth model has a value of

$$V_0 = \frac{D_0(1 + g)}{r - g}, \text{ or } V_0 = \frac{D_1}{r - g} \text{ where } r > g.$$

▶ The value of noncallable fixed-rate perpetual preferred stock is $V_0 = D/r$, where $D$ is the stock's (constant) annual dividend.

▶ Assuming that price equals value, the Gordon growth model estimate of a stock's expected rate of return is

$$r = \frac{D_0(1 + g)}{P_0} + g = \frac{D_1}{P_0} + g$$

▶ Given an estimate of the next-period dividend and the stock's required rate of return, we can use the Gordon growth model to estimate the dividend growth rate implied by the current market price (making a constant growth rate assumption).

▶ The present value of growth opportunities (PVGO) is the part of a stock's total value, $V_0$, that comes from profitable future growth opportunities in contrast to the value associated with assets already in place. The relationship is $V_0 = E_1/r + \text{PVGO}$, where $E_1/r$ is defined as the no-growth value per share.

▶ We can express the leading price–earnings ratio ($P_0/E_1$) and the trailing price–earnings ratio ($P_0/E_0$) in terms of the Gordon growth model as, respectively,

$$\frac{P_0}{E_1} = \frac{D_1/E_1}{r - g} = \frac{1 - b}{r - g} \text{ and } \frac{P_0}{E_0} = \frac{D_0(1 + g)/E_0}{r - g} = \frac{(1 - b)(1 + g)}{r - g}$$

The above expressions give a stock's justified price–earnings ratio based on forecasts of fundamentals (given that the Gordon growth model is appropriate).

▶ The Gordon growth model may be useful for valuing broad-based equity indexes and the stock of businesses with earnings that we expect to grow at a stable rate comparable to or lower than the nominal growth rate of the economy.

▶ Gordon growth model values are very sensitive to the assumed growth rate and required rate of return.

▶ For many companies, growth falls into phases. In the growth phase, a company enjoys an abnormally high growth rate in earnings per share, called supernormal growth. In the transition phase, earnings growth slows. In the mature phase, the company reaches an equilibrium in which factors such as earnings growth and the return on equity stabilize at levels that can be sustained long term. Analysts often apply multistage DCF models to value the stock of a firm with multistage growth prospects.

▶ The two-stage dividend discount model assumes different growth rates in Stage 1 and Stage 2

$$V_0 = \sum_{t=1}^{n} \frac{D_0(1 + g_S)^t}{(1 + r)^t} + \frac{D_0(1 + g_S)^n(1 + g_L)}{(1 + r)^n(r - g_L)}$$

where $g_S$ is the expected dividend growth rate in the first period and $g_L$ is the expected growth rate in the second period.

▶ The terminal stock value, $V_n$, is sometimes found with the Gordon growth model or with some other method, such as applying a P/E multiplier to forecasted EPS as of the terminal date.

▶ The H-model assumes that the dividend growth rate declines linearly from a high supernormal rate to the normal growth rate during Stage 1, and then grows at a constant normal growth rate thereafter:

$$V_0 = \frac{D_0(1 + g_L)}{r - g_L} + \frac{D_0 H(g_S - g_L)}{r - g_L} = \frac{D_0(1 + g_L) + D_0 H(g_S - g_L)}{r - g_L}$$

▶ There are two basic three-stage models. In one version, the growth rate in the middle stage is constant. In the second version, the growth rate declines linearly in Stage 2 and becomes constant and normal in Stage 3.

▶ Spreadsheet models are very flexible, providing the analyst with the ability to value any pattern of expected dividends.

▶ In addition to valuing equities, the IRR of a DDM, assuming assets are correctly priced in the marketplace, has been used to estimate required returns. For simpler models (like the one-period model, the Gordon growth model, and the H-model), well-known formulas may be used to calculate these rates of return. For many dividend streams, however, the rate of return must be found by trial and error, producing a discount rate that equates the present value of the forecasted dividend stream to the current market price.

▶ Multistage DDM models can accommodate a wide variety of patterns of expected dividends. Even though such models may use stylized assumptions about growth, they can provide useful approximations.

▶ Dividend growth rates can be obtained from analyst forecasts, from statistical forecasting models, or from company fundamentals. The sustainable growth rate depends on the ROE and the earnings retention rate, $b$: $g = b \times$ ROE. This expression can be expanded further, using the DuPont formula, as

$$g = \frac{\text{Net income} - \text{Dividends}}{\text{Net income}} \times \frac{\text{Net income}}{\text{Sales}}$$
$$\times \frac{\text{Sales}}{\text{Total assets}} \times \frac{\text{Total assets}}{\text{Shareholders' equity}}$$

## PRACTICE PROBLEMS FOR READING 41

1. The expression for the value of a stock given a single-period investment horizon has four variables: $V_0$, $D_1$, $P_1$, and $r$. Solve for the value of the missing variable for each of the four stocks in the table below.

| Stock | Estimated Value ($V_0$) | Expected Dividend ($D_1$) | Expected Price ($P_1$) | Required Rate of Return ($r$) |
|---|---|---|---|---|
| 1 | | $0.30 | $21.00 | 10.0% |
| 2 | $30.00 | | 32.00 | 10.0 |
| 3 | 92.00 | 2.70 | | 12.0 |
| 4 | 16.00 | 0.30 | 17.90 | |

2. General Motors (NYSE: GM) sells for $66.00 per share. The expected dividend for next year is $2.40. Use the single-period DDM to predict GM's stock price one year from today. The risk-free rate of return is 5.3 percent, the equity risk premium is 6.0 percent, and GM's beta is 0.90.

3. BP PLC (NYSE: BP) has a current stock price of $50 and current dividend of $1.50. The dividend is expected to grow at 5 percent annually. BP's beta is 0.85. The risk-free interest rate is 4.5 percent, and the equity risk premium is 6.0 percent.

   A. What is next year's projected dividend?

   B. What is BP's required rate of return based on the CAPM?

   C. Using the Gordon growth model, what is the value of BP?

   D. Assuming the Gordon growth model is valid, what dividend growth rate would result in a model value of BP equal to its market price?

4. The current market prices of three stocks are given below. The current dividends, dividend growth rates, and required rates of return are also given. The dividend growth rates are perpetual.

| Stock | Current Price | Current Dividend ($t = 0$) | Dividend Growth Rate | Required Rate of Return |
|---|---|---|---|---|
| Que Corp. | $25.00 | $0.50 | 7.0% | 10.0% |
| SHS Company | $40.00 | $1.20 | 6.5 | 10.5 |
| True Corp. | $20.00 | $0.88 | 5.0 | 10.0 |

   A. Find the value of each stock with the Gordon growth model.

   B. Which stock's current market price has the smallest premium or largest discount (in percentage terms) relative to its DDM valuation?

**5.** For five utility stocks, the table below provides the expected dividend for next year, the current market price, the expected dividend growth rate, and the beta. The risk-free rate is currently 5.3 percent, and the equity risk premium is 6.0 percent.

| Stock | Dividend $(D_1)$ | Price $(P_0)$ | Dividend Growth Rate $(g)$ |
|---|---|---|---|
| American Electric (NYSE: AEP) | 2.40 | 46.17 | 5.0% |
| Consolidated Edison (NYSE: ED) | 2.20 | 39.80 | 5.0 |
| Exelon Corp. (NYSE: EXC) | 1.69 | 64.12 | 7.0 |
| Southern Co. (NYSE: SO) | 1.34 | 23.25 | 5.5 |
| Dominion Resources (NYSE: D) | 2.58 | 60.13 | 5.5 |

Calculate the expected rate of return for each stock using the Gordon growth model.

**6.** Vicente Garcia is a buy-side analyst for a large pension fund. He frequently uses dividend discount models such as the Gordon growth model for the consumer noncyclical stocks that he covers. The current dividend for Procter & Gamble Co. (NYSE: PG) is $1.46, and the dividend eight years ago was $0.585. The current stock price is $80.00.

  **A.** What is the historical dividend growth rate for Procter & Gamble?

  **B.** Garcia assumes that the future dividend growth rate will be exactly half of the historical rate. What is Procter & Gamble's expected rate of return using the Gordon growth model?

  **C.** Garcia uses a beta of 0.53 (computed versus the S&P 500 index) for Procter & Gamble. The risk-free rate of return is 5.56 percent and the equity risk premium is 3.71 percent. If Garcia continues to assume that the future dividend growth rate will be exactly half of the historical rate, what is the value of the stock with the Gordon growth model?

**7.** NiSource Preferred B (NYSE: NI-B) is a fixed-rate perpetual preferred stock paying a $3.88 annual dividend. If the required rate of return is 7.88 percent, what is the value of one share? If the price of this preferred stock were $46.00, what would be the yield?

**8.** R. A. Nixon put out a "strong buy" on DuPoTex (DPT). This company has a current stock price of $88.00 per share. The company has sales of $210 million, net income of $3 million, and 300 million outstanding shares. DPT is not paying a dividend. Dorothy Josephson has argued with Nixon that DPT's valuation is excessive relative to its sales, profits, and any reasonable assumptions about future possible dividends. Josephson also asserts that DPT has a market value equal to that of many large blue-chip companies, which it does not deserve. Nixon feels that Josephson's concerns reflect an archaic attitude about equity valuation and a lack of understanding about DPT's industry.

**A.** What is the total market value of DPT's outstanding shares? What are the price-to-earnings and price-to-sales ratios?

**B.** Nixon and Josephson have agreed on a scenario for future earnings and dividends for DPT. Their assumptions are that sales grow at 60 percent annually for four years, and then at 7 percent annually thereafter. In Year 5 and thereafter, earnings will be 10 percent of sales. No dividends will be paid for four years, but in Year 5 and after, dividends will be 40 percent of earnings. Dividends should be discounted at a 12 percent rate. What is the value of a share of DPT using the discounted dividend approach to valuation?

**C.** Nixon and Josephson explore another scenario for future earnings and dividends for DPT. They assume that sales will grow at 7 percent in Year 5 and thereafter. Earnings will be 10 percent of sales, and dividends will be 40 percent of earnings. Dividends will be initiated in Year 5, and dividends should be discounted at 12 percent. What level of sales is required in Year 4 to achieve a discounted dividend valuation equal to the current stock price?

**9.** Dole Food (NYSE: DOL) has a current dividend of $0.40, which is expected to grow at 7 percent forever. Felipe Rodriguez has estimated the required rate of return for Dole using three methods. The methods and the estimates are as follows:

| | |
|---|---|
| Bond yield plus risk premium method | $r = 9.6\%$ |
| CAPM method | $r = 11.2\%$ |
| APT method | $r = 10.4\%$ |

Using the assumed dividend pattern, what is the value of Dole Food using each of the three estimated required rates of return?

**10.** The CFO of B-to-C Inc., a retailer of miscellaneous consumer products, recently announced the objective of paying its first (annual) cash dividend of $0.50 four years from now. Thereafter, the dividend is expected to increase by 7 percent per year for the foreseeable future. The company's required rate of return is 15 percent.

**A.** Assuming that you have confidence in the CFO's dividend target, what is the value of the stock of B-to-C today?

**B.** Suppose that you think that the CFO's outlook is too optimistic. Instead, you believe that the first dividend of $0.50 will not be received until six years from now. What is the value of the stock?

**11.** FPR is expected to pay a $0.60 dividend next year. The dividend is expected to grow at a 50 percent annual rate for Years 2 and 3, at 20 percent annually for Years 4 and 5, and at 5 percent annually for Year 6 and thereafter. If the required rate of return is 12 percent, what is the value per share?

**12.** Hanson PLC (LSE: HNS) is selling for GBP 472. Hansen has a beta of 0.83 against the FTSE 100 index, and the current dividend is GBP 13.80. The risk-free rate of return is 4.66 percent, and the equity risk premium is 4.92 percent. An analyst covering this stock expects the Hanson dividend to grow initially at 14 percent but to decline linearly to 5 percent over a 10-year period. After that, the analyst expects the dividend to grow at 5 percent.

**A.** Compute the value of the Hanson dividend stream using the H-model. According to the H-model valuation, is Hanson overpriced or underpriced?

**B.** Assume that Hanson's dividends follow the H-model pattern the analyst predicts. If an investor pays the current GBP 472 price for the stock, what is the expected rate of return?

**13.** Your supervisor has asked you to evaluate the relative attractiveness of the stocks of two very similar chemical companies: Litchfield Chemical Corp. (LCC) and Aminochem Company (AOC). AOC and LCC have June 30 fiscal year ends. You have compiled the data in the following exhibit for this purpose.

**Selected Data for Litchfield and Aminochem**

|  | Litchfield Chemical (LCC) | Aminochem (AOC) |
|---|---|---|
| Current stock price | $50 | $30 |
| Shares outstanding (millions) | 10 | 20 |
| Projected earnings per share (FY 1996) | $4.00 | $3.20 |
| Projected dividend per share (FY 1996) ($D_1$) | $0.90 | $1.60 |
| Projected dividend growth rate | 8% | 7% |
| Investors' required rate of return | 10% | 11% |
| Balance sheet data (millions) |  |  |
| Long-term debt | $100 | $130 |
| Stockholders' equity | $300 | $320 |

**A.** Calculate the value of the common stock of LCC and AOC using the constant-growth DDM and investors' required rate of return. Show your work.

**B.** Calculate the sustainable growth rate of LCC and AOC. Show your work.

**C.** Recommend LCC *or* AOC for investment. Justify your choice using your answers to A and B and the information in the exhibit.

**14.** Scott Kelly is reviewing MasterToy's financial statements in order to estimate its sustainable growth rate. Using the information presented in the following exhibit,

    **A.**   **i.** Identify the three components of the DuPont formula.

         **ii.** Calculate the ROE for 1999 using the three components of the DuPont formula.

         **iii.** Calculate the sustainable growth rate for 1999.

Kelly has calculated actual and sustainable growth for each of the past four years and finds in each year that its calculated sustainable growth rate substantially exceeds its actual growth rate.

    **B.** Cite one course of action (other than ignoring the problem) Kelly should encourage MasterToy to take, assuming the calculated sustainable growth rate continues to exceed the actual growth rate.

---

**MasterToy Inc.**
**Actual 1998 and Estimated 1999 Financial Statements**
**for FY Ending December 31**
**($ Millions, except Per-Share Data)**

| Income Statement | 1998 | 1999e | Change (%) |
|---|---|---|---|
| Revenue | $4,750 | $5,140 | 8.2 |
| Cost of goods sold | $2,400 | $2,540 | |
| Selling, general, and administrative | 1,400 | 1,550 | |
| Depreciation | 180 | 210 | |
| Goodwill amortization | 10 | 10 | |
|    Operating income | $760 | $830 | 9.2 |
| Interest expense | 20 | 25 | |
|    Income before taxes | $740 | $805 | |
| Income taxes | 265 | 295 | |
|    Net income | $475 | $510 | |
| Earnings per share | $1.79 | $1.96 | 9.5 |
| Average shares outstanding (millions) | 265 | 260 | |

| Balance Sheet | 1998 | 1999e | Change (%) |
|---|---|---|---|
| Cash | $400 | $400 | |
| Accounts receivable | 680 | 700 | |
| Inventories | 570 | 600 | |
| Net property, plant, and equipment | 800 | 870 | |
| Intangibles | 500 | 530 | |
|    Total assets | $2,950 | $3,100 | |
| Current liabilities | $550 | $600 | |
| Long-term debt | 300 | 300 | |
|    Total liabilities | $850 | $900 | |

| | 1998 | 1999e | Change (%) |
|---|---|---|---|
| Stockholders' equity | 2,100 | 2,200 | |
|    Total liabilities and equity | $2,950 | $3,100 | |
| Book value per share | $7.92 | $8.46 | |
| Annual dividend per share | $0.55 | $0.60 | |

**15.** The management of Telluride, an international diversified conglomerate based in the United States, believes that the recent strong performance of its wholly owned medical supply subsidiary, Sundanci, has gone unnoticed. In order to realize Sundanci's full value, Telluride has announced that it will divest Sundanci in a tax-free spin-off.

    Sue Carroll, CFA, is Director of Research at Kesson and Associates. In developing an investment recommendation for Sundanci, Carroll has directed four of her analysts to determine a valuation of Sundanci using various valuation disciplines. To assist her analysts, Carroll has gathered the information shown in the exhibits below.

### Sundanci Actual 1999 and 2000 Financial Statements for FY Ending May 31 ($ Millions, except Per-Share Data)

| Income Statement | 1999 | 2000 |
|---|---|---|
| Revenue | $474 | $598 |
| Depreciation | 20 | 23 |
| Other operating costs | 368 | 460 |
| Income before taxes | 86 | 115 |
| Taxes | 26 | 35 |
| Net income | 60 | 80 |
| Dividends | 18 | 24 |
| Earnings per share | $0.714 | $0.952 |
| Dividends per share | $0.214 | $0.286 |
| Common shares outstanding (millions) | 84.0 | 84.0 |

| Balance Sheet | 1999 | 2000 |
|---|---|---|
| Current assets | $201 | $326 |
| Net property, plant and equipment | 474 | 489 |
|    Total assets | 675 | 815 |
| Current liabilities | 57 | 141 |
| Long-term debt | 0 | 0 |
|    Total liabilities | 57 | 141 |
| Shareholders' equity | 618 | 674 |
|    Total liabilities and equity | 675 | 815 |
| Capital expenditures | 34 | 38 |

### Selected Financial Information

| | |
|---|---|
| Required rate of return on equity | 14% |
| Growth rate of industry | 13% |
| Industry P/E | 26 |

Prior to determining Sundanci's valuation, Carroll analyzes Sundanci's return on equity (ROE) and sustainable growth.

**A.**   **i.** Calculate the *three* components of ROE in the DuPont formula for the year 2000.

  **ii.** Calculate ROE for the year 2000.

  **iii.** Calculate the sustainable rate of growth. Show your work.

Carroll learns that Sundanci's Board of Directors is considering the following policy changes that will affect Sundanci's sustainable growth rate:

▶  Director A proposes an increase in the quarterly dividend of $0.15 per share.

▶  Director B proposes a bond issue of $25 million, the proceeds of which will be used to increase production capacity.

▶  Director C proposes a 2-for-1 stock split.

**B.** Indicate the effect of each of these proposals on Sundanci's sustainable rate of growth, given that the other factors remain unchanged. Identify which components of the sustainable growth model, if any, are directly affected by each proposal.

Helen Morgan, CFA, has been asked by Carroll to determine the potential valuation for Sundanci using the DDM. Morgan anticipates that Sundanci's earnings and dividends will grow at 32 percent for two years and 13 percent thereafter.

**C.** Calculate the current value of a share of Sundanci stock using a two-stage dividend discount model and the data from the exhibits above. Show your work.

**16.** Peninsular Research is initiating coverage of a mature manufacturing industry. John Jones, CFA, head of the research department, gathers the information given below to help in his analysis.

### Fundamental Industry and Market Data

| | |
|---|---|
| Forecasted industry earnings retention rate | 40% |
| Forecasted industry return on equity | 25% |
| Industry beta | 1.2 |
| Government bond yield | 6% |
| Equity risk premium | 5% |

**A.** Compute the price to earnings $(P_0/E_1)$ ratio for the industry based on the fundamental data given. Show your work.

Jones wants to analyze how fundamental P/Es might differ among countries. He gathers the following data:

### Economic and Market Data

| Fundamental Factors | Country A | Country B |
|---|---|---|
| Forecasted growth in real gross domestic product | 5% | 2% |
| Government bond yield | 10% | 6% |
| Equity risk premium | 5% | 4% |

**B.** Determine whether each of the fundamental factors above would cause P/Es to be generally higher for Country A or higher for Country B. Justify each of your conclusions with one reason. *Note*: Consider each fundamental factor in isolation, with all else remaining equal.

**17.** Janet Ludlow's company requires all its analysts to use a two-stage DDM and the CAPM to value stocks. Using these models, Ludlow has valued QuickBrush Company at $63 per share. She now must value SmileWhite Corporation.

| Valuation Information: December 1997 | | |
| --- | --- | --- |
| | **QuickBrush** | **SmileWhite** |
| Beta | 1.35 | 1.15 |
| Market price | $45.00 | $30.00 |
| Intrinsic value | $63.00 | ? |
| Notes: | | |
| Risk-free rate | 4.50% | |
| Expected market return $[E(R_M)]$ | 14.50% | |

**A.** Calculate the required rate of return for SmileWhite using the information given above and the CAPM. Show your work.

Ludlow estimates the following EPS and dividend growth rates for SmileWhite:

| First three years: | 12% per year |
| --- | --- |
| Years thereafter: | 9% per year |

The 1997 dividend per share is $1.72.

**B.** Estimate the intrinsic value of SmileWhite using the data above and the two-stage DDM. Show your work.

**C.** Recommend QuickBrush or SmileWhite stock for purchase by comparing each company's intrinsic value with its current market price. Show your work.

**D.** Describe one strength of the two-stage DDM in comparison with the constant-growth DDM. Describe one weakness inherent in all DDMs.

## The following information relates to Questions 18–23

Bernard Chabot is a recent college graduate and new trainee at Stoneman Private Equity Group. Chabot is asked to estimate the current value of Virgo Company using a two-stage dividend discount model. Virgo's dividend is expected to be $2.50 a share one year from now, grow for two more years at 10 percent per year, and then remain the same thereafter. The discount rate is 12 percent.

Simon Barrow, CFA, suggests that a simple procedure to estimate the discount rate is to begin by using the Gordon growth model to estimate the equity risk premium. Barrow provides Chabot with the following information that might be helpful to complete this task.

▶ Current level of the S&P 500 Index is 1200.

▶ Current dividend on the S&P 500 Index is 30.

▶ Long-term U.S. government bond yield is 4.75 percent.

▶ Future earnings growth rate of the S&P 500 Index is 6.75 percent.

Stoneman selected Virgo Company for analysis because it expects to take the company private, reorganize it, and then eventually recover the investment either by selling Virgo to another private equity group or by an initial public offering. Barrow suggests that the present value of growth opportunities (PVGO) concept might provide insight into what part of a company's current stock is a reflection of the value of assets in place and what part is attributed to future growth opportunities. Stoneman's analysts had reviewed Libra Corporation and Chabot is asked to calculate Libra's PVGO given the following characteristics:

► Current EPS is $2.40.

► Current stock price is $29.

► Cost of equity is 10 percent.

► Return on book equity is 12 percent.

► Sustainable growth rate is 4 percent.

Chabot used the two-stage dividend discount model to estimate the value of Virgo because he is a new employee who only recently received his undergraduate degree, has little experience, and was told by his boss to use that approach. In order to assess whether Chabot is more knowledgeable about valuation models, Barrow enters a conversation with Chabot about the H-model. Chabot makes the following statements about the H-model and dividend discount models.

Statement 1:   The H-model provides a better approximation to the exact DDM model when the extraordinary growth period is longer.

Statement 2:   The H-model reduces to the Gordon model of expected return when the short and long growth rates are equal.

Statement 3:   One of the terms of the H-model provides the exact present value of the portion of the dividend stream attributable to the normal long-term growth rate.

Barrow believes that Chabot should also have some knowledge of price-to-earnings (P/E) ratios and tells Chabot that dividend discount models can be used to estimate the justified P/E ratio for a company. He provides Chabot the following information and asks Chabot to calculate the justified forward P/E ratio.

► Current stock price is €16.00.

► The yield on the company's newly issued long-term debt is 8 percent.

► The risk premium is 4 percent.

► Current earnings per share are €1.00.

► Current dividends per share are €0.45.

► Estimated growth rate of dividends is 10 percent.

Finally, Chabot is asked to answer questions about the sustainable growth rate concept. He makes the following statements.

Statement 1:   If a firm keeps its capital structure and return on equity constant over time, then to grow faster than the sustainable growth rate it must issue additional common stock.

Statement 2:   When using the two and three stage dividend discount models, the sustainable growth concept is useful for estimating the growth rate during the terminal stage.

Statement 3:    Though average ROE is most often used to calculate the sustainable growth rate, the exact relationship assumes ending ROE is used.

**18.** The value of Virgo Company common stock using a two-stage dividend discount model is *closest* to:

    **A.**  $24.20.

    **B.**  $24.52.

    **C.**  $26.97.

**19.** The Gordon growth model estimate of equity risk premium is *closest* to:

    **A.**  4.50%.

    **B.**  4.67%.

    **C.**  7.25%.

**20.**  The estimate of PVGO for Libra Corporation is *closest* to:

    **A.**  $5.

    **B.**  $9.

    **C.**  $11.

**21.** Which of Chabot's statements about the H-model is *least* valid?

    **A.**  Statement 1.

    **B.**  Statement 2.

    **C.**  Statement 3.

**22.** The justified forward P/E ratio for Barrow's example company is *closest* to:

    **A.**  22.50.

    **B.**  24.75.

    **C.**  27.50.

**23.** Which statement by Chabot about the sustainable growth concept is *least* valid?

    **A.**  Statement 1.

    **B.**  Statement 2.

    **C.**  Statement 3.

# STUDY SESSION 12
## EQUITY INVESTMENTS:
### Valuation Models

This study session presents additional valuation methodologies that provide an estimate of a firm's intrinsic value. The discounted dividend model discussed in Study Session 11 remains a baseline model. The free cash flow approach to valuation is an important alternative to the dividend discount model when dividends are not the best representation of a company's value. Price multiples are among the most familiar and widely used valuation measures because of their simplicity and the ease with which they can be used and communicated. Residual income models have become common alternatives to the other models.

## READING ASSIGNMENTS

**Reading 42**    Free Cash Flow Valuation
by John D. Stowe, CFA, Thomas R. Robinson, CFA, Jerald E. Pinto, CFA, and Dennis W. McLeavey, CFA

**Reading 43**    Market-Based Valuation: Price Multiples
*Analysis of Equity Investments: Valuation,* by John D. Stowe, CFA, Thomas R. Robinson, CFA, Jerald E. Pinto, CFA, and Dennis W. McLeavey, CFA

**Reading 44**    U.S. Portfolio Strategy: Seeking Value—Anatomy of Valuation
*Anatomy of Valuation*

**Reading 45**    Residual Income Valuation
by John D. Stowe, CFA, Thomas R. Robinson, CFA, R. Elaine Henry, CFA, and Jerald E. Pinto, CFA

23⅜ 24

4¹¹⁄₁₆

4⅝ 4⅝ − ⅜

5½ **5½** − ⅜

5½ 5½

5½ 20⅝ 21³⁄₁₆ − ¹⁄₁₆

17³⁄₈ **18⅛** + ⅞

18½ 6½ **6½** − ½

7¼ **6½** 6½

15⁄₁₆ 3¹⁄₃₂ − ⅛

1 9⁄₁₆

9⁄₁₆ 9⁄₁₆

15⁄₃₂

7¹⁵⁄₁₆ 7¹³⁄₁₆ 7¹⁵⁄₁₆

2⅝ 2¹¹⁄₃₂ **2½** +

2¾ 2¼ 2¼

11³⁄₈ 11¾ +

6⅛ 12¹⁄₁₆ 11³⁄₈ 11¾ +

87 33¾ 33 33¹⁄₁₆ −

602 25⅝ 24⁹⁄₁₆ 25¾ +

833 12 11⅝ 11⅞ +

16 10½ 10½ 10½ −

78 15⅞ 15¹³⁄₁₆ 15⅞ −

4608 9¹⁄₁₆ 8¼ 8⅞ +

11¼ 10⅛

# FREE CASH FLOW VALUATION

by John D. Stowe, CFA, Thomas R. Robinson, CFA, Jerald E. Pinto, CFA, and Dennis W. McLeavey, CFA

## LEARNING OUTCOMES

| The candidate should be able to: | Mastery |
|---|:---:|
| **a.** define and interpret free cash flow to the firm (FCFF) and free cash flow to equity (FCFE); | ☐ |
| **b.** describe, compare, and contrast the FCFF and FCFE approaches to valuation; | ☐ |
| **c.** contrast the ownership perspective implicit in the FCFE approach to the ownership perspective implicit in the dividend discount approach; | ☐ |
| **d.** discuss the appropriate adjustments to net income, earnings before interest and taxes (EBIT), earnings before interest, taxes, depreciation, and amortization (EBITDA), and cash flow from operations (CFO) to calculate FCFF and FCFE; | ☐ |
| **e.** calculate FCFF and FCFE given a company's financial statements, prepared according to U.S. generally accepted accounting principles (GAAP) or International Financial Reporting Standards (IFRS); | ☐ |
| **f.** discuss approaches for forecasting FCFF and FCFE; | ☐ |
| **g.** contrast the recognition of value in the FCFE model with the recognition of value in dividend discount models; | ☐ |
| **h.** explain how dividends, share repurchases, share issues, and changes in leverage may affect FCFF and FCFE; | ☐ |
| **i.** critique the use of net income and EBITDA as proxies for cash flow in valuation; | ☐ |
| **j.** discuss the single-stage (stable-growth), two-stage, and three-stage FCFF and FCFE models (including assumptions) and explain the company characteristics that would justify the use of each model; | ☐ |
| **k.** calculate the value of a company using the stable-growth, two-stage, and three-stage FCFF and FCFE models; | ☐ |

| l. | explain how sensitivity analysis can be used in FCFF and FCFE valuations; | ☐ |
| m. | discuss approaches for calculating the terminal value in a multistage valuation model; | ☐ |
| n. | describe the characteristics of companies for which the FCFF model is preferred to the FCFE model. | ☐ |

## 1    INTRODUCTION TO FREE CASH FLOWS

Discounted cash flow (DCF) valuation views the intrinsic value of a security as the present value of its expected future cash flows. When applied to dividends, the DCF model is the discounted dividend approach or dividend discount model (DDM). This reading extends DCF analysis to value a company and its equity securities by valuing free cash flow to the firm (FCFF) and free cash flow to equity (FCFE). Whereas dividends are the cash flows actually paid to stockholders, free cash flows are the cash flows *available* for distribution to shareholders.

Unlike dividends, FCFF and FCFE are not readily available data. Analysts need to compute these quantities from available financial information, which requires a clear understanding of free cash flows as well as the ability to interpret and use the information correctly. Forecasting future free cash flows is also challenging. The analyst's understanding of a company's financial statements, its operations and financing, and its industry and role in the economy can pay real "dividends" as he or she studies a stock. Finding current cash flows and forecasting future cash flows is a rich and challenging exercise. Many analysts consider free cash flow models to be more useful than dividend discount models in practice. Free cash flows provide an economically sound basis for valuation.

Analysts like to use free cash flow as return (either FCFF or FCFE) whenever one or more of the following conditions is present:

► The company is not dividend paying;

► The company is dividend paying but dividends differ significantly from the company's capacity to pay dividends;

► Free cash flows align with profitability within a reasonable forecast period with which the analyst is comfortable; or

► The investor takes a control perspective.

If an investor can take control of the company (or expects another investor to do so), dividends can be changed substantially, possibly coming closer to the company's capacity to pay dividends. Such an investor can also apply free cash flows to uses such as servicing the debt incurred in an acquisition.

Common equity can be valued directly using FCFE or indirectly by first computing the value of the firm using a FCFF model and then subtracting the value of non-common-stock capital (usually debt)[1] from FCFF to arrive at the value of equity. The purpose of this reading is to develop the background required to use the FCFF or FCFE approaches to valuing a company's equity. To the extent that free cash flows are more meaningful than dividends and that analysts have a sound economic basis for their free cash flow estimates, free cash flow models have much potential in practical application.

Section 2 defines the concepts of free cash flow to the firm and free cash flow to equity, and then presents the two valuation models based on discounting of FCFF and FCFE. We also explore the constant-growth models for valuing FCFF and FCFE, special cases of the general models, in this section. After reviewing the FCFF and FCFE valuation process in Section 2, in Section 3 we turn to the vital task of calculating and forecasting FCFF and FCFE. Section 4 explains multistage free cash flow valuation models and presents some of the issues associated with their application. Analysts usually value operating assets and nonoperating assets separately and then combine them to find the total value of the firm, an approach described in Section 5.

# FCFF AND FCFE VALUATION APPROACHES                                    2

The purpose of this section is to provide a conceptual understanding of free cash flows and the valuation models based on them. A more detailed accounting treatment of free cash flows and more-complicated valuation models will follow in subsequent sections.

## 2.1 Defining Free Cash Flow

**Free cash flow to the firm** is the cash flow available to the company's suppliers of capital after all operating expenses (including taxes) have been paid and necessary investments in working capital (e.g., inventory) and fixed capital (e.g., equipment) have been made. FCFF is the cash flow from operations minus capital expenditures. To calculate FCFF, analysts may use different equations depending on the accounting information available. As mentioned, the company's suppliers of capital include common stockholders, bondholders and, sometimes, preferred stockholders.

   **Free cash flow to equity** is the cash flow available to the company's common equity holders after all operating expenses, interest, and principal payments

---

[1] A company's suppliers of capital include stockholders, bondholders, and (sometimes) preferred stockholders.

have been paid and necessary investments in working and fixed capital have been made. FCFE is the cash flow from operations minus capital expenditures minus payments to (and plus receipts from) debtholders.

How is free cash flow related to a company's net income, cash flow from operations, and measures such as EBITDA (earnings before interest, taxes, depreciation, and amortization)? This question is important: The analyst must understand the relationship between a company's reported accounting data and free cash flow in order to forecast free cash flow and its expected growth. Although a company reports cash flow from operations (CFO) on the statement of cash flows, CFO is *not* free cash flow. Net income and CFO data can be used, however, in determining a company's free cash flow.

In contrast to earnings and cash flow measures such as CFO, the advantage of FCFF and FCFE is that they can be used directly in a discounted cash flow framework to value the firm or to value equity. Other earnings measures such as net income, EBIT, EBITDA, or CFO do not have this property because they either double-count or omit cash flows in some way. For example, EBIT and EBITDA are before-tax measures, and the cash flows available to investors (in the firm or in equity of the firm) must be after tax. From the stockholders' perspective, these measures do not account for differing capital structures (the after-tax interest expenses or preferred dividends) or for the funds that bondholders supply to finance investments in operating assets. Moreover, these measures do not account for the reinvestment of cash flows that the company makes in capital assets and working capital to maintain or maximize the long-run value of the firm.

Dealing with free cash flow is more challenging than dealing with dividends because the analyst must integrate the cash flows from the company's operations with those from its investing and financing activities. Because FCFF is the after-tax cash flow going to all investors in the firm, the value of the firm is found by discounting FCFF at the weighted-average cost of capital (WACC). The value of equity is then found by subtracting the value of debt from the value of the firm. On the other hand, FCFE is the cash flow going to common stockholders, so the appropriate risk-adjusted discount rate for FCFE is the required rate of return on equity.

Depending on the company being analyzed, an analyst may have reasons to prefer using FCFF or FCFE. If the company's capital structure is relatively stable, FCFE is more direct and simpler to use than FCFF. The FCFF model is often chosen, however, in two types of cases:

▶ *A levered company with negative FCFE.* In this case, working with FCFF to value stock may be easier. The analyst would discount FCFF to find the present value of operating assets, add cash and marketable securities to get total firm value, and then subtract the market value of debt to find the intrinsic value of equity.

▶ *A levered company with a changing capital structure.* First, if the historical data are used to forecast free cash flow growth rates, the FCFF growth may more clearly reflect fundamentals than the FCFE growth, which would reflect fluctuating amounts of net borrowing. Second, in a forward-looking context, the required return on equity may be expected to be more sensitive to changes in financial leverage than changes in the weighted average cost of capital, making the use of a constant discount rate harder to justify.

Specialized DCF approaches are also available to facilitate the equity valuation when capital structure is expected to change.[2]

In the following, we present the general form of these two valuation models: the FCFF valuation model and the FCFE valuation model.

## 2.2 Present Value of Free Cash Flow

The two distinct approaches to valuation using free cash flow are the FCFF valuation approach and the FCFE valuation approach. The general expression for these valuation models is similar to the expression for the general dividend discount model. In that model, the value of a share of stock equals the present value of the dividends from Time 1 through infinity, discounted at the required rate of return for equity.

### 2.2.1 Present Value of FCFF

The FCFF valuation approach estimates the value of the firm as the present value of future FCFF discounted at the weighted average cost of capital (WACC):

$$\text{Firm value} = \sum_{t=1}^{\infty} \frac{FCFF_t}{(1 + WACC)^t} \qquad \text{(42-1)}$$

Because FCFF is the cash flow available to all suppliers of capital, discounting FCFF using WACC gives the total value of all of the company's capital. The value of equity is the value of the firm minus the market value of its debt:

$$\text{Equity value} = \text{Firm value} - \text{Market value of debt} \qquad \text{(42-2)}$$

Dividing the total value of equity by the number of outstanding shares gives the value per share.

The cost of capital is the required rate of return that investors should demand for a cash flow stream like that generated by the company. WACC depends on the risk of these cash flows. The calculation and interpretation of WACC were discussed in the reading on return concepts. To refresh the definition, WACC is the weighted average of the after (corporate) tax required rates of return for debt and equity, where the weights used are the proportions of the firm's total market value from each source, debt and equity. As an alternative, analysts may use the weights of debt and equity in the company's target capital structure when these weights are known and differ from market value weights. The formula for WACC is

$$WACC = \frac{MV(\text{Debt})}{MV(\text{Debt}) + MV(\text{Equity})} r_d (1 - \text{Tax rate}) \qquad \text{(42-3)}$$
$$+ \frac{MV(\text{Equity})}{MV(\text{Debt}) + MV(\text{Equity})} r$$

---

[2] The **adjusted present value** (APV) approach is one example of such models. In the APV approach, firm value is calculated as the sum of the value of the company assuming no use of debt (unlevered firm value), and the net present value of any effects of debt on firm value (such as any tax benefits of using debt and any costs of financial distress). In this approach, we can estimate unlevered company value by discounting FCFF (assuming no debt) at the unlevered cost of equity (the cost of equity assuming no debt). For more details, see Ross, Westerfield, and Jaffe (2002), who explain APV in a capital budgeting context.

MV(Debt) and MV(Equity) are the current market values of debt and equity, not their book or accounting values, and their ratios to the total market value of debt plus equity define the weights in the WACC formula. The quantities $r_d(1 -$ Tax rate) and $r$ are, respectively, the after tax cost of debt and the after tax cost of equity (in the case of equity the before and after tax costs are the same, referring to corporate taxes).

### 2.2.2 Present Value of FCFE

The value of equity can also be found by discounting FCFE at the required rate of return on equity ($r$):

$$\text{Equity value} = \sum_{t=1}^{\infty} \frac{\text{FCFE}_t}{(1 + r)^t} \qquad \text{(42-4)}$$

Because FCFE is the cash flow remaining for equity holders after all other claims have been satisfied, discounting FCFE by $r$ (the required rate of return on equity) gives the value of the firm's equity. Dividing the total value of equity by the number of outstanding shares gives the value per share.

## 2.3 Single-Stage (Constant-Growth) FCFF and FCFE Models

In the DDM approach, the Gordon (constant, or stable growth) model makes the assumption that dividends grow at a constant rate. Assuming that free cash flows grow at a constant rate results in the single-stage (stable growth) FCFF and FCFE models.

### 2.3.1 Constant-Growth FCFF Valuation Model

Assume that FCFF grows at a constant rate $g$, such that FCFF in any period is equal to FCFF in the previous period multiplied by $(1 + g)$:

$$\text{FCFF}_t = \text{FCFF}_{t-1}(1 + g)$$

If FCFF grows at a constant rate,

$$\text{Firm value} = \frac{\text{FCFF}_1}{\text{WACC} - g} = \frac{\text{FCFF}_0(1 + g)}{\text{WACC} - g} \qquad \text{(42-5)}$$

Subtracting the market value of debt from the firm value gives the value of equity.

### EXAMPLE 1

#### Using the Constant-Growth FCFF Valuation Model

Cagiati Enterprises has FCFF of 700 million Swiss francs (CHF) and FCFE of CHF620 million. Cagiati's before-tax cost of debt is 5.7 percent and its required rate of return for equity is 11.8 percent. The company expects a target capital structure consisting of 20 percent debt financing and 80 percent equity financing. The tax rate is 33.33 percent, and FCFF is expected to grow forever at 5.0 percent. Cagiati Enterprises has debt outstanding with a market value of CHF2.2 billion and has 200 million outstanding common shares.

1. What is Cagiati's weighted average cost of capital?
2. What is the value of Cagiati's equity using the FCFF valuation approach?
3. What is the value per share using this FCFF approach?

**Solution to 1:** Using Equation 42-3, WACC is

$$\text{WACC} = 0.20(5.7\%)(1 - 0.3333) + 0.80(11.8\%) = 10.2\%$$

**Solution to 2:** The firm value of Cagiati Enterprises is the present value of FCFF discounted using WACC. For FCFF growing at a constant 5 percent rate, the result is

$$\text{Firm value} = \frac{\text{FCFF}_1}{\text{WACC} - g} = \frac{\text{FCFF}_0(1 + g)}{\text{WACC} - g} = \frac{700(1.05)}{0.102 - 0.05}$$

$$= \frac{735}{0.052} = \text{CHF14,134.6 million}$$

The value of equity is the value of the firm minus the value of debt:

$$\begin{aligned}\text{Equity value} &= \text{CHF14,134.6 million} - \text{CHF2,200 million}\\ &= \text{CHF11,934.6 million}\end{aligned}$$

**Solution to 3:** Dividing CH11,934.6 million by the number of outstanding shares gives the value per share:

$$\begin{aligned}V_0 &= \text{CHF11,934.6 million}/200 \text{ million shares}\\ &= \text{CHF59.67 per share}\end{aligned}$$

### 2.3.2 Constant-Growth FCFE Valuation Model

The constant-growth FCFE valuation model assumes that FCFE grows at a constant rate $g$. FCFE in any period is equal to FCFE in the preceding period multiplied by $(1 + g)$:

$$\text{FCFE}_t = \text{FCFE}_{t-1}(1 + g)$$

The value of equity if FCFE is growing at a constant rate is

$$\text{Equity value} = \frac{\text{FCFE}_1}{r - g} = \frac{\text{FCFE}_0(1 + g)}{r - g} \qquad \textbf{(42-6)}$$

The discount rate is $r$, the required rate of return on equity. Note that the growth rate of FCFF and the growth rate of FCFE are frequently not the same.

## 3

# FORECASTING FREE CASH FLOW

Estimating FCFF or FCFE requires a complete understanding of the company and its financial statements. In order to provide a context for the estimation of FCFF and FCFE, we will first use an extensive example to show the relation between free cash flow and accounting measures of income.

For most of this section, we will assume that the company has two sources of capital, debt and common stock. Once the concepts of FCFF and FCFE are understood for a company financed using only debt and common stock, it is easy to incorporate preferred stock for the relatively small number of companies that actually use it (in Section 3.7, we will incorporate preferred stock as a third source of capital).

## 3.1 Computing FCFF from Net Income

FCFF is the cash flow available to the company's suppliers of capital after all operating expenses (including taxes) have been paid and operating investments have been made. The company's suppliers of capital include bondholders and common stockholders (and occasionally preferred stockholders, which we ignore until later). Understanding that a noncash charge is a charge or expense that does not involve the outlay of cash, the expression for FCFF is as follows:

> FCFF = Net income available to common shareholders
> Plus: Net noncash charges
> Plus: Interest expense × (1 − Tax rate)
> Less: Investment in fixed capital[3]
> Less: Investment in working capital

This equation can be written more compactly as

$$FCFF = NI + NCC + Int(1 - Tax\ rate) - FCInv - WCInv \qquad \textbf{(42-7)}$$

Consider each component of FCFF. The starting point in Equation 42-7 is net income available to common shareholders—the bottom line in an income statement. It represents income after depreciation, amortization, interest expense, income taxes, and the payment of dividends to preferred shareholders (but not payment of dividends to common shareholders).

Net noncash charges represent an adjustment for noncash decreases and increases in net income. This adjustment is the first of several that analysts generally perform on a net basis. If noncash decreases in net income exceed the increases, as is usually the case, the adjustment is positive. If noncash increases exceed noncash decreases, the adjustment is negative. The most common noncash charge is depreciation expense. When a company purchases fixed capital such as equipment, the balance sheet reflects a cash outflow at the time of purchase. In subsequent periods, the company records depreciation expense as the asset is used. The depreciation expense reduces net income but is not a cash outflow. Depreciation expense is thus one (the most common) noncash charge that must be added back in computing FCFF. In the case of intangible assets,

---

[3] In this reading, when we refer to "investment in fixed capital" or "investment in working capital," we are referring to the investments made in the specific period for which the free cash flow is calculated.

there is a similar noncash charge, amortization expense, that must also be added back. Other noncash charges vary from company to company and will be discussed in Section 3.3.

After-tax interest expense must be added back to net income to arrive at FCFF. This step is required because interest expense net of the related tax savings was deducted in arriving at net income, and because interest is a cash flow available to one of the company's capital providers. In the United States and many other countries, interest is tax deductible (reduces taxes) for the company and taxable for the recipient. As we shall see later, when we discount FCFF, we do so using an after-tax cost of capital. For consistency, we thus compute FCFF using the after-tax interest paid.[4]

Similar to after-tax interest expense, if a company has preferred stock, dividends on that preferred stock are deducted in arriving at net income available to common shareholders. Because preferred stock dividends are also a cash flow available to one of the company's capital providers, this item is added back to arrive at FCFF. Further discussion of the effects of preferred stock appears in Section 3.7.

Investments in fixed capital represent the outflow of cash for investments necessary to support the company's current and future operations. These investments are capital expenditures for long-term assets such as property, plant, and equipment (PP&E) necessary to support the company's operations. Necessary capital expenditures can also include intangible assets such as trademarks. In the case of cash acquisition of another company in place of a direct acquisition of PP&E, this cash purchase amount can also be treated as a capital expenditure that reduces the company's free cash flow (note that this is the conservative treatment in that it reduces FCFF). In the case of large acquisitions (and all noncash acquisitions), analysts must take care in evaluating the impact on future free cash flow. If a company receives cash in disposing of any of its fixed capital, the analyst must deduct this cash in arriving at investments in fixed capital. For example, suppose we had a sale of equipment for $100,000. This cash inflow reduces the company's cash outflows for investments in fixed capital.

The company's cash flow statement is an excellent source of information on capital expenditures as well as sales of fixed capital. Analysts should be aware that some companies acquire fixed capital without using cash—for example, through an exchange for stock or debt. Such acquisitions do not appear on a company's cash flow statement but, if material, must be disclosed in the footnotes. Although noncash exchanges do not affect historical FCFF, if the capital expenditures are necessary and may be made in cash in the future, the analyst should use this information in forecasting future FCFF.

Last is an important adjustment for net increases in working capital. As noted in our earlier example, this adjustment represents the net investment in current assets, such as accounts receivable, less current liabilities such as accounts payable. Analysts can find this information by examining either the company's balance sheet or the cash flow statement.

Although working capital is often defined as current assets minus current liabilities, working capital for cash flow and valuation purposes is defined to exclude cash and short-term debt (which includes notes payable and the current portion of long-term debt). When finding the net increase in working capital for the purpose of calculating free cash flow, we define working capital to exclude cash and cash equivalents, as well as notes payable and the current portion of

---

[4] Note that we could compute WACC on a pretax basis and compute FCFF by adding back interest paid with no tax adjustment. It is critical, however, that analysts be consistent in their measures of FCFF and WACC.

long-term debt. Cash and cash equivalents are excluded because a change in cash is what we are trying to explain. Notes payable and the current portion of long-term debt are excluded because they are liabilities with explicit interest costs that make them financing, rather than operating, items.

Example 2 shows all of the adjustments to net income required to find FCFF.

## EXAMPLE 2

### Calculating FCFF from Net Income

Cane Distribution, Inc., is a distribution company incorporated on 31 December 2007 with initial capital infusions of $224,000 of debt and $336,000 of common stock. This initial capital was immediately invested in fixed capital of $500,000 and working capital of $60,000. Working capital initially consists solely of inventory. The fixed capital consists of nondepreciable property of $50,000 and depreciable property of $450,000. The latter has a 10-year useful life with no salvage value. Exhibits 1, 2, and 3 provide Cane's financial statements for the three years following incorporation. Starting with net income, calculate Cane's FCFF for each year.

### EXHIBIT 1 — Cane Distribution, Inc. Income Statement (in Thousands)

| Years Ending 31 December | 2008 | 2009 | 2010 |
|---|---|---|---|
| Earnings before interest, taxes, depreciation, and amortization (EBITDA) | $200.00 | $220.00 | $242.00 |
| Depreciation expense | 45.00 | 49.50 | 54.45 |
| Operating income | 155.00 | 170.50 | 187.55 |
| Interest expense | 15.68 | 17.25 | 18.97 |
| Income before taxes | 139.32 | 153.25 | 168.58 |
| Income taxes (at 30%) | 41.80 | 45.97 | 50.58 |
| Net income | $ 97.52 | $107.28 | $118.00 |

### EXHIBIT 2 — Cane Distribution, Inc. Balance Sheet (in Thousands)

| Years Ending 31 December | 2007 | 2008 | 2009 | 2010 |
|---|---|---|---|---|
| Cash | $ 0.00 | $108.92 | $228.74 | $ 360.54 |
| Accounts receivable | 0.00 | 100.00 | 110.00 | 121.00 |
| Inventory | 60.00 | 66.00 | 72.60 | 79.86 |
| Current assets | 60.00 | 274.92 | 411.34 | 561.40 |
| Fixed assets | 500.00 | 500.00 | 550.00 | 605.00 |
| Less: Accumulated depreciation | 0.00 | 45.00 | 94.50 | 148.95 |
| Total assets | $560.00 | $729.92 | $866.84 | $1,017.45 |

*(Exhibit continued on next page . . .)*

| EXHIBIT 2 | (continued) | | | |
|---|---|---|---|---|
| Years Ending 31 December | 2007 | 2008 | 2009 | 2010 |
| Accounts payable | $ 0.00 | $ 50.00 | $ 55.00 | $ 60.50 |
| Current portion of long-term debt | 0.00 | 0.00 | 0.00 | 0.00 |
| Current liabilities | 0.00 | 50.00 | 55.00 | 60.50 |
| Long-term debt | 224.00 | 246.40 | 271.04 | 298.14 |
| Common stock | 336.00 | 336.00 | 336.00 | 336.00 |
| Retained earnings | 0.00 | 97.52 | 204.80 | 322.80 |
| Total liabilities and equity | $560.00 | $729.92 | $866.84 | $1,017.45 |

| EXHIBIT 3 | Cane Distribution, Inc. Working Capital (in Thousands) | | | |
|---|---|---|---|---|
| Years Ending 31 December | 2007 | 2008 | 2009 | 2010 |
| *Current assets excluding cash* | | | | |
| Accounts receivable | $ 0.00 | $100.00 | $110.00 | $121.00 |
| Inventory | 60.00 | 66.00 | 72.60 | 79.86 |
| Total current assets excluding cash | 60.00 | 166.00 | 182.60 | 200.86 |
| *Current liabilities excluding short-term debt* | | | | |
| Accounts payable | 0.00 | 50.00 | 55.00 | 60.50 |
| Working capital | $60.00 | $116.00 | $127.60 | $140.36 |
| Increase in working capital | | $56.00 | $11.60 | $12.76 |

**Solution:** Following the logic in Equation 42-7, we calculate FCFF from net income as follows: we add noncash charges (here depreciation) and aftertax interest expense to net income, then subtract the investment in fixed capital and the investment in working capital The format for presenting the solution follows the convention that parentheses around a number indicate subtraction.

| Years Ending 31 December | 2008 | 2009 | 2010 |
|---|---|---|---|
| Net income | $97.52 | $107.28 | $118.00 |
| Noncash charges − Depreciation | 45.00 | 49.50 | 54.45 |
| Interest expense × (1 − Tax rate) | 10.98 | 12.08 | 13.28 |
| Investment in fixed capital | (0.00) | (50.00) | (55.00) |
| Investment in working capital | (56.00) | (11.60) | (12.76) |
| Free cash flow to the firm | $97.50 | $107.26 | $117.97 |

## 3.2 Computing FCFF from the Statement of Cash Flows

FCFF is cash flow available to all capital providers (debt and equity). Analysts frequently use cash flow from operations, taken from the statement of cash flows, as a starting point to compute free cash flow because CFO incorporates adjustments for noncash expenses (such as depreciation and amortization) as well as for net investments in working capital.

In a statement of cash flows, cash flows are separated into three components: cash flow from operating activities (or cash flows from operations), cash flows from investing activities, and cash flows from financing activities. Cash flow from operations, which we abbreviate CFO, is the net amount of cash provided from operating activities. The operating section of the cash flow statement shows cash flows related to operating activities, such as cash received from customers and cash paid to suppliers. Investing activities relate to the company's investments in (or sales of) long-term assets, particularly PP&E and long-term investments in other companies. Financing activities relate to the raising or repayment of the company's capital. Interestingly, under U.S. GAAP, interest expense paid to debt capital providers must be classified as part of cash flow from operations (as is interest income), although payment of dividends to equity capital providers is classified as a financing activity. International Financial Reporting Standards (IFRS), on the other hand, allow the company to classify interest paid as either an operating or financing activity. Further, IFRS allow dividends paid to be classified as either an operating or financing activity. Exhibit 4 summarizes U.S. GAAP and IFRS treatment of interest and dividends:

| EXHIBIT 4 | U.S. GAAP versus IFRS Treatment of Interest and Dividends | |
| --- | --- | --- |
| | **U.S. GAAP** | **IFRS** |
| Interest received | Operating | Operating or Investing |
| Interest paid | Operating | Operating or Financing |
| Dividends received | Operating | Operating or Investing |
| Dividends paid | Financing | Operating or Financing |

To estimate FCFF by starting with CFO, we must recognize the treatment of interest paid. If, as with U.S. GAAP, the after-tax interest expense was taken out of net income and out of CFO, after-tax interest expense must be added back in order to get FCFF. In the U.S. case, FCFF can be estimated as follows:

Free cash flow to the firm = Cash flow from operations
Plus: Interest expense × (1 − Tax rate)
Less: Investment in fixed capital

or

$$FCFF = CFO + Int(1 - \text{Tax rate}) - FCInv \qquad \text{(42-8)}$$

The after-tax interest expense is added back because it was previously taken out of net income. The investment in working capital does not appear in Equation 42-8 because CFO already includes investment in working capital. The following example illustrates the calculation of FCFF using CFO. In the following example, CFO is calculated beginning with net income, an approach known as the indirect method.[5]

## EXAMPLE 3

### Calculating FCFF from CFO

Use the information from the statement of cash flows given in Exhibit 5 to calculate FCFF for the three years.

| EXHIBIT 5 | Cane Distribution, Inc. Statement of Cash Flows (in Thousands) Indirect Method | | |
|---|---|---|---|
| **Years Ending 31 December** | **2008** | **2009** | **2010** |
| **Cash Flow from Operations** | | | |
| Net income | $ 97.52 | $107.28 | $118.00 |
| Plus: Depreciation | 45.00 | 49.50 | 54.45 |
| Increase in accounts receivable | (100.00) | (10.00) | (11.00) |
| Increase in inventory | (6.00) | (6.60) | (7.26) |
| Increase in accounts payable | 50.00 | 5.00 | 5.50 |
| Cash flow from operations | 86.52 | 145.18 | 159.69 |
| | | | |
| **Cash Flow from Investing Activities** | | | |
| Purchases of PP&E | 0.00 | (50.00) | (55.00) |
| | | | |
| **Cash Flow from Financing Activities** | | | |
| Borrowing (repayment) | 22.40 | 24.64 | 27.10 |
| Total cash flow | 108.92 | 119.82 | 131.80 |
| Beginning cash | 0.00 | 108.92 | 228.74 |
| Ending cash | $108.92 | $228.74 | $360.54 |
| | | | |
| *Notes*: | | | |
| Cash paid for interest | ($15.68) | ($17.25) | ($18.97) |
| Cash paid for taxes | ($41.80) | ($45.98) | ($50.57) |

---

[5] See Robinson, van Greuning, Henry, and Broihahn, "Understanding the Cash Flow Statement" (2007) for a discussion of the indirect and direct cash flow statement formats.

**Solution:** As shown in Equation 42-8, FCFF equals CFO plus after-tax interest minus the investment in fixed capital:

| Years Ending 31 December | 2008 | 2009 | 2010 |
|---|---|---|---|
| Cash flow from operations | 86.52 | 145.18 | 159.69 |
| Interest expense × (1 − Tax rate) | 10.98 | 12.08 | 13.28 |
| Investment in fixed capital | (0.00) | (50.00) | (55.00) |
| Free cash flow to the firm | 97.50 | 107.26 | 117.97 |

## 3.3 Noncash Charges

The best place to find historical noncash charges is in the company's statement of cash flows. If an analyst wants to use an add-back method, as in FCFF = NI + NCC + Int(1 − Tax rate) − FCInv − WCInv, the analyst should verify the noncash charges to ensure that the FCFF estimate provides a reasonable basis for forecasting. As one example, restructuring charges can involve cash expenditures and noncash charges. For example, severance pay for laid-off employees could be a cash restructuring charge. On the other hand, a write-down in the value of assets as part of a restructuring charge is a noncash item. Example 4 illustrates noncash restructuring charges that must be added back to net income to obtain CFO as well as (noncash) gains from the sale of assets in restructuring which must be subtracted from net income in arriving at CFO.

### EXAMPLE 4

**An Examination of Noncash Charges**

Alberto-Culver Company (NYSE: ACV) develops, manufactures, distributes, and markets branded beauty care products and branded food and household products in more than 100 countries. Jane Everett wants to value Alberto Culver using the FCFF method, and collects information from the company's 10-K for the fiscal year ended 30 September 2007.

     Note that the cash flow statement in Exhibit 6 follows a presentation convention according to which "Less: . . . 50" means "subtract 50" and "Less: . . . (50)" means "add 50," following the logic that "minus a minus equals a plus." The reader will also encounter in practice "Less: . . . (50)" interpreted as "subtract 50."

| EXHIBIT 6 | Alberto Culver Statements of Cash Flows<br>Consolidated Statements of Cash Flows<br>Alberto-Culver Company & Subsidiaries (in US$ Thousands) | | |
|---|---|---|---|
| **Years Ended 30 September** | **2007** | **2006** | **2005** |
| **Cash Flows from Operating Activities:** | | | |
| Net earnings | **78,264** | 205,321 | 210,901 |
| Less: Earnings (loss) from discontinued operations | **(2,963)** | 125,806 | 141,062 |
| Earnings from continuing operations | **81,227** | 79,515 | 69,839 |

*(Exhibit continued on next page . . .)*

| EXHIBIT 6 | (continued) | | | |
|---|---|---|---|---|

| Years Ended 30 September | 2007 | 2006 | 2005 |
|---|---|---|---|
| Adjustments to reconcile earnings from continuing operations to net cash provided by operating activities: | | | |
| Depreciation | 28,824 | 24,642 | 23,420 |
| Amortization of other assets and unearned compensation | 2,811 | 3,403 | 2,774 |
| Restructuring and other—non-cash charges (note 4) | 14,053 | — | — |
| Restructuring and other—gain on sale of assets (note 4) | (5,894) | — | — |
| Non-cash charge related to conversion to one class of common stock (note 5) | — | 4 | 10,456 |
| Stock option expense (note 9) | 3,741 | 10,763 | — |
| Deferred income taxes | (21,064) | 2,196 | 677 |
| Cash effects of changes in (excluding acquisitions and divestitures): | | | |
| Receivables, net | (26,635) | (15,270) | (24,223) |
| Inventories | 4,168 | (13,424) | (13,751) |
| Other current assets | 2,842 | (5,497) | (1,665) |
| Accounts payable and accrued expenses | 15,096 | 4,761 | (14,386) |
| Income taxes | 4,657 | (905) | 9,137 |
| Other assets | (897) | (2,786) | (8,595) |
| Other liabilities | (3,914) | 3,736 | 15,192 |
| Net cash provided by operating activities | 99,015 | 91,138 | 68,875 |

Everett notices that the reconciliation amounts on the cash flow statement for restructuring charges differ from the $34,645 restructuring charge recorded on the income statement. She finds the following discussion of restructuring charges in the Management Discussion and Analysis section.

| EXHIBIT 7 | Management Discussion and Analysis (Excerpt) |
|---|---|

Restructuring and other expenses during the fiscal year ended September 30, 2007 consist of the following (in thousands):

| | |
|---|---|
| Severance and other exit costs | $17,056 |
| Non-cash charges related to the acceleration of vesting of stock options and restricted shares in connection with the Separation | 12,198 |
| Contractual termination benefits for the former President and Chief Executive Officer in connection with the Separation | 9,888 |
| Non-cash charge for the recognition of foreign currency translation loss in connection with the liquidation of a foreign legal entity | 1,355 |
| Legal fees and other expenses incurred to assign the company's trademarks following the closing of the Separation | 42 |
| Gain on sale of assets | (5,894) |
| | $34,645 |

## Severance and Other Exit Costs

On November 27, 2006, the company committed to a plan to terminate employees as part of a reorganization following the Separation. In connection with this reorganization plan, on December 1, 2006 the company announced that it expects to close its manufacturing facility in Dallas, Texas. The company's worldwide workforce is being reduced by approximately 225 employees as a result of the reorganization plan, including 125 employees from the Dallas, Texas manufacturing facility. The changes primarily affect corporate functions or the Consumer Packaged Goods business segment. The company expects to record additional pre-tax restructuring charges of approximately $1.5 million related to this plan in fiscal year 2008, primarily during the first half. These amounts exclude the effect of the sale of the manufacturing facility in Dallas, Texas. Cash payments related to this plan are expected to be substantially completed by the end of the second quarter of fiscal year 2008.

The following table reflects the activity related to the restructuring plan during the fiscal year ended September 30, 2007 (in thousands):

|  | Initial Charges | Cash Payments & Other Settlements | Liability at September 30, 2007 |
|---|---|---|---|
| Severance | $15,405 | (12,774) | 2,631 |
| Contract termination costs | 237 | (237) | — |
| Other | 1,414 | (1,321) | 93 |
|  | $17,056 | (14,332) | 2,724 |

Using the information presented above, answer the following questions:

1. Why is there a difference in the amounts shown for restructuring charges on the income statement and cash flow statement?

2. How should the restructuring charges be treated when forecasting future cash flows?

**Solution to 1:** The difference between restructuring charges on the income statement and the cash flow statement arises because some of the restructuring charges are paid in cash and others are not. The cash flow statement shows the noncash restructuring charges ($14,053) as an amount added back to net income in the process of arriving at net cash provided by operating activities.

You may note that Exhibit 7 discloses two noncash charges totaling $12,198 + $1,355 = $13,553 although the statement of cash flows shows restructuring and other noncash charges of $14,053. MDA provided no explanation for the balance of $14,053 − $13,553 = $500; MDA's disclosure of information was incomplete.

**Solution to 2:** Restructuring charges are generally unpredictable, and would not typically be forecast. However, in Alberto's case there are $2,724 of restructuring-related liabilities remaining (mostly consisting of liabilities for severance pay) that were expected to be paid in early 2008. The forecast for 2008 should reflect these cash expenditures that will be made.

Noncash restructuring charges can also cause an increase in net income in some circumstances, for example when a company reverses part or all of a previous accrual. Gains and losses are another noncash item that can either increase or decrease net noncash charges. If a company sells a piece of equipment with a book value of €60,000 for €100,000, it reports the €40,000 gain as part of net income. The €40,000 gain is not a cash flow, however, and must be subtracted in arriving at FCFF. Note that the €100,000 is a cash flow and is part of the company's net investment in fixed capital. A loss reduces net income and thus must be added back in arriving at FCFF. Aside from depreciation, gains and losses are the most commonly seen noncash charges that require an adjustment to net income. Analysts should examine the company's cash flow statement to identify items particular to a company and to determine what analyst adjustments might be needed to make the accounting numbers useful for forecasting purposes.

Exhibit 8 summarizes the common noncash charges that affect net income and indicates for each item whether to add it to or subtract it from net income in arriving at FCFF.

The case of deferred taxes requires special attention. Deferred taxes result from differences in the timing of reporting income and expenses on the company's financial statements and the company's tax return. The income tax expense deducted in arriving at net income for financial reporting purposes is not the same as the amount of cash taxes paid. Over time, these differences between book and taxable income should offset each other and have no impact on aggregate cash flows. If the analyst's purpose is forecasting and he seeks to identify the persistent components of FCFF, then it is not appropriate to add back deferred tax changes that are expected to reverse in the near future. In some circumstances, however, a company may be able to consistently defer taxes until a much later date. If a company is growing and has the ability to indefinitely defer tax liability, an analyst adjustment (add-back) to net income is warranted. An acquirer must be aware, however, that these taxes may be payable at some time in the future.

Conversely, companies often record expenses for financial reporting purposes (e.g., restructuring charges) that are not deductible for tax purposes. In this instance, current tax payments are higher than reported on the income statement, resulting in a deferred tax asset and a subtraction from net income to arrive at cash flow on the cash flow statement. If the deferred tax asset is

| **EXHIBIT 8** | **Noncash Items and FCFF** |
| --- | --- |
| **Noncash Item** | **Adjustment to NI to Arrive at FCFF** |
| Depreciation | Added back |
| Amortization and impairment of intangibles | Added back |
| Restructuring charges (expense) | Added back |
| Restructuring charges (income resulting from reversal) | Subtracted |
| Losses | Added back |
| Gains | Subtracted |
| Amortization of long-term bond discounts | Added back |
| Amortization of long-term bond premiums | Subtracted |
| Deferred taxes | Added back but warrants special attention |

expected to reverse (e.g., through tax depreciation deductions) in the near future, the analyst would not want to subtract the deferred tax asset in his cash flow forecast to avoid underestimating future cash flows. On the other hand, if the company is expected to have these charges on a continual basis, a subtraction is warranted to lower the forecast of future cash flows.

Employee stock options provide another challenge. Under International Financial Reporting Standards and U.S. GAAP companies must now record an expense for options provided to employees on the income statement. The granting of options themselves does not result in a cash outflow and is therefore a noncash charge; however, there are long-term cash flow implications. When the employee exercises the option the company receives some cash related to the exercise price of the option for the strike price. This cash flow is considered a financing cash flow. Also, in some cases, a company may receive a tax benefit from issuing options that could increase operating cash flow but not net income. Both IFRS and U.S. GAAP require that a portion of the tax effect be recorded as a financing cash flow rather than an operating cash flow in the cash flow statement. The analysts should review the cash flow statement and footnotes to determine the impact of options on operating cash flows. If these cash flows are not expected to persist in the future, analysts should not include them in their forecast of cash flows. An analyst should also consider the impact of stock options on the number of shares outstanding. When computing equity value, the analyst may want to use the number of shares expected to be outstanding based on the exercise of employee stock options rather than use currently outstanding shares.

Example 5 illustrates that when forecasting cash flows for valuation purposes, analysts should consider the sustainability of historical working capital effects on free cash flow.

## EXAMPLE 5

### Sustainability of Working Capital Effects on Free Cash Flow

Ryanair Holdings PLC (LSE: RYAOF) operates a low-fares scheduled passenger airline serving short-haul, point-to-point routes between Ireland, the United Kingdom, Continental Europe, and Morocco. The operating activities section of its cash flow statement and a portion of the investing activities section are presented in Exhibit 9 below. The cash flow statement was prepared in accordance with IFRS.

### EXHIBIT 9    Ryanair Holdings PLC Cash Flow Statement (Excerpt)

| Year Ended March 31 (Thousands of Euros) | 2007 | 2006 | 2005 |
|---|---|---|---|
| Operating activities | | | |
| Profit before tax | 451,037 | 338,888 | 309,196 |
| Adjustments to reconcile profits before tax to net cash provided by operating activities | | | |
| Depreciation | 143,503 | 124,405 | 110,357 |
| Decrease (increase) in inventories | 1,002 | (962) | (424) |
| Decrease (increase) in trade receivables | 6,497 | (9,265) | (5,712) |
| Decrease (increase) in other current assets | (30,849) | (882) | (4,855) |
| (Decrease) increase in trade payables | (24,482) | (12,835) | 24,182 |

*(Exhibit continued on next page . . .)*

| EXHIBIT 9 | (continued) | | |
|---|---|---|---|
| **Year Ended March 31 (Thousands of Euros)** | **2007** | **2006** | **2005** |
| (Decrease) increase in accrued expenses | 233,839 | 150,083 | 89,406 |
| (Decrease) increase in other creditors | 75,351 | 11,403 | (10,986) |
| Increase in maintenance provisions | 11,997 | 9,486 | 714 |
| Loss (gain) on disposal of property, plant, and equipment | (91) | (815) | (47) |
| Decrease (increase) in interest receivable | 48 | (3,959) | (505) |
| Decrease (increase) in interest payable | 2,671 | 1,159 | 3,420 |
| Retirement costs | 589 | 507 | 167 |
| Share based payments | 3,935 | 2,921 | 488 |
| Income tax | (5,194) | 436 | (4,198) |
| Net cash provided by operating activities | 869,853 | 610,570 | 511,203 |
| Investing activities | | | |
| Capital expenditure (purchase of property, plant, and equipment) | (494,972) | (546,225) | (631,994) |

Analysts predict that as Ryanair grows in coming years, depreciation expense should increase substantially.

Based on the information given, address the following:

1. Contrast reported depreciation expense to reported capital expenditures and describe the implications of future growth in depreciation expense on future net income and future cash from operating activities (all else equal).
2. Explain the effects on free cash flow to equity of changes in 2007 in working capital accounts such as inventory, accounts receivable, and accounts payable, and comment on the long-term sustainability of such changes.

**Solution to 1:** In the period 2005 to 2007 depreciation expense has been a small fraction of capital expenditures. For example, in 2007 capital expenditures of €495 million were 3.5 times as large as the €143.5 million depreciation expense.

Depreciation is a deduction to calculate net income. Therefore, as depreciation expense increases in coming years, net income will be reduced. Specifically, net income is reduced by (Depreciation expense) $\times$ (1 − Tax rate). However, depreciation is added back in full to net income in calculating CFO. The difference between depreciation expense—the amount added back to net income to calculate CFO—and the amount by which net income is reduced by depreciation expense, is (Tax rate) $\times$ (Depreciation expense), representing a positive increment to CFO. Thus, the projected increase in depreciation expense is a negative for future net income but a positive for future CFO. (At worst, if the company operates at a loss, depreciation is neutral for CFO.)

**Solution to 2:** In 2007 the decreases in inventory and accounts receivable ("trade receivables") resulted in positive adjustments to net income (i.e., the changes increased cash flow relative to net income). The adjustments are positive because decreases in these accounts (the sale of inventory and collection of accounts receivable) are a source of cash. On the current liabilities side, the increase in accrued expenses and increase in other creditors were also add-backs to net income and sources of cash because such increases represent increase in amounts for which cash payments have yet to be made. On the other hand, the negative adjustment for accounts payable indicates that the accounts payable balance declined: Ryanair spent cash to reduce the amount of trade credit being extended to it by suppliers during the year, resulting in a reduction of cash. Because CFO is a component of FCFE, the items that had a positive (negative) effect on CFO also represent a positive (negative) effect on FCFE.

Declining balances for assets such as inventory or for liabilities such as accounts payable are not sustainable indefinitely. In the extreme case, the balance would decline to zero and no further reduction would be possible. Given the growth in net income and the expansion of plant and equipment evidenced by capital expenditures, Ryanair appears to be growing and investors should expect its working capital requirements to grow accordingly. Thus the components of 2007 FCFE attributable to reduction in inventory and accounts receivable balances is probably not relevant in forecasting future FCFE.

## 3.4 Computing FCFE from FCFF

FCFE is cash flow available to equity holders only. It is thus necessary to reduce FCFF by the aftertax value of interest paid to debtholders and to add any net increase in borrowing[6] (subtract any net decrease in borrowing).

Free cash flow to equity = Free cash flow to the firm
Less: Interest expense × (1 − Tax rate)
Plus: Net borrowing

or

$$\text{FCFE} = \text{FCFF} - \text{Int}(1 - \text{Tax rate}) + \text{Net borrowing} \qquad \text{(42-9)}$$

As Equation 42-9 shows, FCFE is found by starting from FCFF and subtracting after-tax interest expenses and adding net new borrowing. Conversely, the analyst can also find FCFF from FCFE by making the opposite adjustments—by adding after-tax interest expenses and subtracting net borrowing: FCFF = FCFE + Int(1 − Tax rate) − Net borrowing.

Exhibit 10 shows the calculation of FCFE starting with FCFF using the values for FCFF for the Cane Distribution Company calculated in Example 3. To calculate FCFE, aftertax interest expense is subtracted from FCFF then net borrowing (equal to new debt borrowing minus debt repayment) is added.

As stated earlier, FCFE is the cash flow available to common stockholders—the remaining cash flow after all operating expenses (including taxes) have been paid, capital investments have been made, and other transactions with other suppliers of capital have been made. The company's other capital suppliers include creditors, such as bondholders, and preferred stockholders. The cash

---

[6] Net borrowing is net debt issued less debt repayments over the period for which we are calculating free cash flow.

| EXHIBIT 10 | Calculating FCFE from FCFF | | |
|---|---|---|---|
| **Years Ending 31 December** | **2008** | **2009** | **2010** |
| Free cash flow to the firm | 97.50 | 107.26 | 117.97 |
| Interest paid $\times$ (1 − Tax rate) | (10.98) | (12.08) | (13.28) |
| New debt borrowing | 22.40 | 24.64 | 27.10 |
| Debt repayment | (0) | (0) | (0) |
| Free cash flow to equity | 108.92 | 119.82 | 131.79 |

flows (net of taxes) that have been transacted with creditors and preferred stock-holders are deducted from FCFF to arrive at FCFE.

FCFE is the amount that the company can afford to pay out as dividends. In actuality, companies often pay out substantially more or substantially less than FCFE for many reasons, so FCFE often differs from dividends paid. One reason for this difference is that the dividend decision is a discretionary decision of the board of directors. Most corporations "manage" their dividends, preferring to raise them gradually over time, in part because they are very reluctant to cut dividends. Consequently, earnings are much more volatile than dividends. Companies often raise dividends slowly even when their earnings are increasing rapidly, and companies often maintain their current dividends even when their profitability has declined.

In Equations 42-7 and 42-8 above, we showed the calculation of FCFF starting with net income and cash flow from operations, respectively. As Equation 42-9 shows, FCFE = FCFF − Int(1 − Tax rate) + Net borrowing. By subtracting after-tax interest expense and adding net borrowing to Equations 42-7 and 42-8, we then have equations to calculate FCFE starting with net income or CFO, respectively:

$$FCFE = NI + NCC − FCInv − WCInv + Net\ borrowing \qquad \textbf{(42-10)}$$

$$FCFE = CFO − FCInv + Net\ borrowing \qquad \textbf{(42-11)}$$

## EXAMPLE 6

### Adjusting Net Income or CFO to Find FCFF and FCFE

The balance sheet, income statement, and statement of cash flows for the Pitts Corporation are shown in Exhibit 11. The Pitts Corporation has net income of $240 million in 2007. Show the calculations required to do each of the following:

1. Calculate FCFF starting with the net income figure.
2. Calculate FCFE starting from the FCFF calculated in Part 1.
3. Calculate FCFE starting with the net income figure.
4. Calculate FCFF starting with CFO.
5. Calculate FCFE starting with CFO.

| EXHIBIT 11 | Financial Statements for Pitts Corporation (in Millions, except for Per-Share Data) |
|---|---|

| Balance Sheet Year Ended 31 December | 2006 | 2007 |
|---|---|---|
| **Assets** | | |
| **Current assets** | | |
| Cash and equivalents | $ 190 | $ 200 |
| Accounts receivable | 560 | 600 |
| Inventory | 410 | 440 |
| Total current assets | 1,160 | 1,240 |
| Gross fixed assets | 2,200 | 2,600 |
| Accumulated depreciation | (900) | (1,200) |
| Net fixed assets | 1,300 | 1,400 |
| **Total assets** | $2,460 | $2,640 |
| | | |
| **Liabilities and shareholders' equity** | | |
| **Current liabilities** | | |
| Accounts payable | $ 285 | $ 300 |
| Notes payable | 200 | 250 |
| Accrued taxes and expenses | 140 | 150 |
| Total current liabilities | 625 | 700 |
| Long-term debt | 865 | 890 |
| Common stock | 100 | 100 |
| Additional paid-in capital | 200 | 200 |
| Retained earnings | 670 | 750 |
| **Total shareholders' equity** | 970 | 1,050 |
| **Total liabilities and shareholders' equity** | $2,460 | $2,640 |

| Statement of Income Year Ended 31 December | 2007 |
|---|---|
| Total revenues | $3,000 |
| Operating costs and expenses | 2,200 |
| EBITDA | 800 |
| Depreciation | 300 |
| Operating income (EBIT) | 500 |
| Interest expense | 100 |
| Income before tax | 400 |
| Taxes (at 40 percent) | 160 |

*(Exhibit continued on next page . . .)*

| EXHIBIT 11 | (continued) |
|---|---|

**Statement of Income**
| Year Ended 31 December | 2007 |
|---|---|
| Net income | 240 |
| Dividends | 160 |
| Change in retained earnings | 80 |
| Earnings per share | $0.48 |
| Dividends per share | $0.32 |

**Statement of Cash Flows**
| Year Ended 31 December | 2007 |
|---|---|
| **Operating activities** | |
| Net income | $ 240 |
| Adjustments | |
| Depreciation | 300 |
| Changes in working capital | |
| Accounts receivable | (40) |
| Inventories | (30) |
| Accounts payable | 15 |
| Accrued taxes and expenses | 10 |
| Cash provided by operating activities | $ 495 |
| **Investing activities** | |
| Purchases of fixed assets | 400 |
| Cash used for investing activities | $ 400 |
| **Financing activities** | |
| Notes payable | (50) |
| Long-term financing issuances | (25) |
| Common stock dividends | 160 |
| Cash used for financing activities | $ 85 |
| Cash and equivalents increase (decrease) | 10 |
| Cash and equivalents at beginning of year | 190 |
| Cash and equivalents at end of year | $ 200 |
| **Supplemental cash flow disclosures** | |
| Interest paid | $ 100 |
| Income taxes paid | $ 160 |

**Solution to 1:** The analyst can use Equation 42-7 to find FCFF from net income:

| | |
|---|---:|
| Net income available to common shareholders | $240 |
| Plus: Net noncash charges | 300 |
| Plus: Interest expense $\times$ (1 − Tax rate) | 60 |
| Less: Investment in fixed capital | (400) |
| Less: Investment in working capital | (45) |
| Free cash flow to the firm | $155 |

(In the format shown, "Less: . . . (x)" is interpreted as "subtract x" which is one convention that will be encountered.)

This equation can also be written as

$$FCFF = NI + NCC + Int(1 - Tax\ rate) - FCInv - WCInv$$
$$= \$240 + 300 + 60 - 400 - 45 = \$155\ million$$

Some of these items need explanation. Capital spending is $400 million, which is the increase in gross fixed assets shown on the balance sheet as well as capital expenditures shown as an investing activity on the statement of cash flows. The increase in working capital is $45 million, which is the increase in accounts receivable of $40 million ($600 million − $560 million) plus the increase in inventories of $30 million ($440 million − $410 million) minus the increase in accounts payable of $15 million ($300 million − $285 million) minus the increase in accrued taxes and expenses of $10 million ($140 million − $130 million). When finding the increase in working capital, we ignore cash because the change in cash is what we are calculating. Furthermore, we also ignore short-term debt, such as notes payable, because it is part of the capital provided to the company and is not considered an operating item. The after-tax interest cost is the interest expense times (1 − Tax rate), or $100 million $\times$ (1 − 0.40) = $60 million. The values of the remaining items in Equation 42-7 can be taken directly from the financial statements.

**Solution to 2:** Finding FCFE from FCFF can be done with Equation 42-9:

| | |
|---|---:|
| Free cash flow to the firm | $155 |
| Less: Interest expense $\times$ (1 − Tax rate) | 60 |
| Plus: Net borrowing | 75 |
| Free cash flow to equity | $170 |

Or, using

$$FCFE = FCFF - Int(1 - Tax\ rate) + Net\ borrowing$$
$$FCFE = 155 - 60 + 75 = \$170\ million$$

**Solution to 3:** The analyst can use Equation 42-10 to find FCFE from NI.

| | |
|---|---:|
| Net income available to common shareholders | $240 |
| Plus: Net noncash charges | 300 |
| Less: Investment in fixed capital | 400 |
| Less: Investment in working capital | 45 |
| Plus: Net borrowing | 75 |
| Free cash flow to equity | $170 |

Or, using the equation

$$FCFE = NI + NCC - FCInv - WCInv + \text{Net borrowing}$$
$$FCFE = 240 + 300 - 400 - 45 + 75 = \$170 \text{ million}$$

Because notes payable increased by 50 (250 − 200) and long-term debt increased by 25 (890 − 865), net borrowing is 75.

**Solution to 4:** Equation 42-8 can be used to find FCFF from CFO:

| | |
|---|---:|
| Cash flow from operations | $495 |
| Plus: Interest expense × (1 − Tax rate) | 60 |
| Less: Investment in fixed capital | 400 |
| Free cash flow to the firm | $155 |

or

$$FCFF = CFO + Int(1 - \text{Tax rate}) - FCInv$$
$$FCFF = 495 + 60 - 400 = \$155 \text{ million}$$

**Solution to 5:** Equation 42-11 can be used to find FCFE from CFO:

| | |
|---|---:|
| Cash flow from operations | $495 |
| Less: Investment in fixed capital | 400 |
| Plus: Net borrowing | 75 |
| Free cash flow to equity | $170 |

or

$$FCFE = CFO - FCInv + \text{Net borrowing}$$
$$FCFE = 495 - 400 + 75 = \$170 \text{ million}$$

FCFE is usually less than FCFF. In this example, however, FCFE ($170 million) exceeds FCFF ($155 million) because external borrowing was large during this year.

## 3.5 Finding FCFF and FCFE from EBIT or EBITDA

FCFF and FCFE are most frequently calculated from a starting basis of net income or CFO (as shown in Sections 3.1 and 3.2). Two other starting points are EBIT or EBITDA from the income statement.

To show the relationship between EBIT and FCFF, we start with Equation 42-7 and assume that the only noncash charge (NCC) is depreciation (Dep):

$$FCFF = NI + Dep + Int(1 - \text{Tax rate}) - FCInv - WCInv$$

Net income (NI) can be expressed as

$$NI = (EBIT - Int)(1 - Tax\ rate) = EBIT(1 - Tax\ rate) - Int(1 - Tax\ rate)$$

Substituting this equation for NI in Equation 42-7, we have

$$FCFF = EBIT(1 - Tax\ rate) + Dep - FCInv - WCInv \qquad (42\text{-}12)$$

To get FCFF from EBIT, we multiply EBIT by (1 − Tax rate), add back depreciation, and then subtract the investments in fixed capital and working capital.

It is also easy to show the relation between FCFF from EBITDA. Net income can be expressed as

$$NI = (EBITDA - Dep - Int)(1 - Tax\ rate) = EBITDA(1 - Tax\ rate) \\ - Dep(1 - Tax\ rate) - Int(1 - Tax\ rate)$$

Substituting this equation for NI in Equation 42-7 results in

$$FCFF = EBITDA(1 - Tax\ rate) + Dep(Tax\ rate) \\ - FCInv - WCInv \qquad (42\text{-}13)$$

FCFF equals EBITDA times (1 − Tax rate) plus depreciation times the tax rate minus the investments in fixed capital and working capital. In comparing Equations 42-12 and 42-13, note the difference in the handling of depreciation.

Many noncash charge adjustments required to calculate FCFF based on net income are not required when starting from EBIT or EBITDA. In the calculation of net income, many noncash charges are made after computing EBIT or EBITDA, so they do not need to be added back when calculating FCFF based on EBIT or EBITDA. Another important consideration is that some noncash charges, such as depreciation, are tax deductible. A noncash charge that affects taxes must be accounted for. In summary, in calculating FCFF from EBIT or EBITDA, whether an adjustment for a noncash charge is needed depends on where in the income statement the charge has been deducted; furthermore, the form of any needed adjustment depends on whether the noncash charge is a tax-deductible expense.

It is also possible to calculate FCFE (instead of FCFF) from EBIT or EBITDA. An easy way to obtain FCFE from EBIT or EBITDA is to derive FCFF using Equation 42-12 or 42-13, and then subtract Int(1 − Tax rate) and add net borrowing to end up with FCFE as a function of FCFF:[7]

$$FCFE = FCFF - Int(1 - Tax\ rate) + Net\ borrowing$$

Example 7 uses the Pitts Corporation financial statements to find FCFF and FCFE from EBIT and EBITDA.

---

[7] It is also possible to derive equations for FCFE as a function of EBIT or EBITDA. To do so, start with the equation for FCFE as a function of NI (Equation 42-10), again making the assumption that the only noncash charge is depreciation: FCFE = NI + Dep − FCInv − WCInv + Net borrowing. Substituting NI = EBIT(1 − Tax rate) − Int(1 − Tax rate) and NI = EBITDA(1 − Tax rate) − Dep(1 − Tax rate) − Int(1 − Tax rate) into Equation 42-10 yields two equations for FCFE as a function of EBIT or EBITDA, respectively:

FCFE = EBIT(1 − Tax rate) − Int(1 − Tax rate) + Dep − FCInv − WCInv
        + Net borrowing

FCFE = EBITDA(1 − Tax rate) + Dep(Tax rate) − Int(1 − Tax rate) − FCInv
        − WCInv + Net borrowing

## EXAMPLE 7

### Adjusting EBIT and EBITDA to Find FCFF and FCFE

The Pitts Corporation (financial statements provided in Example 6) has EBIT of $500 million and EBITDA of $800 million in 2007. Show the adjustments that would be required to find FCFF and FCFE:

1. starting from EBIT, and
2. starting from EBITDA.

**Solution to 1:** To get FCFF from EBIT using Equation 42-12:

| | |
|---|---:|
| EBIT(1 − Tax rate) = 500(1 − 0.40) | $300 |
| Plus: Net noncash charges | 300 |
| Less: Net investment in fixed capital | 400 |
| Less: Net increase in working capital | 45 |
| Free cash flow to the firm | $155 |

or

$$\text{FCFF} = \text{EBIT}(1 - \text{Tax rate}) + \text{Dep} - \text{FCInv} - \text{WCInv}$$
$$\text{FCFF} = 500(1 - 0.40) + 300 - 400 - 45 = \$155 \text{ million}$$

To obtain FCFE, make the appropriate adjustments to FCFF:

$$\text{FCFE} = \text{FCFF} - \text{Int}(1 - \text{Tax rate}) + \text{Net borrowing}$$
$$\text{FCFE} = 155 - 100(1 - 0.40) + 75 = \$170 \text{ million}$$

**Solution to 2:** To obtain FCFF from EBITDA using Equation 42-13:

| | |
|---|---:|
| EBITDA(1 − Tax rate) = 800(1 − 0.40) | $480 |
| Plus: Depreciation(Tax rate) = 300(0.40) | 120 |
| Less: Net investment in fixed capital | 400 |
| Less: Net increase in working capital | 45 |
| Free cash flow to the firm | $155 |

or

$$\text{FCFF} = \text{EBITDA}(1 - \text{Tax rate}) + \text{Dep}(\text{Tax rate}) - \text{FCInv} - \text{WCInv}$$
$$\text{FCFF} = 800(1 - 0.40) + 300(0.40) - 400 - 45 = \$155 \text{ million}$$

Again, to obtain FCFE, make the appropriate adjustments to FCFF:

$$\text{FCFE} = \text{FCFF} - \text{Int}(1 - \text{Tax rate}) + \text{Net borrowing}$$
$$\text{FCFE} = 155 - 100(1 - 0.40) + 75 = \$170 \text{ million}$$

## 3.6 Forecasting FCFF and FCFE

Computing FCFF and FCFE based on historical accounting data is relatively straightforward. In some cases, these data are used directly to extrapolate free cash flow growth in a single-stage FCF valuation model. On other occasions, the analyst may not expect the future free cash flows to bear a simple relation to the past. The analyst may desire to forecast future FCFF or FCFE directly. In this case, the analyst must forecast the individual components of free cash flow. This section extends our previous presentation on computing FCFF and FCFE to the more complex task of forecasting FCFF and FCFE. We present FCFF and FCFE valuation models in the next section.

One method for forecasting free cash flow involves applying some constant growth rate to a current level of free cash flow (possibly adjusted). The simplest basis for specifying the future growth rate is to assume that a historical growth rate will also apply to the future. This approach would be appropriate if a company's free cash flow tended to grow at a constant rate and if historical relationships between free cash flow and fundamental factors were expected to be maintained.

---

### EXAMPLE 8

**Constant Growth in FCFF**

Use Pitts Corporation data to compute its FCFF for the next three years. Assume growth in FCFF remains at historical levels of 15 percent a year.

|       | 2007A  | 2008E  | 2009E  | 2010E  |
|-------|--------|--------|--------|--------|
| FCFF  | 155.00 | 178.25 | 204.99 | 235.74 |

---

A more complex approach is to forecast the components of free cash flow. This approach can better capture the complex relationships among the components. For example, one popular method[8] is to forecast the individual components of free cash flow—EBIT(1 − Tax rate), net noncash charges, investment in fixed capital, and investment in working capital. EBIT can be forecasted directly or by forecasting sales and the company's EBIT margin based on an analysis of historical data and the current and expected economic environment. Similarly, analysts can examine the historical relationship between increases in sales and investments in fixed and working capital.

In the following, we illustrate a shortcut sales-based forecasting method for FCFF and FCFE based on the major assumption that:

▶   investment in fixed capital in excess of depreciation (FCInv − Dep) and investment in working capital (WCInv) both bear a constant relationship to forecast increases in the size of the company as measured by increases in sales

plus, for FCFE forecasting, the assumption that:

▶   the capital structure represented by the debt ratio (DR)—debt as a percentage of debt plus equity—is constant.

---

[8] See Rappaport (1997) for a variation of this model.

The method involves a simplification in considering depreciation as the only noncash charge and does not work well when that is a not good approximation. If depreciation reflects the annual cost for maintaining the existing capital stock, the difference between fixed capital investment and depreciation—incremental FCInv—should be related to the capital expenditures required for growth. The following inputs are needed:

▶ forecasts of sales growth rates

▶ forecasts of the aftertax operating margin (for FCFF forecasting) or profit margin (for FCFE forecasting)

▶ an estimate of the relationship of incremental FCInv to sales increases

▶ an estimate of the relationship of WCInv to sales increases

▶ an estimate of the debt ratio (DR)

In the case of FCFF forecasting, FCFF is calculated by forecasting EBIT(1 − Tax rate) and subtracting incremental fixed capital expenditures and incremental working capital expenditures.[9] In order to estimate FCInv and WCInv, we multiply their past proportion to sales' increases by the forecasted sales' increases. Incremental fixed capital expenditures as a proportion of sales increases are computed as follows:

$$\frac{\text{Capital expenditures} - \text{Depreciation expense}}{\text{Increase in sales}}$$

Similarly, incremental working capital expenditures as a proportion of sales increases are

$$\frac{\text{Increase in working capital}}{\text{Increase in sales}}$$

When depreciation is the only significant net noncash charge, this method yields the same results as the previous equations for estimating FCFF or FCFE. Rather than adding back all depreciation and subtracting all capital expenditures when starting with EBIT(1 − Tax rate), this approach simply subtracts the net capital expenditures in excess of depreciation.

Although it may not be obvious, this approach recognizes that capital expenditures have two components: those expenditures necessary to maintain existing capacity (fixed capital replacement) and those incremental expenditures necessary for growth. In forecasting, the former are likely to be related to the current level of sales and the latter are likely related to the forecast of sales growth.

When forecasting FCFE, analysts often make an assumption that there is a target ratio of debt financing in the financing of the company. They sometimes assume that a specified percentage of the sum of a) net new investment in fixed capital (new fixed capital minus depreciation expense) and b) the increase in working capital, is financed with a target ratio of debt. This leads to a simplification of FCFE calculations. Assuming that depreciation is the only noncash charge, Equation 42-10, FCFE = NI + NCC − FCInv − WCInv + Net borrowing, becomes

$$\text{FCFE} = \text{NI} - (\text{FCInv} - \text{Dep}) - \text{WCInv} + \text{Net borrowing} \qquad \textbf{(42-14)}$$

---

[9] See Rappaport (1997).

Note that FCInv − Dep represents the incremental fixed capital expenditure net of depreciation. By assuming a target debt ratio (DR), we eliminate the need to forecast net borrowing and can use the expression

$$\text{Net borrowing} = \text{DR}(\text{FCInv} - \text{Dep}) + \text{DR}(\text{WCInv})$$

Using this expression, we do not need to forecast debt issuance and repayment on an annual basis to estimate net borrowing. Equation 42-14 then becomes

$$\text{FCFE} = \text{NI} - (\text{FCInv} - \text{Dep}) - \text{WCInv} + (\text{DR})(\text{FCInv} - \text{Dep}) + (\text{DR})(\text{WCInv})$$

or

$$\text{FCFE} = \text{NI} - (1 - \text{DR})(\text{FCInv} - \text{Dep}) - (1 - \text{DR})(\text{WCInv}) \qquad \textbf{(42-15)}$$

Equation 42-15 says that FCFE equals NI minus the amount of fixed capital expenditure (net of depreciation) and working capital investment that is equity financed. We again assume that the only noncash charge is depreciation.

### EXAMPLE 9

**Free Cash Flow Tied to Sales**

At the end of 2007, Carla Espinosa is an analyst following Pitts Corporation. From Example 6 the company's sales for 2007 were $3,000 million. Assume that sales grew by $300 million from 2006 to 2007. Espinosa expects Pitts Corporation's sales to increase by 10 percent a year thereafter. Furthermore, Pitts is a stable company in many respects, and Espinosa expects it to maintain its historical EBIT margin and proportions of incremental investments in fixed and working capital. Pitts Corporation's EBIT for 2007 is $500 million; its EBIT margin is 16.67 percent (500/3000), and its tax rate is 40 percent.

Note from Pitts Corporation's 2007 cash flow statement (Exhibit 11) the amount for "purchases of fixed assets" (i.e., capital expenditures) of $400 million and depreciation of $300 million. Thus, incremental fixed capital investment in 2007 was

(Capital expenditures − Depreciation expense)/(Increase in sales) or
(400−300)/(300) = 33.33%

Incremental working capital investment in the past year was

(Increase in working capital)/(Increase in sales)
45/300 = 15%

So for every $100 increase in sales, Pitts Corporation invests $33.33 in new equipment in addition to replacement of depreciated equipment and $15 in working capital. Espinosa forecasts FCFF for 2008 as shown below:

| | | |
|---|---|---|
| Sales | $3,300 | Up 10% |
| EBIT | 550 | 16.67% of sales |
| EBIT(1 − Tax rate) | 330 | Adjusted for 40% tax rate |
| Incremental FC | (100) | 33.33% of sales increase |
| Incremental WC | (45) | 15% of sales increase |
| FCFF | $ 185 | |

This model can be used to forecast multiple periods and is flexible enough to allow varying sales growth rates, EBIT margins, tax rates, and incremental capital increase rates.

## EXAMPLE 10

### Free Cash Flow Growth Tied to Sales Growth

Continuing her work, Espinosa wants to forecast FCFF for the next five years. Espinosa is concerned that Pitts will not be able to maintain its historical EBIT margin and that the EBIT margin will decline from the current 16.67 percent to 14.5 percent in the next five years. Exhibit 12 summarizes her forecasts.

| EXHIBIT 12 | Free Cash Flow Growth for Pitts Corporation | | | | |
|---|---|---|---|---|---|
| | Year 1 | Year 2 | Year 3 | Year 4 | Year 5 |
| Sales growth | 10.00% | 10.00% | 10.00% | 10.00% | 10.00% |
| EBIT margin | 16.67% | 16.00% | 15.50% | 15.00% | 14.50% |
| Tax rate | 40.00% | 40.00% | 40.00% | 40.00% | 40.00% |
| Incremental FC investment | 33.33% | 33.33% | 33.33% | 33.33% | 33.33% |
| Incremental WC investment | 15.00% | 15.00% | 15.00% | 15.00% | 15.00% |
| Prior year sales | 3,000.00 | | | | |
| Sales forecast | 3,300.00 | 3,630.00 | 3,993.00 | 4,392.30 | 4,831.53 |
| EBIT forecast | 550.00 | 580.80 | 618.92 | 658.85 | 700.57 |
| EBIT(1 − Tax rate) | 330.00 | 348.48 | 371.35 | 395.31 | 420.34 |
| Incremental FC | (100.00) | (110.00) | (121.00) | (133.10) | (146.41) |
| Incremental WC | (45.00) | (49.50) | (54.45) | (59.90) | (65.88) |
| FCFF | 185.00 | 188.98 | 195.90 | 202.31 | 208.05 |

The model need not begin with sales; it could start with net income, cash flow from operations, or EBITDA.

A similar model can be designed for FCFE. In the case of FCFE, the analyst can begin with net income and must also forecast any net new borrowing or net preferred stock issue.

---

### EXAMPLE 11

**Finding FCFE**

Espinosa decides to forecast FCFE for the year 2008. She uses the same expectations derived in the example above. Additionally, she expects

▶ the profit margin to remain at 8 percent (= 240/3000), and
▶ the company to finance incremental fixed and working capital investments with 50 percent debt—the target debt ratio.

| | | |
|---|---|---|
| Sales | $3,300 | Up 10% |
| NI | 264 | 8.0% of sales |
| Incremental FC | (100) | 33.33% of sales increase |
| Incremental WC | (45) | 15% of sales increase |
| Net borrowing | 72.50 | (100 FCInv + 45 WCInv) × 50% |
| FCFE | $191.50 | |

---

When the company has significant noncash charges other than depreciation expense, the approach just illustrated will result in a less accurate estimate of FCFE than one obtained by forecasting all the individual components of FCFE.

In some cases, the analyst will have specific forecasts of planned components, such as capital expenditures. In other cases, the analyst studies historical relationships, such as previous capital expenditures and sales levels, to develop a forecast.

## 3.7 Other Issues in Free Cash Flow Analysis

We have already presented a number of practical issues that arise in using free cash flow valuation models. Other issues relate to analyst adjustments to CFO, the relation between free cash flow and dividends, and valuation with more complicated financial structures.

### 3.7.1 Analyst Adjustments to CFO

Although corporate financial statements are often straightforward, frequently they are not transparent (i.e., the quality of the reported numbers and of disclosures is not high). Sometimes, difficulties in analysis arise because the companies and their transactions are simply more complicated than the example provided by the Pitts Corporation (above).

For instance, in many corporate financial statements, the changes in balance sheet items (the increase in an asset or the decrease in a liability) differ from those reported on the statement of cash flows. Likewise, depreciation in the statement of cash flows may differ from depreciation expense in the income statement. How do such problems arise?

Two factors can cause discrepancies between changes in balance sheet accounts and the changes reported in the statement of cash flows: acquisitions and divestitures, and foreign subsidiaries. For example, an increase in an inventory account can result from purchases from suppliers (which is an operating activity) or from an acquisition or merger with another company that has inventory on its balance sheet (which is an investing activity). Discrepancies can also occur from currency translations of foreign subsidiaries.

Because the CFO figure from the statement of cash flows may be contaminated by cash flows arising from financing and/or investing activities, when analysts use CFO in a valuation context, ideally they should remove such contaminations. The resulting analyst-adjusted CFO would then be the starting point for free cash flow calculations.

### 3.7.2 Free Cash Flow versus Dividends and Other Earnings Components

Many analysts have a strong preference for free cash flow valuation models over dividend discount models (DDMs). Although perhaps no theoretical advantage exists for one type of model over another, legitimate reasons to prefer one model can arise in the process of applying free cash flow models versus DDMs. First, many corporations pay no, or very low, cash dividends. Using dividend discount models to value these companies puts the analyst in an awkward situation, forcing her to speculate about when dividends will be initiated and established at a material level. Second, dividend payments are at the discretion of the corporation's board of directors. As such, they may imperfectly signal the company's long-run profitability. Some corporations clearly pay dividends that are substantially less than their free cash flow, and others pay dividends that are substantially more. Finally, as mentioned in Section 1, dividends are the cash flow going to shareholders and free cash flow to equity is the cash flow available to shareholders if they controlled the company. If a company is being analyzed as a takeover target, free cash flow is the appropriate cash flow measure; once the company is taken over, the new owners will have discretion over free cash flow.

We have defined FCFF and FCFE and presented alternative (equivalent) ways to calculate both of them. So you should have a good feel for what is included in FCFF or FCFE. You may wonder why some cash flows are not included. Specifically, what role do dividends, share repurchases, share issuance, or leverage changes have on FCFF and FCFE? The simple answer is: not much. Recall two formulas for FCFF and FCFE:

$$FCFF = NI + NCC + Int(1 - Tax\ rate) - FCInv - WCInv$$

$$FCFE = NI + NCC - FCInv - WCInv + Net\ borrowing$$

Notice that dividends and these other transactions are absent from the formulas. The reason is that FCFF and FCFE are the cash flows *available* to investors or to stockholders; dividends and share repurchases are *uses* of these cash flows. So the simple answer is that transactions between the company and its shareholders (through cash dividends, share repurchases and share issuances) do not affect free cash flow. Leverage changes, such as using more debt financing, would have some impact because they would increase the interest tax shield (reduce corporate taxes because of the tax deductibility of interest) and reduce the cash flow available to equity. In the long run, however, investing and financing decisions made today will affect future cash flows.

If all inputs were known and mutually consistent, a dividend discount model and a FCFE model would result in identical valuations for a stock. One possibility is that FCFE equals cash dividends each year. Both cash flow streams are discounted at the required return for equity and would thus have the same present value. Generally, FCFE and dividends will differ. FCFE recognizes value as the cash flow available to stockholders (NI + NCC − FCInv − WCInv + Net borrowing) even if it is not paid out in dividends. The company's board of directors, because of its discretion over dividends, can choose to pay dividends that are lower or higher than FCFE. Generally, however, the same economic forces that lead to low (high) dividends lead to low (high) FCFE. For example, a rapidly growing company with superior investment opportunities will retain a high proportion of earnings and pay low dividends. This same company would have high investments in fixed capital and working capital and have a low FCFE (which is clear from the expression FCFE = NI + NCC − FCInv − WCInv + Net borrowing). Conversely, a mature company that is investing relatively little might have high dividends and high FCFE. In spite of this tendency, however, FCFE and dividends will usually differ.

FCFF and FCFE, as defined in this volume, are measures of cash flow designed for valuation of the firm or its equity. Other definitions of "free cash flow" frequently appear in textbooks, articles, and vendor-supplied databases of financial information on public companies. In many cases, these other definitions of free cash flow are not designed for valuation purposes and thus should not be used for valuation. Using numbers supplied by others without knowing exactly how they are defined increases the likelihood of making errors in valuation. As consumers and producers of research, analysts are well advised to clarify the definition of free cash flow being used because so many versions exist.

Because free cash flow analysis requires considerable care and understanding in its use, some practitioners erroneously use earnings components such as NI, EBIT, EBITDA, or CFO in a discounted cash flow valuation. Such mistakes may lead the analyst to systematically overstate or understate the value of a stock. Shortcuts can be costly.

One common shortcut is to use EBITDA as a proxy for the cash flow to the firm. Equation 42-13 clearly showed the differences between EBITDA and FCFF:

$$FCFF = EBITDA(1 - \text{Tax rate}) + Dep(\text{Tax rate}) - FCInv - WCInv$$

Depreciation charges as a percentage of EBITDA vary substantially for different companies and industries, as does the depreciation tax shield (the depreciation charge times the tax rate). Although FCFF captures this difference, EBITDA does not. EBITDA also does not account for the investments a company makes in fixed capital or working capital. Hence, EBITDA is a very poor measure of the cash flow available to the company's investors. Using EBITDA in a discounted cash flow model (instead of an actual cash flow) has another important aspect as well: EBITDA is a before-tax measure, so the discount rate applied to EBITDA would need to be a before-tax rate. The WACC used to discount FCFF is an after-tax rate.

EBITDA is a poor proxy for FCFF because it does not account for the depreciation tax shield and the investment in fixed capital and working capital, but it is an even poorer proxy for free cash flow to equity. From a stockholder's perspective, additional defects of EBITDA include its failure to account for the after-tax interest costs or cash flows from new borrowing or debt repayments. Example 12 shows the mistakes sometimes made in discussions of cash flows.

## EXAMPLE 12

### The Mistake of Using Net Income for FCFE and EBITDA for FCFF

A recent job applicant made some interesting comments about FCFE and FCFF: "I don't like the definitions for FCFE and FCFF because they are unnecessarily complicated and confusing. The best measure of FCFE, the funds available to pay dividends, is simply net income. You take the net income number straight off the income statement and don't need to make any further adjustments. Likewise, the best measure of FCFF, the funds available to the company's suppliers of capital, is EBITDA. You can take EBITDA straight off the income statement and don't need to consider using anything else."

How would you respond to the job applicant's definition of (1) FCFE and (2) FCFF?

**Solution to 1:** The FCFE is the cash generated by the business's operations less the amounts it must reinvest in additional assets plus the amounts it is borrowing. Equation 42-10, which starts with net income to find FCFE, shows these items:

$$
\begin{aligned}
\text{Free cash flow to equity} = &\text{ Net income available to common} \\
&\text{ shareholders} \\
&\text{Plus: Net noncash charges} \\
&\text{Less: Investment in fixed capital} \\
&\text{Less: Investment in working capital} \\
&\text{Plus: Net borrowing}
\end{aligned}
$$

Net income does not include several cash flows. Investments in fixed or working capital reduce the cash available to stockholders, as do loan repayments. New borrowing increases the cash available. FCFE includes the cash generated from operating the business and also accounts for the investing and financing activities of the company. So, net income tells only part of the overall story. Of course, a special case exists in which net income and FCFE are the same. This case occurs when new investments exactly equal depreciation and the company is not investing in working capital or engaging in any net borrowing.

**Solution to 2:** Assuming that EBITDA equals FCFF introduces several possible mistakes. Equation 42-13 highlights these mistakes:

$$
\begin{aligned}
\text{Free cash flow to the firm} = &\text{ EBITDA}(1 - \text{Tax rate}) \\
&\text{Plus: Depreciation(Tax rate)} \\
&\text{Less: Investment in fixed capital} \\
&\text{Less: Investment in working capital}
\end{aligned}
$$

The applicant is ignoring taxes, which obviously reduce the cash available to the company's suppliers of capital.

### 3.7.3 Free Cash Flow and More-Complicated Capital Structures

For the most part, the discussion of FCFF and FCFE above assumes a simple capital structure in which the company has two sources of capital, debt and equity. Including preferred stock as a third source of capital would cause the analyst to add terms to the equations for FCFF and FCFE for the dividends paid on preferred stock and for the issuance or repurchase of preferred shares. Instead of including those terms in all of the equations, we chose to leave preferred stock out because only a minority of corporations use preferred stock. For companies that do have preferred stock, however, its effects can be incorporated where appropriate.

For example, in Equation 42-7, which calculates FCFF starting with net income available to common shareholders, preferred dividends paid would have to be added to the cash flows to obtain FCFF. In Equation 42-10, which calculates FCFE starting with net income available to common shareholders, if preferred dividends were already subtracted when arriving at net income available, no further adjustment for preferred dividends would be required. Issuing (redeeming) preferred stock increases (decreases) the cash flow available to common stockholders, however, so this term must be added in. In many respects, the existence of preferred stock in the capital structure has many of the same effects as the existence of debt, except that unlike interest payments on debt, preferred stock dividends paid are not tax deductible.

---

### EXAMPLE 13

**FCFF Valuation with Preferred Stock in the Capital Structure**

Welch Corporation uses bond, preferred stock, and common stock financing. The market value of each of these sources of financing and the before-tax required rates of return for each are given in Exhibit 13:

| EXHIBIT 13 | Welch Corporation Capital Structure | |
| --- | --- | --- |
| | **Market Value** | **Required Return** |
| Bonds | $400,000,000 | 8.0% |
| Preferred stock | $100,000,000 | 8.0% |
| Common stock | $500,000,000 | 12.0% |
| Total | $1,000,000,000 | |

Other financial information:

▶ Net income available to common shareholders = $110,000,000
▶ Interest expenses = $32,000,000
▶ Preferred dividends = $8,000,000
▶ Depreciation = $40,000,000
▶ Investment in fixed capital = $70,000,000
▶ Investment in working capital = $20,000,000
▶ Net borrowing = $25,000,000

- ▶ Tax rate = 30 percent
- ▶ Stable growth rate of FCFF = 4.0 percent
- ▶ Stable growth rate of FCFE = 5.0 percent

**1.** Calculate Welch Corporation's WACC.

**2.** Calculate the current value of FCFF.

**3.** Based on forecasted FCFF, what is the total value of the firm and the value of equity?

**4.** Calculate the current value of FCFE.

**5.** Based on forecasted FCFE, what is the value of equity?

**Solution to 1:** Based on the weights and after-tax costs of each source of capital, the WACC is

$$\text{WACC} = \frac{400}{1,000}8\%(1 - 0.30) + \frac{100}{1,000}8\% + \frac{500}{1,000}12\% = 9.04\%$$

**Solution to 2:** If the company did not issue preferred stock, FCFF would be

$$\text{FCFF} = \text{NI} + \text{NCC} + \text{Int}(1 - \text{Tax rate}) - \text{FCInv} - \text{WCInv}$$

If preferred stock dividends have been paid (and net income is income available to common), the preferred dividends must be added back just as after-tax interest expenses are above. The modified equation (including preferred dividends) for FCFF would be

$$\text{FCFF} = \text{NI} + \text{NCC} + \text{Int}(1 - \text{Tax rate}) + \text{Preferred dividends} \\ - \text{FCInv} - \text{WCInv}$$

For Welch Corporation, FCFF is

$$\text{FCFF} = 110 + 40 + 32(1 - 0.30) + 8 - 70 - 20 = \$90.4 \text{ million.}$$

**Solution to 3:** The total value of the firm is

$$\text{Firm} = \frac{\text{FCFF}_1}{\text{WACC} - g} = \frac{90.4(1.04)}{0.0904 - 0.04}$$

$$= \frac{94.016}{0.0504} = \$1,865.40 \text{ million}$$

The value of equity is the total value of the company minus the value of debt and preferred stock:

$$\text{Equity} = 1,865.40 - 400 - 100 = \$1,365.40 \text{ million.}$$

**Solution to 4:** With no preferred stock, FCFE is

$$\text{FCFE} = \text{NI} + \text{NCC} - \text{FCInv} - \text{WCInv} + \text{Net borrowing}$$

If the company has preferred stock, the FCFE equation is essentially the same. Net borrowing would be the total of new debt borrowing and net issuances of new preferred stock. For Welch Corporation, FCFE is

$$FCFE = 110 + 40 - 70 - 20 + 25 = \$85 \text{ million}$$

**Solution to 5:** Valuing FCFE, which is growing at 5.0 percent, we have a value of equity of

$$\text{Equity} = \frac{FCFE_1}{r - g} = \frac{85(1.05)}{0.12 - 0.05} = \frac{89.25}{0.07} = \$1,275.00 \text{ million}$$

Paying cash dividends on common stock does not affect FCFF or FCFE, the amounts of cash *available* to all investors or to common stockholders. It is simply a use of the available cash. Share repurchases of common stock also do not affect FCFF or FCFE. Share repurchases, in many respects, are substitutes for cash dividends. Similarly, issuing shares of common stock does not affect FCFF or FCFE. On the other hand, changing leverage (changing the amount of debt financing in the company's capital structure) does have some effects. An increase in leverage will not affect FCFF (although it might affect the calculations you use to arrive at FCFF). An increase in leverage affects FCFE in two ways. In the year the debt is issued, it increases the FCFE by the amount of debt issued. After the debt is issued, FCFE is then reduced by the after-tax interest expense.

Section 3 has discussed the concepts of FCFF and FCFE and their estimation. The next section presents additional valuation models using forecasts of FCFF or FCFE to value the firm or its equity. These free cash flow models are similar in structure to dividend discount models, although the analyst must face the reality that estimating free cash flows is a more time-consuming exercise than estimating dividends.

# 4    FREE CASH FLOW MODEL VARIATIONS

Section 4 presents several extensions of the FCF models presented earlier. In many cases, especially when inflation rates are volatile, analysts will value real cash flows instead of nominal values. As with dividend discount models, free cash flow models are very sensitive to the data inputs, and analysts routinely perform sensitivity analyses on their valuations. Previously, in Section 2, we presented single-stage free cash flow models, which have a constant growth rate. This section presents two-stage and three-stage free cash flow valuation models.

## 4.1 An International Application of the Single-Stage Model

Valuation using real values instead of nominal values has much appeal when inflation rates are high and volatile. Many analysts use this adaptation for both domestic and foreign stocks, but the use of real values is especially helpful for valuing international stocks. Special challenges to valuing equities from multiple countries include incorporating economic factors such as interest rate, inflation rate, and growth rate differences across countries as well as dealing with variable accounting standards. Furthermore, performing analyses in multiple countries challenges the analyst, and most particularly a team of analysts, to use consistent assumptions for all countries.

Several securities firms have adapted the single-stage FCFE model to address some of these challenges of international valuation. They choose to analyze companies using real cash flows and real discount rates instead of using nominal values. To estimate real discount rates, they use a modification of the build-up method mentioned in the return concepts reading. Starting with a "country return," which is a real required rate of return for stocks from a particular country, they then make adjustments to the country return for the stock's industry, size, and leverage:

| | |
|---|---|
| Country return (real) | x.xx% |
| +/− Industry adjustment | x.xx% |
| +/− Size adjustment | x.xx% |
| +/− Leverage adjustment | x.xx% |
| Required rate of return (real) | x.xx% |

The adjustments in the model should have sound economic justification. They should reflect factors expected to affect the relative risk and return associated with an investment.

The growth rate of FCFE also is predicted in real terms. These securities firms supply all analysts with estimates of the real growth rates for each country. The analyst then chooses a real growth rate for the stock benchmarked against the real country growth rate. This approach is particularly useful for countries with high or variable inflation rates. The value of the stock is found with an equation essentially like Equation 42-6 except that all terms in the equation are in real terms. If $FCFE_0$ is for the current year, say 2008, then the value of the stock will be in 2008 currency.

$$V_0 = \frac{FCFE_0(1 + g_{real})}{r_{real} - g_{real}}$$

Whenever real discount rates and real growth rates can be estimated more reliably than nominal discount rates and nominal growth rates, this method is worth using. Example 14 below shows how this procedure can be applied.

## EXAMPLE 14

### Using Real Cash Flows and Discount Rates for International Stocks

YPF Sociedad Anonima (NYSE: YPF) is an integrated oil and gas company headquartered in Buenos Aires, Argentina. Although cash flows have been volatile, an analyst has estimated a normalized FCFE of 1.05 Argentine pesos (ARS) per share for the year just ended. The real country return for Argentina is 7.30 percent; adjustments to the country return for YPF S.A. are an industry adjustment of +0.80 percent, a size adjustment of −0.33 percent, and a leverage adjustment of −0.12 percent. The long-term real growth rate for Argentina is estimated to be 3.0 percent, and the real growth rate of YPF S.A. is expected to be about 0.5 percent below the country rate. The real required rate of return for YPF S.A. is

| | |
|---|---|
| Country return (real) | 7.30% |
| Industry adjustment | +0.80% |
| Size adjustment | −0.33% |
| Leverage adjustment | −0.12% |
| Required rate of return | 7.65% |

The real growth rate of FCFE is expected to be 2.5 percent (3.0% − 0.5%), so the value of one share is

$$V_0 = \frac{FCFE_0(1 + g_{real})}{r_{real} - g_{real}} = \frac{1.05(1.025)}{0.0765 - 0.025} = \frac{1.07625}{0.0515} = ARS20.90$$

## 4.2  Sensitivity Analysis of FCFF and FCFE Valuations

In large measure, growth in FCFF and in FCFE depend on a company's future profitability. Sales growth and changes in net profit margins dictate future net profits. Sales growth and profit margins depend on the growth phase of the company and the profitability of the industry. A highly profitable company in a growing industry can enjoy years of profit growth. Eventually, its profit margins are likely to be eroded by increased competition, and sales growth is likely to abate as well because of fewer opportunities for expansion of market size and market share. Growth rates and the duration of growth are difficult to forecast.

The base-year values for the FCFF or FCFE growth models are also critical. Given the same required rates of return and growth rates, the value of the firm or the value of equity will increase or decrease proportionately with the initial value of FCFF or FCFE employed.

Valuing a company involves forecasts of the company's future cash flows as well as estimates of the opportunity cost of funds that should be used to find the present value of the future cash flows. Analysts can perform a sensitivity analysis, which shows how sensitive the final valuation is to changes in each of a valuation model's input variables. Some input variables have a much larger impact on stock valuation than others. Example 15 shows the sensitivity of the valuation of Petrobras to four input variables.

### EXAMPLE 15

**Sensitivity Analysis of a FCFE Valuation**

Steve Bono is valuing the equity of Petroleo Brasilieiro (NYSE: PBR), commonly known as Petrobras, in early 2007 using the single-stage (constant growth) FCFE model. Estimated FCFE for 2006 was BRL6.15. Bono's best estimates of input values for the analysis are as follows:

▶  The FCFE growth rate is 7.3 percent.
▶  The risk-free rate is 10.0 percent.

▶ The equity risk premium is 5.5 percent.

▶ Beta is 1.0.

Using the CAPM, Bono estimates that the required rate of return for Petrobras is

$$r = E(R_i) = R_F + \beta_i[E(R_M) - R_F] = 10\% + 1.0(5.5\%) = 15.5\%$$

The estimated value per share is

$$V_0 = \frac{FCFE_0(1 + g)}{r - g} = \frac{6.15(1.073)}{0.155 - 0.073} = BRL80.48$$

Exhibit 14 shows Bono's base case and the highest and lowest reasonable alternative estimates. The column "Valuation with Low Estimate" gives the estimated value of Petrobras using the low estimate for the variable on the same row of the first column and the base case estimates for the remaining three variables. "Valuation with High Estimate" performs a similar exercise using the high estimate for the variable at issue.

| EXHIBIT 14 | Sensitivity Analysis for Petrobras Valuation | | | | |
|---|---|---|---|---|---|
| Variable | Base Case Estimate | Low Estimate | High Estimate | Valuation with Low Estimate | Valuation with High Estimate |
| Beta | 1 | 0.75 | 1.25 | BRL96.69 | BRL68.92 |
| Risk-free rate | 10.00% | 8.00% | 12.00% | BRL106.43 | BRL64.70 |
| Equity risk premium | 5.50% | 4.50% | 6.50% | BRL91.65 | BRL71.73 |
| FCFE growth rate | 7.3% | 5.00% | 9.00% | BRL61.50 | BRL103.13 |

As Exhibit 14 shows, the value of Petrobras is very sensitive to the inputs. Of the four variables presented, the stock valuation was least sensitive to the range of estimates for the equity risk premium and beta. The range of estimates for these variables gave the smallest ranges of stock values (from BRL71.73 to BRL91.65 for the equity risk premium and from BRL68.92 to BRL96.69 for beta). The stock value was most sensitive to the extreme values for the risk-free rate and for the FCFE growth rate. Of course, the variables to which the stock price is most sensitive vary from case to case. A sensitivity analysis gives the analyst a guide as to which variables are most critical to the final valuation.

## 4.3 Two-Stage Free Cash Flow Models

Several two-stage and multistage models exist for valuing FCF streams, just as several such models are available for valuing dividend streams. The free cash flow models are much more complex than the discounted dividend models because the analyst usually incorporates sales, profitability, investments, financing costs, and new financing to find FCFF or FCFE.

In two-stage FCF models, the growth rate in the second stage is a long-run sustainable growth rate. For a declining industry, the second-stage growth rate could be slightly below the GDP growth rate. For an industry that will grow in the future relative to the overall economy, the second-stage growth rate could be slightly greater than the GDP growth rate.

The two most popular versions of the two-stage FCFF and FCFE models are distinguished by the pattern of the growth rates in Stage 1. In one version, the growth rate is constant in Stage 1 before dropping to the long-run sustainable rate in Stage 2. In the other version, the growth rates decline in Stage 1, reaching the sustainable rate at the beginning of Stage 2. The latter model is like the H-model for discounted dividend valuation in which dividend growth rates decline in Stage 1 and are constant in Stage 2.

The growth rates can be applied to different variables. The growth rate could be the growth rate for FCFF or FCFE, or the growth rate for income (such as net income), or the growth rate for sales. If the growth rate were for net income, the changes in FCFF or FCFE would also depend on investments in operating assets and financing of these investments. When the growth rate in income declines, such as between Stage 1 and Stage 2, investments in operating assets will probably decline at the same time. If the growth rate is for sales, changes in net profit margins as well as investments in operating assets and financing policies will determine FCFF and FCFE.

A general expression for the two-stage FCFF valuation model is

$$\text{Firm value} = \sum_{t=1}^{n} \frac{\text{FCFF}_t}{(1 + \text{WACC})^t} + \frac{\text{FCFF}_{n+1}}{(\text{WACC} - g)} \frac{1}{(1 + \text{WACC})^n} \quad \textbf{(42-16)}$$

The summation gives the present value of the first $n$ years of FCFF. The terminal value of the FCFF from Year $n + 1$ onward is $\text{FCFF}_{n+1}/(\text{WACC} - g)$, which is discounted at the WACC for $n$ periods to obtain its present value. Subtracting the value of outstanding debt gives the value of equity. The value per share is then found by dividing the total value of equity by the number of outstanding shares.

The general expression for the two-stage FCFE valuation model is

$$\text{Equity value} = \sum_{t=1}^{n} \frac{\text{FCFE}_t}{(1 + r)^t} + \frac{\text{FCFE}_{n+1}}{r - g} \frac{1}{(1 + r)^n} \quad \textbf{(42-17)}$$

The summation is the present value of the first $n$ years of FCFE, and the terminal value of $\text{FCFE}_{n+1}/(r - g)$ is discounted at the required rate of return on equity for $n$ years. The value per share is found by dividing the total value of equity by the number of outstanding shares.

In Equation 42-17, the terminal value of the stock at $t = n$ is found using the constant-growth FCFE model. In this case, $\text{TV}_n = \text{FCFE}_{n+1}/(r - g)$. Of course, the analyst might choose to estimate the terminal value, $\text{TV}_n$, another way, such as using a P/E multiplied by the company's forecasted EPS. The terminal value estimation is critical for a simple reason: The present value of the terminal value often represents a substantial portion of the total value of the stock. For example, in Equation 42-17 above, when calculating the total present value of the first $n$ cash flows (FCFE) and the present value of the terminal value, the latter is often substantial. In the examples that follow, the terminal value is usually very important. The same is true in practice.

### 4.3.1 Fixed Growth Rates in Stage 1 and Stage 2

The simplest two-stage FCFF or FCFE growth model has a constant growth rate in each stage. Example 16 finds the value of a firm that has a 20 percent sales growth rate in Stage 1 and a 6 percent sales growth rate in Stage 2.

### EXAMPLE 16

## A Two-Stage FCFE Valuation Model with a Constant Growth Rate in Each Stage

Uwe Henschel is doing a valuation of TechnoSchaft using the following information:

▶ Year 0 sales per share = €25.

▶ Sales growth rate = 20 percent annually for three years and 6 percent annually thereafter.

▶ Net profit margin = 10 percent forever.

▶ Net investment in fixed capital (net of depreciation) = 50 percent of the sales increase.

▶ Annual increase in working capital = 20 percent of the sales increase.

▶ Debt financing = 40 percent of the net investments in capital equipment and working capital.

▶ TechnoSchaft beta = 1.20, risk-free rate of return = 7 percent, equity risk premium = 4.5 percent.

The required rate of return for equity is

$$r = E(R_i) = R_F + \beta_i[E(R_M) - R_F] = 7\% + 1.2(4.5\%) = 12.4\%$$

Exhibit 15 shows the calculations for FCFE.

| EXHIBIT 15 | FCFE Estimates for TechnoSchaft | | | | | |
|---|---|---|---|---|---|---|
| Year | 1 | 2 | 3 | 4 | 5 | 6 |
| Sales growth rate | 20% | 20% | 20% | 6% | 6% | 6% |
| Sales per share | 30.000 | 36.000 | 43.200 | 45.792 | 48.540 | 51.452 |
| Net profit margin | 10% | 10% | 10% | 10% | 10% | 10% |
| Earnings per share | 3.000 | 3.600 | 4.320 | 4.579 | 4.854 | 5.145 |
| Net FCInv per share | 2.500 | 3.000 | 3.600 | 1.296 | 1.374 | 1.456 |
| WCInv per share | 1.000 | 1.200 | 1.440 | 0.518 | 0.550 | 0.582 |
| Debt financing per share | 1.400 | 1.680 | 2.016 | 0.726 | 0.769 | 0.815 |
| FCFE per share | 0.900 | 1.080 | 1.296 | 3.491 | 3.700 | 3.922 |
| Growth rate of FCFE | | 20% | 20% | 169% | 6% | 6% |

In the exhibit, sales grow at 20 percent annually for the first three years and then at 6 percent thereafter. Profits, which are 10 percent of sales, grow at the same rates. The net investments in fixed capital and working capital are 50 percent of the increase in sales and 20 percent of the increase in sales, respectively. New debt financing equals 40 percent of the total increase in net fixed capital and working capital. FCFE is EPS minus the net investment in fixed capital per share minus the investment in working capital per share plus the debt financing per share.

Notice that FCFE grows by 20 percent annually for the first three years. Then, between Year 3 and Year 4, when the sales growth rate drops from 20 percent to 6 percent, FCFE increases substantially. In fact, FCFE increases by 169 percent from Year 3 to Year 4. This large increase in FCFE occurs because profits grow at 6 percent but the investments in capital equipment and working capital (and the increase in debt financing) drop substantially from the previous year. In Years 5 and 6 in the table, sales, profit, investments, financing, and FCFE all grow at 6 percent.

The stock value is the present value of the first three years' FCFE plus the present value of the terminal value of the FCFE from Years 4 and later. The terminal value is

$$TV_3 = FCFE_4 / (r - g) = 3.491 / (0.124 - 0.06) = 54.55.$$

The present values are

$$V_0 = \frac{0.900}{1.124} + \frac{1.080}{(1.124)^2} + \frac{1.296}{(1.124)^3} + \frac{54.55}{(1.124)^3} = 0.801 + 0.855$$
$$+ \ 0.913 + 38.415 = €40.98.$$

The estimated value of this stock is €40.98 per share.

As mentioned previously, the terminal value may account for a large fraction of the value of a stock. For this case, the present value of the terminal value is €38.415 out of a total value of €40.98. The present value of the terminal value is almost 94 percent of the total value of TechnoSchaft stock.

### 4.3.2 Declining Growth Rates in Stage 1 and Constant Growth in Stage 2

Growth rates usually do not drop precipitously from one rate to another as they do between the stages in the two-stage model above, but growth rates can decline over time for many reasons. Sometimes, a small company has a high growth rate that is not sustainable as its market share increases. A highly profitable company also can attract competition that makes it harder for the company to sustain its high profit margins.

In this section, we present two examples of the two-stage model with declining growth rates in Stage 1. In the first example, the growth rate of EPS declines during Stage 1. As a company's profitability declines and the company is no longer generating very high returns, the company will usually reduce its net new investment in operating assets. The debt financing accompanying the new investments will also decline. It is not unusual for highly profitable, growing companies to have negative or low cash flows. Later, when growth in profits slows, investments will tend to slow and the company will experience positive cash flows. Of course, the negative cash flows incurred in the high-growth stage help determine the cash flows that occur in future years.

Example 17 below models FCFE per share as a function of EPS, which declines constantly during Stage 1. Because of declining earnings growth rates, the company in the example reduces its new investments over time as well. The value of the company depends on these free cash flows, which are substantial after the high-growth (and high-profitability) period has largely elapsed.

**EXAMPLE 17**

### A Two-Stage FCFE Valuation Model with Declining Net Income Growth in Stage 1

Vishal Noronha needs to prepare a valuation of Sindhuh Enterprises. Noronha has assembled the following information for his analysis. It is now the first day of 2008.

- ▶ EPS for 2007 is $2.40.
- ▶ For the next five years, the growth rate in EPS is given below. After 2012, the growth rate will be 7 percent.

| Year | 2008 | 2009 | 2010 | 2011 | 2012 |
|------|------|------|------|------|------|
| Growth rate for EPS | 30% | 18% | 12% | 9% | 7% |

- ▶ Net investment in fixed capital (net of depreciation) for the next five years are given below. After 2012, capital expenditures are expected to grow at 7 percent annually.

| Year | 2008 | 2009 | 2010 | 2011 | 2012 |
|------|------|------|------|------|------|
| Net capital expenditure per share | 3.000 | 2.500 | 2.000 | 1.500 | 1.000 |

- ▶ The investment in working capital each year will equal 50 percent of the net investment in capital items.
- ▶ Thirty percent of the net investment in fixed capital and investment in working capital will be financed with new debt financing.
- ▶ Current market conditions dictate a risk-free rate of 6.0 percent, an equity risk premium of 4.0 percent, and a beta of 1.10 for Sindhuh Enterprises.

**1.** What is the per-share value of Sindhuh Enterprises on the first day of 2008?

**2.** What should be the trailing P/E on the first day of 2008 and the first day of 2012?

**Solution to 1:** The required return for Sindhuh should be

$$r = E(R_i) = R_F + \beta_i[E(R_M) - R_F] = 6\% + 1.1\ (4\%) = 10.4\%.$$

The FCFEs for the company for years 2008 through 2012 are given in Exhibit 16.

| EXHIBIT 16 | FCFE Estimates for Sindhuh Enterprises | | | | |
|---|---|---|---|---|---|
| Year | 2008 | 2009 | 2010 | 2011 | 2012 |
| Growth rate for EPS | 30% | 18% | 12% | 9% | 7% |
| Earnings per share | $3.120 | $3.682 | $4.123 | $4.494 | $4.809 |
| Net FCInv per share | 3.000 | 2.500 | 2.000 | 1.500 | 1.000 |
| WCInv per share | 1.500 | 1.250 | 1.000 | 0.750 | 0.500 |
| Debt financing per share* | 1.350 | 1.125 | 0.900 | 0.675 | 0.450 |
| FCFE per share** | −0.030 | 1.057 | 2.023 | 2.919 | 3.759 |
| PV of FCFE discounted at 10.4% | −0.027 | 0.867 | 1.504 | 1.965 | |

*30 percent of (Net FCInv + WCInv)

**EPS − Net FCInv per share − WCInv per share + Debt financing per share

Earnings are $2.40 in 2007. Earnings increase each year by the growth rate given in the table. Net capital expenditures (capital expenditures minus depreciation) are the amounts that Noronha assumed. The increase in working capital each year is 50 percent of the increase in net capital expenditures. Debt financing is 30 percent of the total outlays for net capital expenditures and working capital each year. The FCFE each year is net income minus net capital expenditures minus increase in working capital plus new debt financing. Finally, for years 2008 through 2011, the present value of FCFE is found by discounting FCFE by the 10.4 percent required rate of return for equity.

After 2011, FCFE will grow by a constant 7 percent annually, so the constant growth FCFE valuation model can be used to value this cash flow stream. At the end of 2011, the value of the future FCFE is

$$V_{2011} = \frac{FCFE_{2012}}{r - g} = \frac{3.759}{0.104 - 0.07} = \$110.56$$

To find the present value of $V_{2011}$ as of the end of 2007, $V_{2007}$, we discount $V_{2011}$ at 10.4 percent for four years:

$$PV = 110.56/(1.104)^4 = \$74.425$$

The total present value of the company is the present value of the first four years' FCFE plus the present value of the terminal value, or

$$V_{2007} = -0.027 + 0.867 + 1.504 + 1.965 + 74.42 = \$78.73$$

**Solution to 2:** Using the estimated $78.73 stock value, the trailing P/E at the beginning of 2008 would be

$$P/E = 78.73/2.40 = 32.8$$

At the beginning of 2012, the expected stock value is $110.56 and the previous year's earnings per share is $4.494, so the trailing P/E at this time would be

$$P/E = 110.56/4.494 = 24.6$$

After its high-growth phase has ended, the P/E for the company declines substantially.

FCFE in this example was based on forecasts of future earnings per share. Analysts often model a company by forecasting future sales and then estimating the profits, investments, and financing associated with those sales levels. For large companies, analysts may estimate the sales, profitability, investments, and financing for each division or large subsidiary. The free cash flows for all of the divisions or subsidiaries are aggregated to get the free cash flow for the company as a whole.

Example 18 below is a two-stage FCFE model with declining sales growth rates in Stage 1, with profits, investments, and financing keyed to sales. In Stage 1, the growth rate of sales and the profit margin on sales both decline as the company matures and faces more competition and lower growth.

## EXAMPLE 18

### A Two-Stage FCFE Valuation Model with Declining Sales Growth Rates

Medina Werks has a competitive advantage that will probably deteriorate over time. Flavio Torino expects this deterioration to be reflected in declining sales growth rates as well as declining profit margins. To value the company, Torino has accumulated the following information:

▶ Current sales are $600 million. Over the next six years, the annual sales growth rate and the net profit margin are projected to be as follows:

| Year | 1 | 2 | 3 | 4 | 5 | 6 |
|---|---|---|---|---|---|---|
| Sales growth rate | 20% | 16% | 12% | 10% | 8% | 7% |
| Net profit margin | 14% | 13% | 12% | 11% | 10.50% | 10% |

Beginning in Year 6, the 7 percent sales growth rate and 10 percent net profit margin should persist indefinitely.

▶ Capital expenditures (net of depreciation) in the amount of 60 percent of the sales increase will be required each year.

▶ Investments in working capital equal to 25 percent of the sales increase will also be required each year.

▶ Debt financing will be used to fund 40 percent of the investments in net capital items and working capital.

▶ The beta for Medina Werks is 1.10. The risk-free rate of return is 6.0 percent and the equity risk premium is 4.5 percent.

▶ There are 70 million outstanding shares.

What is the estimated total market value of equity and the value per share?

The required return for Medina is

$$r = E(R_i) = R_F + \beta_i[E(R_M) - R_F] = 6\% + 1.10(4.5\%) = 10.95\%$$

The annual sales and net profit can be found readily as shown in Exhibit 17.

| EXHIBIT 17 | FCFE Estimates for Medina Werks | | | | | |
|---|---|---|---|---|---|---|
| **Year** | **1** | **2** | **3** | **4** | **5** | **6** |
| Sales growth rate | 20% | 16% | 12% | 10% | 8% | 7% |
| Net profit margin | 14% | 13% | 12% | 11% | 10.50% | 10% |
| Sales | 720.000 | 835.200 | 935.424 | 1028.966 | 1111.284 | 1189.074 |
| Net profit | 100.800 | 108.576 | 112.251 | 113.186 | 116.685 | 118.907 |
| Net FCInv | 72.000 | 69.120 | 60.134 | 56.125 | 49.390 | 46.674 |
| WCInv | 30.000 | 28.800 | 25.056 | 23.386 | 20.579 | 19.447 |
| Debt financing | 40.800 | 39.168 | 34.076 | 31.804 | 27.988 | 26.449 |
| FCFE | 39.600 | 49.824 | 61.137 | 65.480 | 74.703 | 79.235 |
| PV of FCFE at 10.95% | 35.692 | 40.475 | 44.763 | 43.211 | 44.433 | |

Sales increase each year by the sales growth rate shown. Net profit each year is the year's net profit margin times the year's sales. Capital investment (net of depreciation) equals 60 percent of the sales increase from the previous year. The investment in working capital is 25 percent of the sales increase from the previous year. The debt financing each year is equal to 40 percent of the total net investment in capital items and working capital for that year. FCFE is net income minus the net capital investment minus the working capital investment plus the debt financing. The present value of each year's FCFE is found by discounting FCFE at the required rate of return for equity, 10.95 percent.

In Year 6 and beyond, sales will increase at 7 percent annually. Net income will be 10 percent of sales, so net profit will also grow at a 7 percent annual rate. Because they are pegged to the 7 percent sales increase, the investments in capital items and working capital and debt financing will also grow at the same 7 percent rate. The amounts in Year 6 for net income, investment in capital items, investment in working capital, debt financing, and FCFE will grow at 7 percent.

The terminal value of FCFE in Year 6 and beyond is

$$TV_5 = \frac{FCFE_6}{r - g} = \frac{79.235}{0.1095 - 0.07} = 2{,}005.95 \text{ million}$$

The present value of this amount is

$$PV = 2{,}005.95/(1.1095)^5 = 1{,}193.12 \text{ million}$$

The estimated total market value of the firm is the present value of FCFE for Years 1 through 5 plus the present value of the terminal value: Market value = 35.692 + 40.475 + 44.763 + 43.211 + 44.433 + 1,193.12 = $1,401.69 million. Dividing by the 70 million outstanding shares gives the estimated value per share of $20.02.

## 4.4 Three-Stage Growth Models

Three-stage models are a straightforward extension of the two-stage models. One common version of a three-stage model is to assume a constant growth rate in each of the three stages. The growth rates could be for sales, and profits, investments in fixed and working capital, and external financing could be a function of the level of sales or changes in sales. A more simplistic model would apply the growth rate to FCFF or FCFE.

A second common model is a three-stage model with constant growth rates in Stages 1 and 3 and a declining growth rate in Stage 2. Again, the growth rates could be applied to sales or to FCFF or FCFE. Although it is unlikely that future FCFF and FCFE will follow the assumptions of either of these three-stage growth models, analysts often consider such models to provide useful approximations.

Example 19 is a three-stage FCFF valuation model with declining growth rates in Stage 2. The model is directly forecasting FCFF instead of deriving FCFF from a more complicated model that estimates cash flow from operations and investments in fixed capital and working capital. Because Marathon Oil spun off substantial assets in 2001, the analyst is unsure how much value remains in the company. Hence, he is updating his valuation of the firm with a new model and estimated parameters.

---

### EXAMPLE 19

#### A Three-Stage FCFF Valuation Model with Declining Growth in Stage 2

Charles Jones is evaluating Reliant Home Furnishings using a three-stage growth model. He has accumulated the following information:

► Current FCFF = $745 million

► Outstanding shares = 309.39 million

► Equity beta = 0.90, risk-free rate = 5.04 percent, and equity risk premium = 5.5 percent

► Cost of debt = 7.1 percent

► Marginal tax rate = 34 percent

► Capital structure = 20 percent debt, 80 percent equity

► Long term debt = $1.518 billion

► Growth rate of FCFF =

    ► 8.8 percent annually in Stage 1, Years 1−4

    ► 7.4 percent in Year 5, 6.0 percent in Year 6, 4.6 percent in Year 7

    ► 3.2 percent in Year 8 and thereafter

Using the information that Jones has accumulated, estimate the following:

**1.** WACC.

**2.** Total value of the firm.

**3.** Total value of equity.

**4.** Value per share.

**Solution to 1:** The required return for equity is

$$r = E(R_i) = R_F + \beta_i[E(R_M) - R_F] = 5.04\% + 0.9(5.5\%) = 9.99\%$$

WACC is

$$WACC = 0.20(7.1\%)(1 - 0.34) + 0.80(9.99\%) = 8.93\%$$

**Solution to 2:** Exhibit 18 displays the projected FCFF over the next eight years and the present values of each, discounted at 8.93 percent:

| EXHIBIT 18 | Forecasted FCFF for Reliant Home Furnishings | | | | | | | |
|---|---|---|---|---|---|---|---|---|
| Year | 1 | 2 | 3 | 4 | 5 | 6 | 7 | 8 |
| Growth rate | 8.80% | 8.80% | 8.80% | 8.80% | 7.40% | 6.00% | 4.60% | 3.20% |
| FCFF | 811 | 882 | 959 | 1,044 | 1,121 | 1,188 | 1,243 | 1,283 |
| PV at 8.93% | 744 | 743 | 742 | 741 | 731 | 711 | 683 | |

The terminal value at the end of Year 7 is

$$TV_7 = FCFF_8/(WACC - g) = 1,283/(0.0893 - 0.032) = \$22,391 \text{ million.}$$

The present value of this amount, discounted at 8.93 percent for seven years, is

$$PV \text{ of } TV_7 = 22,391/(1.0893)^7 = \$12,304 \text{ million}$$

The total present value of the first seven years' FCFF is \$5,097 million. The total value of the firm is \$12,304 million + \$5,097 million = \$17,401 million.

**Solution to 3:** The value of equity is the value of the firm minus the market value of debt: \$17,401 million − \$1,518 million = \$15,883 million.

**Solution to 4:** Dividing the equity value by the number of shares yields the value per share: \$15,883 million/309.39 million = \$51.33.

# 5     NON-OPERATING ASSETS AND FIRM VALUE

If a company has significant nonoperating assets such as excess cash, excess marketable securities, or land held for investment, then analysts often calculate the value of the firm as the value of its operating assets plus the value of its nonoperating assets:

$$\text{Value of firm} = \text{Value of operating assets} + \text{Value of nonoperating assets} \tag{42-18}$$

Recall that when calculating FCFF or FCFE, investments in working capital do not include any investments in cash and marketable securities. The value of cash and marketable securities should be added to the value of the company's operating assets to find the total firm value. Some companies have substantial noncurrent investments in stocks and bonds that are not operating subsidiaries but financial investments. These investments should be reflected at their current market value. Those securities reported at book values based on accounting conventions should be revalued to market values.

# SUMMARY

Discounted cash flow models are used widely by analysts to value companies.

▶ Free cash flow to the firm (FCFF) and free cash flow to equity (FCFE) are the cash flows available to all of the investors in the company and to common stockholders, respectively.

▶ Analysts like to use free cash flow as return (either FCFF or FCFE)
  ▶ if the company is not dividend paying,
  ▶ if the company is dividend paying but dividends differ significantly from the company's capacity to pay dividends,
  ▶ if free cash flows align with profitability within a reasonable forecast period with which the analyst is comfortable, or
  ▶ if the investor takes a control perspective.

▶ The FCFF valuation approach estimates the value of the firm as the present value of future FCFF discounted at the weighted average cost of capital (WACC):

$$\text{Firm value} = \sum_{t=1}^{\infty} \frac{\text{FCFF}_t}{(1 + \text{WACC})^t}$$

The value of equity is the value of the firm minus the value of the firm's debt:

$$\text{Equity value} = \text{Firm value} - \text{Market value of debt}$$

Dividing the total value of equity by the number of outstanding shares gives the value per share.

The WACC formula is

$$\text{WACC} = \frac{\text{MV(Debt)}}{\text{MV(Debt)} + \text{MV(Equity)}} r_d (1 - \text{Tax rate})$$

$$+ \frac{\text{MV(Equity)}}{\text{MV(Debt)} + \text{MV(Equity)}} r$$

▶ The value of the firm if FCFF is growing at a constant rate is

$$\text{Firm value} = \frac{\text{FCFF}_1}{\text{WACC} - g} = \frac{\text{FCFF}_0 (1 + g)}{\text{WACC} - g}$$

▶ With the FCFE valuation approach, the value of equity can be found by discounting FCFE at the required rate of return on equity ($r$):

$$\text{Equity value} = \sum_{t=1}^{\infty} \frac{\text{FCFE}_t}{(1 + r)^t}$$

Dividing the total value of equity by the number of outstanding shares gives the value per share.

▶ The value of equity if FCFE is growing at a constant rate is

$$\text{Equity value} = \frac{\text{FCFE}_1}{r - g} = \frac{\text{FCFE}_0 (1 + g)}{r - g}$$

▶ FCFF and FCFE are frequently calculated starting with net income:

FCFF = NI + NCC + Int(1−Tax rate) − FCInv − WCInv

FCFE = NI + NCC − FCInv − WCInv + Net borrowing

▶ FCFF and FCFE are related to each other as follows:

FCFE = FCFF − Int(1 − Tax rate) + Net borrowing

▶ FCFF and FCFE can be calculated starting from cash flow from operations:

FCFF = CFO + Int(1 − Tax rate) − FCInv

FCFE = CFO − FCInv + Net borrowing

▶ FCFF can also be calculated from EBIT or EBITDA

FCFF = EBIT(1 − Tax rate) + Dep − FCInv − WCInv

FCFF = EBITDA(1 − Tax rate) + Dep(Tax rate) − FCInv − WCInv

FCFE can then be found by using FCFE = FCFF − Int(1 − Tax rate) + Net borrowing.

▶ Finding CFO, FCFF, and FCFE can require careful interpretation of corporate financial statements. In some cases, the needed information may not be transparent.

▶ Earnings components such as net income, EBIT, EBITDA, and CFO should not be used as cash flow measures to value a firm. These earnings components either double-count or ignore parts of the cash flow stream.

▶ More-complicated capital structures, such as those with preferred stock, are easily adapted to find FCFF or FCFE.

▶ A general expression for the two-stage FCFF valuation model is

$$\text{Firm value} = \sum_{t=1}^{n} \frac{\text{FCFF}_t}{(1 + \text{WACC})^t} + \frac{\text{FCFF}_{n+1}}{(\text{WACC} - g)} \frac{1}{(1 + \text{WACC})^n}$$

▶ A general expression for the two-stage FCFE valuation model is

$$\text{Equity value} = \sum_{t=1}^{n} \frac{\text{FCFE}_t}{(1 + r)^t} + \frac{\text{FCFE}_{n+1}}{r - g} \frac{1}{(1 + r)^n}$$

▶ One common two-stage model assumes a constant growth rate in each stage, and a second common model assumes declining growth in Stage 1 followed by a long-run sustainable growth rate in Stage 2.

▶ To forecast FCFF and FCFE, analysts build a variety of models of varying complexity. A common approach is to forecast sales, with profitability, investments, and financing derived from changes in sales.

▶ Three-stage models are often considered to be good approximations for cash flow streams that, in reality, fluctuate from year to year.

▶ Nonoperating assets such as excess cash and marketable securities, noncurrent investment securities, and nonperforming assets are usually segregated from the company's operating assets. They are valued separately and then added to the value of the company's operating assets to find total firm value.

# PRACTICE PROBLEMS FOR READING 42

1. Indicate the effect on this period's FCFF and FCFE of a change in each of the items listed below. Assume a $100 increase in each case and a 40 percent tax rate.

   A. Net income.

   B. Cash operating expenses.

   C. Depreciation.

   D. Interest expense.

   E. EBIT.

   F. Accounts receivable.

   G. Accounts payable.

   H. Property, plant, and equipment.

   I. Notes payable.

   J. Cash dividends paid.

   K. Proceeds from issuing new common shares.

   L. Common stock share repurchases.

2. LaForge Systems, Inc. has net income of $285 million for the year 2003. Using information from the company's financial statements below, show the adjustments to net income that would be required to find:

   A. FCFF, and

   B. FCFE.

   C. In addition, show the adjustments to FCFF that would result in FCFE.

## LaForge Systems, Inc. Balance Sheet

| In Millions | 31 December 2007 | 2008 |
|---|---|---|
| **Assets** | | |
| **Current assets** | | |
| Cash and equivalents | $ 210 | $ 248 |
| Accounts receivable | 474 | 513 |
| Inventory | 520 | 564 |
| Total current assets | 1,204 | 1,325 |
| Gross fixed assets | 2,501 | 2,850 |
| Accumulated depreciation | (604) | (784) |
| Net fixed assets | 1,897 | 2,066 |
| **Total assets** | $3,101 | $3,391 |

**Liabilities and shareholders' equity**

**Current liabilities**

| | | |
|---|---|---|
| Accounts payable | $ 295 | $ 317 |
| Notes payable | 300 | 310 |
| Accrued taxes and expenses | 76 | 99 |
| Total current liabilities | 671 | 726 |
| Long-term debt | 1,010 | 1,050 |
| Common stock | 50 | 50 |
| Additional paid-in capital | 300 | 300 |
| Retained earnings | 1,070 | 1,265 |
| Total shareholders' equity | 1,420 | 1,615 |
| Total liabilities and shareholders' equity | $3,101 | $3,391 |

## Statement of Income

| In Millions, except Per Share Data | 31 December 2008 |
|---|---|
| Total revenues | $2,215 |
| Operating costs and expenses | 1,430 |
| EBITDA | 785 |
| Depreciation | 180 |
| EBIT | 605 |
| Interest expense | 130 |
| Income before tax | 475 |
| Taxes (at 40 percent) | 190 |
| Net income | 285 |
| Dividends | 90 |
| Addition to retained earnings | 195 |

## Statement of Cash Flows

| In Millions | 31 December 2008 |
|---|---|
| **Operating activities** | |
| Net income | $ 285 |
| Adjustments | |
| Depreciation | 180 |
| Changes in working capital | |
| Accounts receivable | (39) |
| Inventories | (44) |
| Accounts payable | 22 |
| Accrued taxes and expenses | 23 |
| Cash provided by operating activities | $427 |

**Investing activities**

| | |
|---|---|
| Purchases of fixed assets | 349 |
|   Cash used for investing activities | $349 |

**Financing activities**

| | |
|---|---|
| Notes payable | (10) |
| Long-term financing issuances | (40) |
| Common stock dividends | 90 |
|   Cash used for financing activities | $40 |
| Cash and equivalents increase (decrease) | 38 |
| Cash and equivalents at beginning of year | 210 |
| Cash and equivalents at end of year | $248 |

**Supplemental cash flow disclosures**

| | |
|---|---|
| Interest paid | $130 |
| Income taxes paid | $190 |

**3.** For LaForge Systems, whose financial statements are given in Problem 2 above, show the adjustments from the current levels of CFO (which is 427), EBIT (605), and EBITDA (785) to find

  **A.** FCFF, and

  **B.** FCFE.

**4.** The term "free cash flow" is frequently applied to cash flows that differ from the definition for FCFF that should be used to value a firm. Two such definitions of "free cash flow" are given below. Compare the definitions given for FCF to FCFF.

  **A.** FCF = Net income + Depreciation and amortization − Cash dividends − Capital expenditures.

  **B.** FCF = Cash flow from operations (from the statement of cash flows) − Capital expenditures.

**5.** Proust Company has FCFF of $1.7 billion and FCFE of $1.3 billion. Proust's WACC is 11 percent and its required rate of return for equity is 13 percent. FCFF is expected to grow forever at 7 percent and FCFE is expected to grow forever at 7.5 percent. Proust has debt outstanding of $15 billion.

  **A.** What is the total value of Proust's equity using the FCFF valuation approach?

  **B.** What is the total value of Proust's equity using the FCFE valuation approach?

6. Quinton Johnston is evaluating TMI Manufacturing Co., Ltd. headquartered in Taiwan. In 2008, when Johnston is performing his analysis, the company is unprofitable. Furthermore, TSM pays no dividends on its common shares. Johnston decides to value TSM using his forecasts of FCFE and makes the following assumptions:

   ► The company has 17.0 billion outstanding shares.

   ► Sales will be $5.5 billion in 2009, increasing at 28 percent annually for the next four years (through 2013).

   ► Net income will be 32 percent of sales.

   ► Investment in fixed assets will be 35 percent of sales, investment in working capital will be 6 percent of sales, and depreciation will be 9 percent of sales.

   ► 20 percent of the investment in assets will be financed with debt.

   ► Interest expenses will be only 2 percent of sales.

   ► The tax rate will be 10 percent.

   ► TSM's beta is 2.1, the risk-free government bond rate is 6.4 percent, and the equity risk premium is 5.0 percent.

   ► At the end of 2013, Johnston projects TMI Manufacturing Co. will sell for 18 times earnings.

   What is the value of one ordinary share of TMI Manufacturing Co., Ltd.?

7. Do Pham is evaluating Phaneuf Accelerateur using the FCFF and FCFE valuation approaches. Pham has collected the following information (currency in euros):

   ► Phaneuf has net income of 250 million, depreciation of 90 million, capital expenditures of 170 million, and an increase in working capital of 40 million.

   ► Phaneuf will finance 40 percent of the increase in net fixed assets (capital expenditures less depreciation) and 40 percent of the increase in working capital with debt financing.

   ► Interest expenses are 150 million. The current market value of Phaneuf's outstanding debt is 1,800 million.

   ► FCFF is expected to grow at 6.0 percent indefinitely, and FCFE is expected to grow at 7.0 percent.

   ► The tax rate is 30 percent.

   ► Phaneuf is financed with 40 percent debt and 60 percent equity. The before-tax cost of debt is 9 percent and the before-tax cost of equity is 13 percent.

   ► Phaneuf has 10 million outstanding shares.

   A. Using the FCFF valuation approach, estimate the total value of the firm, the total market value of equity, and the value per share.

   B. Using the FCFE valuation approach, estimate the total market value of equity and the value per share.

**8.** PHB Company currently sells for $32.50 per share. In an attempt to determine if PHB is fairly priced, an analyst has assembled the following information:

▶ The before-tax required rates of return on PHB debt, preferred stock, and common stock are 7.0 percent, 6.8 percent, and 11.0 percent, respectively.

▶ The company's target capital structure is 30 percent debt, 15 percent preferred stock, and 55 percent common stock.

▶ The market value of the company's debt is $145 million, and its preferred stock is valued at $65 million.

▶ PHB's FCFF for the year just ended is $28 million. FCFF is expected to grow at a constant rate of 4 percent for the foreseeable future.

▶ The tax rate is 35 percent.

▶ PHB has 8 million outstanding common shares.

What is PHB's estimated value per share? Is PHB's stock underpriced?

**9.** Watson Dunn is planning to value BCC Corporation using a single-stage FCFF approach. BCC provides a variety of industrial metals and minerals. The financial information Dunn has assembled for his valuation is as follows:

▶ The company has 1,852 million shares outstanding.

▶ Market value of debt is $3.192 billion.

▶ FCFF is currently $1.1559 billion.

▶ Equity beta is 0.90, the equity risk premium is 5.5 percent, and the risk-free rate is 5.5 percent.

▶ The before-tax cost of debt is 7.0 percent.

▶ The tax rate is 40 percent.

▶ To calculate WACC, assume the company is financed 25 percent with debt.

▶ FCFF growth rate is 4 percent.

Using Dunn's information, calculate the following:

**A.** WACC.

**B.** Value of the firm.

**C.** Total market value of equity.

**D.** Value per share.

**10.** Kenneth McCoin is valuing McInish Corporation and performing a sensitivity analysis on his valuation. He uses a single-stage FCFE growth model. The "base case" values for each of the parameters in the model are given in the table below, along with possible "low" and "high" estimates for each variable.

| Variable | Base Case Value | Low Estimate | High Estimate |
|---|---|---|---|
| Normalized $FCFE_0$ | $0.88 | $0.70 | $1.14 |
| Risk-free rate | 5.08% | 5.00% | 5.20% |
| Equity risk premium | 5.50% | 4.50% | 6.50% |
| Beta | 0.70 | 0.60 | 0.80 |
| FCFE growth rate | 6.40% | 4.00% | 7.00% |

**A.** Use the base case values to estimate the current value of McInish Corporation.

**B.** Calculate the range of stock prices that would occur if the base case value for $FCFE_0$ were replaced by the low and high estimate for $FCFE_0$. Similarly, using the base case values for all other variables, calculate the range of stock prices caused by using the low and high values for beta, the risk-free rate, the equity risk premium, and the growth rate. Rank the sensitivity of the stock price to each of the five variables based on these ranges.

**11.** An aggressive financial planner who claims to have a superior method for picking undervalued stocks is courting one of your clients. The planner claims that the best way to find the value of a stock is to divide EBITDA by the risk-free bond rate. The planner is urging your client to invest in NewMarket, Inc. The planner says that NewMarket's EBITDA of $1,580 million divided by the long-term government bond rate of 7 percent gives a total value of $22,571 million. With 318 million outstanding shares, NewMarket's value per share using this method is $70.98. Shares of NewMarket currently trade for $36.50, and the planner wants your client to make a large investment in Alcan through him.

**A.** Provide your client with an alternative valuation of NewMarket based on a two-stage FCFE valuation approach. Use the following assumptions:

▶ Net income is currently $600 million. Net income will grow by 20 percent annually for the next three years.

▶ The net investment in operating assets (capital expenditures less depreciation plus investment in working capital) will be $1,150 million next year and grow at 15 percent for the following two years.

▶ Forty percent of the net investment in operating assets will be financed with net new debt financing.

▶ NewMarket's beta is 1.3, the risk-free bond rate is 7 percent, and the equity risk premium is 4 percent.

▶ After three years, the growth rate of net income will be 8 percent and the net investment in operating assets (capital expenditures minus depreciation plus increase in working capital) each year will drop to 30 percent of net income.

▶ Debt is, and will continue to be, 40 percent of total assets.

▶ NewMarket has 318 million outstanding shares.

Find the value per share of NewMarket.

**B.** Criticize the valuation approach that the aggressive financial planner used.

**12.** Bron has earnings per share of $3.00 in 2002 and expects earnings per share to increase by 21 percent in 2003. Earnings per share are expected to grow at a decreasing rate for the following five years, as shown in the table below. In 2008, the growth rate will be 6 percent and is expected to stay at that rate thereafter. Net capital expenditures (capital expenditures minus depreciation) will be $5.00 per share in 2002 and then follow the pattern predicted in the table. In 2008, net capital expenditures are expected to be $1.50 and will then grow at 6 percent annually. The investment in working capital parallels the increase in net capital expenditures and is predicted to equal 25 percent of net capital expenditures each year. In 2008, investment in working capital will be $0.375 and is predicted to grow at 6 percent thereafter. Bron will use debt financing to fund 40 percent of net capital expenditures and 40 percent of the investment in working capital.

| Year | 2003 | 2004 | 2005 | 2006 | 2007 | 2008 |
|---|---|---|---|---|---|---|
| Growth rate for earnings per share | 21% | 18% | 15% | 12% | 9% | 6% |
| Net capital expenditure per share | $5.00 | $5.00 | $4.50 | $4.00 | $3.50 | $1.50 |

The required rate of return for Bron is 12 percent. Find the value per share using a two-stage FCFE valuation approach.

**13.** The management of Telluride, an international diversified conglomerate based in the United States, believes that the recent strong performance of its wholly owned medical supply subsidiary, Sundanci, has gone unnoticed. To realize Sundanci's full value, Telluride announced that it will divest Sundanci in a tax-free spinoff.

Sue Carroll, CFA, is Director of Research at Kesson and Associates. In developing an investment recommendation for Sundanci, Carroll has gathered the information shown in Exhibits P-1 and P-2 below.

| EXHIBIT P-1 | Sundanci Actual 1999 and 2000 Financial Statements for Fiscal Years Ending 31 May (in Millions, except Per-Share Data) | |
| --- | --- | --- |
| **Income Statement** | **1999** | **2000** |
| Revenue | $474 | $598 |
| Depreciation | 20 | 23 |
| Other operating costs | 368 | 460 |
| Income before taxes | 86 | 115 |
| Taxes | 26 | 35 |
| Net income | 60 | 80 |
| Dividends | 18 | 24 |
| Earnings per share | $0.714 | $0.952 |
| Dividends per share | $0.214 | $0.286 |
| Common shares outstanding | 84.0 | 84.0 |
| **Balance Sheet** | **1999** | **2000** |
| Current assets (includes $5 cash in 1999 and 2000) | $201 | $326 |
| Net property, plant, and equipment | 474 | 489 |
| Total assets | 675 | 815 |
| Current liabilities (all non-interest bearing) | 57 | 141 |
| Long-term debt | 0 | 0 |
| Total liabilities | | |
| Shareholders' equity | 618 | 674 |
| Total liabilities and equity | 675 | 815 |
| Capital expenditures | 34 | 38 |

| EXHIBIT P-2 | Selected Financial Information |
| --- | --- |
| Required rate of return on equity | 14% |
| Industry growth rate | 13% |
| Industry P/E | 26 |

Abbey Naylor, CFA, has been directed by Carroll to determine the value of Sundanci's stock using the FCFE model. Naylor believes that Sundanci's FCFE will grow at 27 percent for two years, and 13 percent thereafter. Capital expenditures, depreciation, and working capital are all expected to increase proportionately with FCFE.

**A.** Calculate the amount of FCFE per share for 2000 using the data from Exhibit P-1 above. Show your work.

**B.** Calculate the current value of a share of Sundanci stock based on the two-stage FCFE model. Show your work.

**C.** Describe limitations that the two-stage DDM and FCFE models have in common.

**14.** John Jones, CFA, is head of the research department of Peninsular Research. One of the companies he is researching, Mackinac Inc., is a U.S.-based manufacturing company. Mackinac has released its June 2001 financial statements, shown in Exhibits P-3, P-4, and P-5.

| EXHIBIT P-3 | Mackinac Inc. Annual Income Statement 30 June 2001 (in Thousands, except Per-Share Data) |
|---|---|

| | |
|---|---|
| Sales | $250,000 |
| Cost of goods sold | 125,000 |
| Gross operating profit | 125,000 |
| Selling, general, and administrative expenses | 50,000 |
| EBITDA | 75,000 |
| Depreciation and amortization | 10,500 |
| EBIT | 64,500 |
| Interest expense | 11,000 |
| Pretax income | 53,500 |
| Income taxes | 16,050 |
| Net income | $37,450 |
| Shares outstanding | 13,000 |
| EPS | $2.88 |

| EXHIBIT P-4 | Mackinac Inc. Balance Sheet 30 June 2001 (in Thousands) |
|---|---|

**Current Assets**

| | | |
|---|---|---|
| Cash and equivalents | $20,000 | |
| Receivables | 40,000 | |
| Inventories | 29,000 | |
| Other current assets | 23,000 | |
| Total current assets | | $112,000 |

*(Exhibit continued on next page . . .)*

| EXHIBIT P-4 | (continued) |
|---|---|

**Noncurrent Assets**

| | | | |
|---|---|---|---|
| Property, plant, and equipment | $145,000 | | |
| Less: Accumulated depreciation | 43,000 | | |
| Net property, plant, and equipment | | 102,000 | |
| Investments | | 70,000 | |
| Other noncurrent assets | | 36,000 | |
| Total noncurrent assets | | | 208,000 |
| Total assets | | | $320,000 |

**Current Liabilities**

| | | |
|---|---|---|
| Accounts payable | $41,000 | |
| Short-term debt | 12,000 | |
| Other current liabilities | 17,000 | |
| Total current liabilities | | $70,000 |

**Noncurrent Liabilities**

| | | |
|---|---|---|
| Long-term debt | 100,000 | |
| Total noncurrent liabilities | | 100,000 |
| Total liabilities | | 170,000 |

**Shareholders' Equity**

| | | |
|---|---|---|
| Common equity | 40,000 | |
| Retained earnings | 110,000 | |
| Total equity | | 150,000 |
| Total liabilities and equity | | $320,000 |

| EXHIBIT P-5 | Mackinac Inc. Cash Flow Statement 30 June 2001 (in Thousands) |
|---|---|

**Cash Flow from Operating Activities**

| | | |
|---|---|---|
| Net income | | $37,450 |
| Depreciation and amortization | | 10,500 |

**Change in Working Capital**

| | | |
|---|---|---|
| (Increase) Decrease in receivables | ($5,000) | |
| (Increase) Decrease in inventories | (8,000) | |
| Increase (Decrease) in payables | 6,000 | |
| Increase (Decrease) in other current liabilities | 1,500 | |
| Net change in working capital | | (5,500) |
| Net cash from operating activities | | $42,450 |

*(Exhibit continued on next page . . .)*

---

**EXHIBIT P-5** **(continued)**

**Cash Flow from Investing Activities**

| | | |
|---|---:|---:|
| Purchase of property, plant, and equipment | ($15,000) | |
| Net cash from investing activities | | ($15,000) |

**Cash Flow from Financing Activities**

| | | |
|---|---:|---:|
| Change in debt outstanding | $4,000 | |
| Payment of cash dividends | (22,470) | |
| Net cash from financing activities | | (18,470) |
| Net change in cash and cash equivalents | | $8,980 |
| Cash at beginning of period | | 11,020 |
| Cash at end of period | | $20,000 |

---

Mackinac has announced that it has finalized an agreement to handle North American production of a successful product currently marketed by a foreign company. Jones decides to value Mackinac using the dividend discount model (DDM) and the free cash flow-to-equity (FCFE) model. After reviewing Mackinac's financial statements above and forecasts related to the new production agreement, Jones concludes the following:

▶ Mackinac's earnings and FCFE are expected to grow 17 percent a year over the next three years before stabilizing at an annual growth rate of 9 percent.

▶ Mackinac will maintain the current payout ratio.

▶ Mackinac's beta is 1.25.

▶ The government bond yield is 6 percent, and the market equity risk premium is 5 percent.

A. Calculate the value of a share of Mackinac's common stock using the two-stage DDM. Show your calculations.

B. Calculate the value of a share of Mackinac's common stock using the two-stage FCFE model. Show your calculations.

C. Jones is discussing with a corporate client the possibility of that client acquiring a 70 percent interest in Mackinac. Discuss whether the DDM or FCFE model is more appropriate for this client's valuation purposes.

**15.** SK Telecom Co. is a cellular telephone paging and computer communication services company in Seoul, South Korea. The company is traded on the Korea, New York, and London stock exchanges (NYSE: SKM). Sol Kim has estimated the normalized FCFE for SK Telecom to be 1,300 Korean won (per share) for the year just ended. The real country return for South Korea is 6.50 percent. To estimate the required return for SK Telecom, the adjustments to the real country return are an industry adjustment of +0.60 percent, a size adjustment of −0.10 percent, and a leverage adjustment of +0.25 percent. The long-term real growth rate for South Korea is estimated at 3.5 percent, and Kim expects the real growth rate of SK Telecom to track the country rate.

  **A.** What is the real required rate of return for SK Telecom?

  **B.** Using the single-stage FCFE valuation model and real values for the discount rate and FCFE growth rate, estimate the value of one share of SK Telecom.

**16.** Lawrence McKibben is preparing a valuation of QuickChange Auto Centers, Inc. McKibben has decided to use a three-stage FCFE valuation model and the following estimates. The FCFE per share for the current year is $0.75. FCFE is expected to grow at 10 percent for next year, then at 26 percent annually for the following three years, and then grow at 6 percent in Year 5 and thereafter. QuickChange's estimated beta is 2.00, and McKibben feels that current market conditions dictate a 4.5 percent risk-free rate of return and a 5.0 percent equity risk premium. Given McKibben's assumptions and approach, what is the value of QuickChange?

**17.** Clay Cooperman has valued the operating assets of Johnson Extrusion at $720 million. The company also has short-term cash and securities with a market value of $60 million. The noncurrent investments have a book value of $30 million and a market value of $45 million. The company also has an overfunded pension plan, with plan assets of $210 million and plan liabilities of $170 million. Johnson Extrusion has $215 million of notes and bonds outstanding and 100 million outstanding shares. What is the value per share?

# Use the following information to answer Questions 18–23

Ryan Leigh is preparing a presentation that analyzes the valuation of the common stock of two companies under consideration as additions to his firm's recommended list. Leigh is using the Gordon growth model to value the common stock of the first company, Emerald Corporation, and a free cash flow to equity (FCFE) model to value the common stock of the second company, Holt Corporation. Holt's 2007 and 2008 financial statements, contained in Exhibits 1 and 2, are prepared in accordance with U.S. GAAP. Holt Corporation currently pays a dividend and has stated that future dividend growth will not exceed growth in free cash flow to equity.

Leigh presents his valuations of the common stock of Emerald and Holt to his supervisor, Alice Smith. Smith has the following questions and comments:

  **1.** "For purpose of establishing Emerald's long-term dividend growth rate, I estimate that Emerald's long-term expected dividend payout rate is 20 percent and its return on equity is 10 percent over the long-term."

  **2.** "Why did you use a FCFE model to value Holt's common stock? Can you use a dividend discount model instead?"

| EXHIBIT 1 | Holt Corporation Consolidated Balance Sheets (US$ Millions) | | | |
|---|---|---|---|---|
| At 31 December | | 2008 | | 2007 |
| **Assets** | | | | |
| **Current assets** | | | | |
| Cash and cash equivalents | | $ 372 | | $ 315 |
| Accounts receivable | | 770 | | 711 |
| Inventories | | 846 | | 780 |
| Total current assets | | 1,988 | | 1,806 |
| Gross fixed assets | 4,275 | | 3,752 | |
| Less: Accumulated depreciation | 1,176 | 3,099 | 906 | 2,846 |
| **Total assets** | | $5,087 | | $4,652 |
| **Liabilities and shareholders' equity** | | | | |
| **Current liabilities** | | | | |
| Accounts payable | | $476 | | $443 |
| Accrued taxes and expenses | | 149 | | 114 |
| Notes payable | | 465 | | 450 |
| Total current liabilities | | 1,090 | | 1,007 |
| Long-term debt | | 1,575 | | 1,515 |
| Common stock | | 525 | | 525 |
| Retained earnings | | 1,897 | | 1,605 |
| **Total liabilities and shareholders' equity** | | $5,087 | | $4,652 |

3. "How did Holt's FCFE for 2008 compare with its free cash flow to the firm (FCFF) for the same year? I recommend you to use a FCFF model to value Holt's common stock instead of using FCFE because Holt has had a history of leverage changes in the past."

4. "In the last three years, about 5 percent of Holt's growth in FCFE has come from decreases in inventory."

Leigh responds to each of Smith's points as follows:

1. "I will use your estimates and calculate Emerald's long-term, sustainable dividend growth rate."

2. "There are two reasons why I used the FCFE model to value Holt's common stock instead of using a dividend discount model. The first reason is that Holt's dividends differ significantly from its capacity to pay dividends. The second reason is that Holt is a takeover target and once the company is taken over, the new owners will have discretion over free cash flow."

3. "I will calculate Holt's FCFF for 2008 and estimate the value of Holt's common stock using a FCFF model."

4. "Holt is a growing company. In forecasting Holt's free cash flow to equity growth rate I will not consider decreases in inventory as being a long-term source of growth in FCFE."

| EXHIBIT 2 | Holt Corporation Consolidated Income Statement for the Year Ended 31 December 2008 (US$ Millions) |
|---|---|

| | 2008 |
|---|---|
| Total revenues | $ 3,323 |
| Cost of goods sold | 1,287 |
| Selling, general, and administrative expenses | 858 |
| Earnings before interest, taxes, depreciation, and amortization (EBITDA) | 1,178 |
| Depreciation expense | 270 |
| Operating income | 908 |
| Interest expense | 195 |
| Pretax income | 713 |
| Income tax (at 32%) | 228 |
| Net income | $ 485 |

**18.** Which of the following long-term free cash flow to equity growth rates is *most* consistent with the facts and stated policies of Emerald?

   **A.** 5 percent or lower.

   **B.** 2 percent or higher.

   **C.** 8 percent or higher.

**19.** Do the reasons provided by Leigh support his use of the FCFE model to value Holt's common stock instead of using a dividend discount model?

   **A.** Yes.

   **B.** No, because Holt's dividend situation argues in favor of using the DDM.

   **C.** No, because FCFE is not appropriate for investors taking a control perspective.

**20.** Holt's FCFF (millions) for 2008 is *closest* to:

   **A.** $308.

   **B.** $370.

   **C.** $422.

**21.** Holt's FCFE (millions) for 2008 is *closest* to:

   **A.** $175.

   **B.** $250.

   **C.** $364.

**22.** Leigh's comment about not considering decreases in inventory to be a source of long-term growth in free cash flow to the firm for Holt is:

    **A.** inconsistent with a forecasting perspective.

    **B.** mistaken because decreases in inventory are a use rather than a source of cash.

    **C.** consistent with a forecasting perspective because inventory reduction has a limit, particularly for a growing firm.

**23.** Smith's recommendation to use a FCFF model to value Holt is:

    **A.** logical, given the prospect of Holt changing capital structure.

    **B.** not logical because the FCFF is only used to value the total firm.

    **C.** not logical because FCFE represents a more direct approach to free cash flow valuation.

## Use the following information to answer Questions 24–29

Gabriela Cervera is a new equity analyst at Mita Asset Management (MAM). Cervera's supervisor has asked her to prepare valuations of two companies—Geo, Inc. and Raylord Corporation—to present at an upcoming investment policy committee meeting. The supervisor states that MAM would like to assess the value that a prospective acquirer would pay to take control of the companies. He asks Cervera to consider the following models and advise the committee as to which model is most appropriate for Geo:

▶ Free cash flow model

▶ Gordon growth model

▶ Residual income model

▶ Two-stage dividend discount model

Geo pays a constant dividend of $2.00 and is expected to do so for the foreseeable future regardless of the growth in earnings or cash flow. Cervera expects Geo's free cash flow to equity to grow at 8 percent per year for the next five years and 4 percent per year thereafter. Geo's financial statements reveal that the clean surplus relation does not hold.

    Cervera estimates that Raylord's dividends will grow at an initial rate of 12 percent with the growth rate declining linearly over a 4-year period to a final and perpetual growth rate of 5 percent. Raylord's free cash flow to equity is expected to grow at 11 percent for the next three years and 4 percent thereafter. Financial data for Raylord are presented in Exhibit 1.

| EXHIBIT 1 | Financial Data for Raylord Corporation |
|---|---|
| Current free cash flow to equity (in millions) | $850 |
| Capital expenditures (in millions) | $150 |
| Current dividend per share | $1.50 |
| Required return for equity | 12.5% |
| Percentage of equity | 100% |
| Percentage of debt | 0% |
| Current price per share | $67 |

Cervera prepares analyses based on the dividend discount model and the discounted free cash flow model for Raylord.

In preparation for the meeting with the investment policy committee, Cervera writes a note on the application of free cash flow models, part of which is reproduced in Exhibit 2.

| EXHIBIT 2 | Free Cash Flow Valuation Note |
|---|---|

The computation of a company's current-year free cash flow to equity is not affected by:

a) paying cash dividends in that year.

b) new debt issuances in that year.

A year later, Geo announces a change in dividend policy from a constant dollar dividend to a constant payout ratio. Cervera decides to perform a computation of sustainable growth to determine whether the current growth rate assumptions are appropriate. Cervera creates a long-term forecast for Geo as presented in Exhibit 3.

| EXHIBIT 3 | Long-Term Forecast Information for Geo, Inc. |
|---|---|

| | |
|---|---|
| Net profit margin | 5% |
| Asset turnover | 1.25 |
| Financial leverage (assets/equity) | 2.00 |
| Dividend payout ratio | 40% |
| Income tax rate | 30% |

**24.** Given Geo's initial circumstances, which model is most appropriate for valuing Geo's equity?

　　**A.** Free cash flow model.

　　**B.** Gordon growth model.

　　**C.** Two-stage dividend discount model.

**25.** Using the H-model version of the discounted dividend approach, Raylord's equity value per share is closest to:

　　**A.** $22.24.

　　**B.** $23.80.

　　**C.** $25.48.

**26.** Compared with free cash flow to equity (FCFE), Raylord's free cash flow to the firm (FCFF) and cash flow from operating activities (CFO), respectively, are most likely to be:

|     | FCFF      | CFO    |
|-----|-----------|--------|
| A.  | higher    | lower  |
| B.  | the same  | lower  |
| C.  | the same  | higher |

**27.** Using a free cash flow to equity model, the total value of Raylord's equity (in millions) is closest to:

A.  $ 9,990.

B.  $11,360.

C.  $12,470.

**28.** Regarding the effect of cash dividends and new debt issuances, respectively, on free cash flow to equity, Cervera's note (Exhibit 2) is:

|     | Cash Dividends | New Debt Issuances |
|-----|----------------|--------------------|
| A.  | correct        | correct            |
| B.  | correct        | incorrect          |
| C.  | incorrect      | incorrect          |

**29.** Based on Exhibit 3, the best estimate of the sustainable growth rate for Geo is:

A.  5.25%.

B.  6.00%.

C.  7.50%.

# Questions 30–35 relate to Alcorp and are based on Readings 41 and 42

Bo Chow and Shen Xue are competing investment bankers presenting acquisition candidates to a private equity investor, Simon Lieu.

Chow: "I recommend Alcorp, a France-based producer of branded luxury goods. Because Alcorp is entering the mature phase of its life cycle, I have used the Gordon growth model, the two-stage dividend discount model, and the H-model for dividends (data provided in Exhibit 1) to estimate its intrinsic value. Not only do all three models indicate that Alcorp is significantly undervalued, the management of Alcorp recently confirmed that fiscal 2009 revenue and earnings growth estimates are on target."

Lieu: "Chow, based on the Gordon growth model, what is your estimate of the market-implied expected rate of return for Alcorp as of 31 December 2008?"

| EXHIBIT 1 | Chow's Input Data and Assumptions for Alcorp |
|---|---|

**Company Data**

▶ Financial statements prepared in accordance with U.S. GAAP.

▶ Required rate of return on equity = 10.00 percent.

▶ 2008 annual dividend €2.00 per share.

▶ Average 5-year ROE (2004 − 2008) = 20.00 percent.

▶ Average 5-year payout ratio (2004 − 2008) = 40.00 percent.

▶ Average 5-year earnings growth (2004 − 2008) = 10.00 percent.

▶ Stock price at 31 December 2008 = €35.00.

**Gordon Growth Model**

▶ Dividends will grow at 8.00 percent per year indefinitely.

**Two Stage Dividend Discount Model**

▶ Dividends grow at 8.00 percent annually from 2009–2011 (3 years), and then by 5.00 percent annually, thereafter.

**H-Model**

▶ Dividends grow at 8.25 percent in 2009.

▶ The dividend growth rate will decline linearly over a 5-year period to a perpetual growth rate of 5.00 percent.

Xue: "I recommend Benido, S.p.A., an Italy-based designer, producer, and marketer of fashion accessories. I used a free cash flow approach to estimate its intrinsic value (Exhibit 2). I think Benido is significantly undervalued on both a free cash flow to the firm (FCFF) and a free cash flow to equity (FCFE) basis. In addition, the company is entering the growth phase of its life cycle."

| EXHIBIT 2 | Xue's Input Data and Assumptions for Benido, S.p.A. |
|---|---|

**Company Data**

- Financial statements are prepared in accordance with U.S. GAAP.
- FCFF in 2008 was €2.2 million.
- Cash flow from operations (CFO) in 2008 was €2 million.
- Benido is financed with 30 percent debt and 70 percent equity based on market value. The pre-tax cost of debt is 7.25 percent and the cost of equity is 10.25 percent.
- Net borrowings in 2008 decreased by €750,000 (debt was reduced).
- The tax rate is 40 percent.
- Investment in fixed capital during 2008 was €320,000.
- The value of Benido's non-operating assets is not significant.
- Market value of debt outstanding is €11.91 million.
- Benido has 230,000 shares outstanding.

**Free Cash Flow Approach**

- FCFF is expected to grow by 3.5 percent indefinitely.
- FCFE is expected to grow by 2.5 percent indefinitely.

---

Lieu asks Xue: "When is it appropriate to use the free cash flow model instead of the dividend discount model?"

**30.** Regarding Lieu's question about the market-implied expected rate of return, Chow's best response is:

   **A.** 14.17%.

   **B.** 16.17%.

   **C.** 16.29%.

**31.** Using the two-stage dividend discount model, the estimated value of Alcorp's common stock (per share) on 31 December 2008 is closest to:

   **A.** 42.00.

   **B.** 45.53.

   **C.** 49.18.

**32.** Using the H-model for dividends, the estimated value of Alcorp's common stock (per share) on 31 December 2008 is closest to:

   **A.** 45.25.

   **B.** 46.55.

   **C.** 48.50.

**33.** Using the FCFF approach, the estimated intrinsic value of Benido's common stock (per share) on 31 December 2008 is closest to:

   **A.** 94.88.

   **B.** 140.29.

   **C.** 147.01.

**34.** Using the FCFE approach, the estimated value of Benido's common stock (per share) on 31 December 2008 is closest to:

   **A.** 52.17.

   **B.** 53.47.

   **C.** 96.61.

**35.** Which of the following is the best response to Lieu's question about the free cash flow and dividend discount models?

   **A.** When the company's payout ratio is low.

   **B.** When the investor takes a control perspective.

   **C.** When the company is entering the growth phase of its life cycle.

$23\frac{3}{8}$  24

$4\frac{5}{8}$  $4\frac{11}{16}$  ...

$5\frac{1}{2}$  $5\frac{1}{2}$ $-$ $\frac{3}{8}$

$5\frac{1}{2}$  $5\frac{1}{2}$ $-$ $\frac{1}{16}$

$20\frac{5}{8}$  $21\frac{13}{16}$ $-$ $\frac{1}{8}$

$17\frac{3}{8}$  $18\frac{1}{8}$ $+$ $\frac{7}{8}$

$6\frac{1}{2}$  $6\frac{1}{2}$ $-$ $\frac{1}{2}$

$7\frac{1}{4}$  $\frac{15}{16}$  $31\frac{1}{32}$ $-$ $\frac{1}{8}$

$\frac{9}{16}$  $\frac{9}{16}$

$1\frac{1}{32}$  $7\frac{13}{16}$  $7\frac{15}{16}$

$7\frac{15}{16}$

$2\frac{5}{8}$  $2\frac{11}{32}$  $2\frac{1}{2}$ $+$

$2\frac{3}{4}$  $2\frac{1}{4}$  $2\frac{1}{4}$

$12\frac{1}{16}$  $11\frac{3}{8}$  $11\frac{3}{4}$ $+$

87  $33\frac{3}{4}$  33  $33\frac{1}{4}$ $-$

$25\frac{5}{8}$  $24\frac{9}{16}$  $25\frac{3}{8}$ $+$

$12$  $11\frac{5}{8}$  $11\frac{5}{8}$ $+$

16  $10\frac{1}{2}$  $10\frac{1}{2}$  $10\frac{1}{4}$ $-$

78  $15\frac{7}{8}$  $15\frac{13}{16}$  $15\frac{7}{8}$ $-$

$9\frac{1}{16}$  $8\frac{1}{4}$  $8\frac{3}{8}$ $+$

$11\frac{1}{4}$  $10\frac{1}{8}$  $10\frac{1}{4}$

# MARKET-BASED VALUATION: PRICE MULTIPLES

by John D. Stowe, CFA, Thomas R. Robinson, CFA, Jerald E. Pinto, CFA, and Dennis W. McLeavey, CFA

## LEARNING OUTCOMES

| The candidate should be able to: | Mastery |
|---|:---:|
| **a.** distinguish between the method of comparables and the method based on forecasted fundamentals as approaches to using price multiples in valuation, and discuss the economic rationales for each approach; | ☐ |
| **b.** define a justified price multiple; | ☐ |
| **c.** discuss rationales for using each price multiple and dividend yield in valuation, discuss possible drawbacks to the use of each price multiple and dividend yield, and calculate each price multiple and dividend yield; | ☐ |
| **d.** calculate underlying earnings given earnings per share (EPS) and nonrecurring items in the income statement and discuss the methods of normalizing EPS, and calculate normalized EPS by each method; | ☐ |
| **e.** explain and justify the use of earnings yield (E/P); | ☐ |
| **f.** discuss the fundamental factors that influence each price multiple and dividend yield; | ☐ |
| **g.** calculate the justified price-to-earnings ratio (P/E), price-to-book ratio (P/B), and price-to-sales ratio (P/S) for a stock, based on forecasted fundamentals; | ☐ |
| **h.** calculate a predicted P/E, given a cross-sectional regression on fundamentals, and explain limitations to the cross-sectional regression methodology; | ☐ |
| **i.** define the benchmark value of a multiple; | ☐ |
| **j.** evaluate a stock by the method of comparables using each of the price multiples and explain the importance of fundamentals in using the method of comparables; | ☐ |
| **k.** calculate the P/E-to-growth ratio (PEG), and explain its use in relative valuation; | ☐ |
| **l.** calculate and explain the use of price multiples in determining terminal value in a multi-stage discounted cash flow (DCF) model; | ☐ |
| **m.** discuss alternative definitions of cash flow used in price multiples, and explain the limitations of each definition; | ☐ |

|  |  |  |
|---|---|---|
| **n.** | discuss the sources of differences in cross-border valuation comparisons; | ☐ |
| **o.** | describe the main types of momentum indicators and their use in valuation. | ☐ |

## 1  INTRODUCTION

Among the most familiar and widely used valuation tools are price multiples. **Price multiples** are ratios of a stock's market price to some measure of value per share. The intuition behind price multiples is that we cannot evaluate a stock's price—judge whether it is fairly valued, overvalued, or undervalued—without knowing what a share buys in terms of assets, earnings, or some other measure of value. As valuation indicators (measures or indicators of value), price multiples have the appealing qualities of simplicity in use and ease in communication. A price multiple summarizes in a single number the valuation relationship between a stock's price and a familiar quantity such as earnings, sales, or book value per share. Among the questions we will study in this reading that will help us use price multiples professionally are the following:

▶ What accounting issues affect particular price multiples, and how can analysts address them?

▶ How do price multiples relate to fundamentals, such as earnings growth rates, and how can analysts use this information when making valuation comparisons among stocks?

▶ For which types of valuation problems is a particular price multiple appropriate or inappropriate?

▶ What challenges arise in applying price multiples internationally?

According to surveys of professional practice, **momentum indicators** are popular. These relate either price or a fundamental (such as earnings) to the time series of its own past values, or in some cases to its expected value. The logic behind the use of momentum indicators is the proposition that such indicators may provide information on future patterns of returns over some time horizon. Because the purpose of valuation is to help select rewarding investments, momentum indicators are also a class of valuation indicators, with a focus different from and complementary to that of price multiples.

The reading is organized as follows: In Section 2, we put the use of price multiples in its economic context and present certain themes common to the use of any price multiple. We then begin a treatment of individual ratios: Section 3 presents price-to-earnings multiples (P/Es), Section 4 presents price-to-book multiples (P/Bs), Section 5 presents price-to-sales multiples (P/Ss), and Section 6 presents price-to-cash flow multiples.

Enterprise value is the total market value of all sources of financing including common stock (a more technical definition will follow); EBITDA (earnings before interest, tax, depreciation, and amortization) is an accounting concept related to cash flow from operations. We present valuation using the ratio of enterprise value to EBITDA in Section 7. Dividends in relation to price have been used as a valuation indicator. Because the ratio of price to dividends is not defined for stocks that do not pay dividends, we discuss valuation in terms of dividend yield (D/P) in Section 8. Section 9 presents issues in using price multiples internationally. In Section 10, we turn to a discussion of momentum valuation indicators. We present some practical aspects of using valuation indicators in investment management in Section 11, and we conclude with a summary of the reading.

# PRICE MULTIPLES IN VALUATION

2

In practice, analysts use price multiples in two ways: the method of comparables and the method based on forecasted fundamentals. Each of these methods relates to a definite economic rationale. In this section, we introduce the two methods and their associated economic rationales.

The idea behind price multiples is that we need to evaluate a stock's price in relation to what it buys in terms of earnings, assets, or some other measure of value. Obtained by dividing price by a measure of value per share, a price multiple gives the price to purchase one unit of value, however value is measured. For example, a price-to-sales ratio of 2 means that it takes two units of currency (for example, €2) to buy one unit of sales (for example, €1 of sales).

This scaling of price per share by value per share also makes comparisons possible among different stocks. For example, an investor pays more for a unit of sales for a stock with a P/S of 2.5 than for another stock with a P/S of 2. If the securities are otherwise closely similar (if they have similar risk, profit margins, and growth prospects, for example), the investor might conclude that the second security is undervalued relative to the first.

So, price multiples are price scaled by a measure of value, which provides the basis for the method of comparables. The **method of comparables** involves using a price multiple to evaluate whether an asset is relatively fairly valued, relatively undervalued, or relatively overvalued when compared to a benchmark value of the multiple. The word *relatively* is necessary. An asset may be undervalued relative to a comparison asset or group of assets, and an analyst may expect the asset to outperform the comparison asset or assets on a relative basis. If the comparison asset or assets themselves are not efficiently priced, however, the stock may not be undervalued—it could be fairly valued or even overvalued (on an absolute basis).

Many choices for the benchmark value of a multiple have appeared in stock valuation, including the multiple of a closely matched individual stock as well as the average or median value of the multiple for the stock's company or industry peer group. The economic rationale underlying the method of comparables is the law of one price—the economic principle that two identical assets should sell at the same price.[1] The method of comparables is perhaps the most widely used approach for analysts reporting valuation judgments on the basis of price multiples.

---

[1] In practice, analysts can at best only approximately match characteristics across companies. To keep our classification simple, we treat comparisons with a market index and with historical values of a stock's multiple under the rubric of the method of comparables. Nevertheless, the law of one price is the idea driving the method of comparables.

Because cash flows are related to fundamentals, we can also relate multiples to company fundamentals through a discounted cash flow (DCF) model. Expressions for price multiples in terms of fundamentals permit analysts to examine how valuation differences across stocks relate to different expectations concerning fundamentals such as earnings growth rates.

Recall that DCF models view the intrinsic value of stock as the present value of all its expected future returns or cash flows. Fundamentals—characteristics of a business related to profitability or financial strength—drive cash flows. Price multiples are calculated with respect to a single value of a fundamental, such as earnings per share (EPS). For example, we calculate what we will later discuss as a leading price–earnings multiple (P/E) on the basis of a forecast of EPS for the next year. Despite being stated with respect to only a single value of a fundamental, we can relate any price multiple to the entire future stream of expected cash flows through its DCF value. We do this by first taking the present value of the stream of expected future cash flows; we then divide that present value by the fundamental (e.g., forecasted EPS).

For example, if the DCF value of a U.K. stock is GBP10.20 and forecasted EPS is GBP1.2, the P/E consistent with the DCF value is GBP10.20/GBP1.2 = 8.5. We can do this exercise using any DCF model (defining cash flows as dividends, free cash flow, or residual income) and any definition of price multiple. We illustrated this concept in the reading on discounted dividend valuation, where we explained P/E in terms of perhaps the simplest DCF model, the Gordon growth dividend discount model, in an expression that includes the expected dividend growth rate (among other variables). We call the approach relating a price multiple to fundamentals through a DCF model the **method based on forecasted fundamentals**.[2] DCF valuation, because it incorporates forecasts of all future returns or cash flows, is the most basic valuation approach in theory. That characteristic of DCF models and the possibility of relating price multiples to DCF models provide the economic rationale for the method based on forecasted fundamentals.

We can also usefully incorporate the insights from the method based on forecasted fundamentals in explaining valuation differences based on comparables, because we seldom find other than approximate comparables. In the sections covering each multiple, we will present the method based on forecasted fundamentals first so we can refer to it when using the method of comparables.

In summary, we can approach valuation using multiples from two perspectives. First, we can use the method of comparables, which involves comparing a stock's multiple to a standard of comparison. Similar assets should sell at similar prices. Second, we can use the method based on forecasted fundamentals, which involves forecasting the stock's fundamentals rather than making comparisons with other stocks. The price multiple of an asset should be related to the prospective cash flows from holding it.

Using either method, how can an analyst express his view of the value of a stock? Of course the analyst can offer just the qualitative judgment that the stock appears to be fairly valued, overvalued, or undervalued (and offer definite reasons for the view). The analyst may also be more precise, communicating a **justified price multiple** for the stock: the estimated fair value of that multiple.[3] An analyst can justify a multiple based on the method of comparables or the method based on forecasted fundamentals.

---

[2] For brevity, we sometimes use the phrase "based on fundamentals" in describing multiples calculated according to this approach.

[3] The justified price multiple is also called the **warranted price multiple** or the **intrinsic price multiple**.

For example, suppose that we are using the price-to-book multiple (P/B) in a valuation and that the mean P/B for the company's peer group, the standard of comparison, is 2.3. The stock's justified P/B, based on the method of comparables, is 2.3 (without making possible adjustments for differences in fundamentals). We can compare the justified with the actual P/B based on market price to form an opinion on value. If the justified P/B is larger (smaller) than the actual P/B, the stock may be undervalued (overvalued). We can also translate the justified P/B based on comparables into an estimate of absolute fair value of the stock, on the assumption that the comparison assets are fairly priced. If the current book value per share is $23, then the fair value of the stock is 2.3 × $23 = $52.90, which can be compared with its market price.

On the other hand, suppose that on the basis of a residual income model valuation, the DCF value of the stock is $46. Then the justified P/B based on forecasted fundamentals is $46/$23 = 2.0, which we can again compare with the actual value of the stock's ratio. We can also state our estimate of the stock's absolute fair value as 2 × $23 = $46. (Note that the analyst could report valuation judgments related to a DCF model in terms of the DCF value directly; however, price multiples are a familiar form in which to state valuations.)

In the next section, we begin our discussion of specific implementations of the price multiple approach to valuation.

## PRICE TO EARNINGS      3

In the first edition of *Security Analysis*, Benjamin Graham and David L. Dodd (1934, p. 351) described common stock valuation based on P/Es as the standard method of that era, and the price-to-earnings ratio is doubtless still the most familiar valuation measure today.

We begin our discussion of the P/E with rationales offered by analysts for its use, as well as possible drawbacks. We then define the two chief variations of the P/E: the trailing P/E and the leading P/E. The multiple's numerator, market price, is (as in other multiples) definitely determinable; it presents no special problems of interpretation. But the denominator, EPS, is based on the complex rules of accrual accounting and presents important interpretation issues. We discuss those issues and the adjustments analysts can make to obtain more meaningful P/Es. Finally, we conclude the section by examining how analysts use P/Es to value a stock using the method of forecasted fundamentals and the method of comparables. As mentioned earlier, we discuss fundamentals first so that we can draw from that discussion's insights when using comparables.

Analysts have offered several rationales for using P/Es:

▶ Earnings power is a chief driver of investment value, and EPS, the denominator of the P/E ratio, is perhaps the chief focus of security analysts' attention. In Block's 1999 survey of AIMR members, earnings ranked first among four variables—earnings, cash flow, book value, and dividends—as an input in valuation.

▶ The P/E ratio is widely recognized and used by investors.

▶ Differences in P/Es may be related to differences in long-run average returns, according to empirical research.[4]

---

[4] Block (1999) documented a belief among AIMR members that low-P/E stocks tend to outperform the market. See Bodie, Kane, and Marcus (2001) for a brief summary of the related academic research, which has wide ramifications and is the subject of continuing active debate.

Drawbacks to using P/Es derive from the characteristics of EPS:

▶ EPS can be negative, and the P/E ratio does not make economic sense with a negative denominator.

▶ The ongoing or recurring components of earnings are the most important in determining intrinsic value. Earnings often have volatile, transient components, however, making the analyst's task difficult.

▶ Management can exercise its discretion within allowable accounting practices to distort EPS as an accurate reflection of economic performance. Distortions can affect the comparability of P/Es across companies.

Analysts have developed methods to attempt to address these potential drawbacks, and we will discuss these methods later. In the next section, we discuss the definition and calculation of EPS for use in P/Es.

## 3.1 Determining Earnings

In calculating a P/E, the current price for publicly traded companies is generally easily obtained and unambiguous. Determining the earnings figure to be used in the denominator, however, is not as straightforward. The following two issues must be considered:

▶ the time horizon over which earnings are measured, which results in two chief alternative definitions of the P/E; and

▶ adjustments to accounting earnings that the analyst may make, so that P/Es can be compared across companies.

The two chief alternative definitions of P/E are trailing P/E and leading P/E. A stock's **trailing P/E** (sometimes referred to as a **current P/E**) is its current market price divided by the most recent four quarters' EPS. In such calculations, EPS is sometimes referred to as trailing 12 months (TTM) EPS. Trailing P/E is the P/E published in financial newspapers' stock listings. The **leading P/E** (also called the **forward P/E** or **prospective P/E**) is a stock's current price divided by next year's expected earnings. Other names and time horizon definitions also exist: First Call/Thomson Financial reports as the "current P/E" a stock's market price divided by the last reported annual EPS; Value Line reports as the "P/E" a stock's market price divided by the sum of the preceding two quarters' trailing earnings and the next two quarters' expected earnings.

In using the P/E, the same definition should be applied to all companies and time periods under examination. Otherwise the P/Es are not comparable, either for a given company over time or for different companies at a specific point in time. The differences in P/E calculated using different methods could be systematic (as opposed to random). For example, for companies with rising earnings, the leading P/E will be smaller than the trailing P/E because the denominator in the leading P/E calculation will be larger.

Logic sometimes indicates that a particular definition of the P/E is not relevant. For example, a major acquisition or divestiture may change the nature of a business so that the trailing P/E based on past EPS is not informative about the future and thus not relevant to a valuation. In such a case, the leading P/E is the appropriate measure. Valuation is a forward-looking process and the analyst, when she has earnings forecasts, usually features the leading P/E in analyses. If a company's future earnings are not readily predictable, however, then a trailing P/E (or alternative valuation metric) may be more appropriate. In the following sections, we address issues that arise in calculating trailing and leading P/Es.

### 3.1.1 Calculating the Trailing P/E

When calculating a P/E using trailing earnings, care must be taken in determining the EPS used in the denominator. An analyst must consider the following:

▶ transitory, nonrecurring components of earnings that are company specific;

▶ transitory components of earnings due to cyclicality (business or industry cyclicality);

▶ differences in accounting methods; and

▶ potential dilution of EPS.

Example 1 illustrates the first bullet point. Items in earnings that are not expected to recur in the future (nonrecurring earnings) are generally removed by analysts. Such items are not expected to reappear in future earnings, and valuation looks to the future as concerns cash flows. The analyst's focus is on estimating **underlying earnings**: earnings excluding nonrecurring components.[5] An increase in underlying earnings reflects an increase in earnings that the analyst expects to persist into the future.

### EXAMPLE 1

**Adjusting EPS for Nonrecurring Items**

You are calculating a trailing P/E for American Electric Power (NYSE: AEP) as of 9 November 2001, when the share price closed at $44.50. In its fiscal year ended 31 December 2000, AEP recorded EPS of $0.83 that included an extraordinary loss of $0.11. Additionally, AEP took an expense of $203 million for merger costs during that calendar year, which are not expected to recur, and had unusual deficits in two out of four quarters. As of November 2001, the trailing twelve months' EPS was $2.16, including three quarters in 2001 and one quarter in 2000. The fourth quarter of calendar year 2000 had $0.69 per share in nonrecurring expenses. Without making an adjustment for nonrecurring items, the trailing P/E was $44.50/$2.16 = 20.6. Adjusting for these items, you arrive at a figure for trailing EPS of $2.85 using an underlying earnings concept, and a trailing P/E of $44.50/$2.85 = 15.6. This number is the P/E an analyst would use in valuation, being consistent in the treatment of earnings for all stocks under review. In the course of this reading, we will illustrate adjustments to earnings in many examples.

The identification of nonrecurring items often requires detailed work, in particular the examination of the income statement, the footnotes to the income statement, and management's discussion and analysis. The analyst cannot rely only on income statement classifications in identifying the nonrecurring components of earnings. Nonrecurring items (for example, gains and losses from the

---

[5] Other names for underlying earnings include **persistent earnings**, **continuing earnings**, and **core earnings**.

sale of assets, asset write-downs, provisions for future losses, and changes in accounting estimates) often appear in the income from continuing operations portion of a business's income statement.[6] An analyst taking the income statement classification at face value could draw incorrect conclusions in a valuation.

Besides company-specific effects such as restructuring costs, transitory effects on earnings can come from business-cycle or industry-cycle influences, as stated in the second bullet point above. These effects are somewhat different in nature. Because business cycles repeat, such effects (although transitory) can be expected to recur over subsequent cycles.

Because of cyclic effects, the most recent four quarters of earnings may not accurately reflect the average or long-term earnings power of the business, particularly for **cyclical businesses**—businesses with high sensitivity to business- or industry-cycle influences. Trailing EPS for such stocks are often depressed or negative at the bottom of the cycle and unusually high at the top of the cycle. Empirically, P/Es for cyclical companies are often highly volatile over a cycle without any change in business prospects: high P/Es on depressed EPS at the bottom of the cycle and low P/Es on unusually high EPS at the top of the cycle, a countercyclical property of P/Es known as the **Molodovsky effect**.[7] Analysts address this problem by normalizing EPS—that is, calculating the level of EPS that the business could achieve currently under mid-cyclical conditions (**normalized earnings per share** or **normal earnings per share**).[8] Two of several available methods to calculate normal EPS are as follows:

▶ *The method of historical average EPS.* Normal EPS is calculated as average EPS over the most recent full cycle.

▶ *The method of average return on equity.* Normal EPS is calculated as the average return on equity (ROE) from the most recent full cycle, multiplied by current book value per share.

The first method is one of several possible statistical approaches to the problem of cyclical earnings; however, this method does not account for changes in the business's size. The second alternative, by using recent book value per share, reflects more accurately the effect on EPS of growth or shrinkage in the company's size. For that reason, the method of average ROE is sometimes preferred.[9] When reported current book value does not adequately reflect company size in relation to past values (because of items such as large write-downs), the analyst can make the appropriate accounting adjustment. The analyst can also estimate normalized earnings by multiplying total assets by an estimate of the long-run return on total assets.[10]

---

[6] An asset **write-down** is a reduction in the value of an asset as stated in the balance sheet. The timing and amount of write-downs often are at least in part discretionary. **Accounting estimates** include the useful lives of assets (depreciable lives), warranty costs, and the amount of uncollectible receivables.

[7] Named after Nicholas Molodovsky, who wrote on this subject in the 1950s. We can state the Molodovsky effect another way: P/Es may be negatively related to the recent earnings growth rate but positively related to the anticipated future growth rate, because of expected rebounds in earnings.

[8] The wording is based on a definition in Kisor and Whitbeck (1963, p. 57). Some writers describe the removal of any one-time or nonrecurring items from earnings as normalizing earnings as well.

[9] This approach has appeared in valuation research, as in Michaud (1999), who calculated a normalized earnings yield rather than a normalized P/E. (Earnings yield is earnings per share divided by price.)

[10] An example of the application of this method is Lee, Myers, and Swaminathan (1999), who used 6 percent of total assets as an estimate of normal earnings levels when current earnings for a company were negative, in their study of the intrinsic value of the Dow Jones Industrial Average, a U.S. equity index. According to the authors, the long-run return on total assets in the United States is approximately 6 percent.

### EXAMPLE 2

#### Normalizing EPS for Business-Cycle Effects

You are researching the valuation of Koninklijke Philips Electronics N.V. (NYSE: PHG), Europe's largest electronics company, as of the beginning of November 2001. On 8 November 2001, PHG stock closed at $25.72. PHG experienced a severe cyclical contraction in its Consumer Electronics division in 2001, resulting in a loss of $1.94 per share; you thus decide to normalize earnings. You believe the 1995–2000 period (which excludes 2001) reasonably captures average profitability over a business cycle. Table 1 supplies data on EPS, book value per share (BVPS), and return on equity (ROE).[11]

| TABLE 1 Koninklijke Philips (EPS and BVPS in U.S. Dollars) | | | | | | | |
|---|---|---|---|---|---|---|---|
| | **2001** | **2000** | **1999** | **1998** | **1997** | **1996** | **1995** |
| EPS | (1.94) | 2.11 | 1.15 | 0.87 | 1.16 | 0.55 | 1.14 |
| BVPS | 13.87 | 16.62 | 9.97 | 11.68 | 6.57 | 6.43 | 6.32 |
| ROE | NM | 0.129 | 0.104 | 0.072 | 0.168 | 0.083 | 0.179 |

NM = not meaningful.
*Sources:* www.philips.com for 2001 data; *The Value Line Investment Survey* for other data.

Using the data in Table 1,

1. Calculate a normal EPS for PHG based on the method of historical average EPS, and then calculate the P/E based on that estimate of normal EPS.

2. Calculate a normal EPS for PHG based on the method of average ROE and the P/E based on that estimate of normal EPS.

3. Explain the source of the differences in the normal EPS calculated by the two methods, and contrast the impact on the estimate of a normal P/E.

**Solution to 1:** Averaging EPS over the 1995–2000 period, we find that ($1.14 + $0.55 + $1.16 + $0.87 + $1.15 + $2.11)/6 = $1.16. According to the method of historical average EPS, PHG's normal EPS is $1.16. The P/E based on this estimate is $25.72/1.16 = 22.2.

**Solution to 2:** Averaging ROE over the 1995–2000 period, we find that (0.179 + 0.083 + 0.168 + 0.072 + 0.104 + 0.129)/6 = 0.1225, or 12.25%. For current BVPS, we use the 2001 value of $13.87. According to the method of average ROE, we have 0.1225 × $13.87 = $1.70 as normal EPS. The P/E based on this estimate is $25.72/$1.70 = 15.1.

---

[11] EPS and BVPS are based on EUR/USD translation rates for 2001 and 2000 and on Dutch guilder/USD translation rates for earlier years, as given by Value Line.

**Solution to 3:** From 1995 to 2001, BVPS increased from $6.32 to $13.87, an increase of about 219 percent. The estimate of $1.70 from the average ROE method compared with $1.16 from the historical average EPS method reflects the use of information on the current size of the company. Because of that difference, PHG appears more conservatively valued (as indicated by a lower P/E) using the method based on average ROE.

We also need to adjust EPS for differences in accounting methods between the company and its standard of comparison or benchmark, so that the P/Es are comparable.

### EXAMPLE 3

**Adjusting for Differences in Accounting Methods**

In late October 1999, Coachmen Industries (NYSE: COA) was trading at a price of $16 per share and had trailing twelve months EPS of $1.99. COA's P/E was thus 8.04. At the same time, Winnebago Industries (NYSE: WGO) was trading at a price of $17 per share and had trailing twelve months EPS of $1.99 for a P/E of 8.54. COA uses the first-in, first-out (FIFO) method of accounting for its inventory. WGO uses the last-in, first-out (LIFO) method of accounting for its inventory. Adjusting WGO's results for differences between the LIFO and FIFO methods produces an adjusted EPS of $2.02 and an adjusted P/E of 8.42. Adjusting EPS for WGO for consistency with COA's inventory accounting method narrows the difference between the two companies' P/Es.

In addition to adjustments for nonrecurring items and accounting methods, the analyst should consider the impact of potential dilution on EPS.[12] Companies are required to present both basic EPS and diluted EPS. **Basic earnings per share** reflects total earnings divided by the weighted-average number of shares actually outstanding during the period. **Diluted earnings per share** reflects division by the number of shares that would be outstanding if holders of securities such as executive stock options, equity warrants, and convertible bonds exercised their options to obtain common stock.

---

[12] Dilution refers to the reduction in the proportional ownership interests as a result of the issuance of new shares.

**EXAMPLE 4**

**Basic versus Diluted Earnings per Share**

For the fiscal year ended 31 June 2001, Microsoft (Nasdaq NMS: MSFT) had basic EPS of $1.38 and diluted EPS of $1.32. Based on a stock price of $60 shortly after the release of the annual report, Microsoft's trailing P/E is 43.5 using basic EPS and 45.5 using diluted EPS.

Two issues concerning P/Es that relate to their use in investment management and research are (1) negative earnings and (2) look-ahead bias in calculating trailing P/Es. (**Look-ahead bias** is the use of information that is not contemporaneously available in computing a quantity.)

Stock selection disciplines that use P/Es or other price multiples often involve ranking stocks from highest value of the multiple to lowest value of the multiple. The security with the lowest positive P/E has the lowest purchase cost per currency unit of earnings among the securities ranked. Negative earnings, however, result in a negative P/E. A negative-P/E security will rank below the lowest positive-P/E security but, because earnings are negative, the negative-P/E security is actually the most costly in terms of earnings purchased.[13]

Negative P/Es are not meaningful. In some cases, an analyst might handle negative EPS by using normal EPS in its place. Also, when trailing EPS is negative, year-ahead EPS and thus the leading P/E may be positive. If the analyst is interested in a ranking, an available solution (applicable to any ratio involving a quantity that can be negative or zero) is to restate the ratio with price in the denominator, because price is never negative.[14] In the case of the P/E, the associated ratio is E/P, the **earnings yield** ratio. Ranked by earnings yields from highest to lowest, the securities are correctly ranked from cheapest to most costly in terms of the amount of earnings one unit of currency buys.

Table 2 illustrates the above points for a group of personal computer manufacturers, three of which have negative EPS. When reporting a P/E based on negative earnings, analysts should report such P/Es as NM (not meaningful).

Investment analysts often research investment strategies involving P/Es and other price multiples using historical data. When doing so, analysts must be aware that time lags in the reporting of financial results create the potential for look-ahead bias in the research. For example, as of early January 2003, most companies have not reported EPS for the last quarter of 2002, so a trailing P/E would be based on EPS for first, second, and third quarters of 2002 and the last quarter of 2001. An investment strategy based on a trailing P/E calculated using actual EPS for the last quarter of 2002 could be examined with hindsight, but because the portfolio manager could not implement the strategy in practice, it would involve look-ahead bias. The correction is to calculate the trailing P/E based on four quarters of EPS, lagged by a sufficient amount of time relative to the time at

---

[13] Some research indicates that stocks with negative P/Es have special risk-return characteristics (see Fama and French 1992), so care should be exercised in interpreting such rankings.

[14] Earnings yield can be based on normal EPS and expected next-year EPS as well as on trailing EPS. In these cases too, earnings yield provides a consistent ranking.

| TABLE 2 | P/E and E/P for Four Personal Computer Manufacturers (as of 13 November 2001; in U.S. Dollars) | | | |
|---|---|---|---|---|
| | Current Price | Trailing EPS | Trailing P/E | E/P |
| Dell Computer Corporation (Nasdaq NMS: DELL) | 26.00 | 0.49 | 53.06 | 1.9% |
| Apple Computer (Nasdaq NMS: AAPL) | 19.20 | −0.11 | NM | −0.6% |
| Compaq Computer Corporation (NYSE: CPQ) | 8.59 | −0.40 | NM | −4.7% |
| Gateway (NYSE: GTW) | 8.07 | −3.15 | NM | −39.0% |

*Source:* Morningstar, Inc.

which stock price is observed, so that the EPS information would be contemporaneously available. The same principle applies to other multiples calculated on a trailing basis.

### 3.1.2 Calculating a Leading P/E

In the definition of leading P/E, analysts have interpreted "next year's expected earnings" as:

► expected EPS for the next four quarters; or

► expected EPS for the next fiscal year.

We can take the first definition, which is closest to how cash flows are dated in our discussion of DCF valuation, as what we understand by leading P/E, unless stated otherwise.[15] To illustrate the calculation, suppose the current market price of a stock is $15 as of 1 March 2003, and the most recently reported quarterly EPS (for the quarter ended 31 December 2002) is $0.22. Your forecasts of EPS are as follows:

► $0.15 for the quarter ending 31 March 2003

► $0.18 for the quarter ending 30 June 2003

► $0.18 for the quarter ending 30 September 2003

► $0.24 for the quarter ending 31 December 2003

The sum of the forecasts for the next four quarters to report is $0.15 + $0.18 + $0.18 + $0.24 = $0.75, and the leading P/E for this stock is $15/$0.75 = 20.0.

For examples of the fiscal year concept, First Call/Thomson Financial reports a stock's "forward P/E" (leading P/E) in two ways: first, based on the

---

[15] Analysts have developed DCF expressions incorporating fractional time periods. In practice, uncertainty in forecasts is the more limiting factor to accuracy in estimating justified P/Es.

## EXAMPLE 5

### Calculating a Leading P/E Ratio (1)

A market price for the common stock of American Electric Power (NYSE: AEP) in mid-November 2001 was $44.55. AEP's fiscal year coincides with the calendar year. According to Zacks Investment Research, the consensus EPS forecast for 2001 (FY1 as of November 2001) was $3.87. The consensus EPS forecast for 2002 (FY2 as of November 2001) was $3.69.

1. Calculate AEP's leading P/E based on a fiscal year definition and FY1 consensus forecasted EPS.
2. Calculate AEP's leading P/E based on a fiscal year definition and FY2 consensus forecasted EPS.

**Solution to 1:** AEP's leading P/E is $44.55/$3.87 = 11.5 based on FY1 forecasted EPS. Note that this EPS number involves the forecast of only one quarter as of November 2001.

**Solution to 2:** AEP's leading P/E is $44.55/$3.69 = 12.1 based on FY2 forecasted EPS.

mean of analysts' current fiscal year (FY1 = Fiscal Year 1) forecasts, in which analysts may have actual EPS in hand for some quarters; and second, based on analysts' following fiscal year (FY2 = Fiscal Year 2) forecasts, which must be based entirely on forecasts. For First Call, "forward P/E" contrasts with "current P/E", which is based on the last reported annual EPS, as mentioned earlier. Clearly, analysts must be consistent in the definition of leading P/E when comparing stocks.

In Example 5, the business's EPS was expected to be relatively stable, and the leading P/Es based on the two different EPS specifications presented did not vary substantially from each other. Example 6 presents the calculation of leading P/Es for the company examined in Example 2, Koninklijke Philips. Valuations according to leading P/E can vary dramatically depending on the definition of earnings for businesses with volatile earnings. The analyst was probably justified in normalizing EPS in Example 2.

## EXAMPLE 6

### Calculating a Leading P/E Ratio (2)

In Example 2, we calculated a normalized EPS for Koninklijke Philips (NYSE: PHG) and a P/E based on normalized EPS. In this example, we compute leading P/Es for PHG using alternative definitions. Table 3 presents PHG's actual and forecasted EPS, which reflect a severe downturn in its Consumer Electronics division.

| TABLE 3 | Quarterly EPS for PHG (in U.S. Dollars, Excluding Nonrecurring Items) | | | |
|---|---|---|---|---|
| | **31 March** | **30 June** | **30 September** | **31 December** |
| 2001 | 0.08 | (0.34) | (0.27) | E0.00 |
| 2002 | E(0.05) | E0.10 | E0.15 | E0.30 |

*Source: The Value Line Investment Survey.*

On 8 November 2001, PHG stock closed at $25.72. PHG's fiscal year ends on 31 December. As of 8 November 2001, solve the following problems using the information in Table 3:

1. Calculate PHG's leading P/E based on the next four quarters of forecasted EPS.
2. Calculate PHG's leading P/E based on a fiscal year definition and current fiscal year (2001) forecasted EPS.
3. Calculate PHG's leading P/E based on a fiscal year definition and next fiscal year (2002) forecasted EPS.

**Solution to 1:** We sum forecasted EPS as follows:

| | |
|---|---|
| 4Q:2001 EPS (estimate) | $0.00 |
| 1Q:2002 EPS (estimate) | ($0.05) |
| 2Q:2002 EPS (estimate) | $0.10 |
| 3Q:2002 EPS (estimate) | $0.15 |
| Sum | $0.20 |

The leading P/E by this definition is $25.72/$0.20 = 128.6.

**Solution to 2:** We sum EPS as follows:

| | |
|---|---|
| 1Q:2001 EPS (actual) | $0.08 |
| 2Q:2001 EPS (actual) | ($0.34) |
| 3Q:2001 EPS (actual) | ($0.27) |
| 4Q:2001 EPS (estimate) | $0.00 |
| Sum | ($0.53) |

The leading P/E is $25.72/($0.53) = −48.5 or not meaningful (NM).

**Solution to 3:** We sum EPS as follows:

| | |
|---|---|
| 1Q:2002 EPS (estimate) | ($0.05) |
| 2Q:2002 EPS (estimate) | $0.10 |
| 3Q:2002 EPS (estimate) | $0.15 |
| 4Q:2002 EPS (estimate) | $0.30 |
| Sum | $0.50 |

The leading P/E by this definition is $25.72/$0.50 = 51.4.

Having explored the issues involved in calculating P/Es, we turn to using them in valuation.

## 3.2 Valuation Based on Forecasted Fundamentals

The analyst who understands DCF valuation models can use them not only in developing an estimate of the justified P/E for a stock but also to gain insight into possible sources of valuation differences using the method of comparables. The simplest of all DCF models is the Gordon growth form of the dividend discount model. In the reading on discounted dividend valuation, we related the P/E to the Gordon growth model value of the stock through the expressions

$$\frac{P_0}{E_1} = \frac{D_1/E_1}{r - g} = \frac{1 - b}{r - g}$$

which was the equation for the leading P/E, and

$$\frac{P_0}{E_0} = \frac{D_0(1 + g)/E_0}{r - g} = \frac{(1 - b)(1 + g)}{r - g}$$

which was the equation for the trailing P/E. Note that both expressions state P/E as a function of two fundamentals: the stock's required rate of return, $r$, reflecting its risk, and the expected (stable) dividend growth rate, $g$. The dividend payout ratio, $1 - b$, also enters into the expression. A particular value of the P/E is associated with a set of forecasts of the fundamentals (and dividend payout ratio). This value is the stock's justified P/E based on forecasted fundamentals (that is, the P/E justified by fundamentals). The higher the expected dividend growth rate or the lower the stock's required rate of return, the higher the stock's intrinsic value and the higher its justified P/E, all else equal. This intuition carries over to more-complex DCF models. Using any DCF model, all else equal, justified P/E is:

▶ inversely related to the stock's required rate of return; and
▶ positively related to the growth rate(s) of future expected cash flows, however defined.

We illustrate the calculation of a justified leading P/E in Example 7.

---

### EXAMPLE 7

**Leading P/E Based on Fundamental Forecasts (1)**

FPL Group (NYSE: FPL) is a southeastern U.S. utility. Jan Unger, a utility analyst, forecasts a long-term earnings retention rate ($b$) of 50 percent and a long-term growth rate of 5 percent. Unger also calculates a required rate of return of 9 percent. Based on Unger's forecasts of fundamentals and the equation above, FPL's justified leading P/E is

$$\frac{P_0}{E_1} = \frac{1 - b}{r - g} = \frac{1 - 0.50}{0.09 - 0.05} = 12.5$$

---

When assuming a complex DCF model for valuing the stock, we may not be able to express the P/E as a function of fundamental variables. Nevertheless, we can still calculate a justified P/E by dividing the DCF value by the fundamental used in the multiple, as illustrated in Example 8.

### EXAMPLE 8

**Leading P/E Based on Fundamental Forecasts (2)**

Hyundai Motor Company Ltd (KSE: 05380.KS) manufactures and sells cars, trucks, and commercial vehicles. As of the beginning of February 2002, you are valuing Hyundai stock (which closed at Korean won 29,300 on that day). Using a spreadsheet free-cash-flow-to-equity model in which you have forecasted FCFE individually for 2002 and 2003, and valuing the final piece using a P/E, you obtain a FCFE value for the stock of KRW31,500. For ease of communication, you want to express your valuation in terms of a leading P/E based on forecasted year 2002 EPS of KRW4,446.

1. What is Hyundai's justified P/E based on forecasted fundamentals?
2. State whether the stock appears to be fairly valued, overvalued, or undervalued, based on your answer to Problem 1.

**Solution to 1:** KRW31,500/KRW4,446 = 7.1 is the justified leading P/E.

**Solution to 2:** The justified P/E of 7.1 is slightly larger than the leading P/E based on market price, KRW29,300/KRW4,446 = 6.6. Consequently, the stock appears to be slightly undervalued.

Although related to a justified P/E, a predicted P/E can be estimated from cross-sectional regressions of P/E on the fundamentals believed to drive security valuation. Kisor and Whitbeck (1963) and Malkiel and Cragg (1970) pioneered this approach. The P/Es, and the stock and company characteristics thought to determine P/E, are measured as of a given year for a group of stocks. The P/Es are regressed against the stock and company characteristics. The estimated equation shows the relationships in the data set between P/E and the characteristics for that group of stocks and for that time period. The Kisor and Whitbeck study included the historical growth rate in earnings, the dividend payout ratio, and the standard deviation of EPS changes as explanatory (independent) variables. Malkiel and Cragg (1970) introduced explanatory variables based on expectations (alongside regressions on historical values). The analyst can in fact conduct such cross-sectional regressions using any set of variables he believes determines investment value. Other DCF models besides the dividend discount model (DDM) can provide ideas for such variables.

The cross-sectional regression method summarizes a large amount of data in a single equation and can provide a useful additional perspective on a valuation.

**EXAMPLE 9**

**Predicted P/E Based on a Cross-Sectional Regression**

You are valuing a food company with a beta of 0.9, a dividend payout ratio of 0.45, and an earnings growth rate of 0.08. The estimated regression for a group of other stocks in the same industry is

$$\text{Predicted P/E} = 12.12 + (2.25 \times \text{DPR}) - (0.20 \times \text{Beta}) + (14.43 \times \text{EGR})$$

where

> DPR = the dividend payout ratio
> Beta = the stock's beta
> EGR = the five-year earnings growth rate

**1.** What is the predicted P/E for the food company based on the above cross-sectional regression?

**2.** If the stock's actual trailing P/E is 18, is the stock fairly valued, overvalued, or undervalued?

**Solution to 1:** Predicted P/E = 12.12 + (2.25 × 0.45) − (0.20 × 0.9) + (14.43 × 0.08) = 14.1. The predicted P/E is 14.1.

**Solution to 2:** Because the predicted P/E of 14.1 is less than the actual P/E of 18, the stock appears to be overvalued (selling at a higher multiple than is justified by its fundamentals).

It is infrequently used as a main tool, however, because it is subject to at least three limitations:

▶ The method captures valuation relationships for a specific time period and sample of stocks. The predictive power of the regression for a different stock and different time period is not known.

▶ The regression coefficients and explanatory power of the regressions tend to change substantially over a number of years. The relationships between P/E and fundamentals may thus change over time.

▶ Because regressions using this method are prone to the problem of multicollinearity (correlation within linear combinations of the independent variables), interpreting individual regression coefficients is difficult.

## 3.3 Valuation Using Comparables

The most common application of the P/E approach to valuation is to compare a stock's price multiple with a benchmark value of the multiple. This section explores these comparisons for P/Es. To apply the method of comparables using any multiple, an analyst must follow these steps:

▶ Select and calculate the price multiple that will be used in the comparison.

▶ Select the comparison asset or assets.

▶ Calculate the value of the multiple for the comparison asset. For a group of comparison assets, calculate a mean or median value of the multiple for the assets. The result in either case is the **benchmark value of the multiple**.

▶ Compare the subject stock's actual multiple with the benchmark value.

▶ When feasible, assess whether differences between the actual and benchmark values of the multiple are explained by differences in the fundamental determinants of the price multiple and modify conclusions about relative valuation accordingly.

The above bullet points provide the structure for this reading's presentation of the method of comparables. Some practitioners will take the benchmark value of the multiple, possibly subjectively adjusted for differences in fundamentals, as the basis for a point estimate of value. This variation is illustrated in Example 11, Problem 2. We can apply this discussion to P/Es. Choices for the P/E benchmark value that have appeared in practice include:

▶ the P/E of the most closely matched individual stock;

▶ the average or median value of the P/E for the company's peer group of companies within an industry;

▶ the average or median value of the P/E for the company's industry or sector;

▶ the P/E for a representative equity index; and

▶ an average past value of the P/E for the stock.

Because of averaging, valuation errors are probably less likely to occur when we use an equity index or a group of stocks than when we use a single stock. Hence, the focus of the following discussion will be the last four methods (we will illustrate a comparison with a closely matched individual stock in the section on price to cash flow).

Economists and investment analysts have long attempted to group companies by similarities and differences in their business operations. A country's economy overall is grouped most broadly into **economic sectors** or large industry groupings. These groupings can change over time. As one example, Standard & Poor's once divided the U.S. economy into 11 sectors, shown in Table 4 (beginning with Basic Materials).[16]

Companies in an economic sector share some characteristics that distinguish them from companies in other sectors; however, a given sector usually contains businesses with very distinct business operations. Analysts thus further

---

[16] Standard & Poor's has since revised its sector classifications to the following 10 sectors: Consumer Discretionary, Consumer Staples, Energy, Financials, Health Care, Industrials, Information Technology, Materials, Telecommunication, and Utilities. Consumer Discretionary, Industrials, and Information Technology largely correspond to the old sectors Consumer Cyclicals, Capital Goods, and Technology, respectively; the former Transportation sector has been folded into the new Industrial sector. Within the sectors, Standard & Poor's has also made revisions to its industry classifications. For more information, visit www.spglobal.com/gics.html.

## TABLE 4  Valuation of U.S. Sectors: P/E (as of 31 May 2001)

|  | 2000 | 2001E | Long-Term Average |
|---|---|---|---|
| S&P 1500 | 22.4 | 23.5 | 26.5 |
| S&P 500 | 25.1 | 23.8 | 17.8 |
| Mid-Cap 400 | 22.6 | 20.4 | 23.8 |
| Small-Cap 600 | 21.9 | 18.8 | 23.8 |
| Basic Materials | 24.7 | 26.4 | 26.3 |
| **Capital Goods** | 28.6 | 24.1 | 33.1 |
| Communications Services | 22.7 | 31.0 | 26.9 |
| Consumer Cyclicals | 24.2 | 22.5 | 21.3 |
| Consumer Staples | 31.7 | 28.9 | 28.7 |
| Energy | 14.7 | 14.3 | 21.6 |
| Financial | 19.4 | 16.7 | 13.0 |
| Health Care | 37.7 | 28.5 | 24.9 |
| Technology | 30.6 | 43.1 | 28.8 |
| Transportation | 18.3 | 16.3 | 20.7 |
| Utilities | 28.6 | 16.5 | 13.4 |

*Source:* Standard & Poor's *Industry Surveys: Monthly Investment Review* (June 2001).

sort companies into industries within a sector. Many different government and investment industry classification schemes exist. According to Standard & Poor's, however, Consumer Cyclicals contains 23 industries, including Textiles with a P/E of 17.9 and Leisure Time Products with a P/E of 46.6.[17] Within Textiles, there is a subgroup—Textiles (Apparel). Within Textiles (Apparel), Standard & Poor's distinguishes peer groups of companies, or companies that are most similar within an industry. For example, one Standard & Poor's peer group in Textiles (Apparel) is Hosiery/Intimate/Bridal Apparel, composed of nine companies that manufacture and sell apparel in these categories.

An analyst could form even more-narrowly defined peer groups within the S&P peer group. One tool for identifying similarities and differences among businesses being used as comparables is financial ratio analysis. Financial ratios can point to contrasts in:

▶ a company's ability to meet short-term financial obligations (liquidity ratios);
▶ the efficiency with which assets are being used to generate sales (asset turnover ratios);
▶ the use of debt in financing the business (leverage ratios);
▶ the degree to which fixed charges such as interest on debt are met by earnings or cash flow (coverage ratios); and
▶ profitability (profitability ratios).

---

[17] According to the June 2001 issue of the *Industry Surveys: Monthly Investment Review.*

With this understanding of terms in hand, we turn to presenting the method of comparables, beginning with industry peer groups and moving to comparison assets that are progressively less closely matched to the stock. We then turn to using historical P/Es in comparisons. Finally, we sketch how both fundamentals- and comparables-driven models for P/Es can be used to calculate a value for the mature phase in a multistage DCF valuation.

### 3.3.1 Peer Company Multiples

A business's peer group of companies is frequently used for comparison assets. The advantage to using a peer group is that the constituent companies are typically similar in their business mix. This approach is consistent with the idea underlying the method of comparables—that similar assets should sell at similar prices. The subject stock's P/E is then compared to the mean or median P/E for the peer group to arrive at a relative valuation. Multiplying the justified P/E by EPS, we can also arrive at an absolute value that can be compared with the stock's market price. The absolute value represents an estimate of intrinsic value if the comparison assets were efficiently (fairly) priced.

---

**EXAMPLE 10**

**A Simple Peer Group Comparison**

As a housing industry analyst at a brokerage firm, you are valuing Lennar Corporation (NYSE: LEN), a U.S. builder of moderately priced homes with nationwide operations. The valuation metric that you have selected is the trailing P/E. You are evaluating the P/E using the median trailing P/E of peer group companies as the benchmark value. LEN is in the homebuilding industry, and its peer group is Homebuilders-National. Table 5 presents the relevant data.

**TABLE 5    Trailing P/Es of U.S. National Homebuilders (as of 9 November 2001)**

| Company | Trailing P/E |
|---|---|
| Beazer Homes USA (NYSE: BZH) | 6.83 |
| Centex Corporation (NYSE: CTX) | 7.36 |
| D.R. Horton (NYSE: DHI) | 7.99 |
| Lennar Corporation (NYSE: LEN) | 7.20 |
| MDC Holdings (NYSE: MDC) | 4.91 |
| Pulte Homes (NYSE: PHM) | 5.94 |
| Ryland Group (NYSE: RYL) | 6.70 |
| Toll Brothers (NYSE: TOL) | 6.29 |
| Mean | 6.65 |
| Median (midway between 6.70 and 6.83) | 6.77 |

*Source:* Morningstar, Inc.

---

Based on the data in Table 5, answer the following questions:

1. Given the definition of the benchmark stated above, state the benchmark value of the P/E for LEN.

2. State whether LEN is relatively fairly valued, relatively overvalued, or relatively undervalued, assuming no differences in fundamentals among the peer group companies. Justify your answer.

3. Which stocks in the Homebuilders-National group appear to be relatively undervalued using the mean trailing P/E as a benchmark? What further analysis may be appropriate to confirm your answer?

**Solution to 1:** The median trailing P/E for the group is 6.77, so 6.77 represents the benchmark value of the multiple (the analyst chose to use the median rather than the mean).

**Solution to 2:** LEN appears to be overvalued because its P/E is greater than the median P/E of 6.77.

**Solution to 3:** MDC, PHM, and TOL appear to be undervalued relative to their peers because their trailing P/Es are lower than the mean P/E of 6.65. The apparent differences in valuation may be explained by differences in risk and expected growth rates compared with their peers. In addition, financial ratio analysis may help analysts determine the precise dimensions along which businesses may differ by risk and expected return.

In actual practice, analysts often find that the stock being valued has some significant differences from the median or mean fundamental characteristics of the comparison assets. In applying the method of comparables, analysts usually attempt to judge whether differences from the benchmark value of the multiple can be explained by differences in the fundamental factors believed to influence the multiple. The following relationships for P/E hold, all else equal:

▶ If the subject stock has higher-than-average (or median) expected earnings growth, a higher P/E than the benchmark P/E is justified.

▶ If the subject stock has higher-than-average (or median) risk (operating or financial), a lower P/E than the benchmark P/E is justified.

Another perspective on the above two points is that for a group of stocks with comparable relative valuations, the stock with the greatest expected growth rate (or the lowest risk) is the most attractively valued, all else equal. Example 11, Problem 1, illustrates this principle.

One metric that appears to address the impact of earnings growth on P/E is the P/E-to-growth (**PEG**) ratio. PEG is calculated as the stock's P/E divided by the expected earnings growth rate. The ratio in effect calculates a stock's P/E per unit of expected growth. Stocks with lower PEGs are more attractive than stocks with higher PEGs, all else equal. PEG is useful but must be used with care for several reasons:

▶ PEG assumes a linear relationship between P/Es and growth. The model for P/E in terms of DDM shows that in theory the relationship is not linear.

▶ PEG does not factor in differences in risk, a very important component of P/Es.

▶ PEG does not account for differences in the duration of growth. For example, dividing P/Es by short-term (five-year) growth forecasts may not capture differences in growth in long-term growth prospects.

The way in which fundamentals can add insight to comparables is illustrated in Example 11.

## EXAMPLE 11

### A Peer Group Comparison Modified by Fundamentals

Continuing with the valuation of homebuilders, you gather information on fundamentals related to risk (beta[18]), profitability (five-year earnings growth forecast), and valuation (trailing and leading P/E). These data are reported in Table 6, which lists companies in order of descending earnings growth forecasts. The use of leading P/Es recognizes that differences in trailing P/Es could be the result of transitory effects on earnings.

| TABLE 6 | Valuation Data for U.S. National Homebuilders (as of 9 November 2001) | | | | |
|---|---|---|---|---|---|
| | Trailing P/E | Leading P/E | Five-Year EPS Growth Forecast | Leading PEG | Beta |
| TOL | 6.29 | 6.43 | 14.60% | 0.44 | 1.05 |
| DHI | 7.99 | 7.37 | 14.20% | 0.52 | 1.40 |
| LEN | 7.20 | 7.12 | 14.00% | 0.51 | 1.45 |
| BZH | 6.83 | 7.29 | 14.00% | 0.52 | 1.00 |
| CTX | 7.36 | 7.63 | 13.30% | 0.57 | 1.20 |
| MDC | 4.91 | 5.93 | 13.30% | 0.45 | 1.05 |
| RYL | 6.70 | 7.76 | 11.80% | 0.66 | 1.20 |
| PHM | 5.94 | 6.08 | 11.70% | 0.52 | 1.05 |
| Mean | 6.65 | 6.95 | 13.36% | 0.52 | 1.18 |
| Median | 6.77 | 7.21 | 13.65% | 0.52 | 1.13 |

*Source:* Morningstar, Inc.

---

[18] In comparables work, analysts may also use other measures of risk, for example financial leverage.

Based on the data in Table 6, answer the following questions:

1. In Example 10, Problem 3, MDC, PHM, and TOL were identified as possibly relatively undervalued compared with the peer group as a whole. Using information relating to profitability and risk, which of the three stocks appears to be the relatively *most* undervalued? Justify your answer with three reasons.

2. TOL has a consensus year-ahead EPS forecast of $5.48. Suppose that the median P/E of 7.21 for the peer group is subjectively adjusted upward to 7.5 for the justified P/E for TOL, reflecting TOL's lower risk and superior fundamentals. Estimate TOL's intrinsic value.

3. TOL's current market price is $35.25. State whether TOL appears to be fairly valued, overvalued, or undervalued on an absolute basis, given your answer to Problem 2 above.

**Solution to 1:** Among MDC, PHM, and TOL, TOL appears to represent the greatest undervaluation, according to the data in Table 6. Of the three stocks, TOL has:

▶ the highest five-year consensus earnings growth forecast;
▶ the lowest PEG based on leading P/E; and
▶ the same level of risk as measured by beta.

**Solution to 2:** $5.48 × 7.50 = $41.10 is an estimate of intrinsic value. Because the adjustment is subjective, we might prefer to say that TOL should trade at a premium to $5.48 × 7.21 = $39.51.

**Solution to 3:** Because $41.10 is greater than $35.25, TOL appears to be undervalued on an absolute basis.

Analysts frequently compare a stock's multiple with the median or mean value of the multiple for larger sets of assets than a company's peer group. As one example, Value Line reports a relative P/E that is calculated as the stock's current P/E divided by the median P/E under Value Line review. The less closely matched the stock is to the comparison assets, the more dissimilarities are likely to be present to complicate the interpretation. Arguably, however, the larger the number of assets, the more likely it is that mispricings of individual assets cancel out. For example, during the 1998–2000 Internet boom, valuation relative to the overall market was more likely to point to the possibility of a crash in 2000–2001 than valuation relative to other Internet stocks alone. The next sections examine these larger groups.

### 3.3.2 Industry and Sector Multiples

Mean or median industry P/Es, as well as economic sector P/Es, are frequently used in relative valuation. The median is insensitive to outliers. Many databases, however, report only mean values of multiples for industries. The mechanics of using industry multiples are identical to the case of peer group comparisons. We make a comparison of a stock's multiple to the mean or median multiple for the company's industry, taking account of relevant fundamental information.

The analyst may want to explore whether the comparison assets themselves are efficiently priced. This will give insight into whether the relative valuation (justified P/E based on comparables) accurately reflects absolute intrinsic value.

---

**EXAMPLE 12**

**Relative Industry Valuation**

In general, the U.S. pharmaceutical industry traded at a substantial premium to the market (S&P 500) in the years 1951 to 1993.[19] In the early 1990s, the industry's relative valuation was at its lowest level and priced at a discount to the market. Had the U.S. pharmaceutical industry prospects changed?

To some extent, the industry outlook had changed due to the prospect of U.S. health care reform and secular changes in the industry in the early 1990s. Nevertheless, stocks in this sector continued to rise dramatically through the year 2000. Recent S&P industry data indicate that as of 31 May 2001, the U.S. pharmaceutical industry was trading at an average P/E of 33.7 compared to an S&P 500 P/E of 25.1—once again, at a premium to the market.

---

### 3.3.3 Overall Market Multiple

Although the logic of the comparables approach points to industry and peer companies as comparison assets, equity market indexes also have been used as comparison assets. The mechanics of using the method of comparables are not changed, although the user should be cognizant of any size differences between the subject stock and the stocks in the selected index. The question of whether the overall market is fairly priced has captured analyst interest over the entire history of investments. We mentioned one approach to market valuation (using a DDM) in the reading on discounted dividend valuation. We end the discussion of using an equity market index as a comparison asset with two topical developments in market valuation.

---

**EXAMPLE 13**

**Valuation Relative to the Market**

You are analyzing three large-cap European stock issues with approximately equal earnings growth prospects and risk. As one step in your analysis, you have decided to check valuations relative to the Financial Times Stock Exchange (FTSE) Eurotop 300, an index of Europe's 300 largest companies. Table 7 provides the data.

**TABLE 7   Comparison with an Index Multiple (Prices and EPS in €)**

| As of 28 February 2002 | Stock A | Stock B | Stock C | FTSE Eurotop 300 |
|---|---|---|---|---|
| Current price | 23 | 50 | 260 | 1229 |
| P/E 2003E | 20 | 25.5 | 20 | 23.2 |
| Five-year average P/E (as a percent of Eurotop 300 P/E) | 80 | 110 | 105 | |

*Source:* Bank Leu *Stock Guide* (March 2002) for FTSE Eurotop 300 data.

---

[19] The example draws on information in Haley (1993).

Based only on the data in Table 7, answer the following questions:

**1.** Which stock appears relatively undervalued against the FTSE Eurotop 300?

**2.** State the assumption underlying the five-year average P/E comparisons.

**Solution to 1:** Stock C appears to be undervalued against the FTSE Eurotop 300. Stock A and Stock C both are trading at a P/E of 20 relative to 2003 estimated earnings, versus a P/E of 23.2 for the market. But Stock A has historically traded at P/E reflecting a 20 percent discount to the market (which would equal a P/E of $0.8 \times 23.2 = 18.6$). In contrast, Stock C has usually traded at a premium to the market P/E but now trades at a discount to it. Stock B trades at a high P/E, in line with its historical relationship to the market P/E
($1.1 \times 23.2 = 25.5$).

**Solution to 2:** Using historical relative valuation information in investment decisions relies on an assumption of stable underlying economic relationships (that the past is relevant for the future).

Because many equity indexes are market capitalization weighted, most vendors report the average market P/E with the individual P/Es weighted by the company's market capitalization. As a consequence, the largest constituent stocks heavily influence the calculated P/E. To the extent there are systematic differences in the P/Es by market capitalization, differences from the index's multiple may be explained by such effects. For stocks in middle capitalization ranges in particular, the analyst should favor using the median P/E for the index as the benchmark value of the multiple.[20]

As with other comparison assets, the analyst may be interested in whether the equity index itself is efficiently priced. A common comparison is the index's P/E in relation to historical values. For example, the current P/E of 27.83 for the Dow Jones Industrial Average as of 31 October 2001 was well above the 10-year average P/E of 17.4 reported by Value Line through 2000. Using a broader index of stocks over the 1871–1996 period, Siegel (1998) computed a long-term median P/E for U.S. stocks of 13.70. Two potential justifications for a higher P/E are lower interest rates and higher expected growth rates. An alternative hypothesis is that the market as a whole is currently overvalued or, alternatively, that earnings are abnormally low. The use of past data relies on the key assumption that the past (sometimes the distant past) is relevant for the future.

Other methods of examining market valuation have been used as well. The reading on evaluating the performance of your hedge funds mentions the use of DCF models. Examples 14 and 15 illustrate other approaches.

---

[20] The differences can be substantial. For example, as of 31 October 2001, including only stocks with positive earnings, the market-cap-weighted mean P/E for the S&P 500 was 25.8 but the median P/E was 22.

## EXAMPLE 14

### The Fed Model

One of the main drivers of P/E for the market as a whole is the level of interest rates. The inverse relationship between value and interest rates can be seen from the expression of P/E in terms of fundamentals, because the risk-free rate is one component of the required rate of return that is inversely related to value. The U.S. Federal Reserve Board of Governors uses one such valuation model that relates the inverse of the S&P 500 P/E, the earnings yield, to the yield to maturity on 10-year Treasury bonds. As already defined in Section 3.1.1, Earnings yield = E/P, where the Fed uses expected earnings for the next 12 months in calculating this ratio.

The model asserts that the market is overvalued when the stock market's current earnings yield is less than the 10-year Treasury bond yield. The intuition is that when Treasury bonds yield more than the earnings yield on the stock market, which is riskier than bonds, stocks are an unattractive investment. Figure 1 shows the historical indications of market overvaluation by performance of this model.

### FIGURE 1   The Fed Stock Valuation Model

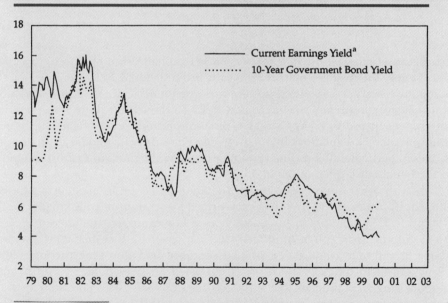

[a] I/B.E.S consensus estimates of earnings over the coming 12 months divided by S&P 500 Index.

*Source:* Reprinted with permission of Dr. Edward Yardeni.

Figure 1 shows that, in general, the earnings yield has tracked the 10-year Treasury bond yield quite closely. Interestingly, the model indicated that the S&P 500 was overvalued at the beginning of 2000, a year in which the S&P 500 returned −9.1 percent. According to the model, the justified or fair-value P/E for the S&P 500 is the reciprocal of the 10-year T-bond yield. As of 1 March 2002, with a 10-year T-bond yielding 4.975 percent, the justified P/E on the S&P 500 was 1/0.04975 = 20.1, according to the model. The leading P/E for the S&P 500 as of same date based on the consensus 2002 EPS from First Call/Thomson Financial was 29.6.

Earlier, we presented an expression for the justified P/E in terms of the Gordon growth model. That expression indicates that the expected growth rate in dividends or earnings is a variable entering into the intrinsic value of a stock (or an index of stocks). That variable is lacking in the Fed model.[21] Example 15 presents a model that takes a step toward addressing these concerns.

---

### EXAMPLE 15

**The Yardeni Model**

Yardeni (2000) developed a model that incorporates the expected growth rate in earnings—a variable that is missing in the Fed model.[22] Yardeni's model is

$$CEY = CBY - b \times LTEG + Residual$$

CEY is the current earnings yield on the market index, CBY is the current Moody's A rated corporate bond yield, and LTEG is the consensus five-year earnings growth rate forecast for the market index. The coefficient $b$ measures the weight the market gives to five-year earnings projections (recall that the expression for P/E in terms of the Gordon growth model is based on the long-term sustainable growth rate and that five-year forecasts of growth may not be sustainable). Note that although CBY incorporates a default risk premium relative to T-bonds, it does not incorporate an equity risk premium per se (for example, in the bond yield plus risk premium model for the cost of equity, presented in the reading on evaluating the performance of your hedge funds, we added 300 to 400 basis points to a corporate bond yield).

Yardeni has found that the historical coefficient $b$ has averaged 0.10. Noting that CEY is E/P and taking the inverse of both sides of this equation, Yardeni obtains the following expression for the justified P/E on the market:

$$\frac{P}{E} = \frac{1}{(CBY - b \times LTEG)}$$

Consistent with valuation theory, in Yardeni's model, higher current corporate bond yields imply a lower justified P/E, and higher expected long-term growth results in a higher justified P/E. Yardeni's model uses a five-year growth forecast as a proxy for longer-term growth. Figure 2 illustrates the fair value predictions of the Yardeni model for the S&P 500. Figure 2 shows that in the years 1997 through 1999, the S&P 500 appeared to be overvalued using the historical weighting of 0.10 on growth; at the end of 1999, the model required a 0.25 weighting on growth to justify the market valuation, possibly indicating too much optimism was built into prices. As of 1 March 2002, with 10-year A rated

---

[21] The earnings yield is in fact the expected rate of return on a no-growth stock (under the assumption that price equals value). See Equation 41-12 in the reading on discounted dividend valuation, setting price equal to value: $P_0 = E/r + PVGO$. Setting the present value of growth opportunities equal to zero and rearranging, $r = E/P_0$.

[22] This model is presented as one example of more-complex models than the Fed model. Economic analysts at most investment companies have their own models that incorporate growth and historical relationships of market indices and government bonds.

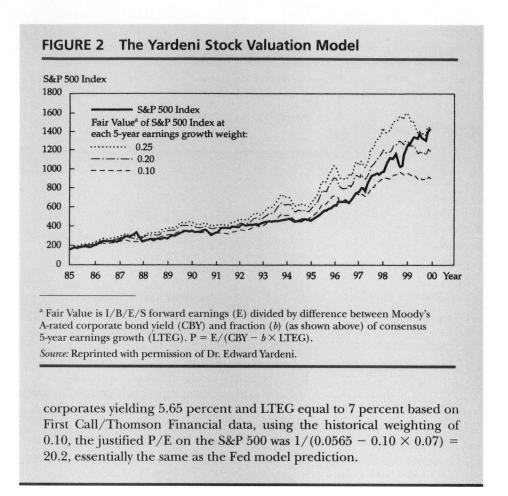

**FIGURE 2    The Yardeni Stock Valuation Model**

S&P 500 Index

Legend:
— S&P 500 Index
Fair Value[a] of S&P 500 Index at each 5-year earnings growth weight:
········· 0.25
—·—·— 0.20
— — — 0.10

[a] Fair Value is I/B/E/S forward earnings (E) divided by difference between Moody's A-rated corporate bond yield (CBY) and fraction ($b$) (as shown above) of consensus 5-year earnings growth (LTEG). $P = E/(CBY - b \times LTEG)$.

*Source:* Reprinted with permission of Dr. Edward Yardeni.

corporates yielding 5.65 percent and LTEG equal to 7 percent based on First Call/Thomson Financial data, using the historical weighting of 0.10, the justified P/E on the S&P 500 was $1/(0.0565 - 0.10 \times 0.07) = 20.2$, essentially the same as the Fed model prediction.

### 3.3.4 Own Historical P/E Comparisons

As an alternative to comparing a stock's valuation with that of other stocks, another tradition uses past values of a stock's own P/E as a basis for comparison. Underlying this use is the idea that a stock's P/E may regress to historical average levels. A benchmark value can be obtained in a variety of ways with this approach. Value Line reports as a "P/E median" a rounded average of four middle values of a stock's average annual P/E for the previous 10 years. The five-year average trailing P/E is another reasonable alternative. In general, trailing P/Es are more commonly used than leading P/Es in such computations. Besides "higher" and "lower" comparisons with this benchmark, justified price based on this approach may be calculated as follows:

Justified price = (Benchmark value of own historical P/Es)
× (Most recent EPS)          (43-1)

Normalized EPS replaces most recent EPS in Equation 43-1 when EPS is negative and as otherwise appropriate (see Section 3.1.1).

Changes in the interest rate environment and economic fundamentals over different time periods are a limitation to using an average past value of P/E for a

**EXAMPLE 16**

**Valuation Relative to Own Historical P/Es**

As of the beginning of 2001, you are valuing the Bank of Nova Scotia (TSE: BNS.TO), Canada's fourth-largest bank in terms of assets. You are investigating the method of comparables using BNS.TO's five-year average P/E as the benchmark value of the multiple. Table 8 presents the data.

**TABLE 8   Historical P/Es for BNS.TO**

|  | 2000 | 1999 | 1998 | 1997 | 1996 | Overall Mean |
|---|---|---|---|---|---|---|
| Average annual P/E | 9.7 | 11.1 | 12.8 | 11.0 | 8.0 | 10.5 |

Source: The Value Line Investment Survey.

1. State a benchmark value for BNS.TO's P/E.
2. Given 2000 EPS of CAD3.55, calculate a justified price for BNS.

**Solution to 1:** From Table 8, this benchmark value is 10.5.

**Solution to 2:** The calculation is $10.5 \times CAD3.55 = CAD37.28$.

stock as a benchmark. One specific caution is that inflation can distort the economic meaning of reported earnings. Consequently, comparisons of own P/E with average P/E, calculated with respect to a period with a different inflationary environment, can be misleading.[23] Further, analysts should be alert to the impact of changes in a company's business mix over time on valuation levels. If the company's business has changed substantially over the time period examined, the method based on own past P/Es is prone to error.

### 3.3.5 Using P/Es to Obtain Terminal Value in Multistage Dividend Discount Models

In valuing a stock using a DDM, whether using a multistage model or modeling within a spreadsheet (forecasting cash flows individually up to some horizon), the accurate estimation of the terminal value of the stock is important. The key condition that must be satisfied is that terminal value reflects earnings growth

---

[23] In the presence of inflation, reported earnings can overstate the real economic value of earnings that investors in principle are concerned about. Investors may value a given amount of reported earnings less during inflationary periods, tending to lower observed P/Es during such periods. For more details, see Bodie, Kane, and Marcus (2001).

that the company can sustain in the long run. Analysts frequently use price multiples to estimate terminal value, in particular P/Es and P/Bs. We can call such multiples **terminal price multiples**. Some choices available to the analyst in the multiples approach (where $n$ is the point in time at which the final stage begins) include the following:

### Terminal Price Multiple Based on Fundamentals

Analysts may restate the Gordon growth model value as a multiple by dividing it by $B_n$ or $E_n$ (for a trailing terminal price multiple) or by $B_{n+1}$ or $E_{n+1}$ (for a leading terminal price multiple). Of course, multiplying by the same value of the fundamental gives estimated terminal value. Because of their familiarity, multiples may be a useful way to communicate an estimate of terminal value.

### Terminal Price Multiple Based on Comparables

The expression for terminal value (using P/E as an example) is

$$V_n = \text{Benchmark value of trailing P/E} \times E_n$$

or

$$V_n = \text{Benchmark value of leading P/E} \times E_{n+1}$$

Analysts have used various choices for the benchmark value, including:

► median industry P/E;

► average industry P/E; and

► average of own past P/Es.

The use of a comparables approach has the strength that it is entirely grounded in market data. In contrast, the Gordon growth model calls for specific estimates (the required rate of return, the dividend payout ratio, and the expected mature growth rate) and is very sensitive to perturbations in those estimates. A possible disadvantage to the comparables approach, however, is that when the benchmark value reflects mispricing (over- or undervaluation), so will the estimate of terminal value.

---

### EXAMPLE 17

**Valuing the Mature Growth Phase Using P/Es**

As an energy analyst, you are valuing the stock of an oil exploration company. You have projected earnings and dividends three years out (to $t = 3$), and you have gathered the following data and estimates:

► required rate of return = 0.10

► average dividend payout rate for mature companies in the market = 0.45

► industry average ROE = 0.13

► $E_3$ = $3.00

► industry average P/E = 14.3

---

On the basis of the above information, answer the following questions:

1. Calculate terminal value based on comparables.
2. Contrast your answer in Problem 1 to an estimate of terminal value using the Gordon growth model.

**Solution to 1:** $V_n$ = Benchmark value of P/E $\times E_n$ = 14.3 $\times$ \$3.00
= \$42.90

**Solution to 2:** In the sustainable growth rate expression, $g = b \times$ ROE, we can use $(1 - 0.45) = 0.55 = b$, and ROE = 0.13 (the industry average), obtaining $g = b \times$ ROE = 0.55 $\times$ 0.13 = 0.0715. Given the required rate of return of 0.10, we obtain the estimate \$3.00 $(0.45)(1.0715)/(0.10 - 0.0715)$ = \$50.76. In this case, the Gordon growth model estimate of terminal value is $(\$50.76 - \$42.90)/\$42.90 = 0.1832$, or 18.3 percent higher than the estimate based on multiples.

# PRICE TO BOOK VALUE

**4**

The ratio of market price per share to book value per share (P/B), like P/E, has a long history of use in valuation practice (as discussed in Graham and Dodd 1934). In Block's 1999 survey of AIMR members, book value ranked distinctly behind earnings and cash flow, but ahead of dividends, of the four factors surveyed.[24] According to the *Merrill Lynch Institutional Factor Survey*, in the years 1989 to 2001, P/B has been only slightly less popular than P/E as a factor consistently used among institutional investors.[25]

In the P/E ratio, the measure of value (EPS) in the denominator is a flow variable relating to the income statement. In contrast, the measure of value in the P/B's denominator (book value per share) is a stock or level variable coming from the balance sheet. Intuitively, book value per share attempts to represent the investment that common shareholders have made in the company, on a per-share basis. (*Book* refers to the fact that the measurement of value comes from accounting records or books, in contrast to market value.) To define book value per share more precisely, we first find **shareholders' equity** (total assets minus total liabilities). Because our purpose is to value common stock, we subtract from shareholders' equity any value attributable to preferred stock; we thus obtain common shareholders' equity or the **book value of equity** (often called simply **book value**).[26] Dividing book value by the number of common stock shares outstanding, we obtain **book value per share**, the denominator in the P/B.

In the balance of this section, we present the reasons analysts have offered for using P/B as well as possible drawbacks to its use. We then illustrate the

---

[24] Earnings received a ranking of 1.55, cash flow a ranking of 1.65, book value a ranking of 3.29, and dividends a ranking of 3.51, where 1, 2, 3, and 4 were assigned to inputs ranked first, second, third, and last in importance in averaging responses.

[25] From 1989 to 2001, an average of 37.3 percent of respondents reported consistently using P/B in valuation, compared with 40.4 percent for earnings yield (the reciprocal of P/E rather than P/E was the actual variable surveyed by Merrill Lynch).

[26] If we were to value a company as a whole, rather than just the common stock, we would not exclude the value of preferred stock from the computation.

calculation of P/B and discuss the fundamental factors that drive P/B. We end the section by showing the use of P/B based on the method of comparables. Analysts have offered several rationales for the use of the P/B:

▶ Because book value is a cumulative balance sheet amount, book value is generally positive even when EPS is negative. We can generally use P/B when EPS is negative, whereas P/E based on a negative EPS is not meaningful.

▶ Because book value per share is more stable than EPS, P/B may be more meaningful than P/E when EPS is abnormally high or low, or is highly variable.

▶ As a measure of net asset value per share, book value per share has been viewed as appropriate for valuing companies composed chiefly of liquid assets, such as finance, investment, insurance, and banking institutions (Wild, Bernstein, and Subramanyam 2001, p. 233). For such companies, book values of assets may approximate market values.

▶ Book value has also been used in the valuation of companies that are not expected to continue as a going concern (Martin 1998, p. 22).

▶ Differences in P/Bs may be related to differences in long-run average returns, according to empirical research.[27]

Possible drawbacks of P/Bs in practice include the following:

▶ Other assets besides those recognized in accounting may be critical operating factors. For example, in many service companies, **human capital**—the value of skills and knowledge possessed by the workforce—is more important than physical capital as an operating factor.

▶ P/B can be misleading as a valuation indicator when significant differences exist among the level of assets used by the companies under examination. Such differences may reflect differences in business models, for example.

▶ Accounting effects on book value may compromise book value as a measure of shareholders' investment in the company. As one example, book value can understate shareholders' investment as a result of the expensing of investment in research and development (R&D). Such expenditures often positively affect income over many periods and in principle create assets. Accounting effects such as these can impair the comparability of P/B across companies and countries.[28]

▶ In the accounting of most countries, including the United States, book value largely reflects the historical purchase costs of assets, as well as accumulated accounting depreciation expenses. Inflation as well as technological change eventually drive a wedge between the book value and the market value of assets. As a result, book value per share often poorly reflects the value of shareholders' investments. Such effects can impair the comparability of P/Bs across companies, for example when significant differences exist in the average age of assets among companies being compared.

Example 18 illustrates one possible disadvantage to using P/B in valuation.

---

[27] See Bodie, Kane, and Marcus (2001) for a brief summary of the empirical research.

[28] For example, in some countries the values of brand name assets created by advertising are recognized on the balance sheet; in the United States, they are not.

## EXAMPLE 18

### Differences in Business Models Reflected in Differences in P/Bs

Dell Computer Corporation (Nasdaq NMS: DELL), Apple Computer (Nasdaq NMS: AAPL), Gateway (NYSE: GTW), and Compaq Computer Corporation (NYSE: CPQ) compete with each other in the personal computer industry. Table 9 gives valuation data for these companies according to P/B, as of the end of 2001.

**TABLE 9    P/Bs for Four Peer Companies**

| Company | P/B |
| --- | --- |
| Dell | 14.42 |
| Apple | 1.76 |
| Gateway | 1.83 |
| Compaq | 1.23 |

*Source:* Morningstar, Inc.

Dell is an assembler rather than a manufacturer, uses a just-in-time inventory system for parts needed in assembly, and sells built-to-order computers directly to the end consumer. Just-in-time inventory systems attempt to minimize the amount of time that parts needed for building computers are held in inventory. How can these practices explain the much higher P/B of Dell compared with the P/Bs of peer group stocks?

Because Dell assembles parts manufactured elsewhere, it requires smaller investments in fixed assets than it would if it were a manufacturer; this translates into a smaller book value per share. The just-in-time inventory system reduces Dell's required investment in working capital. Because Dell does not need to respond to the inventory needs of large resellers, its need to invest in working capital is reduced. The overall effect of this business model is that Dell generates its sales on a comparatively small base of assets. As a result, Dell's P/B is not comparable with those of its peer group, and the question of relative valuation is not resolved by the comparison in Table 9. Using P/B as a valuation indicator effectively penalizes Dell's efficient business model.[29]

## 4.1 Determining Book Value

In this section, we illustrate the calculation of book value and how analysts may adjust book value to improve the comparability of P/B ratios across companies. To compute book value per share, we need to refer to the business's balance

---

[29] There is a second reason for Dell's relatively high P/B; Dell's substantial share repurchases have reduced its book value per share in the years preceding this data.

sheet, which has a shareholders' (or stockholders') equity section. The computation of book value is as follows:

▶ (Shareholders' equity) − (Total value of equity claims that are senior to common stock) = Common shareholders' equity

▶ (Common shareholders' equity)/(Number of common stock shares outstanding) = Book value per share

## EXAMPLE 19

### Computing Book Value per Share

Ennis Business Forms (NYSE: EBF), a wholesale manufacturer of custom business forms and other printed business products, reported the balance sheet given in Table 10 for its fiscal year ending 28 February 2001.

| TABLE 10 | Ennis Business Forms Balance Sheet (in Thousands, except Per-Share Amounts) |
|---|---|
| | **28 Feb 2001** |
| **Assets** | |
| **Current assets** | |
| Cash and cash equivalents | $ 8,964 |
| Short term investments | 980 |
| Net receivables | 29,957 |
| Inventory | 13,088 |
| Unbilled contract revenue | 364 |
| Other current assets | 4,910 |
| Total Current Assets | 58,263 |
| **Noncurrent assets** | |
| Investment securities | 2,170 |
| Net property, plant, and equipment | 57,781 |
| Goodwill | 23,615 |
| Other assets | 1,025 |
| **Total Assets** | **$ 142,854** |
| **Liabilities and Shareholders' Equity** | |
| **Current liabilities** | |
| Current installments of long-term debt | $ 4,176 |
| Accounts payable | 6,067 |
| Accrued expenses | 7,665 |
| Total Current Liabilities | 17,908 |
| **Noncurrent liabilities** | |
| Long-term debt | 23,555 |
| Deferred credits | 9,851 |
| **Total Liabilities** | 51,314 |

*(Table continued on next page . . .)*

| TABLE 10 (continued) | |
|---|---|
| | **28 Feb 2001** |
| **Shareholders' equity** | |
| Common stock | |
| ($2.50 par value. Authorized 40,000,000; issued 21,249,860) | 53,125 |
| Additional paid-in capital | 1,040 |
| Retained earnings | 127,817 |
| Treasury stock | |
| (cost of 4,979,095 shares repurchased in 2001) | (90,442) |
| Total Shareholders' Equity | 91,540 |
| **Total Liabilities and Shareholders' Equity** | **$ 142,854** |

The entries in the balance sheet should be familiar. Treasury stock results from share repurchases (or buybacks) and is a deduction (recorded at cost above) to reach shareholders' equity. For the number of shares to be used in the divisor, we take 21,249,860 shares issued (under Common stock) and subtract 4,979,095 shares repurchased in 2001 to get 16,270,765 shares outstanding.

1. Using the data in Table 10, calculate book value per share as of 28 February 2001.

2. Given a closing price per share for EBF of $8.42 as of 4 June 2001, and your answer to Problem 1, calculate EBF's P/B as of 4 June 2001.

**Solution to 1:** (Common shareholders' equity)/(Number of common stock shares outstanding) = $91,540,000/16,270,765 = $5.63.

**Solution to 2:** P/B = $8.42/$5.63 = 1.5.

Possible senior claims to common stock include the value of preferred stock and dividends in arrears on preferred stock.[30] Example 19 illustrates the calculation.

Example 19 illustrated the calculation of book value per share without any adjustments. Adjusting P/B has two purposes: (1) to make P/B more accurately reflect the value of shareholders' investment and (2) to make P/B more useful for comparisons among different stocks.

▶ Some services and analysts report a **tangible book value per share**. Computing tangible book value per share involves subtracting reported intangible assets from the balance sheet from common shareholders' equity. The analyst should be familiar with the calculation. However, from

---

[30] Some preferred stock issues have the right to premiums (liquidation premiums) if they are liquidated. If present, these premiums should be deducted as well.

the viewpoint of financial theory, the general exclusion of all intangibles may not be warranted. In the case of individual intangible assets such as patents, which can be separated from the entity and sold, exclusion may not be justified. Exclusion may be appropriate, however, for goodwill from acquisitions. **Goodwill** represents the excess of the purchase price of an acquisition over the net asset value of tangible assets and specifically identifiable intangibles. Many analysts feel that goodwill does not represent an asset, because it is not separable and may reflect overpayment for an acquisition.

▶ For book value per share to most accurately reflect current values, the balance sheet should be adjusted for significant off-balance-sheet assets and liabilities and for differences in the fair value of these assets/liabilities from recorded accounting amounts.[31] Internationally, accounting methods currently report some assets/liabilities at historical cost (with some adjustments) and others at fair value.[32] For example, assets such as land or equipment are reported at their historical acquisitions cost, and in the case of equipment are being depreciated over their useful lives. These assets may have appreciated over time, or they may have declined in value more than is reflected in the depreciation computation. Other assets such as investments in marketable securities are reported at fair market value. Reporting assets at fair value would make P/B more relevant for valuation (including comparisons among companies).

▶ Certain adjustments may be appropriate for comparability. For example, one company may use FIFO and a peer company may use LIFO, which in an inflationary environment will generally understate inventory values. To more accurately assess the relative valuation of the two companies, the analyst should restate the book value of the company using LIFO to what it would be on a FIFO basis. Example 20 illustrates this and other adjustments to book value.[33]

Regarding the second bullet point, over the last few years, there has been a trend among accounting standard setters toward a fair value model—more assets/liabilities are stated at fair value. If this trend continues, the need for adjustments will be reduced (but not eliminated).

---

### EXAMPLE 20

#### Adjusting Book Value

Edward Stavros is a junior analyst at a major U.S. pension fund. Stavros is researching Harley Davidson (NYSE: HDI) for the fund's Consumer Cyclical portfolio. Stavros is particularly interested in determining Harley Davidson's relative P/B. He obtains the condensed balance sheet for Harley Davidson from Edgar Online (a computerized database of U.S. SEC filings); his data are shown in Table 11.

---

[31] An example of an off-balance sheet liability is a guarantee to pay a debt of another company in the event of that company's default. See Chapter 11 of White, Sondhi, and Fried (1998).

[32] **Fair value** has been defined as the price at which an asset or liability would change hands between a willing buyer and a willing seller when the former is not under any compulsion to buy and the latter is not under any compulsion to sell.

[33] For a complete discussion of balance sheet adjustments, see "Analysis of Financial Statements: A Synthesis," in White, Sondhi, and Fried (1998).

**TABLE 11   Harley Davidson Condensed Consolidated Balance Sheet (in Thousands)**

| | 31 Dec 2000 |
|---|---|
| **Assets** | |
|   **Current assets** | |
|     Cash and cash equivalents | $ 419,736 |
|     Accounts receivable, net | 98,311 |
|     Finance receivables, net | 530,859 |
|     Inventories | 191,931 |
|     Other current assets | 56,427 |
|   Total Current Assets | 1,297,264 |
|   **Noncurrent assets** | |
|     Finance receivables, net | 234,091 |
|     Property, plant, and equipment, net | 754,115 |
|     Goodwill | 54,331 |
|     Other assets | 96,603 |
| **Total Assets** | **$ 2,436,404** |
| **Liabilities and Shareholders' Equity** | |
|   **Current liabilities** | |
|     Accounts payable | $ 169,844 |
|     Accrued and other liabilities | 238,390 |
|     Current portion of finance debt | 89,509 |
|   Total Current Liabilities | 497,743 |
|   **Noncurrent liabilities** | |
|     Finance debt | 355,000 |
|     Other long-term liabilities | 97,340 |
|     Postretirement health care benefits | 80,666 |
|     Contingencies | |
|   **Shareholders' equity** | 1,405,655 |
| **Total Liabilities and Shareholders' Equity** | **$ 2,436,404** |

Stavros computes book value per share initially by dividing total shareholders' equity ($1,405,655,000) by the number of shares outstanding at 31 December 2000 (302,070,745). The resulting book value per share is $4.65. Stavros then realizes that he must examine the full set of financial statements to assess the impact of accounting methods on balance sheet data. Harley Davidson's footnotes indicate that the company uses the LIFO inventory method. Inventories on a FIFO basis are presented in the company's footnotes at $210,756,000. Additionally, an examination of Harley's pension footnotes indicates that the pension plan is currently overfunded but that accounting rules require the recognition of a net liability of $21,705,000. This overstatement of a liability is somewhat offset by an underfunded postretirement health care plan that understates liabilities by $15,400,000.

Stavros makes the following adjustments on an after-tax basis (HDI's average tax rate is 37 percent) to his book value computation (in dollars):

| | |
|---|---|
| Total shareholders equity | $1,405,655,000 |
| Plus inventory adjustment | 18,825,000 × 0.63 = 11,859,750 |
| Plus pension adjustment | 21,705,000 × 0.63 = 13,674,150 |
| Less post-retirement adjustment | 15,400,000 × 0.63 = (9,702,000) |
| Adjusted book value | $1,421,486,900 |
| Adjusted book value per share | $4.71 |

In the above calculations, the after-tax amount is found by multiplying the pretax amount by $(1 - 0.37) = 0.63$. Stavros is putting all the company's inventory valuation on a FIFO basis for comparability. Using after-tax amounts is necessary because if Harley Davidson were to change its inventory method to FIFO, the change would result in higher taxes as HDI liquidates old inventory. Although inventory on the balance sheet would increase by $18,825,000, taxes payable would also increase (or cash would decrease). As a result, the net effect on book value equals the change in inventory less the associated tax increase.

In conclusion, adjusted book value per share is $4.71.[34] Based on a price of $42.00 shortly after year-end, HDI has a P/B (adjusted basis) of $42/$4.71 = 8.9. Outstanding stock options could dilute both book value per share figures by $0.07, which would have a small impact on these ratios.

## 4.2 Valuation Based on Forecasted Fundamentals

We can use fundamental forecasts to estimate a stock's justified P/B. For example, assuming the Gordon growth model and using the expression $g = b \times$ ROE for the sustainable growth rate, the expression for the justified P/B based on the most recent book value $(B_0)$ is[35]

$$\frac{P_0}{B_0} = \frac{\text{ROE} - g}{r - g}$$

(43-2)

For example, if a business's ROE is 12 percent, its required rate of return is 10 percent, and its expected growth rate is 7 percent, then its justified P/B based on fundamentals is $(0.12 - 0.07)/(0.10 - 0.07) = 1.7$.

---

[34] The calculation of tangible book value per share (adjusted basis for inventory accounting method) is as follows:

| | |
|---|---|
| Adjusted book value | $1,421,486,900 |
| Less goodwill | (54,331,000) |
| Tangible adjusted book value | $1,367,155,900 |
| Tangible adjusted book value per share | $4.53 |

and price to tangible book value is 9.3.

[35] According to the Gordon growth model, $V_0 = E_1 \times (1 - b)/(r - g)$. Defining ROE $= E_1/B_0$, so $E_1 = B_0 \times$ ROE, and substituting for $E_1$ into the prior expression, we have $V_0 = B_0 \times$ ROE $\times (1 - b)/(r - g)$, giving $V_0/B_0 =$ ROE $\times (1 - b)/(r - g)$. The sustainable growth rate expression is $g = b \times$ ROE. Substituting $b = g/$ROE into the expression just given for $V_0/B_0$, we have $V_0/B_0 = (\text{ROE} - g)/(r - g)$. Because justified price is intrinsic value, $V_0$, we obtain Equation 43-2.

Equation 43-2 states that the justified P/B is an increasing function of ROE, all else equal. Because the numerator and denominator are differences of ROE and $r$, respectively, from the same quantity, $g$, what determines the justified P/B in Equation 43-2 is ROE in relation to the required rate of return, $r$. The larger ROE is in relation to $r$, the higher the justified P/B based on fundamentals.[36]

A practical insight from Equation 43-2 is that we cannot evaluate whether a particular value of the P/B reflects undervaluation without taking into account the business's profitability. Equation 43-2 suggests as well that given two stocks with the same P/B, the one with the higher ROE is relatively undervalued, all else equal. These relationships have been confirmed using cross-sectional regression analysis.[37]

Further insight into the P/B comes from the residual income model, which was mentioned in the reading on discounted dividend valuation. The expression for the justified P/B based on the residual income valuation is[38]

$$\frac{P_0}{B_0} = 1 + \frac{\text{Present value of expected future residual earnings}}{B_0} \qquad \textbf{(43-3)}$$

Equation 43-3, which makes no special assumptions about growth, states the following:

▶ If the present value of expected future residual earnings is zero—for example, if the business just earns its required return on investment in every period—the justified P/B is 1.

▶ If the present value of expected future residual earnings is positive (negative), the justified P/B is greater than (less than) 1.

## 4.3 Valuation Using Comparables

To use the method of comparables for valuing stocks using a P/B, we follow the same steps given in Section 3.3, illustrated there with P/Es. In contrast to EPS, however, analysts' forecasts of book value are not aggregated and widely disseminated by vendors such as First Call/Thomson Financial and Zacks; in practice, most analysts use trailing book value in calculating P/Bs.[39] Evaluation of relative P/Bs should consider differences in return on invested capital (as measured by ROE in this context), risk, and expected earnings growth.

---

[36] This relationship can be seen clearly if we set $g = 0$ (the no-growth case): $P_0/B_0 = \text{ROE}/r$.

[37] Harris and Marston (1994) perform a regression of B/MV (book to market, the inverse of the P/B) against variables for growth (mean analyst forecasts) and risk (beta) for a large sample of companies over the period July 1982 to December 1989. The estimated regression was

B/MV = $1.172 - 4.15 \times$ Growth + $0.093 \times$ Risk ($R^2 = 22.9\%$)

The coefficient of $-4.15$ indicates that expected growth was negatively related to B/MV, and, as a consequence, positively related to P/B. Risk was positively related to B/MV and thus negatively related to P/B. Both variables were statistically significant with growth having the greatest impact. Fairfield (1994) also found that P/Bs are related to future expectations of ROE in the predicted fashion.

[38] Noting that (ROE $- r) \times B_0$ would define a level residual income stream, we can show that Equation 43-2 is consistent with Equation 43-3 (a general expression) as follows. In $P_0/B_0 = (\text{ROE} - g)/(r - g)$, we can successively rewrite the numerator (ROE $- g) + r - r = (r - g) +$ (ROE $- r$), so $P_0/B_0 = [(r - g) + (\text{ROE} - r)]/(r - g) = 1 + (\text{ROE} - r)/(r - g)$, which can be written $P_0/B_0 = 1 + [(\text{ROE} - r)/(r - g)] \times B_0/B_0 = 1 + [(\text{ROE} - r) \times B_0/(r - g)]/B_0$; the second term in the final expression is the present value of residual income divided by $B_0$ as in Equation 43-3.

[39] Because equity in successive balance sheets is linked by net income from the income statement, however, the analyst could, given dividend forecasts, translate EPS forecasts into corresponding book value forecasts, taking account of any anticipated ownership transactions.

## EXAMPLE 21

### P/B Comparables Approach

Todd Fisher, CFA, is a portfolio manager with Midland Value, a mid-cap value mutual fund. Recently, a property and casualty company owned by the fund was acquired by a large-cap insurance company. Todd is seeking a mid-cap replacement for this position. Given the fund's value orientation, Todd is particularly interested in mid-cap property and casualty companies selling at a reasonable multiple to book value. Todd's initial research has resulted in a short list of four candidates: Allmerica Financial Corporation (NYSE: AFC), American Financial Group (NYSE: AFG), Safeco Corporation (Nasdaq NMS: SAFC), and Old Republic International Corporation (NYSE: ORI). Table 12 presents information on these companies.[40]

### TABLE 12  P/B Comparables Approach

| | Price to Book Value | | | | | | | Forecasted | |
|---|---|---|---|---|---|---|---|---|---|
| Year | 1996 | 1997 | 1998 | 1999 | 2000 | Five-Year Average | Current | ROE | Beta |
| AFC | 1.0 | 1.1 | 1.4 | 1.4 | 1.6 | 1.3 | 0.8 | 9.5% | 1.10 |
| AFG | 1.5 | 1.5 | 1.6 | 1.2 | 1.0 | 1.4 | 1.0 | 13.5% | 0.95 |
| SAFC | 1.2 | 1.2 | 1.1 | 0.8 | 0.9 | 1.0 | 1.1 | 10% | 1.05 |
| ORI | 1.4 | 1.6 | 1.4 | 0.6 | 1.6 | 1.3 | 1.2 | 11% | 0.90 |
| Property/ casualty industry (mean value) | | | | | | | 2.2 | 11% | |

*Sources:* Morningstar and *The Value Line Investment Survey* for ROE forecasts.

Based only on the information in Table 12, answer the following questions:

1. Discuss the valuation of ORI relative to the industry.
2. Discuss the valuation of AFG relative to the industry and peer companies.

**Solution to 1:** ORI is selling at a P/B that is only 55 percent of the industry mean, although its forecasted ROE equals the mean forecasted ROE for the industry, 11 percent. ORI appears to be relatively undervalued based on an industry benchmark.

**Solution to 2:** AFG is selling at a P/B that is only 45 percent of the industry mean P/B. At the same time, its expected ROE is distinctly higher than the industry's. On the basis of the data given, AFG appears to be undervalued relative to the industry benchmark. AFG also appears to be undervalued

---

[40] Forecasted ROE refers to forecasts for 2004 to 2006.

with respect to SAFC and probably AFC and ORI as well, based on the data given:

▶ AFG zhas a lower P/B, a higher expected ROE, and a lower beta than SAFC.

▶ Although the P/B of AFG is 25 percent higher than that of AFC, its expected ROE is 42 percent higher than AFC, with lower risk as judged by beta.

▶ With a P/B that is about 17 percent smaller than ORI's, a higher expected ROE, and only a 0.05 difference in beta, AFG also may be relatively undervalued with respect to ORI.

# PRICE TO SALES                                            5

Certain types of privately held companies, including investment management companies and companies in partnership form, have long been valued as a multiple of annual revenues. In recent decades, the ratio of price to sales has become well known as a valuation indicator for publicly traded companies as well. According to the *Merrill Lynch Institutional Factor Survey*, from 1989 to 2001, on average, slightly more than one-quarter of respondents consistently used the P/S in their investment process.

Analysts have offered the following rationales for using P/S:

▶ Sales are generally less subject to distortion or manipulation than are other fundamentals, such as EPS or book value. Through discretionary accounting decisions concerning expenses, for example, management can distort EPS as a reflection of economic performance. In contrast, total sales, as the top line in the income statement, is prior to any expenses.

▶ Sales are positive even when EPS is negative. Therefore, analysts can use P/S when EPS is negative, whereas the P/E based on a negative EPS is not meaningful.

▶ Because sales are generally more stable than EPS, which reflects operating and financial leverage, P/S is generally more stable than P/E. P/S may be more meaningful than P/E when EPS is abnormally high or low.

▶ P/S has been viewed as appropriate for valuing the stock of mature, cyclical, and zero-income companies (Martin 1998).

▶ Differences in P/Ss may be related to differences in long-run average returns, according to empirical research.[41]

Possible drawbacks of using P/S in practice include the following:

▶ A business may show high growth in sales even when it is not operating profitably as judged by earnings and cash flow from operations. To have value as a going concern, a business must ultimately generate earnings and cash.

▶ P/S does not reflect differences in cost structures among different companies.

▶ Although relatively robust with respect to manipulation, revenue recognition practices offer the potential to distort P/S.

---

[41] See Nathan, Sivakumar, and Vijayakumar (2001), O'Shaughnessy (1997), and Senchack and Martin (1987).

## 5.1 Determining Sales

P/S is calculated as price per share divided by annual net sales per share (net sales is total sales less returns and customer discounts). Analysts usually use annual sales from the company's most recent fiscal year in the calculation, as illustrated in Example 22. Because valuation is forward-looking in principle, the analyst may also develop and use P/Ss based on forecasts of next year's sales.

### EXAMPLE 22

**Calculating P/S**

In 2001, Abitibi-Consolidated (Toronto Stock Exchange: A.TO), a manufacturer of newsprint and groundwood papers, reported 2001 net sales of CAD6,032,000,000 with 440 million shares outstanding. Calculate the P/S for Abitibi based on a closing price of CAD13.38 on 14 February 2002.

Sales per share = CAD6,032,000,000/440,000,000 = CAD13.71

So, P/S = CAD13.38/CAD13.71 = 0.9759 or 1.0.

Although the determination of sales is more straightforward than the determination of earnings, the analyst should evaluate a company's revenue recognition practices, in particular those tending to speed up the recognition of revenues. An analyst using a P/S approach who does not also assess the quality of accounting for sales may be led to place too high a value on such companies' shares. Example 23 illustrates the problem.

### EXAMPLE 23

**Revenue Recognition Practices (1)**

Analysts label stock markets as *bubbles* when market prices appear to lose contact with intrinsic value. The run-up of the prices of Internet stocks in U.S. markets in the 1998–2000 period, in the view of many, represented a bubble. During this period, many analysts adopted P/S as a metric for valuing Internet stocks with negative earnings and cash flow. Perhaps at least partly as a result of this practice, some Internet companies engaged in questionable revenue recognition practices to justify their high valuations. In order to increase sales, some companies engaged in activities such as bartering website advertising with other Internet companies. For example, Internet Revenue.com might barter $1,000,000 worth of banner advertising with RevenueIsUs.com. Each would show $1,000,000 of revenue and $1,000,000 of expense. Although neither had any net income or cash flow, each company's revenue growth and market valuation was enhanced (at least temporarily). The value placed on the advertising was also questionable. As a result of these and other questionable activities, the U.S. SEC issued a stern warning to companies. International accounting standard setters have begun a study to define revenue recognition principles. The analyst should review footnote disclosures to assess whether the company may be recognizing revenue prematurely or otherwise aggressively.

Example 24 illustrates another instance in which an analyst would need to look behind the accounting numbers.

---

## EXAMPLE 24

### Revenue Recognition Practices (2)

Sales on a **bill-and-hold basis** involve selling products but not delivering those products until a later date.[42] Sales on this basis have the effect of accelerating sales into an earlier reporting period. The following is a case in point. In its Form 10K filed 6 March 1998, for fiscal year ended 28 December 1997, Sunbeam Corporation listed the following footnote:

1. *Operations and significant accounting policies revenue recognition.* The company recognizes revenues from product sales principally at the time of shipment to customers. In limited circumstances, at the customer's request the company may sell seasonal product on a bill and hold basis provided that the goods are completed, packaged and ready for shipment, such goods are segregated and the risks of ownership and legal title have passed to the customer. The amount of such bill and hold sales at 29 December 1997 was approximately 3 percent of consolidated revenues. Net sales are comprised of gross sales less provisions for expected customer returns, discounts, promotional allowances and cooperative advertising.

After internal and SEC investigations, the company restated its financial results, including a restated revenue recognition policy:

*Revenue recognition.* The company recognizes sales and related cost of goods sold from product sales when title passes to the customers which is generally at the time of shipment. Net sales is comprised of gross sales less provisions for estimated customer returns, discounts, promotional allowances, cooperative advertising allowances and costs incurred by the company to ship product to customers. Reserves for estimated returns are established by the company concurrently with the recognition of revenue. Reserves are established based on a variety of factors, including historical return rates, estimates of customer inventory levels, the market for the product and projected economic conditions. The company monitors these reserves and makes adjustment to them when management believes that actual returns or costs to be incurred differ from amounts recorded. In some situations, the company has shipped product with the right of return where the company is unable to reasonably estimate the level of returns and/or the sale is contingent upon the resale of the product. In these situations, the company does not recognize revenue upon product shipment, but rather when it is reasonably expected the product will not be returned.

---

[42] For companies whose reports must conform to U.S. SEC accounting regulations, revenue from bill-and-hold sales cannot be reported unless the risk of loss on the products transfers to the buyer and additional criteria are met (see SEC Staff Accounting Bulletin 101 for criteria).

> The company had originally reported revenue of \$1,168,182,000 for the fiscal year ended 31 December 1997. After restatement, the company reported revenue of \$1,073,000,000 for the same period—a more than 8 percent reduction in revenue. The analyst reading the footnote in the original report would have noted the bill-and-hold practices and reduced revenue by 3 percent. This company engaged in other accounting practices tending to inflate revenue, which did not come to light until the investigation.

Sometimes, as in Example 24, it is not possible to determine precisely by how much sales may be overstated. If a company is engaged in questionable revenue recognition practices of an unknown amount, the analyst may well suggest avoiding that security. At the very least, the analyst should be skeptical and assess a higher risk premium, which would result in a lower justified P/S.

## 5.2 Valuation Based on Forecasted Fundamentals

Like other multiples, P/S can be linked to DCF models. In terms of the Gordon growth model, we can state P/S as[43]

$$\frac{P_0}{S_0} = \frac{(E_0/S_0)(1-b)(1+g)}{r-g} \qquad (43\text{-}4)$$

where $E_0/S_0$ is the business's profit margin $PM_0$. Although the profit margin is stated in terms of trailing sales and earnings, the analyst may use a long-term forecasted profit margin in Equation 43-4. Equation 43-4 states that the justified P/S is an increasing function of its profit margin and earnings growth rate, and the intuition generalizes to more complex DCF models. Profit margin is a determinant of the justified P/S not only directly, but also through its effect on $g$. We can illustrate this concept by restating Equation 41-26 from the reading on discounted dividend valuation for the sustainable growth rate, $g$:

$$g = b \times PM_0 \times \frac{\text{Sales}}{\text{Assets}} \times \frac{\text{Assets}}{\text{Shareholders' equity}}$$

where the last three terms come from the DuPont analysis of ROE. An increase (decrease) in the profit margin produces a higher (lower) sustainable growth rate, so long as sales do not decrease (increase) proportionately.[44]

## 5.3 Valuation Using Comparables

Using the method of comparables for valuing stocks using P/S follows the steps given in Section 3.3, which we earlier illustrated using P/E and P/B. As men-

---

[43] The Gordon growth model is $P_0 = D_0(1 + g)/(r - g)$. Substituting $D_0 = E_0(1 - b)$ into the previous equation produces $P_0 = E_0(1 - b)(1 + g)/(r - g)$. Dividing both sides by $S_0$ gives $P_0/S_0 = (E_0/S_0)(1 - b)(1 + g)/(r - g)$.

[44] That is, it is possible that an increase (decrease) in the profit margin could be offset by a decrease (increase) in total asset turnover (Sales/Assets).

**EXAMPLE 25**

### Justified P/S Based on Forecasted Fundamentals

As an automobile analyst, you are valuing the stocks of three automobile manufacturers including General Motors (NYSE: GM) as of the end of 2001. You estimate that GM's required rate of return is 11 percent based on an average of a capital asset pricing model (CAPM) estimate and a bond yield plus risk premium estimate. Your other forecasts are as follows:

- ▶ long-term profit margin = 3.5 percent;
- ▶ dividend payout ratio = 30 percent; and
- ▶ earnings growth rate = 5 percent.

Although you forecast that GM's profit margin for 2001 will be 1 percent, you recognize that 2001 was a year of economic contraction. A profit margin of 3.5 percent is close to GM's long-term average, and an earnings growth rate of 5 percent is close to the median analyst forecast, according to First Call/Thomson Financial. As a first estimate of GM's justified P/S based on forecasted fundamentals, you decide to use Equation 43-4.

**1.** Based on the above data, calculate GM's justified P/S.

**2.** Given an estimate of GM's sales per share for 2001 of $295, what is the intrinsic value of GM stock?

**3.** Given a market price for GM of $53 as of 6 December 2001, and your answer to Problem 2, state whether GM stock appears to be fairly valued, overvalued, or undervalued.

**Solution to 1:** Using Equation 43-4, we calculate GM's justified P/S as follows:

$$\frac{P_0}{S_0} = \frac{0.035 \times 0.30 \times 1.05}{0.11 - 0.05} = 0.1838$$

**Solution to 2:** An estimate of intrinsic value is $0.1838 \times \$295 = \$54.22$. Rounding P/S to two decimal places, we can calculate intrinsic value as $0.18 \times \$295 = \$53.10$.

**Solution to 3:** GM stock appears to be approximately fairly valued, or slightly undervalued.

tioned earlier, P/Ss are usually reported based on trailing sales. The analyst may also base a relative valuation on P/Ss calculated on forecasted sales, given that the analyst has developed models for forecasting sales.[45] In valuing stocks using the method of comparables, analysts should also gather information on profit margin, expected earnings growth, and risk. As always, the quality of accounting merits investigation as well.

---

[45] Unlike EPS forecasts, analysts' sales forecasts are not generally gathered and disseminated.

## EXAMPLE 26

### P/S Comparables Approach

Continuing with the valuation project, you have compiled the information on GM and peer companies Ford Motor Corporation (NYSE: F) and DaimlerChrysler (NYSE: DCX) given in Table 13.

### TABLE 13    P/S Comparables (as of 6 December 2001)

| | Price to Sales | | | 2000 Profit Margin | Forecast Profit Margin | Median Analyst Long-Term EPS Growth Forecast | Beta |
|---|---|---|---|---|---|---|---|
| | Current Close | YTD High | YTD Low | | | | |
| General Motors (GM) | 0.16 | 0.21 | 0.12 | 3.0% | 2.5% | 5.0% | 1.11 |
| Ford (F) | 0.19 | 0.29 | 0.16 | 2.8% | 3.0% | 5.0% | 0.99 |
| DaimlerChrysler (DCX) | 0.32 | 0.37 | 0.18 | 2.2% | 2.6% | 7.0% | 1.23 |

*Sources:* Bloomberg LLC, *The Value Line Investment Survey* for profit margin and ROE forecasts, and First Call/Thomson Financial for EPS growth forecasts.

Answer the following questions using the data in Table 13:

1. Based on the P/S (using the current close) and referencing no other information, does GM appear to be relatively undervalued?

2. State whether GM or DCX is most closely comparable to Ford. Justify your answer.

3. As of the end of 2001, the S&P 500 had a weighted average P/S of 2.5 and a median P/S of 1.27. GM, F, and DCX have traded at P/Ss that represent discounts of as much as 90 percent from the weighted average P/S for the S&P 500. Can you conclude from this fact alone that, as a group, the three automobile makers were undervalued in absolute terms? Explain your answer.

**Solution to 1:** Because the P/S for GM, 0.16, is the lowest of the three P/Ss, GM appears to be relatively undervalued, referencing no other information.

**Solution to 2:** Ford appears to be more closely matched to GM than to DaimlerChrysler on the basis of the information given. The profit margin, the growth rate *g*, and risk are key fundamentals in the P/S approach. Ford closely matches GM along the dimension of expected growth. The risk of Ford stock as measured by beta is closer to GM than to DaimlerChrysler. The comparison of profit margins, reflecting cost structure, is less conclusive but does not contradict the general conclusion. The current profit margin of Ford is close to that of General Motors (2.8%/3% = 0.933 or 93% of GM's) but well above that of DaimlerChrysler (2.8%/2.2% = 1.27 or 127% of DCX's). The forecast is for Ford to take the lead in profit margin over GM and DCX by about an equal amount.

An interesting point arises here. DCX's actual net profit margin per the unadjusted numbers in its Form 20-F Annual Report filing with the U.S. SEC was 4.86%, and some vendors report that number. Using 4.86%, the analyst might conclude that DCX had the lowest cost structure among the three companies, rather than the highest, in 2000. This percentage, however, includes gains from the sales of business units in 2000, which are nonrecurring. The comparisons in Table 13 better reflect underlying earnings.

**Solution to 3:** No, such a conclusion would not be warranted. Before concluding that the automakers as a group were undervalued in absolute terms, the analyst would need to establish that:

▶ the automakers were relatively undervalued given differences in profit margin, earnings growth prospects, and risk, in relation to the S&P 500; and

▶ the S&P 500 itself was fairly valued at a weighted average P/S of 2.5.

# PRICE TO CASH FLOW

6

Price to cash flow is a widely reported valuation indicator. In Block's 1999 survey of AIMR members, cash flow ranked behind only earnings in importance. According to the *Merrill Lynch Institutional Factor Survey*, price to cash flow on average saw wider use in investment practice than P/E, P/B, P/S, or dividend yield in the 1989–2001 period, among the institutional investors surveyed.[46]

In this section, we present price to cash flow based on alternative major cash flow concepts. With the wide variety of cash flow concepts in use, the analyst should be especially careful that she understands (and communicates, as a writer) the exact definition of *cash flow* that is the basis for the analysis.

Analysts have offered the following rationales for the use of price to cash flow:

▶ Cash flow is less subject to manipulation by management than earnings.[47]

▶ Because cash flow is generally more stable than earnings, price to cash flow is generally more stable than P/E.

▶ Using price to cash flow rather than P/E addresses the issue of differences in accounting conservatism between companies (differences in the quality of earnings).

▶ Differences in price to cash flow may be related to differences in long-run average returns, according to empirical research.[48]

Possible drawbacks to the use of price to cash flow include the following:

---

[46] On average, 46.1 percent of respondents reported consistently using price to cash flow over this period. In one year (2001), price to cash flow ranked first among the 23 factors surveyed.

[47] Cash flow from operations, precisely defined, can be manipulated only through "real" activities, such as the sale of receivables.

[48] See for example O'Shaughnessy (1997), who examined price to cash flow, and Hackel, Livnat, and Rai (1994) and Hackel and Livnat (1991), who examined price to average free cash flow.

## EXAMPLE 27

### Accounting Methods and Cash Flow

One approximation of cash flow in practical use is EPS plus depreciation, amortization, and depletion. Even this simple approximation can point to issues of interest to the analyst in valuation, as this stylized illustration shows. Hypothetical companies A and B have constant cash revenues and cash expenses (as well as a constant number of shares outstanding) in 2000, 2001, and 2002. Company A incurs total depreciation of $15.00 per share during the three-year period, which it spreads out evenly (straight-line depreciation, SLD). Because revenues, expenses, and depreciation are constant over the period, EPS for Business A is also constant, say at $10, as given in Column 1 in Table 14. Business B is identical to Business A except that it uses accelerated depreciation: Depreciation is 150 percent of SLD in 2000, declining to 50 percent of SLD in 2002, as given in Column 5. (We assume both A and B use the same depreciation method for tax purposes.)

### TABLE 14  Earning Growth Rates and Cash Flow (All Amounts per Share)

| Year | Company A | | | Company B | | |
|---|---|---|---|---|---|---|
| | Earnings (1) | Depreciation (2) | Cash Flow (3) | Earnings (4) | Depreciation (5) | Cash Flow (6) |
| 2000 | $10.00 | $5.00 | $15.00 | $7.50 | $7.50 | $15.00 |
| 2001 | $10.00 | $5.00 | $15.00 | $10.00 | $5.00 | $15.00 |
| 2002 | $10.00 | $5.00 | $15.00 | $12.50 | $2.50 | $15.00 |
| | Sum | $15.00 | | Sum | $15.00 | |

Because of different choices in how Company A and B depreciate for financial reporting purposes, Company A's EPS is flat at $10.00 (Column 1) whereas Company B's shows 29 percent compound growth, $(\$12.50/\$7.50)^{1/2} - 1.00 = 0.29$ (Column 4). Company B shows apparent positive earnings momentum. As analysts comparing Companies A and B, we might be misled using EPS numbers as reported (without putting EPS on a comparable basis). For both companies, however, cash flow per share is level at $15. Depreciation may be the simplest noncash charge to understand; write-offs and other noncash charges may offer more latitude for the management of earnings. Hawkins (1998) summarizes many corporate accounting issues for analysts, including how accounting choices can create the effect of earnings momentum.

▶ When the EPS plus noncash charges approximation to cash flow from operations is used, items affecting actual cash flow from operations, such as noncash revenue and net changes in working capital, are ignored.[49]

▶ Theory views free cash flow to equity (FCFE) rather than cash flow as the appropriate variable for valuation. We can use P/FCFE ratios but FCFE does have the possible drawback of being more volatile compared to cash flow, for many businesses. FCFE is also more frequently negative than cash flow.

---

[49] For example, aggressive recognition (front-end loading) of revenue would not be captured in the earnings-plus-noncash-charges definition.

## 6.1 Determining Cash Flow

In practice, analysts and data vendors often use simple approximations to cash flow from operations in calculating cash flow in price to cash flow. For many companies, depreciation and amortization are the major noncash charges regularly added to net income in the process of calculating cash flow from operations by the add-back method. A representative approximation specifies cash flow per share as EPS plus per-share depreciation, amortization, and depletion.[50] We call this estimation the earnings-plus-noncash-charges definition and use the symbol CF for it, understanding that this definition is one common usage in calculating price to cash flow rather than a technically accurate definition from an accounting perspective. We will also introduce more technically accurate cash flow concepts: cash flow from operations (CFO), free cash flow to equity (FCFE), and EBITDA, an estimate of pre-interest, pre-tax operating cash flow.[51]

---

### EXAMPLE 28

**Calculating Earnings-Plus-Noncash Charges (CF)**

In 2000, Koninklijke Philips Electronics N.V. reported net income of €9,602 million, equal to basic EPS of €7.31, as well as depreciation and amortization of €2,320 million or €1.75 per share. Koninklijke Philips trades both on the New York Stock Exchange (NYSE: PHG) and Euronext Amsterdam (AEX: PHIA). An AEX price for Koninklijke Philips as of early March 2001 was €30. Calculate the P/CF ratio for PHIA.

EPS plus per-share depreciation, amortization, and depletion is €7.31 + €1.75 = €9.06 per share. Thus P/CF = €30/€9.06 = 3.31, or 3.3.

---

Most frequently, trailing price to cash flow are reported. A trailing price to cash flow is calculated as the current market price divided by the sum of the most recent four quarters' cash flow per share. A fiscal year definition is also possible, just as in the case of EPS.

Rather than use an approximate EPS-plus-noncash charges concept of cash flow, analysts can use cash flow from operations (CFO) in a price multiple. CFO is found in the statement of cash flows. Careful analysts often adjust CFO as reported to remove the effects of any items related to financing or investing activities. For example, when CFO includes cash outflows for interest expense and cash inflows for interest income, as in U.S. GAAP accounting, one common adjustment is to add back to CFO the quantity (Net cash interest outflow) × (1 − Tax rate).[52] Analysts also adjust CFO for components not expected to persist into future time periods.

---

[50] This representation is, for example, the definition in Value Line (2001). Value Line states its definition of cash flow in terms of "net income minus preferred dividends (if any)," which is net income to common shareholders, to which it adds the above three noncash charges. The resulting sum is then divided by the number of shares outstanding. Note that depletion is an expense only for natural resource companies.

[51] See Grant and Parker (2001). Grant and Parker point out that EBITDA as a cash flow approximation assumes that changes in working capital accounts are immaterial. The EPS-plus-noncash-charges definition makes the same assumption (it is essentially earnings before depreciation and amortization).

[52] Under International Accounting Standards (IAS), interest income and interest expense may or may not be in CFO. Therefore, an adjustment may be necessary to match U.S. GAAP and IAS. Consistency in treatment is important.

In addition, the analyst can relate price to FCFE, the cash flow concept with the strongest link to valuation theory. Because the amount of capital expenditures as a fraction of CFO will generally differ among companies being compared, the analyst may find that rankings by P/CFO (as well as P/CF) will differ from rankings by P/FCFE. Because period-by-period FCFE can be more volatile than CFO (or CF), however, a trailing P/FCFE is not necessarily more informative in a valuation. As an example, consider two similar businesses with the same CFO and capital expenditures over a two-year period. If the first company times the expenditures towards the beginning of the period and the second times the expenditures towards the end, the P/FCFE ratios for the two stocks may differ sharply without pointing to a meaningful economic difference between them.[53] This concern can be addressed at least in part by using price to average free cash flow, as in Hackel, Livnat, and Rai (1994).

Another ratio sometimes reported is P/EBITDA.[54] EBITDA is earnings before interest, taxes, depreciation, and amortization. To calculate EBITDA, as discussed in the reading on free cash flow valuation, analysts usually start with earnings from continuing operations excluding nonrecurring items. To that earnings number, interest, taxes, depreciation, and amortization are added. When per-share price is in the numerator, per-share EBITDA is used in the denominator. EBITDA, as already mentioned, is a pre-tax and pre-interest number. Because EBITDA is pre-interest, it is a flow to both debt and equity. As a result, with EBITDA in the denominator of a ratio, total company value (debt plus equity) is more appropriate than common stock value in the numerator. In Section 7, we present a multiple, enterprise value to EBITDA, that is consistent with this observation.

---

## EXAMPLE 29

### Alternative Price to Cash Flow Concepts

In Example 18, we concluded that the P/B was inappropriate for valuing Dell Computer (Nasdaq NMS: DELL) relative to peer companies. In particular, Dell's relatively efficient use of assets penalizes it in P/B comparisons. Because Dell's business model results in relatively strong cash flow, we might compare Dell with its peers on the basis of one or more cash flow measures or related concepts:

▶ EPS-plus-noncash charges (CF);

▶ CFO;

▶ FCFE; and/or

▶ EBITDA.

In this example, we illustrate the calculation of price multiples based on these concepts from actual financials. The two financial statements needed to calculate any of these concepts are the income statement and the statement of cash flows, given in Tables 15(A) and 15(B).

---

[53] The analyst could appropriately use the FCFE discounted cash flow model value, which incorporates all expected future free cash flows to equity, however.

[54] Another concept that has become popular is cash earnings, which has been defined in various ways, such as earnings plus amortization of intangibles or EBITDA less net financial expenses.

Other information for Dell is as follows:

▶ In the last three years, Dell has had a cash flow "tax benefits of employee stock plans," which it has classified as an operating cash flow. This item, amounting to $929 million in 2001, relates to tax benefits from the exercise of employee stock options during a period of rising stock prices. The amount of such benefits in the future is related to continuing rising stock prices for Dell.

▶ Net investment income of $531 million included $47 million in interest expense. Actual cash interest paid for the year was $49 million. Cash flow from operations as reported incorporates such financing effects. The effective tax rate per the income statement was 30 percent.

▶ Dell stock closed at $27.11 on 16 April 2001.

**TABLE 15(A) Dell Computer Corporation Consolidated Statement of Income (in Millions, except Per-Share Amounts)**

|  | 2 Feb 2001 |
| --- | --- |
| Net revenue | $31,888 |
| Cost of revenue | 25,445 |
| Gross margin | 6,443 |
| Operating expenses |  |
| Selling, general, and administrative | 3,193 |
| Research, development, and engineering | 482 |
| Special charges | 105 |
| Total operating expenses | 3,780 |
| Operating income | 2,663 |
| Investment and other income, net | 531 |
| Income before income taxes and cumulative effect of change in accounting principle | 3,194 |
| Provision for income taxes | (958) |
| Cumulative effect of change in accounting principle, net | (59) |
| Net income | $ 2,177 |
| Earnings per common share: |  |
| Before cumulative effect of change in accounting principle: |  |
| Basic | $ 0.87 |
| Diluted | $ 0.81 |
| After cumulative effect of change in accounting principle: |  |
| Basic | $ 0.84 |
| Diluted | $ 0.79 |
| Weighted average shares outstanding: |  |
| Basic | 2,582 |
| Diluted | 2,746 |

| TABLE 15(B)  Dell Computer Corporation Consolidated Statement of Cash Flows (in Millions) | |
|---|---|
| | **2 Feb 2001** |
| Cash flows from operating activities: | |
| Net income | $ 2,177 |
| Adjustments to reconcile net income to net cash provided by operating activities | |
| Depreciation and amortization | 240 |
| Tax benefits of employee stock plans | 929 |
| Special charges | 105 |
| Gain on sale of investments | (307) |
| Other | 109 |
| Changes in | |
| Operating working capital | 671 |
| Non-current assets and liabilities | 271 |
| Net cash provided by operating activities | 4,195 |
| Cash flows from investing activities: | |
| Investments | |
| Purchases | (2,606) |
| Maturities and sales | 2,331 |
| Capital expenditures | (482) |
| Net cash used in investing activities | (757) |
| Cash flows from financing activities | |
| Purchase of common stock | (2,700) |
| Issuance of common stock under employee plans | 404 |
| Proceeds from issuance of long-term debt, net of issuance costs | — |
| Other | (9) |
| Net cash used in financing activities | (2,305) |
| | |
| Effect of exchange rate changes on cash | (32) |
| Net increase in cash | 1,101 |
| Cash and cash equivalents at beginning of period | 3,809 |
| Cash and cash equivalents at end of period | $4,910 |

Based on the above data, answer the following questions:

1. Calculate P/CF.
2. Calculate P/CFO, adjusting CFO for the "tax benefits of employee stock plans" and for financing effects.
3. Calculate P/FCFE consistent with your work in Problem 2.
4. Calculate P/EBITDA.

**Solution to 1:** Net income = $2,177 million; depreciation and amortization = $240 million; so CF = 2,177 + 240 = $2,417 million. There are 2,582 million shares outstanding. Thus CF = 2,417/2,582 = 0.94 and P/CF = 27.11/0.94 = 28.8.

**Solution to 2:** Cash flow from operations is $4,195 million. Excluding $929 million associated with tax benefits of employee stock plans gives 4,195 − 929 = $3,266. To further adjust CFO for the effect of actual cash interest paid, we have 3,266 + 49(1 − 0.30) = $3,266 + $34.3 = $3,300.3. So $3,300.3/2,582 = $1.28. So P/CFO based on adjusted per-share CFO of $1.28 equals $27.11/$1.28 = 21.2.[55] The logic of excluding the $929 million is that because such tax benefits depend on stock price performance, they may not persist into the future.

**Solution to 3:** Recall that FCFE is cash flow from operations less net investment in fixed capital plus net borrowing. Net cash used in fixed capital (reported above as capital expenditures) was $482 million and net borrowing was zero. Because FCFE is a flow to equity, we must subtract the add-back of $34.3 million that we made in Problem 2. So FCFE is $3,300.3 − $482 − $34.3 = $2,784. Per share we have $2,784/2,582 = $1.08. P/FCFE = $27.11/$1.08 = 25.1.

**Solution to 4:** Net income = $2,177 million, Interest expense = $47 million, Depreciation and amortization = $240 million, Taxes = $958 million. EBITDA = $2,177 + $47 + $240 million + $958 = $3,422. Per share EBITDA = $3,422/2,582 = $1.32. P/EBITDA = $27.11/$1.32 = 20.5.

In summary, this exercise produced multiples ranging from 20.5 for P/EBITDA to 28.8 for P/CF. Consistency in definition is important. Furthermore, if the analyst were featuring diluted EPS in her analysis, she would report cash flow multiples based on 2,746 million diluted shares.

## 6.2 Valuation Based on Forecasted Fundamentals

The relationship between the justified price to cash flow and fundamentals follows from the familiar mathematics of the present value model. The justified price to cash flow is inversely related to the stock's required rate of return and positively related to the growth rate(s) of expected future cash flows (however defined), all else equal. We can find a justified price to cash flow based on fundamentals by finding the value of a stock using the most suitable DCF model and dividing that number by cash flow, using our chosen definition of cash flow. Example 30 illustrates the process.

---

[55] Although 30 percent was the effective tax rate per the income statement, interestingly Dell actually paid no taxes for the year because of the effect of the employee stock options. The adjustment we just illustrated would be appropriate for use in forecasting; adding back the full $49 million (reflecting no taxes) would better reflect actual cash flow for the year purged of financing items.

---

**EXAMPLE 30**

**Justified Price to Cash Flow Based on Forecasted Fundamentals**

As a technology analyst, you are working on the valuation of Dell Computer (Nasdaq NMS: DELL). You have calculated per-share FCFE for DELL of 1.39. As a first estimate of value, you are applying a FCFE model under the assumption of a stable long-term growth rate in FCFE:

$$V_0 = \frac{(1 + g)\,FCFE_0}{r - g}$$

where $g$ is the expected growth rate of FCFE. You estimate trailing FCFE at \$1.39 per share and trailing CF (based on the earnings plus noncash charges definition) at \$0.75. Your other estimates are a 14.5 percent required rate of return and an 8.5 percent expected growth rate of FCFE.

1. What is the intrinsic value of DELL, according to a constant-growth FCFE model?
2. What is the justified P/CF, based on forecasted fundamentals?
3. What is the justified P/FCFE, based on forecasted fundamentals?

**Solution to 1:** Calculate intrinsic value as $(1.085 \times \$1.39)/(0.145 - 0.085) = \$25.14$.

**Solution to 2:** Calculate a justified P/CF based on forecasted fundamentals as \$25.14/\$0.75 = 33.5.

**Solution to 3:** The justified P/FCFE ratio is \$25.14/\$1.39 = 18.1.

---

## 6.3 Valuation Using Comparables

Using the method of comparables for valuing stocks based on price to cash flow follows the steps given in Section 3.3, which we earlier illustrated using P/E, P/B, and P/S.

---

**EXAMPLE 31**

**Price to Cash Flow and Comparables**

As a technology analyst, you have been asked to compare the valuation of Compaq Computer Corporation (NYSE: CPQ) with Gateway, Inc. (NYSE: GTW).[56] One valuation metric you are considering is P/CF. Table 16 gives information on P/CF, P/FCFE, and selected fundamentals as of 16 April 2001.

---

[56] In 2002, Compaq Computer Corporation merged with Hewlett-Packard Corporation.

| TABLE 16 A Comparison between Two Companies (All Amounts per Share) | | | | | | | |
| --- | --- | --- | --- | --- | --- | --- | --- |
| | Current Price | Trailing CF per Share | P/CF | Trailing FCFE per Share | P/FCFE | Consensus Five-Year Growth Forecast | Beta |
| CPQ | $17.98 | $1.84 | 9.8 | $0.29 | 62 | 13.4% | 1.50 |
| GTW | $15.65 | $1.37 | 11.4 | −$1.99 | NM | 10.6% | 1.45 |

*Source: The Value Line Investment Survey.*

Using the information in Table 16, compare the valuations of CPQ and GTW using the P/CF multiple, assuming that the two stocks have approximately equal risk.

CPQ is selling at a P/CF (9.8) approximately 14 percent smaller than the P/CF of GTW (11.4). We would expect on that basis that, all else equal, investors anticipate a higher growth rate for GTW. In fact, the consensus five-year earnings growth forecast for CPQ is 280 basis points higher than for GTW. As of the date of the comparison, CPQ appears to be relatively undervalued compared with GTW, as judged by P/CF. The information in Table 16 on FCFE supports the proposition that CPQ may be relatively undervalued. Positive FCFE for CPQ suggests that growth was funded internally; negative FCFE for GTW suggests the need for external funding of growth.

# ENTERPRISE VALUE TO EBITDA                 7

In Section 6, when presenting the P/EBITDA multiple, we stated that because EBITDA is a flow to both debt and equity, a multiple using total company value in the numerator was logically more appropriate. Enterprise value to EBITDA responds to this need. **Enterprise value (EV)** is total company value (the market value of debt, common equity, and preferred equity) minus the value of cash and investments. Because the numerator is enterprise value, EV/EBITDA is a valuation indicator for the overall company rather than common stock. If the analyst can assume that the business's debt and preferred stock (if any) are efficiently priced, the analyst can also draw an inference about the valuation of common equity. Such an assumption is often reasonable.

Analysts have offered the following rationales for using EV/EBITDA:

► EV/EBITDA may be more appropriate than P/E for comparing companies with different financial leverage (debt), because EBITDA is a pre-interest earnings figure, in contrast to EPS, which is post-interest.

► By adding back depreciation and amortization, EBITDA controls for differences in depreciation and amortization across businesses. For this reason, EV/EBITDA is frequently used in the valuation of capital-intensive businesses (for example, cable companies and steel companies). Such businesses typically have substantial depreciation and amortization expenses.

► EBITDA is frequently positive when EPS is negative.

Possible drawbacks to EV/EBITDA include the following:

▶ EBITDA will overestimate cash flow from operations if working capital is growing. EBITDA also ignores the effects of differences in revenue recognition policy on cash flow from operations.[57]

▶ Free cash flow to the firm (FCFF), which directly reflects the amount of required capital expenditures, has a stronger link to valuation theory than does EBITDA. Only if depreciation expenses match capital expenditures do we expect EBITDA to reflect differences in businesses' capital programs. This qualification to EBITDA comparisons can be meaningful for the capital-intensive businesses to which EV/EBITDA is often applied.

## 7.1 Determining EBITDA

We illustrated the calculation of EBITDA in the reading on free cash flow valuation as well as in Section 6 of this reading. As discussed above, analysts commonly define enterprise value as follows:

| | |
|---|---|
| Market value of common equity | (Number of shares outstanding × Price per share) |
| Plus: | Market value of preferred stock (if any) |
| Plus: | Market value of debt |
| Less: | Cash and investments |
| Equals: | Enterprise value |

Cash and investments (sometimes termed nonearning assets) are subtracted because EV is designed to measure the price an acquirer would pay for a company as a whole. The acquirer must buy out current equity and debt providers but then gets access to the cash and investments, which lower the net cost of the acquisition. The same logic explains the use of market values: In repurchasing debt, an acquirer would have to pay market prices. Some debt, however, may be private and not trade, or be publicly traded but trade infrequently. When the analyst does not have market values, he uses book values (values as given in the balance sheet). Example 32 illustrates the calculation of EV/EBITDA.

---

### EXAMPLE 32

#### Calculating EV/EBITDA

Comcast Corporation is principally engaged in the development, management, and operation of hybrid fiber-coaxial broadband cable networks, cellular and personal communications systems, and the provision of content. Table 17 gives excerpts from the consolidated balance sheet (as of 31 December 2000).

---

[57] See Moody's Investors Service (2000) and Grant and Parker (2001) for additional issues and concerns.

| TABLE 17 | Comcast Corporation Liabilities and Shareholders' Equity (in Millions, except per Share) |
|---|---|
| | **31 Dec 2000** |

| **Liabilities and Shareholders' Equity** | |
|---|---|
| **Current liabilities** | |
| Accounts payable and accrued expenses | $2,852.9 |
| Accrued interest | 105.5 |
| Deferred income taxes | 789.9 |
| Current portion of long-term debt | 293.9 |
| Total Current Liabilities | 4,042.2 |
| **Noncurrent liabilities** | |
| Long-term debt, less current portion | 10,517.4 |
| Deferred income taxes | 5,786.7 |
| Minority interest and other commitments and contingencies | 1,257.2 |
| Common equity put options | 54.6 |
| Total Noncurrent Liabilities | 17,615.9 |
| **Shareholders' equity** | |
| Preferred Stock: Authorized, 20,000,000 shares 5.25% | |
|    Series B mandatorily redeemable convertible, $1,000 par value; issued, 59,450 at redemption value | 59.5 |
| Class A special common stock, $1 par value: Authorized, 2,500,000,000 shares; issued, 931,340,103; outstanding, 908,015,192 | 908.0 |
| Class A common stock, $1 par value: Authorized, 200,000,000 shares; issued and outstanding, 21,832,250 | 21.8 |
| Class B common stock, $1 par value: Authorized, 50,000,000 shares; issued and outstanding, 9,444,375 | 9.4 |
| Additional capital | 11,598.8 |
| Retained earnings (accumulated deficit) | 1,056.5 |
| Accumulated other comprehensive income | 432.4 |
| Total shareholders' equity | 14,086.4 |
| **Total Liabilities and Shareholders' Equity** | **$35,744.5** |

An unusual item in the balance sheet is "common equity put options," which were issued as part of a share repurchase program. Because the value of these puts should be reflected in the price of the common stock, the $54.6 million should not be included in calculating EV. The balance sheet shows that Comcast has three classes of common stock:

▶ Class A Special Common Stock (Nasdaq NMS: CMCSK) is generally nonvoting. This issue is a component of the S&P 500;

▶ Class A (Nasdaq NMS: CMCSA) is entitled to one vote; and

► Class B is entitled to 15 votes and is convertible, share for share, into Class A or Class A Special Common Stock. This issue is not publicly traded.

Closing share prices as of 7 March 2001 were $45.875 for CMCSK and $45.25 for CMCSA. "Minority interest and other" is to be viewed as an equity item.[58]

The asset side of the balance sheet (as of 31 December 2000) gave the following items (in millions):

| | |
|---|---|
| Cash and cash equivalents | $651.5 |
| Investments | $3,059.7 |

The income statement for the year ending 31 December 2000 gave the following items (in millions):

| | |
|---|---|
| Net income | $2,021.5 |
| Net income for common stockholders | $1,998.0 |
| Interest expense | $691.4 |
| Taxes | $1,441.3 |
| Depreciation | $837.3 |
| Amortization | $1,794.0 |

Based on the above information, calculate EV/EBITDA.

**Solution:** We first calculate EBITDA. We always select net income (which is net income available to both preferred and common equity) in the EBITDA calculation:

| | 2000 |
|---|---|
| Net income | $2,021.5 |
| Interest | $691.4 |
| Taxes | $1,441.3 |
| Depreciation | $837.3 |
| Amortization | +$1,794.0 |
| EBITDA | $6,785.5 |

We calculate the value of all equity, adding to it "minority interest and other."

| | Millions |
|---|---|
| CMCSK issue ($45.875 × 908.015192 million shares) | 41,655.20 |
| CMCSA issue ($45.25 × 21.83225 million shares) | 987.91 |
| Class B stock (per books) | 9.4 |
| Common equity value | 42,652.51 |
| Preferred equity (per books) | 59.5 |
| Total equity | 42,712.01 |
| Minority interest and other | 1,257.2 |
| Common equity plus minority interest | 43,969.21 |

[58] Minority interest represents the proportionate stake of minority shareholders in a company's consolidated, majority-owned subsidiary.

The value of long-term debt (per the books) is \$10,517.4 million.

The sum of cash and cash equivalents plus investments is \$651.5 million + \$3,059.7 million = \$3,711.2 million.

So, EV = \$43,969.21 million + \$10,517.4 million − \$3,711.2 million = \$50,775.41 million. We conclude that EV/EBITDA = (\$50,775.41 million)/(\$6,785.5 million) = 7.5.

## 7.2 Valuation Based on Forecasted Fundamentals

As with other multiples, intuition concerning the fundamental drivers of enterprise value to EBITDA can help when applying the method of comparables. All else equal, the justified EV/EBITDA based on fundamentals should be positively related to expected growth rate in FCFF and negatively related to the business's weighted-average cost of capital. The analyst should review the statement of cash flows to get a better picture of the relationship of EBITDA to the company's underlying cash flow from operations.

## 7.3 Valuation Using Comparables

A recent equity research report on the cable industry, excerpted in Table 18, illustrates a format for the presentation of relative valuations using EV/EBITDA, which is informally called a "cash flow multiple" in the report. All else equal, a lower EV/EBITDA value relative to peers indicates relative undervaluation. The analyst's recommendations are clearly not completely determined by relative EV/EBITDA, however; from the analyst's perspective, EV/EBITDA is simply one piece of information to consider.

## DIVIDEND YIELD    8

Total return has a capital appreciation component and a dividend yield component. Dividend yield is frequently reported to supply the investor with an estimate of the dividend yield component of total return. Dividend yield is also used as a valuation indicator. According to the *Merrill Lynch Institutional Factor Survey*, from 1989 to 2001, on average slightly less than one-quarter of respondents reported using dividend yield as a factor in the investment process.

Analysts have offered the following rationales for using dividend yields in valuation:

► Dividend yield is a component of total return.

► Dividends are a less risky component of total return than capital appreciation.

Possible drawbacks of dividend yield include the following:

► Dividend yield is only one component of total return; not using all information related to expected return is suboptimal.

► Dividends paid now displace earnings in all future periods (a concept known as the **dividend displacement of earnings**). Investors trade off future earnings growth to receive higher current dividends.

**TABLE 18  EV/EBITDA Multiples Are Well Below Recent Averages. Calendar 2002E Cash Flow Multiples (in Millions, except per Share)**

|  | CMCSK[c] | CHTR[d] | COX | ADLAC[e] | CVC | MCCC[f] | ICCI[g] | Average |
|---|---|---|---|---|---|---|---|---|
| Rating | Strong Buy | Strong Buy | Buy | Strong Buy | Buy | Buy | Buy |  |
| Size ranking | 3 | 4 | 5 | 6 | 7 | 8 |  |  |
| Price | $33.98 | $17.62 | $39.65 | $28.97 | $40.00 | $16.10 | $20.25 |  |
| *Times*... Diluted shares outstanding[a] | 964 | 657 | 620 | 173 | 178 | 119.9 | 61.3 |  |
| *Equals*... Equity market capitalization | $32,754 | $11,583 | $24,576 | $5,016 | $7,104 | $1,930 | $1,242 |  |
| *Plus*... Debt at 12/02 | $10,852 | $17,618 | $8,988 | $13,936 | $6,147 | $3,059 | $1,055 |  |
| *Plus*... Preferred | $0 | $0 | $281 | $148 | $2,630 | $0 | $0 |  |
| *Less*... Nonearning assets at 12/02 | $15,726 | $144 | $5,792 | ($139) | $3,885 | $7 | $19 |  |
| *Less*... Options exercise | $507 | $0 | $80 | $0 | $481 | $0 | $21 |  |
| *Equals*... Enterprise value | $27,373 | $29,057 | $27,973 | $19,239 | $11,514 | $4,982 | $2,257 |  |
| Adjusted Cable EBITDA[b] | $2,455 | $2,134 | $1,822 | $1,616 | $1,012 | $387 | $185 |  |
| *Equals*... |  |  |  |  |  |  |  |  |
| **Cable Cash Flow Multiple** | **11.1×** | **13.6×** | **15.4×** | **11.9×** | **11.4×** | **12.9×** | **12.2×** | **12.6×** |
| Pro forma subscribers at 12/02 | 8,475 | 7,130 | 6,402 | 5,858 | 3,059 | 1,593 | 592 |  |
| Pro forma homes passed at 12/02 | 13,610 | 12,161 | 10,016 | 9,503 | 4,417 | 2,595 | 1,035 |  |
| **Enterprise value per subscriber** | **$3,230** | **$4,075** | **$4,369** | **$3,284** | **$3,764** | **$3,127** | **$3,809** | **$3,665** |
| **Enterprise value per homes passed** | **$2,011** | **$2,389** | **$2,793** | **$2,024** | **$2,607** | **$1,920** | **$2,181** |  |
| Percent of plant > 550 MHz at 12/02 | 98% | 95% | 96% | 96% | 95% | 86% | 95% |  |

[a] Includes primary shares plus in-the-money employee/management options and convertible instruments.

[b] Adjusted Cable EBITDA includes allocated corporate overhead.

[c] Pro forma the AT&T and Adelphia system swaps and AT&T system acquisitions as if all were completed prior to January 1, 2001.

[d] Pro forma the Kalamazoo and AT&T systems acquisitions as if they occurred January 1, 2000.

[e] Pro forma the Century, Frontier, Harron, Coaxial, Benchmark, Cablevision (Cleveland), Prestige, and GS Communications acquisitions as if they took place on January 1, 2000.

[f] Pro forma the AT&T acquisition as if it occurred before January 1, 2000.

[g] All numbers proportional of Insight's 50% stake in the Insight Midwest JV. Pro forma the JV rollup as if it occurred before January 1, 2000.

*Source:* Shapiro, Savner, and Toobig (2001).

▶ The argument about the relative safety of dividends presupposes that the market prices reflect in a biased way differences in the relative risk of the components of return.

## 8.1 Calculation of Dividend Yield

This reading thus far has presented multiples with market price in the numerator. Price to dividend (P/D) ratios have occasionally appeared in valuation, particularly with respect to indexes. Many stocks, however, do not pay dividends, and the P/D ratio is undefined with zero in the denominator; for such stocks, dividend yield is defined. For practical purposes, dividend yield is the preferred way to present this variable. **Trailing dividend yield** is generally calculated as four times the most recent quarterly per-share dividend divided by the current market price per share. (The most recent quarterly dividend times four is known as the **dividend rate**.) The **leading dividend yield** is calculated as forecasted dividends per share over the next year divided by the current market price per share.

---

**EXAMPLE 33**

**Calculating Dividend Yield**

Table 19 gives dividend data for Ford Motor Company (NYSE: F).

**TABLE 19 Dividend Data for Ford Motor Company**

|  | Dividends per Share |
|---|---|
| 1Q:2002 | $0.10 |
| 4Q:2001 | $0.15 |
| 3Q:2001 | $0.30 |
| 2Q:2001 | $0.30 |
| Total | $0.85 |

*Source:* Standard & Poor's Stock Reports.

---

Given a price per share of $14.62, calculate the trailing dividend yield of Ford.

The dividend rate is $0.10 × 4 = $0.40. The dividend yield is $0.40/$14.62 = 0.0274 or 2.7%. This percentage is the yield reported by Standard & Poor's in a stock report on Ford Motor Company dated 16 February 2002.

---

## 8.2 Valuation Based on Forecasted Fundamentals

The relationship of dividend yield to fundamentals can be illustrated in the context of the Gordon growth model. From that model we obtain the expression

$$\frac{D_0}{P_0} = \frac{r - g}{1 + g}$$

**(43-5)**

Equation 43-5 shows that dividend yield is negatively related to the expected rate of growth in dividends and positively related to the stock's required rate of return. The first point implies that the selection of stocks with relatively high dividend yields is consistent with an orientation to a value rather than growth investment style.

## 8.3  Valuation Using Comparables

Using dividend yield with comparables is similar to the process that has been illustrated for other multiples. An analyst compares a company with its peers to determine whether it is attractively priced considering its dividend yield and risk. The analyst should examine whether differences in expected growth explain difference in dividend yield. Another consideration used by some investors is the security of the dividend (the probability that it will be cut).

### EXAMPLE 34

**Dividend Yield Comparables**

William Leiderman is a portfolio manager for a U.S. pension fund's domestic equity portfolio. The portfolio is exempt from taxes, so any differences in the taxation of dividends and capital gains are not relevant. Leiderman's client has a high current income requirement. Leiderman is considering the purchase of utility stocks for the fund as of early April 2002. He has narrowed down his selection to three large-cap utilities serving the southeastern United States, given in Table 20.

**TABLE 20   Using Dividend Yield to Compare Stocks**

| Company | Consensus Forecast Growth | Beta | Dividend Yield |
|---|---|---|---|
| Florida Power and Light (NYSE: FPL) | 6.95% | 0.13 | 3.7% |
| Progress Energy (NYSE: PGN) | 6.79% | 0.09 | 4.4% |
| Southern Company (NYSE: SO) | 5.44% | −0.06 | 4.7% |

*Source:* First Call/Thomson Financial.

All of the securities exhibit similar and low market risk. Although Southern Company has the highest dividend yield, it also has the lowest expected growth rate. Leiderman determines that Progress Energy provides the greatest combination of dividend yield and growth, amounting to 11.19 percent.

# INTERNATIONAL VALUATION CONSIDERATIONS

Clearly, to perform a relative value analysis, an analyst must use comparable companies and underlying financial data prepared using comparable methods. Using relative valuation methods in an international setting is thus difficult. Comparing companies across borders frequently involves accounting method differences, cultural differences, economic differences, and resulting differences in risk and growth opportunities. P/Es for individual companies in the same industry across borders have been found to vary widely.[59] Furthermore, national market P/Es often vary substantially at any single point in time. As of 30 November 1998, P/Es in 10 markets around the world ranged from a low of 18.1 in Hong Kong to a high of 191.0 in Japan.[60]

Although international accounting standards are beginning to converge, significant differences across borders still exist, making comparisons difficult. Even if harmonization of accounting principles is achieved, the need to adjust accounting data for comparability will always remain. As we have seen in earlier sections, even within a single country's accounting standards, differences between companies result from management's accounting choices (e.g., FIFO versus LIFO). The U.S. SEC requires that foreign companies whose securities trade in U.S. markets provide a reconciliation of their earnings from home country accounting principles to U.S. GAAP. This requirement not only assists the analyst in making necessary adjustments but also provides some insight into appropriate adjustments for other companies not required to provide this data. Table 21 presents a reconciliation from International Accounting Standards to U.S. GAAP for Nokia Corporation (NYSE: NOK).

In a study of companies filing such reconciliations to U.S. GAAP, Harris and Muller (1999) classify common differences into seven categories.

| | Mean Adjustment Direction | |
| --- | --- | --- |
| Category | Earnings | Equity |
| Differences in the treatment of goodwill | Minus | Plus |
| Deferred income taxes | Plus | Plus |
| Foreign exchange adjustments | Plus | Minus |
| Research and development costs | Minus | Minus |
| Pension expense | Minus | Plus |
| Tangible asset revaluations | Plus | Minus |
| Other | Minus | Minus |

Although the mean adjustments are presented above, adjustments for individual companies can vary considerably. This list, however, provides the analyst with common adjustments that should be made.

International accounting differences affect the comparability of all price multiples. Of the price multiples examined in this reading, P/CFO and P/FCFE will generally be least affected by accounting differences. P/Bs and P/Es will

---

[59] Copeland, Koller, and Murrin (1994, p. 375) provide an interesting example.
[60] See Schieneman (2000).

**TABLE 21   Principal Differences between IAS and U.S. GAAP for Nokia Corporation (Years Ended 31 December; in Millions)**

|  | 1999 | 1998 |
|---|---|---|
| Reconciliation of net income |  |  |
| Net income reported under IAS | €2,577 | €1,750 |
| U.S. GAAP adjustments |  |  |
| Deferred income taxes | 0 | −70 |
| Pension expense | 9 | 16 |
| Development costs | −47 | −18 |
| Marketable securities | −15 | 29 |
| Sale-leaseback transaction | 4 | 1 |
| Deferred tax effect of U.S. GAAP adjustments | 14 | −19 |
| Net income under U.S. GAAP | €2,542 | €1,689 |
| Reconciliation of shareholders' equity |  |  |
| Total shareholders' equity reported under IAS | €7,378 | €5,109 |
| U.S. GAAP adjustments |  |  |
| Pension expense | 54 | 45 |
| Development costs | −186 | −138 |
| Marketable securities | 142 | 89 |
| Sale-leaseback transaction | 0 | −4 |
| Deferred tax effect of U.S. GAAP adjustments | −4 | 1 |
| Total shareholders' equity under U.S. GAAP | €7,384 | €5,102 |

*Source:* Nokia Corporation Annual Report, 1999.

generally be more severely affected, as will multiples based on concepts such as EBITDA, which start from accounting earnings.

## 10   MOMENTUM VALUATION INDICATORS

The valuation indicators we call momentum indicators relate either price or a fundamental such as earnings to the time series of their own past values, or in some cases to the fundamental's expected value. One style of growth investing uses positive momentum in various senses as a selection criterion, and practitioners sometimes refer to such strategies as growth/momentum investment strategies. Momentum indicators based on price, such as the relative strength indicator discussed below, have also been referred to as **technical indicators**. According to the *Merrill Lynch Institutional Factor Survey*, momentum indicators were among the most popular valuation indicators over 1989 to 2001.[61] In this

---

[61] During the time period, the percentage of respondents who indicated that they used EPS surprise (surprise relative to consensus forecasts), EPS momentum (defined as 12-month trailing EPS divided by year-ago 12-month trailing EPS), and relative strength (defined as the difference between 3-month and 12-month price performance) was 51.5 percent, 46.3 percent, and 39.1 percent, respectively. EPS surprise was the most popular factor of the 23 surveyed over the entire time period.

section, we review three representative momentum group indicators: earnings surprise, standardized unexpected earnings, and relative strength.

To define standardized unexpected earnings, we define **unexpected earnings** (also called **earnings surprise**) as the difference between reported earnings and expected earnings,

$$UE_t = EPS_t - E(EPS_t)$$

where $UE_t$ is the unexpected earnings for quarter $t$, $EPS_t$ is the reported EPS for quarter $t$, and $E(EPS_t)$ is the expected EPS for the quarter. For example, a stock with reported quarterly earnings of $1.05 and expected earnings of $1.00 would have a positive earnings surprise of $0.05. Often the percent earnings surprise, earnings surprise divided by expected EPS, is reported; in this example, percent earning surprise would be $0.05/$1.00 = 0.05 or 5%. When used directly as a valuation indicator, earnings surprise is generally scaled by a measure reflecting the variability or range in analysts' EPS estimates. The principle is that a given size EPS forecast error in relation to the mean is more meaningful the less the disagreement among analysts' forecasts. A way to accomplish such scaling is to divide unexpected earnings by the standard deviation of analysts' earnings forecasts, which we can call **scaled earnings surprise**.

---

### EXAMPLE 35

#### Calculating Scaled Earnings Surprise Using Analyst Forecasts

As of the end of November, the mean December 2001 quarterly consensus earnings forecast for International Business Machines (NYSE: IBM) was $1.32. For the 18 analysts covering the stock, the low forecast is $1.22 and the high is $1.37, and the standard deviation of the forecasts is $0.03. If reported earnings come in $0.04 above the mean forecast, what is the earnings surprise for IBM, scaled to reflect the dispersion in analysts' forecasts?

In this case, scaled earnings surprise is $0.04/$0.03 = 1.33.

---

The rationale behind using earnings surprises is the thesis that positive surprises may be associated with persistent positive abnormal returns, or alpha. The same rationale lies behind a momentum indicator that is closely related to earnings surprise but more highly researched: **standardized unexpected earnings** (SUE). SUE is defined as

$$SUE_t = \frac{EPS_t - E(EPS_t)}{\sigma[EPS_t - E(EPS_t)]}$$

where the numerator is the unexpected earnings for $t$ and the denominator, $\sigma[EPS_t - E(EPS_t)]$, is the standard deviation of past unexpected earnings over some period prior to time $t$—for example, the 20 quarters prior to $t$ as in Latané and Jones (1979), the article that introduced the SUE concept. In SUE, the magnitude of unexpected earnings is scaled by a measure of the size of historical forecast errors or surprises. The principle is that a given size EPS forecast error is more (less) meaningful the smaller (the larger) the historical size of forecast errors.

Suppose that for a stock that had a $0.05 earnings surprise, the standard deviation of past surprises is $0.20. The $0.05 surprise is relatively small compared to past forecast errors, reflected in a SUE of $0.05/$0.20 = 0.25. If the standard error of past surprises were smaller, say $0.07, the SUE would be $0.05/$0.07 = 0.71. SUE has been the subject of a number of studies.[62]

Another set of indicators, **relative strength (RSTR) indicators**, compare a stock's performance during a particular period either to its own past performance[63] or to the performance of some group of stocks. The simplest relative strength indicator of the first type is the stock's compound rate of return over some specified time horizon, such as six months or one year.[64] Despite its simplicity, this measure has appeared in numerous recent studies including Chan, Jegadeesh, and Lakonishok (1999) and Lee and Swaminathan (2000). The rationale behind its use is the thesis that patterns of persistence or reversal exist in stock returns, which may depend empirically on the investor's time horizon (Lee and Swaminathan 2000).

A simple relative strength indicator of the second type is the stock's performance divided by the performance of an equity index. If the value of this ratio increases, the stock price increases relative to the index and displays positive relative

## EXAMPLE 36

### Relative Strength in Relation to an Equity Index

Table 22 shows the values of the utility and the finance components of the NYSE Common Stock Indexes for the end of each of 12 months from November 2000 through October 2001. Values for the NYSE Composite Index are also given.

#### TABLE 22  NYSE Indexes

|  | Utility | Finance | Composite |
|---|---|---|---|
| November | 434.95 | 592.35 | 629.78 |
| December | 440.54 | 646.95 | 656.87 |
| January | 442.51 | 641.37 | 663.64 |
| February | 406.01 | 603.76 | 626.94 |
| March | 394.69 | 585.48 | 595.66 |
| April | 421.41 | 604.65 | 634.83 |
| May | 406.49 | 625.11 | 641.67 |
| June | 376.61 | 626.65 | 621.76 |
| July | 370.92 | 616.58 | 616.94 |
| August | 346.92 | 585.54 | 597.84 |
| September | 340.74 | 549.41 | 543.84 |
| October | 323.46 | 543.16 | 546.34 |

---

[62] See Reilly and Brown (2000) and Sharpe, Alexander, and Bailey (1999) for a summary.

[63] Other definitions relate a stock's return over a recent period to its return over a longer period that includes the more recent period.

[64] This concept has also been referred to as **price momentum** in the academic literature.

To produce the information for Table 23, we divide each industry index value by the NYSE Composite value for the same month and then scale those results so that relative strength for November 2001 equals 1.0.

### TABLE 23  Relative Strength Indicators

|  | RSTR Utility | RSTR Finance |
|---|---|---|
| November | 1.000 | 1.000 |
| December | 0.971 | 1.047 |
| January | 0.965 | 1.028 |
| February | 0.938 | 1.024 |
| March | 0.959 | 1.045 |
| April | 0.961 | 1.013 |
| May | 0.917 | 1.036 |
| June | 0.877 | 1.072 |
| July | 0.871 | 1.063 |
| August | 0.840 | 1.041 |
| September | 0.907 | 1.074 |
| October | 0.857 | 1.057 |

On the basis of Tables 22 and 23, answer the following questions:

1. State the relative strength of utilities and finance over the entire time period November 2000 through October 2001. Interpret the relative strength for each sector over that period.

2. Discuss the relative performance of utilities and finance in the month of April 2001.

**Solution to 1:** The relative strength of utilities was 0.857. This number represents $1 - 0.857 = 0.143$ or 14.3% underperformance relative to the NYSE Composite over the time period. The relative strength of finance was 1.057. This number represents $1.057 - 1.000 = 0.057$ or 5.7% outperformance relative to the NYSE Composite over the time period.

**Solution to 2:** April 2001 utilities' RSTR at 0.961 was higher than in the prior month, but finance's RSTR at 1.013 was lower than in the prior month. In contrast to performance for the entire period, utilities outperformed finance in April.

strength. Often the relative strength indicator may be scaled to 1.0 at the beginning of the study period. If the stock goes up at a higher (lower) rate than the index, for example, then relative strength will be above (below) 1.0. Relative strength in this sense is often calculated for industries as well as for individual stocks.

Momentum group indicators have substantial followings among professional investors. The rigorous study of the use of such indicators is a subject of current active research both in industry and business schools.

## 11  VALUATION INDICATORS AND INVESTMENT MANAGEMENT

All the valuation indicators discussed in this reading are quantitative aids, but not necessarily solutions, to the problem of security selection. Because each carefully selected and calculated price multiple, momentum indicator, or fundamental may supply some piece of the puzzle of stock valuation, many investors use more than one valuation indicator (in addition to other criteria) in stock selection.[65] The application of a set of criteria to reduce an investment universe to a

---

### EXAMPLE 37

**Using Screens to Find Stocks for a Portfolio**

Janet Larsen manages an institutional portfolio and is currently looking for new stocks to add to the portfolio. Larsen has a commercial database with information on 7,532 U.S. stocks. She has designed several screens to select stocks with low P/E, P/CF, and Enterprise Value/EBITDA multiples. She also wants stocks that are currently paying a cash dividend and have positive earnings, and stocks with a total market capitalization between $1 billion and $5 billion. Table 24 shows the number of stocks that meet each of six screens reflecting these desires, as well as the number of stocks meeting all screens simultaneously, as of January 2002.

#### TABLE 24   A Stock Screen

| Screen | Stocks Meeting Screen | |
| --- | --- | --- |
|  | Number | Percent |
| P/E < 20.0 | 2,549 | 33.8% |
| P/CF < 12.0 | 4,209 | 55.9% |
| Enterprise value/EBITDA < 10.0 | 4,393 | 58.3% |
| Dividends > 0 | 2,411 | 32.0% |
| EPS > 0 | 4,116 | 54.6% |
| Market capitalization from 1 billion to 5 billion | 1,009 | 13.4% |
| All six screens simultaneously | 117 | 1.6% |

---

[65] According to the *Merrill Lynch Institutional Factor Survey* for 2001, from 1989 to 2001 responding institutional investors on average used about 8 factors (of the 23 surveyed) in selecting stocks. The survey factors include not only price multiples, momentum indicators, and DDM, but the fundamentals ROE, debt to equity, projected five-year EPS growth, EPS variability, EPS estimate dispersion, size, beta, foreign exposure, low price, and neglect.

▶ The product of the fractions of stocks passing each screen individually is $0.338 \times 0.559 \times 0.583 \times 0.32 \times 0.546 \times 0.134 = 0.0026$, or 0.26%.

▶ The P/E of the S&P 500 was 24.4, the P/E of S&P 500/BARRA Growth Index was 32.4, and the P/E of the S&P 500/BARRA Value Index was 19.2 as of January 2002, excluding companies with negative earnings from the calculation of P/E.

Answer the following questions using the information supplied above:

1. What type of valuation indicators does Larsen not include in her stock screen?

2. Characterize the overall orientation of Larsen as to investment style.

3. Why is the fraction of stocks passing all six screens simultaneously, 1.6 percent, larger than the product of the fraction of stocks passing each screen individually, 0.26 percent?

4. State two limitations of Larsen's stock screen.

**Solution to 1:** Larsen has not included momentum indicators in the screen.

**Solution to 2:** Larsen can be characterized as a mid-cap value investor. Her screen does not include explicit growth rate criteria or include momentum indicators, such as positive earnings surprise, usually associated with a growth orientation. Larsen also specifies a cutoff for P/E that is consistent with the S&P 500/BARRA Value Index. Note that her multiples criteria are all "less than" criteria.[66]

**Solution to 3:** The fraction of stocks passing all screens simultaneously is greater than 0.26 percent because the criteria are not all independent. For example, we expect that some stocks that pass the P/CF criterion also will pass the P/E criteria because cash flow is positively correlated with earnings, on average.

**Solution to 4:** Larsen does not include any fundamental criteria. This is a limitation because a stock's expected low growth rate or high risk may explain its low P/E. A second limitation of her screen is that the computations of the value indicators in a commercial database may not reflect the appropriate adjustments to inputs. The absence of qualitative criteria is also a possible limitation.

smaller set of investments is called **screening**. Stock screens often include not only criteria based on the valuation measures discussed in this reading but fundamental criteria that may explain differences in such measures. Computerized stock screening is an efficient way to narrow a search for investments and is a part of many stock-selection disciplines. The limitations to such screens usually relate to the lack of control over the calculation of important inputs (such as EPS)

---

[66] In using multiples such as P/E or P/B in this widely used fashion to characterize a portfolio, an analyst should be aware of the limitations. A high-P/E stock is usually labeled as a growth stock but may actually be an overpriced low-growth stock in the sense of future earnings growth.

when using many commercial databases and screening tools; the absence of qualitative factors in most databases is another important limitation.

Investors also apply all the metrics that we have illustrated in terms of individual stocks to industries and economic sectors. For example, average price multiples and momentum indicators can be used in sector rotation strategies to determine relatively under- or overvalued sectors.[67] (A **sector rotation strategy** is an investment strategy that over-weights economic sectors that are anticipated to outperform or lead the overall market.)

---

[67] See Salsman (1997) for an example.

# SUMMARY

In this reading, we have defined and explained the most important valuation indicators in professional use and illustrated their application to a variety of valuation problems.

▶ Price multiples are ratios of a stock's price to some measure of value per share.

▶ Momentum indicators relate either price or a fundamental to the time series of their own past values (or in some cases to their expected value).

▶ Price multiples are most frequently applied to valuation using the method of comparables. This method involves using a price multiple to evaluate whether an asset is relatively undervalued, fairly valued, or overvalued in relation to a benchmark value of the multiple.

▶ The benchmark value of the multiple may be the multiple of a similar company or the median or average value of the multiple for a peer group of companies, an industry, an economic sector, an equity index, or the median or average own past values of the multiple.

▶ The economic rationale for the method of comparables is the law of one price.

▶ Price multiples may also be applied to valuation using the method based on forecasted fundamentals. Discounted cash flow models provide the basis and rationale for this method. Fundamentals also interest analysts who use the method of comparables, because differences between a price multiple and its benchmark value may be explained by differences in fundamentals.

▶ The key idea behind the use of P/Es is that earning power is a chief driver of investment value and EPS is probably the primary focus of security analysts' attention. EPS, however, is frequently subject to distortion, often volatile, and sometimes negative.

▶ The two alternative definitions of P/E are trailing P/E, based on the most recent four quarters of EPS, and leading P/E, based on next year's expected earnings.

▶ Analysts address the problem of cyclicality by normalizing EPS—that is, calculating the level of EPS that the business could achieve currently under mid-cyclical conditions (normal EPS).

▶ Two methods to normalize EPS are the method of historical average EPS (over the most recent full cycle) and the method of average ROE (average ROE multiplied by current book value per share).

▶ Earnings yield (E/P) is the reciprocal of the P/E. When stocks have negative EPS, a ranking by earnings yield is meaningful whereas a ranking by P/E is not.

▶ Historical trailing P/Es should be calculated with EPS lagged a sufficient amount of time to avoid look-ahead bias. The same principle applies to other multiples calculated on a trailing basis.

▶ The fundamental drivers of P/E are expected earnings growth rate(s) and the required rate of return. The justified P/E based on fundamentals bears a positive relationship to the first factor and an inverse relationship to the second factor.

▶ PEG (P/E to growth) is a tool to incorporate the impact of earnings growth on P/E. PEG is calculated as the ratio of the P/E to the consensus growth forecast. Stocks with lower PEGs are more attractive than stocks with higher PEGs, all else equal.

▶ We can estimate terminal value in multistage DCF models using price multiples based on comparables. The expression for terminal value is (using P/E as an example)

$$V_n = \text{Benchmark value of trailing P/E} \times E_n$$

or

$$V_n = \text{Benchmark value of leading P/E} \times E_{n+1}$$

▶ Book value per share attempts to represent the investment that common shareholders have made in the company, on a per-share basis. Inflation, technological change, and accounting distortions, however, can impair book value for this purpose.

▶ Book value is calculated as common shareholders' equity divided by the number of shares outstanding. Analysts adjust book value to more accurately reflect the value of shareholders' investment and to make P/B more useful for comparing different stocks.

▶ The fundamental drivers of P/B are ROE and the required rate of return. The justified P/B based on fundamentals bears a positive relationship to the first factor and an inverse relationship to the second factor.

▶ An important rationale for the price-to-sales ratio (P/S) is that sales, as the top line in an income statement, are generally less subject to distortion or manipulation than other fundamentals such as EPS or book value. Sales are also more stable than earnings and never negative.

▶ P/S fails to take into account differences in cost structure between businesses, may not properly reflect the situation of companies losing money, and can be subject to manipulation through revenue recognition practices.

▶ The fundamental drivers of P/S are profit margin, growth rate, and the required rate of return. The justified P/S based on fundamentals bears a positive relationship to the first two factors and an inverse relationship to the third factor.

▶ A key idea behind the use of price-to-cash-flow ratios is that cash flow is less subject to manipulation than are earnings. Price to cash flow are often more stable than P/E. Some common approximations to cash flow from operations have limitations, however, because they ignore items that may be subject to manipulation.

▶ The major cash flow and related concepts used in multiples are earnings-plus-noncash charges (CF), cash flow from operations (CFO), free cash flow to equity (FCFE), and earnings before interest, taxes, depreciation, and amortization (EBITDA).

▶ In calculating price to cash flow, the earnings-plus-noncash charges concept is traditionally used, although the FCFE has the strongest link to financial theory.

▶ CF and EBITDA are not strictly cash flow numbers because they do not account for noncash revenue and net changes in working capital.

▶ The fundamental drivers of price to cash flow, however defined, are the expected growth rates of future cash flows and the required rate of return. The justified price to cash flow based on fundamentals bears a positive relationship to the first factor and an inverse relationship to the second.

- Enterprise value (EV) is total company value (the market value of debt, common equity, and preferred equity) minus the value of cash and investments.

- EV/EBITDA is preferred to P/EBITDA because EBITDA as a pre-interest number is a flow to all providers of capital.

- EV/EBITDA may be more appropriate than P/E for comparing companies with different amounts of financial leverage (debt).

- EV/EBITDA is frequently used in the valuation of capital-intensive businesses.

- The fundamental drivers of EV/EBITDA are the expected growth rate in free cash flow to the firm and the weighted-average cost of capital. The justified EV/EBITDA based on fundamentals bears a positive relationship to the first factor and an inverse relationship to the second.

- Dividend yield has been used as a valuation indicator because it is a component of total return, and is less risky than capital appreciation. However, investors trade off future earnings growth to receive higher current dividends.

- Trailing dividend yield is calculated as four times the most recent quarterly per-share dividend divided by the current market price.

- The fundamental drivers of dividend yield are the expected growth rate in dividends and the required rate of return.

- Comparing companies across borders frequently involves accounting method differences, cultural differences, economic differences, and resulting differences in risk and growth opportunities.

- Momentum valuation indicators include earnings surprise, standardized unexpected earnings, and relative strength.

- Unexpected earnings (or earnings surprise) equals the difference between reported earnings and expected earnings.

- Standardized unexpected earnings (SUE) is unexpected earnings divided by the standard deviation in past unexpected earnings.

- Relative-strength indicators compare a stock's performance during a period either with its own past performance (first type) or with the performance of some group of stocks (second type). The rationale behind using relative strength is the thesis of patterns of persistence or reversal in returns.

- Screening is the application of a set of criteria to reduce an investment universe to a smaller set of investments and is a part of many stock selection disciplines. In general, limitations of such screens include the lack of control over the calculation of important inputs and the absence of qualitative factors.

## PRACTICE PROBLEMS FOR READING 43

1. As of February 2002, you are researching Smith International (NYSE: SII), an oil field services company subject to cyclical demand for its services. You believe the 1997–2000 period reasonably captures average profitability. SII closed at $57.98 on 2 February 2002.

|        | 2001    | 2000   | 1999   | 1998   | 1997   |
|--------|---------|--------|--------|--------|--------|
| EPS    | E$3.03  | $1.45  | $0.23  | $2.13  | $2.55  |
| BVPS   | E19.20  | 16.21  | 14.52  | 13.17  | 11.84  |
| ROE    | E16%    | 8.9%   | 1.6%   | 16.3%  | 21.8%  |

*Source: The Value Line Investment Survey.*

   A. Define normal EPS.

   B. Calculate a normal EPS for SII based on the method of historical average EPS, and then calculate the P/E based on that estimate of normal EPS.

   C. Calculate a normal EPS for SII based on the method of average ROE and the P/E based on that estimate of normal EPS.

2. An analyst plans to use P/E and the method of comparables as a basis for recommending one of two peer group companies in the personal digital assistant business. Data on the companies' prices, trailing EPS, and expected growth rates in sales (five-year compounded rate) are given in the table below. Neither business has been profitable to date, and neither is anticipated to have positive EPS over the next year.

|            | Price | Trailing EPS | P/E | Expected Growth (Sales) |
|------------|-------|--------------|-----|-------------------------|
| Hand       | $22   | −$2.20       | NM  | 45%                     |
| Somersault | $10   | −$1.25       | NM  | 40%                     |

   Unfortunately, because the earnings for both companies were negative, the P/Es were not meaningful. On the basis of the above information, answer the following questions.

   A. State how the analyst might make a relative valuation in this case.

   B. Which stock should the analyst recommend?

**3.** May Stewart, CFA, a retail analyst, is performing a P/E-based comparison of two jewelry stores as of early 2001. She has the following data for Hallwhite Stores (HS) and Ruffany (RUF).

- ► HS is priced at $44. RUF is priced at $22.50.

- ► HS has a simple capital structure, earned $2.00 per share in 2000, and is expected to earn $2.20 in 2001.

- ► RUF has a complex capital structure as a result of its outstanding stock options. Moreover, it had several unusual items that reduced its basic EPS in 2000 to $0.50 (versus the $0.75 that it earned in 1999).

- ► For 2001, Stewart expects RUF to achieve net income of $30 million. RUF has 30 million shares outstanding and options outstanding for an additional 3,333,333 shares.

- **A.** Which P/E (trailing or leading) should Stewart use to compare the two companies' valuation?

- **B.** Which of the two stocks is relatively more attractively valued on the basis of P/Es (assuming that all other factors are approximately the same for both stock)?

**4.** You are researching the valuation of the stock of a company in the food processing industry. Suppose you intend to use the mean value of the leading P/Es for the food processing industry stocks as the benchmark value of the multiple. That mean P/E is 18.0. The leading or expected EPS for the next year for the stock you are studying is $2.00. You calculate 18.0 × $2.00 = $36, which you take to be the intrinsic value of the stock based only on the information given above. Comparing $36 with the stock's current market price of $30, you conclude the stock is undervalued.

- **A.** Give two reasons why your conclusion that the stock is undervalued may be in error.

- **B.** What additional information about the stock and the peer group would support your original conclusion?

**5. A.** Identify two significant differences between Yardeni's model of stock market valuation and the Fed model.

- **B.** Suppose an analyst uses an equity index as a comparison asset in valuing a stock. Which price multiple(s) would cause concern about the impact of potential overvaluation of the equity index on a decision to recommend purchase of an individual stock?

**6.** Christie Johnson, CFA, has been assigned to analyze Sundanci. Johnson assumes that Sundanci's earnings and dividends will grow at a constant rate of 13 percent. Exhibits P-1 and P-2 provide financial statements and other information for Sundanci.

- **A.** Calculate a justified P/E based on information in Exhibits P-1 and P-2 and on Johnson's assumptions for Sundanci. Show your work.

- **B.** Identify, within the context of the constant dividend growth model, how *each* of the fundamental factors shown below would affect the P/E.

  - **i.** The risk (beta) of Sundanci increases substantially.

  - **ii.** The estimated growth rate of Sundanci's earnings and dividends increases.

  - **iii.** The market risk premium increases.

    Note: A change in a fundamental factor is assumed to happen in isolation; interactive effects between factors are ignored. Every other item of the company is unchanged.

| EXHIBIT P-1 | Sundanci Actual 1999 and 2000 Financial Statements For Fiscal Years Ending 31 May (in Millions, except Per-Share Data) | |
|---|---|---|

| Income Statement | 1999 | 2000 |
|---|---|---|
| Revenue | $474 | $598 |
| Depreciation | 20 | 23 |
| Other operating costs | 368 | 460 |
| Income before taxes | 86 | 115 |
| Taxes | 26 | 35 |
| Net income | 60 | 80 |
| Dividends | 18 | 24 |
| Earnings per share | $0.714 | $0.952 |
| Dividends per share | $0.214 | $0.286 |
| Common shares outstanding | 84.0 | 84.0 |

| Balance Sheet | 1999 | 2000 |
|---|---|---|
| Current assets | $201 | $326 |
| Net property, plant, and equipment | 474 | 489 |
| Total assets | 675 | 815 |
| Current liabilities | 57 | 141 |
| Long-term debt | 0 | 0 |
| Total liabilities | | |
| Shareholders' equity | 618 | 674 |
| Total liabilities and equity | 675 | 815 |
| Capital expenditures | 34 | 38 |

| EXHIBIT P-2 | Selected Financial Information |
|---|---|

| Required rate of return on equity | 14% |
|---|---|
| Growth rate of industry | 13% |
| Industry P/E | 26 |

7. At a meeting of your company's investment policy committee, Bill Yu presents a recommendation based on a P/E analysis. He presents the case for Connie's Sporting Goods (CSG), a small chain of retail stores that receives almost no coverage by analysts. Yu begins by noting that CSG appeared to be fairly valued compared with its peers on a P/E basis. CSG's 10-Q filing revealed, however, that an initiative at CSG to offer sports instruction (e.g., golf lessons) along with equipment should immediately raise the earnings growth rate at the company from 5 percent to 6 percent. Yu thus expects the company's trailing P/E to rise from 10.5 to 13.25, a

26 percent increase, as soon as the investment community recognizes this development. The computations supporting his analysis follow.

Currently the justified P/E based on fundamentals is

$$\frac{P_0}{E_0} = \frac{(1 - b)(1 + g)}{r - g} = \frac{(1 - 0.5)(1.05)}{0.10 - 0.05} = 10.5$$

He points out that when $g$ rises to 0.06, the trailing P/E should increase to 13.25, providing investors with appreciation in excess of 20 percent. When asked if he expects CSG's ROE to improve with the initiative, Yu indicated that it would likely be flat for the first several years. A colleague argues that because of the flat ROE, CSG's justified P/E will not increase to 13.25 because $b$ must increase to be consistent with the sustainable growth rate expression for $g$. Only companies with at least 20 percent near-term appreciation potential are candidates for inclusion on your company's focus list of stocks.

**A.** How would you expect the new initiative to affect the trailing P/E accorded to CSG's stock, assuming Yu's assumptions are correct? (Growth will increase as indicated above and ROE will be steady.)

**B.** Is CSG a good candidate for your company's focus list?

**8.** Tom Smithfield is valuing the stock of a food processing business. He has projected earnings and dividends to four years (to $t = 4$). Other information and estimates are:

▶ Required rate of return = 0.09

▶ Average dividend payout rate for mature companies in the market = 0.45

▶ Industry average ROE = 0.10

▶ $E_3 = \$3.00$

▶ Industry average P/E = 12

On the basis of the above, answer the following questions:

**A.** Compute terminal value based on comparables.

**B.** Contrast your answer in Part A to an estimate of terminal value using the Gordon growth model.

**9.** Discuss three types of stocks or investment problems for which an analyst could appropriately use P/B in valuation.

**10.** Avtech is a multinational distributor of semiconductor chips and related products to businesses. Its leading competitor around the world is Target Electronics. Avtech has a current market price of $10, 20 million shares outstanding, annual sales of $1 billion, and a 5 percent profit margin. Target has a market price of $20, 30 million shares outstanding, annual sales of $1.6 billion, and a profit margin of 4.9 percent. Based on the information given, answer the following questions.

**A.** Which of the two companies has a more attractive valuation based on P/S?

**B.** Identify and explain one advantage of P/S over P/E as a valuation tool.

**11.** Wilhelm Müller, CFA, has organized the selected data on four food companies that appear below (TTM stands for trailing 12 months):

|  | Hormel Foods | Tyson Foods | IBP Corp | Smithfield Foods |
|---|---|---|---|---|
| Stock price | $25.70 | $11.77 | $23.65 | $24.61 |
| Shares out (1,000s) | 138,923 | 220,662 | 108,170 | 103,803 |
| Market cap ($ mil) | 3,570 | 2,597 | 2,558 | 2,523 |
| Sales ($ mil) | 4,124 | 10,751 | 17,388 | 6,354 |
| Net income ($ mil) | 182 | 88 | 122 | 252 |
| TTM EPS | $1.30 | $0.40 | $1.14 | $2.31 |
| Return on equity | 19.20% | 4.10% | 6.40% | 23.00% |
| Net profit margin | 4.41% | 0.82% | 0.70% | 3.99% |

On the basis of the data given, answer the following questions.

**A.** Calculate the trailing P/E and P/S for each company.

**B.** Explain on the basis of fundamentals why these stocks have different P/Ss.

**12.** John Jones, CFA, is head of the research department at Peninsular Research. Peninsular has a client who has inquired about the valuation method best suited for comparison of companies in an industry with the following characteristics:

▶ Principal competitors within the industry are located in the United States, France, Japan, and Brazil.

▶ The industry is currently operating at a cyclical low, with many companies reporting losses.

Jones recommends that the client consider the following valuation ratios:

**1.** P/E.

**2.** P/B.

**3.** P/S.

Determine which *one* of the three valuation ratios is most appropriate for comparing companies in this industry. Support your answer with one reason that makes that ratio superior to either of the other two ratios in this case.

**13.** General Electric (NYSE: GE) is currently selling for $38.50, with trailing 12-month earnings and dividends of $1.36 and $0.64, respectively. P/E is 28.3, P/B is 7.1, and P/S is 2.9. The return on equity is 27.0 percent, and the profit margin on sales is 10.9 percent. The Treasury bond rate is 4.9 percent, the equity risk premium is 5.5 percent, and GE's beta is 1.2.

   **A.** What is GE's required rate of return, based on the capital asset pricing model?

   **B.** Assume that the dividend and earnings growth rates are 9 percent. What P/Es, P/Bs, and P/Ss would be justified given the required rate of return in Part A and current values of the dividend payout ratio, ROE, and profit margin?

   **C.** Given that the assumptions and constant growth model are appropriate, state whether GE appears to be fairly valued, overvalued, or undervalued based on fundamentals.

**14.** Jorge Zaldys, CFA, is researching the relative valuation of two companies in the aerospace/defense industry, NCI Heavy Industries (NCI) and Relay Group International (RGI). He has gathered relevant information on the companies in the table that follows.

   Using the information in the table, answer the following questions:

   **A.** Calculate P/EBITDA for NCI and RGI.

   **B.** Calculate EV/EBITDA for NCI and RGI.

   **C.** Select NCI or RGI for recommendation as relatively undervalued. Justify your selection.

## EBITDA Comparisons (in € Millions except for per Share)

| Company | RGI | NCI |
|---|---|---|
| Price per share | 150 | 100 |
| Shares outstanding | 5 million | 2 million |
| Market value of debt | 50 | 100 |
| Book value of debt | 52 | 112 |
| Cash and investments | 5 | 2 |
| Net income | 49.5 | 12 |
| Net income from continuing operations | 49.5 | 8 |
| Interest expense | 3 | 5 |
| Depreciation and amortization | 8 | 4 |
| Taxes | 2 | 3 |

**15.** Define the major alternative cash flow concepts, and state one limitation of each.

**16.** Data for two hypothetical companies in the pharmaceutical industry, DriveMed and MAT Technology, are given in the table below. For both companies, expenditures in fixed capital and working capital during the previous year reflected anticipated average expenditures over the foreseeable horizon.

|  | DriveMed | MAT Tech. |
| --- | --- | --- |
| Current price | $46.00 | $78.00 |
| Trailing CF per share | $3.60 | $6.00 |
| P/CF | 12.8 | 13.0 |
| Trailing FCFE per share | $1.00 | $5.00 |
| P/FCFE | 46.0 | 15.6 |
| Consensus five-year growth forecast | 15% | 20% |
| Beta | 1.25 | 1.25 |

On the basis of the information supplied, discuss the valuation of MAT Technology relative to DriveMed. Justify your conclusion.

**17.** Your value-oriented investment management company recently hired a new analyst, Bob Westard, because of his expertise in the life sciences and biotechnology areas. At the company's weekly meeting, during which each analyst proposes a stock idea for inclusion on the company's approved list, Westard recommends Human Cloning International (HCI). He bases his recommendation to the Investment Committee on two considerations. First, HCI has pending patent applications but a P/E that he judges to be low given the potential earnings from the patented products. Second, HCI has had high relative strength versus the S&P 500 over the past month.

**A.** Explain the difference between price multiples and relative strength approaches.

**B.** State which, if any, of the bases for Westard's recommendation is consistent with the investment orientation of your company.

**18.** Kirstin Kruse, a portfolio manager, has an important client who wants to alter the composition of her equity portfolio, which is currently a diversified portfolio of 60 global common stocks. The client wants a portfolio that meets the following criteria:

▶ Stocks must be in the Dow Jones Industrial Average, Transportation Average, or Utilities Average.

▶ Stocks must have a dividend yield of at least 5.0 percent.

▶ Stocks must have a P/E no greater than 20.

▶ Stocks must have a total market capitalization of at least $2.0 billion.

The table below shows how many stocks satisfied each screen, which was run in November 2001.

| Screen | Number Satisfying |
|---|---|
| In Dow Jones Industrial Average, Transportation Average, or Utilities Average | 65 |
| Dividend yield of at least 5.0% | 10 |
| P/E less than 20 | 27 |
| Total market cap of at least $2.0 billion | 52 |
| Satisfies all four screens | 6 |

Other facts are:

▶ In total, there are 65 stocks in these three indexes (30 in the Industrial Average, 20 in the Transportation Average, and 15 in the Utilities Average).

▶ The stocks meeting all four screens were Southern Co. (utility), TXU Corporation (utility), Eastman Kodak Co. (consumer goods), Public Service Enterprise Group (utility), Reliant Energy (utility), and Consolidated Edison (utility).

**A.** Which valuation indicator or fundamental in Kruse's screen is most restrictive?

**B.** Critique the construction of the screen.

**C.** Do these screens identify an appropriate replacement portfolio for the client?

## The following information relates to Questions 19–24 and is based on Readings 37 and 43

Cecilia Tan is an equity analyst who is preparing an analysis of two securities for presentation at an upcoming meeting of her firm's portfolio managers.

The first security is the common stock of Diamondback Industries, a manufacturer of household products. Tan decides to use the method of comparables to value Diamondback by comparing Diamondback's price multiples with those of comparable peer companies. Tan collects fundamental data, including price multiples, on Diamondback and the peer companies, which are presented in Exhibit 1. Tan selects the price-to-earnings ratio (P/E) as her primary price multiple for evaluating Diamondback. She also evaluates Diamondback's P/E relative to growth (PEG) and compares it with the PEGs of four peer companies. Diamondback has a required rate of return of 11 percent and a long-term expected return on equity (ROE) of 13 percent.

| EXHIBIT 1 | Fundamental Data for Diamondback Industries and Peer Companies | | | |
|---|---|---|---|---|
| Company | Price per Share ($) | Last Four Quarters Cumulative Earnings per Share ($) | Estimate of Next Four Quarters Cumulative Earnings per Share ($) | Expected Five-Year Annual Growth Rate in Earnings (%) |
| Diamondback | 20 | 1.00 | 1.10 | 10 |
| Peer 1 | 30 | 1.60 | 1.70 | 10 |
| Peer 2 | 26 | 1.35 | 1.50 | 16 |
| Peer 3 | 70 | 3.75 | 4.00 | 9 |
| Peer 4 | 18 | 0.95 | 1.15 | 15 |

The second security is the common stock of Indigo Corporation, a manufacturer of industrial equipment whose sales are strongly tied to the overall economic cycle. Tan plans to evaluate the current P/E of Indigo compared with its P/E over the recent business cycle. For overall valuation purposes, Tan will compute normalized earnings per share. Tan believes that the 2005 results are abnormal and that the period from 2000 to 2004 captures average profitability over a business cycle. Historical data for Indigo are presented in Exhibit 2. Because Indigo has cyclical earnings, Tan also decides to compute a justified price-to-sales ratio (P/S). Tan estimates a long-term profit margin of 6 percent, a long-term dividend payout ratio of 40 percent, an earnings growth rate of 6 percent, and a required rate of return of 10 percent.

| EXHIBIT 2 | Historical Data for Indigo Corporation | | |
|---|---|---|---|
| Year | Earnings per Share ($) | Book Value per Share at End of Period ($) | Return on Equity (%) |
| 2005 | 0.40 | 13.50 | 2.90 |
| 2004 | 1.40 | 13.50 | 10.77 |
| 2003 | 1.00 | 12.50 | 8.20 |
| 2002 | 0.50 | 11.90 | 4.22 |
| 2001 | 0.95 | 11.80 | 8.25 |
| 2000 | 1.76 | 11.25 | 16.40 |
| Average 2000–2004 | 1.12 | 12.19 | 9.57 |
| Average 2000–2005 | 1.00 | 12.41 | 8.46 |

Tan examines the impact of inflation on P/Es. She prepares an example to demonstrate intrinsic P/E values for a hypothetical company that has no growth in real earnings and has a real required rate of return of 6 percent. She assumes the company can only pass 60 percent of inflation through its earnings (a flow-through rate of 60 percent). She computes an intrinsic P/E for an inflation rate of 4 percent.

**19.** The *most* appropriate rationale for Tan's decision to use the method of comparables to value Diamondback is:

    **A.** the law of one price.

    **B.** that intrinsic value is the present value of expected cash flows.

    **C.** that forecasted fundamentals determine justified price multiples.

**20.** What is the *most* appropriate justification for Tan's selection of the P/E as her primary price multiple for Diamondback?

    **A.** Earnings can have volatile, transient components.

    **B.** Earnings power is a chief driver of investment value.

    **C.** Management has discretion over the determination of earnings.

**21.** Based on a leading P/E, which peer company appears to have the *lowest* relative valuation according to the PEG ratio?

    **A.** Peer 2.

    **B.** Peer 3.

    **C.** Peer 4.

**22.** Indigo's 2005 normalized earnings per share under the method of average ROE is *closest* to:

    **A.** $1.12.

    **B.** $1.19.

    **C.** $1.29.

**23.** The year-end 2005 justified P/S ratio for Indigo is *closest* to:

   **A.** 0.600.

   **B.** 0.636.

   **C.** 0.900.

**24.** For an expected inflation rate of 4 percent, what is the prospective (leading) intrinsic P/E of Tan's hypothetical company?

   **A.** 13.16.

   **B.** 16.67.

   **C.** 25.00.

# U.S. PORTFOLIO STRATEGY: SEEKING VALUE—ANATOMY OF VALUATION

by David J. Kostin, Jessica Binder, Robert Koyfman, and Caesar Maasry

## READING
# 44

## LEARNING OUTCOMES

| The candidate should be able to: | Mastery |
|---|:---:|
| **a.** explain why an analyst would use a ten-year moving average as a benchmark in the valuation process; | ☐ |
| **b.** determine the importance of correlation analysis when using a multi-matrix valuation approach; | ☐ |
| **c.** illustrate why the PEG valuation technique must be used with care; | ☐ |
| **d.** indicate the impact of discount rate sensitivity in valuation models. | ☐ |

## INTRODUCTION          1

We dissect the S&P 500 and identify the least and most expensive stocks across the market and within sectors. We highlight a "super-value" portfolio of 50 stocks to buy that trade at low valuations on seven metrics and an "anti-value" portfolio of 50 expensive stocks to sell.

**The S&P 500 is Undervalued on All Metrics from a Bottom-Up Perspective**    On a bottom-up basis, the S&P 500 trades one standard deviation below its 10-year average on EV/Sales, EV/EBITDA, Price/Book, Free Cash Flow Yield, P/E, PEG & Implied Growth. Larger-caps are more undervalued than smaller-caps, particularly in Consumer Discretionary.

**Information Technology and Health Care Are the Most Undervalued Sectors** Information Technology and Health Care are the ONLY sectors that are inexpensive today on ALL seven metrics relative to how they have been valued during the past ten-years. Utilities and Financials are the most overvalued sectors.

> **Note:**
> The Goldman Sachs research report should be studied for the generic features of security analysis rather than for specific characteristics of a company, industry, or country. Candidates are not expected to know details of the companies, industries, or countries, but rather to understand how the analytical techniques can be applied.

### S&P 500 on a Bottom-Up Basis Is Inexpensive Relative to History

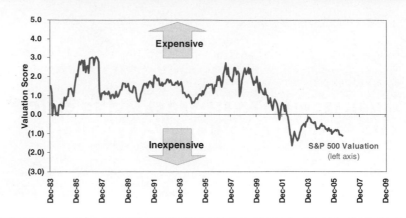

*Sources:* Compustat and Goldman Sachs Research.

**Weatherford International, Stryker and Apollo Are Least Expensive Stocks**
Within the S&P 500, Weatherford International (WFT, Buy), Stryker Corp. (SYK, Buy) and Apollo Group (APOL, NC) are the three most undervalued stocks ranked on seven metrics.

## Introducing Our "Super-Value" and "Anti-Value" Portfolios

We dissect the S&P 500 and identify the least and most expensive stocks across the market and within sectors. We highlight a "super-value" portfolio of 50 stocks to buy that trade at low valuations on seven metrics and an "anti-value" portfolio of 50 expensive stocks to sell.

### "What Looks Cheap in the Market Now?"

We have noticed a significant increase in the number of clients who call to ask the question: "What looks cheap in the market now?" Clients have always asked variations on this theme, such as "what do you like in the market?" but more than the usual suspects are now probing around the topic of valuation. Market participants recognize that the U.S. economy is in transition, and the outlook is less certain now than it was just several months ago. Attractive valuation offers portfolio managers some comfort when selecting stocks in an uncertain market.

### How One Portfolio Strategist Responds

We characterize a stock as "undervalued" if it trades at a discount to its historical average valuation relative to the market on a variety of financial measures. We use a combination of seven metrics to identify an "undervalued" equity security:

► enterprise value/sales (EV/Sales);
► enterprise value/EBITDA (EV/EBITDA);
► price/book;
► free cash flow yield (FCF);

- ► price/earnings (P/E);
- ► P/E-to-long-term growth (PEG); and
- ► implied growth (computed by reversing the dividend discount model).

Obviously, investors use many different techniques to classify a stock as attractively valued. An entire library of academic books has been written on the subject of how to value a stock. We prefer to use several valuation measures to facilitate comparison across sectors. The correlation between the individual metrics ranges from 0.2 to 0.9.

### Just How "Cheap" Is "Cheap"?

We often view the world through the prism of a distribution. In seeking to identify "cheap" stocks, we focused on companies trading at extreme undervaluation across the seven metrics. In fact, on a bottom-up basis, the S&P 500 is trading at roughly one standard deviation below its 10-year average on nearly every one of the seven metrics (see Exhibits 2 and 3). One drawback to this approach is that "broken growth" stocks screen as attractively valued today based on the lofty valuations assigned to them when their growth prospects were much brighter.

### Introducing Our "Super-Value" and "Anti-Value" Portfolios

We have created a 50-stock sector-neutral portfolio of the most "undervalued" stocks in the S&P 500 (see Bloomberg ticker <GSTHSVLU> on <GSSU5>). We created a similar 50-stock sector-neutral basket of "overvalued" stocks in the S&P 500 (see Bloomberg <GSTHAVLU>).

## Taking a Comprehensive Look at Valuation

### A Comprehensive View of Valuation that Incorporates Seven Metrics and History

This reading expands our view of stock valuation to incorporate seven different valuation metrics and also examines how individual stocks are currently valued on these measures relative to how they have been valued over the past decade.

### High Relative P/E Stocks Continue to Underperform

In a report published earlier in 2006 we focused exclusively on P/E as a measure of valuation and looked solely at current relative valuation within a sector. Our February 2006 report entitled *High P/E means high expectations but low returns* noted that high relative P/E stocks have consistently underperformed both low relative P/E stocks and the S&P 500 for most of the past 15 years. In 2006 YTD, a sector-neutral basket of low-relative P/E stocks has beat a high-relative P/E basket by 540 basis points.

### History of Buying "Super-Value" Portfolio and Selling "Anti-Value" Appears Positive

We back-tested our more comprehensive valuation framework by tracking the performance of stocks we would have identified as "Super-value" against stocks we would have identified as "Anti-value." Our analysis shows a positive average return for holdings periods of one, three, six and 12 months (see Exhibit 1).

| EXHIBIT 1 | Return Summary of "Super-Value" versus "Anti-Value" Trade since 1995 as of September 8, 2006 |
|---|---|

| Invest. Horizon: | 1M | 3M | 6M | 12M |
|---|---|---|---|---|
| Observations: | 139 | 137 | 134 | 128 |
| 10 + | 2 % | 9 % | 12 % | 21 % |
| 5 to 10 | 6 | 8 | 13 | 8 |
| 2 to 5 | 17 | 15 | 7 | 8 |
| 1 to 2 | 11 | 9 | 5 | 1 |
| 0 to 1 | 12 | 9 | 7 | 2 |
| (1) to 0 | 20 | 8 | 7 | 2 |
| (2) to (1) | 13 | 7 | 5 | 6 |
| (5) to (2) | 13 | 20 | 16 | 9 |
| (10) to (5) | 6 | 11 | 19 | 21 |
| (10) - | 0 | 4 | 10 | 21 |
| Total | 100 % | 100 % | 100 % | 100 % |
| Positive | 48 | 50 | 43 | 40 |
| Negative | 52 | 50 | 57 | 60 |
| Total | 100 % | 100 % | 100 % | 100 % |

*Probability of Return (%)* (vertical axis label)

| Return Summary | | | | |
|---|---|---|---|---|
| Invest. Horizon: | 1M | 3M | 6M | 12M |
| Max | 18 % | 25 % | 33 % | 46 % |
| 75th %tile | 2 | 4 | 4 | 8 |
| Average | 0.5 % | 0.7 % | 0.4 % | 1.3 % |
| 25th %tile | (2) | (3) | (6) | (10) |
| Min | (9) | (21) | (21) | (28) |

Average return of long "Super-value" and short "Anti-value" trade is positive for all holding periods shown.

*Sources:* Compustat and Goldman Sachs Research.

Our back-tested portfolios were created employing the same methodology we use to construct the current "Super-value" and "Anti-value" portfolios. We constructed the portfolios sector-neutral to the S&P 500 to reduce the influence of thematic trends and to capture valuation-driven returns. We believe money managers will focus increased attention on valuation in the coming months.

## 2  GOLDMAN SACHS U.S. VALUATION MONITOR

On a bottom-up basis the S&P 500 currently trades approximately one standard deviation below the ten-year average on all seven financial metrics we analyzed. In fact, the market is about as inexpensive as at any time over the past 23 years, with the exception of late 2002/early 2003 before the current bull market began (see Exhibit 2).

From a sector perspective, Information Technology and Health Care are notably undervalued relative to how these sectors have traded versus the market over the past ten years (see Exhibit 2). Utilities and Financials are even more dramatically overvalued, trading two standard deviations above their long-term averages.

| EXHIBIT 2 | S&P 500 on a Bottom-Up Basis Is Inexpensive Relative to History as of September 8, 2006 |

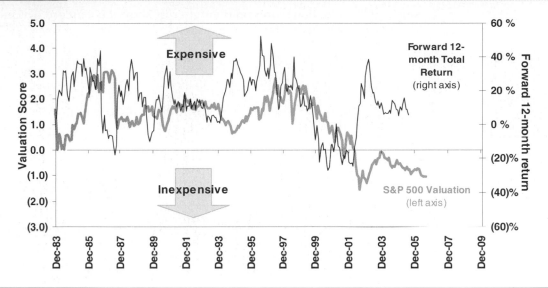

*Sources:* Compustat and Goldman Sachs Research.

| EXHIBIT 3 | Information Technology and Health Care Are the Most Attractively Valued Sectors as of September 8, 2006 |

### Goldman Sachs US Valuation Monitor

| | EV/ Sales | EV/ EBITDA | Price/ Book | FCF Yield | P/E | PEG Ratio | Implied Growth | Average | |
|---|---|---|---|---|---|---|---|---|---|
| **S&P 500** | **(1.4)** | **(1.9)** | **(1.0)** | **(0.7)** | **(1.3)** | **(0.9)** | **(0.6)** | **(1.1)** | |
| | | | | | | | | | |
| Information Technology | (0.4) | (0.9) | (0.5) | (1.9) | (0.9) | (0.6) | (4.3) | **(1.3)** | INEXPENSIVE |
| Health Care | (1.3) | (0.8) | (1.1) | (1.6) | (0.1) | 0.3 | (0.8) | **(0.8)** | |
| Energy | (0.6) | (1.1) | 1.6 | (0.5) | (1.2) | (1.8) | 0.1 | **(0.5)** | |
| Telecommunication Services | (0.7) | 1.3 | 0.2 | (0.5) | 0.0 | 0.4 | 1.4 | **0.3** | |
| Materials | 1.1 | 0.5 | 1.3 | 0.9 | (0.4) | (1.7) | 1.0 | **0.4** | |
| Industrials | 1.3 | 0.7 | 0.5 | (0.5) | 0.9 | 0.3 | 0.7 | **0.6** | |
| Consumer Staples | 1.0 | 0.4 | (1.5) | 0.3 | 1.3 | 2.5 | 0.2 | **0.6** | |
| Consumer Discretionary | 1.5 | 0.7 | 0.1 | 1.7 | 1.0 | 0.9 | 1.1 | **1.0** | |
| Utilities | | 2.2 | 2.4 | 0.8 | 2.0 | (0.0) | 4.4 | **2.0** | |
| Financials | | | 0.2 | | 1.5 | 1.3 | 4.9 | **2.0** | EXPENSIVE |

*Note:* S&P valuation calculated on an absolute basis, sector valuations calculated relative to S&P 500. Valuation score calculated as the average number of standard deviations seven valuation metrics differ from 10-year averages: EV/Sales, EV/EBITDA, P/B, FCF yield, P/E, PEG, and Implied Growth.

*Sources:* Compustat and Goldman Sachs Research.

## Bottom-Up Valuation of the S&P 500: A Look at Seven Metrics

On an absolute basis the S&P 500 appears most undervalued on an EV/ EBITDA, trading almost two standard deviations below the average of the past decade. The S&P 500 appears least undervalued in terms of implied 5-year EPS growth that we compute by reversing the dividend discount model.

The Exhibits on the left side provide the absolute level of the seven metrics since 1983. Valuation scores on the right side show the standard deviations from the 10-year average.

---

**EXHIBIT 4** | **S&P 500 Bottom-Up Valuation on Seven Key Financial Metrics as of September 8, 2006**

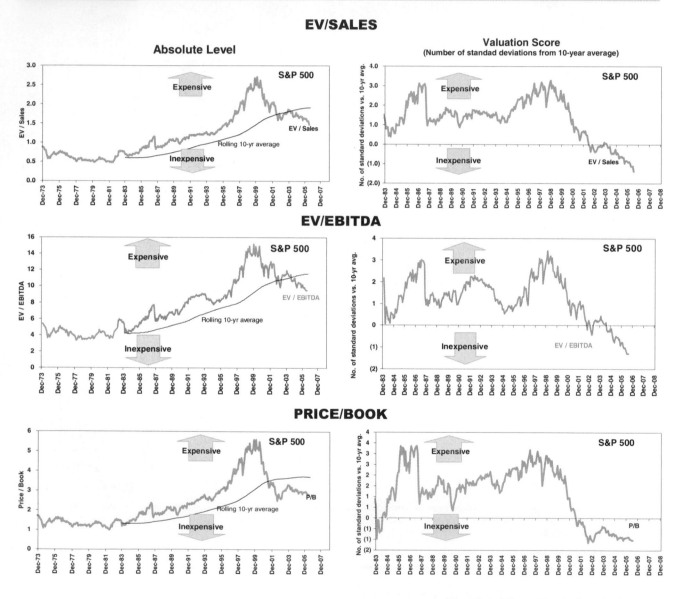

*(Exhibit continued on next page . . .)*

**EXHIBIT 4**    (continued)

# FREE CASH FLOW YIELD

**Absolute Level**

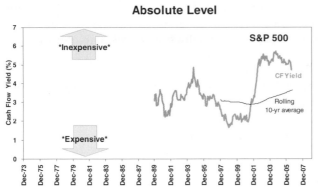

**Valuation Score**
(Number of standad deviations from 10-year average)

## P/E

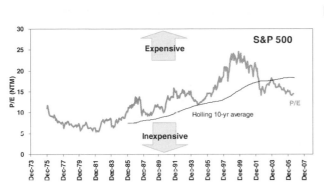

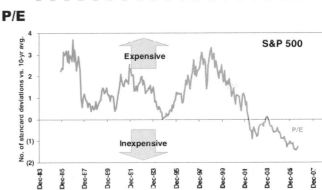

## P/E-to-GROWTH (PEG)

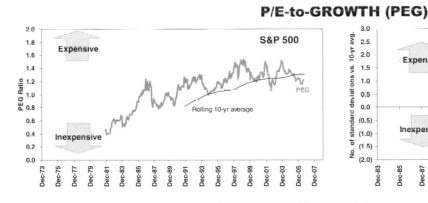

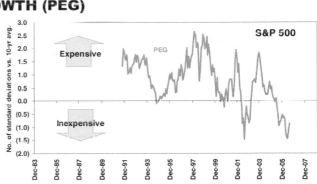

## IMPLIED GROWTH (reverse DDM)

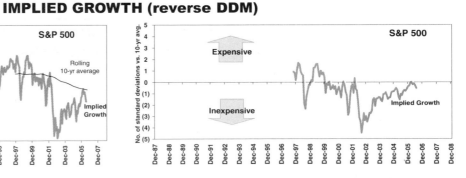

*Sources:* Compustat and Goldman Sachs Research.

## Mean versus Median (Larger-Cap Stocks Are More Undervalued)

Within the S&P 500, the magnitude of the current undervaluation of larger-cap stocks relative to their history appears greater than the degree of undervaluation of the smaller-cap stocks in the index relative to their history (see Exhibit 1).

The equal-weighted average of company valuation scores is greater than the market-cap weighted average in every sector, suggesting that the smaller-cap stocks are more expensive vs. larger-cap stocks across the S&P.

Note that the overall S&P 500 on a bottom-up basis is more undervalued (less expensive) than small-cap stocks in the Russell 2000 Index.

The larger-cap stocks appear valued most similarly to smaller-cap stocks in Utilities, where the difference appears negligible.

Within Consumer Discretionary and Health Care, the equal-weighted average of valuation scores suggests stocks are slightly expensive compared with history. But the market-cap weighted average suggests stocks are inexpensive. This disparity indicates that the larger-cap names in these two sectors are undervalued (see Exhibit 5).

| EXHIBIT 5 | Number of Standard Deviations from 10-Year Average: Market-Cap Weighted versus Equal-Weighted Average as of September 8, 2006 |
|---|---|

| | Average Valuation | | |
| | Mkt Cap. Weighted | Equal Weighted | Difference |
|---|---|---|---|
| **S&P 500** | 0.1 | 0.3 | **(0.20)** |
| | | | |
| **Utilities** | 1.6 | 1.6 | **(0.00)** |
| **Financials** | 0.6 | 0.7 | **(0.08)** |
| **Telecommunication Services** | 0.6 | 0.7 | **(0.11)** |
| **Energy** | (0.4) | (0.3) | **(0.11)** |
| **Materials** | 0.4 | 0.6 | **(0.14)** |
| **Consumer Staples** | 0.5 | 0.7 | **(0.16)** |
| **Industrials** | 0.1 | 0.3 | **(0.18)** |
| **Information Technology** | (0.7) | (0.4) | **(0.22)** |
| **Health Care** | (0.1) | 0.2 | **(0.31)** |
| **Consumer Discretionary** | (0.2) | 0.1 | **(0.34)** |

**Larger-caps INEXPENSIVE vs. Smaller-caps**

Positive equal weighted average suggests that stocks are slightly expensive relative to history, but negative market-cap weighted averages suggest stocks are inexpensive.

Larger-cap stocks appear relatively undervalued vs. smaller-cap stocks.

*Note:* S&P valuation calculated on an absolute basis, sector valuations calculated relative to S&P 500. Valuation score calculated as the average number of standard deviations seven valuation metrics differ from 10-year averages: EV/Sales, EV/EBITDA, P/B, FCF yield, P/E, PEG, and Implied Growth.

*Sources:* Compustat and Goldman Sachs Research.

# THE GOLDMAN SACHS "SUPER-VALUE" AND "ANTI-VALUE" PORTFOLIOS

## 3

We ranked the individual stocks in the S&P 500 based on the difference between current and historical valuations using the seven financial metrics discussed previously. Taking the current sector composition of the S&P 500 Index, we created two 50-stock sector-neutral portfolios comprised of the least and most expensive stocks in each sector. The stocks and their historical relative valuation scores appear in Exhibits 8 and 10 respectively, and the current valuation ratios appear in Exhibits 9 and 11, respectively.

Exhibit 6 shows the performance of the Goldman Sachs "Super-value" and "Anti-value" portfolios and the S&P 500 over the past 10 years.

| EXHIBIT 6 | Goldman Sachs "Super-Value" and "Anti-Value" Portfolios and S&P 500 Total Returns, 1995–2006 YTD as of September 8, 2006 |
|---|---|

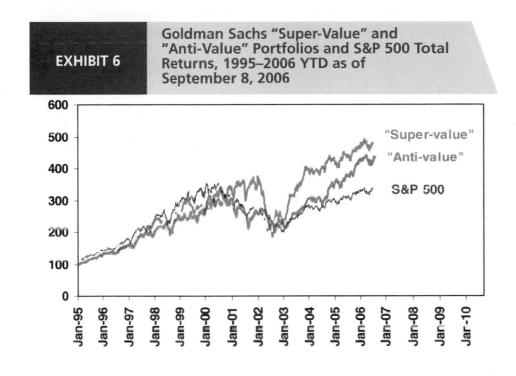

*Sources:* Compustat and Goldman Sachs Research.

Appendix 44A contains a list of the 25 least and more expensive stocks in the S&P 500.

Appendix 44B contains the 50 largest stocks in the S&P 500 ranked by valuation scores.

| EXHIBIT 7 | Valuation of "Super-Value" and "Anti-Value" Portfolios as of September 8, 2006 |

### Historical Relative Valuation

| | EV/ Sales | EV/ EBITDA | Price/ Book | FCF Yield | P/E (NTM) | PEG Ratio | Implied Growth | Valuation Score 8-Sep-06 |
|---|---|---|---|---|---|---|---|---|
| "Super-value" portfolio | (1.2) | (1.0) | (0.7) | (1.3) | (1.1) | (0.8) | (1.5) | (1.0) |
| "Anti-value" portfolio | 1.4 | 1.3 | 1.2 | 0.6 | 1.6 | 1.3 | 2.4 | 1.5 |
| S&P 500 (median) | 0.0 | (0.0) | 0.1 | (0.0) | 0.4 | 0.0 | 1.1 | 0.3 |

### Current Valuation Metrics

| | EV/ Sales | EV/ EBITDA | Price/ Book | FCF Yield | P/E (NTM) | PEG Ratio | Implied Growth |
|---|---|---|---|---|---|---|---|
| "Super-value" portfolio | 2.7 | 9.6 | 3.4 | 4.7 % | 16.3 | 1.2 | (6.6) pp |
| "Anti-value" portfolio | 2.3 | 10.3 | 3.4 | 4.2 | 17.1 | 1.7 | 11.2 |
| S&P 500 (median) | 1.7 | 9.1 | 2.8 | 4.7 | 16.1 | 1.4 | 3.7 |

*Sources:* Compustat and Goldman Sachs Research.

## The Goldman Sachs "Super-Value" Portfolio

| EXHIBIT 8 | Our Sector-Neutral Portfolio of the 50 Most Undervalued Stocks in the S&P 500 as of September 8, 2006 |
|---|---|

| Weight (%) | Company | Ticker | Rating | Sub-Sector | Equity Cap ($ Bill) | Total Return YTD | Valuation Score 8-Sep-06 |
|---|---|---|---|---|---|---|---|
| **10%** | **Consumer Discretionary** | | | | | | |
| 2 | Apollo Group | APOL | NC | Education Services | 8 | (21)% | (2.0) |
| 2 | Home Depot | HD | Buy | Home Improvement Retail | 71 | (14) | (1.8) |
| 2 | News Corporation | NWS.A | Neutral | Movies & Entertainment | 60 | 22 | (1.5) |
| 2 | Bed Bath & Beyond | BBBY | Neutral | Homefurnishing Retail | 10 | (6) | (1.5) |
| 2 | Gap, Inc. | GPS | Neutral | Apparel Retail | 14 | (3) | (1.5) |
| **10%** | **Consumer Staples** | | | | | | |
| 2 | Wal-Mart Stores | WMT | Buy | Hypermarkets & Super Centers | 195 | 1% | (1.8) |
| 2 | Coca-Cola Co. | KO | Neutral | Soft Drinks | 105 | 12 | (0.9) |
| 2 | Wrigley (Wm) Jr. | WWY | NC | Packaged Foods & Meats | 13 | (12) | (0.7) |
| 2 | Coca-Cola Enterprises | CCE | Neutral | Soft Drinks | 10 | 13 | (0.4) |
| 2 | Walgreen Co. | WAG | Buy | Drug Retail | 51 | 16 | (0.4) |
| **10%** | **Energy** | | | | | | |
| 2 | Weatherford International Ltd. | WFT | Buy | Oil & Gas Equipment & Services | 14 | 13% | (2.7) |
| 2 | National Oilwell Varco | NOV | Buy | Oil & Gas Equipment & Services | 11 | (1) | (1.4) |
| 2 | BJ Services | BJS | Neutral | Oil & Gas Equipment & Services | 10 | (12) | (1.2) |
| 2 | Nabors Industries Ltd. | NBR | Neutral | Oil & Gas Drilling | 10 | (17) | (0.9) |
| 2 | Rowan Cos. | RDC | Neutral | Oil & Gas Drilling | 4 | (5) | (0.8) |
| **22%** | **Financials** | | | | | | |
| 2 | American Int'l. Group | AIG | Buy | Multi-line Insurance | 167 | (5)% | (1.2) |
| 2 | Simon Property Group, Inc | SPG | Buy | Retail REITs | 19 | 16 | (0.9) |
| 2 | Fifth Third Bancorp | FITB | Neutral | Regional Banks | 22 | 6 | (0.8) |
| 2 | Charles Schwab | SCHW | Neutral | Investment Banking & Brokerage | 21 | 12 | (0.8) |
| 2 | Synovus Financial | SNV | NC | Regional Banks | 9 | 8 | (0.5) |
| 2 | Capital One Financial | COF | Buy | Consumer Finance | 22 | (16) | (0.4) |
| 2 | Northern Trust Corp. | NTRS | Neutral | Asset Management & Custody Banks | 12 | 10 | (0.4) |
| 2 | CIT Group | CIT | NC | Specialized Finance | 9 | (12) | (0.4) |
| 2 | ProLogis | PLD | Buy | Industrial REITs | 14 | 24 | (0.3) |
| 2 | E*Trade Financial Corp. | ET | Neutral | Investment Banking & Brokerage | 10 | 8 | (0.3) |
| 2 | Prudential Financial | PRU | Neutral | Life & Health Insurance | 35 | (2) | (0.2) |
| **12%** | **Health Care** | | | | | | |
| 2 | Stryker Corp. | SYK | Buy | Health Care Equipment | 20 | 10% | (2.2) |
| 2 | Medtronic Inc. | MDT | Neutral | Health Care Equipment | 56 | (18) | (1.5) |
| 2 | Zimmer Holdings | ZMH | NC | Health Care Equipment | 17 | (0) | (1.3) |
| 2 | BIOGEN IDEC Inc. | BIIB | Neutral | Biotechnology | 15 | (3) | (1.0) |
| 2 | Amgen | AMGN | Buy | Biotechnology | 80 | (14) | (1.0) |
| 2 | Genzyme Corp. | GENZ | Neutral | Biotechnology | 17 | (7) | (0.9) |
| **10%** | **Industrials** | | | | | | |
| 2 | Cintas Corporation | CTAS | NC | Diversified Commercial & Professional Services | 6 | (8)% | (1.8) |
| 2 | United Parcel Service | UPS | NC | Air Freight & Logistics | 75 | (6) | (1.5) |
| 2 | L-3 Communications Holdings | LLL | Buy | Aerospace & Defense | 9 | 2 | (1.2) |
| 2 | Robert Half International | RHI | Neutral | Human Resource & Employment Services | 5 | (19) | (1.1) |
| 2 | Southwest Airlines | LUV | NC | Airlines | 13 | 0 | (0.8) |
| **16%** | **Information Technology** | | | | | | |
| 2 | eBay Inc. | EBAY | Buy | Internet Software & Services | 40 | (34)% | (1.9) |
| 2 | Linear Technology Corp. | LLTC | Buy | Semiconductors | 10 | (8) | (1.6) |
| 2 | Xilinx, Inc | XLNX | Neutral | Semiconductors | 7 | (16) | (1.5) |
| 2 | Maxim Integrated Prod | MXIM | Neutral | Semiconductors | 9 | (20) | (1.5) |
| 2 | Microsoft Corp. | MSFT | Buy | Systems Software | 261 | (1) | (1.4) |
| 2 | Altera Corp. | ALTR | Neutral | Semiconductors | 7 | 4 | (1.3) |
| 2 | Analog Devices | ADI | Neutral | Semiconductors | 11 | (16) | (1.3) |
| 2 | Jabil Circuit | JBL | Buy | Electronic Manufacturing Services | 6 | (28) | (1.2) |
| **2%** | **Materials** | | | | | | |
| 2 | Newmont Mining Corp. (Hldg. Co.) | NEM | Neutral | Gold | 22 | (9)% | (0.6) |
| **4%** | **Telecommunication Services** | | | | | | |
| 2 | AT & T Inc. | T | Not Rated | Integrated Telecommunication Services | 122 | 33% | 0.0 |
| 2 | Sprint Nextel Corp. | S | Buy | Wireless Telecommunication Services | 49 | (22) | 0.1 |
| **4%** | **Utilities** | | | | | | |
| 2 | AES Corp. | AES | NC | Independent Power Producers & Energy Traders | 13 | 29% | 0.4 |
| 2 | DTE Energy Co. | DTE | NC | Multi-Utilities | 7 | (2) | 0.7 |
| **100%** | **Total** | | | | | | |
| | "Super-value" portfolio (average) | | | | | (2.4)% | (1.0) |
| | S&P 500 | | | | | 5.4% | (1.2) |

*Note:* S&P valuation calculated on an absolute basis, sector valuations calculated relative to S&P 500. Valuation score calculated as the average number of standard deviations seven valuation metrics differ from 10-year averages: EV/Sales, EV/EBITDA, P/B, FCF yield, P/E, PEG, and Implied Growth.

*Sources:* Compustat, Lionshare via FactSet, and Goldman Sachs Research.

| EXHIBIT 9 | Current Valuation Data for Our Sector-Neutral Portfolio of 50 Most Undervalued Stocks in the S&P 500 as of September 8, 2006 |
|---|---|

| Weight (%) | Company | Ticker | Rating | Price 8-Sep-06 | EV/ Sales | EV/ EBITDA | Price/ Book | FCF Yield | P/E (NTM) | PEG Ratio | Implied Growth |
|---|---|---|---|---|---|---|---|---|---|---|---|
| **10%** | **Consumer Discretionary** | | | | | | | | | | |
| 2 | Apollo Group | APOL | NC | $47.87 | 2.9 | 7.7 | 10.7 | 9.6% | 16.7 | 1.1 | (10.3) pp |
| 2 | Home Depot | HD | Buy | 34.28 | 0.8 | 6.2 | 2.7 | 4.5 | 10.8 | 0.8 | (16.6) |
| 2 | News Corporation | NWS.A | Neutral | 18.87 | 2.5 | 8.5 | 1.5 | 5.1 | 18.0 | 1.0 | (4.0) |
| 2 | Bed Bath & Beyond | BBBY | Neutral | 34.11 | 1.3 | 8.6 | 4.1 | 4.0 | 15.2 | 1.0 | (11.3) |
| 2 | Gap, Inc. | GPS | Neutral | 16.90 | 0.7 | 3.4 | 1.7 | 13.2 | 14.1 | 1.2 | (7.1) |
| **10%** | **Consumer Staples** | | | | | | | | | | |
| 2 | Wal-Mart Stores | WMT | Buy | 46.72 | 0.7 | 6.0 | 2.2 | 3.0 | 15.3 | 1.2 | (8.0) |
| 2 | Coca-Cola Co. | KO | Neutral | 44.60 | 4.3 | 11.4 | 5.5 | 4.9 | 18.4 | 2.3 | (8.3) |
| 2 | Wrigley (Wm) Jr. | WWY | NC | 46.05 | 2.9 | 11.1 | 4.4 | 2.6 | 22.4 | 2.0 | 0.2 |
| 2 | Coca-Cola Enterprises | CCE | Neutral | 21.46 | 1.3 | 6.8 | 1.1 | 7.6 | 15.7 | 1.9 | (1.6) |
| 2 | Walgreen Co. | WAG | Buy | 50.91 | 1.0 | NM | 5.6 | 2.4 | 26.4 | 1.7 | 4.8 |
| **10%** | **Energy** | | | | | | | | | | |
| 2 | Weatherford International Ltd. | WFT | Buy | 41.01 | 2.1 | 10.8 | 3.0 | 0.6 | 13.6 | 0.5 | (7.0) |
| 2 | National Oilwell Varco | NOV | Buy | 62.16 | 1.4 | 12.4 | 2.5 | 2.9 | 14.7 | 0.5 | (9.6) |
| 2 | BJ Services | BJS | Neutral | 32.26 | 1.9 | 8.1 | 4.2 | 3.8 | 10.3 | 0.5 | (16.7) |
| 2 | Nabors Industries Ltd. | NBR | Neutral | 31.61 | 2.1 | 6.7 | 3.1 | (0.6) | 7.0 | 0.2 | (21.9) |
| 2 | Rowan Cos. | RDC | Neutral | 33.53 | 2.0 | 6.5 | 2.3 | (0.6) | 7.2 | 0.2 | (21.3) |
| **22%** | **Financials** | | | | | | | | | | |
| 2 | American Int'l. Group | AIG | Buy | 64.24 | NM | NM | 1.9 | NM | 10.9 | 0.8 | (8.1) |
| 2 | Simon Property Group, Inc | SPG | Buy | 86.62 | NM | NM | 4.9 | NM | 15.8 | 2.0 | (13.9) |
| 2 | Fifth Third Bancorp | FITB | Neutral | 39.05 | NM | NM | 2.3 | NM | 13.9 | 1.4 | (5.0) |
| 2 | Charles Schwab | SCHW | Neutral | 16.28 | NM | NM | 3.8 | NM | 18.9 | 1.3 | (3.6) |
| 2 | Synovus Financial | SNV | NC | 28.87 | NM | NM | 3.0 | NM | 15.2 | 1.2 | (1.1) |
| 2 | Capital One Financial | COF | Buy | 72.46 | NM | NM | 1.7 | NM | 9.8 | 0.8 | (3.7) |
| 2 | Northern Trust Corp. | NTRS | Neutral | 56.49 | NM | NM | 2.9 | NM | 17.5 | 1.5 | 0.4 |
| 2 | CIT Group | CIT | NC | 44.90 | NM | NM | 1.3 | NM | 9.1 | 1.1 | (6.1) |
| 2 | ProLogis | PLD | Buy | 56.57 | NM | NM | 3.4 | NM | 17.9 | 4.0 | (2.0) |
| 2 | E*Trade Financial Corp. | ET | Neutral | 22.61 | NM | NM | 3.1 | NM | 14.0 | 1.0 | (1.8) |
| 2 | Prudential Financial | PRU | Neutral | 72.00 | NM | NM | 1.6 | NM | 11.8 | 0.8 | NM |
| **12%** | **Health Care** | | | | | | | | | | |
| 2 | Stryker Corp. | SYK | Buy | 48.82 | 3.3 | 9.8 | 4.2 | 4.2 | 22.2 | 1.1 | (2.0) |
| 2 | Medtronic Inc. | MDT | Neutral | 46.66 | 4.6 | 13.3 | 5.5 | 4.2 | 19.3 | 1.3 | (7.4) |
| 2 | Zimmer Holdings | ZMH | NC | 67.37 | 4.5 | 12.6 | 3.6 | 4.5 | 18.4 | 1.1 | (1.2) |
| 2 | BIOGEN IDEC Inc. | BIIB | Neutral | 43.98 | 5.1 | 11.2 | 2.2 | 3.6 | 20.3 | 1.4 | (5.7) |
| 2 | Amgen | AMGN | Buy | 67.93 | 5.5 | 13.4 | 4.4 | 5.3 | 17.5 | 1.2 | (6.5) |
| 2 | Genzyme Corp. | GENZ | Neutral | 65.79 | 5.4 | 17.0 | 3.3 | 2.9 | 21.4 | 1.2 | (0.7) |
| **10%** | **Industrials** | | | | | | | | | | |
| 2 | Cintas Corporation | CTAS | NC | 37.53 | 1.8 | 7.7 | 2.5 | 5.9 | 17.2 | 1.2 | (6.2) |
| 2 | United Parcel Service | UPS | NC | 69.56 | 1.5 | 9.1 | 4.5 | 4.1 | 17.2 | 1.4 | (4.4) |
| 2 | L-3 Communications Holdings | LLL | Buy | 75.26 | 1.0 | 9.0 | 2.0 | 8.9 | 14.1 | 1.2 | (0.3) |
| 2 | Robert Half International | RHI | Neutral | 30.42 | 1.1 | 9.6 | 5.4 | 5.1 | 17.7 | 0.9 | (21.2) |
| 2 | Southwest Airlines | LUV | NC | 16.48 | 1.3 | 6.2 | 1.8 | 9.5 | 18.5 | 1.2 | 7.3 |
| **16%** | **Information Technology** | | | | | | | | | | |
| 2 | eBay Inc. | EBAY | Buy | 28.51 | 5.5 | 15.1 | 3.5 | 5.1 | 25.2 | 1.2 | (7.7) |
| 2 | Linear Technology Corp. | LLTC | Buy | 32.59 | 6.4 | 12.1 | 4.8 | 4.5 | 20.4 | 1.0 | (15.1) |
| 2 | Xilinx, Inc | XLNX | Neutral | 21.07 | 3.1 | 11.4 | 2.7 | 5.9 | 19.3 | 1.3 | (16.8) |
| 2 | Maxim Integrated Prod | MXIM | Neutral | 28.56 | 3.5 | 11.3 | 3.5 | 4.5 | 17.5 | 1.0 | (19.6) |
| 2 | Microsoft Corp. | MSFT | Buy | 25.60 | 4.4 | 9.3 | 5.1 | 5.7 | 17.7 | 1.5 | (12.5) |
| 2 | Altera Corp. | ALTR | Neutral | 19.33 | 4.2 | 14.9 | 5.3 | 5.6 | 19.5 | 1.0 | (13.7) |
| 2 | Analog Devices | ADI | Neutral | 29.63 | 2.9 | 9.2 | 2.9 | 5.1 | 16.1 | 0.8 | (20.8) |
| 2 | Jabil Circuit | JBL | Buy | 26.46 | 0.4 | 7.8 | 2.1 | 3.5 | 15.5 | 0.6 | (12.0) |
| **2%** | **Materials** | | | | | | | | | | |
| 2 | Newmont Mining Corp. (Hldg. Co.) | NEM | Neutral | 48.19 | 3.6 | 11.0 | 2.6 | 0.4 | 22.2 | 0.6 | (5.7) |
| **4%** | **Telecommunication Services** | | | | | | | | | | |
| 2 | AT & T Inc. | T | Not Rated | 31.35 | 1.8 | 8.1 | 2.5 | 6.4 | 13.6 | 1.4 | (2.6) |
| 2 | Sprint Nextel Corp. | S | Buy | 16.51 | 1.5 | 4.7 | 1.4 | 10.3 | 12.6 | 0.9 | 14.3 |
| **4%** | **Utilities** | | | | | | | | | | |
| 2 | AES Corp. | AES | NC | 20.45 | NM | 8.1 | 7.3 | 7.9 | 22.5 | 1.4 | 13.6 |
| 2 | DTE Energy Co. | DTE | NC | 41.17 | NM | 8.6 | 1.3 | (0.9) | 10.6 | 2.4 | 8.3 |
| **100%** | **Total** | | | | | | | | | | |
| | "Super-value" portfolio (average) | | | | 2.7 | 9.6 | 3.4 | 4.7% | 16.3 | 1.2 | (6.6) pp |
| | S&P 500 | | | | 1.5 | 8.4 | 2.8 | 4.7% | 14.3 | 1.2 | |

*Sources:* Compustat, Lionshare via FactSet, and Goldman Sachs Research.

# The Goldman Sachs "Anti-Value" Portfolio

**EXHIBIT 10**    **Our Sector-Neutral Portfolio of the 50 Most Overvalued Stocks in the S&P 500 as of September 8, 2006**

| Weight (%) | Company | Ticker | Rating | Sub-Sector | Equity Cap ($ Bill) | Total Return YTD | Valuation Score 8-Sep-06 |
|---|---|---|---|---|---|---|---|
| 10% | **Consumer Discretionary** | | | | | | |
| 2 | Wendy's International | WEN | Neutral | Restaurants | 7 | 16 % | 2.1 |
| 2 | McGraw-Hill | MHP | Neutral | Publishing | 20 | 11 | 1.7 |
| 2 | Snap-On Inc. | SNA | NC | Household Appliances | 3 | 18 | 1.6 |
| 2 | Federated Dept. Stores | FD | Buy | Department Stores | 22 | 20 | 1.6 |
| 2 | V.F. Corp. | VFC | NC | Apparel Accessories & Luxury Goods | 8 | 32 | 1.5 |
| 10% | **Consumer Staples** | | | | | | |
| 2 | Altria Group, Inc. | MO | Neutral | Tobacco | 173 | 14% | 2.2 |
| 2 | UST Inc. | UST | Sell | Tobacco | 9 | 36 | 1.9 |
| 2 | Sara Lee Corp. | SLE | NC | Packaged Foods & Meats | 11 | (8) | 1.7 |
| 2 | Archer-Daniels-Midland | ADM | NC | Agricultural Products | 26 | 62 | 1.7 |
| 2 | Constellation Brands | STZ | Buy | Distillers & Vintners | 6 | 6 | 1.4 |
| 10% | **Energy** | | | | | | |
| 2 | Murphy Oil | MUR | Buy | Integrated Oil & Gas | 9 | (12)% | 1.0 |
| 2 | Occidental Petroleum | OXY | Neutral | Integrated Oil & Gas | 40 | 19 | 0.7 |
| 2 | El Paso Corp. | EP | NC | Oil & Gas Storage & Transportation | 10 | 16 | 0.7 |
| 2 | Devon Energy Corp. | DVN | Neutral | Oil & Gas Exploration & Production | 30 | 8 | 0.5 |
| 2 | Sunoco., Inc. | SUN | Neutral | Oil & Gas Refining & Marketing | 9 | (16) | 0.3 |
| 22% | **Financials** | | | | | | |
| 2 | Chubb Corp. | CB | Neutral | Property & Casualty Insurance | 21 | 4% | 2.1 |
| 2 | AmSouth Bancorporation | ASO | Not Rated | Regional Banks | 10 | 12 | 2.0 |
| 2 | T. Rowe Price Group | TROW | Neutral | Asset Management & Custody Banks | 12 | 23 | 2.0 |
| 2 | Mellon Bank Corp. | MEL | Neutral | Asset Management & Custody Banks | 16 | 12 | 2.0 |
| 2 | Aon Corp. | AOC | NC | Insurance Brokers | 11 | (4) | 1.8 |
| 2 | Loews Corp. | LTR | Neutral | Multi-line Insurance | 21 | 21 | 1.8 |
| 2 | PNC Bank Corp. | PNC | Neutral | Regional Banks | 21 | 19 | 1.8 |
| 2 | KeyCorp | KEY | Neutral | Regional Banks | 15 | 14 | 1.8 |
| 2 | First Horizon National | FHN | Sell | Regional Banks | 5 | 1 | 1.7 |
| 2 | Principal Financial Group | PFG | Sell | Life & Health Insurance | 15 | 12 | 1.6 |
| 2 | Huntington Bancshares | HBAN | Sell | Regional Banks | 6 | 3 | 1.6 |
| 12% | **Health Care** | | | | | | |
| 2 | Becton, Dickinson | BDX | Neutral | Health Care Equipment | 17 | 15% | 2.0 |
| 2 | Bard (C.R.) Inc. | BCR | NC | Health Care Equipment | 8 | 15 | 1.9 |
| 2 | Laboratory Corp. of America Holt | LH | NC | Health Care Services | 8 | 24 | 1.8 |
| 2 | Manor Care Inc. | HCR | NC | Health Care Facilities | 4 | 32 | 1.7 |
| 2 | Humana Inc. | HUM | Buy | Managed Health Care | 10 | 13 | 1.6 |
| 2 | Thermo Electron | TMO | NC | Life Sciences Tools & Services | 6 | 30 | 1.2 |
| 10% | **Industrials** | | | | | | |
| 2 | United Technologies | UTX | Buy | Aerospace & Defense | 64 | 15% | 1.9 |
| 2 | CSX Corp. | CSX | NC | Railroads | 13 | 20 | 1.8 |
| 2 | General Dynamics | GD | Buy | Aerospace & Defense | 28 | 23 | 1.5 |
| 2 | Allied Waste Industries | AW | NC | Environmental & Facilities Services | 4 | 17 | 1.4 |
| 2 | Cooper Industries, Ltd. | CBE | Neutral | Electrical Components & Equipment | 7 | 13 | 1.3 |
| 16% | **Information Technology** | | | | | | |
| 2 | Electronic Arts | ERTS | NC | Home Entertainment Software | 16 | 0% | 1.1 |
| 2 | Autodesk, Inc. | ADSK | Neutral | Application Software | 8 | (22) | 0.9 |
| 2 | Apple Computer | AAPL | Buy | Computer Hardware | 62 | 1 | 0.7 |
| 2 | Freescale Semiconductor Inc. | FSL.B | Neutral | Semiconductors | 13 | 23 | 0.6 |
| 2 | Unisys Corp. | UIS | Neutral | IT Consulting & Other Services | 2 | (8) | 0.6 |
| 2 | Convergys Corp. | CVG | Sell | Data Processing & Outsourced Services | 3 | 30 | 0.5 |
| 2 | Intuit, Inc. | INTU | NC | Application Software | 11 | 17 | 0.5 |
| 2 | NVIDIA Corp. | NVDA | Neutral | Semiconductors | 10 | 52 | 0.5 |
| 2% | **Materials** | | | | | | |
| 2 | Pactiv Corp. | PTV | NC | Metal & Glass Containers | 4 | 21% | 1.8 |
| 4% | **Telecommunication Services** | | | | | | |
| 2 | ALLTEL Corp. | AT | Neutral | Wireless Telecommunication Services | 21 | 9% | 1.2 |
| 2 | BellSouth | BLS | Not Rated | Integrated Telecommunication Services | 75 | 56 | 1.0 |
| 4% | **Utilities** | | | | | | |
| 2 | Entergy Corp. | ETR | Buy | Electric Utilities | 16 | 16% | 2.2 |
| 2 | Keyspan Energy | KSE | NC | Multi-Utilities | 7 | 20 | 2.2 |
| 100% | **Total** | | | | | | |
| | "Anti-value" portfolio (average) | | | | | 15.5% | 1.5 |
| | S&P 500 | | | | | 5.4% | (1.2) |

*Note:* S&P valuation calculated on an absolute basis, sector valuations calculated relative to S&P 500. Valuation score calculated as the average number of standard deviations seven valuation metrics differ from 10-year averages: EV/Sales, EV/EBITDA, P/B, FCF yield, P/E, PEG, and Implied Growth.

*Sources:* Compustat and Goldman Sachs Research.

| EXHIBIT 11 | Current Valuation Data for Our Sector-Neutral Portfolio of 50 Most Overvalued Stocks in the S&P 500 as of September 8, 2006 |
|---|---|

| | | | | | Current Valuation Metrics | | | | | | |
|---|---|---|---|---|---|---|---|---|---|---|---|
| Weight (%) | Company | Ticker | Rating | Price 8-Sep-06 | EV/ Sales | EV/ EBITDA | Price/ Book | FCF Yield | P/E (NTM) | PEG Ratio | Implied Growth |
| **10%** | **Consumer Discretionary** | | | | | | | | | | |
| 2 | Wendy's International | WEN | Neutral | $63.59 | 1.9 | 12.8 | 3.4 | 0.5% | 25.5 | 2.1 | 24.4 pp |
| 2 | McGraw-Hill | MHP | Neutral | 56.55 | 3.1 | 11.2 | 8.1 | 7.5 | 22.8 | 1.8 | 10.0 |
| 2 | Snap-On Inc. | SNA | NC | 43.36 | 1.1 | 10.3 | 2.5 | 8.1 | 21.2 | 1.8 | 19.4 |
| 2 | Federated Dept. Stores | FD | Buy | 39.58 | 1.0 | 7.9 | 2.2 | 22.9 | 15.7 | 1.3 | 15.5 |
| 2 | V.F. Corp. | VFC | NC | 71.42 | 1.2 | 7.1 | 2.3 | 6.2 | 13.8 | 1.4 | 11.4 |
| **10%** | **Consumer Staples** | | | | | | | | | | |
| 2 | Altria Group, Inc. | MO | Neutral | 82.97 | 2.7 | 10.2 | 4.7 | 6.3 | 15.1 | 1.9 | 15.4 |
| 2 | UST Inc. | UST | Sell | 54.05 | 5.0 | 10.1 | NM | 6.2 | 16.9 | 2.4 | 19.5 |
| 2 | Sara Lee Corp. | SLE | NC | 14.50 | 1.3 | 10.7 | 3.7 | 4.9 | 18.4 | 2.4 | 12.5 |
| 2 | Archer-Daniels-Midland | ADM | NC | 39.59 | 0.8 | 9.8 | 2.8 | 2.4 | 16.0 | 1.8 | 12.0 |
| 2 | Constellation Brands | STZ | Buy | 27.74 | 1.8 | 8.9 | 1.9 | 4.3 | 15.3 | 1.2 | 4.4 |
| **10%** | **Energy** | | | | | | | | | | |
| 2 | Murphy Oil | MUR | Buy | 47.34 | 4.5 | 4.4 | 2.3 | (4.1) | 11.8 | 1.2 | 2.9 |
| 2 | Occidental Petroleum | OXY | Neutral | 46.79 | 2.4 | 4.3 | 2.6 | 8.7 | 8.4 | 0.8 | 1.6 |
| 2 | El Paso Corp. | EP | NC | 14.01 | 4.6 | 10.8 | 2.9 | (14.9) | 12.5 | 1.6 | 5.0 |
| 2 | Devon Energy Corp. | DVN | Neutral | 67.56 | 3.0 | 4.7 | 2.0 | (2.6) | 9.4 | 1.2 | 6.1 |
| 2 | Sunoco., Inc. | SUN | Neutral | 65.50 | 0.3 | 4.2 | 4.2 | 10.8 | 7.6 | 0.8 | 1.8 |
| **22%** | **Financials** | | | | | | | | | | |
| 2 | Chubb Corp. | CB | Neutral | 50.41 | NM | NM | 1.8 | NM | 10.2 | 1.0 | 2.2 |
| 2 | AmSouth Bancorporation | ASO | Not Rated | 28.86 | NM | NM | 2.8 | NM | 13.1 | 1.7 | 10.6 |
| 2 | T. Rowe Price Group | TROW | Neutral | 44.15 | NM | NM | 5.9 | NM | 22.2 | 1.8 | 11.0 |
| 2 | Mellon Bank Corp. | MEL | Neutral | 37.55 | NM | NM | 3.7 | NM | 16.7 | 1.6 | 7.6 |
| 2 | Aon Corp. | AOC | NC | 34.04 | NM | NM | 2.0 | NM | 13.3 | 1.9 | 8.7 |
| 2 | Loews Corp. | LTR | Neutral | 38.05 | NM | NM | 1.1 | NM | 10.5 | 1.3 | 9.8 |
| 2 | PNC Bank Corp. | PNC | Neutral | 71.72 | NM | NM | 2.5 | NM | 13.6 | 1.5 | 9.5 |
| 2 | KeyCorp | KEY | Neutral | 36.62 | NM | NM | 2.0 | NM | 12.5 | 1.6 | 9.6 |
| 2 | First Horizon National | FHN | Sell | 38.10 | NM | NM | 2.0 | NM | 13.7 | 1.7 | 5.5 |
| 2 | Principal Financial Group | PFG | Sell | 53.07 | NM | NM | 2.0 | NM | 15.4 | 1.3 | 8.1 |
| 2 | Huntington Bancshares | HBAN | Sell | 23.90 | NM | NM | 2.1 | NM | 13.0 | 1.9 | 7.0 |
| **12%** | **Health Care** | | | | | | | | | | |
| 2 | Becton, Dickinson | BDX | Neutral | 68.60 | 2.8 | 11.0 | 5.0 | 4.2 | 19.5 | 1.6 | 10.2 |
| 2 | Bard (C.R.) Inc. | BCR | NC | 75.44 | 3.6 | 13.3 | 4.9 | 3.5 | 21.9 | 1.6 | 14.4 |
| 2 | Laboratory Corp. of America Holdings | LH | NC | 67.01 | 2.5 | 10.5 | 4.0 | 6.6 | 19.8 | 1.5 | 6.7 |
| 2 | Manor Care Inc. | HCR | NC | 51.96 | 1.2 | 9.9 | 4.8 | 5.6 | 20.5 | 1.4 | 14.3 |
| 2 | Humana Inc. | HUM | Buy | 61.46 | 0.3 | 10.3 | 4.1 | 16.9 | 19.5 | 1.2 | 18.3 |
| 2 | Thermo Electron | TMO | NC | 39.29 | 2.3 | 14.2 | 2.4 | 3.6 | 21.2 | 1.4 | 10.0 |
| **10%** | **Industrials** | | | | | | | | | | |
| 2 | United Technologies | UTX | Buy | 63.34 | 1.5 | 10.5 | 3.8 | 4.8 | 16.4 | 1.5 | 6.9 |
| 2 | CSX Corp. | CSX | NC | 30.30 | 1.9 | 7.0 | 1.7 | 0.0 | 13.2 | 0.8 | 10.9 |
| 2 | General Dynamics | GD | Buy | 69.37 | 1.2 | 10.7 | 3.4 | 7.1 | 15.7 | 1.6 | 9.4 |
| 2 | Allied Waste Industries | AW | NC | 10.26 | 2.5 | 6.7 | 0.9 | (0.7) | 20.3 | 1.7 | 20.8 |
| 2 | Cooper Industries, Ltd. | CBE | Neutral | 81.15 | 1.6 | 11.3 | 3.2 | 6.4 | 16.2 | 1.5 | 14.2 |
| **16%** | **Information Technology** | | | | | | | | | | |
| 2 | Electronic Arts | ERTS | NC | 52.51 | 4.5 | 26.2 | 4.9 | 2.9 | NM | NM | 47.3 |
| 2 | Autodesk, Inc. | ADSK | Neutral | 33.49 | 3.8 | 16.2 | 10.0 | 5.4 | 21.1 | 1.3 | 26.8 |
| 2 | Apple Computer | AAPL | Buy | 72.52 | 2.5 | 21.0 | 7.6 | 1.5 | 29.6 | 1.7 | 8.9 |
| 2 | Freescale Semiconductor Inc. | FSLB | Neutral | 30.94 | 1.8 | 7.4 | 2.8 | 7.4 | 15.7 | 1.6 | (6.7) |
| 2 | Unisys Corp. | UIS | Neutral | 5.39 | 0.4 | 7.9 | 1.4 | (3.2) | 30.8 | 3.4 | 28.3 |
| 2 | Convergys Corp. | CVG | Sell | 20.59 | 1.1 | 7.4 | 2.1 | 6.1 | 17.6 | 1.5 | 8.1 |
| 2 | Intuit, Inc. | INTU | NC | 31.16 | 3.7 | 13.0 | 6.2 | 5.0 | 22.2 | 1.5 | (2.3) |
| 2 | NVIDIA Corp. | NVDA | Neutral | 27.70 | 3.0 | 17.8 | 6.9 | 3.3 | 20.7 | 1.1 | (4.2) |
| **2%** | **Materials** | | | | | | | | | | |
| 2 | Pactiv Corp. | PTV | NC | 26.70 | 1.6 | 8.6 | 4.2 | 3.4 | 17.6 | 1.7 | 15.8 |
| **4%** | **Telecommunication Services** | | | | | | | | | | |
| 2 | ALLTEL Corp. | AT | Neutral | 55.24 | 2.8 | 6.1 | 1.9 | 7.3 | 20.7 | 3.4 | 14.2 |
| 2 | BellSouth | BLS | Not Rated | 41.19 | 2.5 | 9.9 | 3.1 | 3.4 | 17.2 | 2.6 | 9.2 |
| **4%** | **Utilities** | | | | | | | | | | |
| 2 | Entergy Corp. | ETR | Buy | 78.11 | NM | 8.1 | 2.0 | (2.6) | 17.0 | 2.3 | 16.6 |
| 2 | Keyspan Energy | KSE | NC | 41.28 | NM | 8.7 | 1.6 | (1.9) | 17.0 | 4.5 | 9.7 |
| **100%** | **Total** | | | | | | | | | | |
| | "Anti-value" portfolio (average) | | | | 2.3 | 10.3 | 3.4 | 4.2% | 17.1 | 1.7 | 11.2 pp |
| | S&P 500 | | | | 1.5 | 8.4 | 2.8 | 4.7% | 14.3 | 1.2 | |

*Sources:* Compustat and Goldman Sachs Research.

# APPENDIX 44A

| EXHIBIT A-1 | Correlation of Valuation Metrics as of September 8, 2006 |

| S&P 500 | P/E | PEG | EV/ Sales | EV/ EBITDA | Cash Flow Yield | P/B | Growth | Valuation Score |
|---|---|---|---|---|---|---|---|---|
| P/E | | 0.7 | 0.6 | 0.6 | 0.5 | 0.3 | 0.7 | **0.9** |
| PEG | 0.7 | | 0.4 | 0.3 | 0.2 | 0.1 | 0.4 | **0.6** |
| EV/Sales | 0.6 | 0.4 | | 0.5 | 0.3 | 0.5 | 0.5 | **0.7** |
| EV/EBITDA | 0.6 | 0.3 | 0.5 | | 0.4 | 0.5 | 0.5 | **0.8** |
| Cash Flow Yield | 0.5 | 0.2 | 0.3 | 0.4 | | 0.4 | 0.3 | **0.6** |
| P/B | 0.3 | 0.1 | 0.5 | 0.5 | 0.4 | | 0.2 | **0.6** |
| Growth | 0.7 | 0.4 | 0.5 | 0.5 | 0.3 | 0.2 | | **0.8** |
| **Valuation Score** | **0.9** | **0.6** | **0.7** | **0.8** | **0.6** | **0.6** | **0.8** | |

*Sources:* Compustat and Goldman Sachs Research.

## APPENDIX 44B

**EXHIBIT B-1** — The 25 Least and Most Expensive Stocks in the S&P 500 as of September 8, 2006

**25 Least Expensive Stocks**

| Company | Ticker | Rating | Price 8-Sep | MktCap ($ Bill) | YTD Return | EV/ Sales | EV/ EBITDA | Price/ Book | FCF Yield | P/E | PEG Ratio | Implied Growth | Average |
|---|---|---|---|---|---|---|---|---|---|---|---|---|---|
| Weatherford International Ltd. | WFT | Buy | $41.01 | 14 | 13 | NM | NM | NM | NM | (3.8) | (2.2) | (2.2) | (2.7) |
| Stryker Corp. | SYK | Buy | 48.82 | 14 | 10 | (1.0) | (3.3) | (2.5) | (3.8) | (1.4) | (1.5) | NM | (2.2) |
| Apollo Group | APOL | NC | 47.87 | 7 | (21) | (2.0) | (2.3) | (1.2) | NM | (1.8) | 0.8 | (3.7) | (2.0) |
| eBay Inc. | EBAY | Buy | 28.51 | 33 | (34) | (2.1) | (2.3) | (2.2) | (1.2) | (2.3) | (1.2) | NM | (1.9) |
| Cintas Corporation | CTAS | NC | 37.53 | 5 | (8) | (1.5) | (2.0) | (1.7) | (2.1) | (1.6) | (1.9) | NM | (1.8) |
| Wal-Mart Stores | WMT | Buy | 46.72 | 117 | 1 | (1.2) | (3.1) | (2.4) | (0.1) | (1.6) | (1.4) | (2.6) | (1.8) |
| Home Depot | HD | Buy | 34.28 | 71 | (14) | (1.6) | (1.4) | (1.5) | (1.5) | (1.7) | (1.6) | (3.0) | (1.8) |
| Linear Technology Corp. | LLTC | Buy | 32.59 | 10 | (8) | (1.8) | (1.3) | (1.3) | (2.5) | (1.2) | (1.2) | NM | (1.6) |
| Xilinx, Inc. | XLNX | Neutral | 21.07 | 7 | (16) | (1.4) | (1.4) | (1.2) | (3.2) | (1.5) | (0.5) | NM | (1.5) |
| News Corporation | NWS.A | Neutral | 18.87 | 45 | 22 | 1.7 | (3.1) | (2.1) | (3.4) | (1.1) | (1.2) | NM | (1.5) |
| Bed Bath & Beyond | BBBY | Neutral | 34.11 | 10 | (6) | (1.8) | (1.4) | (1.4) | (1.7) | (1.8) | (1.0) | NM | (1.5) |
| United Parcel Service | UPS | NC | 69.56 | 75 | (6) | (0.3) | (1.2) | (1.5) | (0.7) | (1.9) | (1.1) | (3.8) | (1.5) |
| Maxim Integrated Prod | MXIM | Neutral | 28.56 | 9 | (20) | (2.2) | (0.6) | (1.7) | (2.1) | (1.5) | (0.9) | NM | (1.5) |
| Medtronic Inc. | MDT | Neutral | 46.66 | 56 | (18) | (2.2) | (0.6) | (1.7) | (1.1) | (2.0) | (1.3) | NM | (1.5) |
| Gap, Inc. | GPS | Neutral | 16.90 | 9 | (3) | (1.1) | (1.7) | (1.3) | (3.7) | (0.7) | (0.4) | (1.3) | (1.5) |
| Coach, Inc. | COH | Buy | 31.88 | 12 | (4) | (1.7) | (0.4) | (0.1) | (1.2) | (2.0) | (1.9) | (2.8) | (1.4) |
| Microsoft Corp. | MSFT | Buy | 25.60 | 225 | (1) | (1.4) | (1.6) | (0.7) | (0.7) | (1.1) | (1.3) | (3.1) | (1.4) |
| National Oilwell Varco | NOV | Buy | 62.16 | 11 | (1) | NM | (1.7) | 0.1 | NM | (3.2) | (0.7) | NM | (1.4) |
| Sears Holding Corp. | SHLD | NC | 151.50 | 15 | 31 | (0.1) | (1.2) | (2.8) | NM | (1.1) | (1.6) | NM | (1.4) |
| Altera Corp. | ALTR | Neutral | 19.33 | 7 | 4 | (1.0) | (0.6) | (0.4) | (1.7) | (1.2) | (0.9) | (3.7) | (1.3) |
| Analog Devices | ADI | Neutral | 29.63 | 11 | (16) | (1.4) | (1.3) | (1.1) | (1.2) | (1.4) | (1.5) | NM | (1.3) |
| Zimmer Holdings | ZMH | NC | 67.37 | 17 | (0) | (0.8) | (0.6) | (0.7) | (1.9) | (1.4) | (1.3) | (2.5) | (1.3) |
| American Int'l. Group | AIG | Neutral | 64.24 | 167 | (5) | NM | NM | (1.1) | NM | (1.5) | (1.1) | (1.3) | (1.2) |
| Jabil Circuit | JBL | Buy | 26.46 | 5 | (28) | (2.4) | (0.8) | (1.4) | 0.6 | (1.5) | (1.9) | NM | (1.2) |
| Paychex Inc. | PAYX | Neutral | 35.22 | 12 | (6) | (1.2) | (1.1) | (1.4) | (1.2) | (1.4) | (0.7) | NM | (1.2) |
| **S&P 500** | | | | 11751 | 5 | (1.4) | (2.0) | (1.0) | (0.7) | (1.3) | (0.9) | (1.0) | (1.2) |
| **(Median)** | | | | 11 | 4 | 0.0 | (0.0) | 0.1 | (0.0) | 0.4 | 0.0 | 1.1 | 0.3 |
| PNC Bank Corp. | PNC | Neutral | 71.72 | 21 | 19 | NM | NM | 2.1 | NM | 2.0 | 1.3 | NM | 1.8 |
| American Electric Power | AEP | Sell | 35.91 | 14 | (0) | NM | 1.6 | 1.1 | 3.9 | 1.2 | (0.0) | 3.1 | 1.8 |
| Peoples Energy | PGL | NC | 41.05 | 2 | 21 | NM | 2.7 | 1.5 | 1.0 | 2.6 | 1.3 | NM | 1.8 |
| Loews Corp. | LTR | Neutral | 38.05 | 15 | 21 | NM | NM | 1.0 | NM | 2.2 | 2.3 | NM | 1.8 |
| Aon Corp. | AOC | NC | 34.04 | 11 | (4) | NM | NM | 0.3 | NM | 0.8 | 2.4 | 3.8 | 1.8 |
| Constellation Energy Group | CEG | NC | 59.62 | 11 | 6 | NM | 2.4 | 2.8 | 2.4 | 1.2 | (1.3) | 3.6 | 1.8 |
| Pinnacle West Capital | PNW | NC | 44.89 | 4 | 13 | NM | 2.2 | 1.1 | 2.8 | 1.5 | 0.3 | 3.3 | 1.9 |
| Bard (C.R.) Inc. | BCR | NC | 75.44 | 8 | 15 | 2.0 | 2.4 | 1.5 | 1.1 | 2.0 | 1.3 | 2.7 | 1.9 |
| Consolidated Edison | ED | Sell | 45.29 | 11 | 2 | NM | 2.4 | 1.2 | NM | 1.7 | 0.4 | 3.8 | 1.9 |
| UST Inc. | UST | Sell | 54.05 | 9 | 36 | 2.2 | 0.1 | NM | 0.3 | 2.8 | 2.2 | 3.8 | 1.9 |
| FPL Group | FPL | NC | 44.25 | 18 | 9 | NM | 2.2 | 1.6 | 3.0 | 1.4 | (0.4) | 3.7 | 1.9 |
| PPL Corp. | PPL | NC | 33.57 | 13 | 17 | NM | 2.5 | 1.1 | 2.5 | 2.2 | (0.4) | 3.6 | 1.9 |
| United Technologies | UTX | Buy | 63.34 | 64 | 15 | 2.0 | 3.2 | 1.0 | 1.1 | 1.9 | 1.8 | 2.6 | 1.9 |
| Mellon Bank Corp. | MEL | Neutral | 37.55 | 16 | 12 | NM | NM | 1.3 | NM | 2.1 | 1.4 | 3.1 | 2.0 |
| T. Rowe Price Group | TROW | Neutral | 44.15 | 12 | 23 | NM | NM | 2.6 | NM | 1.9 | 2.0 | 1.3 | 2.0 |
| Becton, Dickinson | BDX | Neutral | 68.60 | 17 | 15 | 2.1 | 2.6 | 2.2 | 1.8 | 1.6 | 1.2 | 2.4 | 2.0 |
| Southern Co. | SO | NC | 34.05 | 25 | 2 | NM | 2.8 | 1.2 | NM | 1.5 | 0.6 | 4.0 | 2.0 |
| Public Serv. Enterprise Inc. | PEG | NC | 67.46 | 17 | 7 | NM | 1.9 | 2.0 | 3.0 | 2.9 | 0.3 | NM | 2.0 |
| AmSouth Bancorporation | ASO | Not Rated | 28.86 | 10 | 12 | NM | NM | 1.3 | NM | 1.5 | 1.8 | 3.5 | 2.0 |
| Xcel Energy Inc. | XEL | NC | 20.29 | 8 | 13 | NM | 1.3 | 1.2 | 2.0 | 2.6 | 1.5 | 3.8 | 2.1 |
| Wendy's International | WEN | Neutral | 63.59 | 7 | 16 | 2.7 | NM | 1.8 | 0.4 | 2.8 | 2.8 | NM | 2.1 |
| Chubb Corp. | CB | Neutral | 50.41 | 21 | 4 | NM | NM | 1.5 | NM | 1.7 | 1.9 | 3.3 | 2.1 |
| Keyspan Energy | KSE | NC | 41.28 | 7 | 20 | NM | 2.8 | (0.1) | 2.9 | 2.1 | 1.7 | 3.6 | 2.2 |
| Entergy Corp. | ETR | Buy | 78.11 | 16 | 16 | NM | 2.1 | 2.2 | 3.5 | 2.8 | 0.3 | NM | 2.2 |
| Altria Group, Inc. | MO | Neutral | 82.97 | 173 | 14 | 2.4 | 2.9 | 0.5 | 0.8 | 2.3 | 3.1 | 3.6 | 2.2 |

**25 Most Expensive Stocks**

*Inexpensive* ↓ *Expensive*

*Note:* S&P valuation calculated on an absolute basis, sector valuations calculated relative to S&P 500. Valuation score calculated as the average number of standard deviations seven valuation metrics differ from 10-year averages: EV/Sales, EV/EBITDA, P/B, FCF yield, P/E, PEG, and Implied Growth.

*Sources:* Compustat and Goldman Sachs Research.

# APPENDIX 44C

| EXHIBIT C-1 | Valuation of Largest 50 Stocks in S&P 500 as of September 8, 2006 |

| Company | Ticker | Rating | Price 8-Sep-06 | Mkt Cap ($ Bill) | YTD Return | EV/ Sales | EV/ EBITDA | Price/ Book | FCF Yield | P/E | PEG Ratio | Implied Growth | Average |
|---|---|---|---|---|---|---|---|---|---|---|---|---|---|
| Wal-Mart Stores | WMT | Buy | 46.72 | 195 | 1 | (1.2) | (3.1) | (2.4) | (0.1) | (1.6) | (1.4) | (2.6) | **(1.8)** |
| Home Depot | HD | Buy | 34.28 | 71 | (14) | (1.6) | (1.4) | (1.5) | (1.5) | (1.7) | (1.6) | (3.0) | **(1.8)** |
| News Corporation | NWS.A | Neutral | 18.87 | 60 | 22 | 1.7 | (3.1) | (2.1) | (3.4) | (1.1) | (1.2) | NM | **(1.5)** |
| United Parcel Service | UPS | NC | 69.56 | 75 | (6) | (0.3) | (1.2) | (1.5) | (0.7) | (1.9) | (1.1) | (3.8) | **(1.5)** |
| Medtronic Inc. | MDT | Neutral | 46.66 | 56 | (18) | (2.2) | (0.6) | (1.7) | (1.1) | (2.0) | (1.3) | NM | **(1.5)** |
| Microsoft Corp. | MSFT | Buy | 25.60 | 261 | (1) | (1.4) | (1.6) | (0.7) | (0.7) | (1.1) | (1.3) | (3.1) | **(1.4)** |
| American Int'l. Group | AIG | Buy | 64.24 | 167 | (5) | NM | NM | (1.1) | NM | (1.5) | (1.1) | (1.3) | **(1.2)** |
| Cisco Systems | CSCO | Buy | 21.75 | 133 | 27 | (0.9) | (0.6) | (0.5) | (1.0) | (1.0) | (0.6) | (3.3) | **(1.1)** |
| QUALCOMM Inc. | QCOM | Buy | 36.54 | 61 | (15) | (0.3) | (0.8) | (0.5) | (2.0) | (1.8) | (1.0) | NM | **(1.1)** |
| Amgen | AMGN | Buy | 67.93 | 80 | (14) | (1.0) | (0.5) | (0.9) | (1.0) | (0.9) | (0.8) | (1.9) | **(1.0)** |
| Oracle Corp. | ORCL | Neutral | 15.91 | 85 | 30 | (0.1) | (0.6) | (1.1) | (1.7) | (0.8) | (0.3) | (2.2) | **(1.0)** |
| Coca-Cola Co. | KO | Neutral | 44.60 | 105 | 12 | (0.8) | (0.7) | (1.2) | (1.1) | (1.0) | 0.4 | (2.2) | **(0.9)** |
| Walt Disney Co. | DIS | Buy | 29.58 | 65 | 23 | 0.2 | (0.0) | 0.4 | (1.3) | (1.4) | (0.7) | (3.2) | **(0.8)** |
| International Bus. Machines | IBM | Neutral | 80.66 | 125 | (1) | 0.2 | (0.7) | (0.8) | (2.3) | (0.6) | (1.2) | (0.2) | **(0.8)** |
| Time Warner Inc. | TWX | Neutral | 16.87 | 69 | (2) | (0.7) | (0.5) | (0.6) | 0.6 | (0.4) | (0.5) | (2.7) | **(0.7)** |
| Exxon Mobil Corp. | XOM | Buy | 66.81 | 404 | 21 | (1.0) | (0.7) | 1.8 | (1.3) | (1.9) | (1.6) | 0.2 | **(0.6)** |
| Lilly (Eli) & Co. | LLY | Buy | 55.26 | 62 | (0) | (1.2) | (0.9) | (1.2) | 1.5 | (1.0) | (0.4) | (1.4) | **(0.6)** |
| Pfizer, Inc. | PFE | Not Rated | 27.59 | 202 | 22 | (0.7) | (0.9) | (1.4) | (2.2) | (1.0) | 3.1 | (1.2) | **(0.6)** |
| Chevron Corp. | CVX | Neutral | 64.22 | 142 | 16 | (1.0) | (0.9) | 0.6 | (0.7) | (1.3) | (1.7) | 0.8 | **(0.6)** |
| Intel Corp. | INTC | Buy | 19.45 | 113 | (21) | (1.1) | (0.9) | (1.2) | (0.0) | 0.2 | 0.2 | (0.9) | **(0.6)** |
| General Electric | GE | Buy | 34.01 | 354 | (2) | 1.5 | (0.3) | (1.5) | 0.3 | (0.9) | (0.4) | (1.8) | **(0.4)** |
| Comcast Corp. | CMCSA | Neutral | 34.90 | 74 | 35 | (0.5) | (0.3) | (0.6) | 0.5 | (0.8) | (0.7) | NM | **(0.4)** |
| Johnson & Johnson | JNJ | Not Rated | 63.59 | 188 | 8 | (0.0) | 0.0 | (0.7) | (0.5) | (0.7) | 0.1 | (0.8) | **(0.4)** |
| Wyeth | WYE | Neutral | $48.25 | 65 | 6 | (0.4) | (0.9) | (0.5) | (0.5) | (0.5) | 0.0 | 0.4 | **(0.3)** |
| Motorola Inc. | MOT | Neutral | 23.70 | 59 | 5 | 0.2 | 0.1 | 1.9 | (1.0) | (0.9) | (0.2) | (1.9) | **(0.2)** |
| Hewlett-Packard | HPQ | Buy | 36.17 | 101 | 27 | 0.1 | (0.3) | 0.5 | (1.0) | 0.2 | (0.4) | 0.6 | **(0.0)** |
| Schlumberger Ltd. | SLB | Buy | 57.95 | 68 | 20 | 0.8 | (0.0) | 2.1 | (0.2) | 0.4 | (0.8) | (2.3) | **0.0** |
| ConocoPhillips | COP | Buy | 60.34 | 100 | 5 | (0.6) | (0.8) | (0.4) | 0.6 | 0.1 | (0.3) | 1.7 | **0.0** |
| AT & T Inc. | T | Not Rated | 31.35 | 122 | 33 | (1.4) | 2.9 | (0.7) | (0.0) | 0.2 | (0.7) | 0.1 | **0.0** |
| Morgan Stanley | MS | Buy | 66.69 | 71 | 19 | NM | NM | 0.2 | NM | NM | NM | NM | **0.2** |
| Merck & Co. | MRK | Sell | 41.06 | 90 | 33 | 0.7 | (0.7) | (1.0) | (0.9) | 0.8 | 1.9 | 0.8 | **0.3** |
| Abbott Labs | ABT | Neutral | 48.90 | 75 | 27 | (0.1) | 0.5 | (0.9) | (1.1) | 1.0 | 0.9 | 1.7 | **0.3** |
| Merrill Lynch | MER | Neutral | 72.71 | 67 | 8 | NM | NM | 0.7 | NM | (0.2) | (1.2) | 1.9 | **0.3** |
| Citigroup Inc. | C | Neutral | 48.72 | 242 | 4 | NM | NM | (0.8) | NM | 0.0 | 0.6 | 1.9 | **0.4** |
| PepsiCo Inc. | PEP | Neutral | 64.73 | 107 | 11 | 1.4 | (0.2) | 0.7 | 0.7 | 1.0 | 0.6 | (0.9) | **0.5** |
| Boeing Company | BA | Neutral | 72.80 | 58 | 5 | 1.1 | 0.3 | 2.2 | (0.4) | 0.5 | (0.1) | 1.2 | **0.7** |
| Apple Computer | AAPL | Buy | 72.52 | 62 | 1 | 2.0 | 0.7 | 2.5 | 0.5 | 0.1 | (0.5) | (0.4) | **0.7** |
| Procter & Gamble | PG | Neutral | 61.14 | 201 | 7 | 1.7 | 2.4 | (0.9) | 0.9 | 0.7 | (0.5) | 0.6 | **0.7** |
| United Health Group Inc. | UNH | Sell | 50.90 | 69 | (18) | 0.2 | 1.1 | 0.4 | (0.1) | 1.4 | 1.3 | 0.9 | **0.7** |
| American Express | AXP | NC | 52.62 | 65 | 3 | NM | NM | 1.7 | NM | 1.0 | (0.3) | 1.1 | **0.9** |
| Verizon Communications | VZ | Neutral | 35.40 | 103 | 22 | (0.3) | 1.0 | (1.1) | (0.4) | 1.4 | 2.8 | 2.8 | **0.9** |
| Wachovia Corp. | WB | Buy | 54.34 | 87 | 6 | NM | NM | 0.1 | NM | 0.9 | 0.0 | 2.7 | **0.9** |
| JPMorgan Chase & Co. | JPM | Neutral | 45.26 | 157 | 17 | NM | NM | (0.5) | NM | 1.8 | 1.5 | NM | **1.0** |
| BellSouth | BLS | Not Rated | 41.19 | 75 | 56 | (0.1) | NM | 0.7 | 1.2 | 2.2 | 1.1 | NM | **1.0** |
| U.S. Bancorp | USB | Buy | 32.19 | 57 | 10 | NM | NM | 0.7 | NM | 0.7 | 0.9 | 3.3 | **1.4** |
| Bank of America Corp. | BAC | Buy | 51.66 | 236 | 16 | NM | NM | 0.6 | NM | 0.9 | 1.2 | 3.5 | **1.5** |
| United Technologies | UTX | Buy | 63.34 | 64 | 15 | 2.0 | 3.2 | 1.0 | 1.1 | 1.9 | 1.8 | 2.6 | **1.9** |
| Altria Group, Inc. | MO | Neutral | 82.97 | 173 | 14 | 2.4 | 2.9 | 0.5 | 0.8 | 2.3 | 3.1 | 3.6 | **2.2** |
| Wells Fargo | WFC | Buy | 34.98 | 118 | 14 | NM | NM | 0.7 | NM | NM | NM | 3.9 | **2.3** |
| Google Inc. | GOOG | Buy | 377.85 | 115 | (9) | NM | NM | NM | NM | NM | NM | NM | **NM** |

*Note:* S&P valuation calculated on an absolute basis, sector valuations calculated relative to S&P 500. Valuation score calculated as the average number of standard deviations seven valuation metrics differ from 10-year averages: EV/Sales, EV/EBITDA, P/B, FCF yield, P/E, PEG, and Implied Growth.

*Sources:* Compustat and Goldman Sachs Research.

The Equities Division of the firm has previously introduced a basket of securities discussed in this report. The Equity Analyst may have been consulted as to the composition of the basket prior to its launch. However, the views expressed in this research and its timing were not shared with the Equities Division.

4⅝ 4⅞ ⅜
5½ 5½ —
5½ 21¹³/₁₆ — ¹/₁₆
20⅝ 21¹³/₁₆ — ¼
17⅜ 18⅛ + ⅞
6½ 6½ — ½
7¼ 6½
3¹/₃₂ — ⅛
15/16
9/16 ⁹/₁₆
9/16
1⅓/₃₂ 7¹⁵/₁₆
7¹⁵/₁₆ 7¹³/₁₆ 7¹⁵/₁₆
2⅝ 2¹¹/₃₂ 2½ +
2¾ 2¼ 2¼
6½ 12¹/₁₆ 11⅜ 11¾ +
67 33¾ 33 33¼ —
602 25⅝ 24⁹/₁₆ 25¾ +
833 12 11⅝ 11⅞ +
16 10½ 10½ 10½ —
78 15⅞ 15¹³/₁₆ 15¾ —
508 9¹/₁₆ 8¼ 8⅛
430 11¼ 10⅛ 10⅛
4⅞ 4

# RESIDUAL INCOME VALUATION

by John D. Stowe, CFA, Thomas R. Robinson, CFA, R. Elaine Henry, CFA, and Jerald E. Pinto, CFA

## LEARNING OUTCOMES

| The candidate should be able to: | Mastery |
|---|:---:|
| **a.** calculate and interpret residual income and related measures (e.g., economic value added and market value added); | ☐ |
| **b.** discuss the uses of residual income models; | ☐ |
| **c.** calculate future values of residual income given current book value, earnings growth estimates, and an assumed dividend payout ratio, calculate the intrinsic value of a share of common stock using the residual income model, and contrast the recognition of value in the residual income model to value recognition in other present value models; | ☐ |
| **d.** discuss the fundamental determinants or drivers of residual income; | ☐ |
| **e.** explain the relationship between residual income valuation and the justified price-to-book ratio based on forecasted fundamentals; | |
| **f.** calculate and interpret the intrinsic value of a share of common stock using a single-stage (constant-growth) residual income model; | ☐ |
| **g.** calculate an implied growth rate in residual income given the market price-to-book ratio and an estimate of the required rate of return on equity; | ☐ |
| **h.** explain continuing residual income, list the common assumptions regarding continuing residual income, and justify an estimate of continuing residual income at the forecast horizon given company and industry prospects; | ☐ |
| **i.** calculate and interpret the intrinsic value of a share of common stock using a multistage residual income model, given the required rate of return, forecasted earnings per share over a finite horizon, and forecasted continuing residual earnings; | ☐ |
| **j.** explain the relationship of the residual income model to the dividend discount and free cash flow to equity models; | ☐ |

|  |  |
|---|---|
| **k.** discuss the strengths and weaknesses of the residual income model; | ☐ |
| **l.** justify the selection of the residual income model for equity valuation, given characteristics of the company being valued; | ☐ |
| **m.** discuss the major accounting issues in applying residual income models. | ☐ |

**1**

# INTRODUCTION

Residual income models of equity value have become widely recognized tools in both investment practice and research. Conceptually, residual income is net income less a charge (deduction) for common shareholders' opportunity cost in generating net income. It is the residual or remaining income after considering the costs of all the company's capital. The appeal of residual income models stems from a shortcoming of traditional accounting. Specifically, although a company's income statement includes a charge for the cost of debt capital in the form of interest expense, it does not include a charge for the cost of equity capital. A company can have positive net income but may still not be adding value for shareholders if it does not earn more than its cost of equity capital. Residual income models explicitly recognize the costs of all the capital employed in generating income.

As an economic concept, residual income has a long history. As far back as the 1920s, General Motors employed the concept in evaluating business segments.[1] More recently, residual income has received renewed attention and interest, sometimes under names such as economic profit, abnormal earnings, or economic value added. Although residual income concepts have been used in a variety of contexts, including the measurement of internal corporate performance, this reading will focus on the residual income model for estimating the intrinsic value of common stock. Among the questions we will study to help us use residual income models professionally are the following:

▶ How is residual income measured, and how can an analyst use residual income in valuation?
▶ How does residual income relate to fundamentals, such as return on equity and earnings growth rates?
▶ How is residual income linked to other valuation methods, such as a price-multiple approach?
▶ What accounting-based challenges arise in applying residual income valuation?

The reading is organized as follows: In Section 2, we develop the concept of residual income, introduce the use of residual income in valuation, and briefly

---

[1] See, for example, Young (1999) and Lo and Lys (2000).

present alternative measures used in practice. In Section 3, we derive the residual income valuation model and illustrate its use in valuing common stock. We then illustrate practical applications, including the single-stage (constant-growth) residual income model, and a multistage residual income model. In Section 4, we describe the relative strengths and weaknesses of residual income valuation compared to other valuation methods. Section 5 addresses accounting issues in the use of residual income valuation. We conclude with a summary of the reading.

# RESIDUAL INCOME 2

Traditional financial statements, particularly the income statement, are prepared to reflect earnings available to owners. As a result, the income statement shows net income after deducting an expense for the cost of debt capital, i.e., interest expense. The income statement does not, however, deduct dividends or other charges for equity capital. Thus, traditional financial statements essentially let the owners decide whether earnings cover their opportunity costs. The economic concept of residual income, on the other hand, explicitly deducts the estimated cost of equity capital, the finance concept that measures shareholders' opportunity costs. Example 1 illustrates, in a stylized setting, the calculation and interpretation of residual income.[2]

## EXAMPLE 1

### The Calculation of Residual Income

Axis Manufacturing Company, Inc. (AXCI), a very small company in terms of market capitalization, has total assets of €2,000,000 financed 50 percent with debt and 50 percent with equity capital. The cost of debt capital is 7 percent before taxes (4.9 percent after taxes) and the cost of equity capital is 12 percent. The company has earnings before interest and taxes (EBIT) of €200,000 and a tax rate of 30 percent. Net income for AXCI can be determined as follows:

| | |
|---|---|
| EBIT | €200,000 |
| Less: Interest expense | 70,000 |
| Pretax income | €130,000 |
| Less: Income tax expense | 39,000 |
| Net income | €91,000 |

With earnings of €91,000, AXCI is clearly profitable in an accounting sense. But was the company's profitability adequate return for its owners? Unfortunately, it was not. To incorporate the cost of equity capital,

---

[2] To simplify the following introduction, we assume here that net income accurately reflects *clean surplus accounting*, which we will explain later in this reading. Our discussions in this reading assume that companies' financing consists of common equity and debt only. In the case of a company that also has preferred stock financing, the calculation of residual income would reflect the deduction of preferred stock dividends from net income.

we compute residual income. One approach to calculating residual income is to deduct an **equity charge** (the estimated cost of equity capital in money terms) from net income. We compute the equity charge as follows:

$$\text{Equity charge} = \text{Equity capital} \times \text{Cost of equity capital in percent}$$
$$= €1{,}000{,}000 \times 12\%$$
$$= €120{,}000.$$

As stated, residual income is equal to net income minus the equity charge:

| | |
|---|---|
| Net income | €91,000 |
| Less: Equity charge | 120,000 |
| Residual income | €(29,000) |

AXCI did not earn enough to cover the cost of equity capital. As a result, it has negative residual income. Although AXCI is profitable in an accounting sense, it is not profitable in an economic sense.

In Example 1, we calculated residual income based on net income and a charge for the cost of equity capital. Analysts will also encounter another approach to calculating residual income that yields the same results under certain assumptions. In this second approach, which takes the perspective of all providers of capital (both debt and equity), we subtract a **capital charge** (the company's total cost of capital in money terms) from the company's after-tax operating profit. In the case of AXCI in Example 1, net operating profit after taxes (NOPAT) is €140,000 (= €200,000 less 30% taxes). AXCI's after-tax weighted-average cost of capital (WACC) is 8.45 percent, computed as 50 percent (capital structure weight of equity) times the cost of equity of 12 percent plus 50 percent (capital structure weight of debt) times the after-tax cost of debt, 4.9 percent.[3] The capital charge is €169,000 (= 8.45% × €2,000,000), which is higher than its after-tax operating profit of €140,000 by €29,000, the same figure obtained in Example 1.

As illustrated in the following table, both approaches yield the same results in this example because of two assumptions. First, this example assumes that the cost of debt capital equals the cost of debt capital used in determining net income, i.e., the reported interest expense. Specifically, in this example, the after-tax interest expense incorporated in net income (€49,000 = €70,000 times 1 minus 30%) is equal to the cost of debt incorporated into the capital charge using the after-tax weighted-average cost of capital (WACC). Second, this example assumes that the weights used in calculating the WACC are derived from the book value of debt and equity. Specifically, this example uses the weights of 50 percent debt and 50 percent equity.

Note that the approaches will yield different results unless both of these assumptions are made. Specifically, the two approaches will yield different

---

[3] This example of the weighted-average cost of capital assumes that interest is tax deductible. In countries where corporate interest is not tax deductible, the after-tax cost of debt would equal the pretax cost of debt. In the rest of the reading, we will refer to *after-tax cost of capital* or *after-tax WACC* as *cost of capital* and *WACC*, respectively, for brevity.

results if the charge for debt capital used in a residual income calculation (based on the cost of debt capital going forward) differs from the interest expense used in net income (based on the reported cost of debt capital.) The two approaches will also yield different results if the weights used in calculating the WACC are not based on the book value of the company's debt and equity. If, for example, the weights are based on a company's target capital structure or on the current market value of the company's debt and/or equity, the results under the two approaches will differ.

| Approach 1 | | | Approach 2 | |
|---|---|---|---|---|
| Net income | €91,000 | Plus the after-tax interest expense of €49,000 | Net operating profit after tax | €140,000 |
| Less: Equity charge | 120,000 | Plus the after-tax capital charge for debt of €49,000 | Less: Capital charge | (169,000) |
| Residual income | €(29,000) | | Residual income | €(29,000) |

That the company is not profitable in an economic sense can also be seen by comparing the company's cost of capital to its return on capital. Specifically, the company's WACC, 8.45 percent, is greater than its after-tax return on total assets or capital. The after-tax net operating return on total assets or capital is calculated as profits divided by total assets (or total capital). In this example, the after-tax net operating return on total assets is 7 percent (= €140,000/€2,000,000), which is 1.45 percentage points less than the company's WACC.[4]

## 2.1 The Use of Residual Income in Equity Valuation

A company that is generating more income than its cost of obtaining capital—i.e., one with positive residual income—is creating value. Conversely, a company that is not generating enough income to cover its cost of capital—i.e., one with negative residual income—is destroying value. Thus, all else equal, higher (lower) residual income should be associated with higher (lower) valuations.

We can illustrate the impact of residual income on equity valuation using the case of AXCI presented in Example 1. Assume the following:

▶ Initially, AXCI equity is selling for book value or 1,000,000, with 100,000 shares outstanding. Thus, AXCI's book value per share and initial share price are both €10.

▶ Earnings per share (EPS) are €0.91(= €91,000/100,000 shares).

▶ Earnings will continue at the current level indefinitely.

▶ All net income is distributed as dividends.

Because AXCI is not earning its cost of equity, as shown in Example 1, the company's share price should fall. Given the information, we know that AXCI is

---

[4] After-tax net operating profits as a percent of total assets or capital has been called **return on invested capital** (ROIC). Residual income can also be calculated as (ROIC – WACC) × (Beginning capital).

destroying €29,000 of value per year, which equals €0.29 per share (= €29,000/100,000 shares). Discounted at 12 percent cost of equity, the present value of the perpetuity is €2.42 (= €0.29/12%). The current share price minus the present value of the value being destroyed equals €7.58 (= €10 − €2.42). Another way to look at this is to note that the earnings yield (E/P) for a no-growth company, as here, is an estimate of the expected rate of return. Therefore, when price reaches the point at which E/P equals the required rate of return on equity, an investment in the stock is expected to just cover the stock's required rate of return. With EPS of €0.91, the earnings yield is exactly 12 percent (AXCI's cost of equity) when its share price is €7.58333 (i.e., €0.91/€7.58333 = 12%). At a share price of €7.58333, the total market value of AXCI's equity is €758,333. When a company has negative residual income, we expect shares to sell at a discount to book value. In this example, AXCI's price-to-book ratio (P/B) at this level of discount from book value would be 0.7583. In contrast, if AXCI instead were earning positive residual income, we would conclude that its shares would sell at a premium to book value. In summary, we expect higher residual income to be associated with higher market prices (and higher P/Bs), all else equal.

Residual income models have been used to value both individual stocks[5] and the Dow Jones Industrial Average[6] and have been proposed as a solution to measuring goodwill impairment by accounting standard setters.[7] Residual income models have been found more useful than some other major present value models of equity value in explaining stock prices (American Accounting Association, 2001).

Residual income and residual income valuation models have been referred to by a variety of names. Residual income has sometimes been called **economic profit** because it represents the economic profit of the company after deducting the cost of all capital: debt and equity. In forecasting future residual income, the term **abnormal earnings** is also used. Assuming that in the long term the company is expected to earn its cost of capital (from all sources), any earnings in excess of the cost of capital can be termed abnormal earnings. The residual income valuation model has also been called the **discounted abnormal earnings model** (DAE model) and the **Edwards–Bell–Ohlson model** (EBO model) after the names of researchers in the field. This reading focuses on a presentation of a general residual income valuation model that can be used by analysts using publicly available data and nonproprietary accounting adjustments. A number of commercial implementations of the approach are also very well known, however. Before returning to the general residual income valuation model in Section 3, we briefly discuss one such commercial implementation and the related concept of market value added.

## 2.2 Commercial Implementations

One example of several competing commercial implementations of the residual income concept is **economic value added** (EVA®), trademarked by Stern Stewart & Company.[8] In the previous section, we illustrated a calculation of residual

---

[5] See Fleck, Craig, Bodenstab, Harris, and Huh (2001).

[6] See Lee and Swaminathan (1999) and Lee, Myers, and Swaminathan (1999).

[7] See American Accounting Association Financial Accounting Standards Committee (2001). **Impairment** in an accounting context means downward adjustment. **Goodwill**, in this context, is an intangible asset that may appear on a company's balance sheet as a result of its purchase of another company.

[8] For a complete discussion, see Stern (1991) and Peterson and Peterson (1996).

income starting from net operating profit after taxes, and EVA takes the same broad approach. Specifically, EVA is computed as

$$\text{EVA} = \text{NOPAT} - (\text{C\%} \times \text{TC}) \qquad \textbf{(45-1)}$$

where NOPAT is the company's net operating profit after taxes, C% is the cost of capital and TC is total capital. In this model, both NOPAT and TC determined under generally accepted accounting principles are adjusted for a number of items.[9] Some of the more common adjustments follow:

▶ Research and development expenses are capitalized and amortized rather than expensed (R&D expense is added back to earnings to compute NOPAT).

▶ In the case of strategic investments that are not expected to generate a return immediately, a charge for capital is suspended until a later date.

▶ Goodwill is capitalized and not amortized (amortization expense is added back in arriving at NOPAT, and accumulated amortization is added back to capital).

▶ Deferred taxes are eliminated such that only cash taxes are treated as an expense.

▶ Any inventory LIFO reserve is added back to capital and any increase in the LIFO reserve is added in arriving at NOPAT.

▶ Operating leases are treated as capital leases, and nonrecurring items are adjusted.

Because of the adjustments made under EVA, a different numerical result will be obtained, in general, than that resulting from the use of the simple computation presented in Example 1. In practice, general (nonbranded) residual income (RI) valuation also considers the impact of accounting methods on reported results. However, analysts' adjustments to reported accounting results in estimating residual income will generally reflect some differences from the set specified for EVA. Section 5 of this reading will explore accounting considerations in more detail.

Over time, a company must generate EVA in order for its market value to increase. A related concept is market value added (MVA):

$$\text{MVA} = \text{Market value of the company} - \text{Total capital} \qquad \textbf{(45-2)}$$

A company that generates positive EVA should have a market value in excess of the accounting book value of its capital.

Research on the ability of value-added concepts to explain equity value and stock returns has reached mixed conclusions. Peterson and Peterson (1996) found that value-added measures are slightly more highly correlated with stock returns than traditional measures such as return on assets and return on equity. Bernstein and Pigler (1997) and Bernstein, Bayer, and Pigler (1998) found that value-added measures are no better at predicting stock performance than are measures such as earnings growth.

---

[9] See, for example, Ehrbar (1998).

A variety of commercial models related to the residual income concept have been marketed by other major accounting and consulting firms. Interestingly, the application focus of these models is not, in general, equity valuation. Rather, these implementations of the residual income concept are marketed primarily for measuring internal corporate performance and determining executive compensation.

## 3    THE RESIDUAL INCOME VALUATION MODEL

In Section 2, we discussed the concept of residual income and briefly introduced the relationship of residual income to equity value. In the long term, companies that earn more than the cost of capital should sell for more than book value, and companies that earn less than the cost of capital should sell for less than book value. The **residual income model** (RIM) of valuation analyzes the intrinsic value of equity as two components:

▶ the current book value of equity, plus

▶ the present value of expected future residual income.

Note that when we turn from valuing total shareholders' equity to directly valuing an individual common share, we work with earnings per share rather than net income. According to the residual income model, the intrinsic value of common stock can be expressed as follows:

$$V_0 = B_0 + \sum_{t=1}^{\infty} \frac{RI_t}{(1 + r)^t} = B_0 + \sum_{t=1}^{\infty} \frac{E_t - rB_{t-1}}{(1 + r)^t}$$     **(45-3)**

where

$V_0$ = value of a share of stock today ($t = 0$)
$B_0$ = current per-share book value of equity
$B_t$ = expected per-share book value of equity at any time $t$
$r$ = required rate of return on equity investment (cost of equity)
$E_t$ = expected EPS for period $t$
$RI_t$ = expected per-share residual income, equal to $E_t - rB_{t-1}$

The per-share residual income in period $t$, $RI_t$, is the EPS for the period, $E_t$, minus the per-share equity charge for the period, which is the required rate of return on equity times the book value per share at the beginning of the period, or $rB_{t-1}$. Whenever earnings per share exceed the per-share cost of equity, per-share residual income is positive; and whenever earnings are less, per-share residual income is negative. Example 2 illustrates the calculation of per-share residual income.

### EXAMPLE 2

#### Per-Share Residual Income Forecasts

David Smith is evaluating the expected residual income of Carrefour SA (NYSE Euronext Paris: FR0000120172), a France-based operator of hypermarkets and other store formats in Europe, the Americas, and

Asia, as of the end of September 2007. Using an adjusted beta of 0.72 relative to the CAC 40 Index, a 10-year government bond yield of 4.3 percent and an estimated equity risk premium of 7 percent, Smith uses the capital asset pricing model to estimate Carrefour's required rate of return $r$ at $4.3\% + 0.72(7\%) = 9.3$ percent. Smith obtains the following data from Bloomberg as of the close on 24 September 2007:

| | |
|---|---|
| Current market price: | €48.83 |
| Book value per share as of 31 December 2006: | €13.46 |
| Consensus annual earnings estimates | |
| FY 2007 (ending December): | €2.71 |
| FY 2008: | €2.86 |
| Annualized dividend per share forecast | |
| FY 2007 | €1.03 |
| FY 2008 | €1.06 |

What is the forecast residual income for fiscal years ended December 2007 and December 2008?

Solution:

| EXHIBIT 1 | Carrefour SA, Amounts in € | |
|---|---|---|
| **Year** | **2007** | **2008** |
| *Forecasting book value per share* | | |
| Beginning book value ($B_{t-1}$) | 13.46 | 15.14 |
| Earnings per share forecast ($E_t$) | 2.71 | 2.86 |
| Less: Dividend forecast ($D_t$) | 1.03 | 1.06 |
| Add: Change in retained earnings ($E_t - D_t$) | 1.68 | 1.80 |
| Forecast ending book value per share ($B_{t-1} + E_t - D_t$) | 15.14 | 16.94 |
| *Calculating the equity charge* | | |
| Beginning ending book value per share | 13.46 | 15.14 |
| Multiply: Cost of equity | × 0.093 | × 0.093 |
| Per-share equity charge ($r \times B_{t-1}$) | 1.25 | 1.41 |
| *Estimating per share residual income* | | |
| EPS forecast | 2.71 | 2.86 |
| Less: Equity charge | 1.25 | 1.41 |
| Per-share residual income | 1.46 | 1.45 |

We illustrate the use of Equation 45-3, the expression for the estimated intrinsic value of common stock, in Example 3.

## EXAMPLE 3

### Using the Residual Income Model (1)

Bugg Properties' expected EPS is $2.00, $2.50, and $4.00 for the next three years, respectively. Analysts expect that Bugg will pay dividends of $1.00, $1.25, and $12.25 for the three years. The last dividend is anticipated to be a liquidating dividend; analysts expect Bugg will cease operations after Year 3. Bugg's current book value is $6.00 per share, and its required rate of return on equity is 10 percent.

1. Calculate per-share book value and residual income for the next three years.

2. Estimate the stock's value using the residual income model given in Equation 45-3:

$$V_0 = B_0 + \sum_{t=1}^{\infty} \frac{E_t - rB_{t-1}}{(1 + r)^t}$$

3. Confirm your valuation estimate in Part 2 using the discounted dividend approach (i.e., estimating the value of a share as the present value of expected future dividends).

**Solution to 1:** The book values and residual incomes for the next three years are as follows:

| EXHIBIT 2 | Bugg Properties, Amounts in $ | | |
|---|---|---|---|
| **Year** | **1** | **2** | **3** |
| Beginning book value per share ($B_{t-1}$) | 6.00 | 7.00 | 8.25 |
| Net income per share (EPS) | 2.00 | 2.50 | 4.00 |
| Less: Dividends per share ($D$) | 1.00 | 1.25 | 12.25 |
| Change in retained earnings (EPS − $D$) | 1.00 | 1.25 | −8.25 |
| Ending book value per share ($B_{t-1}$ + EPS − $D$) | 7.00 | 8.25 | 0.00 |
| Net income per share (EPS) | 2.00 | 2.50 | 4.000 |
| Less: Per share equity charge ($rB_{t-1}$) | 0.60 | 0.70 | 0.825 |
| Residual income (EPS − Equity charge) | 1.40 | 1.80 | 3.175 |

**Solution to 2:** The value using the residual income model is

$$V_0 = 6.00 + \frac{1.40}{(1.10)} + \frac{1.80}{(1.10)^2} + \frac{3.175}{(1.10)^3}$$

$$= 6.00 + 1.2727 + 1.4876 + 2.3854$$

$$= \$11.15$$

**Solution to 3:** The value using a discounted dividend approach is

$$V_0 = \frac{1.00}{(1.10)} + \frac{1.25}{(1.10)^2} + \frac{12.25}{(1.10)^3}$$

$$= 0.9091 + 1.0331 + 9.2036$$

$$= \$11.15$$

Example 3 illustrates two important points about residual income models. First, the residual income model is fundamentally similar to other valuation models such as the dividend discount model (DDM), and given consistent assumptions will yield equivalent results. Second, recognition of value typically occurs earlier in residual income models than in dividend discount models. In Example 3, the residual income model attributes $6.00 of the $11.15 total value to the *first* time period. In contrast, the DDM model attributes $9.2036 of the $11.15 total value to the *final* time period. The balance of Section 3 develops the most familiar general expression for the residual income model and illustrates the model's application.

## 3.1 The General Residual Income Model

The residual income model has a clear relationship to other valuation models, such as the dividend discount model. In fact, the residual income model given in Equation 45-3 can be derived from the dividend discount model. The general expression for the dividend discount model is

$$V_0 = \frac{D_1}{(1+r)^1} + \frac{D_2}{(1+r)^2} + \frac{D_3}{(1+r)^3} + \ldots$$

The **clean surplus relation** states the relationship among earnings, dividends, and book value as follows:

$$B_t = B_{t-1} + E_t - D_t$$

In other terms, the ending book value of equity equals the beginning book value plus earnings less dividends, apart from ownership transactions. The condition that income (earnings) reflects all changes in the book value of equity other than ownership transactions is known as clean surplus accounting. Rearranging the clean surplus relation, the dividend for each period can be viewed as the net income minus the earnings retained for the period, or net income minus the increase in book value:

$$D_t = E_t - (B_t - B_{t-1}) = E_t + B_{t-1} - B_t$$

Substituting $E_t + B_{t-1} - B_t$ for $D_t$ in the expression for $V_0$ results in

$$V_0 = \frac{E_1 + B_0 - B_1}{(1 + r)^1} + \frac{E_2 + B_1 - B_2}{(1 + r)^2} + \frac{E_3 + B_2 - B_3}{(1 + r)^3} + \cdots$$

This equation can be re-written as follows:

$$V_0 = B_0 + \frac{E_1 - rB_0}{(1 + r)^1} + \frac{E_2 - rB_1}{(1 + r)^2} + \frac{E_3 - rB_2}{(1 + r)^3} + \cdots$$

Expressed with summation notation, the following equation restates the residual income model that we gave in Equation 45-3 above:

$$V_0 = B_0 + \sum_{t=1}^{\infty} \frac{RI_t}{(1 + r)^t} = B_0 + \sum_{t=1}^{\infty} \frac{E_t - rB_{t-1}}{(1 + r)^t}$$

According to the above expression, the value of a stock equals its book value per share plus the present value of expected future per-share residual income. Note that when the present value of expected future per-share residual income is positive (negative), intrinsic value $V_0$ is greater (smaller) than book value per share, $B_0$.

The residual income model used in practice today has largely developed from the academic work of Ohlson (1995) and Feltham and Ohlson (1995) and the earlier work of Edwards and Bell (1961), although in the United States this method has been used to value small businesses in tax cases since the 1920s.[10] The general expression for the residual income model based on this work[11] can also be stated as

$$V_0 = B_0 + \sum_{t=1}^{\infty} \frac{(ROE_t - r)B_{t-1}}{(1 + r)^t} \qquad \text{(45-4)}$$

Equation 45-4 is equivalent to the expressions for $V_0$ given earlier because in any year $t$, $RI_t = (ROE_t - r)B_{t-1}$. Other than the required rate of return on common stock, the inputs to the residual income model come from accounting data. Note that ROE in this context uses beginning book value of equity in the denominator, whereas in financial statement analysis ROE is frequently calculated using the average book value of equity in the denominator. Example 4 illustrates the estimation of value using Equation 45-4.

### EXAMPLE 4

#### Using the Residual Income Model (2)

To recap the data from Example 3, Bugg Properties has expected earnings per share of $2.00, $2.50, and $4.00, and expected dividends per share of $1.00, $1.25, and $12.25 over the next three years. Analysts expect that the last dividend will be a liquidating dividend and that Bugg

---

[10] In tax valuation, the method is known as the excess earnings method. For example, see Hitchner (2006) and U.S. IRS Revenue Ruling 68-609.

[11] See, for example, Hirst and Hopkins (2000).

will cease operating after Year 3. Bugg's current book value per share is $6.00, and its estimated required rate of return on equity is 10 percent.

Using the above data, estimate the value of Bugg Properties stock using a residual income model of the form

$$V_0 = B_0 + \sum_{t=1}^{\infty} \frac{(\text{ROE}_t - r)B_{t-1}}{(1 + r)^t}$$

**Solution:** To value the stock, we need to forecast residual income. Exhibit 3 illustrates the calculation of residual income. (Note that Exhibit 3 arrives at the same estimates of residual income as did Exhibit 2 in Example 3.)

### EXHIBIT 3

| Year | 1 | 2 | 3 |
|---|---|---|---|
| Earnings per share | $ 2.00 | $ 2.50 | $ 4.00 |
| Divided by: Beginning book value per share | ÷ 6.00 | ÷ 7.00 | ÷ 8.25 |
| ROE | 0.3333 | 0.3571 | 0.4848 |
| Less: Required rate of return on equity | −0.1000 | −0.1000 | −0.1000 |
| Abnormal rate of return (ROE − $r$) | 0.2333 | 0.2571 | 0.3848 |
| Multiply by: Beginning book value per share | ×6.00 | ×7.00 | ×8.25 |
| Residual income (ROE − $r$) × Beginning BV | $ 1.400 | $ 1.800 | $ 3.175 |

We estimate the stock value as follows:

$$V_0 = 6.00 + \frac{1.40}{(1.10)} + \frac{1.80}{(1.10)^2} + \frac{3.175}{(1.10)^3}$$

$$= 6.00 + 1.2727 + 1.4876 + 2.3854$$

$$= \$11.15$$

Note that the value is identical to the estimate obtained using Equation 45-3, as illustrated in Example 3, because the assumptions are the same and Equations 45-3 and 45-4 are equivalent expressions:

$$\underbrace{V_0 = B_0 + \sum_{t=1}^{\infty} \frac{E_1 - rB_{t-1}}{(1 + r)^t}}_{\text{Equation 45-3}} = \underbrace{B_0 + \sum_{t=1}^{\infty} \frac{(\text{ROE}_t - r)B_{t-1}}{(1 + r)^t}}_{\text{Equation 45-4}}$$

Example 4 showed that residual income value can be estimated using current book value, forecasts of earnings, forecasts of book value, and an estimate of the required rate of return on equity. The forecasts of earnings and book value translate into ROE forecasts.

**EXAMPLE 5**

### Valuing a Company Using the General Residual Income Model

Robert Sumargo, an equity analyst, is considering the valuation of Cisco Systems (NasdaqGS:CSCO), which closed on 11 December 2007 at $28.02. Sumargo notes that CSCO has generally had fairly high ROE over the past 10 years and that consensus analyst forecasts for EPS for the next two fiscal years reflect expected ROE of around 29 percent. Sumargo expects that high ROEs may not be sustainable in the future. Sumargo often takes a present value approach to valuation. As of the date of the valuation, CSCO does not pay dividends; although a discounted dividend valuation is possible, Sumargo does not feel confident about predicting the date of dividend initiation. He decides to apply the residual income model to value CSCO, using the following data and assumptions:

▶ According to the capital asset pricing model (CAPM), CSCO has a required rate of return of approximately 10.5 percent.

▶ CSCO's book value per share at 28 July 2007 was $5.02.

▶ ROE is expected to be 29 percent for fiscal year-end July 2008. Because of competitive pressures, Sumargo expects CSCO's ROE to decline in the following years and incorporates an assumed decline of slightly less than 1 percent (0.9%) each year until it reaches the CAPM required rate of return.

▶ CSCO does not currently pay a dividend. Sumargo does not expect the company to pay a dividend in the foreseeable future, so that all earnings will be reinvested. In addition, Sumargo expects that share repurchases will approximately offset new share issuances.

Compute the value of CSCO using the residual income model (Equation 45-4).

**Solution:** Book value per share is initially $5.02. Based on a ROE forecast of 29 percent in the first year, the forecast EPS would be $1.46. Because no dividends are paid and the clean surplus relation is assumed to hold, book value at the end of the period is forecast at $6.48 (= $5.02 + $1.46). For 2008, residual income is measured as projected EPS of $1.46 minus an equity charge of $0.53, or $0.93. This is equivalent to the beginning book value per share of $5.02 times the difference between ROE of 29 percent and $r$ of 10.5 percent (i.e., $5.02(0.29 − 0.105) = $0.93). The present value of $0.93 at 10.5 percent for one year is $0.84. This process is continued year by year as presented in Exhibit 4. The value of CSCO under this residual income model would be the present value of each year's residual income plus the current book value per share. Because residual income is zero starting in 2029, no forecast is required beyond that period. The estimated value under this model is $27.79, as shown in Exhibit 4.

| | EXHIBIT 4 | | Valuation of CSCO Using the Residual Income Model | | | | | |
|---|---|---|---|---|---|---|---|---|
| Year | Projected Income EPS $ | Projected Dividend per Share $ | Book Value per Share $ | Forecast ROE On (Beginning Book Value) (%) | Cost of Equity (%) | Equity Charge $ | Residual Income (RI) $ | PV of BV and RI $ |
| | [Plus] | [Minus] | 5.02 | | | | | 5.02 |
| 2008 | 1.46 | 0.00 | 6.48 | 29.0 | 10.5 | 0.53 | 0.93 | 0.84 |
| 2009 | 1.82 | 0.00 | 8.30 | 28.1 | 10.5 | 0.68 | 1.14 | 0.93 |
| 2010 | 2.26 | 0.00 | 10.56 | 27.2 | 10.5 | 0.87 | 1.39 | 1.03 |
| 2011 | 2.78 | 0.00 | 13.34 | 26.3 | 10.5 | 1.11 | 1.67 | 1.12 |
| 2012 | 3.39 | 0.00 | 16.73 | 25.4 | 10.5 | 1.40 | 1.99 | 1.21 |
| 2013 | 4.10 | 0.00 | 20.83 | 24.5 | 10.5 | 1.76 | 2.34 | 1.29 |
| 2014 | 4.91 | 0.00 | 25.74 | 23.6 | 10.5 | 2.19 | 2.73 | 1.36 |
| 2015 | 5.84 | 0.00 | 31.58 | 22.7 | 10.5 | 2.70 | 3.14 | 1.41 |
| 2016 | 6.89 | 0.00 | 38.47 | 21.8 | 10.5 | 3.32 | 3.57 | 1.45 |
| 2017 | 8.04 | 0.00 | 46.51 | 20.9 | 10.5 | 4.04 | 4.00 | 1.47 |
| 2018 | 9.30 | 0.00 | 55.81 | 20.0 | 10.5 | 4.88 | 4.42 | 1.47 |
| 2019 | 10.66 | 0.00 | 66.47 | 19.1 | 10.5 | 5.86 | 4.80 | 1.45 |
| 2020 | 12.10 | 0.00 | 78.57 | 18.2 | 10.5 | 6.98 | 5.12 | 1.40 |
| 2021 | 13.59 | 0.00 | 92.16 | 17.3 | 10.5 | 8.25 | 5.34 | 1.32 |
| 2022 | 15.11 | 0.00 | 107.28 | 16.4 | 10.5 | 9.68 | 5.44 | 1.22 |
| 2023 | 16.63 | 0.00 | 123.91 | 15.5 | 10.5 | 11.26 | 5.36 | 1.09 |
| 2024 | 18.09 | 0.00 | 142.00 | 14.6 | 10.5 | 13.01 | 5.08 | 0.93 |
| 2025 | 19.45 | 0.00 | 161.45 | 13.7 | 10.5 | 14.91 | 4.54 | 0.75 |
| 2026 | 20.67 | 0.00 | 182.11 | 12.8 | 10.5 | 16.95 | 3.71 | 0.56 |
| 2027 | 21.67 | 0.00 | 203.79 | 11.9 | 10.5 | 19.12 | 2.55 | 0.35 |
| 2028 | 22.42 | 0.00 | 226.20 | 11.0 | 10.5 | 21.40 | 1.02 | 0.13 |
| 2029 | 23.75 | 0.00 | 249.95 | 10.5 | 10.5 | 23.75 | 0.00 | 0.00 |
| Total | | | | | | | | $27.79 |

*Note*: This table was created in Excel, so numbers may differ from what will be obtained using a calculator, because of rounding.

Example 5 refers to the assumption of clean surplus accounting. The residual income model, as stated earlier, assumes clean surplus accounting. The clean surplus accounting assumption is illustrated in Exhibit 4, for example, where ending book value per share is computed as beginning book value plus net income minus dividends. Under both IFRS and U.S. GAAP, several items of income and expense occurring during a period, such as changes in the market value of certain securities, bypass the income statement and affect a company's book value of equity directly.[12] Strictly speaking, in using residual income models we are concerned with all items of income and expense (income under clean surplus accounting). If an analyst can reliably estimate material differences from clean surplus accounting expected in the future, an adjustment to net income may be appropriate. Section 5.1 explores violations of the clean surplus accounting assumption in more detail.

## 3.2 Fundamental Determinants of Residual Income

The residual income model in general makes no assumptions about future earnings and dividend growth. If we assume constant earnings and dividend growth, we can derive a version of the residual income model that usefully illustrates the fundamental drivers of residual income. We use the following expression for justified price to book (P/B) based on forecasted fundamentals, assuming the Gordon (constant growth) DDM and the sustainable growth rate equation, $g = b \times$ ROE:[13]

$$\frac{P_0}{B_0} = \frac{ROE - g}{r - g}$$

which is mathematically equivalent to

$$\frac{P_0}{B_0} = 1 + \frac{ROE - r}{r - g}$$

The justified price is the stock's intrinsic value ($P_0 = V_0$). Therefore, using the previous equation, we can express a stock's intrinsic value under the residual income model, assuming constant growth, as

$$V_0 = B_0 + \frac{ROE - r}{r - g} B_0 \qquad\qquad \textbf{(45-5)}$$

Under this model, the estimated value of a share is thus the book value per share ($B_0$) plus the present value $(ROE - r)B_0/(r - g)$ of the expected stream of residual income. In the case of a company for which ROE exactly equals the cost of equity, the intrinsic value should equal the book value per share. We call Equation 45-5 the single-stage (or constant-growth) residual income model.

In an ideal world, where the book value of equity represents the fair value of net assets and clean surplus accounting prevails, the term $B_0$ reflects the value of assets owned by the company less its liabilities. The second term, $(ROE - r)B_0/(r - g)$, represents additional value expected because of the company's ability to generate returns in excess of its cost of equity; the second term is the present value of the company's expected economic profits. Unfortunately, both U.S. and international accounting rules enable companies to exclude some liabilities from their balance sheets, and neither set of rules reflects the fair value of many

---

[12] Under international financial reporting standards (IFRS), income and expense items that bypass the income statement include revaluation surpluses, particular gains and losses arising on translating the financial statements of a foreign operation, and gains or losses on re-measuring available-for-sale financial assets. In U.S. financial statements, items that bypass the income statement (dirty surplus items) are referred to as **other comprehensive income** (OCI). The relationship is Comprehensive income = Net income + Other comprehensive income.

[13] Note that the sustainable growth rate formula itself can be derived from the clean surplus relation.

corporate assets. There is, however, a move internationally toward fair value accounting, particularly for financial assets. Further, controversies, such as the failure of Enron Corporation in the United States, have highlighted the importance of identifying off-balance-sheet financing techniques.

The residual income model is most closely related to the P/B ratio. A stock's justified P/B ratio is directly related to expected future residual income. Another closely related concept is **Tobin's** $q$, the ratio of the market value of debt and equity to the replacement cost of total assets:[14]

$$\text{Tobin's } q = \frac{\text{Market value of debt and equity}}{\text{Replacement cost of total assets}}$$

Although similar to P/B, Tobin's $q$ also has some obvious differences: The numerator includes the market value of total capital (debt as well as equity). The denominator uses total assets rather than equity. Further, assets are valued at replacement cost rather than a historical accounting cost; replacement costs take account of the effects of inflation. All else equal, we expect Tobin's $q$ to be higher, the greater the productivity of a company's assets.[15] One difficulty in computing Tobin's $q$ is the lack of information on assets' replacement costs. If available, market values of assets or replacement costs can be more useful in a valuation than historical costs.

## 3.3 Single-Stage Residual Income Valuation

The single-stage (constant-growth) residual income model assumes that a company has a constant return on equity and constant earnings growth rate over time. This model was given in Equation 45-5, repeated below:

$$V_0 = B_0 + \frac{\text{ROE} - r}{r - g} B_0$$

### EXAMPLE 6

**Single-Stage Residual Income Model (1)**

Joseph Yoh is evaluating a purchase of Canon, Inc. (NYSE: CAJ). Current book value per share is $18.81, and the current price per share is $51.90 (from Value Line, 2 November 2007). Yoh expects long-term ROE to be 16 percent and long-term growth to be 8 percent. Assuming a cost of equity of 11 percent, what is the intrinsic value of Canon stock using a single-stage residual income model?

**Solution:**

$$V_0 = \$18.81 + \frac{0.16 - 0.11}{0.11 - 0.08} \$18.81$$
$$= \$50.16$$

---

[14] See Tobin (1969) or more recent work such as Landsman and Shapiro (1995).

[15] Tobin theorized that $q$ would average to 1 over all companies, as the economic rents or profits earned by assets would average to zero.

Similar to the Gordon growth DDM, the single-stage residual income model can be used to assess the market expectations of residual income growth, i.e., an implied growth rate, by inputting the current price into the model and solving for $g$.

---

### EXAMPLE 7

**Single-Stage Residual Income Model (2)**

Joseph Yoh is curious about the market-perceived growth rate, given that he is comfortable with his other inputs. Using the current price per share of $51.90 for Canon, Yoh solves the following equation for $g$:

$$\$51.90 = \$18.81 + \frac{0.16 - 0.11}{0.11 - g}\$18.81$$

He finds an implied growth rate of 8.16 percent.

---

In the above example, the company was valued at more than twice its book value because its ROE exceeded its cost of equity. If ROE were equal to the cost of equity, the company would be valued at book value. If ROE were lower than the cost of equity, the company would have negative residual income and be valued at less than book value. (When a company has no prospect of being able to cover its cost of capital, a liquidation of the company and redeployment of assets may be appropriate.)

In many applications, a drawback to the single-stage model is that it assumes the excess ROE above the cost of equity will persist indefinitely. More likely, a company's ROE will revert to a mean value of ROE over time, and at some point, the company's residual income will be zero. If a company or industry has an abnormally high ROE, other companies will enter the marketplace, increasing competition and lowering returns for all companies. Similarly, if an industry has a low ROE, companies will exit the industry (through bankruptcy or otherwise) and ROEs will tend to rise over time. As with the single-stage DDM, the single-stage residual income model also assumes a constant growth rate over time. In light of these considerations, the residual income model has been adapted in practice to handle declining residual income. For example, Lee and Swaminathan (1999) and Lee, Myers, and Swaminathan (1999) used a residual income model to value the Dow 30 assuming that ROE fades (reverts) to the industry mean over time. Lee and Swaminathan found that the residual income model had more ability than traditional price multiples to predict future returns. Fortunately, other models are available that enable us to relax the assumption of indefinite persistence of excess returns. The following section describes a multistage residual income model.

## 3.4 Multistage Residual Income Valuation

As with other valuation approaches (DDM and DCF), a multistage residual income approach can be used which forecasts residual income for a certain time horizon and then estimates a terminal value based on continuing residual income at the end of that time horizon. **Continuing residual income** is residual income after the forecast horizon. As with other valuation models, the forecast horizon for the initial stage should be based on the ability to explicitly forecast inputs into the model. Because ROEs have been found to revert to mean levels over time and may decline to the cost of equity in a competitive environment, residual income approaches often model ROE fading toward the cost of equity. As ROE approaches the cost of equity, residual income approaches zero. An ROE equal to the cost of equity would result in residual income of zero.

In residual income valuation, the current book value often captures a large portion of total value and the terminal value may not be a large component of total value both because book value is larger than the periodic residual income and because ROE may fade over time toward the cost of equity. This contrasts with other multistage approaches (DDM and DCF), in which the present value of the terminal value is frequently a significant portion of total value.

Analysts make a variety of assumptions concerning continuing residual income. Frequently, one of the following assumptions is made:

▶ Residual income continues indefinitely at a positive level;

▶ Residual income is zero from the terminal year forward;

▶ Residual income declines to zero as ROE reverts to the cost of equity over time; or

▶ Residual income reflects the reversion of ROE to some mean level.

We illustrate several of these approaches below.

One finite-horizon model of residual income valuation assumes that at the end of time horizon $T$, there is a certain premium over book value ($P_T - B_T$) for the company, in which case, current value equals the following:[16]

$$V_0 = B_0 + \sum_{t=1}^{T} \frac{(F_t - rB_{t-1})}{(1 + r)^t} + \frac{P_T - B_T}{(1 + r)^T} \qquad \textbf{(45-6)}$$

Alternatively,

$$V_0 = B_0 + \sum_{t=1}^{T} \frac{(\text{ROE}_t - r)B_{t-1}}{(1 + r)^t} + \frac{P_T - B_T}{(1 + r)^T} \qquad \textbf{(45-7)}$$

The last component in both specifications represents the premium over book value at the end of the forecast horizon. The longer the forecast period, the greater the chance that the company's residual income will converge to zero. For long forecast periods, this last term may thus be treated as zero. For shorter forecast periods, a forecast of the premium should be calculated.

## EXAMPLE 8

### Multistage Residual Income Model (1)

Diana Rosato, CFA, is considering an investment in Taiwan Semiconductor Manufacturing Ltd., a manufacturer and marketer of integrated circuits. Listed on the Taiwan Stock Exchange (2330), the company's stock

---

[16] See Bauman (1999).

is also traded on the New York Stock Exchange (NYSE: TSM). Rosato obtained the following facts and estimates as of early 2007:

► Current price = TWD62.9.

► Cost of equity = 15 percent.

► Taiwan Semiconductor's ROE has ranged from 18.4 percent to 22.7 percent over the period 2004–2006, reflecting a recovery from the difficult period of 2001–2003 when it averaged 7.1 percent.

► In 2005 the company instituted a cash dividend of TWD2.9846 for 2006.

► Book value per share (BVPS) stood at TWD19.59 at the end of 2006.

► Rosato's forecasts of EPS are TWD4.256 for 2007 and TWD5.566 for 2008. She expects dividends of TWD3.000 for 2007 and TWD3.284 for 2008.

► Rosato expects Taiwan Semiconductor's ROE to be 25 percent from 2009 through 2016 and then decline to 20 percent through 2026.

► For the period after 2008, Rosato assumes an earnings retention ratio of 70 percent.

► Rosato assumes that after that 2026, ROE will be 15 percent and thus residual income will be zero; therefore, the terminal value would thus be zero. Rosato's residual income model is as follows:

### EXHIBIT 5    Taiwan Semiconductor

| Year | Book Value (TWD) | Projected Income (TWD) | Dividend per Share (TWD) | Forecasted ROE (Beg. Equity, %) | COE (%) | COE (TWD) | Residual Income (TWD) | Present Value of Residual Income |
|------|------|------|------|------|------|------|------|------|
| 2006 | 19.5900 | | | | | | | 19.59 |
| 2007 | 20.8460 | 4.2560 | 3.0000 | 21.73 | 15.00 | 2.9385 | 1.3175 | 1.15 |
| 2008 | 23.1180 | 5.5560 | 3.2840 | 26.65 | 15.00 | 3.1269 | 2.4291 | 1.84 |
| 2009 | 27.1637 | 5.7795 | 1.7339 | 25.00 | 15.00 | 3.4677 | 2.3118 | 1.52 |
| 2010 | 31.9173 | 6.7909 | 2.0373 | 25.00 | 15.00 | 4.0745 | 2.7164 | 1.55 |
| 2011 | 37.5028 | 7.9793 | 2.3938 | 25.00 | 15.00 | 4.7876 | 3.1917 | 1.59 |
| 2012 | 44.0658 | 9.3757 | 2.8127 | 25.00 | 15.00 | 5.6254 | 3.7503 | 1.62 |
| 2013 | 51.7773 | 11.0164 | 3.3049 | 25.00 | 15.00 | 6.6099 | 4.4066 | 1.66 |
| 2014 | 60.8385 | 12.9443 | 3.8833 | 25.00 | 15.00 | 7.7666 | 5.1777 | 1.69 |
| 2015 | 71.4851 | 15.2096 | 4.5629 | 25.00 | 15.00 | 9.1258 | 6.0838 | 1.73 |
| 2016 | 83.9950 | 17.8713 | 5.3614 | 25.00 | 15.00 | 10.7228 | 7.1485 | 1.77 |
| 2017 | 95.7543 | 16.7990 | 5.0397 | 20.00 | 15.00 | 12.5992 | 4.1997 | 0.90 |
| 2018 | 109.1598 | 19.1509 | 5.7453 | 20.00 | 15.00 | 14.3631 | 4.7877 | 0.89 |
| 2019 | 124.4422 | 21.8320 | 6.5496 | 20.00 | 15.00 | 16.3740 | 5.4580 | 0.89 |
| 2020 | 141.8641 | 24.8884 | 7.4665 | 20.00 | 15.00 | 18.6663 | 6.2221 | 0.88 |
| 2021 | 161.7251 | 28.3728 | 8.5118 | 20.00 | 15.00 | 21.2796 | 7.0932 | 0.87 |
| 2022 | 184.3666 | 32.3450 | 9.7035 | 20.00 | 15.00 | 24.2588 | 8.0863 | 0.86 |
| 2023 | 210.1779 | 36.8733 | 11.0620 | 20.00 | 15.00 | 27.6550 | 9.2183 | 0.86 |
| 2024 | 239.6029 | 42.0356 | 12.6107 | 20.00 | 15.00 | 31.5267 | 10.5089 | 0.85 |
| 2025 | 273.1473 | 47.9206 | 14.3762 | 20.00 | 15.00 | 35.9404 | 11.9801 | 0.84 |
| 2026 | 311.3879 | 54.6295 | 16.3888 | 20.00 | 15.00 | 40.9721 | 13.6574 | 0.83 |

Present value   TWD 44.38

Terminal Premium = 0.00

The market price of TWD62.9 exceeds the estimated value of TWD44.38. The market price reflects either higher forecasts of residual income over the period to 2026, a higher terminal premium than Rosato forecasts, and/or a lower cost of equity. If Rosato is confident in her forecasts she may conclude that the company is overvalued in the current marketplace.

Lee and Swaminathan (1999) and Lee, Myers, and Swaminathan (1999) have presented a residual income model based on explicit forecasts of residual income for three years. Thereafter, ROE is forecast to fade to the industry mean value of ROE. The terminal value at the end of the forecast horizon ($T$) is estimated as the terminal-year residual income discounted in perpetuity. Lee and Swaminathan stated that this assumes that any growth in earnings after $T$ is value neutral. Exhibit 6 presents sector ROE data from Hemscott Americas, retrieved from Yahoo.com. (ROE data for specific industries can be retrieved from the same source.) In forecasting a fading ROE, the analyst should also consider any trends in industry ROE.

| EXHIBIT 6 | U.S. Sector ROEs |
|---|---|
| **Sectors** | **ROE %** |
| Basic Materials | 23.21 |
| Conglomerates | 20.10 |
| Consumer Goods | 20.83 |
| Financial | 20.22 |
| Healthcare | 15.49 |
| Industrial Goods | 17.37 |
| Services | 14.55 |
| Technology | 14.37 |
| Utilities | 14.44 |

*Source*: Based on Hemscott Americas data retrieved from http://biz.yahoo.com on 22 January 2008.

**EXAMPLE 9**

**Multistage Residual Income Model (2)**

Rosato's supervisor questions her assumption that Taiwan Semiconductor will have no premium at the end of her forecast period. Rosato assesses the impact of a terminal value based on a perpetuity of Year 2026 residual income. She computes the following terminal value:

$$TV = TWD13.6574/0.15 = TWD91.0491$$

The present value of this terminal value is as follows:

$$PV = TWD91.04901/(1.15)^{20} = TWD5.5631$$

Adding TWD5.56 to the previous value of TWD44.38 (for which the terminal value was zero) yields a total value of TWD49.94. Because the current market price of TWD62.9 is greater than TWD49.94, market participants either expect a positive continuing residual income at an even higher level than her new assumptions and/or are forecasting a higher interim ROEs. Again, if Rosato is confidence in her forecasts, she may conclude that the company is overvalued.

Another multistage model assumes that ROE fades over time to the cost of equity. In this approach, ROE can be explicitly forecast each period until reaching the cost of equity. The forecast would then end and the terminal value would be zero.

Dechow, Hutton, and Sloan (1998) presented an analysis of a residual income model in which residual income fades over time:[17]

$$V_0 = B_0 + \sum_{t=1}^{T-1} \frac{(E_t - rB_{t-1})}{(1+r)^t} + \frac{E_T - rB_{T-1}}{(1+r-\omega)(1+r)^{T-1}} \qquad (45\text{-}8)$$

This model adds a persistence factor, $\omega$, which is between 0 and 1. A persistence factor of 1.0 implies that residual income will not fade at all; rather it will continue at the same level indefinitely (i.e., in perpetuity). A persistence factor of 0 implies that residual income will not continue after the initial forecast horizon. The higher the value of the persistence factor, the higher the higher the stream of residual income in the final stage, and the higher the valuation, all else equal. Dechow et al. found that in a large sample of company data from 1976 to 1995, the persistence factor equaled 0.62, which was interpreted by Bauman (1999) as equivalent to residual income decaying at an average rate of 38 percent a year. The persistence factor considers the long-run mean-reverting nature of ROE, assuming that over time ROE regresses towards $r$ and that resulting residual income fades toward zero. Clearly, the persistence factor varies from company to company. For example, a company with a strong market leadership position would have a lower expected rate of decay (Bauman, 1999). Dechow et al. provided insight into some characteristics that can indicate a lower or higher level of persistence, listed in Exhibit 7.

---

[17] See Dechow, Hutton, and Sloan (1998) and Bauman (1999).

| EXHIBIT 7 | Final-Stage Residual Income Persistence |
|---|---|
| **Lower Residual Income Persistence** | **Higher Residual Income Persistence** |
| Extreme accounting rates of return (ROE) | Low dividend payout |
| Extreme levels of special items (e.g., nonrecurring items) | High historical persistence in the industry |
| Extreme levels of accounting accruals | |

Example 10 illustrates the assumption that continuing residual income will decline to zero as ROE approaches the required rate of return on equity.

---

### EXAMPLE 10

**Multistage Residual Income Model (3)**

Rosato extends her analysis to consider the possibility that ROE will slowly decay after 2027 toward $r$, rather than using a perpetuity of Year 2026 residual income. Rosato estimates a persistence parameter of 0.60. The present value of the terminal value is determined as

$$\frac{E_T - rB_{T-1}}{(1 + r - \omega)(1 + r)^{T-1}}$$

with $T = 21$ and 2027 residual income equal to $13.6574 \times 1.14 = 15.5714$ percent, where the 1.14 growth factor reflects a 14 percent growth rate calculated as the retention ratio times ROE, or $(0.70)(20\%) = 0.14$.

$$\frac{15.57}{(1 + 0.15 - 0.60)(1.15)^{20}} = 1.73$$

Total value is TWD46.11 calculated by adding the present value of the terminal value, TWD1.73, to TWD44.38. Rosato concludes that if Taiwan Semiconductor's residual income does not persist at a stable level past 2026 and deteriorates over time, the shares are even more overvalued.

---

# RESIDUAL INCOME VALUATION IN RELATION TO OTHER APPROACHES

**4**

Before proceeding to the next section, which addresses accounting issues in using the residual income model, we briefly summarize the relationship of the residual income model to other valuation models.

Valuation models based on discounting dividends (DDM) or on discounting free cash flows (FCF) are theoretically sound models, as is the residual income model. Unlike the residual income model, however, DDM and FCF models forecast future cash flows and find the value of stock by discounting them back to the present using the required return. (Recall that the required return is the cost of equity for both the DDM and the free cash flows to equity model (FCFE). For the free cash flow to the firm model (FCFF), the required return is the overall weighted average cost of capital. The RI model approaches this process differently. It starts with a value based on the balance sheet, the book value of equity, and adjusts this value by adding the present values of expected future residual income. Thus, the recognition of value is different, but the total present value, whether using expected dividends, expected free cash flow, or book value plus expected residual income, should be consistent, in theory.[18]

Example 11 again illustrates the important point that the recognition of value in residual income models typically occurs earlier than in dividend discount models. In other words, residual income models tend to assign a relatively small portion of a security's total present value to the earnings that occur in later years. Note also that this example makes use of the fact that the present value of a perpetuity in the amount of $X$ can be calculated as $X/r$.

---

### EXAMPLE 11

**Valuing a Perpetuity with the Residual Income Model**

Assume the following data:

▶ A company will earn $1.00 per share forever.
▶ The company pays out all earnings as dividends.
▶ Book value per share is $6.00.
▶ The required rate of return on equity (or the percent cost of equity) is 10 percent.

1. Calculate the value of this stock using the dividend discount model (DDM).
2. Calculate the level amount of per-share residual income that will be earned each year.
3. Calculate the value of the stock using a residual income valuation model.
4. Create a table summarizing the year-by-year valuation using the dividend discount model and the residual income model.

**Solution to 1:** Because the dividend $D$ is a perpetuity, the present value of $D$ can be calculated as $D/r$.

$$V_0 = D/r = \$1.00/0.10 = \$10.00 \text{ per share.}$$

**Solution to 2:** Because each year all net income is paid out as dividends, book value per share will be constant at $6.00. Therefore, with a required rate of return on equity of 10 percent, for all future years, per share residual income will be as follows:

$$RI_t = E_t - rB_{t-1} = \$1.00 - 0.10(\$6.00) = \$1.00 - \$0.60 = \$0.40$$

---

[18] See, for example, Shrieves and Wachowicz (2001).

**Solution to 3:** Using a residual income model, the estimated value equals the current book value per share plus the present value of future expected residual income (which here can be valued as a perpetuity):

$V_0$ = Book value + PV of expected future per-share residual
income
= $6.00 + $0.40/0.10
= $6.00 + $4.00 = $10.00

**Solution to 4:** Exhibit 8 below summarizes the year-by-year valuation using the DDM and the RI valuation models.

| EXHIBIT 8 | Value Recognition in DDM and RIM Valuation | | | |
|---|---|---|---|---|
| | **Dividend Discount Model** | | **Residual Income Model** | |
| Year | $D_t$ | PV of $D_t$ | $B_0$ or $RI_t$ | PV of $B_0$ or $RI_t$ |
| 0 | | | 6.00 | 6.000 |
| 1 | 1.00 | 0.909 | 0.40 | 0.364 |
| 2 | 1.00 | 0.826 | 0.40 | 0.331 |
| 3 | 1.00 | 0.751 | 0.40 | 0.301 |
| 4 | 1.00 | 0.683 | 0.40 | 0.273 |
| 5 | 1.00 | 0.621 | 0.40 | 0.248 |
| 6 | 1.00 | 0.564 | 0.40 | 0.226 |
| 7 | 1.00 | 0.513 | 0.40 | 0.205 |
| 8 | 1.00 | 0.467 | 0.40 | 0.187 |
| . . . | . . . | . . . | . . . | . . . |
| Total | | $10.00 | | $10.00 |

In the residual income valuation, most of the total value of the stock is attributed to the earlier periods. Specifically, in the residual income valuation, current book value of $6.00 represents 60 percent of the stock's total present value of $10.

In contrast, in the DDM, value is derived from the receipt of dividends and typically a smaller proportion of value is attributed to the earlier periods. Less than $1.00 of the total $10 derives from the first year's dividend, and collectively, the first five years' dividends ($3.79 = $0.909 + $0.826 + $0.751 + $0.683 + $0.621) contribute only about 38 percent of the total present value of $10.

As shown earlier and illustrated again in Example 11, the dividend discount and residual income models are in theory mutually consistent. Because of the real-world uncertainty in forecasting distant cash flows, however, we may find that the earlier recognition of value in a residual income approach relative to other present value approaches is a practical advantage. In the dividend discount and free cash flow models (discussed in earlier readings), we often model a stock's value as the sum of the present values of individually forecasted dividends or free cash flows up to some terminal point plus the present value of the expected terminal value of the stock. In practice, a large fraction of a stock's total present value, using either the DDM or FCF model, is represented by the present value of the expected terminal value. However, substantial uncertainty often surrounds the terminal value. In contrast, residual income valuations typically are relatively less sensitive to terminal value estimates. (As discussed, in some residual income valuation contexts the terminal value may actually be set equal to zero.) The derivation of value from the earlier portion of a forecast horizon is one reason residual income valuation can be a useful analytical tool.

## 4.1 Strengths and Weaknesses of the Residual Income Model

Now that we have illustrated the implementation of the residual income model with several examples, we summarize the strengths and weaknesses of the residual income approach. The strengths of the residual income models include the following:

▶ Terminal values do not make up a large portion of the total present value, relative to other models.

▶ The RI models use readily available accounting data.

▶ The models can be readily applied to companies that do not pay dividends or to companies that do not have positive expected near-term free cash flows.

▶ The models can be used when cash flows are unpredictable.

▶ The models have an appealing focus on economic profitability.

The potential weaknesses of residual income models include the following:

▶ The models are based on accounting data that can be subject to manipulation by management.

▶ Accounting data used as inputs may require significant adjustments.

▶ The models require that the clean surplus relation holds, or that the analyst makes appropriate adjustments when the clean surplus relation does not hold. Section 5.1 discusses the clean surplus relation (or clean surplus accounting).

▶ The residual income's model use of accounting income assumes that the cost of debt capital is reflected appropriately by interest expense.

## 4.2 Broad Guidelines for Using a Residual Income Valuation Model

The above list of potential weaknesses helps explain the reading's focus in the following section on accounting considerations. In light of its strengths and weaknesses, we state the following broad guidelines for using a residual income model in common stock valuation. A residual income model is most appropriate when

- a company does not pay dividends, or its dividends are not predictable;

- a company's expected free cash flows are negative within the analyst's comfortable forecast horizon; or

- there is great uncertainty in forecasting terminal values using an alternative present value approach.

Residual income models are least appropriate when

- there are significant departures from clean surplus accounting; or

- significant determinants of residual income, such as book value and ROE, are not predictable.

Because the various valuation models can all be derived from the same underlying theoretical model, when fully consistent assumptions are used to forecast earnings, cash flow, dividends, book value, and residual income through a full set of pro forma (projected) financial statements, and the same required rate of return on equity is used as the discount rate, the same estimate of value should result using each model. Practically speaking, however, it may not be possible to forecast each of these items with the same degree of certainty.[19] For example, if a company has near-term negative free cash flow and forecasts for the terminal value are uncertain, a residual income model may be more appropriate. On the other hand, a company with positive, predictable cash flow that does not pay a dividend would be well suited for a discounted free cash flow valuation.

Residual income models, just like the DDM and FCF models, can also be used to establish justified market multiples, such as P/E or P/B. For example, the value can be determined using a residual income model and divided by earnings to arrive at a justified P/E.

A residual income model can also be used in conjunction with other models to assess the consistency of results. If a wide variation of estimated value is found and each model appears appropriate, the inconsistency may lie with the assumptions used in the models. The analyst would need to perform additional work to determine whether the assumptions are mutually consistent and which model is most appropriate for the subject company.

## ACCOUNTING AND INTERNATIONAL CONSIDERATIONS

## 5

To most accurately apply the residual income model in practice, the analyst may need to adjust book value of common equity for off-balance-sheet items and adjust reported net income to obtain **comprehensive income** (as defined in U.S. GAAP, all changes in equity other than contributions by, and distributions to, owners). In this section, we will discuss issues relating to these tasks.

Bauman (1999) has noted that the strength of the residual income valuation model is that the two components (book value and future earnings) of the model have a balancing effect on each other, provided that the clean surplus relationship is followed:

All other things held constant, companies making aggressive (conservative) accounting choices will report higher (lower) book values and

---

[19] For a lively debate on this issue, see Penman and Sougiannis (1998), Penman (2001), Lundholm and O'Keefe (2001a), and Lundholm and O'Keefe (2001b).

lower (higher) future earnings. In the model, the present value of differences in future income is exactly offset by the initial differences in book
value. (Baumann 1999, page 31)

Unfortunately, this argument has several problems in practice because the clean
surplus relationship does not prevail, and analysts often use past earnings to predict future earnings. International Financial Reporting Standards (IFRS) and
U.S. GAAP permit a variety of items to bypass the income statement and be
reported directly in stockholders' equity. Further, off-balance-sheet liabilities or
non-operating and nonrecurring items of income may obscure a company's
financial performance. The analyst must thus be aware of such items when evaluating the book value of equity and return on equity to be used as inputs into a
residual income model.

With regard to the possibility that aggressive accounting choices will lead to
lower reported future earnings, consider an example in which a company
chooses to capitalize an expenditure in the current year rather than to expense
it. Doing so overstates current-year earnings as well as current book value. If an
analyst uses current earnings (or ROE) naively in predicting future residual
earnings, the residual income model will overestimate the value of the company.
Take, for example, a company with $1,000,000 of book value and $200,000 of
earnings before taxes, after expensing an expenditure of $50,000. Ignoring
taxes, this company has a ROE of 20 percent. If the company capitalized the
expenditure rather than expensing it immediately, it would have a ROE of 23.81
percent ($250,000/$1,050,000). Although at some time in the future this capitalized item will likely be amortized or written off, thus reducing realized future
earnings, analysts' expectations often rely on historical data. If capitalization of
expenditures persists over time for a stable size company, ROE can decline
because net income will normalize over the long term, but book value will be
overstated. For a growing company, for which the expenditure in question is
increasing, ROE can continue at high levels over time. In practice, because the
residual income model uses primarily accounting data as inputs, the model can
be sensitive to accounting choices, and aggressive accounting methods (e.g.,
accelerating revenues or deferring expenses) can result in valuation errors. The
analyst must therefore be particularly careful in analyzing a company's reported
data for use in a residual income model.

As we have seen, two principal drivers of residual earnings are ROE and
book value. The analyst must understand how to use historical reported accounting data for these items to the extent he uses historical data in forecasting future
ROE and book value. Earlier readings explained the DuPont analysis of ROE,
which can be used as a tool in forecasting, and discussed the calculation of book
value. We extend these previous discussions below with specific application to
residual income valuation, particularly in addressing the following accounting
considerations:

► violations of the clean surplus relationship,

► balance sheet adjustments for fair value,

► intangible assets,

► nonrecurring items,

► aggressive accounting practices, and

► international considerations.

In any valuation, we must pay close attention to the accounting practices of the
company being valued. In the following sections, we address the above issues as
they particularly affect residual income valuation.

## 5.1 Violations of the Clean Surplus Relationship

One potential accounting issue in applying a residual income model is a violation of clean surplus accounting. Violations may occur when accounting standards permit charges directly to stockholders' equity, bypassing the income statement. An example is the case of changes in the market value of available-for-sale investments. Under both IFRS (IAS 39, paragraph 55(b) and U.S. GAAP (SFAS No. 115, paragraph 13), investments considered to be "available for sale" are shown on the balance sheet at market value; however, any change in their market value is reflected directly in stockholders' equity rather than as income on the income statement.

As stated earlier, comprehensive income is defined in U.S. GAAP as all changes in equity other than contributions by, and distributions to, owners. Comprehensive income includes: (a) net income reported on the income statement and (b) *Other comprehensive income* (previously defined), which is the result of other events and transactions that result in a change to equity but are not reported on the income statement. Items that commonly bypass the income statement include[20]

- foreign currency translation adjustments,
- certain pension adjustments, and
- fair value changes of some financial instruments.

An identical concept exists in IFRS, although the terminology "other comprehensive income" is not used. Under both U.S. and International standards, items such as fair value changes for some financial instruments and foreign currency translation adjustments bypass the income statement. In addition, under IFRS, which unlike U.S. GAAP permits revaluation of fixed assets (IAS 16, paragraph 39-42), some changes in the fair value of fixed assets also bypass the income statement and directly affect equity.

In all of these cases where items bypass the income statement, the book value of equity is stated accurately, but net income is not from the perspective of residual income valuation. The analyst should be most concerned with the impact of these items on forecasts of net income and ROE (which has net income in the numerator), and hence also residual income.[21] Because some items (including those listed above) bypass the income statement, they are excluded from historical ROE data. As noted by Frankel and Lee (1999), bias will be introduced into the valuation only if the present expected value of the clean surplus violations do not net to zero. In other words, reductions in income from some periods may be offset by increases from other periods. The analyst must examine the equity section of the balance sheet and the related statements of shareholders' equity and comprehensive income carefully for items that have bypassed the income statement; the analyst can then assess whether amounts are likely to be offsetting and can assess the impact on future ROE.

---

[20] See Frankel and Lee (1999).

[21] The analyst should most precisely calculate historical ROE at the aggregate level (e.g., as net income divided by shareholders' equity) rather than as earnings per share divided by book value per share, because actions such as share issuance and share repurchases can distort ROE calculated on a per-share basis.

## EXAMPLE 12

### Evaluating Clean Surplus Violations

Excerpts from two companies' statements of changes in stockholders' equity are shown below. The first statement, prepared under IFRS as of 31 December 2006, is for Nokia Corporation (NYSE: NOK), a Finland-headquartered leading manufacturer of mobile phones, with operations in four business segments: mobile phones, multimedia, enterprise solutions, and networks. The second statement, prepared under U.S. GAAP as of 31 December 2006, is for SAP AG (NYSE: SAP), a Germany-headquartered worldwide provider of enterprise application software including enterprise resource planning (ERP), customer relationship management (CRM), and supply chain management (SCM) software.

| **EXHIBIT 9** | **Nokia Corporation Statement of Changes in Stockholders' Equity (Excerpt) (€ Millions)** | | | | | | | | |
|---|---|---|---|---|---|---|---|---|---|
| Group | Share Capital | Share Issue Premium | Treasury Shares | Translation Differences | Fair Value and Other Reserves | Retained Earnings | Before Minority Interests | Minority Interests | Total |
| Balance at December 31, 2005 | 266 | 2,458 | −3,616 | 69 | −176 | 13,308 | 12,309 | 205 | 12,514 |
| Tax benefit on stock options exercised | | 23 | | | | | 23 | | 23 |
| Excess tax benefit on share-based compensation | | 14 | | | | | 14 | | 14 |
| Translation differences | | | | −141 | | | −141 | −13 | −154 |
| Net investment hedge gains, net of tax | | | | 38 | | | 38 | | 38 |
| Cash flow hedges, net of tax | | | | | 171 | | 171 | | 171 |
| Available-for-sale investments, net of tax | | | | | −9 | | −9 | | −9 |
| Other decrease, net | | | | | | −52 | −52 | −1 | −53 |
| Profit | | | | | | 4,306 | 4,306 | 60 | 4,366 |
| Total recognized income and expense | 0 | 37 | 0 | −103 | 162 | 4,254 | 4,350 | 46 | 4,396 |
| Total of other equity movements | −20 | 212 | 1,556 | 0 | 0 | −6,439 | −4,691 | −159 | −4,850 |
| Balance at December 31, 2006 | 246 | 2,707 | −2,060 | −34 | −14 | 11,123 | 11,968 | 92 | 12,060 |

*Source*: www.nokia.com/A4126243

**EXHIBIT 10**

**SAP AG and Subsidiaries**
**Consolidated Statements of Shareholders' Equity and Comprehensive Income (Excerpt)**
**U.S. GAAP for the Years Ended December 31**

| | Additional Paid-In Capital €(000) | Retained Earnings €(000) | Accumulated Other Comprehensive Income/ Loss | | | | | Treasury Stock €(000) | Total €(000) |
| --- | --- | --- | --- | --- | --- | --- | --- | --- | --- |
| | | | Foreign Currency Translation Adjustment €(000) | Unrealized Gains/Losses on Marketable Securities €(000) | Unrecognized Pension Plan Cost €(000) | Unrealized Gains/Losses on Hedges €(000) | Currency Effects from Inter-Company Long-Term Investment Transactions €(000) | | |
| December 31, 2005 | 372,767 | 5,986,186 | −202,260 | 11,168 | −9,975 | 42,449 | 40,763 | −775,318 | 5,782,238 |
| Net income | | 1,871,377 | | | | | | | 1,871,377 |
| Other comprehensive income/loss, net of tax | | | −148,568 | −6,692 | | −28,420 | −26,022 | | −209,702 |
| Total comprehensive income/loss | | | | | | | | | 1,661,675 |
| Stock-based compensation | 17,611 | | | | | | | | 17,611 |
| Dividends | | −447,219 | | | | | | | −447,219 |
| Treasury stock transactions | 44,434 | | | | | | | −966,492 | −922,058 |
| Convertible bonds and stock options exercised | 48,940 | | | | | | | | 49,366 |
| Issuance of common stock | −134,768 | −815,885 | | | | | | | 0 |
| Other | 3,658 | 350 | | | | | | | 4,008 |
| Impact of first-time adoption of SFAS 158 | | | | | | −9,766 | | | −9,766 |
| December 31, 2006 | 352,642 | 6,594,809 | −350,828 | 4,476 | −19,741 | 14,029 | 14,741 | −1,741,810 | 6,135,855 |

*Source:* www.sap.com/about/investor/index.epx

For Nokia, items that have bypassed the income statement in 2006 are those that are summed to obtain "Total recognized income and expense" in the columns labeled "Share issue premium," "Translation differences," and "Fair value and other reserves." For SAP, the amounts that bypassed the income statement in 2006 appear in the five columns below the heading "Accumulated other comprehensive income/loss."

To illustrate the issues in interpreting these items, consider the columns "Translation differences" (Nokia) and "Foreign currency translation adjustment" (SAP). The amounts in these columns reflect currency translation adjustments to equity that have bypassed the income statement. For Nokia, the adjustment for the year 2006 was minus €103 million. Because this is a negative adjustment to stockholders' equity, this item would have decreased income if it had been reported on the income statement. However, the balance is not increasing, i.e., it appears to be reversing to zero over time. For SAP, the translation adjustment for the year 2006 was minus €148 million. Again, because this is a negative adjustment to stockholders' equity, this item would have decreased income if it had been reported on the income statement. In this case, the negative balance appears to be accumulating, i.e., it does not appear to be reversing (netting to zero) over time. If the analyst expects this trend to continue and has used historical data as the basis for initial estimates of ROE to be used in residual income valuation, a downward adjustment in that estimated future ROE might be warranted. It is possible, however, that future exchange rate movements will reverse this accumulation.

The examples in this reading have used the actual beginning equity and a forecasted level of ROE (return on beginning equity) to compute the forecasted net income. Because equity includes accumulated other comprehensive income (AOCI), the assumptions about future OCI will affect forecasted net income and thus residual income. To illustrate, Exhibit 11 shows a hypothetical company's financials for a single previous year, labeled year $t - 1$, followed by three different forecasts for the following two years. In year $t - 1$, the company reports net income of 120, which is a 12 percent return on beginning equity of $1,000. The company paid no dividends, so ending retained earnings equal $120. In year $t - 1$, the company also reports other comprehensive income of minus $100, i.e. a loss, so the ending amount shown in AOCI is a negative $100. (Companies typically label this line item "accumulated other comprehensive income (loss)," indicating that the amount is an accumulated loss when given in parentheses.)

All three forecasts in Exhibit 11 assume that ROE will be 12 percent and use this assumption to forecast net income for year $t$ and $t + 1$ using the expression $0.12 \times$ Beginning BV. However, each forecast incorporates different assumptions about future OCI. Forecast A assumes that the company will have no OCI in year $t$ or year $t + 1$, such that the amount of AOCI does not change. Forecast B assumes that the company will continue to have the same amount of OCI in year $t$ and year $t + 1$ as it had in the prior year, so that the amount of AOCI becomes more negative each year. Forecast C assumes that the company's OCI will reverse in year $t$, such that at the end of year $t$, AOCI will be zero. As shown, because the forecasts use the assumed ROE to compute forecasted net income, the forecasts for net income and residual income in year $t + 1$ vary significantly.

Because this example assumes all earnings are retained, a forecast of 12 percent ROE also implies that net income and residual income will grow at 12 percent. Only the year $t$ to year $t + 1$ under Forecast A, which assumes no future OCI, correctly reflects that relationship. Specifically, in Forecast A, both net income and residual income increase by 12 percent from year $t$ to year $t + 1$. Net income grows from \$122.40 to \$137.09, an increase of (\$137.09/\$122.40) $- 1 =$ 12 percent; and residual income grows from \$20.40 to \$22.85, an increase of (\$22.85/\$20.40) $- 1 = 12$ percent. In contrast with Forecast A, neither Forecast B nor Forecast C correctly reflects the relationship between ROE and growth in income (net and residual). Growth in residual income from year $t$ to year $t + 1$ was 2.2 percent under Forecast B and 21.8 percent under Forecast C.

If, alternatively, the forecasts of future ROE and the residual income computation had incorporated total comprehensive income (net income plus other comprehensive income) the results of the residual income computation would have differed significantly. For example, assume that Forecast B, which assumes the company will continue to have the same amount of OCI, had estimated future ROE of 2.0 percent, using total comprehensive income [(\$120 $-$ \$100)/\$1,000 = \$20/\$1,000 = 2 percent]. If the residual income computation had then also used forecasted total comprehensive income at time $t$, the amount of residual income would be negative. Specifically, for time $t$, forecast comprehensive income would be \$22.40 (ROE of 2.0 percent times beginning equity of \$1,020 = \$22.40), the equity charge would be \$102 (required return of 10 percent times beginning equity of \$1,020), and residual income would be $-$\$79.86 (comprehensive income of \$22.40 minus equity charge of \$102 = $-$\$79.86). Clearly, residual income on that basis significantly falls short of the positive \$20.40 when the violation of clean surplus is ignored. As this example demonstrates, using an ROE forecast or a net income forecast that ignores violations of clean surplus accounting will distort estimates of residual income. Unless the present value of such distortions net to zero, using those forecasts will also distort valuations.

| EXHIBIT 11 | Hypothetical Company Alternative Forecasts with Different Assumptions about Comprehensive Income | | | | | | |
|---|---|---|---|---|---|---|---|
| | **Actual** | **Forecast A** | | **Forecast B** | | **Forecast C** | |
| **Year** | **$t-1$** | **$t$** | **$t+1$** | **$t$** | **$t+1$** | **$t$** | **$t+1$** |
| **Beginning Balance Sheet** | | | | | | | |
| Assets | 1,000.00 | 1,020.00 | 1,142.40 | 1,020.00 | 1,042.40 | 1,020.00 | 1,242.40 |
| Liabilities | — | — | — | — | — | — | — |
| Common stock | 1,000.00 | 1,000.00 | 1,000.00 | 1,000.00 | 1,000.00 | 1,000.00 | 1,000.00 |
| Retained earnings | — | 120.00 | 242.40 | 120.00 | 242.40 | 120.00 | 242.40 |
| AOCI | — | (100.00) | (100.00) | (100.00) | (200.00) | (100.00) | — |
| Total equity | 1,000.00 | 1,020.00 | 1,142.40 | 1,020.00 | 1,042.40 | 1,020.00 | 1,242.40 |
| Total liabilities and total equity | 1,000.00 | 1,020.00 | 1,142.40 | 1,020.00 | 1,042.40 | 1,020.00 | 1,242.40 |
| Net income | 120.00 | 122.40 | 137.09 | 122.40 | 125.09 | 122.40 | 149.09 |
| Dividends | — | — | — | — | — | — | — |
| Other comprehensive income | (100.00) | — | — | (100.00) | (100.00) | 100.00 | — |

*(Exhibit continued on next page . . . .)*

| EXHIBIT 11 | (continued) | | | | | | |
|---|---|---|---|---|---|---|---|
| | **Actual** | **Forecast A** | | **Forecast B** | | **Forecast C** | |
| Year | *t* −1 | *t* | *t* +1 | *t* | *t* +1 | *t* | *t* +1 |
| **Ending Balance Sheet** | | | | | | | |
| Assets | 1,020.00 | 1,142.40 | 1,279.49 | 1,042.40 | 1,067.49 | 1,242.40 | 1,391.49 |
| Liabilities | — | — | — | — | — | — | — |
| Common stock | 1,000.00 | 1,000.00 | 1,000.00 | 1,000.00 | 1,000.00 | 1,000.00 | 1,000.00 |
| Retained earnings | 120.00 | 242.40 | 379.49 | 242.40 | 367.49 | 242.40 | 391.49 |
| AOCI | (100.00) | (100.00) | (100.00) | (200.00) | (300.00) | — | — |
| Total equity | 1,020.00 | 1,142.40 | 1,279.49 | 1,042.40 | 1,067.49 | 1,242.40 | 1,391.49 |
| Total Liabilities and total equity | 1,020.00 | 1,142.40 | 1,279.49 | 1,042.40 | 1,067.49 | 1,242.40 | 1,391.49 |
| Residual income calculation based on beginning total equity | | | | | | | |
| Net income | 120.00 | 122.40 | 137.09 | 122.40 | 125.09 | 122.40 | 149.09 |
| Equity charge @ 10% | 100.00 | 102.00 | 114.24 | 102.00 | 104.24 | 102.00 | 124.24 |
| Residual income | 20.00 | 20.40 | 22.85 | 20.40 | 20.85 | 20.40 | 24.85 |

What are the implications for implementing a residual-income-based valuation? If future OCI is expected to be significant relative to net income and if the year-to-year amounts of OCI are not expected to net to zero the analyst should attempt to incorporate such items so that residual income forecasts are closer to what they would be if the clean surplus relation held. Specifically, where possible, the analyst can incorporate explicit assumptions about future amounts of OCI. Lacking a basis for explicit assumptions about future amounts of OCI, the analyst should nonetheless be aware of the potential impact of other comprehensive income on residual income and adjust ROE accordingly. Finally, as noted above, the analyst may decide that an alternative valuation model is more appropriate.

## 5.2 Balance Sheet Adjustments for Fair Value

In order to have a reliable measure of book value of equity, an analyst should identify and scrutinize significant off-balance-sheet assets and liabilities. Additionally, reported assets and liabilities should be adjusted to fair value when possible. Off-balance-sheet assets and liabilities may become apparent by an examination of the financial statement footnotes. Examples include the use of operating leases and the use of special purpose entities to remove both debt and assets from the balance sheet. Some items, such as operating leases, may not affect the amount of equity (because leases involve both off-balance-sheet assets which offset the off-balance-sheet liabilities) but can impact an assessment of future earnings for the residual income component of value. Other assets and liabilities may be stated at other than fair value. For example, inventory may be stated at LIFO and require adjustment to restate to current value. (LIFO is not permitted under IFRS.) Presented below are some common items to review for balance sheet adjustments. Note, however, that this list is not all-inclusive:[22]

- ▶ inventory,
- ▶ deferred tax assets and liabilities,
- ▶ operating leases,
- ▶ special-purpose entities,
- ▶ reserves and allowances (for example, bad debts), and
- ▶ intangible assets.

Additionally, the analyst should examine the financial statements and footnotes for items unique to the subject company.

## 5.3 Intangible Assets

Intangible assets can have a significant impact on book value. In the case of specifically identifiable intangibles that can be separated from the entity (e.g., sold), it is appropriate to include these in the determination of book value of equity. If these assets are wasting (declining in value over time), they will be amortized over time as an expense. Intangible assets, however, require special consideration because they are often not recognized as an asset unless they are obtained in an acquisition. For example, advertising expenditures can create a highly valuable brand, which is clearly an intangible asset; however, advertising expenditures are shown as an expense and the value of a brand would not appear as an asset on the financial statements unless the company owning the brand was acquired.

To demonstrate this, consider a simplified example involving two companies, Alpha and Beta, with the following summary financial information (all amounts in thousands, except per-share data):

|  | Alpha | Beta |
| --- | --- | --- |
| Cash | €1,600 | €100 |
| Property, plant, and equipment | €3,400 | €900 |
| Total assets | €5,000 | €1,000 |
| Equity | €5,000 | €1,000 |
| Net income | €600 | €150 |

Each company pays out all net income as dividends (no growth), and the clean surplus relation holds. Alpha has a 12 percent ROE and Beta has a 15 percent ROE, both expected to continue indefinitely. Each has a 10 percent required rate of return. The fair market value of each company's property, plant, and equipment is the same as its book value. What is the value of each company in a residual income framework?

---

[22] See also Chapter 17 of White, Sondhi, and Fried (1998).

Using total book value rather than per-share data, the value of Alpha would be €6,000, determined as follows:[23]

$$V_0 = B_0 + \frac{ROE - r}{r - g} B_0 = 5,000 + \frac{0.12 - 0.10}{0.10 - 0.00} 5,000 = 6,000$$

Similarly, the value of Beta would be €1,500:

$$V_0 = B_0 + \frac{ROE - r}{r - g} B_0 = 1,000 + \frac{0.15 - 0.10}{0.10 - 0.00} 1,000 = 1,500$$

The value of the companies on a combined basis would be €7,500. Note that both companies are valued more highly than the book value of equity because they have ROEs in excess of the required rate of return. Absent an acquisition transaction, the financial statements of Alpha and Beta do not reflect this value. If either is acquired, however, an acquirer would allocate the purchase price to the acquired assets, with any excess of the purchase price above the acquired assets shown as goodwill.

Suppose Alpha acquires Beta by paying Beta's former shareholders €1,500 in cash. Alpha has just paid €500 in excess of the value of Beta's total reported assets of (€1,000). Assume that Beta's property, plant and equipment was already shown at its fair market value of €1,000, and that the €500 is considered to be the fair value of a license owned by Beta, say an exclusive right to provide a service. Assume further that the original cost of obtaining the license was an immaterial application fee, which does not appear on Beta's balance sheet, and that the license covers a period of 10 years. Because the entire purchase price of €1,500 is allocated to identifiable assets, no goodwill is reported. The balance sheet of Alpha immediately after the acquisition would be[24]

|                                  | Alpha   |
| -------------------------------- | ------- |
| Cash                             | €200    |
| Property, plant, and equipment   | €4,300  |
| License                          | €500    |
| Total assets                     | €5,000  |
| Equity                           | €5,000  |

Note that the total book value of Alpha's equity did not change, because the acquisition was made for cash and thus did not require Alpha to issue any new shares.

Assuming that the license is amortized over a 10-year period, the combined company's expected net income would be €700 (€600 + €150 − €50 amortization). If this net income number is used to derive expected ROE, the expected ROE would be 14 percent. Under a residual income model with no adjustment for amortization, the value of the combined company would be

$$V_0 = B_0 + \frac{ROE - r}{r - g} B_0 = 5,000 + \frac{0.14 - 0.10}{0.10 - 0.00} 5,000 = 7,000$$

---

[23] Results would be the same if done on a per-share basis.

[24] For example, cash at €200 is calculated as €1,600 (cash of Alpha) + €100 (cash of Beta) − €1,500 (purchase price of Beta).

Why should the combined company be worth less than the two separate companies? Assuming that a fair price was paid to Beta's former shareholders, the combined value should not be lower. The lower value using the residual income model results from a reduction in ROE due to the amortization of the intangible license asset. If this asset were not amortized (or if we added back the amortization expense before computing ROE), net income would be €750 and ROE would be 15 percent. The value of the combined entity would be

$$V_0 = B_0 + \frac{\text{ROE} - r}{r - g} B_0 = 5,000 + \frac{0.15 - 0.10}{0.10 - 0.00} 5,000 = 7,500$$

This amount, €7,500, is the same as the sum of the values of the companies on a separate basis.

Would the answer be different if the acquiring company used newly issued stock rather than cash in the acquisition? The form of currency used to pay for the transaction should not impact the total value. If Alpha used €1,500 of newly issued stock to acquire Beta, its balance sheet would be

|                              | Alpha   |
|------------------------------|---------|
| Cash                         | €1,700  |
| Property, plant, and equipment | €4,300  |
| License                      | €500    |
| Total assets                 | €6,500  |
| Equity                       | €6,500  |

Projected earnings, excluding the amortization of the license, would be €750, and projected ROE would be 11.538 percent. Value under the residual income model would be

$$V_0 = B_0 + \frac{\text{ROE} - r}{r - g} B_0 = 6,500 + \frac{0.11538 - 0.10}{0.10 - 0.00} 6,500 = 7,500$$

The overall value remains unchanged. The book value of equity is higher but offset by the impact on ROE. Once again, this assumes that the buyer paid a fair value for the acquisition. If an acquirer overpays for an acquisition, this should become evident in a reduction in future residual income.

Research and development costs provide another example of an intangible asset that must be given careful consideration. Under U.S. GAAP, R&D is generally expensed to the income statement directly (except in certain cases such as SFAS No. 87 which permits capitalization of R&D expenses related to software development once product feasibility has been established). Also, under IFRS, some R&D costs can be capitalized and amortized over time. R&D expenditures are reflected in a company's ROE, and hence residual income, over time. If a company engages in unproductive R&D expenditures, these will lower residual income through the expenditures made. If a company engages in productive R&D expenditures, these should result in higher revenues to offset the expenditures over time. In summary, on an ongoing basis for a mature company, ROE should reflect the productivity of R&D expenditures.

IFRS and U.S. GAAP differ in accounting for in-process R&D, which can be recognized as an acquired finite-life intangible asset or as part of goodwill under

IFRS, but must be expensed immediately under U.S. GAAP. Does the difference matter? Bauman (1999) found that when purchased in-process R&D is capitalized and then amortized over a short period, there is no impact on overall value compared with immediate expensing of R&D in a residual income framework. Further, Lundholm and Sloan (2007) explain that including and subsequently amortizing an asset that was omitted from a company's reported assets has no impact on valuation under a residual income model. Such an adjustment would increase the estimated equity value by adding the asset to book value at time zero but decrease the estimated value by an equivalent amount comprised of (a) the present value of the asset when amortized in the future and (b) the present value of a periodic capital charge based on the amount of the asset times the cost of equity. However, expensing of R&D results in an immediately lower ROE vis-à-vis capitalizing R&D, but will result in a slightly higher ROE relative to capitalizing R&D in future years as this capitalized R&D is amortized.[25] Because ROE is used in a number of expressions derived from the residual income model and may also be used in forecasting net income, the analyst should carefully consider the company's R&D expenditures and their impact on long-term ROE.

## 5.4 Nonrecurring Items

In applying a residual income model, it is important to develop a forecast of future residual income based on recurring items. Often, companies report nonrecurring charges as part of earnings or classify nonoperating income (e.g., sale of assets) as part of operating income. These misclassifications can lead to overestimates and underestimates of future residual earnings if no adjustments are made. No adjustments to book value are necessary for these items, however, because nonrecurring gains and losses are reflected in the value of assets in place. Hirst and Hopkins (2000) noted that nonrecurring items sometimes result from accounting rules and at other times result from "strategic" management decisions. Regardless, they highlighted the importance of examining the financial statement notes and other sources for items that may warrant adjustment in determining recurring earnings, such as

- ▶ unusual items,
- ▶ extraordinary items,
- ▶ restructuring charges,
- ▶ discontinued operations, and
- ▶ accounting changes.

In some cases, management may record restructuring or unusual charges in every period. In these cases, the item may be considered an ordinary operating expense and may not require adjustment.

Companies sometimes inappropriately classify nonoperating gains as a reduction in operating expenses (such as selling, general, and administrative expenses). If material, this inappropriate classification can usually be uncovered by a careful reading of financial statement footnotes and press releases. Analysts should consider whether these items are likely to continue and contribute to residual income over time. More likely, they should be removed from operating earnings when forecasting residual income.

---

[25] See Henry and Gordon "Long-lived Assets" (2008), in particular the case of NOW Inc. in Example 1, for an illustration of the principles involved.

## 5.5 Other Aggressive Accounting Practices

Companies may engage in accounting practices that result in the overstatement of assets (book value) and/or overstatement of earnings. We discussed many of these practices in the preceding sections. Other activities that a company may engage in include accelerating revenues to the current period or deferring expenses to a later period.[26] Both activities simultaneously increase earnings and book value. For example, a company might ship unordered goods to customers at year-end, recording revenues and a receivable. As another example, a company could capitalize rather than expense a cash payment, resulting in lower expenses and an increase in assets.

Conversely, companies have also been criticized for the use of "cookie jar" reserves (reserves saved for future use), in which excess losses or expenses are recorded in an *earlier* period (for example, in conjunction with an acquisition or restructuring) and then used to reduce expense and increase income in future periods. The analyst should carefully examine the use of reserves when assessing residual earnings. Overall, the analyst must evaluate a company's accounting policies carefully and consider the integrity of management in assessing the inputs in a residual income model.

## 5.6 International Considerations

Accounting standards differ internationally. These differences result in different measures of book value and earnings internationally and suggest that valuation models based on accrual accounting data might not perform as well as other present value models in international contexts. It is interesting to note, however, that Frankel and Lee (1999) found that the residual income model works well in valuing companies on an international basis. Using a simple residual income model without any of the adjustments discussed in this reading, they found that their residual income valuation model accounted for 70 percent of the cross-sectional variation of stock prices across 20 countries. Exhibit 12 shows the model's explanatory power by country.

| EXHIBIT 12 | International Application of Residual Income Models |
|---|---|
| **Explanatory Power** | **Country** |
| 40–50 percent | Germany |
| | Japan (Parent company reporting) |
| 60–70 percent | Australia |
| | Canada |
| | Japan (Consolidated reporting) |
| | United Kingdom |
| More than 70 percent | France |
| | United States |

*Source*: Frankel and Lee (1999).

---

[26] See, for example, Schilit (1993).

Germany had the lowest explanatory power. Japan had low explanatory power for companies reporting only parent company results; the explanatory power for Japanese companies reporting on a consolidated basis was considerably higher. Explanatory power was highest in France, the United Kingdom, and the United States. Frankel and Lee concluded that there are three primary considerations in applying a residual income model internationally:

▶ the availability of reliable earnings forecasts,

▶ systematic violations of the clean surplus assumption, and

▶ "poor quality" accounting rules that result in delayed recognition of value changes.

Analysts should expect the model to work best in situations in which earnings forecasts are available, clean surplus violations are limited, and accounting rules do not result in delayed recognition. Because Frankel and Lee found good explanatory power for a residual income model using unadjusted accounting data, it should be expected that if adjustments are made to the reported data to correct for clean surplus and other violations, international comparisons should result in comparable valuations. For circumstances in which clean surplus violations exist, accounting choices result in delayed recognition, or accounting disclosures do not permit adjustment, the residual income model would not be appropriate and the analyst should consider a model less dependent on accounting data, such as a FCFE model.

It should be noted, however, that IFRS is becoming increasingly widely used. By 2011, the number of countries that either require or permit the use of IFRS in preparation of financial statements in their countries is expected to reach 150. Furthermore, standard setters in numerous countries have undertaken to achieve convergence between IFRS and home-country GAAP. Over time, concerns about the use of different accounting standards should become less severe. Nonetheless, even within a single set of accounting standards, companies make choices and estimates that can affect valuation.

## SUMMARY

This reading has discussed the use of residual income models in valuation. Residual income is an appealing economic concept because it attempts to measure economic profit: profits after accounting for all opportunity costs of capital.

▶ Residual income is calculated as net income minus a deduction for the cost of equity capital. The deduction is called the equity charge, and is equal to equity capital multiplied by the required rate of return on equity (the cost of equity capital in percent).

▶ Economic value added (EVA) is a commercial implementation of the residual income concept. EVA = NOPAT − (C% × TC), where NOPAT is net operating profit after taxes, C% is the percent cost of equity capital, and TC is total capital.

▶ Residual income models (including commercial implementations) are used not only for equity valuation but also to measure internal corporate performance and for determining executive compensation.

▶ We can forecast per-share residual income as forecasted earnings per share minus the required rate of return on equity multiplied by beginning book value per share. Alternatively, we can forecast per-share residual income as beginning book value per share multiplied by the difference between forecasted ROE and the required rate of return on equity.

▶ According to the residual income model, the intrinsic value of a share of common stock is the sum of book value per share and the present value of expected future per-share residual income. According to the residual income model, equivalent mathematical expressions for intrinsic value of a common stock are

$$V_0 = B_0 + \sum_{t=1}^{\infty} \frac{RI_t}{(1+r)^t} = B_0 + \sum_{t=1}^{\infty} \frac{E_t - rB_{t-1}}{(1+r)^t}$$

$$= B_0 + \sum_{t=1}^{\infty} \frac{(ROE_t - r)B_{t-1}}{(1+r)^t}$$

where
$V_0$ = value of a share of stock today ($t = 0$)
$B_0$ = current per-share book value of equity
$B_t$ = expected per-share book value of equity at any time $t$
$r$ = required rate of return on equity (cost of equity)
$E_t$ = expected earnings per share for period $t$
$RI_t$ = expected per-share residual income, equal to $E_t - rB_{t-1}$ or to $(ROE - r) \times B_{t-1}$

▶ In most cases, value is recognized earlier in the residual income model compared with other present value models of stock value such as the dividend discount model.

▶ Strengths of the residual income model include the following:

  ▶ Terminal values do not make up a large portion of the value relative to other models.

  ▶ The models use readily available accounting data.

- ▶ The models can be used in the absence of dividends and near-term positive free cash flows.
- ▶ The models can be used when cash flows are unpredictable.
- ▶ Weaknesses of the residual income model include the following:
  - ▶ These models are based on accounting data that can be subject to manipulation by management.
  - ▶ Accounting data used as inputs may require significant adjustments.
  - ▶ The models require that the clean surplus relation holds, or that the analyst makes appropriate adjustments when the clean surplus relation does not hold.
- ▶ The residual income model is most appropriate in the following cases:
  - ▶ A company is not paying dividends or if it exhibits an unpredictable dividend pattern.
  - ▶ A company has negative free cash flow many years out but is expected to generate positive cash flow at some point in the future.
  - ▶ There is a great deal of uncertainty in forecasting terminal values.
- ▶ The fundamental determinants or drivers of residual income are book value of equity and return on equity.
- ▶ Residual income valuation is most closely related to P/B. When the present value of expected future residual income is positive (negative), the justified P/B based on fundamentals is greater than (less than) 1.
- ▶ When fully consistent assumptions are used to forecast earnings, cash flow, dividends, book value, and residual income through a full set of pro forma (projected) financial statements, and the same required rate of return on equity is used as the discount rate, the same estimate of value should result from a residual income, dividend discount, or free cash flow valuation. In practice, however, analysts may find one model much easier to apply and possibly arrive at different valuations using the different models.
- ▶ Continuing residual income is residual income after the forecast horizon. Frequently, one of the following assumptions concerning continuing residual income is made:
  - ▶ Residual income continues indefinitely at a positive level.
  - ▶ Residual income is zero from the terminal year forward.
  - ▶ Residual income declines to zero as ROE reverts to the cost of equity over time.
  - ▶ Residual income declines to some mean level.
- ▶ The residual income model assumes the clean surplus relation $B_t = B_{t-1} + E_t - D_t$. In other terms, the ending book value of equity equals the beginning book value plus earnings less dividends, apart from ownership transactions.
- ▶ In practice, to apply the residual income model most accurately, the analyst may need to
  - ▶ adjust book value of common equity for
    - ▶ off-balance-sheet items.
    - ▶ discrepancies from fair value.
    - ▶ the amortization of certain intangible assets.
  - ▶ adjust reported net income to reflect clean surplus accounting.
  - ▶ adjust reported net income for nonrecurring items misclassified as recurring items.

## PRACTICE PROBLEMS FOR READING 45

**1.** Based on the following information, determine whether Vertically Integrated Manufacturing (VIM) earned any residual income for its shareholders:

▶ VIM had total assets of $3,000,000, financed with twice as much debt capital as equity capital.

▶ VIM's pretax cost of debt is 6 percent and cost of equity capital is 10 percent.

▶ VIM had EBIT of $300,000 and was taxed at a rate of 40 percent.

Calculate residual income using the method based deducting an equity charge.

**2.** Using the following information, estimate the intrinsic value of VIM's common stock using the residual income model:

▶ VIM had total assets of $3,000,000, financed with twice as much debt capital as equity capital.

▶ VIM's pretax cost of debt is 6 percent and cost of equity capital is 10 percent.

▶ VIM had EBIT of $300,000 and was taxed at a rate of 40 percent. EBIT is expected to continue at $300,000 indefinitely.

▶ VIM's book value per share is $20.

▶ VIM has 50,000 shares of common stock outstanding.

**3.** Palmetto Steel, Inc. (PSI) maintains a dividend payout ratio of 80 percent because of its limited opportunities for expansion. Its return on equity is 15 percent. The required rate of return on PSI equity is 12 percent, and its long-term growth rate is 3 percent. Compute the justified P/B based on forecasted fundamentals, consistent with the residual income model and a constant growth rate assumption.

**4.** Because NewMarket Products (NMP) markets consumer staples, it is able to make use of considerable debt in its capital structure; specifically, 90 percent of the company's total assets of $450,000,000 are financed with debt capital. Its cost of debt is 8 percent before taxes, and its cost of equity capital is 12 percent. NMP achieved a pretax income of $5.1 million in 2006 and had a tax rate of 40 percent. What was NMP's residual income?

**5.** In 2007, Smithson-Williams Investments (SWI) achieved an operating profit after taxes of €10 million on total assets of €100 million. Half of its assets were financed with debt with a pretax cost of 9 percent. Its cost of equity capital is 12 percent, and its tax rate is 40 percent. Did SWI achieve a positive residual income?

6. Calculate the economic value added (EVA) or residual income, as requested, for each of the following:

   A. NOPAT = $100

      Beginning book value of debt = $200

      Beginning book value of equity = $300

      WACC = 11 percent

      Calculate EVA.

   B. Net income = €5.00

      Dividends = €1.00

      Beginning book value of equity = €30.00

      Required rate of return on equity = 11 percent

      Calculate residual income.

   C. Return on equity = 18 percent

      Required rate of return on equity = 12 percent

      Beginning book value of equity = €30.00

      Calculate residual income.

7. Jim Martin is using economic value added (EVA) and market value added (MVA) to measure the performance of Sundanci. Martin uses the fiscal 2000 information below for his analysis.

   ▶ Adjusted net operating profit after tax (NOPAT) is $100 million.

   ▶ Total capital is $700 million (no debt).

   ▶ Closing stock price is $26.

   ▶ Sundanci has 84 million shares outstanding.

   ▶ The cost of equity is 14 percent.

   Calculate the following for Sundanci. Show your work.
   A. EVA for fiscal 2000.

   B. MVA as of fiscal year-end 2000.

8. Protected Steel Corporation (PSC) has a book value of $6 per share. PSC is expected to earn $0.60 per share forever and pays out all of its earnings as dividends. The required rate of return on PSC's equity is 12 percent. Calculate the value of the stock using the following:

   A. Dividend discount model.

   B. Residual income model.

9. Notable Books (NB) is a family-controlled company that dominates the retail book market. NB has book value of $10 per share, is expected to earn $2.00 forever, and pays out all of its earnings as dividends. Its required return on equity is 12.5 percent. Value the stock of NB using the following:

   A. Dividend discount model.

   B. Residual income model.

10. Simonson Investment Trust International (SITI) is expected to earn $4.00, $5.00, and $8.00 for the next three years. SITI will pay annual dividends of $2.00, $2.50, and $20.50 in each of these years. The last dividend includes the liquidating payment to shareholders at the end of Year 3 when the trust terminates. SITI's book value is $8 per share and its required return on equity is 10 percent.

   A. What is the current value per share of SITI according to the dividend discount model?

   B. Calculate per-share book value and residual income for SITI for each of the next 3 years and use those results to find the stock's value using the residual income model.

   C. Calculate return on equity and use it as an input to the residual income model to calculate SITI's value.

11. Foodsco Incorporated (FI), a leading distributor of food products and materials to restaurants and other institutions, has a remarkably steady track record in terms of both return on equity and growth. At year-end 2007, FI had a book value of $30 per share. For the foreseeable future, you expect the company to achieve a ROE of 15 percent (on trailing book value) and to pay out one-third of its earnings in dividends. Your required return is 12 percent. Forecast FI's residual income for the year ending 31 December 2012.

12. Lendex Electronics (LE) has had a great deal of turnover of top management for several years and was not followed by analysts during this period of turmoil. Because the company's performance has been improving steadily for the past three years, technology analyst Steve Kent recently reinitiated coverage of LE. A meeting with management confirmed Kent's positive impression of LE's operations and strategic plan. Kent decides LE merits further analysis.

   Careful examination of LE's financial statements revealed that the company had negative other comprehensive income from changes in the value of available-for-sale securities in each of the past five years. How, if at all, should this observation about LE's other comprehensive income affect the figures that Kent uses for the company's ROE and book value for those years?

13. Retail fund manager Seymour Simms is considering the purchase of shares in upstart retailer Hot Topic Stores (HTS). The current book value of HTS is $20 per share, and its market price is $35. Simms expects long-term ROE to be 18 percent, long-term growth to be 10 percent, and cost of equity to be 14 percent. What conclusion would you expect Simms to arrive at if he uses a single-stage residual income model to value these shares?

14. Dayton Manufactured Homes (DMH) builds prefabricated homes and mobile homes. Both favorable demographics and the likelihood of slow, steady increases in market share should enable DMH to maintain its ROE of 15 percent and growth rate of 10 percent over time. DMH has a book value of $30 per share and the required rate of return on its equity is 12 percent. Compute the value of its equity using the single-stage residual income model.

15. Use the following inputs and the finite horizon form of the residual income model to compute the value of Southern Trust Bank (STB) shares as of 31 December 2007:

   ▶ ROE will continue at 15 percent for the next five years (and 10 percent thereafter) with all earnings reinvested (no dividends paid).

   ▶ Cost of equity = 10 percent.

   ▶ $B_0$ = $10 per share (at year-end 2007).

   ▶ Premium over book value at the end of five years will be 20 percent.

## For Questions 16–17, use the following data for Taiwan Semiconductor Manufacturing Ltd. (TSM). Refer to Equation 45-8 in the text

   ▶ Current price = TWD81.

   ▶ Cost of equity = 14.33 percent.

   ▶ Five-year forecast of growth in book value = 22 percent.

   ▶ Book value per share = TWD16.47.

   ▶ Analyst EPS forecasts are TWD2.07 for 2008 and TWD4.81 for 2009.

   ▶ Analysts expect ROE to stabilize at 25 percent from 2008 through 2017, and then decline to 20 percent through 2028 in Problem 16 and 2029 in Problem 17.

   ▶ As of the beginning of 2008, an analyst estimates the intrinsic value using the residual income model as TWD59.18 with the zero premium shown in Example 8.

16. In the above analysis, the analyst uses the multistage residual income model and assumes that TSM's ROE will fade toward the cost of equity capital after 2028. How would her conclusion about TSM's valuation change if she believed that the persistence parameter for this company should be 0.90 (rather than 0.60) because of patent protection for some of TSM's technology?

17. Having completed the revised analysis, which gives TSM greater credit for its patented technology, the analyst realizes that the changes warrant an additional adjustment. Although she generally employs a 20-year time frame when implementing the multistage residual income model, she believes that the TSM's ROE will remain at 20 percent through 2029 before fading toward the cost of equity capital. (Recall she is now using a persistence parameter of 0.90.) How does this extension of the period with above-normal ROE alter her valuation of TSM?

**18.** Shunichi Kobayashi is valuing United Parcel Service (NYSE: UPS). Kobayashi has made the following assumptions:

▶ Book value per share is estimated at $9.62 on 31 December 2007.

▶ EPS will be 22 percent of the beginning book value per share for the next eight years.

▶ Cash dividends paid will be 30 percent of EPS.

▶ At the end of the eight-year period, the market price per share will be three times the book value per share.

▶ The beta for UPS is 0.60, the risk-free rate is 5.00 percent, and the equity risk premium is 5.50 percent.

The current market price of UPS is $59.38, which indicates a current P/B of 6.2.

**A.** Prepare a table showing the beginning and ending book values, net income, and cash dividends annually for the eight-year period.

**B.** Estimate the residual income and the present value of residual income for the eight years.

**C.** Estimate the value per share of UPS stock using the residual income model.

**D.** Estimate the value per share of UPS stock using the dividend discount model. How does this value compare with the estimate from the residual income model?

**19.** Boeing Company (NYSE: BA) has a current stock price of $49.86. It also has a P/B of 3.57 and book value per share of $13.97. Assume that the single-stage growth model is appropriate for valuing the company. Boeing's beta is 0.80, the risk-free rate is 5.00 percent, and the equity risk premium is 5.50 percent.

**A.** If the growth rate is 6 percent and the ROE is 20 percent, what is the justified P/B for Boeing?

**B.** If the growth rate is 6 percent, what ROE is required to yield Boeing's current P/B?

**C.** If the ROE is 20 percent, what growth rate is required for Boeing to have its current P/B?

## The following information relates to Questions 20–25

Eiko Takada, Mikado Suzuki, and Masumi Uchida are principals and owners of Far East Investment Consulting Group (FEICG). They are discussing equity valuation models for use in their consulting activities. Takada wishes to focus on residual income valuation models. She asks Suzuki and Uchida to compare the residual income model with the dividend discount and free cash flow models. Suzuki replies "Residual income methods are most appropriate when the firm does not pay dividends or has negative free cash flow, and when clean surplus accounting does not hold."

Uchida asks, "What does clean surplus accounting mean?" Takada responds "Clean surplus accounting refers to the condition in which any transaction reflected in the balance sheet, other than ownership transactions, first goes through the income statement. Uchida then asks whether the residual income method can be used for a company that reports using "dirty surplus"?

Takada has information for Thor Corporation to illustrate the residual income concept.

| EXHIBIT 1 | Selected Financial Data for Thor Corporation |
|---|---|
| Total assets | $10,000,000 |
| Equity-to-total assets ratio | 0.25 |
| Net income | $560,000 |
| Required return on equity | 12% |
| Dividends | $200,000 |

Takada asks her associates to calculate the intrinsic value of a share of Scorpio Corporation common stock using a single-stage residual income model. Scorpio has the following characteristics:

▶ Current book value per share is $16.00.

▶ Over the long term, earnings growth is expected to be 5 percent.

▶ Cost of equity capital is expected to be 11 percent.

▶ Over the long term, return on equity is expected to be 14 percent.

Suzuki informs the others that application of a multistage residual income model may result in assuming the terminal residual income is equal to zero. He asks Takada and Uchida what this implies for the terminal value.

Takada concludes by mentioning that accounting issues can have a great impact on the residual income valuation process. Takada asks "When a company has nonrecurring charges, should analysts adjust book value and net income?"

**20.** Is Suzuki's statement about residual income valuation correct?

  **A.** Yes.

  **B.** No, residual income models require dividends or positive free cash flow.

  **C.** No, residual income models require clean surplus accounting or appropriate adjustments.

**21.** The *best* response to Uchida's question about whether the residual method can be used when dirty surplus exists is:

  **A.** No.

  **B.** Yes, by replacing net income with comprehensive income.

  **C.** Yes, by replacing net income with the change in book value.

**22.** The residual income for Thor Corporation is *closest* to:

  **A.** $260,000.

  **B.** $360,000.

  **C.** $650,000.

**23.** The intrinsic value of Scorpio Company common stock using the single-stage residual income model is *closest* to:

  **A.** $21.33.

  **B.** $24.00.

  **C.** $40.00.

**24.** The *best* response to Suzuki's question to Takada and Uchida is that the terminal value will:

   **A.** be insignificant.

   **B.** equal book value.

   **C.** no longer grow in value.

**25.** The *best* response to Takada's question is:

   **A.** book value should be adjusted.

   **B.** net income should be adjusted.

   **C.** adjustments are unnecessary because the charges are non-recurring.

## The following information relates to Questions 26–31 and is based on Readings 43 and 45

Ernesto Carrillo, CFA, is an equity analyst assessing the valuations of Tropical Manufacturing, Inc. (TMI) and Barry Financial, Inc. (BFI) to prepare for a meeting with his firm's portfolio managers.

    Carrillo decides to use a market multiple approach, focusing on the price-to-earnings (P/E) ratio for TMI. He computes a justified leading P/E ratio based on the constant growth (Gordon) dividend discount model and the following assumptions:

▶ The industry (leading) P/E ratio is 18.

▶ The required rate of return for equity investments is 11.2 percent based on a beta of 1.30 and a market risk premium of 4 percent.

▶ Estimated long-term growth in earnings and dividends is 9.2 percent.

▶ The dividend payout ratio is 30 percent.

Carrillo wants to understand how each of the assumptions impacts the justified leading P/E, and he performs a sensitivity analysis to assess the impact of each factor.

    Carrillo also wants to contrast the P/E valuation with multiples based on cash flow measures. He prepares an alternative valuation of TMI using an enterprise value to earnings before interest, taxes, depreciation, and amortization (EBITDA) multiple and gathers relevant data shown in Exhibit 1.

| EXHIBIT 1 | Tropical Manufacturing, Inc. |
| --- | --- |
| Price per share | $30 |
| Shares outstanding | 5 million |
| Market value of debt | $50 million |
| Book value of debt | $60 million |
| Cash and investments | $8 million |
| Net income | $8 million |
| Interest expense | $4 million |
| Depreciation and amortization | $2 million |
| Taxes | $3 million |

For BFI, Carrillo uses a residual income approach based on the following assumptions:

► Current book value per share is $25.
► Current price per share is $40.
► Cost of equity is 12 percent.
► Return on equity (ROE) is expected to be 20 percent for the next five years.
► After five years, ROE will slowly decay towards the cost of equity with a persistence parameter of 0.50. Carrillo estimates that book value per share at the end of five years will be $62.21.
► BFI will not pay a dividend.

When Carrillo presents his analysis, one portfolio manager asks the following question regarding residual income valuation: "I understand that Economic Value Added (EVA) is a commonly used residual income measure. How does EVA differ from traditional accounting measures such as net income?"

**26.** Holding all other factors equal, Carrillo's sensitivity analysis will *most likely* indicate a lower justified leading P/E ratio for TMI if he changes his estimate of:

   **A.** beta to 1.2.

   **B.** market risk premium to 3.5%.

   **C.** long-term growth rate of earnings and dividends to 9.0%.

**27.** Carrillo's chosen cash-flow-based alternative valuation multiple is *most likely* to be inappropriate if TMI:

   **A.** has growing working capital needs.

   **B.** and the industry are capital intensive.

   **C.** has peer companies with varying proportions of debt capital.

**28.** Based on the data in Exhibit 1, TMI's enterprise value to EBITDA multiple is *closest* to:

   **A.** 11.29.

   **B.** 11.76.

   **C.** 13.71.

**29.** Based on Carrillo's assumptions, BFI's residual income per share in Year 2 is *closest* to:

   **A.** $2.00.

   **B.** $2.16.

   **C.** $2.40.

**30.** Based on Carrillo's assumptions, BFI's terminal value (premium over book value) at the end of year five will be *closest* to:

   **A.** $3.07.

   **B.** $4.44.

   **C.** $8.03.

**31.** Carrillo's *best* response to the portfolio manager's question is that:

   **A.** EVA does not require adjustments to reported accounting measures.

   **B.** EVA considers the costs of both debt and equity, whereas traditional net income does not.

   **C.** traditional accounting measures such as net income reflect economic profits, whereas EVA does not.

# APPENDIX A

**Appendix A**    Solutions to End-of-Reading Problems

## SOLUTIONS FOR READING 34

**1. A.** A satisfactory answer includes any four of the following uses of valuation models: (1) stock selection, (2) inferring market expectations (about variables such as future growth), (3) evaluating corporate events, (4) fairness opinions, (5) evaluating business strategies and models, (6) communication with analysts and shareholders, or (7) appraisal of private businesses.

    **B.** A portfolio manager's most important use of valuation models is stock selection.

    **C.** A corporate officer would be most directly concerned with using valuation concepts and models to evaluate corporate events, evaluate business strategies and models, and communicate with analysts and shareholders. To the extent that the corporate officer's company had a program of acquisitions, the use of valuation models in fairness opinions would also be relevant.

**2. A.** If Cornell had used a higher discount rate, the revenue growth rate consistent with a price of $61.50 would have been higher than 20 percent a year.

    **B.** In any present value model, present value is inversely related to the discount rate applied to expected future cash flows. The higher the discount rate applied, the greater the future cash flows needed to equal a given value such as $61.50. To obtain the higher future revenue estimates needed to obtain a present value of $61.50 assuming a higher discount rate, a higher revenue growth rate assumption must be made. Therefore, if Cornell had assumed a higher discount rate, he would have concluded that the market expected Intel's revenue growth rate to be even higher than 20 percent.

**3. A.** As part of the planning step (after specification of investment objectives), the investor will generally elaborate on his approach to investment analysis and security selection. An active investor may specify in substantial detail the valuation models and/or criteria that he plans to use.

    **B.** In the execution step, investment strategies are integrated with expectations to select a portfolio. In selecting a portfolio, the investor is continually put to the test to make accurate valuations of securities. Therefore, skill in valuation plays a key role in this step of the portfolio management process.

**4.** An investor trying to replicate a stock index does not need to make valuation judgments about securities. For example, the manager of an account indexed to the S&P 500, a type of passive investment strategy, seeks only to replicate the returns on the S&P 500, whether or not the index is fairly valued. In contrast, active investors attempt to identify mispriced securities—in particular, securities expected to earn a positive excess risk-adjusted return.

**5. A.** The *ex ante* alpha is the expected return minus the required return for a stock. Because the analysts feel their stocks are undervalued, the expected returns should exceed the required rates of return and the *ex ante* alphas should be positive (greater than zero).

Solutions to 1–10 taken from *Analysis of Equity Investments: Valuation*, by John D. Stowe, CFA, Thomas R. Robinson, CFA, Jerald E. Pinto, CFA, and Dennis W. McLeavey, CFA. Copyright © 2002 by AIMR. Reprinted with permission. All other solutions copyright © CFA Institute.

**B.** The *ex post* alpha is the actual return minus the contemporaneous required return.

For KMG, the *ex post* alphas are as follows:

1998: $-34.0\% - 26.6\% = -60.6\%$
1999: $65.4\% - 19.6\% = 45.8\%$
2000: $20.9\% - (-8.5\%) = 29.4\%$
2001: $-12.9\% - (-11.0\%) = -1.9\%$

For NUE, the *ex post* alphas are as follows:

1998: $-8.5\% - 29.2\% = -37.7\%$
1999: $29.4\% - 21.5\% = 7.9\%$
2000: $-25.3\% - (-9.3\%) = -16.0\%$
2001: $37.3\% - (-12.1\%) = 49.4\%$

**6. A.** Wal-Mart's expected return consists of the following:

Price correction $= 56.00 - 53.12 = \$2.88$
Additional price appreciation      4.87
Cash dividends      0.28
Total return      $\overline{\$8.03}$

The expected rate of return is the expected dollar return divided by the price, or $8.03/53.12 = 15.1$ percent.

**B.** *Ex ante* alpha = Expected holding-period return − Required return

*Ex ante* alpha $= 15.1 - 9.2 = 5.9$ percent

**C.** *Ex post* alpha = Actual holding-period return − Contemporaneous required return

*Ex post* alpha $= 8.9 - (-10.4) = 19.3$ percent

**7. A.** *Ex ante* alpha is the expected holding-period return on a security minus the security's required return. An asset with a positive (negative) expected alpha is undervalued (overvalued).

**B.** Alpha of Security $1 = 0.20 - 0.21 = -0.01$ or $-1$ percent
Alpha of Security $2 = 0.18 - 0.08 = 0.10$ or 10 percent
Alpha of Security $3 = 0.11 - 0.10 = 0.01$ or 1 percent

The ranking is:

Security 2, alpha $= 10\%$ (most attractive)
Security 3, alpha $= 1\%$
Security 1, alpha $= -1\%$ (least attractive)

**C.** According to Part B, Security 2 and Security 3 offer positive expected alphas. We might thus decide to invest in Security 2 and Security 3. The risks in such a decision include the following:

▶ We may have made an incorrect or incomplete adjustment for risk. We may not have accounted for all sources of risk reflected in the prices of the securities.

▶ Our own expectations may be biased or otherwise flawed.

▶ Even if our expectations are more accurate than the expectations reflected in the prices of the securities, there is no assurance that the mispricing will be corrected during our investment horizon, if at all.

It is also possible to enumerate other risks.

**8. A.** The analyst collects, organizes, analyzes, and communicates corporate information to investors and then recommends appropriate investment actions based on his analysis. When an analyst does his work well, clients are helped in reaching their investment objectives.

**B.** When well executed, the work of analysts promotes informed buy and sell decisions. Such informed decisions make asset prices better reflections of underlying value, with the result that capital flows to its highest-valued uses. By monitoring managers' actions, investment analysts can also help prevent managers from exploiting corporate resources for their own benefit.

**9.** We need to know (1) the time horizon for the price target and (2) the required rate of return on MBFG.MI. The price target of €9.20 represents a rate of return to investing in the stock calculated as (€9.20 + 0.05)/ €7.73 − 1.0 = 0.197, or 20 percent. Without a time frame, we cannot evaluate how attractive that rate is. Suppose that the time horizon is one year. To further interpret a 20 percent expected one-year rate of return, we need to adjust it for risk. Subtracting the required rate of return from 20 percent would give the share's expected alpha. This number would allow us to conclude whether the stock was fairly valued.

Another acceptable answer is that we would need to know the analyst's current estimate of intrinsic value for MBFG.MI. This may or may not be the target price of €9.20.

**10. A.** XMI's expensing policies with respect to acquisitions inflate its earnings per share growth rate. By pushing down pre-acquisition EPS to an artificially low number, XMI can show unusual post-acquisition earnings growth rates.

**B.** Based on both expensing and revenue recognition policies, earnings clearly do not accurately reflect underlying economics. As noted in Part A, XMI attempts to manipulate the expensing policy of acquisitions to benefit its own earnings growth rate. In speeding up the recognition of revenue in its telecommunications subsidiary, XMI's revenue recognition policy is aggressive. In summary, the quality of XMI earnings is poor. (Note that the quality of XMI's disclosures is also poor, but disclosure was treated under the rubric of accounting risk factors in the reading.)

**C.** The statement is a comparison of value, based on XMI's P/E relative to the P/Es of similar stocks. The underlying model is a relative valuation model (or the method of comparables).

**D.** Risk factors might include:

▶ Possible negative regulatory and legal developments. When and if XMI's accounting and business practices become known, XMI may be subject to legal and regulatory action.

▶ Risks in the forecasts. Because of the poor quality of XMI's earnings and the poor quality of its accounting disclosures, there is great uncertainty in any forecasts in a valuation of XMI.

▶ Other risks. A downward revision to the market price of XMI could occur if the extent of its quality of earnings issues and management's policies were to become known.

**11.** A is correct. The valuation process comprises the following five steps:

**1.** Understanding the business.

**2.** Forecasting company performance.

**3.** Selecting the appropriate valuation model.

**4.** Converting forecasts to a valuation.

**5.** Making the investment decision (recommendation).

**12.** B is correct. Statement 1 correctly asserts that valuation is more important to actively managed portfolios. Passive or index strategies likely do not involve making valuation judgments about individual securities, but for active investment strategies, valuation is relevant and critical. Statement 2 is incorrect because both qualitative and quantitative factors should be considered in the valuation process.

**13.** C is correct. The *ex ante* alpha is the expected rate of return minus the required rate of return. Of the four stocks, STR Home Health has the highest alpha:

| | | |
|---|---|---|
| Care-Rx | $(0.21 - 0.18) =$ | $0.03$ |
| Homecare | $(0.16 - 0.18) =$ | $-0.02$ |
| Leland Services | $(0.09 - 0.15) =$ | $-0.06$ |
| STR Home Health | $(0.20 - 0.15) =$ | $0.05$ |

**14.** A is correct. Houseman's second valuation analysis employs a price-earnings multiple valuation model to specify an asset's value relative to similar assets that should sell at similar price multiples. Price multiples are an example of relative valuation models.

**15.** B is correct. His valuation would be adjusted downward to reflect adjustment for the control premium and lack of liquidity. The required rate of return would increase and the value decrease.

**16.** C is correct. Conflicting results are possible when using a relative valuation model versus using an absolute valuation model. Because of their differing methodologies, different valuations are very possible.

## SOLUTIONS FOR READING 35

1. III is not correct. The central electronic limit order book is the hub of those automated markets that are order-driven (not price-driven.)

2. **A.** The market order will be executed against the best matching order(s). Accordingly, Vincent Jacquet will buy 500 shares at €146 each, 500 shares at €147 each, and the remaining 500 shares at €149 each.

   **B.** Again, the market order will be executed against the best matching order(s). Accordingly, Vincent Jacquet will sell 500 shares at €145 each and 500 shares at €143 each.

3. On the Paris Bourse, the investor who placed the limit order at €24 stands to lose. Informed market participants can sell the share to this investor at €24, although the share is truly worth only €21. In contrast, the dealer is exposed to lose on Nasdaq. The dealer quote is $23.90 − 24.45, which is equivalent to €24.90 − 25.47 at the prevailing exchange rate. Informed market participants can sell the share to the Nasdaq dealer at the bid price of $23.90, although the share is truly worth only €21 or $20.16.

4. Small orders are generally market orders (buy or sell at the best price available in the market). In an order-driven system without developed market making, the automated limit order book generally shows a huge spread between the lowest ask and the highest bid of the orders currently in the system. When a new market order reaches the system, it is unlikely that a matching opposing market order will reach the system at exactly the same time. So, the market order will be executed against the limit order book. Given the wide spread, this will generally imply a transaction at a price that is very different from that of the previous transaction. To avoid this problem, one could have a periodic auction system in which all small orders are stored for a while and an auction takes place infrequently. Another alternative is the "trading halt" used in Tokyo.

   Very large orders (such as block trades—trades of 10,000 shares or more) run a serious risk of being "picked off" on an order-driven system. A large limit order is likely to remain posted for a long time on the computer system. The client is exposed to the risk that someone gets some news about the company or the market before the client is able to revise the posted limit price on the order. Buyers or sellers of large blocks of shares do not wish to be exposed to such a risk. Hence, special procedures have been put into place. Generally, block trades take place off the automated system and are reported only after some accepted delay.

5. Each of the three statements about ECNs is true.

6. **A.** There are not enough buy orders to meet the minimum fill requirement of Participant C, and his order would not be fulfilled. Participant A would buy 50,000 shares at €37 each, and Participant B would sell 50,000 shares at €37 each. Half of Participant A's order would remain unfulfilled. Because the prevailing price is €37, Participant D's order to buy at €36 would remain unfulfilled. All unfulfilled orders of Participants A, C, and D would be resubmitted to the next crossing session because they are all GFD orders.

**B.** Taking into account the trading activity in the first crossing session and the new orders submitted to the next session, the following orders would be there for the next session:

Participant A: a market order to buy 50,000 shares.

Participant C: a market order to sell 150,000 shares, with a minimum fill of 125,000 shares.

Participant D: an order to buy 20,000 shares at €36.

Participant E: a market order to buy 150,000 shares.

Participant F: a market order to sell 50,000 shares.

In this session, the orders of Participants A, C, E, and F would be completely filled. Participants A and E would buy 50,000 and 150,000 shares, respectively. Participants C and F would sell 150,000 and 50,000 shares, respectively. All the transactions would be at €38 per share. Participant D's order would still not be executed and would be resubmitted to the next crossing session later that day.

**7.** B is correct. Unlike U.S. banks, it is common for European banks to own shares of their client banks.

**8.** Because there are no cross-holdings by either Beta or Gamma in Alpha, IWF for Alpha = 100%. For Beta, IWF = $100 - 5 - 15 = 80\%$. For Gamma, IWF = $100 - 5 = 95\%$.

**9.** The apparent market capitalization of these four companies taken together is 50 million × 4 = 200 million. But because of their cross-holdings, there is some double counting. The usual free-float adjustment would be to retain only the portion that is not owned by other companies within the group.

**A.** The adjusted market capitalization is as follows:

Company A: $50 \times (1 - 0.10) = \$45$ million (because 10% of Company A is held by Company C).

Company B: $50 \times (1 - 0.20 - 0.10) = \$35$ million (because 20% of Company B is held by Company A and 10% of Company B is held by Company C).

Company C: $50 \times (1 - 0.10 - 0.15) = \$37.5$ million (because 10% of Company C is held by Company A and 15% of Company C is held by Company B).

Company D: $50 \times (1 - 0.05) = \$47.5$ million (because 5% of Company D is held by Company C).

**B.** From A above, the total adjusted market capitalization = 45 + 35 + 37.5 + 47.5 = \$165 million. Because the unadjusted market capitalization of each company is the same, the total adjusted market cap can also be computed by subtracting the total cross-holdings from 200 million. The total cross-holdings are $50 \times (0.20 + 0.10 + 0.15 + 0.10 + 0.10 + 0.05) = \$35$ million. Thus, the total adjusted market cap = 200 − 35 = \$165 million.

**10. A.** Net dividend in euros, after deducting withholding tax = €0.50 per share × 1,000 shares × (1 − 0.15) = €425. So, the net dividend in dollars = €425 × \$0.9810 per € = \$416.93.

**B.** The investor bought the shares for €56.91 per share × 1,000 shares = €56,910, or €56,910 × \$0.9795 per € = \$55,743.35.

The investor sold the shares for €61.10 per share × 1,000 shares = €61,100, or €61,100 × \$0.9810 per € = \$59,939.1.

Thus, capital gains = 59,939.1 − 55,743.35 = \$4,195.75.

C.  The investor would need to declare the total dividends, that is, without deducting the withholding tax, as dividend income. So, the dividend income to be declared is €0.50 per share × 1,000 shares × $0.9810 per € = $490.50.

Note that because of the tax treaty between the U.S. and Germany, however, the investor can deduct from income tax a tax credit for the dividends withheld in Germany; the tax credit is 490.50 − 416.93 = $73.57. (The tax credit can be computed alternatively as €0.50 per share × 1,000 shares × 0.15 × $0.9810 per € = $73.57.)

**11. A.**  Initial investment = 41 × 100 = $4,100

Gross dividend = 2 × 100 = $200

Selling value = 51 × 100 = $5,100

Gross return in dollars = (5,100 + 200 − 4,100)/4,100 = 0.2927, or 29.27%

**B.**  Initial investment = $4,100 × Skr 9.4188 per $ = Skr 38,617.08

Gross dividend = $200 × Skr 9.8710 per $ = Skr 1,974.20

Selling value = $5,100 × Skr 9.8710 per $ = Skr 50,342.10

Gross return in kroners = (50,342.10 + 1,974.20 − 38,617.08)/ 38,617.08 = 0.3547, or 35.47%

**C.**  Capital gains = Selling value − Initial investment = 50,342.10 − 38,617.08 = Skr 11,725.02
Capital gains tax = 0.15 × 11,725.02 = Skr 1,758.75

Though 15 percent of the dividend was withheld in the United States, income tax in Sweden would be levied on the gross dividend of Skr 1,974.20. So, income tax = 0.50 × 1,974.20 = Skr 987.10. The effect of the dividends withheld in the U.S. is exactly offset by the withholding tax credit. So, we could use the gross dividend (net of Swedish income taxes) in computing the net return. Accordingly, rate of return, in kroners, net of taxes = (Capital gains + Gross dividend − Capital gains tax − Income tax)/Initial investment = (11,725.02 + 1,974.20 − 1,758.75 − 987.10)/38,617.08 = 0.2836, or 28.36%.

**12.**  C is correct. Investors in nondomestic common stock normally avoid double taxation on dividend income by receiving a tax credit for taxes paid to the country where the investment is made.

**13.**  Cost in U.S. dollars per share = $24.37 × 4 = $97.48 (because one Lafarge ADR is equivalent to one-fourth of a Lafarge share). Therefore,

Cost in U.S. dollars for 10,000 shares = $974,800

Cost of purchasing in London = £67.17 × $1.4580 per £ × 10,000 = $979,338.60

Cost of purchasing in Paris = €100.30 × $0.9695 per € × 10,000 = $972,408.50

Thus, it is the cheapest to buy the shares in Paris.

**14.**  The German firm is considering a Level III ADR program. Accordingly, it must satisfy the requirements of both the NYSE and the U.S. Securities and Exchange Commission (SEC). This could impose substantial dual-listing costs on the German firm. The SEC will require the German firm to file a Form 20-F annually. On this form, the firm will have to provide a reconciliation of earnings and shareholder equity under German and U.S. GAAP. This implies that the company will have to supply all information necessary to comply with U.S. GAAP. Furthermore, the NYSE will require timely disclosure of various information, including quarterly accounting statements.

Overall, the disclosure requirements may cause considerable concern, as German and U.S. accounting practices differ substantially. Also, German firms are not accustomed to disclosing as much information in Germany as is required in the United States. They are also not used to producing frequent reports in English. The firm may face another hurdle if it is accustomed to smoothening reported earnings by using various hidden reserves. Another concern that the German firm may have is that cross-listing may increase the volatility of its share prices. It may feel that the U.S. investors may be quicker in selling their shares of the German firm in response to bad news than would the German investors.

15. The cost in British pounds, including commission and transaction tax, would be £3.60/share × 10,000 shares × (1 + 0.0010 + 0.0050) = £36,216. So, the cost in dollars would be £36,216 × $1.5010 per £ = $54,360.22.

16. The receipt in TW$, after excluding commission and transaction tax, would be TW$150.35/share × 20,000 shares × (1 − 0.0010 − 0.0030) = TW$2,994,972. So, the receipt in euros would be TW$2,994,972 / (TW$ 32.88 per €) = €91,087.96.

17. Each of the three statements is true.

18. The creation of WEBS for a country creates an additional option for an investor seeking to invest in equities in that country. Having an additional method by which to participate in a foreign market is likely to cause the premium on an existing closed-end country fund to narrow if the fund is trading at a premium. Or, if the existing closed-end country fund is trading at a discount, the launching of WEBS for that country is likely to make it even less attractive, leading to a widening of the discount.

19. The announcement of foreign investment restrictions increases the importance of closed-end country funds for U.S. investors who want exposure to that country in their investment portfolios. Therefore, all other things constant, these restrictions are likely to increase the premium or decrease the discount on the country fund's shares. That is, the price-net asset value ratio is likely to increase.

20. The cost of 20,000 shares in the United States is $43.65 per share × 20,000 shares = $873,000. The cost in Germany in euros, including a 0.10% commission, would be €44.95 × 20,000 shares × 1.0010 = €899,899. So, the cost in dollars is €899,899 × $ 0.9710 per € = $873,801.93. Thus, it is better to buy the shares traded on the NYSE, saving 873,801.93 − 873,000.00 = $801.93.

21. During the six-hour time period when London is trading but the United States is not, the NAV of the fund in British pounds would be fluctuating in accordance with how the prices of the stocks in the index are changing. Because the U.S. market is closed, the most recent reported dollar price of the fund in the United States would not have changed. Then the U.S. market opens, and the fund's shares in the United States would open at a price based on the NAV in the United Kingdom at that time and the prevailing dollar-to-pound exchange rate. During the two-hour overlapping time period when both markets are open, the NAV in pounds would continue to change. The price of the fund in dollars would also be changing consistent with the changes in NAV and exchange rate. During

the subsequent 4.5-hour time period when the New York market is open but the London market is not, the most recent reported NAV in pounds would remain the same. However, the price of the fund in the United States could change as the exchange rate changes and as new information comes in that affects investors' expectations about future stock prices in the United Kingdom. Then, the U.S. market closes, and during the time period when both markets are closed, the most recent reported U.S. prices and NAV in pounds also stay the same.

# SOLUTIONS FOR READING 36

1. **A.** The expected holding was one year. The actual holding period was from 15 October 2007 to 5 November 2007, which is three weeks.

   **B.** Given fair pricing, the expected return equals the required return, 8.7 percent. The expected price appreciation return over the initial anticipated one-year holding period must be equal to the required return minus the dividend yield, $2.11/72.08 = 0.0293$ or 2.93 percent. Thus expected price appreciation return was $8.7\% - 2.93\% = 5.77$ percent.

   **C.** The realized return was $(\$69.52 - \$72.08)/\$72.08 = -0.03552$ or negative 3.55 percent over three weeks. There was no dividend yield return over the actual holding period.

   **D.** The required return over a three-week holding period was $(1.00161)^3 - 1 = 0.484$ percent. Using the answer to C, the realized alpha was $-3.552 - 0.484 = -4.036$ percent or $-4.04$ percent.

2. For AOL Time Warner, the required return is

   $$r = R_F + \beta[E(R_M) - R_F] = 4.35\% + 2.50(8.04\%) = 4.35\% + 20.10\% = 24.45\%$$

   For J.P. Morgan Chase, the required return is

   $$r = R_F + \beta[E(R_M) - R_F] = 4.35\% + 1.50(8.04\%) = 4.35\% + 12.06\% = 16.41\%$$

   For Boeing, the required return is

   $$r = R_F + \beta[E(R_M) - R_F] = 4.35\% + 0.80(8.04\%) = 4.35\% + 6.43\% = 10.78\%$$

3. **A.** The Fama–French model gives the required return as

   = T-bill rate + (Sensitivity to equity market factor × Equity risk premium) + (Sensitivity to size factor × Size risk premium) + (Sensitivity to value factor × Value risk premium)

   For TerraNova Energy, the required return is

   $$r = 4.7\% + (1.20 \times 4.5\%) + (-0.50 \times 2.7\%) + (-0.15 \times 4.3\%)$$
   $$= 4.7\% + 5.4\% - 1.35\% - 0.645\%$$
   $$= 8.1\%$$

   **B.** TerraNova Energy appears to be a large-cap, growth-oriented, high market risk stock as indicated by its negative size beta, negative value beta, and market beta above 1.0.

4. The required return is given by

   $$r = 0.045 + (-0.2)(0.075) = 4.5\% - 1.5\% = 3.0\%$$

   This example indicates that Newmont Mining has a required return of 3 percent. When beta is negative, an asset has a CAPM required rate of return that is below the risk-free rate. Cases of equities with negative betas are relatively rare.

**5.** B is correct. The Fama–French model incorporates market, size, and value risk factors. One possible interpretation of the value risk factor is that it relates to financial distress.

**6.** Larsen & Toubro Ltd's WACC is 13.64 percent calculated as follows:

|  | **Equity** | | **Debt** | **WACC** |
|---|---|---|---|---|
| Weight | 0.80 | | 0.20 | |
| After-Tax Cost | 15.6% | | $(1 - 0.30)8.28\%$ | |
| Weight × Cost | 12.48% | + | 1.16% | = 13.64% |

**7.** A is correct. The backfilling of index returns using companies that have survived to the index construction date is expected to introduce a positive survivorship bias into returns.

**8.** B is correct. The events of 2004 to 2006 depressed share returns but 1) are not a persistent feature of the stock market environment, 2) were not offset by other positive events within the historical record, and 3) have led to relatively low valuation levels, which are expected to rebound.

**9.** A is correct. The required return reflects the magnitude of the historical equity risk premium, which is generally higher when based on a short-term interest rate (as a result of the normal upward sloping yield curve), and the current value of the rate being used to represent the risk-free rate. The short-term rate is currently higher than the long-term rate, which will also increase the required return estimate. The short-term interest rate, however, overstates the long-term expected inflation rate. Using the short-term interest rate, estimates of the long-term required return on equity will be biased upwards.

**10.** C is correct. According to this model, the equity risk premium is

$$\text{Equity risk premium} = \{[(1 + \text{EINFL})(1 + \text{EGREPS})(1 + \text{EGPE}) - 1.0] + \text{EINC}\} - \text{Expected risk-free return}$$

Here:

| EINFL | = 4 percent per year (long-term forecast of inflation) |
|---|---|
| EGREPS | = 5 percent per year (growth in real earnings) |
| EGPE | = 1 percent per year (growth in market P/E ratio) |
| EINC | = 1 percent per year (dividend yield or the income portion) |

Risk-free return = 7 percent per year (for 10-year maturities)

By substitution, we get:

$$\{[(1.04)(1.05)(1.01) - 1.0] + 0.01\} - 0.07$$
$$= 0.113 - 0.07 = 0.043 \text{ or } 4.3 \text{ percent.}$$

11. C is correct. Based on a long-term government bond yield of 7 percent, a beta of 1, and any of the risk premium estimates that can be calculated from the givens (e.g., a 2 percent historical risk premium estimate or 4.3 percent supply side equity risk premium estimate), the required rate of return would be at least 9 percent. Based on using a short-term rate of 9 percent, C is the correct choice.

12. B is correct. All else equal, the first issue's greater liquidity would tend to make its required return lower than the second issue's. However, the required return on equity increases as leverage increases. The first issue's higher required return must result from its higher leverage, more than offsetting the effect of its greater liquidity, given that both issues have the same market risk.

## SOLUTIONS FOR READING 37

1. The book value represents mostly the historical value of the firm. Most assets and liabilities are carried at their historical cost, allowing for possible depreciation. The stock market price reflects the future earning power of the firm. If rapid growth in earnings is expected, the stock price could be well above the book value.

2. General provisions ("hidden reserves") appear as a liability, although they are in fact equity reserves. These provisions are "hidden" as a liability to allow the firm to use them in the future to smoothen earnings. Accordingly, the true book value is greater than the reported book value by the amount of these reserves. Thus, the practice of allowing corporations to build general provisions leads to an understatement of the reported book value, and an overstatement of the ratio of market price to book value.

3. Some of the reasons why German earnings are understated compared with U.S. earnings are as follows:

   German firms take provisions quite generously, and they are deducted from the reported earnings when initially taken.

   Reported earnings are tax earnings that are subject to many actions taken to reduce taxation.

   Many German firms tend to publish separately the nonconsolidated financial statements of the various companies belonging to the same group.

4. **A.** Without expensing the options, the firm's pretax earnings per share are $2,000,000/500,000 = $4 per share.

   **B.** The expense due to the options is $20,000 \times \$4 = \$80,000$. The pretax income per share would be ($2,000,000 − $80,000)/500,000 = $3.84 per share.

   **C.** The expense due to the options based on the different valuation is $20,000 \times \$5.25 = \$105,000$. The pretax income per share would be ($2,000,000 − $105,000)/500,000 = $3.79 per share.

5. **A.** Consolidated earnings are as follows:

   Company A: 10 million + 10% of 30 million = 13 million

   Company B: 30 million + 20% of 10 million = 32 million

   **B.** The P/E ratios are as follows:

   |  | Company A | Company B |
   |---|---|---|
   | Nonconsolidated | 200/10 = 20 | 450/30 = 15 |
   | Consolidated | 200/13 = 15.4 | 450/32 = 14.1 |

   Due to nonconsolidation, the earnings are understated. Thus, the P/E ratios are overstated due to nonconsolidation. As seen here, the consolidation of earnings adjusts the P/E ratios downward.

*Solutions Manual* to accompany *Global Investments*, Sixth Edition, by Bruno Solnik and Dennis McLeavey, CFA. Copyright © 2009 by Pearson Education. Reprinted with permission of Pearson Education, publishing as Pearson Addison Wesley.

**6.** Under the assumption that the total worldwide revenue of all firms in this industry was $250 billion, the market shares of the top five corporations are the following:

AOL Time Warner: $38 billion/$250 billion = 15.2%

Walt Disney: 25/250 = 10.0%

Vivendi Universal: 25/250 = 10.0%

Viacom: 23/250 = 9.2%

News Corporation: 13/250 = 5.2%

**A.** The three-firm concentration ratio is the combined market share of the largest three firms in the industry = 15.2 + 10 + 10 = 35.2%.

The five-firm concentration ratio is the combined market share of the largest five firms in the industry = 15.2 + 10 + 10 + 9.2 + 5.2 = 49.6%.

**B.** The three-firm Herfindahl index is the sum of the squared market shares of the largest three firms in the industry = $0.152^2 + 0.10^2 + 0.10^2 = 0.043$, or 430% squared. The five-firm Herfindahl index is the sum of the squared market shares of the largest five firms in the industry = $0.152^2 + 0.10^2 + 0.10^2 + 0.092^2 + 0.052^2 = 0.054$.

**C.** The combined market share of the top five firms, as computed in Part A, is 49.6%. Therefore, the combined market share of the 40 other firms is $100 - 49.6 = 50.4\%$. Assuming that each of them has the same share, the share of each is 50.4/40 = 1.26%. So, the Herfindahl index for the industry, which is the sum of the squared market shares of all the firms in the industry, is $0.152^2 + 0.10^2 + 0.10^2 + 0.092^2 + 0.052^2 + 0.0126^2 + \ldots + 0.0126^2 = 0.054 + 40 \times 0.0126^2 = 0.0603$.

**D.** The combined market share of the 10 other firms is $100 - 49.6 = 50.4\%$. Assuming that each of them has the same share, the share of each is 50.4/10 = 5.04%. So, the Herfindahl index for the industry, which is the sum of the squared market shares of all the firms in the industry, is $0.152^2 + 0.10^2 + 0.10^2 + 0.092^2 + 0.052^2 + 0.0504^2 + \ldots + 0.0504^2 = 0.054 + 10 \times 0.0504^2 = 0.0794$.

**E.** There is greater competition in the scenario in Part C than in Part D. The Herfindahl index in Part C is smaller than that in Part D, reflecting a more competitive industry structure in Part C. Also, the reciprocal of the Herfindahl index is 16.6 in Part C and 12.6 in Part D. Thus, the market structure in Part C is equivalent to having 16.6 firms of the same size, and the market structure in Part D is equivalent to having 12.6 firms of the same size. This reflects that the market structure in Part D is relatively more oligopolistic, or less competitive, than in Part C.

**7. A.** Though News Corporation is based in Australia, it is really a global conglomerate, and a majority of its businesses are outside of Australia. About 77 percent of its revenues are in the United States, 15 percent in Europe, and only 8 percent in Australia and Asia together. Its major competitors include firms headquartered in the United States and Vivendi Universal, a firm headquartered in France. In view of the global characteristics of News Corporation, its valuation should be done primarily relative to the global industry.

**B.** Due to differences in accounting standards and practices among countries, the analyst would be concerned if he were comparing ratios of News Corporation, computed as per Australian GAAP, with those of

Vivendi Universal, computed as per French GAAP. However, both firms trade in the United States as registered ADRs and prepare statements as per U.S. GAAP. Therefore, the analyst could simply compare ratios computed based on these statements.

**8. A.** ROE = NI/Equity. So,

ROE for Walt Disney = 1,300/20,975 = 0.062
ROE for News Corporation = 719/16,374 = 0.044

Clearly, Walt Disney did better than News Corporation in terms of ROE.

**B.** One version of the DuPont model breaks down ROE into three contributing elements, as follows:

ROE = Net profit margin $\times$ Asset turnover $\times$ Leverage

where

Net profit margin = NI/Sales
Asset turnover = Sales/Assets
Leverage = Assets/Equity

The three contributing elements for both the companies are computed based on the data given in the problem, and are given in the following table:

|  | Walt Disney | News Corp. |
| --- | --- | --- |
| Net profit margin | 0.056 | 0.050 |
| Asset turnover | 0.536 | 0.403 |
| Leverage | 2.082 | 2.179 |

The numbers in the table indicate that the main reason Walt Disney did better than News Corporation is that it had a better asset turnover. That is, it utilized its assets more efficiently than did News Corporation. Walt Disney also had a higher net profit margin than did News Corporation. The only contributing element that is higher for News Corporation is leverage, implying that News Corporation levered its operating results using more debt than did Walt Disney.

To analyze why the net profit margin for Walt Disney is a little higher than that for News Corporation, the net profit margin is broken down as follows:

Net profit margin = NI/EBT $\times$ EBT/EBIT $\times$ EBIT/Sales.

The breakdown of net profit margin is given in the following table:

|  | Walt Disney | News Corp. |
| --- | --- | --- |
| NI/EBT | 0.562 | 0.593 |
| EBT/EBIT | 0.762 | 0.666 |
| EBIT/Sales | 0.130 | 0.126 |

The data in the table suggest that the net profit margin for Walt Disney was higher than that for News Corporation because of a higher EBT/EBIT ratio (i.e., a lower debt burden, because a higher value of EBT/EBIT implies a lower debt burden). This is not unexpected, because we saw in the breakdown earlier that Walt Disney had a lower leverage than did News Corporation.

9. In an efficient market, all available information is already incorporated in current stock prices. The fact that economic growth is currently higher in Country A than in Country B implies that current stock prices are already "higher" in A than in B. Only unanticipated news about future growth rates should affect future stock prices. Current growth rates can explain past performance of stock prices, but only differences in future growth rates from their current anticipated levels should guide your country selection. Hence, you should decide whether your own economic growth forecasts differ from those implicit in current stock prices.

10. The intrinsic value is given by:

$$P_0 = \frac{D_1}{r - g} = \frac{E_1(1 - b)}{r - g}$$

where

$E_1$ is next year's earnings = €4 per share
$1 - b$ is the earnings payout ratio = 0.70
$r$ is the required rate of return on the stock = 0.12
$g$ is the growth rate of earnings = $1.25 \times 2.8\% = 3.5\%$ or 0.035

so,

$P_0 = 4 \times 0.70/(0.12 - 0.035) = €32.94$ per share
$P_0/E_1 = 0.70/(0.12 - 0.035) = 8.24$

11. **A.** Intrinsic P/E ratio $= \dfrac{P_0}{E_1} = \dfrac{1}{r}\left[1 + \dfrac{b(\text{ROE} - r)}{r - \text{ROE} \times b}\right]$.

In this case, $b = 0$, because the company pays out all its earnings. So, $P_0/E_1 = 1/r = 1/0.13 = 7.69$.

**B.** Again, $P_0/E_1 = 1/r = 1/0.13 = 7.69$.

**C.** It is clear from the expression in Part A that if $b = 0$, the intrinsic P/E value is independent of ROE. To further explore this, realize that the intrinsic P/E value can also be expressed as $P_0/E_1 = (1/r) + \text{FF} \times G$, where the franchise factor is FF = $(\text{ROE} - r)/(\text{ROE} \times r)$ or $1/r - 1/\text{ROE}$, and the growth factor is G = $g/(r - g)$. If $b = 0$, then $g = 0$, and therefore, the growth factor G = 0. Thus, regardless of how big the ROE—and consequently the franchise factor FF—is, the franchise value, FF $\times$ G, is zero, and the intrinsic P/E value is simply $1/r$.

**D.** Again, $P_0/E_1 = 1/r = 1/0.13 = 7.69$.

**E.** In Part D, ROE = $r$ = 13%. It is clear from the expression in Part A that if ROE = $r$, the intrinsic P/E value is independent of the retention ratio, $b$. To further explore this, let us again look at the expression for intrinsic P/E value discussed in Part C. If ROE = $r$, then the franchise factor FF = 0. Thus, regardless of how large the retention ratio—and consequently the growth factor G—is, the franchise value, FF $\times$ G, is zero, and the intrinsic P/E value is simply $1/r$.

**12. A.**  Franchise factor $= 1/r - 1/\text{ROE} = 1/0.10 - 1/0.12 = 1.67$.

**B.**  Growth factor $= g/(r - g) = (b \times \text{ROE})/(r - b \times \text{ROE}) = (0.70 \times 0.12)/(0.10 - 0.70 \times 0.12) = 5.25$.

**C.**  Franchise P/E value $=$ Franchise factor $\times$ Growth factor $= 1.67 \times 5.25 = 8.77$.

**D.**  Tangible P/E value $= 1/r = 1/0.10 = 10$.

**E.**  Intrinsic P/E value $=$ Franchise P/E value $+$ Tangible P/E value $= 8.77 + 10 = 18.77$. We can also verify that intrinsic P/E value $= (1 - b)/(r - g) = (1 - 0.70)/(0.10 - 0.70 \times 0.12) = 18.75$ (the slight difference is due to rounding).

**13.** The P/E is equal to

$$P_0/E_1 = \frac{1}{r + (1 - l)I}$$

where

$I =$ Rate of inflation $= 3\%$
$\rho =$ Real required rate of return $= 8\% - 3\% = 5\%$

**A.**  $\lambda = 1$: $P_0/E_1 = 1/\rho = 1/0.05 = 20$.

**B.**  $\lambda = 0.4$: $P_0/E_1 = 1/(0.05 + 0.60 \times 0.03) = 1/0.068 = 14.71$.

**C.**  $\lambda = 0$: $P_0/E_1 = 1/(\rho + I) = 1/0.08 = 12.50$.

We observe that the higher the inflation flow-through rate, the higher the P/E ratio. In other words, the less a firm is able to pass inflation through its earnings, the more it is penalized.

**14.** For both Company B and Company U, $\lambda = 0.60$, or $1 - \lambda = 0.40$. Also, $\rho = 0.08$ for both.

$$P_0/E_1 \text{ for Company B} = \frac{1}{\rho + (1 - \lambda)I} = 1/(0.08 + 0.40 \times 0.09) = 8.62$$

$$P_0/E_1 \text{ for Company U} = \frac{1}{\rho + (1 - \lambda)I} = 1/(0.08 + 0.40 \times 0.025) = 11.11$$

P/E for Company B, which is subject to a higher inflation rate, is smaller than that for Company U. Thus, if full inflation pass-through cannot be achieved, then the higher the inflation rate, the more negative the influence on the stock price.

**15. A.**  If the company can completely pass inflation through its earnings, P/E $= 1/\rho = 1/0.07 = 14.29$ in each of the years. Inflation has no effect on the P/E ratio, because the firm can completely pass inflation through its earnings.

**B.**  P/E $= \dfrac{1}{\rho + (1 - \lambda)I} = 1/(0.07 + 0.50 \times I)$

| Year | Inflation (%) | P/E |
|------|---------------|-------|
| 1995 | 22.0 | 5.56 |
| 1996 | 9.1 | 8.66 |
| 1997 | 4.3 | 10.93 |
| 1998 | 2.5 | 12.12 |
| 1999 | 8.4 | 8.93 |

C. As mentioned in Part A, inflation has no effect on the P/E ratio if the firm can completely pass inflation through its earnings. However, if the firm cannot completely pass inflation through its earnings as in Part B, then the higher the inflation rate (e.g., in the year 1995), the more severe the influence on the stock price.

16. Due to the appreciation of the euro relative to the dollar, the French goods will become more expensive in terms of the dollar. If the French company is able to completely pass through this increase to its U.S.-based customers, its P/E ratio will not suffer. Regardless of the extent of the appreciation of the euro, the company's P/E ratio will be unaffected if it is able to completely pass the appreciation through to its customers. However, if the company is able to only partially pass the euro appreciation through to its U.S.-based customers, the P/E ratio will go down. The higher the euro appreciation, the more severe will be the decline in the P/E ratio.

17. A. Because the portfolio is equally invested in the two stocks, the factor exposures of the portfolio would be equally weighted averages of the factor exposures of the two stocks. So, the factor exposures of the portfolio would be as follows:

|                | Portfolio |
| --- | --- |
| Confidence | 0.4 |
| Time horizon | 0.7 |
| Inflation | −0.3 |
| Business cycle | 3.0 |
| Market timing | 0.85 |

B. The stocks have a positive exposure to business cycle and a negative exposure to inflation. Also, you expect strong economic growth and an increase in inflation. Therefore, you should overweigh the stock with a greater exposure to business cycle and a smaller exposure (in absolute terms) to inflation. Stock A satisfies both, and accordingly you should overweigh Stock A.

18. It is clear by looking at the table that in each of the three size categories, the low price-to-book value stock (P/BV) outperforms the high P/BV stock. Thus, there seems to be a *value effect,* as the value firms seem to outperform the growth firms. That is, the value factor seems to be significant.

To clearly see the *size effect,* we rearrange the stocks in the two P/BV categories, as follows:

| Stock | Size | P/BV | Return (%) |
| --- | --- | --- | --- |
| A | Huge | High | 4 |
| C | Medium | High | 9 |
| E | Small | High | 13 |
| B | Huge | Low | 6 |
| D | Medium | Low | 12 |
| F | Small | Low | 15 |

In both P/BV categories, smaller firms outperform bigger firms. Thus, there seems to be a *size effect*, and the size factor seems to be significant.

**19.** We first compute the changes in the two factors and the returns on each stock. The following table has the numbers. Because we are computing the changes, we lose one observation.

| Period | Change in Interest Rate | Change in Approval | Return on Stock A | B | C |
|---|---|---|---|---|---|
| 2 | −2.1 | 5 | −0.12 | −0.49 | −0.45 |
| 3 | 0.3 | −1 | −0.22 | 0.39 | 0.39 |
| 4 | 1.7 | −2 | 0.40 | 0.42 | 0.21 |
| 5 | −1.8 | 19 | −0.33 | −0.33 | −0.19 |
| 6 | −0.2 | −19 | −0.16 | −0.30 | −0.22 |
| 7 | 2.3 | 23 | 1.10 | 1.14 | 0.96 |
| 8 | 0.1 | −27 | 0.01 | 0.14 | −0.25 |
| 9 | −2.3 | 2 | −0.50 | −0.48 | −0.23 |
| 10 | −0.2 | 20 | −0.14 | −0.15 | −0.24 |

We now estimate the following factor model for each of the three stocks, using the respective nine observations from the preceding table.

$$R_i = a_i + \beta_{1i}f_1 + \beta_{2i}f_2 + \varepsilon_i$$

where

$R_i$ is the rate of return on stock $i$

$\alpha$ is a constant

$f_1$ and $f_2$ are the two factors common to the three stocks ($f_1$ is the change in interest rate, and $f_2$ is the change in approval rating)

$\beta_{1i}$ and $\beta_{2i}$ are the risk exposures of stock $i$ to each of the two factors

$\varepsilon_i$ is a random term specific to stock $i$

The results of the estimation are as follows:

| | Stock A | Stock B | Stock C |
|---|---|---|---|
| $\alpha$ | 0.05 | 0.10 | 0.03 |
| (*t*-statistic) | (0.56) | (1.31) | (0.36) |
| $\beta_1$ | 0.25*** | 0.31*** | 0.22*** |
| (*t*-statistic) | (4.32) | (6.20) | (3.89) |
| $\beta_2$ | 0.01 | 0.01 | 0.01 |
| (*t*-statistic) | (1.27) | (1.18) | (1.66) |

***Statistically significant at the 99% level.

The values of $\beta_1$ are highly statistically significant, with a *p*-value of less than 0.01, for each of the three stocks. In contrast, none of the values of $\beta_2$ are statistically significant (each of the *p*-values is greater than 0.10). The magnitudes of $\beta_1$ are several times bigger than the magnitudes of $\beta_2$. Clearly, the first factor (change in interest rate) influences stock returns in this country, while the second factor (change in approval) does not.

**20. A.**   $R_f = 4\%$, $RP_w = 5\%$, and $RP_{SFr} = 1\%$

So $E(R_i) = 4\% + \beta_1 \times 5\% + \beta_2 \times 1\%$

Accordingly,

$E(R_A) = 4\% + 1 \times 5\% + 1 \times 1\% = 10\%$
$E(R_B) = 4\% + 1 \times 5\% + 0 \times 1\% = 9\%$
$E(R_C) = 4\% + 1.2 \times 5\% + 0.5 \times 1\% = 10.5\%$
$E(R_D) = 4\% + 1.4 \times 5\% - 0.5 \times 1\% = 10.5\%$

**B.**   Stocks that should be purchased are those with a forecasted return, higher than their theoretical expected return, given the stock's risk exposures. Because the forecasted returns given in the problem are the returns in Swiss francs, we need to convert them to dollar returns first. We expect the Swiss franc to appreciate relative to the dollar by 2 percent. Therefore, using a linear approximation, the dollar return is the return in Swiss francs + 2 percent. The following table summarizes the forecasted returns in francs and in dollars, and the theoretical expected returns in dollars [computed in Part A].

|  | Stock A | Stock B | Stock C | Stock D |
|---|---|---|---|---|
| Forecasted return (in francs) | 8% | 9% | 11% | 7% |
| Forecasted return (in dollars) | 10% | 11% | 13% | 9% |
| Theoretical expected return (in dollars) | 10% | 9% | 10.5% | 10.5% |

Looking at this table, we find that the broker forecasts superior returns for Stocks B and C. Therefore, they should be bought. Conversely, Stock D should be sold.

## SOLUTIONS FOR READING 38

1. C is correct. The Swiss watch industry is in the mature life cycle phase, with growth in sales corresponding to the economic growth of its three largest distribution (primary export) regions. In terms of the business cycle, cyclical industries are those whose earnings track the cycle. The profits of the Swiss watch industry, "benefit from economic upturns, but suffer in a down turn." Therefore, JQC is a cyclical industry stock.

2. C is correct. Duvalier states that high barriers to entry are the primary determinant of industry profitability. Industry economic and technical characteristics that are important determinants of high entry barriers include economies of scale, proprietary product differences, brand identity, switching costs, capital requirements, access to distribution, absolute cost advantages, government policy and expected retaliation. Supplier concentration is not a determinant of entry barriers, but it is a determinant of the bargaining power of suppliers.

3. C is correct. A fundamental question about profitability is whether firms can capture the value they create for buyers, or whether this value is competed away to others. The structure of the industry determines who captures the value. The threat of entry determines the likelihood that new firms will enter an industry and compete away the value. They can do this either passing value on to buyers in the form of lower prices or dissipating value by raising the costs of competing. In this case, the barriers to entry are high and, therefore, the threat of entry is low. Thus, the value that Swiss watchmakers create for buyers is kept by companies in the industry in the form of higher prices. This conclusion is supported by the fact that 80 percent of the watches sold worldwide are manufactured in Hong Kong and Japan, but more than half of the value is generated by the Swiss watch industry.

4. A is correct. Because entry barriers are high in the Swiss watch making industry, new entrants are unlikely to enter the industry and bid down prices.

5. A is correct. The sustainability of a generic strategy requires that a company possess some barriers that make imitation of the strategy difficult. One risk of a differentiation strategy is that cost proximity or parity relative to competitors is lost.

6. A is correct. Newly passed regulations, or changes to old laws, can affect an industry's sales and earnings. In this case, the Swiss Government passed a law in 1992 regulating the use of the term "Swiss made" for watches. In addition, the Swiss watch industry has been able to effectively segment their product offerings by reputation.

## SOLUTIONS FOR READING 41

**1.** The equation for the single-period DDM is $V_0 = \dfrac{D_1 + P_1}{1 + r}$

For Stock 1, $V_0 = \dfrac{0.30 + 21.00}{1.10} = \$19.36$

For Stock 2, $30.00 = \dfrac{D_1 + 32.00}{1.10}$, $D_1 = 1.10(30.00) - 32.00 = \$1.00$

For Stock 3, $92.00 = \dfrac{2.70 + P_1}{1.12}$, $P_1 = 92.00(1.12) - 2.70 = \$100.34$

For Stock 4, $16.00 = \dfrac{0.30 + 17.90}{1 + r}$, $r = \dfrac{0.30 + 17.90}{16.00} - 1 = 0.1375 = 13.75\%$

**2.** Using the CAPM, GM's required rate of return is

$$r = R_F + \beta[E(R_M) - R_F] = 5.3\% + 0.90(6.00\%) = 5.3\% + 5.4\% = 10.7\%$$

Substituting the values into the single-period DDM, we obtain

$$V_0 = \frac{D_1 + P_1}{(1 + r)^1}, \text{ or } 66.00 = \frac{2.40 + P_1}{(1.107)^1}$$

The expected price is $P_1 = 66.00(1.107) - 2.40 = 73.06 - 2.40 = \$70.66$.

**3. A.**  The projected dividend is $D_1 = D_0(1 + g) = 1.50(1.05) = \$1.575$.

**B.**  $r = R_F + \beta[E(R_M) - R_F] = 4.5\% + 0.85(6.0\%) = 4.5\% + 5.1\% = 9.6\%$

**C.**  $V_0 = D_1/(r - g) = 1.575/(0.096 - 0.05) = 1.575/0.046 = \$34.24$

**D.**  The stock price predicted by the Gordon growth model ($\$34.24$) is below the market price of $\$50$. A $g > 5$ percent is required for the value estimated with the model to be $\$50$. To find the $g$ that would yield a $\$50$ price, we solve

$$50 = \frac{1.50(1 + g)}{0.096 - g}, \text{ which simplifies to}$$

$4.8 - 50g = 1.5 + 1.5g$

$51.5g \quad\;\; = 3.3$

$g \qquad\quad\; = 0.06408, \text{ or } g = 6.408\%$

To verify that this growth rate results in a value of $\$50$, substitute $g = 6.408$ percent into the Gordon growth model equation:

$$V_0 = \frac{D_0(1 + g)}{r - g} = \frac{1.50(1.06408)}{0.096 - 0.06408} = \frac{1.59612}{0.03192} = \$50.00$$

**4. A.**   The value of each stock using the Gordon growth model is

$$V_{Que} = \frac{0.50(1.07)}{0.10 - 0.07} = \frac{0.535}{0.03} = \$17.83$$

$$V_{SHS} = \frac{1.20(1.065)}{0.105 - 0.065} = \frac{1.278}{0.04} = \$31.95$$

$$V_{True} = \frac{0.88(1.05)}{0.10 - 0.05} = \frac{0.924}{0.05} = \$18.48$$

**B.**   All three stocks are selling at a premium above their DDM estimated values. The percentage premiums are

Premium (Que) = $(25 - 17.83)/17.83 = 7.17/17.83 = 40.2\%$

Premium (SHS) = $(40 - 31.95)/31.95 = 8.05/31.95 = 25.2\%$

Premium (True) = $(20 - 18.48)/18.48 = 1.52/18.48 = 8.2\%$

True Corporation is selling for the smallest relative premium over its estimated value found with the Gordon growth model.

**5.**   In the Gordon growth model, the expected rate of return is $r = D_1/P_0 + g$.

| | |
|---|---|
| AEP | $r = 2.40/46.17 + 5.0\% = 5.20\% + 5.0\% = 10.2\%$ |
| Consolidated Edison | $r = 2.20/39.80 + 5.0\% = 5.53\% + 5.0\% = 10.53\%$ |
| Exelon | $r = 1.69/64.12 + 7.0\% = 2.64\% + 7.0\% = 9.64\%$ |
| Southern Co. | $r = 1.34/23.25 + 5.5\% = 5.76\% + 5.5\% = 11.26\%$ |
| Dominion Resources | $r = 2.58/60.13 + 5.5\% = 4.29\% + 5.5\% = 9.79\%$ |

**6. A.**   Compounded for eight years, $0.585(1 + g)^8 = 1.46$. Solving for $g$, we get $g = 12.11\%$.

**B.**   For the future dividend growth rate, use $g = 12.11\%/2 = 6.06\%$. The expected rate of return is

$$r = \frac{D_1}{P_0} + g = \frac{1.46(1.0606)}{80.00} + 0.0606 = 0.0800 = 8.00\%$$

(If the growth rate is not rounded, an answer of $r = 7.99$ percent results.)

**C.**   The required rate of return for PG using the CAPM is

$$r = R_F + \beta[E(R_M) - R_F] = 5.56\% + 0.53(3.71\%) = 7.53\%$$

$$V_0 = \frac{D_1}{r - g} = \frac{1.46(1.0606)}{0.0753 - 0.0606} = \$105.34$$

**7.**   The value of one share of NiSource Preferred B is $V_0 = D/r = 3.88/0.0788 = \$49.24$. If the price is \$46.00, the yield is $r = D/P_0 = 3.88/46.00 = 0.0843 = 8.43\%$.

**8. A.**   Total market value = (Price per share) × (Number of shares) = $88.00(300,000,000) = \$26.4$ billion.

Earnings per share = EPS = $\$3,000,000/300,000,000$ shares = \$0.01 per share

P/E = $88.00/0.01 = 8,800$

Sales per share = $\$210,000,000/300,000,000$ shares = \$0.70

Price/Sales = $88.00/0.70 = 125.7$

**B.**   Sales in Year 0 (the current year) are $210 million

Sales in Year 4 = Sales$_4$ = 210 million × $(1.60)^4$ = $1,376.26 million

Sales in Year 5 = Sales$_5$ = Sales$_4$ × $(1.07)$ = 1,376.26 million $(1.07)$ = $1,472.59 million

Earnings in Year 5 = 10% × Sales$_5$ = 0.10 $(1,472.59)$ = $147.26 million

Finally, dividends in Year 5 = 0.40 × 147.26 million = $58.90 million

The dividend per share is 58.90 million/300 million = $0.1963 per share

Using the Gordon growth model, the value of one share at the end of Year 4 would be $V_4 = D_5/(r - g)$ = 0.1963/(0.12 − 0.07) = $3.93 per share.

$V_0$, the present value of $V_4$, is $V_0 = 3.93/(1.12)^4$ = $2.50, which is far less than the current market value of $88.00 per share.

**C.**   We solve this problem by finding the sales and dividend per share in Year 4 that would be required to produce the current $88.00 price. Then we multiply this sales per share figure by the number of outstanding shares to get the total sales figure.

$$88.00 = \frac{1}{(1.12)^4} V_4 = \frac{1}{(1.12)^4}\left(\frac{D_5}{0.12 - 0.07}\right)$$

Solving this expression, we find that $D_5$ = $6.92. Because dividends are growing at 7 percent, $D_4$ = 6.92/1.07 = $6.47. Because dividends are 40 percent of earnings, EPS$_4$ = 6.47/0.40 = $16.175. Because earnings are 10 percent of sales, Sales per share = 16.175/0.10 = $161.75.

Finally, the total sales of the company is $161.75 × 300 million = $48.53 billion. In this scenario, the current valuation of the stock is justified if sales can increase from $210 million to $48.53 billion in four years.

**9.** In the Gordon (constant dividend growth) model, $V_0 = D_0(1 + g)/(r - g)$. With the bond yield plus risk premium method, with $r$ = 9.6%, the value of Dole is

$V_0 = 0.40(1 + 0.07)/(0.096 - 0.07) = 0.428/0.026 = \$16.46.$

With the CAPM method, $r$ = 11.2% and the value of Dole is

$V_0 = 0.40(1 + 0.07)/(0.112 - 0.07) = 0.428/0.042 = \$10.19.$

With the APT, $r$ = 10.4% and the value of Dole is

$V_0 = 0.40(1 + 0.07)/(0.104 - 0.07) = 0.428/0.034 = \$12.59.$

**10. A.**   Counting four years from today, $t$ = 0, the first dividend is expected at $t$ = 4. An analyst accepting the CFO's dividend target would compute the value as follows:

$V_3 = D_4/(r - g)$
$V_3 = 0.50/(0.15 - 0.07) = \$6.25$
$V_0 = V_3/(1 + r)^3$
$V_0 = \$6.25/(1.15)^3 = \$4.11$

**B.** Counting six years from today, $t = 0$, the first dividend is expected at $t = 6$. An analyst extending the dividend target would compute the value as follows:

$$V_5 = D_6/(r - g)$$
$$V_5 = 0.50/(0.15 - 0.07) = \$6.25$$
$$V_0 = V_5/(1 + r)^5$$
$$V_0 = \$6.25/(1.15)^5 = \$3.11$$

**11.** The table below calculates the first five dividends and also finds their present values discounted at 12 percent. The value of the dividends for Year 6 and after is found using the Gordon growth model, where the value at time $t = 5$ depends on the dividend at $t = 6$. $D_6$ is found by growing the $D_1$ dividend at 50 percent for two years, at 20 percent for two more years, and at 5 percent for one year:

$$D_6 = 0.60(1.50)^2(1.20)^2(1.05) = \$2.0412$$

$V_5$ is

$$V_5 = \frac{D_6}{r - g} = \frac{2.0412}{0.12 - 0.05} = \frac{2.0412}{0.07} = \$29.16$$

The present values of $V_5$ and the dividends for $t = 1$ through $t = 5$ are in the far right column of the table.

| Time | Value | Calculation | $D_t$ or $V_t$ | Present Values $D_t/(1.12)^t$ or $V_t/(1.12)^t$ |
|---|---|---|---|---|
| 1 | $D_1$ | 0.60 | 0.60 | 0.536 |
| 2 | $D_2$ | 0.60(1.50) | 0.90 | 0.717 |
| 3 | $D_3$ | $0.60(1.50)^2$ | 1.35 | 0.961 |
| 4 | $D_4$ | $0.60(1.50)^2(1.20)$ | 1.62 | 1.030 |
| 5 | $D_5$ | $0.60(1.50)^2(1.20)^2$ | 1.944 | 1.103 |
| 5 | $V_5$ | $0.60(1.50)^2(1.20)^2(1.05)/(0.12 - 0.05)$ | 29.16 | 16.546 |
| Total | | | | 20.893 |

The dividend for FPR grows at different rates for three time periods. The total present value of the stock's dividends is $20.89.

**12. A.** The required rate of return for Hanson is $r = R_F + \beta[E(R_M) - R_F] = 4.66\% + 0.83(4.92\%) = 8.74\%$. Using the H-model, the value of Hanson PLC is

$$V_0 = \frac{D_0(1 + g_L)}{r - g_L} + \frac{D_0 H(g_S - g_L)}{r - g_L} = \frac{13.80(1 + 0.05)}{0.0874 - 0.05}$$

$$+ \frac{13.80(5)(0.14 - 0.05)}{0.0874 - 0.05}$$

$$V_0 = \frac{14.49}{0.0374} + \frac{6.21}{0.0374} = 387.43 + 166.04 = \text{GBP } 553.47$$

The market price of GBP 472 is below the H-model price of GBP 553.47, so Hanson seems to be underpriced.

**B.** For the H-model the expected rate of return can be derived as

$$r = \left(\frac{D_0}{P_0}\right)[(1 + g_L) + H(g_S - g_L)] + g_L$$

$$r = \left(\frac{13.80}{472}\right)[(1 + 0.05) + 5(0.14 - 0.05)] + 0.05$$

$$= 0.0439 + 0.05 = 0.0939 = 9.39\%$$

Hanson will return 9.39 percent to the investor if all of these assumptions hold.

**13. A.** Using the constant-growth dividend discount model, $V_0 = D_1/(r - g)$

> For LCC: $V_0 = \$0.90/(0.10 - 0.08) = \$45.00$
> For AOC: $V_0 = \$1.60/(0.11 - 0.07) = \$40.00$

**B.** The sustainable growth rate is $g = b \times \text{ROE} = [(E - D)/E] \times (E/BV)$

> For LCC: BV $= \$300/10 = \$30$
> $g = [(\$4.00 - \$0.90)/\$4.00] \times (\$4.00/\$30)$
> $= 0.775 \times 13.33\% = 10.33\%$

> For AOC: BV $= \$320/20 = \$16$
> $g = [(\$3.20 - \$1.60)/\$3.20] \times (\$3.20/\$16)$
> $= 0.50 \times 20\% = 10.00\%$

**C.** *Recommendation*: Aminochem (AOC) is a more attractive investment than Litchfield (LCC) based on the answers to parts A and B and the information provided in the exhibit.

*Justification*: Using the constant-growth dividend discount model (DDM), the price of AOC stock at $30 is well below its DDM value of $40, whereas the price of LCC stock at $50 exceeds its DDM value of $45. AOC stock appears to be undervalued while LCC stock appears to be overvalued. LCC's sustainable growth rate (computed in part B) is higher than that of AOC, but LCC's higher forward P/E of 12.5 ($50/$4) versus 9.4 ($30/$3.20) for AOC is not justified by the small difference in growth rates.

**14. A.** i. Return on equity (ROE) = Profit margin × Asset turnover × Financial leverage

$$\text{ROE} = \frac{\text{Net income}}{\text{Sales}} \times \frac{\text{Sales}}{\text{Total assets}} \times \frac{\text{Total assets}}{\text{Shareholders' equity}}$$

      **ii.** ROE = $(510/5{,}140) \times (5{,}140/3{,}100) \times (3{,}100/2{,}200) = 23.18\%$

        This calculation used end-of-year (1999e) values. Slightly different and acceptable values would be obtained if balance sheet averages were used for assets and equity or if the beginning value for equity were used.

      **iii.** Sustainable growth rate   = ROE × Retention rate

        The retention rate      = 1 − Dividend payout ratio

        Dividend payout ratio   = $0.60/1.96 = 0.306$

        Retention rate         = $1 − 0.306 = 0.694$

        Sustainable growth rate = $23.18\% \times 0.694 = 16.09\%$

**B.** The sustainable growth rate (of 16.09 percent) exceeds MasterToy's actual growth rate. If the problem were temporary, management could simply accumulate resources in anticipation of future growth. Assuming this trend continues longer term (as the question states), however, management has at least two alternative courses of action when actual growth is below sustainable growth:

▶ Return money to shareholders by increasing the dividend or the dividend payout ratio.

▶ Return money to shareholders by buying back stock.

**15. A.**   **i.** Return on equity is the product of three components: profitability (net profit margin), asset turnover ratio (sales/assets), and financial leverage or equity multiplier (asset-to-equity ratio).

      Net profit margin    = Net income/Sales = $80/598 = 13.378\%$

      Total asset turnover = Sales/Total assets = $598/815 = 0.7337$

      Financial leverage   = Total assets/Shareholders' equity = $815/674$
                           = 1.2092

      **ii.** Return on equity = Net income/Shareholders' equity = $80/674 =$
           11.87%

        Or, ROE = $13.378\% \times 0.7337 \times 1.2092 = 11.87\%$

      **iii.** If the company maintains the current capital structure and a stable dividend payout rate, the sustainable rate of growth is defined by the product of ROE, which was calculated above, and the retention rate (1 minus the dividend payout rate), which can be determined from the exhibit. Sustainable growth rate = ROE × Retention rate = $11.87\% \times (1 − 24/80) = 8.31\%$

**B.**

| Proposal | Effect on Sustainable Growth Rate | Component Directly Affected (If Any) |
|---|---|---|
| Increase in quarterly dividend | Decrease | Retention rate. Assuming no change in ROE, an increase in the dividend payout rate lowers the retention rate and thus decreases the sustainable growth rate. |
| Bond issue | Increase | Financial leverage or equity multiplier. An increase in the debt ratio raises financial leverage or the equity multiplier and thus increases sustainable growth. |
| Stock split | No effect | None. A stock split affects none of the components and thus does not affect the sustainable growth rate. |

**C.** Using a two-stage dividend discount model, the current value of a share of Sundanci is calculated as follows:

Year 1 dividend per share $(D_1)$ = \$0.286 (1.32) = \$0.37752

Year 2 dividend per share $(D_2)$ = \$0.286 (1.32)$^2$ = \$0.49833

Year 3 dividend per share $(D_3)$ = \$0.286 (1.32)$^2$ (1.13) = \$0.56311

Terminal value $(V_2) = D_3/(r - g) = 0.56311/(0.14 - 0.13) = \$56.311$

The value of one share is the present value of the first two dividends plus the present value of the terminal share value:

$$V_0 = \frac{0.37752}{1.14} + \frac{0.49833}{(1.14)^2} + \frac{56.311}{(1.14)^2} = 0.331 + 0.383$$

$$+\ 43.329 = \$44.04$$

**16. A.** The industry's estimated P/E can be computed using the following model:

$$P_0/E_1 = \text{Payout ratio}/(r - g)$$

Because $r$ and $g$ are not explicitly given, however, they must be computed. The growth rate is

$$g = \text{ROE} \times \text{Retention rate} = 0.25 \times 0.40 = 0.10$$

The required rate of return is

$$r = R_F + \beta[E(R_M) - R_F] = 0.06 + 1.2(0.05) = 0.06$$
$$+ 0.06 + 0.12$$
$$P_0/E_1 = 0.60/(0.12 - 0.10) = 30.0$$

**B.**

| Fundamental Factor | P/Es Higher for Country A or Country B? | Justification |
|---|---|---|
| Forecasted growth in real gross domestic product (GDP) | P/E should be higher for Country A. | Higher expected growth in GDP implies higher earnings growth and a higher P/E. |
| Government bond yield | P/E should be higher for Country B. | A lower government bond yield implies a lower risk-free rate and a higher P/E. |
| Equity risk premium | P/E should be higher for Country B. | A lower equity risk premium implies a lower required return and a higher P/E. |

**17. A.** The required rate of return is the Risk-free rate + Beta × (Expected market rate of return − Risk-free rate):

$$r = R_F + \beta[E(R_M) - R_F] = 0.045 + 1.15(0.145 - 0.045) = 16.0\%$$

**B.** The formula for the two-stage DDM is

$$V_0 = \sum_{t=1}^{3} \frac{D_t}{(1 + r)^t} + \frac{V_3}{(1 + r)^3}$$

The estimated future dividends are

$D_1 = 1.72 \times 1.12 = 1.93$
$D_2 = 1.93 \times 1.12 = 2.16$
$D_3 = 2.16 \times 1.12 = 2.42$
$D_4 = 2.42 \times 1.09 = 2.64$

The terminal stock price at $t = 3$ is

$$V_3 = D_4/(r - g) = 2.64/(0.16 - 0.09) = 37.71$$

The present values of the first three dividends and the terminal value are

$1.93 \times 1/(1.16)^1 \quad = 1.66$

$2.16 \times 1/(1.16)^2 \quad = 1.61$

$2.42 \times 1/(1.16)^3 \quad = 1.55$

$37.71 \times 1/(1.16)^3 \quad = 24.16$

Total present value $= 28.98$

C.  Recommendation: Janet Ludlow should recommend QuickBrush for purchase because it is selling below Ludlow's intrinsic value estimate, whereas SmileWhite is selling above Ludlow's intrinsic value estimate. QuickBrush should have an expected return above its required rate of return, whereas SmileWhite should have an expected return below its required return.

QuickBrush has an intrinsic value of $63.00 versus a current market price of $45.00, or an intrinsic value of 40% above the market price. SmileWhite has an intrinsic value of $28.98 versus a current market price of $30.00, an intrinsic value of 3.40% below the market price.

D.  *Strengths of the two-stage DDM in comparison with the constant-growth DDM.* The DDM is extremely sensitive to the estimated growth rate, *g*. The two-stage model allows for a separate valuation of two distinct periods in a company's future. As a result, a company such as QuickBrush can be evaluated in light of an anticipated change in sustainable growth. Industries have distinct life cycles in which they typically move from a period of rapid growth to a period of normal growth and then to declining growth. The two-stage model has many of the same problems as the constant-growth model, but it is probably a more realistic approach than assuming a constant growth rate for all time. The use of a two-stage model is a key valuation tool, in that analysts with superior insight into a potential shift in a company's growth rate at a future date can use that expectation to assess the proper valuation at each stage.

*Weaknesses inherent in all DDMs.* All dividend discount models are extremely sensitive to input values. For example, small changes in the growth rate estimates, *g*, and/or the required rate of return, *r*, lead to large changes in a stock's estimated value. These inputs are difficult to estimate and may be based on unrealistic assumptions.

**18.**  B is correct.

$$\text{Value} = \frac{2.50}{1.12} + \frac{2.50 \times 1.10}{1.12^2} + \frac{2.50 \times 1.10^2}{1.12^3} + \frac{3.025}{.12 - 0.0} \times \frac{1.0}{1.12^3}$$
$$= 2.232 + 2.192 + 2.153 + 17.943 = \$24.52$$

**19.**  B is correct.

$$\text{Risk premium} = \frac{30(1.0675)}{1200} + .0675 - .0475 = .0267 + .02 = .0467$$

**20.**  A is correct.

$$\text{PVGO} = Value_0 - \frac{EPS}{r} = \$29 - \frac{2.40}{.10} = 29 - 24 = \$5$$

**21.** A is correct. Statement 1 is inaccurate. Lengthening the above-normal growth period increases the inaccuracy of the approximation. Statements 2 and 3 are true statements.

**22.** A is correct.

$$\frac{P_0}{E_1} = \frac{1-b}{r-g}; b = \frac{.55}{1.00}; r = 8 + 4 = 12\%; \frac{P_0}{E_1} = \frac{.45}{.12 - .10} = 22.50$$

**23.** C is correct. It is the least valid statement. The model assumes beginning of period return on shareholder's equity. A and B are valid statements.

# SOLUTIONS FOR READING 42

**1.**

| $100 Increase in: | Change in FCFF | Change in FCFE |
|---|:---:|:---:|
| A. Net income | +100 | +100 |
| B. Cash operating expenses | −60 | −60 |
| C. Depreciation | +40 | +40 |
| D. Interest expense | 0 | −60 |
| E. EBIT | +60 | +60 |
| F. Accounts receivable | −100 | −100 |
| G. Accounts payable | +100 | +100 |
| H. Property, plant, and equipment | −100 | −100 |
| I. Notes payable | 0 | +100 |
| J. Cash dividends paid | 0 | 0 |
| K. Shares issued | 0 | 0 |
| L. Share repurchases | 0 | 0 |

**2. A.** Free cash flow to the firm, found with Equation 42-7, is

$$FCFF = NI + NCC + Int(1 - Tax\ rate) - FCInv - WCInv$$
$$FCFF = 285 + 180 + 130(1 - 0.40) - 349 - (39 + 44 - 22 - 23)$$
$$FCFF = 285 + 180 + 78 - 349 - 38 = \$156\ million$$

**B.** Free cash flow to equity, found with Equation 42-10, is

$$FCFE = NI + NCC - FCInv - WCInv + Net\ borrowing$$
$$FCFE = 285 + 180 - 349 - (39 + 44 - 22 - 23) + (10 + 40)$$
$$FCFE = 285 + 180 - 349 - 38 + 50 = \$128\ million$$

**C.** To find FCFE from FCFF, use the relationship in Equation 42-9

$$FCFE = FCFF - Int(1 - Tax\ rate) + Net\ borrowing$$
$$FCFE = 156 - 130(1 - 0.40) + (10 + 40)$$
$$FCFE = 156 - 78 + 50 = \$128\ million$$

**3. A.** To find FCFF from CFO, EBIT, or EBITDA, the analyst can use Equations 42-8, 42-12, and 42-13.

To get FCFF from CFO:

$$FCFF = CFO + Int(1 - Tax\ rate) - FCInv$$
$$FCFF = 427 + 130(1 - 0.40) - 349 = 427 + 78 - 349 = \$156\ million$$

To get FCFF from EBIT:

$$FCFF = EBIT(1 - \text{Tax rate}) + Dep - FCInv - WCInv$$
$$FCFF = 605(1 - 0.40) + 180 - 349 - 38$$
$$FCFF = 363 + 180 - 349 - 38 = \$156 \text{ million}$$

Finally, to obtain FCFF from EBITDA:

$$FCFF = EBITDA(1 - \text{Tax rate}) + Dep(\text{Tax rate}) - FCInv - WCInv$$
$$FCFF = 785(1 - 0.40) + 180(0.40) - 349 - 38$$
$$FCFF = 471 + 72 - 349 - 38 = \$156 \text{ million}$$

**B.** The simplest approach is to calculate FCFF from CFO, EBIT, or EBITDA as was done in Part A above, and then to find FCFE by making the appropriate adjustments to FCFF:

$$FCFE = FCFF - Int(1 - \text{Tax rate}) + \text{Net borrowing.}$$
$$FCFE = 156 - 130(1 - 0.40) + 50 = 156 - 78 + 50$$
$$= \$128 \text{ million}$$

You can also find FCFE using CFO, EBIT, or EBITDA directly. Starting with CFO, using Equation 42-11, FCFE is

$$FCFE = CFO - FCInv + \text{Net borrowing}$$
$$FCFE = 427 - 349 + 50 = \$128 \text{ million}$$

Starting with EBIT, FCFE (found with an equation derived in Footnote 7) is

$$FCFE = EBIT(1 - \text{Tax rate}) + Dep - Int(1 - \text{Tax rate})$$
$$- FCInv - WCInv + \text{Net borrowing}$$
$$FCFE = 605(1 - 0.40) + 180 - 130(1 - 0.40) - 349 - 38 + 50$$
$$FCFE = 363 + 180 - 78 - 349 - 38 + 50 = \$128 \text{ million}$$

Finally, starting with EBITDA, FCFE (found with an equation derived in Footnote 7) is

$$FCFE = EBITDA(1 - \text{Tax rate}) + Dep(\text{Tax rate}) - Int$$
$$(1 - \text{Tax rate}) - FCInv - WCInv + \text{Net borrowing}$$
$$FCFE = 785(1 - 0.40) + 180(0.40) - 130(1 - 0.40) - 349$$
$$- 38 + 50$$
$$FCFE = 471 + 72 - 78 - 349 - 38 + 50 = \$128 \text{ million}$$

**4. A.** FCF = Net income + Depreciation and amortization − Cash dividends − Capital expenditures. This definition of FCF is sometimes used to determine how much "discretionary" cash flow management has at its disposal. Management discretion concerning dividends is limited by investor expectations that dividends will be maintained. Comparing this definition with Equation 42-7,

$$FCFF = NI + NCC + Int(1 - \text{Tax rate}) - FCInv - WCInv$$

FCFF includes a reduction for investments in working capital and the addition of after-tax interest expense. Common stock dividends are not subtracted from FCFF because doing so represents a distribution of the cash *available* to investors. (If a company pays preferred dividends, they are added back in Equation 42-7 to include them in FCFF if they had previously been taken out when calculating net income available to common.)

**B.** FCF = Cash flow from operations (from the statement of cash flows) − Capital expenditures. Comparing this definition of FCF with Equation 42-8, FCFF = CFO + Int(1 − Tax rate) − FCInv, can highlight the relation to FCFF: The primary difference is that using Equation 42-8 after-tax interest is added back in order to arrive at the cash flow available to all investors. If preferred dividends had been subtracted to obtain net income (in CFO), they would also have to be added back in. This definition is commonly used to approximate FCFF, and it generally understates the actual FCFF by the amount of after-tax interest expense.

**5. A.** The firm value is the present value of FCFF discounted at the weighted-average cost of capital (WACC), or

$$\text{Firm} = \frac{\text{FCFF}_1}{\text{WACC} - g} = \frac{\text{FCFF}_0(1 + g)}{\text{WACC} - g} = \frac{1.7(1.07)}{0.11 - 0.07}$$

$$= \frac{1.819}{0.04} = 45.475$$

The market value of equity is the value of the firm minus the value of debt:

Equity = 45.475 − 15 = $30.475 billion

**B.** Using the FCFE valuation approach, the present value of FCFE, discounted at the required rate of return on equity, is

$$\text{PV} = \frac{\text{FCFE}_1}{r - g} = \frac{\text{FCFE}_0(1 + g)}{r - g} = \frac{1.3(1.075)}{0.13 - 0.075}$$

$$= \frac{1.3975}{0.055} = 25.409$$

The value of equity using this approach is $25.409 billion.

**6.** The required rate of return found with the CAPM is

$$r = E(R_i) = R_F + \beta_i[E(R_M) - R_F] = 6.4\% + 2.1\,(5.0\%) = 16.9\%$$

The table below shows the values of Sales, Net income, Capital expenditures less depreciation, and Investments in working capital. FCFE equals net income less the investments financed with equity:

FCFE = Net income − (1 − DR)(Capital expenditures
 − Depreciation) − (1 − DR)(Investment in working
 capital)

Because 20 percent of new investments are financed with debt, 80 percent of the investments are financed with equity, reducing FCFE by 80 percent of (Capital expenditures − Depreciation) and 80 percent of the investment in working capital.

| (All Data in $ Billions) | 2009 | 2010 | 2011 | 2012 | 2013 |
|---|---|---|---|---|---|
| Sales (growing at 28%) | 5.500 | 7.040 | 9.011 | 11.534 | 14.764 |
| Net Income = 32% of sales | 1.760 | 2.253 | 2.884 | 3.691 | 4.724 |
| FCInv − Dep = (35% − 9%) × Sales | 1.430 | 1.830 | 2.343 | 2.999 | 3.839 |
| WCInv = (6% of Sales) | 0.330 | 0.422 | 0.541 | 0.692 | 0.886 |
| 0.80 × (FCInv − Dep + WCInv) | 1.408 | 1.802 | 2.307 | 2.953 | 3.780 |
| FCFE = NI−0.80 × (FCInv − Dep + WCInv) | 0.352 | 0.451 | 0.577 | 0.738 | 0.945 |
| PV of FCFE discounted at 16.9% | 0.301 | 0.330 | 0.361 | 0.395 | 0.433 |
| Terminal stock value | | 85.032 | | | |
| PV of Terminal value discounted at 16.9% | | 38.950 | | | |
| Total PV of FCFE | | 1.820 | | | |
| Total value of firm | | 40.770 | | | |

The terminal stock value is 18.0 times the earnings in 2013, or 18 × 4.724 = $85.03 billion. The present value of the terminal value (TWD38.95 billion) plus the present value of the first five years' FCFE (TWD1.82 billion) is TWD40.77 billion. Because there are 17 billion outstanding shares, the value per ordinary share is TWD2.398.

**7. A.** The free cash flow to the firm is

$$\text{FCFF} = \text{NI} + \text{NCC} + \text{Int}(1 − \text{Tax rate}) − \text{FCInv} − \text{WCInv}$$
$$\text{FCFF} = 250 + 90 + 150(1 − 0.30) − 170 − 40$$
$$\text{FCFF} = 250 + 90 + 105 − 170 − 40 = 235 \text{ million}$$

The weighted-average cost of capital is

$$\text{WACC} = 9\%(1 − 0.30)(0.40) + 13\%(0.60) = 10.32\%$$

The value of the firm is

$$\text{Firm value} = \frac{\text{FCFF}_1}{\text{WACC} − g} = \frac{\text{FCFF}_0(1 + g)}{\text{WACC} − g} = \frac{235(1.06)}{0.1032 − 0.06}$$
$$= \frac{249.1}{0.0432} = 5{,}766.20$$

The total value of equity is the total firm value minus the value of debt, Equity = 5,766.20 million − 1,800 million = 3,966.20 million. Dividing by the number of shares gives the per share estimate of $V_0$ = 3,966.20 million/10 million = 396.62 per share.

**B.** The free cash flow to equity is

$$\text{FCFE} = \text{NI} + \text{NCC} − \text{FCInv} − \text{WCInv} + \text{Net borrowing}$$
$$\text{FCFE} = 250 + 90 − 170 − 40 + 0.40(170 − 90 + 40)$$
$$\text{FCFE} = 250 + 90 − 170 − 40 + 48 = 178.$$

Because the company is borrowing 40 percent of the increase in net capital expenditures ($170 - 90$) and working capital (40), net borrowing is 48.

The total value of equity is the FCFE discounted at the required rate of return of equity,

$$\text{Equity value} = \frac{\text{FCFE}_1}{r - g} = \frac{\text{FCFE}_0(1 + g)}{r - g} = \frac{178(1.07)}{0.13 - 0.07}$$

$$= \frac{190.46}{0.06} = 3{,}174.33$$

The value per share is $V_0 = 3{,}174.33$ million$/10$ million $= 317.43$ per share.

**8.** The weighted-average cost of capital for PHB Company is

$$\text{WACC} = 0.30(7.0\%)(1 - 0.35) + 0.15(6.8\%) + 0.55(11.0\%)$$
$$= 8.435\%$$

The firm value is

$$\text{Firm value} = \text{FCFF}_0(1 + g)/(\text{WACC} - g)$$
$$\text{Firm value} = 28(1.04)/(0.08435 - 0.04) = 29.12/0.04435$$
$$= \$656.60 \text{ million}$$

The value of equity is the firm value minus the value of debt minus the value of preferred stock: Equity $= 656.60 - 145 - 65 = \$446.60$ million. Dividing this by the number of shares gives the estimated value per share of $\$446.60$ million$/8$ million shares $= \$55.82$. The estimated value for the stock is greater than the market price of $\$32.50$, so the stock appears to be undervalued.

**9. A.** The required return on equity is

$$r = E(R_i) = R_F + \beta_i[E(R_M) - R_F] = 5.5\% + 0.90(5.5\%) = 10.45\%$$

The weighted-average cost of capital is

$$\text{WACC} = 0.25(7.0\%)(1 - 0.40) + 0.75(10.45\%) = 8.89\%$$

**B.** Firm value $= \text{FCFF}_0(1 + g)/(\text{WACC} - g)$
Firm value $= 1.1559(1.04)/(0.0889 - 0.04) = \$24.583$ billion

**C.** Equity value $=$ Firm value $-$ Market value of debt
Equity value $= 24.583 - 3.192 = \$21.391$ billion

**D.** Value per share $=$ Equity value$/$Number of shares
Value per share $= 21.391/1.852 = \$11.55$.

**10. A.** The required rate of return for McInish found with the CAPM is

$$r = E(R_i) = R_F + \beta_i[E(R_M) - R_F] = 5.08\% + 0.70(5.50\%)$$
$$= 8.93\%.$$

The value per share is

$$V_0 = \frac{FCFE_0(1 + g)}{r - g} = \frac{0.88(1.064)}{0.0893 - 0.064} = \$37.01$$

**B.**   The table below shows the calculated price for McInish using the base case values for all values except for the variable being changed from the base case value.

| Variable | Estimated Price with Low Value | Estimated Price with High Value | Range (Rank) |
|---|---|---|---|
| Normalized $FCFE_0$ | $29.44 | $47.94 | $18.50 (3) |
| Risk-free rate | $38.22 | $35.33 | $2.89 (5) |
| Equity risk premium | $51.17 | $28.99 | $22.18 (2) |
| Beta | $47.29 | $30.40 | $16.89 (4) |
| FCFE perpetual growth rate | $18.56 | $48.79 | $30.23 (1) |

As the table shows, the value of McInish is most sensitive to the changes in the FCFE growth rate, with the price moving over a very wide range. McDonald's stock price is least sensitive to alternative values of the risk-free rate. Alternative values of beta, the equity risk premium, or the initial FCFE value also have a large impact on the value of the stock, although the impacts of these variables are smaller than that of the growth rate.

**11. A.**   Using the CAPM, the required rate of return for NewMarket is

$$r = E(R_i) = R_F + \beta_i[E(R_M) - R_F] = 7\% + 1.3(4\%) = 12.2\%$$

To estimate FCFE, use Equation 42-14:

$$FCFE = \text{Net income} - (1 - DR)(FCInv - \text{Depreciation}) - (1 - DR)(WCInv)$$

where DR is the debt ratio—that is, new debt financing as a percentage of the net new investments in fixed capital and the increase in working capital. The table below shows net income, which grows at 20 percent annually for Years 1, 2, and 3, and then at 8 percent for Year 4. Investment (Capital expenditures − Depreciation + Investment in WC) are 1,150 in Year 1 and grow at 15 percent annually for Years 2 and 3. Debt financing is 40 percent of this investment. FCFE is NI − Investments + Financing. Finally, the present value of FCFE for Years 1, 2, and 3 is found by discounting at 12.2 percent.

| Year | 1 | 2 | 3 | 4 |
|---|---|---|---|---|
| Net income | $720.00 | $864.00 | $1,036.80 | $1,119.74 |
| Investment in operating assets | 1,150.00 | 1,322.50 | 1,520.88 | 335.92 |
| New debt financing | 460.00 | 529.00 | 608.35 | 134.37 |
| Free cash flow to equity | 30.00 | 70.50 | 124.27 | 918.19 |
| PV of FCFE discounted at 12.2% | 26.74 | 56.00 | 87.98 | |

In Year 4, net income is 8 percent larger than in Year 3. In Year 4, the investment in operating assets is 30 percent of net income, and debt financing is 40 percent of this investment. The FCFE in Year 4 is $918.19 million. The value of FCFE after Year 3 is found using the constant-growth model:

$$V_3 = \frac{FCFE_4}{r - g} = \frac{918.19}{0.122 - 0.08} = \$21,861.67 \text{ million}$$

The present value of $V_3$ discounted at 12.2 percent is $15,477.64 million. The total value of equity, the present value of the first three years' FCFE plus the present value of $V_3$, is $15,648.36 million. Dividing this by the number of outstanding shares (318 million) gives a value per share of $49.21. For the first three years, Alcan has a small FCFE because of the large investments it is making during the high-growth phase. In the normal-growth phase, FCFE is much larger because the investments required are much smaller.

B. The planner's estimate of the share value of $70.98 is much higher than the FCFE model estimate of $49.21 for several reasons. First, taxes and interest expenses have a prior claim to the company's cash flow and should be taken out because these cash flows are not available to equity holders. The planner did not do this.

Second, EBITDA does not account for the company's reinvestments in operating assets. So, EBITDA overstates the funds available to stockholders if reinvestment needs exceed depreciation charges, which is the case for growing companies such as Alcan.

Third, EBITDA does not account for the company's capital structure. Using EBITDA to represent a benefit to stockholders (as opposed to stockholders and bondholders combined) is a mistake.

Finally, dividing EBITDA by the bond rate commits major errors as well. The risk-free bond rate is an inappropriate discount rate for risky equity cash flows; the proper measure is the required rate of return on the company's equity. Dividing by a fixed rate also assumes erroneously that the cash flow stream is a fixed perpetuity. EBITDA cannot be a perpetual stream because, if it were distributed, the stream would eventually decline to zero (lacking capital investments). NewMarket is actually a growing company, so assuming it to be a nongrowing perpetuity is a mistake.

**12.** The table below develops the information to calculate FCFE.

| Year | 2003 | 2004 | 2005 | 2006 | 2007 | 2008 |
|---|---|---|---|---|---|---|
| Growth rate for EPS | 21% | 18% | 15% | 12% | 9% | 6% |
| EPS | 3.630 | 4.283 | 4.926 | 5.517 | 6.014 | 6.374 |
| Capital expenditure per share | 5.000 | 5.000 | 4.500 | 4.000 | 3.500 | 1.500 |
| Investment in WC per share | 1.250 | 1.250 | 1.125 | 1.000 | 0.875 | 0.375 |
| New debt financing = 40% of (Capital expenditure + WCInv) | 2.500 | 2.500 | 2.250 | 2.000 | 1.750 | 0.750 |
| FCFE = NI − Capital expenditure − WCInv + New debt financing | −0.120 | 0.533 | 1.551 | 2.517 | 3.389 | 5.249 |
| PV of FCFE discounted at 12% | 20.107 | 0.425 | 1.104 | 1.600 | 1.923 | |

Earnings for 2002 are $3.00, and the EPS estimates for 2003 through 2008 in the table are found by increasing the previous year's earnings per share by that year's growth rate. The net capital expenditures each year were specified by the analyst. The increase in working capital per share is equal to 25 percent of net capital expenditures. Finally, debt financing is 40 percent of that year's total net capital expenditures and investment in working capital. For example, in 2003, net capital expenditures plus investment in working capital is $5.00 plus $1.25 = $6.25. Debt financing is 40 percent of $6.25, or $2.50. Debt financing for 2004 through 2008 is found in the same way.

FCFE equals net income minus net capital expenditures minus investment in working capital plus new debt financing. Notice that FCFE is initially negative in 2003 because of large capital investments and investments in working capital. As these investments decline relative to net income, FCFE becomes very substantial and positive.

The present values of FCFE from 2003 through 2007 are given in the bottom row of the table. These five present values sum to $4.944. Because the FCFE from 2008 onward will grow at a constant 6 percent, the constant-growth model can be used to value these cash flows.

$$V_{2007} = \frac{FCFE_{2008}}{r - g} = \frac{5.249}{0.12 - 0.06} = \$87.483$$

The present value of this stream is $\$87.483/(1.12)^5 = \$49.640$. The value per share is the value of the first five FCFE (2003 through 2007) plus the present value of the FCFE after 2007, or $4.944 + $49.640 = $54.58.

**13. A.** FCFE is defined as the cash flow remaining after the company meets all financial obligations, including debt payment, and covers all capital expenditure and working capital needs. FCFE measures how much a company can afford to pay out as dividends, but in a given year, FCFE may be more or less than the amount actually paid out. Sundanci's FCFE for the year 2000 is calculated as follows:

| | |
|---|---|
| Net income | = $80 million |
| Plus: Depreciation expense | = 23 |
| Less: Capital expenditures | = 38 |
| Less: Investment in WC | = 41 |
| Equals: FCFE | = $24 million |
| Number of shares | = 84 million |
| FCFE per share | = $0.286 |

At the given dividend payout ratio, Sundanci's FCFE equals the dividends paid.

B. The FCFE model requires forecasts of FCFE for the high-growth years (2001 and 2002) plus a forecast for the first year of stable growth (2003) to allow for an estimate of the terminal value in 2002 based on perpetual growth. Because all of the components of FCFE are expected to grow at the same rate, the values can be obtained by projecting the FCFE at the common rate. (Alternatively, the components of FCFE can be projected and aggregated for each year.)

The following template shows the process for estimating Sundanci's current value on a per share basis.

### Free Cash Flow to Equity

Basc Assumptions

| | |
|---|---|
| Shares outstanding (millions) | 84 |
| Required return on equity ($r$) | 14% |

| | | | Actual 2000 | Projected 2001 | Projected 2002 | Projected 2003 |
|---|---|---|---|---|---|---|
| Growth rate ($g$) | | | | 27% | 27% | 13% |
| | Total | Per share | | | | |
| Earnings after tax | $80 | $0.952 | | $1.2090 | $1.5355 | $1.7351 |
| Plus: Depreciation expense | $23 | $0.274 | | $0.3480 | $0.4419 | $0.4994 |
| Less: Capital expenditures | $38 | $0.452 | | $0.5740 | $0.7290 | $0.8238 |
| Less: Increase in net working capital | $41 | $0.488 | | $0.6198 | $0.7871 | $0.8894 |
| Equals: FCFE | $24 | $0.286 | | $0.3632 | $0.4613 | $0.5213 |
| Terminal value[a] | | | | | $52.1300 | |
| Total cash flows to equity[b] | | | | $0.3632 | $52.5913 | |
| Discounted value[c] | | | | $0.3186 | $40.4673 | |
| Current value per share[d] | | | | | $40.7859 | |

[a] Projected 2002 terminal value = Projected 2003 FCFE/($r - g$)

[b] Projected 2002 total cash flows to equity = Projected 2002 FCFE plus Projected 2002 Terminal value

[c] Discounted values obtained using $r$ = 14 percent

[d] Current value per share = Discounted value 2001 plus Discounted value 2002.

C.  The following limitations of the DDM *are* addressed by the FCFE model: The DDM uses a strict definition of cash flows to equity; that is, the expected dividends on the common stock. The FCFE model expands the definition of cash flows to include the balance of residual cash flows after all financial obligations and investment needs have been met. Thus the FCFE model explicitly recognizes the company's investment and financing policies as well as its dividend policy. In instances of a change of corporate control, and thus the possibility of changing dividend policy, the FCFE model provides a better estimate of value.

Both two-stage valuation models allow for two distinct phases of growth, an initial finite period where the growth is abnormal, followed by a stable growth period that is expected to last forever. These two-stage models share the same limitations with respect to the growth assumptions.

First, there is the difficulty of defining the duration of the extraordinary growth period. For example, a longer period of high growth will lead to a higher valuation, and analysts may be tempted to assume an unrealistically long period of extraordinary growth.

Second, an assumption of a sudden shift from high growth to lower, stable growth is unrealistic. The transformation more likely will occur gradually over a period of time.

Third, because value is quite sensitive to the steady-state growth assumption, overestimating or underestimating this rate can lead to large errors in value. The two models share other limitations as well, notably difficulties in accurately estimating required rates of return.

14. A.  Using a two-stage dividend discount model, the value of a share of Mackinac is calculated as follows:

$DPS_0$ = Cash dividends/Shares outstanding = \$22,470/13,000
    = \$1.7285

$DPS_1 = DPS_0 \times 1.17 = \$2.0223$

$DPS_2 = DPS_0 \times 1.17^2 = \$2.3661$

$DPS_3 = DPS_0 \times 1.17^3 = \$2.7683$

$DPS_4 = DPS_0 \times 1.17^3 \times 1.09 = \$3.0175$

Using the CAPM, the required return on equity is

Cost of equity $(r)$ = Government bond rate + (Beta $\times$ Equity risk
        premium)
        = 0.06 + (1.25 \times 0.05) = 0.1225 or 12.25 percent

Value per share = $DPS_1/(1 + r) + DPS_2/(1 + r)^2 + DPS_3/(1 + r)^3$
        $+ [DPS_4/(r - g_{stable})]/(1 + r)^3$

Value per share = \$2.0223/1.1225 + \$2.3661/1.1225^2
        + \$2.7683/1.1225^3
        + [\$3.0175/(0.1225 - 0.09)]/1.1225^3
        = \$1.8016 + \$1.8778 + \$1.9573 + \$65.6450 = \$71.28

**B.** Using the two-stage FCFE model, the value of a share of Mackinac is calculated as follows:

Net income = $37,450

Depreciation = $10,500

Capital expenditures = $15,000

Change in working capital = $5,500

New debt issuance − Principal repayments = Change in debt outstanding = $4,000

$FCFE_0$ = Net income + Depreciation − Capital expenditures − Change in working Capital − Principal repayments + New debt issues

$FCFE_0$ = $37,450 + $10,500 − $15,000 − $5,500 + $4,000 = $31,450

$FCFE_0$ per share = $31,450/13,000 = $2.4192

$FCFE_1 = FCFE_0 \times 1.17 = \$2.8305$

$FCFE_2 = FCFE_0 \times 1.17^2 = \$3.3117$

$FCFE_3 = FCFE_0 \times 1.17^3 = \$3.8747$

$FCFE_4 = FCFE_0 \times 1.17^3 \times 1.09 = \$4.2234$

Cost of equity ($r$) = Government bond rate + (Beta × Equity risk premium)

$\qquad$ = 0.06 + (1.25 × 0.05) = 0.1225 or 12.25 percent

Value per share = $FCFE_1/(1 + r) + FCFE_2/(1 + r)^2 + FCFE_3/(1+ r)^3$

$\qquad + [FCFE_4/(r - g_{stable})]/(1 + r)^3$

Value per share = $\$2.8305/1.1225 + \$3.3117/1.1225^2$

$\qquad + \$3.8747/1.1225^3$

$\qquad + [\$4.2234/(0.1225 - 0.09)]/1.1225^3$

$\qquad$ = $2.5216 + $2.6283 + $2.7395 + $91.8798 = $99.77

**C.** The FCFE model is best for valuing firms for takeovers or in situations that have a reasonable chance for a change in corporate control. Because controlling stockholders can change the dividend policy, they are interested in estimating the maximum residual cash flow after meeting all financial obligations and investment needs. The dividend discount model is based on the premise that the only cash flows received by stockholders are dividends. FCFE uses a more expansive definition to measure what a company can afford to pay out as dividends.

**15. A.** The real required rate of return for SK Telecom Co. is

| | |
|---|---|
| Country return (real) | 6.50% |
| Industry adjustment | +0.60% |
| Size adjustment | −0.10% |
| Leverage adjustment | +0.25% |
| Required rate of return | 7.25% |

**B.** The real growth rate of FCFE is expected to be the same as the country rate of 3.5 percent. The value of one share is

$$V_0 = \frac{FCFE_0(1 + g_{real})}{r_{real} - g_{real}} = \frac{1,300(1.035)}{0.0725 - 0.035} = 35,880 \text{ Korean won}$$

16. The required return for QuickChange, found with the CAPM, is $r =$ $E(R_i) = R_F + \beta_i[E(R_M) - R_F] = 4.5\% + 2.0(5.0\%) = 14.5\%$. The estimated future values of FCFE are given in the table below.

| Year $t$ | Variable | Calculation | Value in Year $t$ | Present Value at 14.5% |
|---|---|---|---|---|
| 1 | $FCFE_1$ | $0.75(1.10)$ | 0.825 | 0.721 |
| 2 | $FCFE_2$ | $0.75(1.10)(1.26)$ | 1.040 | 0.793 |
| 3 | $FCFE_3$ | $0.75(1.10)(1.26)^2$ | 1.310 | 0.873 |
| 4 | $FCFE_4$ | $0.75(1.10)(1.26)^3$ | 1.650 | 0.960 |
| 4 | $TV_4$ | $FCFE_5/(r - g)$ | 20.580 | 11.974 |
|  |  | $= 0.75(1.10)(1.26)^3(1.06)/(0.145 - 0.06)$ |  |  |
|  |  | $= 1.749/0.085$ |  |  |
| 0 | | Total value = PV of FCFE for Years 1–4 | | |
|  | | + PV of Terminal value | | 15.32 |

The FCFE grows at 10 percent for Year 1 and then at 26 percent for Years 2−4. These calculated values for FCFE are shown in the table. The present values of the FCFE for the first four years discounted at the required rate of return are given in the last column of the table. After Year 4, FCFE will grow at 6 percent forever, so the constant-growth FCFE model is used to find the terminal value at Time 4, which is $TV_4 =$ $FCFE_5/(r - g)$. $TV_4$ is discounted at the required return for four periods to find its present value, as shown in the table. Finally, the total value of the stock, $15.32, is the sum of the present values of the first four years' FCFE plus the present value of the terminal value.

17. The total value of non-operating assets is

> $ 60 million short-term securities
>
> $ 45 million market value of noncurrent assets
>
> $ 40 million pension fund surplus
>
> $145 million non-operating assets

The total value of the firm is the value of the operating assets plus the value of the non-operating assets, or $720 million plus $145 million = $865 million. The equity value is the value of the firm minus the value of debt, or $865 million − $215 million = $650 million. The value per share is $650 million/100 million shares = $6.50 per share.

18. C is correct. The sustainable growth rate is ROE multiplied by the retention ratio. ROE is 10 percent, and the retention ratio is 1 − payout ratio, or 1 − 0.2 = 0.8. The sustainable growth rate is 0.8 × 10% = 8%. Because Emerald's policy states that dividend growth will not exceed FCFE growth, FCFE growth should be at least 8 percent per year in the long term.

**19.** A is correct. Justifications for choosing the FCFE model over the DDM include:

  ► The company is dividend paying but dividends differ significantly from the company's capacity to pay dividends (the first reason given by Leigh);

  ► The investor takes a control perspective (the second reason given by Leigh).

**20.** A is correct. FCFF = Net income (NI) + Net noncash charges (NCC) + Interest expense (1 − Tax rate) − Investment in fixed capital (FCInv) − Investment in working capital (WCInv). In this case:

NI = \$485

NCC = Depreciation expense = 270

Interest expense (1 − Tax rate) = 195 (1 − 0.32) = 132.6

  FCInv = Net purchase of fixed assets = Increase in gross fixed assets
          = 4,275 − 3,752 = 523

WCInv = Incr in AR + Incr in Inventory − Incr in AP − Incr in Accr Liab
        = (770 − 711) + (846 − 780) − (476 − 443) − (149 − 114) = 57

  FCFF = 485 + 270 + 132.6 − 523 − 57 = 307.6 or 308

**21.** B is correct. FCFE = Net income (NI) + Net noncash charges (NCC) − Investment in fixed capital (FCInv) − Investment in working capital (WCInv) + Net borrowing. In this case:

| | |
|---|---|
| NI | = \$485 |
| NCC | = Depreciation expense − 270 |
| FCInv | = Net purchase of fixed assets = Increase in gross fixed assets |
| | = 4,275 − 3,752 = 523 |
| WCInv | − Incr in AR + Incr in Inventory − Incr in AP − Inc in Accr Liab |
| | = (770 − 711) + (846 − 780) − (476 − 443) − (149 − 114) = 57 |
| Net borrowing | = Incr in notes payable + Incr in LT debt = (465 − 450) + (1,575 − 1,515) = 75 |
| FCFE | = 485 + 270 − 523 − 57 + 75 = 250 |

As an alternative calculation, FCFE = FCFF − Int (1 − Tax rate) + Net borrowing

FCFE = 307.6 − 195 (1 − 0.32) + (15 + 60) = 250

**22.** C is correct. Inventory cannot be reduced below zero. Furthermore, sales growth is a force tending to increase inventory.

**23.** A is correct. The FCFF model is often selected when the capital structure is expected to change because FCFF estimation may be easier than FCFE estimation given changing financial leverage.

**24.** A is correct. The company's free cash flow is aligned with profitability and the investor is taking a control perspective. Furthermore, while the company is dividend paying, in the long run the dividend will fall short of free cash flow.

**25.** B is correct. The value under the H-model is:

$$V_0 = \frac{D_0(1 + g_L)}{r - g_L} + \frac{D_0 H(g_S - g_L)}{r - g_L}$$

$$V_0 = \frac{1.5 \times 1.05}{0.125 - 0.05} + \frac{1.5 \times 2 \times (0.12 - 0.05)}{0.125 - 0.05}$$

$$V_0 = \frac{1.575}{0.075} + \frac{0.21}{0.075}$$

$$V_0 = \$23.80$$

**26.** C is correct. Because Raylord has no debt, FCFE = FCFF. Furthermore, FCFE is equal to CFO − FCInv when there is no debt, so CFO = FCFE + FCInv and CFO is higher than FCFE.

**27.** C is correct. FCFE is expected to grow at 11% for 3 years and 4% thereafter. In a two-stage model, the calculation is as follows.

|                       | Current | Year 1  | Year 2  | Year 3  |
|-----------------------|---------|---------|---------|---------|
| Growth                | NA      | 11%     | 11%     | 11%     |
| FCFE                  | 850     | 943.50  | 1047.28 | 1162.49 |
| Present Value at 12.5%| NA      | 838.67  | 827.48  | 816.45  |

FCFE in Year 4 = 1,162.49 × 1.04 = 1,208.99.

Terminal value = 1,208.99/ (0.125 − 0.04) = \$14,223.36.

Present value of terminal value = 9,989.52 (discounted at 12.5% for three years).

$$PV = \frac{943.50}{1.125} + \frac{1047.28}{1.125^2} + \frac{1162.49}{1.125^3} + \frac{1162.49(1.04)/(0.125 - 0.04)}{1.125^3}$$

$$PV = 838.67 + 827.48 + 816.45 + 9,989.52 = \$12,472.15$$

**28.** B is correct. Payment of cash dividends does not affect free cash flow to equity but changing leverage (new debt issuances) does, as is indicated in the FCFE equation:

$$FCFE = NI + NCC - FCInv - WCInv + \text{Net borrowing}$$

**29.** C is correct. The sustainable growth rate is:

g    = b × ROE
ROE = Profit margin × Asset turnover × Financial leverage
ROE = 5% × 1.25 × 2.00 = 12.5%
b    = 1 − Dividend payout = 0.60
g    = 0.60 × 12.5% = 7.5%

**30.** A is correct. When the Gordon growth model is solved for $r$, the expected return is:

$$r = \frac{D_0(1+g)}{P_0} + g = \frac{D_1}{P_0} + g$$

$$r = \frac{2(1+.08)}{35} + 0.08 = \frac{2.16}{35} + 0.08 = 0.1417 = 14.17\%$$

**31.** B is correct. The formula for the value of a stock using a two stage dividend discount model is:

$$V_0 = \sum_{t=1}^{n} \frac{D_0 \times (1+g_s)^t}{(1+r)^t} + \frac{D_0 \times (1+g_s)^n \times (1+g_L)}{(1+r)^n \times (r-g_L)}$$

$$V_0 = \sum_{t=1}^{3} \frac{2.00 \times (1+0.08)^t}{(1+0.10)^t} + \frac{2.00 \times (1+0.08)^3 \times (1+0.05)}{(1+0.10)^3 \times (0.10-0.05)}$$

Where:

$n$ = initial growth period = 3 years
$D_0$ = the initial dividend per share = 2.00
$g_s$ = growth rate of dividends in the initial growth period = 8%
$g_L$ = growth rate of dividends in the second growth period = 5%
$r$ = required rate of return on equity = 10.00%

| Time | Value | Calculation | $D_t$ or $V_t$ | $(D_t$ or $V_t)/1.10^t$ | Present Values |
|------|-------|-------------|----------------|------------------------|----------------|
| 1 | $D_1$ | $2.00 \times 1.08$ | 2.16 | $(1.10)^1 = 1.10$ | 1.9636 |
| 2 | $D_2$ | $2.00 \times (1.08)^2$ | 2.3328 | $(1.10)^2 = 1.21$ | 1.9279 |
| 3 | $D_3$ | $2.00 \times (1.08)^3$ | 2.5194 | $(1.10)^3 = 1.331$ | 1.8929 |
| 3 | $V_3$ | $[2.00 \times (1.08)^3 \times 1.05]/(0.10-0.05)$ | 52.9079 | $(1.10)^3 = 1.331$ | 39.7505 |
| Total | | | | | 45.5349 |

**32.** A is correct. The value of the dividend stream in the H-model is:

$$V_0 = \frac{D_0 \times (1+g_L)}{(r-g_L)} + \frac{D_0 H(g_s - g_L)}{(r-g_L)}$$

Where:

$V_0$ = value per share at t = 0
$D_0$ = the initial dividend per share = 2.00
$g_s$ = initial short-term dividend growth rate = 8.25%
$g_L$ = normal long-term dividend growth rate = 5.00%
$r$ = required rate of return on equity = 10.00%
$H$ = half-life in years of the high growth period (i.e., high growth period = $2H$ years) = 2.5

$$V_0 = \frac{2.00 \times (1+0.05)}{(0.10-0.05)} + \frac{2.00(2.5)(0.0825-0.05)}{(0.10-0.05)} = 45.25$$

**33.** C is correct.

$$\text{WACC} = 7.25\% \, (1 - 0.40)(.30) + 10.25\% \, (.70) = 1.305 + 7.175 = 8.48\%$$
$$\text{FCFF}_1 \, (000) = \text{FCFF}_0 \times (1 + g) - 2{,}200 \times (1 + 0.035) = 2{,}277$$

$$\text{Firm value} = \frac{FCFF_1}{WACC - g} = \frac{2{,}277}{(0.0848 - 0.035)} = 45{,}723$$

Value of equity = Firm value − Market value of debt
Value of equity (000) = 45,723 − 11,910 = 33,813

$$V_0 = \frac{\text{Market value of equity}}{\text{Number of shares outstanding}} = \frac{33{,}813}{230} = 147.01$$

**34.** B is correct.

$$\text{FCFE} \, (000) = \text{CFO} - \text{FCInv} + \text{Net Borrowing} = 2{,}000 - 320$$
$$+ \, (-750) = 930$$

$$\text{FCFE}_1 \, (000) = \text{FCFE}_0 \times (1 + g) = 930 \times (1.025) = 953.25$$

$$\text{Equity value} \, (000) = \frac{FCFE_1}{r - g} = \frac{953.25}{(0.1025 - 0.025)} = 12{,}300$$

Equity value per share = 12,300/230 = 53.47

**35.** B is correct. An investor purchasing a small ownership share does not have the ability to meaningfully influence the timing or magnitude of the distribution of the company's cash to shareholders. That perspective is the one taken in applying a dividend discount model. Free cash flow to equity also represents cash flow that can be redeployed outside of the company without affecting the company's capital investments. A controlling equity interest can effect such a redeployment. As a result, free cash flow valuation is appropriate for investors who want to take a control perspective. In this case, the DDM would be inappropriate because Simon plans to acquire control.

# SOLUTIONS FOR READING 43

**1. A.** Normal EPS is the level of earnings per share that the company could currently achieve under mid-cyclical conditions.

**B.** Averaging EPS over the 1997–2000 period, we find that ($2.55 + $2.13 + $0.23 + $1.45)/4 = $1.59. According to the method of historical average EPS, SII's normal EPS is $1.59. The P/E based on this estimate is $57.98/1.59 = 36.5.

**C.** Averaging ROE over the 1997–2000 period, we find that (0.218 + 0.163 + 0.016 + 0.089)/4 = 0.1215. For current BVPS, we use the estimated value of $19.20. According to the method of average ROE, we have 0.1215 × $19.20 = $2.33 as normal EPS. The P/E based on this estimate is $57.98/$2.33 = 24.9.

**2. A.** The analyst can rank the two stocks by earnings yield (E/P). Whether EPS is positive or negative, a lower E/P reflects a richer valuation and a ranking from high to low E/P has a meaningful interpretation.

In some cases, an analyst might handle negative EPS by using normal EPS in its place. Neither business, however, has a history of profitability. When year-ahead EPS is expected to be positive, leading P/E is positive. Thus the use of leading P/Es sometimes addresses the problem of trailing negative EPS. Leading P/E is not meaningful in this case, however, because next year's earnings are expected to be negative.

**B.** Hand has an E/P of −0.100, and Somersault has an E/P of 0.125. A higher earnings yield has a similar interpretation to a lower P/E, and Hand appears to be relatively undervalued. The difference in earnings yield cannot be explained by differences in sales growth forecasts. In fact, Hand has a higher expected sales growth rate than Somersault. Therefore, the analyst should recommend Hand.

**3. A.** Because investing looks to the future, analysts often feature leading P/E when earnings forecasts are available, as they are here. But a specific reason to use leading P/Es based on the facts given is that RUF had some unusual items affecting EPS for 2000. The data to make appropriate adjustments to RUF's 2000 EPS are not given. In summary, Stewart should use leading P/Es.

**B.** Because RUF has a complex capital structure, the P/Es of the two companies must be compared on the basis of diluted EPS.

> For HS: leading P/E = $44/2.20 = 20
> For RUF: leading P/E per diluted share
> = $22.50/(30,000,000/33,333,333) = 25

Therefore, HS has the more attractive valuation at present. The problem illustrates some of the considerations that should be taken into account in using the P/Es and the method of comparables.

**4. A.** Your conclusion may be in error because of the following:

▶ The peer group stocks themselves may be overvalued. Stated another way, the mean P/E of 18 may be too high in terms of intrinsic value. If that is the case, using 18 as a multiplier of the stock's expected EPS will lead to an estimate of stock value in excess of intrinsic value.

▶ The stock's fundamentals may differ from those of the mean food processing industry stock. For example, if the stock's expected growth rate is lower than the mean industry growth rate and its risk is higher than the mean, the stock may deserve a lower P/E than the mean.

In addition, mean P/E may be influenced by outliers.

**B.** The following evidence supports the original conclusion:

▶ Evidence that stocks in the industry are at least on average fairly valued (that stock prices reflect fundamentals).

▶ Evidence that no significant differences exist in the fundamental drivers of P/E for comparing the stock with the average industry stock.

**5. A.** Yardeni's model uses corporate, rather than U.S. government, bond yields and incorporates an estimate of earnings growth to arrive at an estimate of the fair value of stock market.

**B.** In principle, the use of any of this readings price multiples for valuation is vulnerable to this problem in comparing a company's characteristics to the overall market. If the stock market is overvalued, an asset that appears to be comparably valued may also be overvalued.

**6. A.** The formula for calculating P/E for a stable-growth company is the payout ratio divided by the difference between the required rate of return and the growth rate of dividends. If the P/E is being calculated on trailing earnings (Year 0), the payout ratio is increased by the growth rate.

P/E based on trailing earnings:
$$P/E = [\text{Payout ratio } (1 + g)]/(r - g)$$
$$= (0.30 \; 3 \times 1.13)/(0.14 - 0.13) = 33.9$$

P/E based on next year's earnings:
$$P/E = \text{Payout ratio}/(r - g)$$
$$= 0.30/(0.14 - 0.13) = 30$$

**B.**

| Fundamental Factor | Effect on P/E | Explanation (Not Required in Question) |
|---|---|---|
| The risk (beta) of Sundanci increases substantially. | Decrease | P/E is a decreasing function of risk—as risk increases, the P/E decreases. Increases in the risk of Sundanci stock would be expected to lower the P/E. |
| The estimated growth rate of Sundanci's earnings and dividends increases. | Increase | P/E is an increasing function of the growth rate of the company—the higher the expected growth the higher the P/E. Sundanci would command a higher P/E if analysts increase the expected growth rate. |
| The market risk premium increases. | Decrease | P/E is a decreasing function of the market risk premium. An increased market risk premium would increase the required rate of return, lowering the price of a stock relative to its earnings. A higher market risk premium would be expected to lower Sundanci's P/E. |

**7. A.** We would expect the trailing P/E accorded to CSG to increase to 13.25 as anticipated by Yu. The colleague is referring to the sustainable growth rate expression $g = b \times \text{ROE}$. The colleague's argument is that if ROE is level over the next several years, $b$ will need to increase (dividend payout will need to decrease) to support a higher (6 percent) growth rate. The idea is that if $b$ increases when growth becomes 6 percent, the P/E does not increase to 13.25. The argument concerning a change in dividend payout is incorrect. Any of the following arguments may be made:

- ▶ Although ROE is expected to be flat only for several years, long-term ROE is the proper value to use in the sustainable growth rate expression.

- ▶ If $b$ actually increases, $g$ will increase above 6 percent, offsetting the effect of $b$.

- ▶ The sustainable growth rate expression assumes no external equity financing and keeping the capital structure constant. CSG can borrow, either short term while ROE is flat or even long term (possibly increasing debt's weight in the capital structure) to fund this growth. The company can also issue new stock. The sustainable growth rate formula cannot realistically serve as a basis to predict a cut in dividends.

- ▶ Dividend payout, which is a discretionary decision of the board of directors, is not an economic fundamental. Investors look to the underlying cash flow of the business in valuation.

**B.** Because Yu is correct, CSG should be added to the focus list.

**8. A.** $V_n$ = Benchmark value of P/E $\times E_n$ = 12 $\times$ \$3.00 = \$36.0

**B.** In the sustainable growth rate expression $g = b \times \text{ROE}$, we can use $(1 - 0.45) = 0.55 = b$, and ROE = 0.10 (the industry average), obtaining $0.55 \times 0.10 = 0.055$. Given the required rate of return of 0.09, we obtain the estimate \$3.00(0.45) (1.055)/(0.09 − 0.055) = \$40.69. In this case the Gordon growth model estimate of terminal value is higher than the estimate based on multiples. The two estimates may differ for a number of reasons, including the sensitivity of the Gordon growth model to the values of inputs.

**9.** Although the measurement of book value has a number of widely recognized shortcomings, it can still be applied fruitfully in several categories of circumstances:

- ▶ The company is not expected to continue as a going concern. When a company is likely to be liquidated (so that ongoing earnings and cash flow are not relevant) the value of its assets less its liabilities is of utmost importance. Naturally, the analyst must establish the fair value of these assets.

- ▶ The company is composed mainly of liquid assets, such as finance, investment, insurance, and banking institutions.

- ▶ The company's EPS is highly variable or negative.

**10. A.** Avtech: P/S = (\$10 price per share)/[(\$1 billion sales)/(20 million shares)] = \$10/(\$1,000,000,000/20,000,000) = 0.2

Target: P/S = (\$20 price per share)/[(\$1.6 billion sales)/(30 million shares)] = 20/(\$1,600,000,000/\$30,000,000) = 0.375

Avtech has a more attractive valuation based on its lower P/S but comparable profit margins.

**B.** One advantage of P/S over P/E is that companies' accounting decisions can have a much greater impact on reported earnings than they are likely to have on reported sales. Although companies are able to make a number of legitimate business and accounting decisions that affect earnings, their discretion over reported sales (revenue recognition) is more limited.

**11. A.** The P/Es are

| | |
|---|---|
| Hormel | $25.70/1.30 = 19.8$ |
| Tyson | $11.77/0.40 = 29.4$ |
| IBP | $23.65/1.14 = 20.7$ |
| Smithfield | $24.61/2.31 = 10.7$ |

Sales per share are found by dividing sales by shares outstanding. Dividing this into the share price gives the P/Ss:

| | |
|---|---|
| Hormel | $25.70/(4,124/138.923) = 25.70/29.69 = 0.866$ |
| Tyson | $11.77/(10,751/220.662) = 11.77/48.72 = 0.242$ |
| IBP | $23.65/(17,388/108.170) = 23.65/160.75 = 0.147$ |
| Smithfield | $24.61/(6,354/103.803) = 24.61/61.21 = 0.402$ |

**B.** If we rank the stocks by P/S from highest to lowest, we have

| | P/S | Profit Margin |
|---|---|---|
| Hormel | 0.866 | 4.41% |
| Smithfield | 0.402 | 3.99% |
| Tyson | 0.242 | 0.82% |
| IBP | 0.147 | 0.70% |

The differences in P/S appear to be explained, at least in part, by differences in cost structure as measured by profit margin.

**12.** For companies in the industry described, P/S would be superior to either of the other two ratios. Among other considerations, P/S is:

▶ More useful in valuing companies with negative earnings.

▶ Better able to compare companies in different countries that are likely to use different accounting standards (a consequence of the multinational nature of the industry).

▶ Less subject to manipulation (i.e., managing earnings by management, a frequent consequence when companies are in a cyclical low and likely to report losses).

▶ Not as volatile as P/E multiples and hence may be more reliable for use in valuation.

**13. A.** Using the CAPM, the required rate of return is $4.9\% + 1.2 \times 5.5\% = 11.5\%$.

**B.** The dividend payout ratio is \$0.64/\$1.36 = 0.47. The justified values for the three valuation ratios should be

$$\frac{P_0}{E_0} = \frac{(1 - b) \times (1 + g)}{r - g} = \frac{0.47 \times 1.09}{0.115 - 0.09} = \frac{0.5123}{0.025} = 20.5$$

$$\frac{P_0}{B_0} = \frac{\text{ROE} - g}{r - g} = \frac{0.27 - 0.09}{0.115 - 0.09} = \frac{0.18}{0.025} = 7.2$$

$$\frac{P_0}{S_0} = \frac{PM \times (1 - b) \times (1 + g)}{r - g} = \frac{0.109 \times 0.47 \times 1.09}{0.115 - 0.09}$$

$$= \frac{0.05584}{0.025} = 2.2$$

**C.** The justified P/E is lower than the trailing P/E (20.5 versus 28.3), the justified P/B is higher than actual P/B (7.2 versus 7.1), and the justified P/S is lower than the actual P/S (2.2 versus 2.9). Therefore, based on P/E and P/S, GE appears to be over-valued but, based on P/B, appears to be slightly undervalued.

**14. A.** EBITDA = Net income (from continuing operations) + Interest expense + Taxes + Depreciation + Amortization

| | |
|---|---|
| EBITDA for RGI | = €49.5 million + €3 million + €2 million + €8 million = €62.5 million |
| Per-share EBITDA | = (€62.5 million)/(5 million shares) = €12.5 |
| P/EBITDA for RG | = €150/€12.5 = 12 |
| EBITDA for NCI | = €8 million + €5 million + €3 million + €4 million = €20 million |
| Per-share EBITDA | = (€20 million)/(2 million shares) = €10 |
| P/EBITDA for NCI | = €100/€10 = 10 |

**B.** Market value of equity for RGI = €150 × 5 million = €750 million

Market value of debt for RGI = €50
Total market value of RGI = €750 million + €50 = €800 million
Enterprise value (EV) = €800 million − €5 million (cash and investments) = €795 million

Now we divide EV by total (as opposed to per-share) EBITDA:

▶ EV/EBITDA for RGI = (€795 million)/(€62.5 million) = 12.72

Market value of equity for NCI = €100 × 2 million = €200 million
Market value of debt for NCI = €100
Total market value of NCI = €200 million + €100 = €300 million
Enterprise value (EV) = €300 million − €2 million (cash and investments) = €298 million

Now we divide EV by total (as opposed to per-share) EBITDA:

▶ EV/EBITDA for NCI = (€298 million)/(€20 million) = 14.9

C. Zaldys should select RGI as relatively undervalued.

First, it is correct that NCI *appears* to be relatively undervalued based on P/EBITDA, because NCI has a lower P/EBITDA multiple:
- ▶ P/EBITDA = €150/€12.5 = 12 for RGI
- ▶ P/EBITDA = €100/€10 = 10 for NCI

RGI is relatively undervalued based on EV/EBITDA, however, because RGI has the lower EV/EBITDA multiple:
- ▶ EV/EBITDA = (€795 million)/(€62.5 million) = 12.72 for RGI
- ▶ EV/EBITDA = (€298 million)/(€20 million) = 14.9 for NCI

EBITDA is a pre-interest flow; therefore, it is a flow to both debt and equity and the EV/EBITDA multiple is more appropriate than the P/EBITDA multiple. Zaldys would rely on EV/EBITDA to reach his decision when the two ratios conflicted. Note that P/EBITDA does not take into account differences in the use of financial leverage. Substantial differences in leverage exist in this case (NCI uses much more debt), so the preference for EV/EBITDA over P/EBITDA is increased.

15. The major concepts are as follows:

- ▶ EPS plus per-share depreciation, amortization, and depletion (CF)

  *Limitation:* Ignores changes in working capital and noncash revenue. Not a free cash flow concept.

- ▶ Cash flow from operations (CFO)

  *Limitation:* Not a free cash flow concept, so not directly linked to theory.

- ▶ Free cash flow to equity (FCFE)

  *Limitation:* Often more variable and more frequently negative than other cash flow concepts.

- ▶ Earnings before interest, taxes, depreciation, and amortization (EBITDA)

  *Limitation:* Ignores changes in working capital and noncash revenue. Not a free cash flow concept. Relative to its use in P/EBITDA, EBITDA is mismatched with the numerator because it is a pre-interest concept.

16. MAT Technology is relatively undervalued compared with DriveMed based on a P/FCFE multiple that is 34 percent the size of DriveMed's FCFE multiple (15.6/46 = 0.34, or 34%). The only comparison slightly in DriveMed's favor, or approximately equal, is that based on P/CF (12.8 for DriveMed versus 13.0 for MAT Technology). However, FCFE is more strongly grounded in valuation theory than P/CF. Because DriveMed and MAT Technology's expenditures in fixed capital and working capital during the previous year reflected anticipated average expenditures over the foreseeable horizon, we have additional confidence with the P/FCFE comparison.

17. A. Relative strength is based strictly on price movement (a technical indicator). As used by Westard, the comparison is between the returns on HCI and the returns on the S&P 500. In contrast, the price-multiple approaches are based on the relationship of current price not to past prices but to some measure of value such as EPS, book value, sales, or cash flow.

   B. Only the reference to the P/E in relationship to the pending patent applications in Westard's recommendation is consistent with the company's value orientation, because it addresses HCI's P/E in relationship to expected future earnings.

18. **A.** The most restrictive criterion as judged by the number of stocks meeting it is the dividend yield criterion, which results in only 10 eligible investments. The screen strongly emphasizes dividend yield as a valuation indicator.

    **B.** The screen may be too narrowly focused on dividend yield. It did not include variables related to expected growth, required rate of return or risk, or financial strength.

    **C.** The screen results in a very concentrated portfolio. Except for Eastman Kodak, the companies are all utilities, which typically pay high dividends. They belong to a very small segment of the investment universe and would constitute a narrowly focused and non-diversified portfolio.

19. A is correct. Tan's use of the method of comparables to value Diamondback by comparing Diamondback's price multiples with those of comparable peer companies is consistent with the law of one price.

20. B is correct. This is one of the rationales for using the P/E multiple, while both A and C are criticisms of using the P/E multiple.

21. C is correct. Peer 4 has the lowest leading PEG. PEG = Price ÷ EPS ÷ Expected growth rate:

| | Price | Next 4 Quarters EPS | Leading P/E | Expected Growth | Leading PEG |
|---|---|---|---|---|---|
| Peer 1 | $30 | 1.70 | 17.65 | 10 | 1.765 |
| Peer 2 | $26 | 1.50 | 17.33 | 16 | 1.083 |
| Peer 3 | $70 | 4.00 | 17.50 | 9 | 1.944 |
| Peer 4 | $18 | 1.15 | 15.65 | 15 | 1.043 |

22. C is correct.

    Normalized EPS = Average ROE × Current book value

    The average ROE over 2000–2004 is:

    $(10.77\% + 8.20\% + 4.22\% + 8.25\% + 16.4\%)/5 = 9.568\%$. 9.57% was given in the problem.
    Normalized EPS = 9.57% × $13.50 = $1.29

23. B is correct. The justified P/S ratio is

$$\frac{P_0}{S_0} = \frac{(E_0/S_0)(1-b)(1+g)}{r-g} = \frac{(0.06)(0.40)(1.06)}{0.10 - 0.06} = 0.636$$

24. A is correct. This question is based on the earlier reading, on equity: concepts and techniques. The formula for the prospective (leading) intrinsic $P_0/E_1$ is $P/E = 1/[\rho + (1 - \lambda)I]$ where $I$ is inflation, $\lambda$ is the inflation passthrough rate, and $\rho$ is the real required rate of return. Therefore,

$$P_0/E_1 = 1/[0.06 + (1 - 0.60)0.04] = 13.16$$

The P/E for a firm with 0% passthrough (real earnings declining) would be $1/0.10 = 10\times$. The P/E for a firm with a 100% passthrough (real earnings constant) would be $1/0.06 = 16.67 \times$. The correct answer of 13.16 is the only choice between 10 and 16.67.

## SOLUTIONS FOR READING 45

**1.** Yes, VIM earned a positive residual income of $8,000:

| | | |
|---|---|---|
| EBIT | $ 300,000 | |
| Interest | 120,000 | ($2,000,000 × 6%) |
| Pretax income | $180,000 | |
| Tax expense | 72,000 | |
| Net income | $108,000 | |

$$\text{Equity charge} = \text{Equity capital} \times \text{Required return on equity}$$
$$= (1/3)(\$3,000,000) \times 0.10$$
$$= \$1,000,000 \times 0.10 = \$100,000$$

$$\text{Residual income} = \text{Net income} - \text{Equity charge}$$
$$= \$108,000 - \$100,000 = \$8,000$$

**2.** According to the residual income model, the intrinsic value of a share of common stock equals book value per share plus the present value of expected future per-share residual income. Book value per share was given as $20. Noting that debt is $(2/3)(\$3,000,000) = \$2,000,000$ so that interest is $\$2,000,000 \times 6\% = \$120,000$, we find that VIM has residual income of $8,000 calculated (as in Problem 1) as follows:

$$\text{Residual income} = \text{Net income} - \text{Equity charge}$$
$$= [(\text{EBIT} - \text{Interest})(1 - \text{Tax rate})]$$
$$\quad - [(\text{Equity capital})(\text{Required return on equity})]$$
$$= [(\$300,000 - \$120,000)(1 - 0.40)]$$
$$\quad - [(\$1,000,000)(0.10)]$$
$$= \$108,000 - \$100,000$$
$$= \$8,000$$

Therefore, residual income per share is $8,000/50,000 shares = $0.16 per share. Because EBIT is expected to continue at the current level indefinitely, we treat the expected per-share residual income of $0.16 as a perpetuity. The present value of $0.16 discounted at the required return on equity of 10 percent, the present value of the residual income is $1.60 (= $0.16/0.10).

$$\text{Intrinsic value} = \text{Book value per share} + \text{PV of expected future}$$
$$\text{per-share residual income}$$
$$= \$20 + \$1.60 = \$21.60$$

**3.** With $g = b \times \text{ROE} = (1 - 0.80)(0.15) = (0.20)(0.15) = 0.03$,

$$\text{P/B} = (\text{ROE} - g)/(r - g)$$
$$= (0.15 - 0.03)/(0.12 - 0.03)$$
$$= 0.12/0.09 = 1.33$$

or

$$\text{P/B} = 1 + (\text{ROE} - r)/(r - g)$$
$$= 1 + (0.15 - 0.12)/(0.12 - 0.03)$$
$$= 1.33$$

**4.** In this problem (unlike Problems 1 and 2 above), interest expense has already been deducted in arriving at NMP's pretax income of $5.1 million. Therefore,

Net income    $=$ Pretax income $\times$ (1 − Tax rate)
$=$ $5.1 million $\times$ (1 − 0.4)
$=$ $5.1 $\times$ 0.6 $=$ $3.06 million

Equity charge: Total equity $\times$ Cost of equity capital
$=$ (0.1 $\times$ $450 million) $\times$ 12%
$=$ $45 million $\times$ 0.12 $=$ $5,400,000

Residual income $=$ Net income − Equity charge
$=$ $3,060,000 − $5,400,000 $=$ −$2,340,000

NMP had negative residual income of −$2,340,000.

**5.** To achieve a positive residual income, a company's net operating profit after taxes as a percentage of its total assets can be compared with the weighted-average cost of its capital. For SWI:

NOPAT/Assets    $=$ €10 million/€100 million $=$ 10%
WACC    $=$ (Percent of debt) $\times$ (After-tax cost of debt)
$+$ (Percent of equity) $\times$ (Cost of equity)
$=$ (0.5)(0.09) (0.6) $+$ (0.5)(0.12)
$=$ (0.5)(0.054) $+$ (0.5)(0.12) $=$ 0.027 $+$ 0.06 $=$ 0.087
$=$ 8.7%

Therefore, SWI's residual income was positive. Specifically, residual income equals (0.10 − 0.087) $\times$ €100 million $=$ €1.3 million.

**6. A.** EVA $=$ NOPAT − WACC $\times$ (Beginning book value of assets)
$=$ $100 − (11%) $\times$ ($200 $+$ $300) − $100 − (11%)($500) $=$ $45

**B.** $RI_t = E_t - rB_{t-1}$
$=$ €5.00 − (11%)(€30.00) $=$ €5.00 − €3.30 $=$ €1.70

**C.** $RI_t = (ROE_t - r) \times B_{t-1}$
$=$ (18%  12%) $\times$ (€30) − €1.80

**7. A.** Economic value added $=$ Net operating profit after taxes − (Cost of capital $\times$ Total capital) $=$ $100 million − (14% $\times$ $700 million) $=$ $2 million. In the absence of information that would be required to calculate the weighted average cost of debt and equity, and given that Sundanci has no long-term debt, the only capital cost used is the required rate of return on equity of 14 percent.

**B.** Market value added $=$ Market value of capital − Total capital
$26 stock price $\times$ 84 million shares − $700 million $=$ $1.48 billion

**8. A.** Because the dividend is a perpetuity, the no-growth form of the DDM is applied as follows:

$V_0 = D/r$
$=$ $0.60/0.12 $=$ $5 per share

**B.** According to the residual income model, $V_0$ = Book value per share + Present value of expected future per-share residual income.

Residual income is calculated as:

$$RI_t = E - rB_{t-1}$$
$$= \$0.60 - (0.12)(\$6) = -\$0.12$$

Present value of perpetual stream of residual income is calculated as:

$$RI_t/r = -\$0.12/0.12 = -\$1.00$$

The value is calculated as:

$$V_0 = \$6.00 - \$1.00 = \$5.00 \text{ per share}$$

**9. A.** According to the DDM, $V_0 = D/r$ for a no-growth company.

$$V_0 = \$2.00/0.125 = \$16 \text{ per share}$$

**B.** Under the residual income model, $V_0 = B_0$ + Present value of expected future per-share residual income.

Residual income is calculated as:

$$RI_t = E - rB_{t-1}$$
$$= \$2 - (0.125)(\$10) = \$0.75$$

Present value of stream of residual income is calculated as:

$$RI_t/r = 0.75/0.125 = \$6$$

The value is calculated as:

$$V_0 = \$10 + \$6 = \$16 \text{ per share}$$

**10. A.** $V_0$ = Present value of the future dividends
$$= \$2/1.10 + \$2.50/(1.1)^2 + \$20.50/(1.1)^3$$
$$= \$1.818 + \$2.066 + \$15.402 = \$19.286$$

**B.** The book values and residual incomes for the next three years are as follows:

| Year | 1 | 2 | 3 |
|---|---|---|---|
| Beginning book value | $8.00 | $10.00 | $12.50 |
| Retained earnings (Net income − Dividends) | 2.00 | 2.50 | (12.50) |
| Ending book value | $10.00 | $12.50 | $0.00 |
| Net income | $4.00 | $5.00 | $8.00 |
| Less equity charge ($r \times$ Book value) | 0.80 | 1.00 | 1.25 |
| Residual income | $ 3.20 | $4.00 | $ 6.75 |

Under the residual income model,

$V_0 = B_0$ + Present value of expected future per-share residual income.

$V_0 = \$8.00 + \$3.20/1.1 + \$4.00/(1.1)^2 + \$6.75/(1.1)^3$

$V_0 = 8.00 + \$2.909 + \$3.306 + \$5.071 = \$19.286$

C.

| Year | 1 | 2 | 3 |
|---|---|---|---|
| Net income (NI) | 4.00 | 5.00 | 8.00 |
| Beginning book value (BV) | 8.00 | 10.00 | 12.50 |
| Return on equity (ROE) = NI/BV | 50% | 50% | 64% |
| ROE − $r$ | 40% | 40% | 54% |
| Residual income (ROE − $r$) × BV | 3.20 | 4.00 | 6.75 |

Under the residual income model,

$V_0 = B_0$ + Present value of expected future per-share residual income.

$V_0 = \$8.00 + \$3.20/1.1 + \$4.00/(1.1)^2 + \$6.75/(1.1)^3$

$V_0 = 8.00 + \$2.909 + \$3.306 + \$5.071 = \$19.286$

*Note*: Because the residual incomes for each year are necessarily the same in Parts B and C, the results for stock valuation are identical.

11.

| Year | 2008 | 2009 | 2012 |
|---|---|---|---|
| Beginning book value | 30.00 | 33.00 | 43.92 |
| Net income = ROE × Book value | 4.50 | 4.95 | 6.59 |
| Dividends = Payout × Net income | 1.50 | 1.65 | 2.20 |
| Equity charge ($r$ × Book value) | 3.60 | 3.96 | 5.27 |
| Residual income = Net income − Equity charge | 0.90 | 0.99 | 1.32 |
| Ending book value | 33.00 | 36.30 | 48.32 |

The table shows that residual income in Year 2008 is $0.90, which equals Beginning book value × (ROE − $r$) = $30 × (0.15 − 0.12) = $0.90. The Year 2009 column shows that residual income grew by 10 percent to $0.99, which follows from the fact that growth in residual income relates directly to the growth in net income as this example is configured. When both net income and dividends are a function of book value and return on equity is constant, then growth can be predicted from $g$ = (ROE)(1 − Dividend payout ratio). In this case, $g = 0.15 × (1 − 0.333) = 0.10$ or 10 percent. Net income and residual income will grow by 10 percent annually.

Therefore, residual income in Year 2012 = (Residual income in Year 2008) × $(1.1)^4 = 0.90 × 1.4641 = \$1.32$.

12. When items such as changes in the value of available-for-sale securities bypass the income statement, they are generally assumed to be non-operating items that will fluctuate from year to year, although averaging to zero over a period of years. The evidence suggests, however, that changes in the value of available-for-sale securities are not averaging to zero but are

persistently negative. Furthermore, these losses are bypassing the income statement. It appears that the company is either making an inaccurate assumption or misleading investors in one way or another. Accordingly, Kent might adjust LE's income downward by the amount of loss for other comprehensive income for each of those years. ROE would then decline commensurately. LE's book value would *not* be misstated because the decline in the value of these securities was already recognized and appears in the shareholders' equity account "Accumulated Other Comprehensive Income."

**13.** $V_0 = B_0 + (\text{ROE} - r) B_0 / (r - g)$
$= \$20 + (0.18 - 0.14)(\$20)/(0.14 - 0.10)$
$= \$20 + \$20 = \$40$

Given the current market price is \$35 and the estimated value is \$40, Simms will probably conclude that the shares are somewhat undervalued.

**14.** $V_0 = B_0 + (\text{ROE} - r) B_0 / (r - g)$
$= \$30 + (0.15 - 0.12)(\$30)/(0.12 - 0.10)$
$= \$30 + \$45 = \$75 \text{ per share}$

**15.**

| Year | Net Income (Projected) | Ending Book Value | ROE (%) | Equity Charge (in Currency) | Residual Income | PV of RI |
|------|------------------------|-------------------|---------|-----------------------------|-----------------|----------|
| 2007 |                        | 10.00             |         |                             |                 |          |
| 2008 | 1.50                   | 11.50             | 15      | 1.00                        | 0.50            | 0.45     |
| 2009 | 1.73                   | 13.23             | 15      | 1.15                        | 0.58            | 0.48     |
| 2010 | 1.99                   | 15.22             | 15      | 1.32                        | 0.67            | 0.50     |
| 2011 | 2.29                   | 17.51             | 15      | 1.52                        | 0.77            | 0.53     |
| 2012 | 2.63                   | 20.14             | 15      | 1.75                        | 0.88            | 0.55     |
|      |                        |                   |         |                             |                 | $2.51    |

Using the finite horizon form of residual income valuation,

$V_0 = B_0$ + Sum of discounted RIs + Premium (also discounted to present)
$= \$10 + \$2.51 + (0.20)(20.14)/(1.10)^5$
$= \$10 + \$2.51 + \$2.50 = \$15.01$

**16.** The present value of the terminal value would then be

$\text{RI}_T / (1 + r - \omega)(1 + r)^{T-1} = 48.86/(1 + 0.1433 - 0.90)(1.1433)^{20}$
$= 13.79$

Total value is $59.18 + 13.79 = \text{TWD}72.97$. The analyst would again conclude that TSM's shares are overvalued.

**17.** The value of TSM for the forecast period would be the sum of the beginning book value, the present value of residual income, and the terminal value.

| Year | Net Income (Projected) | Book Value | Forecast ROE (Beg. Equity, %) | Cost of Equity (%) | Equity Charge TWD | Residual Income | PV of RI | Total |
|---|---|---|---|---|---|---|---|---|
| 2008 | | 16.47 | | | | | 16.47 | 62.11 |
| 2009 | 2.07 | 18.54 | 12.57 | 14.33 | 2.36 | −0.29 | (0.25) | |
| 2010 | 4.81 | 23.35 | 25.94 | 14.33 | 2.66 | 2.15 | 1.65 | |
| 2011 | 5.84 | 29.19 | 25.00 | 14.33 | 3.35 | 2.49 | 1.67 | |
| 2012 | 7.30 | 36.48 | 25.00 | 14.33 | 4.18 | 3.11 | 1.82 | |
| 2013 | 9.12 | 45.61 | 25.00 | 14.33 | 5.23 | 3.89 | 1.99 | |
| 2014 | 11.40 | 57.01 | 25.00 | 14.33 | 6.54 | 4.87 | 2.18 | |
| 2015 | 14.25 | 71.26 | 25.00 | 14.33 | 8.17 | 6.08 | 2.38 | |
| 2016 | 17.81 | 89.07 | 25.00 | 14.33 | 10.21 | 7.60 | 2.60 | |
| 2017 | 22.27 | 111.34 | 25.00 | 14.33 | 12.76 | 9.50 | 2.85 | |
| 2018 | 27.84 | 139.18 | 25.00 | 14.33 | 15.96 | 11.88 | 3.11 | |
| 2019 | 27.84 | 167.01 | 20.00 | 14.33 | 19.94 | 7.89 | 1.81 | |
| 2020 | 33.40 | 200.41 | 20.00 | 14.33 | 23.93 | 9.47 | 1.90 | |
| 2021 | 40.08 | 240.50 | 20.00 | 14.33 | 28.72 | 11.36 | 1.99 | |
| 2022 | 48.10 | 288.60 | 20.00 | 14.33 | 34.46 | 13.64 | 2.09 | |
| 2023 | 57.72 | 346.32 | 20.00 | 14.33 | 41.36 | 16.36 | 2.20 | |
| 2024 | 69.26 | 415.58 | 20.00 | 14.33 | 49.63 | 19.64 | 2.30 | |
| 2025 | 83.12 | 498.70 | 20.00 | 14.33 | 59.55 | 23.56 | 2.42 | |
| 2026 | 99.74 | 598.43 | 20.00 | 14.33 | 71.46 | 28.28 | 2.54 | |
| 2027 | 119.69 | 718.12 | 20.00 | 14.33 | 85.76 | 33.93 | 2.66 | |
| 2028 | 143.62 | 861.75 | 20.00 | 14.33 | 102.91 | 40.72 | 2.80 | |
| 2029 | 172.35 | 1034.10 | 20.00 | 14.33 | 123.49 | 48.86 | 2.93 | |
| 2030 | 206.82 | 1240.91 | 20.00 | 14.33 | 148.19 | 58.63 | | |

The present value of the terminal value would be

$$\text{RI}_T/(1 + r - \omega)(1 + r)^{T-1} = 58.63/(1 + 0.1433 - 0.90)(1.1433)^{21}$$
$$= 14.47$$

Total value is 62.11 + 14.47 = TWD76.58.

Based on a current price of TWD81, the analyst would again conclude that TSM's shares are overvalued.

**18. A.** Columns (a) through (d) in the table below show calculations for beginning book value, net income, dividends, and ending book value.

| Year | (a) Beginning Book Value | (b) Net Income | (c) Dividends | (d) Ending Book Value | (e) Residual Income | (f) PV of RI |
|---|---|---|---|---|---|---|
| 1 | 9.620 | 2.116 | 0.635 | 11.101 | 1.318 | 1.217 |
| 2 | 11.101 | 2.442 | 0.733 | 12.811 | 1.521 | 1.297 |
| 3 | 12.811 | 2.818 | 0.846 | 14.784 | 1.755 | 1.382 |
| 4 | 14.784 | 3.252 | 0.976 | 17.061 | 2.025 | 1.472 |
| 5 | 17.061 | 3.753 | 1.126 | 19.688 | 2.337 | 1.569 |
| 6 | 19.688 | 4.331 | 1.299 | 22.720 | 2.697 | 1.672 |
| 7 | 22.720 | 4.998 | 1.500 | 26.219 | 3.113 | 1.781 |
| 8 | 26.219 | 5.768 | 1.730 | 30.257 | 3.592 | 1.898 |
| Total | | | | | | 12.288 |

For each year above, net income is 22 percent of beginning book value. Dividends are 30 percent of net income. The ending book value equals the beginning book value plus net income minus dividends.

**B.** Column (e) shows Residual income, which equals Net income minus Cost of equity (%) times Beginning book value.

To find the cost of equity, using the CAPM:

$$r = R_F + \beta_i[E(R_M) - R_F] = 5\% + (0.60)(5.5\%) = 8.30\%$$

For Year 1 in the table above,

$$\begin{aligned} \text{Residual income} = \text{RI}_t &= E - rB_{t-1} \\ &= 2.116 - (8.30\%)(9.62) \\ &= 2.116 - 0.798 = \$1.318 \end{aligned}$$

This same calculation is repeated for Years 2 through 8.

The final column of the table, (f), gives the present value of the calculated residual income, discounted at 8.30 percent.

**C.** To find the stock value with the residual income method, we use the equation

$$V_0 = B_0 + \sum_{t=1}^{T} \frac{(E_t - rB_{t-1})}{(1 + r)^t} + \frac{P_T - B_T}{(1 + r)^T}$$

▶ In this equation, $B_0$ is the current book value per share of $9.62.
▶ The second term, the sum of the present values of the eight years' residual income is shown in the table above, $12.288.
▶ To estimate the final term, the present value of the excess of the terminal stock price over the terminal book value, use the assumption that the terminal stock price is assumed to be 3.0 times

the terminal book value. So, by assumption, the terminal stock price $P_T = 3.0(30.257) = \$90.771$. $P_T - B_T$ is $90.771 - 30.257 = \$60.514$, and the present value of this amount discounted at 8.30 percent for eight years is $31.976.

▶ Summing the relevant terms gives a stock price of $V_0 = 9.62 + 12.288 + 31.976 = \$53.884$.

**D.** The appropriate DDM expression expresses the value of the stock as the sum of the present value of the dividends plus the present value of the terminal value:

$$V_0 = \sum_{t=1}^{T} \frac{D_t}{(1 + r)^t} + \frac{P_T}{(1 + r)^T}$$

Discounting the dividends from the table shown in the solution to Part A above at 8.30 percent gives:

| Year | Dividend | PV of Dividend |
|------|----------|----------------|
| 1 | 0.635 | 0.586 |
| 2 | 0.733 | 0.625 |
| 3 | 0.846 | 0.666 |
| 4 | 0.976 | 0.709 |
| 5 | 1.126 | 0.756 |
| 6 | 1.299 | 0.805 |
| 7 | 1.500 | 0.858 |
| 8 | 1.730 | 0.914 |
| All | | 5.919 |

▶ The present value of the eight dividends is $5.92. The estimated terminal stock price, calculated in the solution to Part C above is $90.771, which equals $47.964 discounted at 8.30 percent for eight years.

▶ The value for the stock, the present value of the dividends plus the present value of the terminal stock price, is $V_0 = 5.92 + 47.964 = \$53.884$.

▶ The stock values estimated with the residual income model and the dividend discount model are identical. Because they are based on similar financial assumptions, this equivalency is expected. Even though the two models differ in their timing of the recognition of value, their final results are the same.

**19. A.** The justified P/B can be found with the following formula:

$$\frac{P_0}{B_0} = 1 + \frac{\text{ROE} - r}{r - g}$$

ROE is 20%, $g$ is 6%, and $r = R_F + \beta_i[E(R_M) - R_F] = 5\% + (0.80)(5.5\%) = 9.4\%$. Substituting in the values gives a justified P/B of

$$\frac{P_0}{B_0} = 1 + \frac{0.20 - 0.094}{0.094 - 0.06} = 4.12$$

The assumed parameters give a justified P/B of 4.12, slightly above the current P/B of 3.57.

**B.** To find the ROE that would result in a P/B of 3.57, we substitute 3.57, $r$, and $g$ into the following equation:

$$\frac{P_0}{B_0} = 1 + \frac{\text{ROE} - r}{r - g}$$

This yields

$$3.57 = 1 + \frac{\text{ROE} - 0.094}{0.094 - 0.06}$$

Solving for ROE, after several steps we finally derive a ROE of 0.18138 or 18.1 percent. This value of ROE is consistent with a P/B of 3.57.

**C.** To find the growth rate that would result in a P/B of 3.57, we use the expression given in Part B, solving for $g$ instead of ROE:

$$\frac{P_0}{B_0} = 1 + \frac{\text{ROE} - r}{r - g}$$

Substituting in the values, we have

$$3.57 = 1 + \frac{0.20 - 0.094}{0.094 - g}$$

Solving for $g$, after several steps we obtain a growth rate of 0.05275 or 5.3 percent. Assuming that the single-stage growth model is applicable to Boeing, the current P/B and current market price can be justified with values for ROE or $g$ that are not much different from our starting values of 20 percent and 6 percent, respectively.

**20.** C is correct. Residual models are least appropriate when significant departures from clean surplus accounting exist.

**21.** B is correct. Comprehensive income includes items that bypass the income statement. The change in book value fails to account for dividends and share repurchases.

**22.** A is correct.

Equity = $0.25 \times \$10,000,000 = \$2,500,000$
Net income = $\$560,000$
Equity charge = $12\% \times \$2,500,000 = \$300,000$
Residual income = $\$560,000 - \$300,000 = \$260,000$

**23.** B is correct.

$$V_0 = B_0 \times \left[1.0 + \frac{\text{ROE} - r}{r - g}\right] = 16 \times \left[1.0 + \frac{0.14 - 0.11}{0.11 - 0.05}\right]$$

$$= 16 \times (1.0 + 0.5) = \$24$$

**24.** B is correct. A terminal residual value of zero implies a zero premium over book value at the end of the forecast horizon. In such a case, when the premium over book value is insignificant, the terminal value equals book value at the end of the forecast horizon. However, the terminal value will continue to grow (unless dividend payout is 100%) because net income is positive and equal to the cost of equity.

**25.** B is correct. There will be no change to book value, but net income will have to be adjusted if the charge was included in operating income.

**26.** C is correct. Lowering the growth rate to 9% from 9.2% will result in a lower justified P/E where justified leading P/E = Payout/$(r - g)$. The original justified leading P/E = Payout/$(r - g)$ = 0.30/(0.112 − 0.092) = 15. New justified leading P/E = 0.30/(0.112 − 0.09) = 13.64 which is lower than 15. The other two changes (lowering the beta and lowering the equity risk premium) would result in a higher, not lower, P/E.

**27.** A is correct. EBITDA will overstate cash flows if working capital is growing.

**28.** A is correct.

Enterprise value:

| | |
|---|---|
| Market value of common stock | $150 million |
| + Market value of preferred stock | 0 |
| + Market value of debt | 50 million |
| − Cash and investments | (8) million |
| = Enterprise value | $192 million |

EBITDA is:

| | |
|---|---|
| Net income | $8 million |
| + taxes | 3 million |
| + interest | 4 million |
| + depreciation and amortization | 2 million |
| EBITDA | $17 million |

Enterprise value/EBITDA = $192/$17 = 11.29

**29.** C is correct.

Beginning book value $25

Residual income = Earnings minus the required return times beginning book value.

Year 1 projected earnings = $25 book value times ROE of 20% = $5.00

Year 1 beginning book value times required return = $25 times 12% = $3.00

Year 1 residual income $2.00 ($5−$3)

Ending book value $30 (beginning plus $5 or increase of 20%)

Year 2 projected income $30 times 20% = $6.00

Year 2 cost of equity $30 times 12% = $3.60

Year 2 residual income $2.40

**30.** C is correct. Terminal value is Residual income in year 6 / $(1 + r -$ Persistence factor) 62.21 (0.20 − 0.12) / (1 + 0.12 − 0.50) = $8.03

**31.** B is correct. EVA explicitly considers the cost of equity in addition to the cost of debt. Net income only considers the cost of debt.

| | | | |
|---|---|---|---|
| 4⅝ | 4¹¹/₁₆ | ⅜ | |
| 5½ | 5½ | − ⅞ | |
| 20⅝ | 2¹³/₁₆ | − ⅛ | |
| 17⅜ | 18⅛ | + ⅞ | |
| 6½ | 6½ | − ½ | |
| 7¼ | 3¹/₃₂ | − ⅛ | |
| 1 | 15/₁₆ | | |
| | 9/₁₆ | 9/₁₆ | |
| 7¹⁵/₁₆ | 7¹³/₁₆ | 7¹⁵/₁₆ | |
| 2⅝ | 2¹¹/₃₂ | 2½ + | |
| 2¾ | 2¼ | 2¼ | |
| 12¹/₁₆ | 11⅜ | 11¾ + | |
| 33¾ | 33 | 33⅛ − | |
| 25⅝ | 24⁹/₁₆ | 25⅛ + | |
| 12 | 11⅝ | 11⅞ + | |
| 10½ | 10½ | 10½ − | |
| 15⅞ | 15¹³/₁₆ | 15⅞ − | |
| 9¹/₁₆ | 8¼ | 8⅛ − | |
| 11¼ | 10⅛ | | |

**A priori probability** A probability based on logical analysis rather than on observation or personal judgment.

**Abandonment option** The ability to terminate a project at some future time if the financial results are disappointing.

**Abnormal earnings** See "*Residual income.*"

**Absolute dispersion** The amount of variability present without comparison to any reference point or benchmark.

**Absolute frequency** The number of observations in a given interval (for grouped data).

**Absolute valuation model** A model that specifies an asset's intrinsic value.

**Accelerated methods of depreciation** Depreciation methods that allocate a relatively large proportion of the cost of an asset to the early years of the asset's useful life.

**Account** With the accounting systems, a formal record of increases and decreases in a specific asset, liability, component of owners' equity, revenue, or expense.

**Account format** A method of presentation of accounting transactions in which effects on assets appear at the left and effects on liabilities and equity appear at the right of a central dividing line; also known as T-account format.

**Accounting estimates** Estimates of items such as the useful lives of assets, warranty costs, and the amount of uncollectible receivables.

**Accounting profit (income before taxes or pretax income)** Income as reported on the income statement, in accordance with prevailing accounting standards, before the provisions for income tax expense.

**Accounting risk** The risk associated with accounting standards that vary from country to country or with any uncertainty about how certain transactions should be recorded.

**Accounts payable** Amounts that a business owes to its vendors for goods and services that were purchased from them but which have not yet been paid.

**Accounts receivable turnover** Ratio of sales on credit to the average balance in accounts receivable.

**Accrual basis** Method of accounting in which the effect of transactions on financial condition and income are recorded when they occur, not when they are settled in cash.

**Accrued expenses (accrued liabilities)** Liabilities related to expenses that have been incurred but not yet paid as of the end of an accounting period—an example of an accrued expense is rent that has been incurred but not yet paid, resulting in a liability "rent payable."

**Accrued interest** Interest earned but not yet paid.

**Accumulated benefit obligation** Under U.S. GAAP, a measure used in estimating a defined-benefit pension plan's liabilities, defined as "the actuarial present value of benefits (whether vested or nonvested) attributed by the pension benefit formula to employee service rendered before a specified date and based on employee service and compensation (if applicable) prior to that date."

**Accumulated depreciation** An offset to property, plant, and equipment (PPE) reflecting the amount of the cost of PPE that has been allocated to current and previous accounting periods.

**Acquiring company, or acquirer** The company in a merger or acquisition that is acquiring the target.

**Acquisition** The purchase of some portion of one company by another; the purchase may be for assets, a definable segment of another entity, or the purchase of an entire company.

**Acquisition method** A method of accounting for a business combination where the acquirer is required to measure each identifiable asset and liability at fair value. This method was the result of a joint project of the IASB and FASB aiming at convergence in standards for the accounting of business combinations.

**Active factor risk** The contribution to active risk squared resulting from the portfolio's different-than-benchmark exposures relative to factors specified in the risk model.

**Active investment managers** Managers who hold portfolios that differ from their benchmark portfolio in an attempt to produce positive risk-adjusted returns.

**Active portfolio** In the context of the Treynor-Black model, the portfolio formed by mixing analyzed stocks of perceived nonzero alpha values. This portfolio is ultimately mixed with the passive market index portfolio.

**Active return** The return on a portfolio minus the return on the portfolio's benchmark.

**Active risk** The standard deviation of active returns.

**Active risk squared** The variance of active returns; active risk raised to the second power.

**Active specific risk or asset selection risk** The contribution to active risk squared resulting from the portfolio's active weights on individual assets as those weights interact with assets' residual risk.

**Active strategy** In reference to short-term cash management, an investment strategy characterized by monitoring and attempting to capitalize on market conditions to optimize the risk and return relationship of short-term investments.

**Activity ratios (asset utilization or operating efficiency ratios)** Ratios that measure how efficiently a company performs day-to-day tasks, such as the collection of receivables and management of inventory.

**Addition rule for probabilities** A principle stating that the probability that $A$ or $B$ occurs (both occur) equals the probability that $A$ occurs, plus the probability that $B$ occurs, minus the probability that both $A$ and $B$ occur.

**Add-on interest** A procedure for determining the interest on a bond or loan in which the interest is added onto the face value of a contract.

**Adjusted beta** Historical beta adjusted to reflect the tendency of beta to be mean reverting.

**Adjusted present value (APV)** As an approach to valuing a company, the sum of the value of the company, assuming no use of debt, and the net present value of any effects of debt on company value.

**Adjusted $R^2$** A measure of goodness-of-fit of a regression that is adjusted for degrees of freedom and hence does not automatically increase when another independent variable is added to a regression.

**After-tax cash flow (ATCF)** Net operating income less debt service and less taxes payable on income from operations.

**After-tax equity reversion (ATER)** Sales price less disposition costs, amortized mortgage loan balance, and capital gains taxes.

**Agency costs** Costs associated with the conflict of interest present when a company is managed by non-owners. Agency costs result from the inherent conflicts of interest between managers and equity owners.

**Agency costs of equity** The smaller the stake that managers have in the company, the less is their share in bearing the cost of excessive perquisite consumption or not giving their best efforts in running the company.

**Agency problem**, **or principal-agent problem** A conflict of interest that arises when the agent in an agency relationship has goals and incentives that differ from the principal to whom the agent owes a fiduciary duty.

**Agency relationships** An arrangement whereby someone, an agent, acts on behalf of another person, the principal.

**Aging schedule** A breakdown of accounts into categories of days outstanding.

**Allowance for bad debts** An offset to accounts receivable for the amount of accounts receivable that are estimated to be uncollectible.

**Alpha (or abnormal return)** The return on an asset in excess of the asset's required rate of return; the risk-adjusted return.

**Alternative hypothesis** The hypothesis accepted when the null hypothesis is rejected.

**American option** An option contract that can be exercised at any time until its expiration date.

**Amortization** The process of allocating the cost of intangible long-term assets having a finite useful life to accounting periods; the allocation of the amount of a bond premium or discount to the periods remaining until bond maturity.

**Amortizing and accreting swaps** A swap in which the notional principal changes according to a formula related to changes in the underlying.

**Analysis of variance (ANOVA)** The analysis of the total variability of a dataset (such as observations on the dependent variable in a regression) into components representing different sources of variation; with reference to regression, ANOVA provides the inputs for an $F$-test of the significance of the regression as a whole.

**Annual percentage rate** The cost of borrowing expressed as a yearly rate.

**Annuity** A finite set of level sequential cash flows.

**Annuity due** An annuity having a first cash flow that is paid immediately.

**Anticipation stock** Excess inventory that is held in anticipation of increased demand, often because of seasonal patterns of demand.

**Antidilutive** With reference to a transaction or a security, one that would increase earnings per share (EPS) or result in EPS higher than the company's basic EPS—antidilutive securities are not included in the calculation of diluted EPS.

**Arbitrage** (1) The simultaneous purchase of an undervalued asset or portfolio and sale of an overvalued but equivalent asset or portfolio, in order to obtain a riskless profit on the price differential. Taking advantage of a market inefficiency in a risk-free manner. (2) A trading strategy designed to generate a guaranteed profit from a transaction that requires no capital commitment or risk bearing on the part of the trader. A simple example of an arbitrage trade would be the simultaneous purchase and sale of the same security in different markets at different prices. (3) The condition in a financial market in which equivalent assets or combinations of assets sell for two different prices, creating an opportunity to profit at no risk with no commitment of money. In a well-functioning financial market, few arbitrage opportunities are possible. (4) A risk-free operation that earns an expected positive net profit but requires no net investment of money.

**Arbitrage opportunity** An opportunity to conduct an arbitrage; an opportunity to earn an expected positive net profit without risk and with no net investment of money.

**Arbitrage portfolio** The portfolio that exploits an arbitrage opportunity.

**Arithmetic mean** The sum of the observations divided by the number of observations.

**Arrears swap** A type of interest rate swap in which the floating payment is set at the end of the period and the interest is paid at that same time.

**Asian call option** A European-style option with a value at maturity equal to the difference between the stock price at maturity and the average stock price during the life of the option, or $0, whichever is greater.

**Asset beta** The unlevered beta; reflects the business risk of the assets; the asset's systematic risk.

**Asset purchase** An acquisition in which the acquirer purchases the target company's assets and payment is made directly to the target company.

**Asset retirement obligations (AROs)** The fair value of the estimated costs to be incurred at the end of a tangible asset's service life. The fair value of the liability is determined on the basis of discounted cash flows.

**Assets** Resources controlled by an enterprise as a result of past events and from which future economic benefits to the enterprise are expected to flow.

**Asset-based loan** A loan that is secured with company assets.

**Asset-based valuation** An approach to valuing natural resource companies that estimates company value on the basis of the market value of the natural resources the company controls.

**Assignment of accounts receivable** The use of accounts receivable as collateral for a loan.

**Asymmetric information** The differential of information between corporate insiders and outsiders regarding the company's performance and prospects. Managers typically have more informa-

tion about the company's performance and prospects than owners and creditors.

**At the money** An option in which the underlying value equals the exercise price.

**Autocorrelation** The correlation of a time series with its own past values.

**Automated Clearing House** An electronic payment network available to businesses, individuals, and financial institutions in the United States, U.S. Territories, and Canada.

**Autoregressive (AR) model** A time series regressed on its own past values, in which the independent variable is a lagged value of the dependent variable.

**Available-for-sale investments** Debt and equity securities not classified as either held-to-maturity or held-for-trading securities. The investor is willing to sell but not actively planning to sell. In general, available-for-sale securities are reported at fair value on the balance sheet.

**Backtesting** With reference to portfolio strategies, the application of a strategy's portfolio selection rules to historical data to assess what would have been the strategy's historical performance.

**Backward integration** A merger involving the purchase of a target ahead of the acquirer in the value or production chain; for example, to acquire a supplier.

**Backwardation** A condition in the futures markets in which the benefits of holding an asset exceed the costs, leaving the futures price less than the spot price.

**Balance of payments accounts** A country's record of international trading, borrowing, and lending.

**Balance sheet (statement of financial position or statement of financial condition)** The financial statement that presents an entity's current financial position by disclosing resources the entity controls (its assets) and the claims on those resources (its liabilities and equity claims), as of a particular point in time (the date of the balance sheet).

**Balance sheet ratios** Financial ratios involving balance sheet items only.

**Balance-sheet-based accruals ratio** The difference between net operating assets at the end and the beginning of the period compared to the average net operating assets over the period.

**Balance-sheet-based aggregate accruals** The difference between net operating assets at the end and the beginning of the period.

**Band-of-investment method** A widely used approach to estimate an overall capitalization rate. It is based on the premise that debt and equity financing is typically involved in a real estate transaction.

**Bank discount basis**   A quoting convention that annualizes, on a 360-day year, the discount as a percentage of face value.

**Bargain purchase**   When a company is acquired and the purchase price is less than the fair value of the net assets. The current treatment of the excess of fair value over the purchase price is different under IFRS and U.S. GAAP. The excess is never accounted for as negative goodwill.

**Basic earnings per share (EPS)**   Net earnings available to common shareholders (i.e., net income minus preferred dividends) divided by the weighted average number of common shares outstanding during the period.

**Basis point value (BPV)**   Also called *present value of a basis point* or *price value of a basis point* (PVBP), the change in the bond price for a 1 basis point change in yield.

**Basis swap**   (1) An interest rate swap involving two floating rates. (2) A swap in which both parties pay a floating rate.

**Bayes' formula**   A method for updating probabilities based on new information.

**Bear hug**   A tactic used by acquirers to circumvent target management's objections to a proposed merger by submitting the proposal directly to the target company's board of directors.

**Bear spread**   An option strategy that involves selling a put with a lower exercise price and buying a put with a higher exercise price. It can also be executed with calls.

**Before-tax cash flow**   A measure of the expected annual cash flow from the operation of a real estate investment after all expenses but before taxes.

**Benchmark**   A comparison portfolio; a point of reference or comparison.

**Benchmark value of the multiple**   In using the method of comparables, the value of a price multiple for the comparison asset; when we have comparison assets (a group), the mean or median value of the multiple for the group of assets.

**Bernoulli random variable**   A random variable having the outcomes 0 and 1.

**Bernoulli trial**   An experiment that can produce one of two outcomes.

**Beta**   A standardized measure of systematic risk based upon an asset's covariance with the market portfolio.

**Bill-and-hold basis**   Sales on a bill-and-hold basis involve selling products but not delivering those products until a later date.

**Binomial model**   A model for pricing options in which the underlying price can move to only one of two possible new prices.

**Binomial random variable**   The number of successes in $n$ Bernoulli trials for which the probability of success is constant for all trials and the trials are independent.

**Binomial tree**   The graphical representation of a model of asset price dynamics in which, at each period, the asset moves up with probability $p$ or down with probability $(1 - p)$.

**Block**   Orders to buy or sell that are too large for the liquidity ordinarily available in dealer networks or stock exchanges.

**Bond equivalent yield**   A calculation of yield that is annualized using the ratio of 365 to the number of days to maturity. Bond equivalent yield allows for the restatement and comparison of securities with different compounding periods.

**Bond indenture**   A legal contract specifying the terms of a bond issue.

**Bond option**   An option in which the underlying is a bond; primarily traded in over-the-counter markets.

**Bond yield plus risk premium approach**   An estimate of the cost of common equity that is produced by summing the before-tax cost of debt and a risk premium that captures the additional yield on a company's stock relative to its bonds. The additional yield is often estimated using historical spreads between bond yields and stock yields.

**Bond-equivalent basis**   A basis for stating an annual yield that annualizes a semiannual yield by doubling it.

**Bond-equivalent yield**   The yield to maturity on a basis that ignores compounding.

**Bonding costs**   Costs borne by management to assure owners that they are working in the owners' best interest (e.g., implicit cost of non-compete agreements).

**Book value equity per share**   The amount of book value (also called carrying value) of common equity per share of common stock, calculated by dividing the book value of shareholders' equity by the number of shares of common stock outstanding.

**Book value of equity (or book value)**   Shareholders' equity (total assets minus total liabilities) minus the value of preferred stock; common shareholders' equity.

**Bootstrapping earnings**   An increase in a company's earnings that results as a consequence of the idiosyncrasies of a merger transaction itself rather than because of resulting economic benefits of the combination.

**Bottom-up analysis** With reference to investment selection processes, an approach that involves selection from all securities within a specified investment universe, i.e., without prior narrowing of the universe on the basis of macroeconomic or overall market considerations.

**Bottom-up forecasting approach** A forecasting approach that involves aggregating the individual company forecasts of analysts into industry forecasts, and finally into macroeconomic forecasts.

**Bottom-up investing** An approach to investing that focuses on the individual characteristics of securities rather than on macroeconomic or overall market forecasts.

**Box spread** An option strategy that combines a bull spread and a bear spread having two different exercise prices, which produces a risk-free payoff of the difference in the exercise prices.

**Break point** In the context of the weighted average cost of capital (WACC), a break point is the amount of capital at which the cost of one or more of the sources of capital changes, leading to a change in the WACC.

**Breakeven point** The number of units produced and sold at which the company's net income is zero (revenues = total costs).

**Breakup value (or private market value)** The value of a business calculated as the sum of the expected value of the business's parts if the parts were independent entities; the value that can be achieved if a company's assets are divided and sold separately.

**Breusch–Pagan test** A test for conditional heteroskedasticity in the error term of a regression.

**Broker** (1) An agent who executes orders to buy or sell securities on behalf of a client in exchange for a commission. (2) *See* Futures commission merchants.

**Brokerage** The business of acting as agents for buyers or sellers, usually in return for commissions.

**Build-up method** A method for determining the required rate of return on equity as the sum of risk premiums, in which one or more of the risk premiums is typically subjective rather than grounded in a formal equilibrium model.

**Built-up method** A method of identifying the basic elements of the overall capitalization rate.

**Bull spread** An option strategy that involves buying a call with a lower exercise price and selling a call with a higher exercise price. It can also be executed with puts.

**Business risk** The risk associated with operating earnings. Operating earnings are uncertain because total revenues and many of the expendi-tures contributed to produce those revenues are uncertain.

**Butterfly spread** An option strategy that combines two bull or bear spreads and has three exercise prices.

**Buy-side analysts** Analysts who work for investment management firms, trusts, and bank trust departments, and similar institutions.

**Call** An option that gives the holder the right to buy an underlying asset from another party at a fixed price over a specific period of time.

**Cannibalization** Cannibalization occurs when an investment takes customers and sales away from another part of the company.

**Cap** (1) A contract on an interest rate, whereby at periodic payment dates, the writer of the cap pays the difference between the market interest rate and a specified cap rate if, and only if, this difference is positive. This is equivalent to a stream of call options on the interest rate. (2) A combination of interest rate call options designed to hedge a borrower against rate increases on a floating-rate loan.

**Capital account** A record of foreign investment in a country minus its investment abroad.

**Capital allocation line (CAL)** A graph line that describes the combinations of expected return and standard deviation of return available to an investor from combining the optimal portfolio of risky assets with the risk-free asset.

**Capital asset pricing model (CAPM)** An equation describing the expected return on any asset (or portfolio) as a linear function of its beta relative to the market portfolio.

**Capital budgeting** The allocation of funds to relatively long-range projects or investments.

**Capital charge** The company's total cost of capital in money terms.

**Capital market line (CML)** The line with an intercept point equal to the risk-free rate that is tangent to the efficient frontier of risky assets; represents the efficient frontier when a risk-free asset is available for investment.

**Capital rationing** A capital rationing environment assumes that the company has a fixed amount of funds to invest.

**Capital structure** The mix of debt and equity that a company uses to finance its business; a company's specific mixture of long-term financing.

**Capitalization rate** The divisor in the expression for the value of a perpetuity.

**Capitalized inventory costs** Costs of inventories including costs of purchase, costs of conversion, other costs to bring the inventories to their present location and condition, and the allocated portion of fixed production overhead costs.

**Caplet**   Each component call option in a cap.

**Capped swap**   A swap in which the floating payments have an upper limit.

**Captive finance subsidiary**   A wholly-owned subsidiary of a company that is established to provide financing of the sales of the parent company.

**Capture hypothesis**   A theory of regulatory behavior that predicts that the regulators will eventually be captured by the special interests of the industry being regulated.

**Carrying amount (book value)**   The amount at which an asset or liability is valued according to accounting principles.

**Cash**   In accounting contexts, cash on hand (e.g., petty cash and cash not yet deposited to the bank) and demand deposits held in banks and similar accounts that can be used in payment of obligations.

**Cash basis**   Accounting method in which the only relevant transactions for the financial statements are those that involve cash.

**Cash conversion cycle (net operating cycle)**   A financial metric that measures the length of time required for a company to convert cash invested in its operations to cash received as a result of its operations; equal to days of inventory on hand + days of sales outstanding − number of days of payables.

**Cash equivalents**   Very liquid short-term investments, usually maturing in 90 days or less.

**Cash flow additivity principle**   The principle that dollar amounts indexed at the same point in time are additive.

**Cash flow at risk (CFAR)**   A variation of VAR that reflects the risk of a company's cash flow instead of its market value.

**Cash flow from operations (cash flow from operating activities or operating cash flow)**   The net amount of cash provided from operating activities.

**Cash flow statement (statement of cash flows)**   A financial statement that reconciles beginning-of-period and end-of-period balance sheet values of cash; consists of three parts: cash flows from operating activities, cash flows from investing activities, and cash flows from financing activities.

**Cash offering**   A merger or acquisition that is to be paid for with cash; the cash for the merger might come from the acquiring company's existing assets or from a debt issue.

**Cash price or spot price**   The price for immediate purchase of the underlying asset.

**Cash ratio**   A liquidity ratio calculated as (cash + short-term marketable investments) divided by current liabilities; measures a company's ability to meet its current obligations with just the cash and cash equivalents on hand.

**Cash settlement**   A procedure used in certain derivative transactions that specifies that the long and short parties engage in the equivalent cash value of a delivery transaction.

**Cash-flow-statement-based accruals ratio**   The difference between reported net income on an accrual basis and the cash flows from operating and investing activities compared to the average net operating assets over the period.

**Cash-flow-statement-based aggregate accruals**   The difference between reported net income on an accrual basis and the cash flows from operating and investing activities.

**Catalyst**   An event or piece of information that causes the marketplace to re-evaluate the prospects of a company.

**Central limit theorem**   A result in statistics that states that the sample mean computed from large samples of size $n$ from a population with finite variance will follow an approximate normal distribution with a mean equal to the population mean and a variance equal to the population variance divided by $n$.

**Centralized risk management or companywide risk management**   When a company has a single risk management group that monitors and controls all of the risk-taking activities of the organization. Centralization permits economies of scale and allows a company to use some of its risks to offset other risks. See also *enterprise risk management*.

**Chain rule of forecasting**   A forecasting process in which the next period's value as predicted by the forecasting equation is substituted into the right-hand side of the equation to give a predicted value two periods ahead.

**Chart of accounts**   A list of accounts used in an entity's accounting system.

**Cheapest to deliver**   A bond in which the amount received for delivering the bond is largest compared with the amount paid in the market for the bond.

**Cherry-picking**   When a bankrupt company is allowed to enforce contracts that are favorable to it while walking away from contracts that are unfavorable to it.

**Classical growth theory**   A theory of economic growth based on the view that the growth of real GDP per person is temporary and that when it rises above subsistence level, a population explosion eventually brings it back to subsistence level.

**Classified balance sheet**  A balance sheet organized so as to group together the various assets and liabilities into subcategories (e.g., current and noncurrent).

**Clean surplus accounting**  Accounting that satisfies the condition that all changes in the book value of equity other than transactions with owners are reflected in income. The bottom-line income reflects all changes in shareholders' equity arising from other than owner transactions. In the absence of owner transactions, the change in shareholders' equity should equal net income. No adjustments such as translation adjustments bypass the income statement and go directly to shareholders equity.

**Clean surplus relation**  The relationship between earnings, dividends, and book value in which ending book value is equal to the beginning book value plus earnings less dividends, apart from ownership transactions.

**Clearinghouse**  An entity associated with a futures market that acts as middleman between the contracting parties and guarantees to each party the performance of the other.

**Clientele effect**  The preference some investors have for shares that exhibit certain characteristics.

**Closeout netting**  Netting the market values of *all* derivative contracts between two parties to determine one overall value owed by one party to another in the event of bankruptcy.

**Coefficient of variation (CV)**  The ratio of a set of observations' standard deviation to the observations' mean value.

**Cointegrated**  Describes two time series that have a long-term financial or economic relationship such that they do not diverge from each other without bound in the long run.

**Collar**  An option strategy involving the purchase of a put and sale of a call in which the holder of an asset gains protection below a certain level, the exercise price of the put, and pays for it by giving up gains above a certain level, the exercise price of the call. Collars also can be used to provide protection against rising interest rates on a floating-rate loan by giving up gains from lower interest rates.

**Combination**  A listing in which the order of the listed items does not matter.

**Commercial paper**  Unsecured short-term corporate debt that is characterized by a single payment at maturity.

**Committed lines of credit**  A bank commitment to extend credit up to a pre-specified amount; the commitment is considered a short-term liability and is usually in effect for 364 days (one day short of a full year).

**Commodity forward**  A contract in which the underlying asset is oil, a precious metal, or some other commodity.

**Commodity futures**  Futures contracts in which the underlying is a traditional agricultural, metal, or petroleum product.

**Commodity option**  An option in which the asset underlying the futures is a commodity, such as oil, gold, wheat, or soybeans.

**Commodity swap**  A swap in which the underlying is a commodity such as oil, gold, or an agricultural product.

**Common size statements**  Financial statements in which all elements (accounts) are stated as a percentage of a key figure such as revenue for an income statement or total assets for a balance sheet.

**Common-size analysis**  The restatement of financial statement items using a common denominator or reference item that allows one to identify trends and major differences; an example is an income statement in which all items are expressed as a percent of revenue.

**Company fundamental factors**  Factors related to the company's internal performance, such as factors relating to earnings growth, earnings variability, earnings momentum, and financial leverage.

**Company share-related factors**  Valuation measures and other factors related to share price or the trading characteristics of the shares, such as earnings yield, dividend yield, and book-to-market value.

**Comparable company**  A company that has similar business risk; usually in the same industry and preferably with a single line of business.

**Comparative advantage**  A person or country has a comparative advantage in an activity if that person or country can perform the activity at a lower opportunity cost than anyone else or any other country.

**Complement**  In probability, with reference to an event *S*, the event that *S* does not occur; in economics, a good that is used in conjunction with another good.

**Completed contract**  A method of revenue recognition in which the company does not recognize any revenue until the contract is completed; used particularly in long-term construction contracts.

**Component cost of capital**   The rate of return required by suppliers of capital for an individual source of a company's funding, such as debt or equity.

**Compounding**   The process of accumulating interest on interest.

**Comprehensive income**   All changes in equity other than contributions by, and distributions to, owners; income under clean surplus accounting; includes all changes in equity during a period except those resulting from investments by owners and distributions to owners; comprehensive income equals net income plus other comprehensive income.

**Conditional expected value**   The expected value of a stated event given that another event has occurred.

**Conditional heteroskedasticity**   Heteroskedasticity in the error variance that is correlated with the values of the independent variable(s) in the regression.

**Conditional probability**   The probability of an event given (conditioned on) another event.

**Conditional variances**   The variance of one variable, given the outcome of another.

**Confidence interval**   A range that has a given probability that it will contain the population parameter it is intended to estimate.

**Conglomerate merger**   A merger involving companies that are in unrelated businesses.

**Consistent**   With reference to estimators, describes an estimator for which the probability of estimates close to the value of the population parameter increases as sample size increases.

**Consolidation**   The combining of the results of operations of subsidiaries with the parent company to present financial statements as if they were a single economic unit. The asset, liabilities, revenues and expenses of the subsidiaries are combined with those of the parent company, eliminating intercompany transactions.

**Constant maturity swap or CMT swap**   A swap in which the floating rate is the rate on a security known as a constant maturity treasury or CMT security.

**Constant maturity treasury or CMT**   A hypothetical U.S. Treasury note with a constant maturity. A CMT exists for various years in the range of 2 to 10.

**Contango**   A situation in a futures market where the current futures price is greater than the current spot price for the underlying asset.

**Contingent claims**   Derivatives in which the payoffs occur if a specific event occurs; generally referred to as options.

**Continuing residual income**   Residual income after the forecast horizon.

**Continuous random variable**   A random variable for which the range of possible outcomes is the real line (all real numbers between ($-\infty$ and $+\infty$) or some subset of the real line.

**Continuous time**   Time thought of as advancing in extremely small increments.

**Continuously compounded return**   The natural logarithm of 1 plus the holding period return, or equivalently, the natural logarithm of the ending price over the beginning price.

**Contra account**   An account that offsets another account.

**Contribution margin**   The amount available for fixed costs and profit after paying variable costs; revenue minus variable costs.

**Control premium**   An increment or premium to value associated with a controlling ownership interest in a company.

**Controlling interest**   An investment where the investor exerts control over the investee, typically by having a greater than 50 percent ownership in the investee.

**Convenience yield**   The nonmonetary return offered by an asset when the asset is in short supply, often associated with assets with seasonal production processes.

**Conventional cash flow**   A conventional cash flow pattern is one with an initial outflow followed by a series of inflows.

**Conversion factor**   An adjustment used to facilitate delivery on bond futures contracts in which any of a number of bonds with different characteristics are eligible for delivery.

**Convertible debt**   Debt with the added feature that the bondholder has the option to exchange the debt for equity at prespecified terms.

**Corporate governance**   The system of principles, policies, procedures, and clearly defined responsibilities and accountabilities used by stakeholders to overcome the conflicts of interest inherent in the corporate form.

**Corporate raider**   A person or organization seeking to profit by acquiring a company and reselling it, or seeking to profit from the takeover attempt itself (e.g., greenmail).

**Corporation**   A legal entity with rights similar to those of a person. The chief officers, executives, or top managers act as agents for the firm and are legally entitled to authorize corporate activities and to enter into contracts on behalf of the business.

**Correlation** A number between −1 and +1 that measures the co-movement (linear association) between two random variables.

**Correlation analysis** The analysis of the strength of the linear relationship between two data series.

**Cost approach to value** A method of valuing property based on site value plus current construction costs less accrued depreciation.

**Cost averaging** The periodic investment of a fixed amount of money.

**Cost leadership** The competitive strategy of being the lowest cost producer while offering products comparable to those of other firms, so that products can be priced at or near the industry average.

**Cost of capital** The rate of return that suppliers of capital require as compensation for their contribution of capital.

**Cost of carry** The cost associated with holding some asset, including financing, storage, and insurance costs. Any yield received on the asset is treated as a negative carrying cost.

**Cost of carry model** A model for pricing futures contracts in which the futures price is determined by adding the cost of carry to the spot price.

**Cost of debt** The cost of debt financing to a company, such as when it issues a bond or takes out a bank loan.

**Cost of equity** The required rate of return on common stock.

**Cost of goods sold** For a given period, equal to beginning inventory minus ending inventory plus the cost of goods acquired or produced during the period.

**Cost of preferred stock** The cost to a company of issuing preferred stock; the dividend yield that a company must commit to pay preferred stockholders.

**Cost recovery method** A method of revenue recognition in which the seller does not report any profit until the cash amounts paid by the buyer—including principal and interest on any financing from the seller—are greater than all the seller's costs for the merchandise sold.

**Cost structure** The mix of a company's variable costs and fixed costs.

**Cost-of-service regulation** Regulation based on allowing prices to reflect only the actual cost of production and no monopoly profits.

**Covariance** A measure of the co-movement (linear association) between two random variables.

**Covariance matrix** A matrix or square array whose entries are covariances; also known as a variance–covariance matrix.

**Covariance stationary** Describes a time series when its expected value and variance are constant and finite in all periods and when its covariance with itself for a fixed number of periods in the past or future is constant and finite in all periods.

**Covered call** An option strategy involving the holding of an asset and sale of a call on the asset.

**Covered interest arbitrage** A transaction executed in the foreign exchange market in which a currency is purchased (sold) and a forward contract is sold (purchased) to lock in the exchange rate for future delivery of the currency. This transaction should earn the risk-free rate of the investor's home country.

**Crawling peg** A policy regime is one that selects a target path for the exchange rate with intervention in the foreign exchange market to achieve that path.

**Creative response** Behavior on the part of a firm that allows it to comply with the letter of the law but violates the spirit, significantly lessening the law's effects.

**Credit** With respect to double-entry accounting, a credit records increases in liability, owners' equity, and revenue accounts or decreases in asset accounts; with respect to borrowing, the willingness and ability of the borrower to make promised payments on the borrowing.

**Credit analysis** The evaluation of credit risk; the evaluation of the creditworthiness of a borrower or counterparty.

**Credit derivatives** A contract in which one party has the right to claim a payment from another party in the event that a specific credit event occurs over the life of the contract.

**Credit risk or default risk** The risk of loss caused by a counterparty's or debtor's failure to make a promised payment.

**Credit scoring model** A statistical model used to classify borrowers according to creditworthiness.

**Credit spread option** An option on the yield spread on a bond.

**Credit swap** A type of swap transaction used as a credit derivative in which one party makes periodic payments to the other and receives the promise of a payoff if a third party defaults.

**Credit VAR, default VAR, or credit at risk** A variation of VAR that reflects credit risk.

**Credit-linked notes** Fixed-income securities in which the holder of the security has the right to withhold payment of the full amount due at maturity if a credit event occurs.

**Creditor nation**   A country that during its entire history has invested more in the rest of the world than other countries have invested in it.

**Creditworthiness**   The perceived ability of the borrower to pay what is owed on the borrowing in a timely manner; it represents the ability of a company to withstand adverse impacts on its cash flows.

**Cross-product netting**   Netting the market values of all contracts, not just derivatives, between parties.

**Cross-sectional analysis**   Analysis that involves comparisons across individuals in a group over a given time period or at a given point in time.

**Cross-sectional data**   Observations over individual units at a point in time, as opposed to time-series data.

**Cumulative distribution function**   A function giving the probability that a random variable is less than or equal to a specified value.

**Cumulative relative frequency**   For data grouped into intervals, the fraction of total observations that are less than the value of the upper limit of a stated interval.

**Currency forward**   A forward contract in which the underlying is a foreign currency.

**Currency option**   An option that allows the holder to buy (if a call) or sell (if a put) an underlying currency at a fixed exercise rate, expressed as an exchange rate.

**Currency swap**   A swap in which each party makes interest payments to the other in different currencies.

**Current account**   A record of receipts from exports of goods and services, payments for imports of goods and services, net income and net transfers received from the rest of the world.

**Current assets**, **or liquid assets**   Assets that are expected to be consumed or converted into cash in the near future, typically one year or less.

**Current cost**   With reference to assets, the amount of cash or cash equivalents that would have to be paid to buy the same or an equivalent asset today; with reference to liabilities, the undiscounted amount of cash or cash equivalents that would be required to settle the obligation today.

**Current credit risk**   The risk associated with the possibility that a payment currently due will not be made.

**Current exchange rate**   For accounting purposes, the spot exchange rate on the balance sheet date.

**Current liabilities**   Short-term obligations, such as accounts payable, wages payable, or accrued liabil-

ities, that are expected to be settled in the near future, typically one year or less.

**Current rate method**   Approach to translating foreign currency financial statements for consolidation in which all assets and liabilities are translated at the current exchange rate. The current rate method is the prevalent method of translation.

**Current ratio**   A liquidity ratio calculated as current assets divided by current liabilities.

**Current taxes payable**   Tax expenses that have been recognized and recorded on a company's income statement but which have not yet been paid.

**Cyclical businesses**   Businesses with high sensitivity to business- or industry-cycle influences.

**Daily settlement**   See *marking to market*.

**Data mining**   The practice of determining a model by extensive searching through a dataset for statistically significant patterns.

**Day trader**   A trader holding a position open somewhat longer than a scalper but closing all positions at the end of the day.

**Days of inventory on hand (DOH)**   An activity ratio equal to the number of days in the period divided by inventory turnover over the period.

**Days of sales outstanding (DSO)**   An activity ratio equal to the number of days in period divided by receivables turnover.

**Dead-hand provision**   A poison pill provision that allows for the redemption or cancellation of a poison pill provision only by a vote of continuing directors (generally directors who were on the target company's board prior to the takeover attempt).

**Dealing securities**   Securities held by banks or other financial intermediaries for trading purposes.

**Debit**   With respect to double-entry accounting, a debit records increases of asset and expense accounts or decreases in liability and owners' equity accounts.

**Debt covenants**   Agreements between the company as borrower and its creditors.

**Debt incurrence test**   A financial covenant made in conjunction with existing debt that restricts a company's ability to incur additional debt at the same seniority based on one or more financial tests or conditions.

**Debt rating approach**   A method for estimating a company's before-tax cost of debt based upon the yield on comparably rated bonds for maturities that closely match that of the company's existing debt.

**Debt ratings**   An objective measure of the quality and safety of a company's debt based upon an analysis of the company's ability to pay the promised cash flows, as well as an analysis of any indentures.

**Debt with warrants** Debt issued with warrants that give the bondholder the right to purchase equity at prespecified terms.

**Debtor nation** A country that during its entire history has borrowed more in the rest of the world than other countries have lent in it.

**Debt-to-assets ratio** A solvency ratio calculated as total debt divided by total assets.

**Debt-to-capital ratio** A solvency ratio calculated as total debt divided by total debt plus total shareholders' equity.

**Debt-to-equity ratio** A solvency ratio calculated as total debt divided by total shareholders' equity.

**Decentralized risk management** A system that allows individual units within an organization to manage risk. Decentralization results in duplication of effort but has the advantage of having people closer to the risk be more directly involved in its management.

**Deciles** Quantiles that divide a distribution into 10 equal parts.

**Decision rule** With respect to hypothesis testing, the rule according to which the null hypothesis will be rejected or not rejected; involves the comparison of the test statistic to rejection point(s).

**Declaration date** The day that the corporation issues a statement declaring a specific dividend.

**Deductible temporary differences** Temporary differences that result in a reduction of or deduction from taxable income in a future period when the balance sheet item is recovered or settled.

**Deep in the money** Options that are far in-the-money.

**Deep out of the money** Options that are far out-of-the-money.

**Default risk premium** An extra return that compensates investors for the possibility that the borrower will fail to make a promised payment at the contracted time and in the contracted amount.

**Defensive interval ratio** A liquidity ratio that estimates the number of days that an entity could meet cash needs from liquid assets; calculated as (cash + short-term marketable investments + receivables) divided by daily cash expenditures.

**Deferred tax assets** A balance sheet asset that arises when an excess amount is paid for income taxes relative to accounting profit. The taxable income is higher than accounting profit and income tax payable exceeds tax expense. The company expects to recover the difference during the course of future operations when tax expense exceeds income tax payable.

**Deferred tax liabilities** A balance sheet liability that arises when a deficit amount is paid for income taxes relative to accounting profit. The taxable income is less than the accounting profit and income tax payable is less than tax expense. The company expects to eliminate the liability over the course of future operations when income tax payable exceeds tax expense.

**Defined-benefit pension plans** Plan in which the company promises to pay a certain annual amount (defined benefit) to the employee after retirement. The company bears the investment risk of the plan assets.

**Defined-contribution pension plans** Individual accounts to which an employee and typically the employer makes contributions, generally on a tax-advantaged basis. The amounts of contributions are defined at the outset, but the future value of the benefit is unknown. The employee bears the investment risk of the plan assets.

**Definitive merger agreement** A contract signed by both parties to a merger that clarifies the details of the transaction, including the terms, warranties, conditions, termination details, and the rights of all parties.

**Degree of confidence** The probability that a confidence interval includes the unknown population parameter.

**Degree of financial leverage (DFL)** The ratio of the percentage change in net income to the percentage change in operating income; the sensitivity of the cash flows available to owners when operating income changes.

**Degree of operating leverage (DOL)** The ratio of the percentage change in operating income to the percentage change in units sold; the sensitivity of operating income to changes in units sold.

**Degree of total leverage** The ratio of the percentage change in net income to the percentage change in units sold; the sensitivity of the cash flows to owners to changes in the number of units produced and sold.

**Degrees of freedom (df)** The number of independent observations used.

**Delivery** A process used in a deliverable forward contract in which the long pays the agreed-upon price to the short, which in turn delivers the underlying asset to the long.

**Delivery option** The feature of a futures contract giving the short the right to make decisions about what, when, and where to deliver.

**Delta** The relationship between the option price and the underlying price, which reflects the sensitivity of the price of the option to changes in the price of the underlying.

**Delta hedge** An option strategy in which a position in an asset is converted to a risk-free position with a position in a specific number of options. The number of options per unit of the underlying changes through time, and the position must be revised to maintain the hedge.

**Delta-normal method** A measure of VAR equivalent to the analytical method but that refers to the use of delta to estimate the option's price sensitivity.

**Dependent** With reference to events, the property that the probability of one event occurring depends on (is related to) the occurrence of another event.

**Dependent variable** The variable whose variation about its mean is to be explained by the regression; the left-hand-side variable in a regression equation.

**Depreciation** The process of systematically allocating the cost of long-lived (tangible) assets to the periods during which the assets are expected to provide economic benefits.

**Deregulation** The elimination or phasing out of regulations on economic activity.

**Derivative** A financial instrument whose value depends on the value of some underlying asset or factor (e.g., a stock price, an interest rate, or exchange rate).

**Derivatives dealers** Commercial and investment banks that make markets in derivatives.

**Descriptive statistics** The study of how data can be summarized effectively.

**Designated fair value instruments** Financial instruments that an entity chooses to measure at fair value per IAS 39 or SFAS 159. Generally, the election to use the fair value option is irrevocable.

**Diff swaps** A swap in which the payments are based on the difference between interest rates in two countries but payments are made in only a single currency.

**Differential expectations** Expectations that differ from consensus expectations.

**Differentiation** The competitive strategy of offering unique products or services along some dimensions that are widely valued by buyers so that the firm can command premium prices.

**Diffuse prior** The assumption of equal prior probabilities.

**Diluted earnings per share (diluted EPS)** Net income, minus preferred dividends, divided by the number of common shares outstanding considering all dilutive securities (e.g., convertible debt and options); the EPS that would result if all dilutive securities were converted into common shares.

**Diluted shares** The number of shares that would be outstanding if all potentially dilutive claims on common shares (e.g., convertible debt, convertible preferred stock, and employee stock options) were exercised.

**Diminishing balance method** An accelerated depreciation method, i.e., one that allocates a relatively large proportion of the cost of an asset to the early years of the asset's useful life.

**Direct debit program** An arrangement whereby a customer authorizes a debit to a demand account; typically used by companies to collect routine payments for services.

**Direct financing lease** A type of finance lease, from a lessor perspective, where the present value of the lease payments (lease receivable) equals the carrying value of the leased asset. The revenues earned by the lessor are financing in nature.

**Direct format (direct method)** With reference to the cash flow statement, a format for the presentation of the statement in which cash flow from operating activities is shown as operating cash receipts less operating cash disbursements.

**Direct income capitalization approach** Division of net operating income by an overall capitalization rate to arrive at market value.

**Direct sales-comparison approach** Method of valuing property based on recent sales prices of similar properties.

**Direct write-off method** An approach to recognizing credit losses on customer receivables in which the company waits until such time as a customer has defaulted and only then recognizes the loss.

**Dirty surplus accounting** Accounting in which some income items are reported as part of stockholders' equity rather than as gains and losses on the income statement; certain items of comprehensive income bypass the income statement and appear as direct adjustments to shareholders' equity.

**Dirty surplus items** Items that affect comprehensive income but which bypass the income statement.

**Disbursement float** The amount of time between check issuance and a check's clearing back against the company's account.

**Discount** To reduce the value of a future payment in allowance for how far away it is in time; to calculate the present value of some future amount. Also, the amount by which an instrument is priced below its face value.

**Discount interest**  A procedure for determining the interest on a loan or bond in which the interest is deducted from the face value in advance.

**Discount rate**  Any rate used in finding the present value of a future cash flow.

**Discounted cash flow analysis**  In the context of merger analysis, it is an estimate of a target company's value found by discounting the company's expected future free cash flows to the present.

**Discrete random variable**  A random variable that can take on at most a countable number of possible values.

**Discrete time**  Time thought of as advancing in distinct finite increments.

**Discriminant analysis**  A multivariate classification technique used to discriminate between groups, such as companies that either will or will not become bankrupt during some time frame.

**Dispersion**  The variability around the central tendency.

**Divestiture**  The sale, liquidation, or spin-off of a division or subsidiary.

**Dividend discount model (DDM)**  A present value model of stock value that views the intrinsic value of a stock as present value of the stock's expected future dividends.

**Dividend discount model based approach**  An approach for estimating a country's equity risk premium. The market rate of return is estimated as the sum of the dividend yield and the growth rate in dividends for a market index. Subtracting the risk-free rate of return from the estimated market return produces an estimate for the equity risk premium.

**Dividend displacement of earnings**  The concept that dividends paid now displace earnings in all future periods.

**Dividend payout policy**  The strategy a company follows with regard to the amount and timing of dividend payments.

**Dividend payout ratio**  The ratio of cash dividends paid to earnings for a period.

**Dividend rate**  The most recent quarterly dividend multiplied by four.

**Dividends per share**  The dollar amount of cash dividends paid during a period per share of common stock.

**Double declining balance depreciation**  An accelerated depreciation method that involves depreciating the asset at double the straight-line rate. This rate is multiplied by the book value of the asset at the beginning of the period (a declining balance) to calculate depreciation expense.

**Double taxation**  Corporate earnings are taxed twice when paid out as dividends. First, corporate earnings are taxed regardless of whether they will be distributed as dividends or retained at the corporate level, and second, dividends are taxed again at the individual shareholder level.

**Double-entry accounting**  The accounting system of recording transactions in which every recorded transaction affects at least two accounts so as to keep the basic accounting equation (assets = liabilities + owners' equity) in balance.

**Down transition probability**  The probability that an asset's value moves down in a model of asset price dynamics.

**Downstream**  A transaction between two affiliates, an investor company and an associate company such that the investor company records a profit on its income statement. An example is a sale of inventory by the investor company to the associate.

**Drag on liquidity**  When receipts lag, creating pressure from the decreased available funds.

**Due diligence**  Investigation and analysis in support of a recommendation; the failure to exercise due diligence may sometimes result in liability according to various securities laws.

**Dummy variable**  A type of qualitative variable that takes on a value of 1 if a particular condition is true and 0 if that condition is false.

**Dumping**  The sale by a foreign firm of exports at a lower price than the cost of production.

**DuPont analysis**  An approach to decomposing return on investment, e.g., return on equity, as the product of other financial ratios.

**Duration**  A measure of an option-free bond's average maturity. Specifically, the weighted average maturity of all future cash flows paid by a security, in which the weights are the present value of these cash flows as a fraction of the bond's price. A measure of a bond's price sensitivity to interest rate movements.

**Dutch Book theorem**  A result in probability theory stating that inconsistent probabilities create profit opportunities.

**Dynamic hedging**  A strategy in which a position is hedged by making frequent adjustments to the quantity of the instrument used for hedging in relation to the instrument being hedged.

**Earnings at risk (EAR)**  A variation of VAR that reflects the risk of a company's earnings instead of its market value.

**Earnings expectation management**  Attempts by management to encourage analysts to forecast a slightly lower number for expected earnings than the analysts would otherwise forecast.

**Earnings game**  Management's focus on reporting earnings that meet consensus estimates.

**Earnings management activity**  Deliberate activity aimed at influencing reporting earnings numbers, often with the goal of placing management in a favorable light; the opportunistic use of accruals to manage earnings.

**Earnings per share**  The amount of income earned during a period per share of common stock.

**Earnings yield**  Earnings per share divided by price; the reciprocal of the P/E ratio.

**Economic exposure**  The risk associated with changes in the relative attractiveness of products and services offered for sale, arising out of the competitive effects of changes in exchange rates.

**Economic growth**  The expansion of production possibilities that results from capital accumulation and technological change.

**Economic growth rate**  The annual percentage change in real GDP.

**Economic order quantity–reorder point**  An approach to managing inventory based on expected demand and the predictability of demand; the ordering point for new inventory is determined based on the costs of ordering and carrying inventory, such that the total cost associated with inventory is minimized.

**Economic profit**  See *"Residual income."*

**Economic sectors**  Large industry groupings.

**Economic value added (EVA®)**  A commercial implementation of the residual income concept; the computation of EVA® is the net operating profit after taxes minus the cost of capital, where these inputs are adjusted for a number of items.

**Economies of scale**  In reference to mergers, it is the savings achieved through the consolidation of operations and elimination of duplicate resources.

**Effective annual rate**  The amount by which a unit of currency will grow in a year with interest on interest included.

**Effective annual yield (EAY)**  An annualized return that accounts for the effect of interest on interest; EAY is computed by compounding 1 plus the holding period yield forward to one year, then subtracting 1.

**Efficiency**  In statistics, a desirable property of estimators; an efficient estimator is the unbiased estimator with the smallest variance among unbiased estimators of the same parameter.

**Efficient frontier**  The portion of the minimum-variance frontier beginning with the global minimum-variance portfolio and continuing above it; the graph of the set of portfolios offering the maximum expected return for their level of variance of return.

**Efficient portfolio**  A portfolio offering the highest expected return for a given level of risk as measured by variance or standard deviation of return.

**Elasticity**  A measure of sensitivity; the incremental change in one variable with respect to an incremental change in another variable.

**Electronic funds transfer**  The use of computer networks to conduct financial transactions electronically.

**Empirical probability**  The probability of an event estimated as a relative frequency of occurrence.

**Enhanced derivatives products companies (EDPC)**  A type of subsidiary engaged in derivatives transactions that is separated from the parent company in order to have a higher credit rating than the parent company.

**Enterprise risk management**  A form of *centralized risk management* that typically encompasses the management of a broad variety of risks, including insurance risk.

**Enterprise value (EV)**  Total company value (the market value of debt, common equity, and preferred equity) minus the value of cash and investments.

**Equilibrium**  The condition in which supply equals demand.

**Equitizing cash**  A strategy used to replicate an index. It is also used to take a given amount of cash and turn it into an equity position while maintaining the liquidity provided by the cash.

**Equity**  Assets less liabilities; the residual interest in the assets after subtracting the liabilities.

**Equity carve-out**  A form of restructuring that involves the creation of a new legal entity and the sale of equity in it to outsiders.

**Equity charge**  The estimated cost of equity capital in money terms.

**Equity dividend rate**  Income rate that reflects the relationship between equity income and equity capital.

**Equity forward**  A contract calling for the purchase of an individual stock, a stock portfolio, or a stock index at a later date at an agreed-upon price.

**Equity method**  A basis for reporting investment income in which the investing entity recognizes a share of income as earned rather than as dividends when received. These transactions are typically reflected in Investments in Associates or Equity Method Investments.

**Equity options**  Options on individual stocks; also known as stock options.

**Equity risk premium** The expected return on equities minus the risk-free rate; the premium that investors demand for investing in equities.

**Equity swap** A swap transaction in which at least one cash flow is tied to the return to an equity portfolio position, often an equity index.

**Error autocorrelation** The autocorrelation of the error term.

**Error term** The portion of the dependent variable that is not explained by the independent variable(s) in the regression.

**Estimate** The particular value calculated from sample observations using an estimator.

**Estimated (or fitted) parameters** With reference to regression analysis, the estimated values of the population intercept and population slope coefficient(s) in a regression.

**Estimation** With reference to statistical inference, the subdivision dealing with estimating the value of a population parameter.

**Estimator** An estimation formula; the formula used to compute the sample mean and other sample statistics are examples of estimators.

**Eurodollar** A dollar deposited outside the United States.

**European-style option or European option** An option contract that can only be exercised on its expiration date.

**Event** Any outcome or specified set of outcomes of a random variable.

**Excess kurtosis** Degree of peakedness (fatness of tails) in excess of the peakedness of the normal distribution.

**Exchange for physicals (EFP)** A permissible delivery procedure used by futures market participants, in which the long and short arrange a delivery procedure other than the normal procedures stipulated by the futures exchange.

**Exchange rate** The value of the U.S. dollar in terms of other currencies in the foreign exchange market.

**Exchange ratio** The number of shares that target stockholders are to receive in exchange for each of their shares in the target company.

**Ex-dividend** Trading ex-dividend refers to shares that no longer carry the right to the next dividend payment.

**Ex-dividend date** The first date that a share trades without (i.e., "ex") the dividend.

**Exercise or exercising the option** The process of using an option to buy or sell the underlying.

**Exercise date** The day that employees actually exercise the options and convert them to stock.

**Exercise price (strike price, striking price, or strike)** The fixed price at which an option holder can buy or sell the underlying.

**Exercise rate or strike rate** The fixed rate at which the holder of an interest rate option can buy or sell the underlying.

**Exhaustive** Covering or containing all possible outcomes.

**Expectational arbitrage** Investing on the basis of differential expectations.

**Expected holding-period return** The expected total return on an asset over a stated holding period; for stocks, the sum of the expected dividend yield and the expected price appreciation over the holding period.

**Expected value** The probability-weighted average of the possible outcomes of a random variable.

**Expensed** Taken as a deduction in arriving at net income.

**Expenses** Outflows of economic resources or increases in liabilities that result in decreases in equity (other than decreases because of distributions to owners); reductions in net assets associated with the creation of revenues.

**Expiration date** The date on which a derivative contract expires.

**Exports** The goods and services that we sell to people in other countries.

**Exposure to foreign exchange risk** The risk of a change in value of an asset or liability denominated in a foreign currency due to a change in exchange rates.

**External growth** Company growth in output or sales that is achieved by buying the necessary resources externally (i.e., achieved through mergers and acquisitions).

**Externality** The effect of an investment on other things besides the investment itself.

**Face value (also principal, par value, stated value, or maturity value)** The amount of cash payable by a company to the bondholders when the bonds mature; the promised payment at maturity separate from any coupon payment.

**Factor** A common or underlying element with which several variables are correlated.

**Factor risk premium (or factor price)** The expected return in excess of the risk-free rate for a portfolio with a sensitivity of 1 to one factor and a sensitivity of 0 to all other factors.

**Factor sensitivity (also factor betas or factor loadings)** An asset's sensitivity to a particular factor; a measure of the response of return to each unit of increase in a factor, holding all other factors constant.

**Fair market value** The market price of an asset or liability that trades regularly.

**Fair value** The price at which an asset or liability would change hands between a willing buyer and a willing seller when the former is not under any compulsion to buy and the latter is not under any compulsion to sell; the price that would be received to sell an asset or paid to transfer a liability in an orderly transaction between market participants.

**Fiduciary call** A combination of a European call and a risk-free bond that matures on the option expiration day and has a face value equal to the exercise price of the call.

**FIFO method** The first in, first out, method of accounting for inventory, which matches sales against the costs of items of inventory in the order in which they were placed in inventory.

**Finance lease (capital lease)** Essentially, the purchase of some asset by the buyer (lessee) that is directly financed by the seller (lessor).

**Financial analysis** The process of selecting, evaluating, and interpreting financial data in order to formulate an assessment of a company's present and future financial condition and performance.

**Financial distress** Heightened uncertainty regarding a company's ability to meet its various obligations because of lower or negative earnings.

**Financial flexibility** The ability to react and adapt to financial adversities and opportunities.

**Financial futures** Futures contracts in which the underlying is a stock, bond, or currency.

**Financial leverage** The extent to which a company can effect, through the use of debt, a proportional change in the return on common equity that is greater than a given proportional change in operating income; also, short for the financial leverage ratio.

**Financial leverage ratio** A measure of financial leverage calculated as average total assets divided by average total equity.

**Financial reporting quality** The accuracy with which a company's reported financials reflect its operating performance and their usefulness for forecasting future cash flows.

**Financial risk** The risk that environmental, social, or governance risk factors will result in significant costs or other losses to a company and its shareholders; the risk arising from a company's obligation to meet required payments under its financing agreements.

**Financing activities** Activities related to obtaining or repaying capital to be used in the business (e.g., equity and long-term debt).

**First-differencing** A transformation that subtracts the value of the time series in period $t - 1$ from its value in period $t$.

**First-order serial correlation** Correlation between adjacent observations in a time series.

**Fixed asset turnover** An activity ratio calculated as total revenue divided by average net fixed assets.

**Fixed charge coverage** A solvency ratio measuring the number of times interest and lease payments are covered by operating income, calculated as (EBIT + lease payments) divided by (interest payments + lease payments).

**Fixed costs** Costs that remain at the same level regardless of a company's level of production and sales.

**Fixed exchange rate** An exchange rate pegged at a value decided by the government or central bank and that blocks the unregulated forces of demand and supply by direct intervention in the foreign exchange market.

**Fixed-income forward** A forward contract in which the underlying is a bond.

**Fixed-rate perpetual preferred stock** Nonconvertible, noncallable preferred stock with a specified dividend rate that has a claim on earnings senior to the claim of common stock, and no maturity date.

**Flexible exchange rate** An exchange rate is determined by demand and supply with no direct intervention in the foreign exchange market by the central bank.

**Flip-in pill** A poison pill takeover defense that dilutes an acquirer's ownership in a target by giving other existing target company shareholders the right to buy additional target company shares at a discount.

**Flip-over pill** A poison pill takeover defense that gives target company shareholders the right to purchase shares of the acquirer at a significant discount to the market price, which has the effect of causing dilution to all existing acquiring company shareholders.

**Float** In the context of customer receipts, the amount of money that is in transit between payments made by customers and the funds that are usable by the company.

**Float factor** An estimate of the average number of days it takes deposited checks to clear; average daily float divided by average daily deposit.

**Floating-rate loan** A loan in which the interest rate is reset at least once after the starting date.

**Floor** A combination of interest rate put options designed to hedge a lender against lower rates on a floating-rate loan.

**Floor traders or locals**  Market makers that buy and sell by quoting a bid and an ask price. They are the primary providers of liquidity to the market.

**Floored swap**  A swap in which the floating payments have a lower limit.

**Floorlet**  Each component put option in a floor.

**Flotation cost**  Fees charged to companies by investment bankers and other costs associated with raising new capital.

**Focus**  The competitive strategy of seeking a competitive advantage within a target segment or segments of the industry, either on the basis of cost leadership (**cost focus**) or differentiation (**differentiation focus**).

**Foreign currency**  The money of other countries regardless of whether that money is in the form of notes, coins, or bank deposits.

**Foreign currency transactions**  Transactions that are denominated in a currency other than a company's functional currency.

**Foreign exchange market**  The market in which the currency of one country is exchanged for the currency of another.

**Forward contract**  An agreement between two parties in which one party, the buyer, agrees to buy from the other party, the seller, an underlying asset at a later date for a price established at the start of the contract.

**Forward integration**  A merger involving the purchase of a target that is farther along the value or production chain; for example, to acquire a distributor.

**Forward price or forward rate**  The fixed price or rate at which the transaction scheduled to occur at the expiration of a forward contract will take place. This price is agreed on at the initiation date of the contract.

**Forward rate agreement (FRA)**  A forward contract calling for one party to make a fixed interest payment and the other to make an interest payment at a rate to be determined at the contract expiration.

**Forward swap**  A forward contract to enter into a swap.

**Free cash flow**  The actual cash that would be available to the company's investors after making all investments necessary to maintain the company as an ongoing enterprise (also referred to as free cash flow to the firm); the internally generated funds that can be distributed to the company's investors (e.g., shareholders and bondholders) without impairing the value of the company.

**Free cash flow hypothesis**  The hypothesis that higher debt levels discipline managers by forcing them to make fixed debt service payments and by reducing the company's free cash flow.

**Free cash flow to equity**  The cash flow available to a company's common shareholders after all operating expenses, interest, and principal payments have been made, and necessary investments in working and fixed capital have been made.

**Free cash flow to equity model**  A model of stock valuation that views a stock's intrinsic value as the present value of expected future free cash flows to equity.

**Free cash flow to the firm**  The cash flow available to the company's suppliers of capital after all operating expenses (including taxes) have been paid and necessary investments in working and fixed capital have been made.

**Free cash flow to the firm model**  A model of stock valuation that views the value of a firm as the present value of expected future free cash flows to the firm.

**Frequency distribution**  A tabular display of data summarized into a relatively small number of intervals.

**Frequency polygon**  A graph of a frequency distribution obtained by drawing straight lines joining successive points representing the class frequencies.

**Friendly transaction**  A potential business combination that is endorsed by the managers of both companies.

**Full price**  The price of a security with accrued interest.

**Functional currency**  The currency of the primary economic environment in which an entity operates.

**Fundamental beta**  A beta that is based at least in part on fundamental data for a company.

**Fundamental factor models**  A multifactor model in which the factors are attributes of stocks or companies that are important in explaining cross-sectional differences in stock prices.

**Fundamentals**  Economic characteristics of a business such as profitability, financial strength, and risk.

**Future value (FV)**  The amount to which a payment or series of payments will grow by a stated future date.

**Futures commission merchants (FCMs)**  Individuals or companies that execute futures transactions for other parties off the exchange.

**Futures contract**  A variation of a forward contract that has essentially the same basic definition but with some additional features, such as a clearinghouse guarantee against credit losses, a daily settlement of gains and losses, and an organized electronic or floor trading facility.

**Futures exchange** A legal corporate entity whose shareholders are its members. The members of the exchange have the privilege of executing transactions directly on the exchange.

**Gains** Asset inflows not directly related to the ordinary activities of the business.

**Gamma** A numerical measure of how sensitive an option's delta is to a change in the underlying.

**General Agreement on Tariffs and Trade** An international agreement signed in 1947 to reduce tariffs on international trade.

**Generalized least squares** A regression estimation technique that addresses heteroskedasticity of the error term.

**Geometric mean** A measure of central tendency computed by taking the $n$th root of the product of $n$ non-negative values.

**Giro system** An electronic payment system used widely in Europe and Japan.

**Going-concern assumption** The assumption that the business will maintain its business activities into the foreseeable future.

**Going-concern value** A business's value under a going-concern assumption.

**Goodwill** An intangible asset that represents the excess of the purchase price of an acquired company over the value of the net assets acquired.

**Government sector surplus or deficit** An amount equal to net taxes minus government expenditure on goods and services.

**Grant date** The day that options are granted to employees; usually the date that compensation expense is measured if both the number of shares and option price are known.

**Greenmail** The purchase of the accumulated shares of a hostile investor by a company that is targeted for takeover by that investor, usually at a substantial premium over market price.

**Gross domestic product** A money measure of the goods and services produced within a country's borders over a stated time period.

**Gross income multiplier (GIM)** A ratio derived from the market; sales price divided by annual gross income equals GIM.

**Gross profit (gross margin)** Sales minus the cost of sales (i.e., the cost of goods sold for a manufacturing company).

**Gross profit margin** The ratio of gross profit to revenues.

**Grouping by function** With reference to the presentation of expenses in an income statement, the grouping together of expenses serving the same function, e.g., all items that are costs of good sold.

**Grouping by nature** With reference to the presentation of expenses in an income statement, the grouping together of expenses by similar nature, e.g., all depreciation expenses.

**Growth accounting** A tool that calculates the contribution to real GDP growth of each of its sources.

**Growth investors** With reference to equity investors, investors who seek to invest in high-earnings-growth companies.

**Growth option or expansion option** The ability to make additional investments in a project at some future time if the financial results are strong.

**Growth phase** A stage of growth in which a company typically enjoys rapidly expanding markets, high profit margins, and an abnormally high growth rate in earnings per share.

**Harmonic mean** A type of weighted mean computed by averaging the reciprocals of the observations, then taking the reciprocal of that average.

**Hedge ratio** The relationship of the quantity of an asset being hedged to the quantity of the derivative used for hedging.

**Hedging** A general strategy usually thought of as reducing, if not eliminating, risk.

**Held-for-trading securities (trading securities)** Debt or equity financial assets bought with the intention to sell them in the near term, usually less than three months; securities that a company intends to trade.

**Held-to-maturity investments** Debt (fixed-income) securities that a company intends to hold to maturity; these are presented at their original cost, updated for any amortization of discounts or premiums.

**Herfindahl–Hirschman Index** A measure of market concentration that is calculated by summing the squared market shares for competing companies in an industry; high HHI readings or mergers that would result in large HHI increases are more likely to result in regulatory challenges.

**Heteroskedastic** With reference to the error term of a regression, having a variance that differs across observations.

**Heteroskedasticity** The property of having a non-constant variance; refers to an error term with the property that its variance differs across observations.

**Heteroskedasticity-consistent standard errors** Standard errors of the estimated parameters of a regression that correct for the presence of heteroskedasticity in the regression's error term.

**Histogram** A bar chart of data that have been grouped into a frequency distribution.

**Historical cost** In reference to assets, the amount paid to purchase an asset, including any costs of acquisition and/or preparation; with reference to liabilities, the amount of proceeds received in exchange in issuing the liability.

**Historical equity risk premium approach** An estimate of a country's equity risk premium that is based upon the historical averages of the risk-free rate and the rate of return on the market portfolio.

**Historical exchange rates** For accounting purposes, the exchange rates that existed when the assets and liabilities were initially recorded.

**Historical method** A method of estimating VAR that uses data from the returns of the portfolio over a recent past period and compiles this data in the form of a histogram.

**Historical simulation (or back simulation)** Another term for the historical method of estimating VAR. This term is somewhat misleading in that the method involves not a *simulation* of the past but rather what *actually happened* in the past, sometimes adjusted to reflect the fact that a different portfolio may have existed in the past than is planned for the future.

**Holder-of-record date** The date that a shareholder listed on the corporation's books will be deemed to have ownership of the shares for purposes of receiving an upcoming dividend; two business days after the ex-dividend date.

**Holding period return** The return that an investor earns during a specified holding period; a synonym for total return.

**Holding period yield (HPY)** The return that an investor earns during a specified holding period; holding period return with reference to a fixed-income instrument.

**Homogenization** Creating a contract with standard and generally accepted terms, which makes it more acceptable to a broader group of participants.

**Homoskedasticity** The property of having a constant variance; refers to an error term that is constant across observations.

**Horizontal analysis** Common-size analysis that involves comparing a specific financial statement with that statement in prior or future time periods; also, cross-sectional analysis of one company with another.

**Horizontal common-size analysis** A form of common-size analysis in which the accounts in a given period are used as the benchmark or base period, and every account is restated in subse-

quent periods as a percentage of the base period's same account.

**Horizontal merger** A merger involving companies in the same line of business, usually as competitors.

**Hostile transaction** An attempt to acquire a company against the wishes of the target's managers.

**Human capital** The value of skills and knowledge possessed by the workforce.

**Hurdle rate** The rate of return that must be met for a project to be accepted.

**Hypothesis** With reference to statistical inference, a statement about one or more populations.

**Hypothesis testing** With reference to statistical inference, the subdivision dealing with the testing of hypotheses about one or more populations.

**Identifiable intangible** An intangible that can be acquired singly and is typically linked to specific rights or privileges having finite benefit periods (e.g., a patent or trademark).

**If-converted method** A method for accounting for the effect of convertible securities on earnings per share (EPS) that specifies what EPS would have been if the convertible securities had been converted at the beginning of the period, taking account of the effects of conversion on net income and the weighted average number of shares outstanding.

**Impairment** Diminishment in value as a result of carrying (book) value exceeding fair value and/or recoverable value.

**Impairment of capital rule** A legal restriction that dividends cannot exceed retained earnings.

**Implied repo rate** The rate of return from a cash-and-carry transaction implied by the futures price relative to the spot price.

**Implied volatility** The volatility that option traders use to price an option, implied by the price of the option and a particular option-pricing model.

**Implied yield** A measure of the yield on the underlying bond of a futures contract implied by pricing it as though the underlying will be delivered at the futures expiration.

**Imports** The goods and services that we buy from people in other countries.

**Imputation** In reference to corporate taxes, a system that imputes, or attributes, taxes at only one level of taxation. For countries using an imputation tax system, taxes on dividends are effectively levied only at the shareholder rate. Taxes are paid at the corporate level but they are *attributed* to the shareholder. Shareholders deduct from their tax bill their portion of taxes paid by the company.

**Income** Increases in economic benefits in the form of inflows or enhancements of assets, or decreases of liabilities that result in an increase in equity (other than increases resulting from contributions by owners).

**Income statement (statement of operations or profit and loss statement)** A financial statement that provides information about a company's profitability over a stated period of time.

**Income tax paid** The actual amount paid for income taxes in the period; not a provision, but the actual cash outflow.

**Income tax payable** The income tax owed by the company on the basis of taxable income.

**Income tax recoverable** The income tax expected to be recovered, from the taxing authority, on the basis of taxable income. It is a recovery of previously remitted taxes or future taxes owed by the company.

**Incremental cash flow** The cash flow that is realized because of a decision; the changes or increments to cash flows resulting from a decision or action.

**Independent** With reference to events, the property that the occurrence of one event does not affect the probability of another event occurring.

**Independent and identically distributed (IID)** With respect to random variables, the property of random variables that are independent of each other but follow the identical probability distribution.

**Independent projects** Independent projects are projects whose cash flows are independent of each other.

**Independent variable** A variable used to explain the dependent variable in a regression; a right-hand-side variable in a regression equation.

**Index amortizing swap** An interest rate swap in which the notional principal is indexed to the level of interest rates and declines with the level of interest rates according to a predefined scheduled. This type of swap is frequently used to hedge securities that are prepaid as interest rates decline, such as mortgage-backed securities.

**Index option** An option in which the underlying is a stock index.

**Indexing** An investment strategy in which an investor constructs a portfolio to mirror the performance of a specified index.

**Indirect format (indirect method)** With reference to cash flow statements, a format for the presentation of the statement which, in the operating cash flow section, begins with net income then shows additions and subtractions to arrive at operating cash flow.

**Industry structure** An industry's underlying economic and technical characteristics.

**Infant-industry argument** The argument that it is necessary to protect a new industry to enable it to grow into a mature industry that can compete in world markets.

**Inflation premium** An extra return that compensates investors for expected inflation.

**Information ratio (IR)** Mean active return divided by active risk; or alpha divided by the standard deviation of diversifiable risk.

**Initial margin requirement** The margin requirement on the first day of a transaction as well as on any day in which additional margin funds must be deposited.

**Initial public offering (IPO)** The initial issuance of common stock registered for public trading by a formerly private corporation.

**In-sample forecast errors** The residuals from a fitted time-series model within the sample period used to fit the model.

**Instability in the minimum-variance frontier** The characteristic of minimum-variance frontiers that they are sensitive to small changes in inputs.

**Installment** Said of a sale in which proceeds are to be paid in installments over an extended period of time.

**Installment method (installment-sales method)** With respect to revenue recognition, a method that specifies that the portion of the total profit of the sale that is recognized in each period is determined by the percentage of the total sales price for which the seller has received cash.

**Intangible assets** Assets lacking physical substance, such as patents and trademarks.

**Interest coverage** A solvency ratio calculated as EBIT divided by interest payments.

**Interest rate** A rate of return that reflects the relationship between differently dated cash flows; a discount rate.

**Interest rate call** An option in which the holder has the right to make a known interest payment and receive an unknown interest payment.

**Interest rate cap or cap** A series of call options on an interest rate, with each option expiring at the date on which the floating loan rate will be reset, and with each option having the same exercise rate. A cap in general can have an underlying other than an interest rate.

**Interest rate collar** A combination of a long cap and a short floor, or a short cap and a long floor. A collar in general can have an underlying other than an interest rate.

**Interest rate floor or floor** A series of put options on an interest rate, with each option expiring at the date on which the floating loan rate will be reset,

**Interest rate forward**  (See *forward rate agreement*)

**Interest rate option**  An option in which the underlying is an interest rate.

**Interest rate parity**  A formula that expresses the equivalence or parity of spot and forward rates, after adjusting for differences in the interest rates.

**Interest rate put**  An option in which the holder has the right to make an unknown interest payment and receive a known interest payment.

**Interest rate swap**  A swap in which the underlying is an interest rate. Can be viewed as a currency swap in which both currencies are the same and can be created as a combination of currency swaps.

**Intergenerational data mining**  A form of data mining that applies information developed by previous researchers using a dataset to guide current research using the same or a related dataset.

**Internal rate of return (IRR)**  Rate of return that discounts future cash flows from an investment to the exact amount of the investment; the discount rate that makes the present value of an investment's costs (outflows) equal to the present value of the investment's benefits (inflows).

**Interquartile range**  The difference between the third and first quartiles of a dataset.

**Interval**  With reference to grouped data, a set of values within which an observation falls.

**Interval scale**  A measurement scale that not only ranks data but also gives assurance that the differences between scale values are equal.

**In-the-money**  Options that, if exercised, would result in the value received being worth more than the payment required to exercise.

**Intrinsic value or exercise value**  The value of an asset given a hypothetically complete understanding of the asset's investment characteristics; the value obtained if an option is exercised based on current conditions.

**Inventory**  The unsold units of product on hand.

**Inventory blanket lien**  The use of inventory as collateral for a loan. Though the lender has claim to some or all of the company's inventory, the company may still sell or use the inventory in the ordinary course of business.

**Inventory turnover**  An activity ratio calculated as cost of goods sold divided by average inventory.

**Inverse floater**  A floating-rate note or bond in which the coupon is adjusted to move opposite to a benchmark interest rate.

**Investing activities**  Activities which are associated with the acquisition and disposal of property, plant, and equipment; intangible assets; other long-term assets; and both long-term and short-term investments in the equity and debt (bonds and loans) issued by other companies.

**Investment constraints**  Internal or external limitations on investments.

**Investment objectives**  Desired investment outcomes; includes risk objectives and return objectives.

**Investment opportunity schedule**  A graphical depiction of a company's investment opportunities ordered from highest to lowest expected return. A company's optimal capital budget is found where the investment opportunity schedule intersects with the company's marginal cost of capital.

**Investment strategy**  An approach to investment analysis and security selection.

**IRR rule**  An investment decision rule that accepts projects or investments for which the IRR is greater than the opportunity cost of capital.

**Joint probability**  The probability of the joint occurrence of stated events.

**Joint probability function**  A function giving the probability of joint occurrences of values of stated random variables.

**Joint venture**  An entity (partnership, corporation, or other legal form) where control is shared by two or more entities called venturers.

**Justified (fundamental) P/E**  The price to earnings ratio that is fair, warranted, or justified on the basis of forecasted fundamentals.

**Justified price multiple (or warranted price multiple or intrinsic price multiple)**  The estimated fair value of the price multiple, usually based on forecasted fundamentals or comparables.

**Just-in-time method**  Method of managing inventory that minimizes in-process inventory stocks.

**$k$th Order autocorrelation**  The correlation between observations in a time series separated by $k$ periods.

**Kurtosis**  The statistical measure that indicates the peakedness of a distribution.

**Labor productivity**  The quantity of real GDP produced by an hour of labor.

**Laddering strategy**  A form of active strategy which entails scheduling maturities on a systematic basis within the investment portfolio such that investments are spread out equally over the term of the ladder.

**Law of one price**  The condition in a financial market in which two equivalent financial instruments or combinations of financial instruments can sell for only one price. Equivalent to the principle that no arbitrage opportunities are possible.

**Leading dividend yield** Forecasted dividends per share over the next year divided by current stock price.

**Leading P/E (or forward P/E or prospective P/E)** A stock's current price divided by the next year's expected earnings.

**Legal risk** The risk that failures by company managers to effectively manage a company's environmental, social, and governance risk exposures will lead to lawsuits and other judicial remedies, resulting in potentially catastrophic losses for the company; the risk that the legal system will not enforce a contract in case of dispute or fraud.

**Legislative and regulatory risk** The risk that governmental laws and regulations directly or indirectly affecting a company's operations will change with potentially severe adverse effects on the company's continued profitability and even its long-term sustainability.

**Leptokurtic** Describes a distribution that is more peaked than a normal distribution.

**Lessee** The party obtaining the use of an asset through a lease.

**Lessor** The owner of an asset that grants the right to use the asset to another party.

**Level of significance** The probability of a Type I error in testing a hypothesis.

**Leverage** In the context of corporate finance, leverage refers to the use of fixed costs within a company's cost structure. Fixed costs that are operating costs (such as depreciation or rent) create operating leverage. Fixed costs that are financial costs (such as interest expense) create financial leverage.

**Leveraged buyout (LBO)** A transaction whereby the target company management team converts the target to a privately held company by using heavy borrowing to finance the purchase of the target company's outstanding shares.

**Leveraged floating-rate note or leveraged floater** A floating-rate note or bond in which the coupon is adjusted at a multiple of a benchmark interest rate.

**Leveraged recapitalization** A post-offer takeover defense mechanism that involves the assumption of a large amount of debt that is then used to finance share repurchases; the effect is to dramatically change the company's capital structure while attempting to deliver a value to target shareholders in excess of a hostile bid.

**Liabilities** Present obligations of an enterprise arising from past events, the settlement of which is expected to result in an outflow of resources embodying economic benefits; creditors' claims on the resources of a company.

**LIFO layer liquidation (LIFO liquidation)** With respect to the application of the LIFO inventory method, the liquidation of old, relatively low-priced inventory; happens when the volume of sales rises above the volume of recent purchases so that some sales are made from relatively old, low-priced inventory.

**LIFO method** The last in, first out, method of accounting for inventory, which matches sales against the costs of items of inventory in the reverse order the items were placed in inventory (i.e., inventory produced or acquired last are assumed to be sold first).

**LIFO reserve** The difference between inventory reported as FIFO and inventory reported as LIFO (FIFO inventory value less LIFO inventory value).

**Likelihood** The probability of an observation, given a particular set of conditions.

**Limit down** A limit move in the futures market in which the price at which a transaction would be made is at or below the lower limit.

**Limit move** A condition in the futures markets in which the price at which a transaction would be made is at or beyond the price limits.

**Limit up** A limit move in the futures market in which the price at which a transaction would be made is at or above the upper limit.

**Linear association** A straight-line relationship, as opposed to a relationship that cannot be graphed as a straight line.

**Linear interpolation** The estimation of an unknown value on the basis of two known values that bracket it, using a straight line between the two known values.

**Linear regression** Regression that models the straight-line relationship between the dependent and independent variable(s).

**Linear trend** A trend in which the dependent variable changes at a constant rate with time.

**Liquidation** To sell the assets of a company, division, or subsidiary piecemeal, typically because of bankruptcy; the form of bankruptcy that allows for the orderly satisfaction of creditors' claims after which the company ceases to exist.

**Liquidation value** The value of a company if the company were dissolved and its assets sold individually.

**Liquidity** A company's ability to satisfy its short-term obligations using assets that are most readily converted into cash; the ability to trade a futures contract, either selling a previously purchased contract or purchasing a previously sold contract.

**Liquidity discount** A reduction or discount to value that reflects the lack of depth of trading or liquidity in that asset's market.

**Liquidity premium** An extra return that compensates investors for the risk of loss relative to an investment's fair value if the investment needs to be converted to cash quickly.

**Liquidity ratios** Financial ratios measuring the company's ability to meet its short-term obligations.

**Liquidity risk** The risk that a financial instrument cannot be purchased or sold without a significant concession in price due to the size of the market.

**Local currency** The currency of the country where a company is located.

**Lockbox system** A payment system in which customer payments are mailed to a post office box and the banking institution retrieves and deposits these payments several times a day, enabling the company to have use of the fund sooner than in a centralized system in which customer payments are sent to the company.

**Locked limit** A condition in the futures markets in which a transaction cannot take place because the price would be beyond the limits.

**Logit model** A qualitative-dependent-variable multiple regression model based on the logistic probability distribution.

**Log-linear model** With reference to time-series models, a model in which the growth rate of the time series as a function of time is constant.

**Log-log regression model** A regression that expresses the dependent and independent variables as natural logarithms.

**London Interbank Offer Rate (LIBOR)** The Eurodollar rate at which London banks lend dollars to other London banks; considered to be the best representative rate on a dollar borrowed by a private, high-quality borrower.

**Long** The buyer of a derivative contract. Also refers to the position of owning a derivative.

**Longitudinal data** Observations on characteristic(s) of the same observational unit through time.

**Long-lived assets (or long-term assets)** Assets that are expected to provide economic benefits over a future period of time, typically greater than one year.

**Long-term contract** A contract that spans a number of accounting periods.

**Long-term debt-to-assets ratio** The proportion of a company's assets that is financed with long-term debt.

**Long-term equity anticipatory securities (LEAPS)** Options originally created with expirations of several years.

**Long-term liability** An obligation that is expected to be settled, with the outflow of resources embody-ing economic benefits, over a future period generally greater than one year.

**Look-ahead bias** A bias caused by using information that was not available on the test date.

**Losses** Asset outflows not directly related to the ordinary activities of the business.

**Lower bound** The lowest possible value of an option.

**Macaulay duration** The duration without dividing by 1 plus the bond's yield to maturity. The term, named for one of the economists who first derived it, is used to distinguish the calculation from modified duration. See also *modified duration*.

**Macroeconomic factor** A factor related to the economy, such as the inflation rate, industrial production, or economic sector membership.

**Macroeconomic factor model** A multifactor model in which the factors are surprises in macroeconomic variables that significantly explain equity returns.

**Maintenance margin requirement** The margin requirement on any day other than the first day of a transaction.

**Management buyout (MBO)** A corporate transaction in which management repurchases all outstanding common stock, usually using the proceeds of debt issuance.

**Managerialism theories** Theories that posit that corporate executives are motivated to engage in mergers to maximize the size of their company rather than shareholder value.

**Manufacturing resource planning (MRP)** The incorporation of production planning into inventory management. A MRP analysis provides both a materials acquisition schedule and a production schedule.

**Margin** The amount of money that a trader deposits in a margin account. The term is derived from the stock market practice in which an investor borrows a portion of the money required to purchase a certain amount of stock. In futures markets, there is no borrowing so the margin is more of a down payment or performance bond.

**Market efficiency** A finance perspective on capital markets that deals with the relationship of price to intrinsic value. The **traditional efficient markets formulation** asserts that an asset's price is the best available estimate of its intrinsic value. The **rational efficient markets formulation** asserts that investors should expect to be rewarded for the costs of information gathering and analysis by higher gross returns.

**Market-extraction method** Method used to estimate the overall capitalization rate by dividing the sale price of a comparable income property into the net operating income.

**Market price of risk**   The slope of the capital market line, indicating the market risk premium for each unit of market risk.

**Market rate**   The rate demanded by purchasers of bonds, given the risks associated with future cash payment obligations of the particular bond issue.

**Market risk**   The risk associated with interest rates, exchange rates, and equity prices.

**Market risk premium**   The expected excess return on the market over the risk-free rate.

**Market share test**   The percentage of a market that a particular firm supplies, used as the primary measure of monopoly power.

**Market timing**   Asset allocation in which the investment in the market is increased if one forecasts that the market will outperform T-bills.

**Marketability discount**   A reduction or discount to value for shares that are not publicly traded.

**Market-oriented investors**   With reference to equity investors, investors whose investment disciplines cannot be clearly categorized as value or growth.

**Marking to market**   A procedure used primarily in futures markets in which the parties to a contract settle the amount owed daily. Also known as the *daily settlement*.

**Markowitz decision rule**   A decision rule for choosing between two investments based on their means and variances.

**Mark-to-market**   The revaluation of a financial asset or liability to its current market value or fair value.

**Matching principle**   The accounting principle that expenses should be recognized when the associated revenue is recognized.

**Matching strategy**   An active investment strategy that includes intentional matching of the timing of cash outflows with investment maturities.

**Materiality**   The condition of being of sufficient importance so that omission or misstatement of the item in a financial report could make a difference to users' decisions.

**Matrix pricing**   In the fixed income markets, to price a security on the basis of valuation-relevant characteristics (e.g., debt-rating approach).

**Mature growth rate**   The earnings growth rate in a company's mature phase; an earnings growth rate that can be sustained long term.

**Mature phase**   A stage of growth in which the company reaches an equilibrium in which investment opportunities on average just earn their opportunity cost of capital.

**Maturity premium**   An extra return that compensates investors for the increased sensitivity of the market value of debt to a change in market interest rates as maturity is extended.

**Mean**   The sum of all values in a distribution or dataset, divided by the number of values summed; a synonym of arithmetic mean.

**Mean absolute deviation**   With reference to a sample, the mean of the absolute values of deviations from the sample mean.

**Mean excess return**   The average rate of return in excess of the risk-free rate.

**Mean reversion**   The tendency of a time series to fall when its level is above its mean and rise when its level is below its mean; a mean-reverting time series tends to return to its long-term mean.

**Mean–variance analysis**   An approach to portfolio analysis using expected means, variances, and covariances of asset returns.

**Measure of central tendency**   A quantitative measure that specifies where data are centered.

**Measure of location**   A quantitative measure that describes the location or distribution of data; includes not only measures of central tendency but also other measures such as percentiles.

**Measurement scales**   A scheme of measuring differences. The four types of measurement scales are nominal, ordinal, interval, and ratio.

**Median**   The value of the middle item of a set of items that has been sorted into ascending or descending order; the 50th percentile.

**Merger**   The absorption of one company by another; two companies become one entity and one or both of the pre-merger companies ceases to exist as a separate entity.

**Mesokurtic**   Describes a distribution with kurtosis identical to that of the normal distribution.

**Method based on forecasted fundamentals**   An approach to using price multiples that relates a price multiple to forecasts of fundamentals through a discounted cash flow model.

**Method of comparables**   An approach to valuation that involves using a price multiple to evaluate whether an asset is relatively fairly valued, relatively undervalued, or relatively overvalued when compared to a benchmark value of the multiple.

**Minimum-variance frontier**   The graph of the set of portfolios that have minimum variance for their level of expected return.

**Minimum-variance portfolio**   The portfolio with the minimum variance for each given level of expected return.

**Minority active investments**   Investments in which investors exert significant influence, but not control, over the investee. Typically, the investor has 20 to 50 % ownership in the investee.

**Minority interest (noncontrolling interest)** The proportion of the ownership of a subsidiary not held by the parent (controlling) company.

**Minority passive investments (passive investments)** Investments in which the investor has no significant influence or control over the operations of the investee.

**Mismatching strategy** An active investment strategy whereby the timing of cash outflows is not matched with investment maturities.

**Mispricing** Any departure of the market price of an asset from the asset's estimated intrinsic value.

**Mixed factor models** Factor models that combine features of more than one type of factor model.

**Mixed offering** A merger or acquisition that is to be paid for with cash, securities, or some combination of the two.

**Modal interval** With reference to grouped data, the most frequently occurring interval.

**Mode** The most frequently occurring value in a set of observations.

**Model risk** The use of an inaccurate pricing model for a particular investment, or the improper use of the right model.

**Model specification** With reference to regression, the set of variables included in the regression and the regression equation's functional form.

**Modified duration** A measure of a bond's price sensitivity to interest rate movements. Equal to the Macaulay duration of a bond divided by one plus its yield to maturity.

**Molodovsky effect** The observation that P/Es tend to be high on depressed EPS at the bottom of a business cycle, and tend to be low on unusually high EPS at the top of a business cycle.

**Momentum indicators** Valuation indicators that relate either price or a fundamental (such as earnings) to the time series of their own past values (or in some cases to their expected value).

**Monetary assets and liabilities** Assets and liabilities with value equal to the amount of currency contracted for, a fixed amount of currency. Examples are cash, accounts receivable, mortgages receivable, accounts payable, bonds payable, and mortgages payable. Inventory is not a monetary asset. Most liabilities are monetary.

**Monetary/nonmonetary method** Approach to translating foreign currency financial statements for consolidation in which monetary assets and liabilities are translated at the current exchange rate. Nonmonetary assets and liabilities are translated at historical exchange rates (the exchange rates that existed when the assets and liabilities were acquired).

**Money market** The market for short-term debt instruments (one-year maturity or less).

**Money market yield (or CD equivalent yield)** A yield on a basis comparable to the quoted yield on an interest-bearing money market instrument that pays interest on a 360-day basis; the annualized holding period yield, assuming a 360-day year.

**Moneyness** The relationship between the price of the underlying and an option's exercise price.

**Money-weighted rate of return** The internal rate of return on a portfolio, taking account of all cash flows.

**Monitoring costs** Costs borne by owners to monitor the management of the company (e.g., board of director expenses).

**Monopolization** The possession of monopoly power in the relevant market and the willful acquisition or maintenance of that power, as distinguished from growth or development as a consequence of a superior product, business acumen, or historical accident.

**Monte Carlo simulation method** An approach to estimating a probability distribution of outcomes to examine what might happen if particular risks are faced. This method is widely used in the sciences as well as in business to study a variety of problems.

**Multicollinearity** A regression assumption violation that occurs when two or more independent variables (or combinations of independent variables) are highly but not perfectly correlated with each other.

**Multiple linear regression** Linear regression involving two or more independent variables.

**Multiple linear regression model** A linear regression model with two or more independent variables.

**Multiple R** The correlation between the actual and forecasted values of the dependent variable in a regression.

**Multiplication rule for probabilities** The rule that the joint probability of events A and B equals the probability of A given B times the probability of B.

**Multi-step format** With respect to the format of the income statement, a format that presents a subtotal for gross profit (revenue minus cost of goods sold).

**Multivariate distribution** A probability distribution that specifies the probabilities for a group of related random variables.

**Multivariate normal distribution** A probability distribution for a group of random variables that is completely defined by the means and variances of the variables plus all the correlations between pairs of the variables.

**Mutually exclusive events**   Events such that only one can occur at a time.

**Mutually exclusive projects**   Mutually exclusive projects compete directly with each other. For example, if Projects A and B are mutually exclusive, you can choose A or B, but you cannot choose both.

**$n$ Factorial**   For a positive integer $n$, the product of the first $n$ positive integers; 0 factorial equals 1 by definition. $n$ factorial is written as $n!$.

**Negative serial correlation**   Serial correlation in which a positive error for one observation increases the chance of a negative error for another observation, and vice versa.

**Neoclassical growth theory**   A theory of economic growth that proposes that real GDP per person grows because technological change induces a level of saving and investment that makes capital per hour of labor grow.

**Net asset balance sheet exposure**   When assets translated at the current exchange rate are greater in amount than liabilities translated at the current exchange rate. Assets exposed to translation gains or losses exceed the exposed liabilities.

**Net book value**   The remaining (undepreciated) balance of an asset's purchase cost. For liabilities, the face value of a bond minus any unamortized discount, or plus any unamortized premium.

**Net borrower**   A country that is borrowing more from the rest of the world than it is lending to it.

**Net exports**   The value of exports of goods and services minus the value of imports of goods and services.

**Net income (loss)**   The difference between revenue and expenses; what remains after subtracting all expenses (including depreciation, interest, and taxes) from revenue.

**Net lender**   A country that is lending more to the rest of the world than it is borrowing from it.

**Net liability balance sheet exposure**   When liabilities translated at the current exchange rate are greater than assets translated at the current exchange rate. Liabilities exposed to translation gains or losses exceed the exposed assets.

**Net operating assets**   The difference between operating assets (total assets less cash) and operating liabilities (total liabilities less total debt).

**Net operating cycle**   An estimate of the average time that elapses between paying suppliers for materials and collecting cash from the subsequent sale of goods produced.

**Net operating profit less adjusted taxes, or NOPLAT**   A company's operating profit with adjustments to normalize the effects of capital structure.

**Net present value (NPV)**   The present value of an investment's cash inflows (benefits) minus the present value of its cash outflows (costs).

**Net profit margin (profit margin or return on sales)**   An indicator of profitability, calculated as net income divided by revenue; indicates how much of each dollar of revenues is left after all costs and expenses.

**Net realizable value**   Estimated selling price in the ordinary course of business less the estimated costs necessary to make the sale.

**Net revenue**   Revenue after adjustments (e.g., for estimated returns or for amounts unlikely to be collected).

**Netting**   When parties agree to exchange only the net amount owed from one party to the other.

**New growth theory**   A theory of economic growth based on the idea that real GDP per person grows because of the choices that people make in the pursuit of profit and that growth can persist indefinitely.

**Node**   Each value on a binomial tree from which successive moves or outcomes branch.

**No-growth company**   A company without positive expected net present value projects.

**No-growth value per share**   The value per share of a no-growth company, equal to the expected level amount of earnings divided by the stock's required rate of return.

**Nominal exchange rate**   The value of the U.S. dollar expressed in units of foreign currency per U.S. dollar.

**Nominal rate**   A rate of interest based on the security's face value.

**Nominal risk-free interest rate**   The sum of the real risk-free interest rate and the inflation premium.

**Nominal scale**   A measurement scale that categorizes data but does not rank them.

**Nonconventional cash flow**   In a nonconventional cash flow pattern, the initial outflow is not followed by inflows only, but the cash flows can flip from positive (inflows) to negative (outflows) again (or even change signs several times).

**Noncurrent**   Not due to be consumed, converted into cash, or settled within one year after the balance sheet date.

**Noncurrent assets**   Assets that are expected to benefit the company over an extended period of time (usually more than one year).

**Nondeliverable forwards (NDFs)**   Cash-settled forward contracts, used predominately with respect to foreign exchange forwards.

**Nonlinear relation** An association or relationship between variables that cannot be graphed as a straight line.

**Nonmonetary assets and liabilities** Assets and liabilities that are not monetary assets and liabilities. Nonmonetary assets include inventory, fixed assets, and intangibles, and nonmonetary liabilities include deferred revenue.

**Nonparametric test** A test that is not concerned with a parameter, or that makes minimal assumptions about the population from which a sample comes.

**Nonstationarity** With reference to a random variable, the property of having characteristics such as mean and variance that are not constant through time.

**Nontariff barrier** Any action other than a tariff that restricts international trade.

**Normal backwardation** The condition in futures markets in which futures prices are lower than expected spot prices.

**Normal contango** The condition in futures markets in which futures prices are higher than expected spot prices.

**Normal distribution** A continuous, symmetric probability distribution that is completely described by its mean and its variance.

**Normalized earnings per share (or normal earnings per share)** The earnings per share that a business could achieve currently under mid-cyclical conditions.

**North American Free Trade Agreement** An agreement, which became effective on January 1, 1994, to eliminate all barriers to international trade between the United States, Canada, and Mexico after a 15-year phasing-in period.

**Notes payable** Amounts owed by a business to creditors as a result of borrowings that are evidenced by (short-term) loan agreements.

**$n$-Period moving average** The average of the current and immediately prior $n - 1$ values of a time series.

**NPV rule** An investment decision rule that states that an investment should be undertaken if its NPV is positive but not undertaken if its NPV is negative.

**Null hypothesis** The hypothesis to be tested.

**Number of days of inventory** An activity ratio equal to the number of days in a period divided by the inventory ratio for the period; an indication of the number of days a company ties up funds in inventory.

**Number of days of payables** An activity ratio equal to the number of days in a period divided by the payables turnover ratio for the period; an estimate of the average number of days it takes a company to pay its suppliers.

**Number of days of receivables** Estimate of the average number of days it takes to collect on credit accounts.

**Objective probabilities** Probabilities that generally do not vary from person to person; includes a priori and objective probabilities.

**Off-balance sheet financing** Arrangements that do not result in additional liabilities on the balance sheet but nonetheless create economic obligations.

**Official settlements account** A record of the change in official reserves, which are the government's holdings of foreign currency.

**Off-market FRA** A contract in which the initial value is intentionally set at a value other than zero and therefore requires a cash payment at the start from one party to the other.

**Offsetting** A transaction in exchange-listed derivative markets in which a party re-enters the market to close out a position.

**One third rule** The rule that, on the average, with no change in technology, a 1 percent increase in capital per hour of labor brings a 1/3 percent increase in labor productivity.

**One-sided hypothesis test (or one-tailed hypothesis test)** A test in which the null hypothesis is rejected only if the evidence indicates that the population parameter is greater than (smaller than) $\theta_0$. The alternative hypothesis also has one side.

**Operating activities** Activities that are part of the day-to-day business functioning of an entity, such as selling inventory and providing services.

**Operating breakeven** The number of units produced and sold at which the company's operating profit is zero (revenues = operating costs).

**Operating cycle** A measure of the time needed to convert raw materials into cash from a sale; it consists of the number of days of inventory and the number of days of receivables.

**Operating lease** An agreement allowing the lessee to use some asset for a period of time; essentially a rental.

**Operating leverage** The use of fixed costs in operations.

**Operating profit (operating income)** A company's profits on its usual business activities before deducting taxes.

**Operating profit margin (operating margin)** A profitability ratio calculated as operating income (i.e., income before interest and taxes) divided by revenue.

**Operating return on assets (operating ROA)**   A profitability ratio calculated as operating income divided by average total assets.

**Operating risk**   The risk attributed to the operating cost structure, in particular the use of fixed costs in operations; the risk arising from the mix of fixed and variable costs; the risk that a company's operations may be severely affected by environmental, social, and governance risk factors.

**Operations risk or operational risk**   The risk of loss from failures in a company's systems and procedures (for example, due to computer failures or human failures) or events completely outside of the control of organizations (which would include "acts of God" and terrorist actions).

**Opportunity cost**   The value that investors forgo by choosing a particular course of action; the value of something in its best alternative use.

**Opportunity set**   The set of assets available for investment.

**Optimal capital structure**   The capital structure at which the value of the company is maximized.

**Optimizer**   A specialized computer program or a spreadsheet that solves for the portfolio weights that will result in the lowest risk for a specified level of expected return.

**Option**   A financial instrument that gives one party the right, but not the obligation, to buy or sell an underlying asset from or to another party at a fixed price over a specific period of time. Also referred to as contingent claims.

**Option price, option premium, or premium**   The amount of money a buyer pays and seller receives to engage in an option transaction.

**Ordinal scale**   A measurement scale that sorts data into categories that are ordered (ranked) with respect to some characteristic.

**Ordinary annuity**   An annuity with a first cash flow that is paid one period from the present.

**Ordinary least squares (OLS)**   An estimation method based on the criterion of minimizing the sum of the squared residuals of a regression.

**Ordinary shares (common stock or common shares)**   Equity shares that are subordinate to all other types of equity (e.g., preferred equity).

**Organic growth**   Company growth in output or sales that is achieved by making investments internally (i.e., excludes growth achieved through mergers and acquisitions).

**Orthogonal**   Uncorrelated; at a right angle.

**Other comprehensive income**   Changes to equity that bypass (are not reported in) the income statement; the difference between comprehensive income and net income.

**Other post-retirement benefits**   Promises by the company to pay benefits in the future, other than pension benefits, such as life insurance premiums and all or part of health care insurance for its retirees.

**Other receivables**   Amounts owed to the company from parties other than customers.

**Outcome**   A possible value of a random variable.

**Outliers**   Small numbers of observations at either extreme (small or large) of a sample.

**Out-of-sample forecast errors**   The differences between actual and predicted value of time series outside the sample period used to fit the model.

**Out-of-sample test**   A test of a strategy or model using a sample outside the time period on which the strategy or model was developed.

**Out-of-the-money**   Options that, if exercised, would require the payment of more money than the value received and therefore would not be currently exercised.

**Overall capitalization rate**   A ratio in property valuation; net operating income divided by sale price. Also known as the going-in rate.

**Overnight index swap (OIS)**   A swap in which the floating rate is the cumulative value of a single unit of currency invested at an overnight rate during the settlement period.

**Owners' equity**   The excess of assets over liabilities; the residual interest of shareholders in the assets of an entity after deducting the entity's liabilities.

**Paired comparisons test**   A statistical test for differences based on paired observations drawn from samples that are dependent on each other.

**Paired observations**   Observations that are dependent on each other.

**Pairs arbitrage**   A trade in two closely related stocks that involves buying the relatively undervalued stock and selling short the relatively overvalued stock.

**Pairs arbitrage trade**   A trade in two closely related stocks involving the short sale of one and the purchase of the other.

**Panel data**   Observations through time on a single characteristic of multiple observational units.

**Parameter**   A descriptive measure computed from or used to describe a population of data, conventionally represented by Greek letters.

**Parameter instability**   The problem or issue of population regression parameters that have changed over time.

**Parametric test**   Any test (or procedure) concerned with parameters or whose validity depends on assumptions concerning the population generating the sample.

**Partial regression coefficients or partial slope coefficients** The slope coefficients in a multiple regression.

**Partnership** A business owned and operated by more than one individual.

**Passive portfolio** A market index portfolio.

**Passive strategy** In reference to short-term cash management, it is an investment strategy characterized by simple decision rules for making daily investments.

**Payables turnover** An activity ratio calculated as purchases divided by average trade payables.

**Payer swaption** A swaption that allows the holder to enter into a swap as the fixed-rate payer and floating-rate receiver.

**Payment date** The day that the company actually mails out (or electronically transfers) a dividend payment.

**Payment netting** A means of settling payments in which the amount owed by the first party to the second is netted with the amount owed by the second party to the first; only the net difference is paid.

**Payoff** The value of an option at expiration.

**Payout ratio** The percentage of total earnings paid out in dividends in any given year (in per-share terms, DPS/EPS).

**Pecking order theory** The theory that managers take into account how their actions might be interpreted by outsiders and thus order their preferences for various forms of corporate financing. Forms of financing that are least visible to outsiders (e.g., internally generated funds) are most preferable to managers and those that are most visible (e.g., equity) are least preferable.

**PEG** The P/E-to-growth ratio, calculated as the stock's P/E divided by the expected earnings growth rate.

**Per unit contribution margin** The amount that each unit sold contributes to covering fixed costs—that is, the difference between the price per unit and the variable cost per unit.

**Percentage-of-completion** A method of revenue recognition in which, in each accounting period, the company estimates what percentage of the contract is complete and then reports that percentage of the total contract revenue in its income statement.

**Percentiles** Quantiles that divide a distribution into 100 equal parts.

**Perfect collinearity** The existence of an exact linear relation between two or more independent variables or combinations of independent variables.

**Performance appraisal** The evaluation of risk-adjusted performance; the evaluation of investment skill.

**Performance guarantee** A guarantee from the clearinghouse that if one party makes money on a transaction, the clearinghouse ensures it will be paid.

**Performance measurement** The calculation of returns in a logical and consistent manner.

**Period costs** Costs (e.g., executives' salaries) that cannot be directly matched with the timing of revenues and which are thus expensed immediately.

**Periodic rate** The quoted interest rate per period; the stated annual interest rate divided by the number of compounding periods per year.

**Permanent differences** Differences between tax and financial reporting of revenue (expenses) that will not be reversed at some future date. These result in a difference between the company's effective tax rate and statutory tax rate and do not result in a deferred tax item.

**Permutation** An ordered listing.

**Perpetuity** A perpetual annuity, or a set of never-ending level sequential cash flows, with the first cash flow occurring one period from now.

**Pet projects** Projects in which influential managers want the corporation to invest. Often, unfortunately, pet projects are selected without undergoing normal capital budgeting analysis.

**Plain vanilla swap** An interest rate swap in which one party pays a fixed rate and the other pays a floating rate, with both sets of payments in the same currency.

**Platykurtic** Describes a distribution that is less peaked than the normal distribution.

**Point estimate** A single numerical estimate of an unknown quantity, such as a population parameter.

**Point of sale** Systems that capture transaction data at the physical location in which the sale is made.

**Poison pill** A pre-offer takeover defense mechanism that makes it prohibitively costly for an acquirer to take control of a target without the prior approval of the target's board of directors.

**Poison puts** A pre-offer takeover defense mechanism that gives target company bondholders the right to sell their bonds back to the target at a pre-specified redemption price, typically at or above par value; this defense increases the need for cash and raises the cost of the acquisition.

**Pooled estimate** An estimate of a parameter that involves combining (pooling) observations from two or more samples.

**Pooling of interests accounting method** A method of accounting in which combined companies were portrayed as if they had always operated as a single economic entity. Called pooling of interests under U.S. GAAP and uniting of interests under IFRS. (No longer allowed under U.S. GAAP or IFRS.)

**Population**  All members of a specified group.

**Population mean**  The arithmetic mean value of a population; the arithmetic mean of all the observations or values in the population.

**Population standard deviation**  A measure of dispersion relating to a population in the same unit of measurement as the observations, calculated as the positive square root of the population variance.

**Population variance**  A measure of dispersion relating to a population, calculated as the mean of the squared deviations around the population mean.

**Portfolio implementation problem**  The part of the execution step of the portfolio management process that involves the implementation of portfolio decisions by trading desks.

**Portfolio performance attribution**  The analysis of portfolio performance in terms of the contributions from various sources of risk.

**Portfolio possibilities curve**  A graphical representation of the expected return and risk of all portfolios that can be formed using two assets.

**Portfolio selection/composition problem**  The part of the execution step of the portfolio management process in which investment strategies are integrated with expectations to select a portfolio of assets.

**Position trader**  A trader who typically holds positions open overnight.

**Positive serial correlation**  Serial correlation in which a positive error for one observation increases the chance of a positive error for another observation, and a negative error for one observation increases the chance of a negative error for another observation.

**Posterior probability**  An updated probability that reflects or comes after new information.

**Potential credit risk**  The risk associated with the possibility that a payment due at a later date will not be made.

**Power of a test**  The probability of correctly rejecting the null—that is, rejecting the null hypothesis when it is false.

**Precautionary stocks**  A level of inventory beyond anticipated needs that provides a cushion in the event that it takes longer to replenish inventory than expected or in the case of greater than expected demand.

**Pre-investing**  The strategy of using futures contracts to enter the market without an immediate outlay of cash.

**Prepaid expense**  A normal operating expense that has been paid in advance of when it is due.

**Present value (PV)**  The present discounted value of future cash flows: For assets, the present discounted value of the future net cash inflows that the asset is expected to generate; for liabilities, the present discounted value of the future net cash outflows that are expected to be required to settle the liabilities.

**Present (price) value of a basis point (PVBP)**  The change in the bond price for a 1 basis point change in yield. Also called *basis point value* (BPV).

**Present value of growth opportunities (or value of growth)**  The difference between the actual value per share and the no-growth value per share.

**Present value model or discounted cash flow model**  A model of intrinsic value that views the value of an asset as the present value of the asset's expected future cash flows.

**Presentation currency**  The currency in which financial statement amounts are presented.

**Pretax margin**  A profitability ratio calculated as earnings before taxes divided by revenue.

**Price discovery**  A feature of futures markets in which futures prices provide valuable information about the price of the underlying asset.

**Price limits**  Limits imposed by a futures exchange on the price change that can occur from one day to the next.

**Price momentum**  A valuation indicator based on past price movement.

**Price multiple**  The ratio of a stock's market price to some measure of value per share.

**Price relative**  A ratio of an ending price over a beginning price; it is equal to 1 plus the holding period return on the asset.

**Price to book value**  A valuation ratio calculated as price per share divided by book value per share.

**Price to cash flow**  A valuation ratio calculated as price per share divided by cash flow per share.

**Price to sales**  A valuation ratio calculated as price per share divided by sales per share.

**Priced risk**  Risk for which investors demand compensation for bearing (e.g., equity risk, company-specific factors, macroeconomic factors).

**Price-setting option**  The operational flexibility to adjust prices when demand varies from forecast. For example, when demand exceeds capacity, the company could benefit from the excess demand by increasing prices.

**Principal** The amount of funds originally invested in a project or instrument; the face value to be paid at maturity.

**Prior probabilities** Probabilities reflecting beliefs prior to the arrival of new information.

**Private sector surplus or deficit** An amount equal to saving minus investment.

**Probability** A number between 0 and 1 describing the chance that a stated event will occur.

**Probability density function** A function with non-negative values such that probability can be described by areas under the curve graphing the function.

**Probability distribution** A distribution that specifies the probabilities of a random variable's possible outcomes.

**Probability function** A function that specifies the probability that the random variable takes on a specific value.

**Probit model** A qualitative-dependent-variable multiple regression model based on the normal distribution.

**Production-flexibility** The operational flexibility to alter production when demand varies from forecast. For example, if demand is strong, a company may profit from employees working overtime or from adding additional shifts.

**Profitability ratios** Ratios that measure a company's ability to generate profitable sales from its resources (assets).

**Project sequencing** To defer the decision to invest in a future project until the outcome of some or all of a current project is known. Projects are sequenced through time, so that investing in a project creates the option to invest in future projects.

**Projected benefit obligation** Under U.S. GAAP, a measure used in estimating a defined-benefit pension plan's liabilities, defined as "the actuarial present value as of a date of all benefits attributed by the pension benefit formula to employee service rendered prior to that date. The projected benefit obligation is measured using assumptions as to future compensation if the pension benefit formula is based on those future compensation levels."

**Proportionate consolidation** A method of accounting for joint ventures where the venturer's share of the assets, liabilities, income and expenses of the joint venture are combined on a line-by-line basis with similar items on the venturer's financial statements.

**Protective put** An option strategy in which a long position in an asset is combined with a long position in a put.

**Provision** In accounting, a liability of uncertain timing or amount.

**Proxy fight** An attempt to take control of a company through a shareholder vote.

**Proxy statement** A public document that provides the material facts concerning matters on which shareholders will vote.

**Pseudo-random numbers** Numbers produced by random number generators.

**Pull on liquidity** When disbursements are paid too quickly or trade credit availability is limited, requiring companies to expend funds before they receive funds from sales that could cover the liability.

**Purchase method** A method of accounting for a business combination where the acquiring company allocates the purchase price to each asset acquired and liability assumed at fair value. If the purchase price exceeds the allocation, the excess is recorded as goodwill.

**Purchased in-process research and development costs** Costs of research and development in progress at an acquired company; often, part of the purchase price of an acquired company is allocated to such costs.

**Purchasing power gain** A gain in value caused by changes in price levels. Monetary liabilities experience purchasing power gains during periods of inflation.

**Purchasing power loss** A loss in value caused by changes in price levels. Monetary assets experience purchasing power losses during periods of inflation.

**Purchasing power parity** The equal value of different monies.

**Pure discount instruments** Instruments that pay interest as the difference between the amount borrowed and the amount paid back.

**Pure factor portfolio** A portfolio with sensitivity of 1 to the factor in question and a sensitivity of 0 to all other factors.

**Pure-play method** A method for estimating the beta for a company or project; it requires using a comparable company's beta and adjusting it for financial leverage differences.

**Put** An option that gives the holder the right to sell an underlying asset to another party at a fixed price over a specific period of time.

**Put–call parity** An equation expressing the equivalence (parity) of a portfolio of a call and a bond with a portfolio of a put and the underlying, which leads to the relationship between put and call prices

**Put–call–forward parity**  The relationship among puts, calls, and forward contracts.

**p-Value**  The smallest level of significance at which the null hypothesis can be rejected; also called the marginal significance level.

**Pyramiding**  Controlling additional property through reinvestment, refinancing, and exchanging.

**Qualifying special purpose entities**  Under U.S. GAAP, a special purpose entity structured to avoid consolidation that must meet qualification criteria.

**Qualitative dependent variables**  Dummy variables used as dependent variables rather than as independent variables.

**Quality of earnings analysis**  The investigation of issues relating to the accuracy of reported accounting results as reflections of economic performance; quality of earnings analysis is broadly understood to include not only earnings management, but also balance sheet management.

**Quantile (or fractile)**  A value at or below which a stated fraction of the data lies.

**Quartiles**  Quantiles that divide a distribution into four equal parts.

**Quick assets**  Assets that can be most readily converted to cash (e.g., cash, short-term marketable investments, receivables).

**Quick ratio, or acid test ratio**  A stringent measure of liquidity that indicates a company's ability to satisfy current liabilities with its most liquid assets, calculated as (cash + short-term marketable investments + receivables) divided by current liabilities.

**Quintiles**  Quantiles that divide a distribution into five equal parts.

**Quota**  A quantitative restriction on the import of a particular good, which specifies the maximum amount that can be imported in a given time period.

**Random number**  An observation drawn from a uniform distribution.

**Random number generator**  An algorithm that produces uniformly distributed random numbers between 0 and 1.

**Random variable**  A quantity whose future outcomes are uncertain.

**Random walk**  A time series in which the value of the series in one period is the value of the series in the previous period plus an unpredictable random error.

**Range**  The difference between the maximum and minimum values in a dataset.

**Rate-of-return regulation**  Regulation that seeks to keep the rate of return in the industry at a com-petitive level by not allowing excessive prices to be charged.

**Ratio scales**  A measurement scale that has all the characteristics of interval measurement scales as well as a true zero point as the origin.

**Ratio spread**  An option strategy in which a long position in a certain number of options is offset by a short position in a certain number of other options on the same underlying, resulting in a risk-free position.

**Rational efficient markets formulation**  See *"Market efficiency."*

**Real exchange rate**  The relative price of foreign-made goods and services to U.S.-made goods and services.

**Real GDP per person**  Real GDP divided by the population.

**Real risk-free interest rate**  The single-period interest rate for a completely risk-free security if no inflation were expected.

**Realizable value (settlement value)**  With reference to assets, the amount of cash or cash equivalents that could currently be obtained by selling the asset in an orderly disposal; with reference to liabilities, the undiscounted amount of cash or cash equivalents expected to be paid to satisfy the liabilities in the normal course of business.

**Recapture premium**  Provision for a return of investment, net of value appreciation.

**Receivables turnover**  An activity ratio equal to revenue divided by average receivables.

**Receiver swaption**  A swaption that allows the holder to enter into a swap as the fixed-rate receiver and floating-rate payer.

**Reconciliation**  Resolving differences in indications of value when estimating market value.

**Regime**  With reference to a time series, the underlying model generating the times series.

**Regression coefficients**  The intercept and slope coefficient(s) of a regression.

**Regulatory risk**  The risk associated with the uncertainty of how derivative transactions will be regulated or with changes in regulations.

**Rejection point (or critical value)**  A value against which a computed test statistic is compared to decide whether to reject or not reject the null hypothesis.

**Relative dispersion**  The amount of dispersion relative to a reference value or benchmark.

**Relative frequency**  With reference to an interval of grouped data, the number of observations in the interval divided by the total number of observations in the sample.

**Relative strength (RSTR) indicators**  Valuation indicators that compare a stock's performance during a period either to its own past performance or to the performance of some group of stocks.

**Relative valuation models**  A model that specifies an asset's value relative to the value of another asset.

**Rent seeking**  The pursuit of wealth by capturing economic rent—consumer surplus, producer surplus, or economic profit.

**Reorganization**  Agreements made by a company in bankruptcy under which a company's capital structure is altered and/or alternative arrangements are made for debt repayment; U.S. Chapter 11 bankruptcy. The company emerges from bankruptcy as a going concern.

**Replacement value**  The market value of a swap.

**Report format**  With respect to the format of a balance sheet, a format in which assets, liabilities, and equity are listed in a single column.

**Reputational risk**  The risk that a company will suffer an extended diminution in market value relative to other companies in the same industry due to a demonstrated lack of concern for environmental, social, and governance risk factors.

**Required rate of return**  The minimum rate of return required by an investor to invest in an asset, given the asset's riskiness.

**Residual autocorrelations**  The sample autocorrelations of the residuals.

**Residual claim**  The owners' remaining claim on the company's assets after the liabilities are deducted.

**Residual dividend approach**  A dividend payout policy under which earnings in excess of the funds necessary to finance the equity portion of company's capital budget are paid out in dividends.

**Residual income (or economic profit or abnormal earnings)**  Earnings for a given time period, minus a deduction for common shareholders' opportunity cost in generating the earnings.

**Residual income model (RIM) (also discounted abnormal earnings model or Edwards-Bell-Ohlson model)**  A model of stock valuation that views intrinsic value of stock as the sum of book value per share plus the present value of the stock's expected future residual income per share.

**Residual loss**  Agency costs that are incurred despite adequate monitoring and bonding of management.

**Retail method**  An inventory accounting method in which the sales value of an item is reduced by the gross margin to calculate the item's cost.

**Return on assets (ROA)**  A profitability ratio calculated as net income divided by average total assets; indicates a company's net profit generated per dollar invested in total assets.

**Return on common equity (ROCE)**  A profitability ratio calculated as (net income − preferred dividends) divided by average common equity; equal to the return on equity ratio when no preferred equity is outstanding.

**Return on equity (ROE)**  A profitability ratio calculated as net income divided by average shareholders' equity.

**Return on invested capital (ROIC)**  The after-tax net operating profits as a percent of total assets or capital.

**Return on total capital**  A profitability ratio calculated as EBIT divided by the sum of short- and long-term debt and equity.

**Revaluation**  The process of valuing long-lived assets at fair value, rather than at cost less accumulated depreciation. Any resulting profit or loss is either reported on the income statement and/or through equity under revaluation surplus.

**Revenue**  The amount charged for the delivery of goods or services in the ordinary activities of a business over a stated period; the inflows of economic resources to a company over a stated period.

**Reverse stock split**  A reduction in the number of shares outstanding with a corresponding increase in share price, but no change to the company's underlying fundamentals.

**Revolving credit agreements**  The strongest form of short-term bank borrowing facilities; they are in effect for multiple years (e.g., 3–5 years) and may have optional medium-term loan features.

**Rho**  The sensitivity of the option price to the risk-free rate.

**Risk budgeting**  The establishment of objectives for individuals, groups, or divisions of an organization that takes into account the allocation of an acceptable level of risk.

**Risk governance**  The setting of overall policies and standards in risk management

**Risk management**  The process of identifying the level of risk an entity wants, measuring the level of risk the entity currently has, taking actions that bring the actual level of risk to the desired level of risk, and monitoring the new actual level of risk so that it continues to be aligned with the desired level of risk.

**Risk premium**  The expected return on an investment minus the risk-free rate.

**Risk-neutral probabilities**  Weights that are used to compute a binomial option price. They are the probabilities that would apply if a risk-neutral investor valued an option.

**Risk-neutral valuation**   The process by which options and other derivatives are priced by treating investors as though they were risk neutral.

**Robust**   The quality of being relatively unaffected by a violation of assumptions.

**Robust standard errors**   Standard errors of the estimated parameters of a regression that correct for the presence of heteroskedasticity in the regression's error term.

**Root mean squared error (RMSE)**   The square root of the average squared forecast error; used to compare the out-of-sample forecasting performance of forecasting models.

**Roy's safety first criterion**   A criterion asserting that the optimal portfolio is the one that minimizes the probability that portfolio return falls below a threshold level.

**Rule of 70**   A rule that states that the number of years it takes for the level of a variable to double is approximately 70 divided by the annual percentage growth rate of the variable.

**Rule of 72**   The principle that the approximate number of years necessary for an investment to double is 72 divided by the stated interest rate.

**Safety stock**   A level of inventory beyond anticipated needs that provides a cushion in the event that it takes longer to replenish inventory than expected or in the case of greater than expected demand.

**Safety-first rules**   Rules for portfolio selection that focus on the risk that portfolio value will fall below some minimum acceptable level over some time horizon.

**Sales**   Generally, a synonym for revenue; "sales" is generally understood to refer to the sale of goods, whereas "revenue" is understood to include the sale of goods or services.

**Sales returns and allowances**   An offset to revenue reflecting any cash refunds, credits on account, and discounts from sales prices given to customers who purchased defective or unsatisfactory items.

**Sales risk**   Uncertainty with respect to the quantity of goods and services that a company is able to sell and the price it is able to achieve; the risk related to the uncertainty of revenues.

**Sales-type lease**   A type of finance lease, from a lessor perspective, where the present value of the lease payments (lease receivable) exceeds the carrying value of the leased asset. The revenues earned by the lessor are operating (the profit on the sale) and financing (interest) in nature.

**Salvage value**   The amount the company estimates that it can sell the asset for at the end of its useful life.

**Sample**   A subset of a population.

**Sample excess kurtosis**   A sample measure of the degree of a distribution's peakedness in excess of the normal distribution's peakedness.

**Sample kurtosis**   A sample measure of the degree of a distribution's peakedness.

**Sample mean**   The sum of the sample observations, divided by the sample size.

**Sample selection bias**   Bias introduced by systematically excluding some members of the population according to a particular attribute—for example, the bias introduced when data availability leads to certain observations being excluded from the analysis.

**Sample skewness**   A sample measure of degree of asymmetry of a distribution.

**Sample standard deviation**   The positive square root of the sample variance.

**Sample statistic or statistic**   A quantity computed from or used to describe a sample.

**Sample variance**   A sample measure of the degree of dispersion of a distribution, calculated by dividing the sum of the squared deviations from the sample mean by the sample size ($n$) minus 1.

**Sampling**   The process of obtaining a sample.

**Sampling distribution**   The distribution of all distinct possible values that a statistic can assume when computed from samples of the same size randomly drawn from the same population.

**Sampling error**   The difference between the observed value of a statistic and the quantity it is intended to estimate.

**Sampling plan**   The set of rules used to select a sample.

**Sandwich spread**   An option strategy that is equivalent to a short butterfly spread.

**Sarbanes–Oxley Act**   An act passed by the U.S. Congress in 2002 that created the Public Company Accounting Oversight Board (PCAOB) to oversee auditors.

**Scaled earnings surprise**   Unexpected earnings divided by the standard deviation of analysts' earnings forecasts.

**Scalper**   A trader who offers to buy or sell futures contracts, holding the position for only a brief period of time. Scalpers attempt to profit by buying at the bid price and selling at the higher ask price.

**Scatter plot**   A two-dimensional plot of pairs of observations on two data series.

**Scenario analysis**   Analysis that shows the changes in key financial quantities that result from given (economic) events, such as the loss of customers, the loss of a supply source, or a catastrophic event; a risk management technique involving examination of the performance of a portfolio under specified situations. Closely related to stress testing.

**Screening**   The application of a set of criteria to reduce a set of potential investments to a smaller set having certain desired characteristics.

**Seats**   Memberships in a derivatives exchange.

**Sector neutral**   Said of a portfolio for which economic sectors are represented in the same proportions as in the benchmark, using market-value weights.

**Sector neutralizing**   Measure of financial reporting quality by subtracting the mean or median ratio for a given sector group from a given company's ratio.

**Sector rotation strategy**   A type of top-down investing approach that involves emphasizing different economic sectors based on considerations such as macroeconomic forecasts.

**Securities Act of 1933**   An act passed by the U.S. Congress in 1933 that specifies the financial and other significant information that investors must receive when securities are sold, prohibits misrepresentations, and requires initial registration of all public issuances of securities.

**Securities Exchange Act of 1934**   An act passed by the U.S. Congress in 1934 that created the Securities and Exchange Commission (SEC), gave the SEC authority over all aspects of the securities industry, and empowered the SEC to require periodic reporting by companies with publicly traded securities.

**Securities offering**   A merger or acquisition in which target shareholders are to receive shares of the acquirer's common stock as compensation.

**Security market line (SML)**   The graph of the capital asset pricing model.

**Segment debt ratio**   Segment liabilities divided by segment assets.

**Segment margin**   Segment profit (loss) divided by segment revenue.

**Segment ROA**   Segment profit (loss) divided by segment assets.

**Segment turnover**   Segment revenue divided by segment assets.

**Sell-side analysts**   Analysts who work at brokerages.

**Semideviation**   The positive square root of semivariance (sometimes called semistandard deviation).

**Semilogarithmic**   Describes a scale constructed so that equal intervals on the vertical scale represent equal rates of change, and equal intervals on the horizontal scale represent equal amounts of change.

**Semivariance**   The average squared deviation below the mean.

**Sensitivity analysis**   Analysis that shows the range of possible outcomes as specific assumptions are changed.

**Serially correlated**   With reference to regression errors, errors that are correlated across observations.

**Service period**   The period benefited by the employee's service, usually the period between the grant date and the vesting date.

**Settlement date** or **payment date**   The date on which the parties to a swap make payments.

**Settlement period**   The time between settlement dates.

**Settlement price**   The official price, designated by the clearinghouse, from which daily gains and losses will be determined and marked to market.

**Settlement risk**   When settling a contract, the risk that one party could be in the process of paying the counterparty while the counterparty is declaring bankruptcy.

**Share repurchase**   A transaction in which a company buys back its own shares. Unlike stock dividends and stock splits, share repurchases use corporate cash.

**Shareholders' equity**   Total assets minus total liabilities.

**Share-the-gains, share-the-pains theory**   A theory of regulatory behavior in which the regulators must take account of the demands of three groups: legislators, who established and who oversee the regulatory agency; members of the regulated industry; and consumers of the regulated industry's products or services.

**Shark repellents**   A pre-offer takeover defense mechanism involving the corporate charter (e.g., staggered boards of directors and supermajority provisions).

**Sharpe ratio**   The average return in excess of the risk-free rate divided by the standard deviation of return; a measure of the average excess return earned per unit of standard deviation of return.

**Sharpe's measure**   Reward-to-volatility ratio; ratio of portfolio excess return to standard deviation.

**Short**   The seller of a derivative contract. Also refers to the position of being short a derivative.

**Shortfall risk**   The risk that portfolio value will fall below some minimum acceptable level over some time horizon.

**Simple interest**   The interest earned each period on the original investment; interest calculated on the principal only.

**Simple random sample**   A subset of a larger population created in such a way that each element of the population has an equal probability of being selected to the subset.

**Simple random sampling**   The procedure of drawing a sample to satisfy the definition of a simple random sample.

**Simulation**   Computer-generated sensitivity or scenario analysis that is based on probability models for the factors that drive outcomes.

**Simulation trial**   A complete pass through the steps of a simulation.

**Single-payment loan**   A loan in which the borrower receives a sum of money at the start and pays back the entire amount with interest in a single payment at maturity.

**Single-step format**   With respect to the format of the income statement, a format that does not subtotal for gross profit (revenue minus cost of goods sold).

**Sinking fund factor**   Amount that must be set aside each period to have $1 at some future point in time.

**Skewed**   Not symmetrical.

**Skewness**   A quantitative measure of skew (lack of symmetry); a synonym of skew.

**Sole proprietorship**   A business owned and operated by a single person.

**Solvency**   With respect to financial statement analysis, the ability of a company to fulfill its long-term obligations.

**Solvency ratios**   Ratios that measure a company's ability to meet its long-term obligations.

**Sovereign yield spread**   An estimate of the country spread (country equity premium) for a developing nation that is based on a comparison of bonds yields in country being analyzed and a developed country. The sovereign yield spread is the difference between a government bond yield in the country being analyzed, denominated in the currency of the developed country, and the Treasury bond yield on a similar maturity bond in the developed country.

**Spearman rank correlation coefficient**   A measure of correlation applied to ranked data.

**Special purpose entity (special purpose vehicle or variable interest entity)**   A non-operating entity created to carry out a specified purpose, such as leasing assets or securitizing receivables; can be a corporation, partnership, trust, limited liability, or partnership formed to facilitate a specific type of business activity.

**Specific identification method**   An inventory accounting method that identifies which specific inventory items were sold and which remained in inventory to be carried over to later periods.

**Spin-off**   A form of restructuring in which shareholders of a parent company receive a proportional number of shares in a new, separate entity; shareholders end up owning stock in two different companies where there used to be one.

**Split-off**   A form of restructuring in which shareholders of the parent company are given shares in a newly created entity in exchange for their shares of the parent company.

**Split-rate**   In reference to corporate taxes, a split-rate system taxes earnings to be distributed as dividends at a different rate than earnings to be retained. Corporate profits distributed as dividends are taxed at a lower rate than those retained in the business.

**Spread**   An option strategy involving the purchase of one option and sale of another option that is identical to the first in all respects except either exercise price or expiration.

**Spreadsheet modeling**   As used in this book, the use of a spreadsheet in executing a dividend discount model valuation, or other present value model valuation.

**Spurious correlation**   A correlation that misleadingly points towards associations between variables.

**Standard cost**   With respect to inventory accounting, the planned or target unit cost of inventory items or services.

**Standard deviation**   The positive square root of the variance; a measure of dispersion in the same units as the original data.

**Standard normal distribution (or unit normal distribution)**   The normal density with mean equal to 0 and standard deviation ($\sigma$) equal to 1.

**Standardized beta**   With reference to fundamental factor models, the value of the attribute for an asset minus the average value of the attribute across all stocks, divided by the standard deviation of the attribute across all stocks.

**Standardized unexpected earnings (SUE)**   Unexpected earnings per share divided by the standard deviation of unexpected earnings per share over a specified prior time period.

**Standardizing**   A transformation that involves subtracting the mean and dividing the result by the standard deviation.

**Stated annual interest rate or quoted interest rate**   A quoted interest rate that does not account for compounding within the year.

**Stated rate (nominal rate or coupon rate)**   The rate at which periodic interest payments are calculated.

**Statement of cash flows (cash flow statement)** A financial statement that reconciles beginning-of-period and end-of-period balance sheet values of cash; provides information about an entity's cash inflows and cash outflows as they pertain to operating, investing, and financing activities.

**Statement of changes in shareholders' equity (statement of owners' equity)** A financial statement that reconciles the beginning-of-period and end-of-period balance sheet values of shareholders' equity; provides information about all factors affecting shareholders' equity.

**Statement of retained earnings** A financial statement that reconciles beginning-of-period and end-of-period balance sheet values of retained income; shows the linkage between the balance sheet and income statement.

**Static trade-off theory of capital structure** A theory pertaining to a company's optimal capital structure; the optimal level of debt is found at the point where additional debt would cause the costs of financial distress to increase by a greater amount than the benefit of the additional tax shield.

**Statistic** A quantity computed from or used to describe a sample of data.

**Statistical factor models** A multifactor model in which statistical methods are applied to a set of historical returns to determine portfolios that best explain either historical return covariances or variances.

**Statistical inference** Making forecasts, estimates, or judgments about a larger group from a smaller group actually observed; using a sample statistic to infer the value of an unknown population parameter.

**Statistically significant** A result indicating that the null hypothesis can be rejected; with reference to an estimated regression coefficient, frequently understood to mean a result indicating that the corresponding population regression coefficient is different from 0.

**Statistics** The science of describing, analyzing, and drawing conclusions from data; also, a collection of numerical data.

**Statutory merger** A merger in which one company ceases to exist as an identifiable entity and all its assets and liabilities become part of a purchasing company.

**Stock grants** The granting of stock to employees as a form of compensation.

**Stock options (stock option grants)** The granting of stock options to employees as a form of compensation.

**Stock purchase** An acquisition in which the acquirer gives the target company's shareholders some combination of cash and securities in exchange for shares of the target company's stock.

**Stock-out losses** Profits lost from not having sufficient inventory on hand to satisfy demand.

**Storage costs or carrying costs** The costs of holding an asset, generally a function of the physical characteristics of the underlying asset.

**Straddle** An option strategy involving the purchase of a put and a call with the same exercise price. A straddle is based on the expectation of high volatility of the underlying.

**Straight-line method** A depreciation method that allocates evenly the cost of a long-lived asset less its estimated residual value over the estimated useful life of the asset.

**Strangle** A variation of a straddle in which the put and call have different exercise prices.

**Strap** An option strategy involving the purchase of two calls and one put.

**Stratified random sampling** A procedure by which a population is divided into subpopulations (strata) based on one or more classification criteria. Simple random samples are then drawn from each stratum in sizes proportional to the relative size of each stratum in the population. These samples are then pooled.

**Stress testing** A set of techniques for estimating losses in extremely unfavorable combinations of events or scenarios.

**Strip** An option strategy involving the purchase of two puts and one call.

**Structured note** A variation of a floating-rate note that has some type of unusual characteristic such as a leverage factor or in which the rate moves opposite to interest rates.

**Subjective probability** A probability drawing on personal or subjective judgment.

**Subsidiary merger** A merger in which the company being purchased becomes a subsidiary of the purchaser.

**Subsistence real wage rate** The minimum real wage rate needed to maintain life.

**Sunk cost** A cost that has already been incurred.

**Supernormal growth** Above average or abnormally high growth rate in earnings per share.

**Surprise** The actual value of a variable minus its predicted (or expected) value.

**Survey approach** An estimate of the equity risk premium that is based upon estimates provided by a panel of finance experts.

**Survivorship bias**    Bias that may result when failed or defunct companies are excluded from membership in a group.

**Sustainable growth rate**    The rate of dividend (and earnings) growth that can be sustained over time for a given level of return on equity, keeping the capital structure constant and without issuing additional common stock.

**Swap**    An agreement between two parties to exchange a series of future cash flows.

**Swap spread**    The difference between the fixed rate on an interest rate swap and the rate on a Treasury note with equivalent maturity; it reflects the general level of credit risk in the market.

**Swaption**    An option to enter into a swap.

**Synthetic call**    The combination of puts, the underlying, and risk-free bonds that replicates a call option.

**Synthetic forward contract**    The combination of the underlying, puts, calls, and risk-free bonds that replicates a forward contract.

**Synthetic index fund**    An index fund position created by combining risk-free bonds and futures on the desired index.

**Synthetic put**    The combination of calls, the underlying, and risk-free bonds that replicates a put option.

**Systematic factors**    Factors that affect the average returns of a large number of different assets.

**Systematic sampling**    A procedure of selecting every $k$th member until reaching a sample of the desired size. The sample that results from this procedure should be approximately random.

**Takeover**    A merger; the term may be applied to any transaction, but is often used in reference to hostile transactions.

**Takeover premium**    The amount by which the takeover price for each share of stock must exceed the current stock price in order to entice shareholders to relinquish control of the company to an acquirer.

**Tangible assets**    Long-term assets with physical substance that are used in company operations, such as land (property), plant, and equipment.

**Tangible book value per share**    Common shareholders' equity minus intangible assets from the balance sheet, divided by the number of shares outstanding.

**Target balance**    A minimum level of cash to be held available—estimated in advance and adjusted for known funds transfers, seasonality, or other factors.

**Target capital structure**    A company's chosen proportions of debt and equity.

**Target company, or target**    The company in a merger or acquisition that is being acquired.

**Target payout ratio**    A strategic corporate goal representing the long-term proportion of earnings that the company intends to distribute to shareholders as dividends.

**Target semideviation**    The positive square root of target semivariance.

**Target semivariance**    The average squared deviation below a target value.

**Tariff**    A tax that is imposed by the importing country when an imported good crosses its international boundary.

**Tax base (tax basis)**    The amount at which an asset or liability is valued for tax purposes.

**Tax expense**    An aggregate of an entity's income tax payable (or recoverable in the case of a tax benefit) and any changes in deferred tax assets and liabilities. It is essentially the income tax payable or recoverable if these had been determined based on accounting profit rather than taxable income.

**Tax loss carry forward**    A taxable loss in the current period that may be used to reduce future taxable income.

**Tax risk**    The uncertainty associated with tax laws.

**Taxable income**    The portion of an entity's income that is subject to income taxes under the tax laws of its jurisdiction.

**Taxable temporary differences**    Temporary differences that result in a taxable amount in a future period when determining the taxable profit as the balance sheet item is recovered or settled.

***t*-Distribution**    A symmetrical distribution defined by a single parameter, degrees of freedom, that is largely used to make inferences concerning the mean of a normal distribution whose variance is unknown.

**Technical indicators**    Momentum indicators based on price.

**Temporal method**    A variation of the monetary/nonmonetary translation method that requires not only monetary assets and liabilities, but also nonmonetary assets and liabilities that are measured at their current value on the balance sheet date to be translated at the current exchange rate. Assets and liabilities are translated at rates consistent with the timing of their measurement value. This method is typically used when the functional currency is other than the local currency.

**Tender offer**    A public offer whereby the acquirer invites target shareholders to submit ("tender") their shares in return for the proposed payment.

**Tenor**    The original time to maturity on a swap.

**Terminal price multiple** The price multiple for a stock assumed to hold at a stated future time.

**Terminal share price** The share price at a particular point in the future.

**Terminal value of the stock (or continuing value of the stock)** The analyst's estimate of a stock's value at a particular point in the future.

**Termination date** The date of the final payment on a swap; also, the swap's expiration date.

**Terms of trade** The quantity of goods and services that a country exports to pay for its imports of goods and services.

**Test statistic** A quantity, calculated based on a sample, whose value is the basis for deciding whether or not to reject the null hypothesis.

**Theory of contestable markets** A hypothesis concerning pricing behavior that holds that even though there are only a few firms in an industry, they are forced to price their products more or less competitively because of the ease of entry by outsiders. The key aspect of a contestable market is relatively costless entry into and exit from the industry.

**Theta** The rate at which an option's time value decays.

**Time series** A set of observations on a variable's outcomes in different time periods.

**Time to expiration** The time remaining in the life of a derivative, typically expressed in years.

**Time value decay** The loss in the value of an option resulting from movement of the option price toward its payoff value as the expiration day approaches.

**Time value of money** The principles governing equivalence relationships between cash flows with different dates.

**Time value or speculative value** The difference between the market price of the option and its intrinsic value, determined by the uncertainty of the underlying over the remaining life of the option.

**Time-period bias** The possibility that when we use a time-series sample, our statistical conclusion may be sensitive to the starting and ending dates of the sample.

**Time-series data** Observations of a variable over time.

**Time-weighted rate of return** The compound rate of growth of one unit of currency invested in a portfolio during a stated measurement period; a measure of investment performance that is not sensitive to the timing and amount of withdrawals or additions to the portfolio.

**Tobin's $q$** The ratio of the market value of debt and equity to the replacement cost of total assets.

**Top-down analysis** With reference to investment selection processes, an approach that starts with macro selection (i.e., identifying attractive geographic segments and/or industry segments) and then addresses selection of the most attractive investments within those segments.

**Top-down forecasting approach** A forecasting approach that involves moving from international and national macroeconomic forecasts to industry forecasts and then to individual company and asset forecasts.

**Top-down investing** An approach to investing that typically begins with macroeconomic forecasts.

**Total asset turnover** An activity ratio calculated as revenue divided by average total assets.

**Total invested capital** The sum of market value of common equity, book value of preferred equity, and face value of debt.

**Total probability rule** A rule explaining the unconditional probability of an event in terms of probabilities of the event conditional on mutually exclusive and exhaustive scenarios.

**Total probability rule for expected value** A rule explaining the expected value of a random variable in terms of expected values of the random variable conditional on mutually exclusive and exhaustive scenarios.

**Total return swap** A swap in which one party agrees to pay the total return on a security. Often used as a credit derivative, in which the underlying is a bond.

**Tracking error** The standard deviation of the difference in returns between an active investment portfolio and its benchmark portfolio; also called tracking error volatility, tracking risk, and active risk.

**Tracking portfolio** A portfolio having factor sensitivities that are matched to those of a benchmark or other portfolio.

**Tracking risk** The standard deviation of the differences between a portfolio's returns and its benchmark's returns; a synonym of active risk.

**Trade credit** A spontaneous form of credit in which a purchaser of the goods or service is financing its purchase by delaying the date on which payment is made.

**Trade receivables (commercial receivables or accounts receivable)** Amounts customers owe the company for products that have been sold as well as amounts that may be due from suppliers (such as for returns of merchandise).

**Trade-weighted index** The average exchange rate, with individual currencies weighted by their importance in U.S. international trade.

**Trading securities (held-for-trading securities)** Securities held by a company with the intent to trade them.

**Traditional efficient markets formulation** See *"Market efficiency."*

**Trailing dividend yield** Current market price divided by the most recent quarterly per-share dividend multiplied by four.

**Trailing P/E (or current P/E)** A stock's current market price divided by the most recent four quarters of earnings per share.

**Transaction exposure** The risk of a change in value between the transaction date and the settlement date of an asset or liability denominated in a foreign currency.

**Transactions motive** In the context of inventory management, the need for inventory as part of the routine production–sales cycle.

**Transition phase** The stage of growth between the growth phase and the mature phase of a company in which earnings growth typically slows.

**Translation exposure** The risk associated with the conversion of foreign financial statements into domestic currency.

**Treasury shares** Shares that were issued and subsequently repurchased by the company.

**Treasury stock method** A method for accounted for the effect of options (and warrants) on earnings per share (EPS) that specifies what EPS would have been if the options and warrants had been exercised and the company had used the proceeds to repurchase common stock.

**Tree diagram** A diagram with branches emanating from nodes representing either mutually exclusive chance events or mutually exclusive decisions.

**Trend** A long-term pattern of movement in a particular direction.

**Trimmed mean** A mean computed after excluding a stated small percentage of the lowest and highest observations.

**Trust receipt arrangement** The use of inventory as collateral for a loan. The inventory is segregated and held in trust, and the proceeds of any sale must be remitted to the lender immediately.

**$t$-Test** A hypothesis test using a statistic ($t$-statistic) that follows a $t$-distribution.

**Two-sided hypothesis test (or two-tailed hypothesis test)** A test in which the null hypothesis is rejected in favor of the alternative hypothesis if the evidence indicates that the population parameter is either smaller or larger than a hypothesized value.

**Type I error** The error of rejecting a true null hypothesis.

**Type II error** The error of not rejecting a false null hypothesis.

**U.S. interest rate differential** The U.S. interest rate minus the foreign interest rate.

**U.S. official reserves** The government's holding of foreign currency.

**Unbiasedness** Lack of bias. A desirable property of estimators, an unbiased estimator is one whose expected value (the mean of its sampling distribution) equals the parameter it is intended to estimate.

**Unbilled revenue (accrued revenue)** Revenue that has been earned but not yet billed to customers as of the end of an accounting period.

**Unclassified balance sheet** A balance sheet that does not show subtotals for current assets and current liabilities.

**Unconditional heteroskedasticity** Heteroskedasticity of the error term that is not correlated with the values of the independent variable(s) in the regression.

**Unconditional probability (or marginal probability)** The probability of an event *not* conditioned on another event.

**Underlying** An asset that trades in a market in which buyers and sellers meet, decide on a price, and the seller then delivers the asset to the buyer and receives payment. The underlying is the asset or other derivative on which a particular derivative is based. The market for the underlying is also referred to as the spot market.

**Underlying earnings (or persistent earnings, continuing earnings, or core earnings)** Earnings excluding nonrecurring components.

**Unearned fees** Unearned fees are recognized when a company receives cash payment for fees prior to earning them.

**Unearned revenue (deferred revenue)** A liability account for money that has been collected for goods or services that have not yet been delivered; payment received in advance of providing a good or service.

**Unexpected earnings (also earnings surprise)** The difference between reported earnings per share and expected earnings per share.

**Unidentifiable intangible** An intangible that cannot be acquired singly and that typically possesses an indefinite benefit period; an example is accounting goodwill.

**Unit root** A time series that is not covariance stationary is said to have a unit root.

**Uniting of interests method** A method of accounting in which combined companies were portrayed as if they had always operated as a single economic entity. Called pooling of interests under U.S. GAAP and uniting of interests under IFRS. (No longer allowed under U.S. GAAP or IFRS.)

**Units-of-production method** A depreciation method that allocates the cost of a long-lived asset based on actual usage during the period.

**Univariate distribution** A distribution that specifies the probabilities for a single random variable.

**Unlimited funds** An unlimited funds environment assumes that the company can raise the funds it wants for all profitable projects simply by paying the required rate of return.

**Up transition probability** The probability that an asset's value moves up.

**Upstream** A transaction between two affiliates, an investor company and an associate company such that the associate company records a profit on its income statement. An example is a sale of inventory by the associate to the investor company.

**Valuation** The process of determining the value of an asset or service on the basis of variables perceived to be related to future investment returns, or on the basis of comparisons with closely similar assets.

**Valuation allowance** A reserve created against deferred tax assets, based on the likelihood of realizing the deferred tax assets in future accounting periods.

**Valuation ratios** Ratios that measure the quantity of an asset or flow (e.g., earnings) in relation to the price associated with a specified claim (e.g., a share or ownership of the enterprise).

**Value** The amount for which one can sell something, or the amount one must pay to acquire something.

**Value at risk (VAR)** A money measure of the minimum value of losses expected during a specified time period at a given level of probability.

**Value investors** With reference to equity investors, investors who are focused on paying a relatively low share price in relation to earnings or assets per share.

**Variable costs** Costs that fluctuate with the level of production and sales.

**Variance** The expected value (the probability-weighted average) of squared deviations from a random variable's expected value.

**Variation margin** Additional margin that must be deposited in an amount sufficient to bring the balance up to the initial margin requirement.

**Vega** The relationship between option price and volatility.

**Venturers** The owners of a joint venture. Each is active in the management and shares control of the joint venture.

**Vertical analysis** Common-size analysis using only one reporting period or one base financial statement; for example, an income statement in which all items are stated as percentages of sales.

**Vertical common-size analysis** The most common type of common-size analysis, in which the accounts in a given period are compared to a benchmark item in that same year.

**Vertical merger** A merger involving companies at different positions of the same production chain; for example, a supplier or a distributor.

**Vested benefit obligation** Under U.S. GAAP, a measure used in estimating a defined-benefit pension plan's liabilities, defined as the "actuarial present value of vested benefits."

**Vested benefits** Future benefits promised to the employee regardless of continuing service. Benefits typically vest after a specified period of service or a specified period of service combined with age.

**Vesting date** The date that employees can first exercise stock options; vesting can be immediate or over a future period.

**Visibility** The extent to which a company's operations are predictable with substantial confidence.

**Volatility** As used in option pricing, the standard deviation of the continuously compounded returns on the underlying asset.

**Voluntary export restraint** An agreement between two governments in which the government of the exporting country agrees to restrain the volume of its own exports.

**Warehouse receipt arrangement** The use of inventory as collateral for a loan; similar to a trust receipt arrangement except there is a third party (i.e., a warehouse company) that supervises the inventory.

**Weighted average cost method** An inventory accounting method that averages the total cost of available inventory items over the total units available for sale.

**Weighted mean** An average in which each observation is weighted by an index of its relative importance.

**Weighted-average cost of capital (WACC)** A weighted average of the after-tax required rates of return on a company's common stock, preferred stock, and long-term debt, where the weights are the fraction of each source of financing in the company's target capital structure.

**White knight**   A third party that is sought out by the target company's board to purchase the target in lieu of a hostile bidder.

**White squire**   A third party that is sought out by the target company's board to purchase a substantial minority stake in the target—enough to block a hostile takeover without selling the entire company.

**White-corrected standard errors**   A synonym for robust standard errors.

**Winner's curse**   The tendency for the winner in certain competitive bidding situations to overpay, whether because of overestimation of intrinsic value, emotion, or information asymmetries.

**Winsorized mean**   A mean computed after assigning a stated percent of the lowest values equal to one specified low value, and a stated percent of the highest values equal to one specified high value.

**Working capital**   The difference between current assets and current liabilities.

**Working capital management**   The management of a company's short-term assets (such as inventory) and short-term liabilities (such as money owed to suppliers).

**Working capital turnover**   A comparison of revenues with working capital to produce a measure that shows how efficiently working capital is employed.

**World Trade Organization**   An international organization that places greater obligations on its member countries to observe the GATT rules.

**Write-down**   A reduction in the value of an asset as stated in the balance sheet.

**Yield**   The actual return on a debt security if it is held to maturity.

**Yield beta**   A measure of the sensitivity of a bond's yield to a general measure of bond yields in the market that is used to refine the hedge ratio.

**Yield spread**   The difference between the yield on a bond and the yield on a default-free security, usually a government note, of the same maturity. The yield spread is primarily determined by the market's perception of the credit risk on the bond.

**Yield to maturity**   The annual return that an investor earns on a bond if the investor purchases the bond today and holds it until maturity.

**Zero-cost collar**   A transaction in which a position in the underlying is protected by buying a put and selling a call with the premium from the sale of the call offsetting the premium from the purchase of the put. It can also be used to protect a floating-rate borrower against interest rate increases with the premium on a long cap offsetting the premium on a short floor.

# INDEX

diversification, V1: 204
impartiality, V1: 204
initial review, V1: 204
loyalty, V1: 204
risk/reward, V1: 202
strategy, V1: 202–203
Prudent Investor Rule,
V1: 199–201, 206
caution, V1: 201
diversification, V1: 201
duty to conform to fiduciary
standards, V1: 200
inflation, V1: 200n1
risk management, V1: 201
Prudent Man Rule, V1: 196–199
PSA. *See* Public Securities Association
public appearances, V1: 156, 160
public companies, V1: 23–24
public good, V1: 458
Public Market Equivalent, V5: 69
Public Securities Association,
V5: 334, 369
public standardized transactions,
futures markets, V6: 57–58
purchase price less than fair value,
V2: 43
purchasing power, V1: 631
purchasing power parity, V1: 530–531,
584, 586–588, 586n7, 596
absolute, V1: 586
adjusted dollar exchange rates,
V4: 255
defined, V1: 586
exchange rate, V1: 530–531
relative, V1: 586
purchasing power protection, V5: 7
purchasing power risk, V6: 439
pure expectations theory, V5: 234–241
local expectations form,
V5: 236–239
put–call parity, options, V6: 157–163,
202–205
put option, V6: 128, 160, 294n5
protective, V6: 157–159
putable bond
nodes, V5: 291
valuing, V5: 290–293
PV. *See* present value
PVGO. *See* present value of growth
opportunities

**Q**
QIBs. *See* qualified institutional buyers
QQQ. *See* Nasdaq
QSPEs. *See* qualified special purpose
entities; qualifying special
purpose entities
quadratic programming, V6: 344n13
quadratic relationships, V1: 226n4

qualified institutional buyers, V4: 77
qualified special purpose entities,
V2: 28n4
qualifying special purpose entities,
V2: 28n4, 49–50
quality of earnings, V2: 315–316
quality of seller/servicer, V5: 187–188
quality option, V6: 290
quantitative methods, valuation,
V1: 217–429
Qubes. *See* Nasdaq
quiet period, defined, V1: 156
quotas, V1: 501–502
effects of, V1: 502
quotation conventions, V1: 553–554,
553n1
quotations, exchange rates,
V1: 550–560
quote-driven market, V4: 52

**R**
RAM. *See* Risk Attribute Model
Ramsey, Frank, V1: 455
random event at node, V5: 275
random walks, V1: 388–392
rapid amortization provision, V5: 406
ratchet, V5: 61
rate covenant, V5: 192
rates. *See* interest; interest rates
rating transition matrix, V5: 165n7
rational investor assumption,
economic-being assumption,
distinguished, V5: 7–8
raw land, V5: 8–9
raw materials
downstream, V4: 162
upstream, V4: 162
real equity returns, V1: 250
real estate investment, V5: 6–7
control of owners, V5: 7
entrepreneurial profit, V5: 7
leverage, V5: 6
pride of ownership, V5: 7
purchasing power protection, V5: 7
tax shelter, V5: 7
real exchange appreciation, V6: 454
real exchange rate, V1: 518, 531–532
real exchange rate risk, V6: 439
real foreign currency risk, V6: 439
real GDP growth rates, V4: 296–297
real GDP per person, United States,
V1: 435
real interest rates, changes in,
V1: 578–579
real option analysis, V3: 54–55, V5: 45
real options, V3: 53–57, V5: 45
Black–Scholes–Merton model,
V3: 57
types, V3: 54

real property investment types,
V5: 10–11
real-terms financial projection,
V4: 258–263
realized capital gains, losses, V2: 310
realized return, V4: 95
reasonable basis, V1: 186
responsibility, V1: 13, 80–84
rebalancing of position, V4: 13
receivables turnover ratio, V2: 3
receiver swaption, V6: 257
recession, V4: 159, 167
recommendations, investment,
V1: 54–55, 80–89
record keeping, V1: 148
soft dollar arrangements,
V1: 138, 148
record retention, V1: 14, 88–89
recovery, V4: 159, 167
redividing profitability, V4: 215
reduced form models, V5: 197,
197n59, 197n62
credit risk models, V5: 197
reference to CFA Institute, V1: 14,
103–109
reference to CFA membership, V1: 104
reference to CFA program, V1: 14,
103–109
referral fees, V1: 14, 99–101
refinancing burnout, V5: 342
regional jurisdiction tax structure,
V6: 496
Registered Retirement Savings Plans,
V6: 517
regression coefficients
autoregressive time-series models,
instability, V1: 386–388
linear regression, V1: 240–265
regression errors, V1: 244n25
regression with heteroskedasticity,
V1: 304
regression with homoskedasticity,
V1: 304
regressions with more than one time
series, V1: 411–415
Dickey-Fuller test, V1: 411
regular dividends, V3: 137
regulation, V1: 468–471, 482–483
antitrust law enforcement,
V1: 480–483
cross-border mergers,
V1: 481–483
monopoly power, V1: 480–481
Sherman Act, V1: 480
antitrust policy, V1: 477–480
Clayton Act of 1914, V1: 478
exemptions from, V1: 479–480
Federal Trade Commission,
V1: 479